LAW AND POPULAR CULTURE:
TEXT, NOTES, AND QUESTIONS

LAW AND POPULAR CULTURE: TEXT, NOTES, AND QUESTIONS

Second Edition

DAVID RAY PAPKE
Professor of Law
Marquette University Law School

CHRISTINE ALICE CORCOS
Associate Professor of Law
Paul M. Hebert Law Center, Louisiana State University

PETER HENRY HUANG
DeMuth Chair Professor of Business Law
University of Colorado Law School

LENORA P. LEDWON
Professor of Law
St. Thomas University School of Law

CARRIE MENKEL-MEADOW
Chancellor's Professor of Law
University of California, Irvine School of Law, and
A.B. Chettle, Jr. Professor of Law, Dispute Resolution and Civil Procedure
Georgetown University Law Center

PHILIP N. MEYER
Professor of Law
Vermont Law School

BINNY MILLER
Professor of Law and Director, Criminal Justice Clinic
American University
Washington College of Law

SEAN O'BRIEN
Associate Professor of Law
UMKC School of Law

ISBN: 978-0-7698-4753-5

Library of Congress Cataloging-in-Publication Data

Law and popular culture : text, notes, and questions / David Ray Papke ... [et al.]. -- 2nd ed.
   p. cm.
Includes index.
ISBN 978-0-7698-4753-5
1. Culture and law. 2. Popular culture. 3. Law--Interpretation and construction. I. Papke, David Ray, 1947-
K487.C8L3895 2012
340'.115--dc23
2011052282

NOTE TO USERS

To ensure that you are using the latest materials available in this area, please be sure to periodically check the LexisNexis Law School web site for downloadable updates and supplements at www.lexisnexis.com/lawschool.

Editorial Offices
121 Chanlon Rd., New Providence, NJ 07974 (908) 464-6800
201 Mission St., San Francisco, CA 94105-1831 (415) 908-3200
www.lexisnexis.com

MATTHEW◆BENDER

Dedication

For those willing to find law in not only their law books but also their culture.

Preface

My co-authors and I are pleased to present the Second Edition of *Law and Popular Culture: Text, Notes and Questions*. We are struck, both individually and collectively, by the immense array of contemporary law-related American popular culture, and we believe pop cultural images and portrayals influence what Americans expect from their laws, lawyers, legal institutions, and government.

The Second Edition maintains the most appreciated features of the First Edition. Each chapter begins with a list of five films which the chapter then addresses along with other works related to a given subject area. Instructors using the Second Edition might want to screen one or more of a chapter's listed films while teaching the chapter. Then, too, the Second Edition includes well over one hundred excerpts from articles by the leading law and popular culture scholars. A majority of these excerpts appeared in the First Edition, but many appear for the first time in the Second. Excerpts are reprinted in edited form and largely without footnotes, but citations accompany the excerpts, allowing readers to consult the complete articles if they are so inclined.

The Second Edition also has new features. An original chapter on "Punishment" explores the surprisingly large body of pop cultural works related to imprisonment and capital punishment. Although film remains the most prominent medium in the Second Edition, law-related imagery and portrayals in such other media as television, inexpensive fiction, children's literature, and the comics receive much greater attention in the text's notes and comments sections than was the case in the First Edition. Most subtly, the Second Edition emphasizes the reasons, forms, and ramifications of law-related popular culture, moving away to some extent from attempts either to point out the legal errors in popular culture or to teach the law using popular culture.

The authors of *Law and Popular Culture: Text, Notes, and Questions* wish to thank Jennifer A. Beszley, the loyal editor of both the First and now the Second Edition at LexisNexis, and also Tulita Papke, our own editorial assistant, whose excellent research, attention to detail, and mastery of computerized formatting greatly improved the quality of the text. My co-authors and I hope teachers and students alike will delight as much as we do in critically considering the interrelationships of law and popular culture. This is one course of study that is demanding and lots of fun as well.

David Ray Papke

Summary Table of Contents

Table of Contents

Table of Contents

Table of Contents

Table of Contents

Table of Contents

Table of Contents

Table of Contents

Table of Contents

Table of Contents

Table of Contents

Table of Contents

Table of Contents

Acknowledgments

Excerpts from the following publications are reprinted with permission in the Second Edition of *Law and Popular Culture: Text, Notes, and Questions*. In general, the excerpts appear without their original footnotes. Full citations are provided for readers who might wish to consult those footnotes or read the articles from which the excerpts are taken.

Chapter 1: Studying Law and Popular Culture

Bergman, Paul, *Teaching Evidence the "Reel" Way*, 21 Quinnipiac L. Rev. 973 (2003).

Denvir, John, *What Movies Teach Law Students*, Picturing Justice; 2003, http://www.usfca.edu/pj.

Freedman, Monroe H., *Atticus Finch – Right and Wrong*, 45 Ala. L. Rev. 404 (1994).

Friedman, Lawrence M., *Law, Lawyers, and Popular Culture*, 98 Yale L.J. 1579 (1989).

Mezey, Naomi & Niles, Mark C., *Screening the Law: Ideology and Law in American Popular Culture*, 28 Colum. J. of Law & the Arts 91 (2005).

Papke, David Ray, *The American Courtroom Trial: Pop Culture, Courthouse Realities, and the Dream World of Justice*, 40 S. Tex. L. Rev. 919 (1999).

Wagner, Kenneth, *A Man for All Seasons*, Picturing Justice; 2005, http://www.usfca.edu/pj.

Chapter 2: Legal Education

Corcos, Christine Alice, *"We Don't Want Advantages": The Woman Lawyer Hero and Her Quest for Power in Popular Culture*, 53 Syracuse L. Rev. 1225 (2003).

LOUISIANA STATE UNIVERSITY, CODE OF STUDENT PROFESSIONAL RESPONSIBILITY (2011).

Papke, David Ray, *Crusading Hero, Devoted Teacher, and Sympathetic Failure: The Self-Image of the Law Professor in Hollywood Cinema and in Real Life, Too*, 28 Vt. L. Rev. 957 (2004).

Rosato, Jennifer, *The Socratic Method and Women Law Students: Humanize, Don't Feminize*, 7 S. Cal. Rev. L. & Women's Stud. 37 (1997).

Torrey, Morrison, *You Call That Education?*, 19 Wis. Women's L.J. 93 (2004).

Vitiello, Michael, Professor Kingsfield: *The Most Misunderstood Character in Literature*, 33 Hofstra L. Rev. 955 (2005).

Chapter 3: Lawyers

Asimow, Michael, *Bad Lawyers in the Movies*, 24 Nova L. Rev. 531 (2000).

Asimow, Michael, *Embodiment of Evil: Law Firms in the Movies*, 48 UCLA L. Rev. 1339 (2001).

Bergman, Paul, *The Movie Lawyers' Guide to Redemptive Legal Practice*, 48 UCLA L. Rev. 1393 (2001).

Menkel-Meadow, Carrie, *Can They Do That? Legal Ethics in Popular Culture: Of Character and Acts*, 48 UCLA L. Rev. 1305 (2001).

Acknowledgments

Simon, William H., *Moral Pluck: Legal Ethics in Popular Culture*, 101 Colum. L. Rev. 421 (2001).

Chapter 4: Clients

Cook, Nancy, *Legal Fictions: Clinical Experiences, Lace Collars, and Boundless Stories*, 1 Clinical L. Rev. 41 (1994).

Dinerstein, Robert D., *Client-Centered Counseling: Reappraisal and Refinement*, 32 Ariz. L. Rev. 501 (1990).

Kruse, Katherine R., *Fortress in the Sand: The Plural Values of Client-Centered Representation*, 12 Clinical L. Rev. 369 (2006).

Margulies, Peter, *Representation of Domestic Violence Survivors as a New Paradigm of Poverty Law: In Search of Access, Connection, and Voice*, 63 Geo. Wash. L. Rev. 1071 (1995).

Miller, Binny, *Teaching Case Theory*, 9 Clinical L. Rev. 293 (2002).

Ogletree, Charles, *Beyond Justifications: Seeking Motivations to Sustain Public Defenders*, 106 Harv. L. Rev. 1239 (1992).

Polikoff, Nancy D., *Am I My Client? The Role Confusion of a Lawyer Activist*, 31 Harv. C.R.-C.L. L. Rev. 443 (1996).

Smith, Abbe, *The Difference in Criminal Defense and the Difference It Makes*, 11 Wash. U. J.L. & Pol'y 83 (2003).

Spinak, Jane, *Reflections on a Case (of Motherhood)*, 95 Colum. L. Rev. 1990 (1995).

White, Lucie E., *Seeking ". . . The Faces of Otherness . . . ": A Response to Professors Sarat, Felstiner, and Cahn*, 77 Cornell L. Rev. 1499 (1992).

White, Lucie E., *To Learn and Teach: Lessons from Driefontein on Lawyering and Power*, 1988 Wis. L. Rev. 699.

Chapter 5: Witnesses

Carey, James, *Charles Laughton, Marlene Dietrich, and the Prior Inconsistent Statement*, 36 Loy. U. Chi. L.J. 433 (2005).

Corcos, Christine Alice, *Legal Fictions: Irony, Storytelling, Truth, and Justice in the Modern Courtroom Drama*, 25 U. Ark. Little Rock L. Rev. 503 (2003).

Covey, Russell Dean, *Beating the Prisoner at Prisoner's Dilemma: The Evidentiary Value of a Witness's Refusal to Testify*, 47 Am. U. L. Rev. 105 (1997).

Hallisey, Robert, *Experts on Eyewitness Testimony in Court – A Short Historical Perspective*, 39 How. L.J. 237 (1995).

Moriarty, Jane Campbell, *Wonders of the Invisible World: Prosecutorial Syndrome and Profile Evidence in the Salem Witchcraft Trials*, 26 Vt. L. Rev. 43 (2001).

Rentschler, Carrie A., *The Physiogomic Turn*, 4 Int'l J. of Comm. 231 (2010).

Chapter 6: Judges

Goldman, Sheldon, *Judicial Confirmation Wars: Ideology and the Battle for the Federal Courts*, 39 U. Rich. L. Rev. 871 (2005).

Greenfield, Steve & Osborn, Guy, *Film, Law and the Delivery of Justice: The Case of*

Acknowledgments

Judge Dredd and the Disappearing Courtroom, 6(2) J. of Criminal Justice and Popular Culture 35 (1999).

Papke, David Ray, *From Flat to Round: Changing Portrayals of the Judge in American Popular Culture*, 31 J. of the Legal Profession 127 (2007).

Podlas, Kimberlianne, *Blame Judge Judy: The Effects of Syndicated Television Courtrooms on Jurors*, 25 Am. J. Trial Advoc. 557 (2002).

Posner, Richard A., *What Do Judges and Justices Maximize? (The Same Thing Everybody Else Does)*, 3 Sup. Ct. Econ. Rev. 1 (1993).

Rendell, Marjorie O., *What Is the Role of the Judge in Our Litigious Society?*, 40 Vill. L. Rev. 1115 (1995).

Resnik, Judith, *On the Bias: Feminist Reconsiderations of the Aspirations for Our Judges*, 61 So. Cal. L. Rev. 1877 (1988).

Rosenbloom, Jonathan D., *Social Ideology As Seen Through Courtroom and Courthouse Architecture*, 22 Colum.-VLA J. of Law & the Arts 463 (1998).

Shale, Suzanne, *The Conflicts of Law and the Character of Men: Writing* Reversal of Fortune *and* Judgment at Nuremberg, 30 U.S.F. L. Rev. 991 (1996).

Tuma, Shawn, *Law in Texas Literature: Texas Justice – Judge Roy Bean Style*, 21 Rev. Litig. 551 (2002).

Chapter 7: Juries

Abramson, Jeffrey, *The Jury and Popular Culture*, 50 DePaul L. Rev. 497 (2000).

Asimow, Michael, *12 Angry Men: A Revisionist View*, 82 Chi.-Kent L. Rev. 711 (2007).

Ball, Milner, *Just Stories*, 12 Cardozo Stud. L. & Literature 37 (2000).

Clover, Carol J., *Movie Juries*, 48 DePaul L. Rev. 389 (1998).

Farrar-Myers, Victoria A. & Myers, Jason B., *Echoes of the Founding: The Jury in Civil Cases as Conferrer of Legitimacy*, 54 SMU L. Rev. 1857 (2001).

Gershman, Bennett L., *Contaminating the Verdict: The Problem of Juror Misconduct*, 50 S.D. L. Rev. 322 (2005).

Gildin, Gary S., *Reality Programming Lessons for Twenty-First Century Trial Lawyering*, 31 Stetson L. Rev. 61 (2001).

Griffin, Lisa Kern, *"The Image We See Is Our Own": Defending the Jury's Territory at the Heart of the Democratic Process*, 75 Neb. L. Rev. 332 (1996).

Gupta, Rajani, *Trial and Errors: Comedy's Quest for the Truth*, 9 UCLA Ent. L. Rev. 113 (2001).

Haddon, Phoebe A., *Rethinking the Jury*, 3 Wm. & Mary Bill Rts. J. 29 (1994).

Hastie, Reid, *Emotions in Jurors' Decisions*, 66 Brook. L. Rev. 991 (2001).

Lane, Maureen E., *Twelve Carefully Selected Not So Angry Men: Are Jury Consultants Destroying the American Legal System?*, 32 Suffolk U. L. Rev. 463 (1999).

Marder, Nancy S., *Introduction to the 50th Anniversary of* 12 Angry Men, 82 Chi.-Kent L. Rev. 557 (2007).

Acknowledgments

Marder, Nancy S., *Introduction to the Jury at a Crossroad: The American Experience*, 78 Chi.-Kent L. Rev. 909 (2003).

Marks, Patricia D., *Magic in the Movies – Do Courtroom Scenes Have Real-Life Parallels?*, N.Y. St. B.J., Vol. 73, No. 5, 40 (June 2001).

Meyer, Philip N., *"Desperate for Love II": Further Reflections on the Interpenetration of Legal and Popular Storytelling in Closing Arguments to a Jury in a Complex Criminal Case*, 30 U.S.F. L. Rev. 931 (1996).

Nichols, Bill, *The Unseen Jury*, 30 U.S.F. L. Rev. 1055 (1996).

Chapter 8: Punishment

Colb, Sherry F., *Oil and Water: Why Retribution and Repentance Do Not Mix*, 22 Quinnipiac L. Rev. 59 (2003).

Dow, David R., *Fictional Documentaries and Truthful Fictions: The Death Penalty in Recent American Film*, 17 Const. Comment. 511 (2000).

Farber, Daniel A., *Stretching the Adjudicative Paradigm: Another Look at Judicial Policy Making and the Modern State*, 24 L. & Soc. Inquiry 751 (1999).

Foster, Teree E., I Want to Live! *Federal Judicial Values in Death Penalty Cases: Preservation of Rights or Punctuality of Execution?* 22 Okla. City L. Rev. 63 (1997).

Gutterman, Melvin, *"Failure to Communicate": The Reel Prison Experience*, 55 SMU L. Rev. 1515 (2002).

Haney, Craig, *The Social Context of Capital Murder: Social Histories and the Logic of Mitigation*, 35 Santa Clara L. Rev. 547 (1995).

Mezey, Naomi & Niles, Mark C., *Screening the Law: Ideology and Law in American Popular Culture*, 28 Colum. J. of Law & the Arts 91 (2005).

Sarat, Austin, *The Cultural Life of Capital Punishment: Responsibility and Representation in* Dead Man Walking *and* Last Dance, 11 Yale J. L. & Human. 153 (1999).

Shapiro, Carole, *Do or Die: Does* Dead Man Walking *Run?* 30 U.S.F. L. Rev. 1143 (1996).

Chapter 9: Tort Law

Abramson, Jeffrey, *The Jury and Popular Culture*, 50 DePaul L. Rev. 497 (2000).

Bender, Leslie, *Feminist (Re)torts: Thoughts on the Liability Crisis, Mass Torts, Power, and Responsibilities*, 1990 Duke L.J. 848.

Chase, Anthony, *Civil Action Cinema*, 1999 L. Rev. Mich. St. Univ. Detroit College L. 945 (1999).

Dixon, Helen G., et. al., *Public Reaction to the Portrayal of the Tobacco Industry in the Film* The Insider, 10 Tobacco Control 285 (2001).

Finley, Lucinda M., *Guarding the Gate to the Courthouse: How Trial Judges Are Using Their Evidentiary Screening Role to Remake Tort Causation Rules*, 49 DePaul L. Rev. 335 (1999).

Silbey, Jessica, *Patterns of Courtroom Justice*, 28 J. L. & Soc'y 97 (2001).

Acknowledgments

Vidmar, Neil, *The American Civil Jury for Aüslander (Foreigners)*, 13 Duke J. Comp. & Int'l L. 95 (2003).

Chapter 10: Criminal Law

Corcos, Christine Alice, *Legal Fictions: Irony, Storytelling, Truth, and Justice in the Modern Courtroom Drama*, 25 U. Ark. Little Rock L. Rev. 503 (2003).

Corcos, Christine Alice, *Prosecutors, Prejudices, and Justice: Observations on Presuming Innocence in Popular Culture and Law*, 34 U. Tol. L. Rev. 793 (2003).

Donovan, Jeremiah, *Some Off-the-Cuff Remarks About Lawyers as Storytellers*, 18 Vt. L. Rev. 751 (1994).

Elkins, James R., *Profane Lawyering*; 2001, http://www.wvu.edu/~lawfac/jelkins/mythweb99/profane.html.

Hyland, William G., Jr., *Creative Malpractice: The Cinematic Lawyer*, 9 Texas Rev. of Ent. and Sports L. 231 (2008).

Meade, Christopher J., *Reading Death Sentences: The Narrative Construction of Capital Punishment*, 71 N.Y.U. L. Rev. 732 (1996).

Meyer, Phillip N., *Are the Characters in a Death Penalty Brief Like the Characters in a Movie?* 32 Vt. L. Rev. 877 (2008).

Meyer, Philip N., *Convicts, Criminals, Prisoners, and Outlaws: A Course in Popular Storytelling*, 42 J. Leg. Educ. 129 (1992).

Meyer, Philip N., *Visual Literacy and the Legal Culture: Reading Film as Text in the Law School Setting*, 17 Leg. Stud. Forum 73 (1993).

Meyer, Philip N., *Why a Jury Trial Is More Like a Movie Than a Novel*, 28 J.L. & Soc'y 133 (2001).

Miller, Carolyn L., *"What a Waste: Beautiful, Sexy Gal, Hell of a Lawyer": Film and the Female Attorney*, 4 Colum. J. of Gender and L. 203 (1994).

Sherwin, Richard K., *Law Frames: Historical Truth and Narrative Necessity in a Criminal Case*, 47 Stan. L. Rev. 39 (1994).

Smith, Abbe, *Defending the Innocent*, 32 Conn. L. Rev. 485 (2000).

Yankah, Ekow N., *Good Guys and Bad Guys: Punishing Character, Equality, and the Irrelevance of Moral Character to Criminal Punishment*, 25 Cardozo L. Rev. 1019 (2004).

Chapter 11: Constitutional Law

Burton, Adam, *Pay No Attention to the Men Behind the Curtain: The Supreme Court, Popular Culture, and the Countermajoritarian Problem*, 73 UMKC L. Rev. 53 (2004).

Lain, Corinna Barrett, *Countermajoritarian Hero or Zero? Rethinking the Warren Court's Role in the Criminal Procedure Revolution*, 152 U. Pa. L. Rev. 1361 (2004).

Peterson, Jennifer, *Freedom of Expression as Liberal Fantasy: The Debate Over* The People vs. Larry Flynt, 29 Media, Culture, & Soc'y 377 (2007).

Ray, Laura Krugman, *Judicial Fictions: Images of Supreme Court Justices in the Novel, Drama, and Film*, 39 Ariz. L. Rev. 151 (1997).

Acknowledgments

Ray, Laura Krugman, *Laughter at the Court: The Supreme Court as a Source of Humor*, 79 So. Cal. L. Rev. 1397 (2006).

Chapter 12: Family Law

Asimow, Michael, *Divorce in the Movies: From the Hays Code to* Kramer vs. Kramer, 24 Leg. Stud. Forum 221 (2000).

Gil, Alexandra, *Great Expectations: Content Regulation in Film, Radio, and Television*, 2009 U. of Denv. Sports & Ent. Law J. 31.

Gillers, Stephen, *Taking* L.A. Law *More Seriously*, 98 Yale L.J. 1606 (1989).

Lurvy, Ira & Eiseman, Selise E., *Divorce Goes to the Movies*, 30 U.S.F. L. Rev. 1209 (1996).

Papke, David Ray, *Peace Between the Sexes: Law and Gender in* Kramer vs. Kramer, 30 U.S.F. L. Rev. 1199 (1996).

Perry, Twila L., *Transracial and International Adoption: Mothers, Hierarchy, Race, and Feminist Legal Theory*, 10 Yale J.L. & Feminism 101 (1998).

Chapter 13: Business Law

Baldassare, Michael A., *Cruella De Vil, Hades, and Ursula the Sea-Witch: How Disney Films Teach Our Children the Basics of Contract Law*, 48 Drake L. Rev. 333 (2000).

Griffith, Sean J., *Deal Protection Provisions in the Last Period of Play*, 71 Fordham L. Rev. 1899 (2001).

Huang, Peter H., *Dangers of Monetary Commensurability: A Psychological Game Model of Contagion*, 146 U. Pa. L. Rev. 1701 (1998).

Huang, Peter H., Kraviek, Kimberly D. & Partnoy, Frank, *Derivatives on TV: A Tale of Two Derivatives Debacles in Prime-time*, 4 Green Bay 2d 257 (2001).

Hurt, Christine, *Moral Hazard and the Initial Public Offering*, 26 Cardozo L. Rev. 711 (2005).

Malloy, Robin Paul, *Framing the Market: Representations of Meaning and Value in Law, Markets, and Culture*, 51 Buff. L. Rev. 1 (2003).

Stout, Lynn A., *The Mechanisms of Market Inefficiency: An Introduction to the New Finance*, 28 J. Corp. L. 635 (2003).

Stout, Lynn A., *On the Proper Motives of Corporate Directors (Or, Why You Don't Want to Invite Homo Economicus to Join Your Board)*, 28 Del. J. Corp. L. 1 (2003).

White, Barbara, *Conflicts in the Regulation of Hostile Business Takeovers in the United States and The European Union*, 9 Ius Gentium 161 (2003).

Chapter 14: International Law

Greenfield, Steve & Osborn, Guy, *Pulped Fiction? Cinematic Parables of (In)justice*, 30 U.S.F. L. Rev. 1181 (1996).

Luban, David, *On Dorfman's* Death and the Maiden, 10 Yale J.L. & Human. 115 (1998).

Roach, Kent & Trotter, Gary, *Miscarriages of Justice in the War Against Terror*, 109 Penn St. L. Rev. 967 (2005).

Shale, Suzanne, *The Conflicts of Law and the Character of Men: Writing* Reversal of

Acknowledgments

Fortune *and* Judgment at Nuremberg, 30 U.S.F. L. Rev. 991 (1996).

Part I

INTRODUCTION

Chapter 1

STUDYING LAW AND POPULAR CULTURE

A. FILMOGRAPHY

Anatomy of a Murder (1959)

A Few Good Men (1992)

Inherit the Wind (1960)

A Man for All Seasons (1966)

To Kill a Mockingbird (1962)

B. LAW-RELATED AMERICAN POPULAR CULTURE

Since the founding of the Republic, law, lawyers, and legal institutions have had special importance in America. In the early decades of the nineteenth century the citizenry not only rejected demands to throw off the English common law but also began developing what would become a huge statutory law. The legal profession grew rapidly, and lawyers became the leading figures in civic and political affairs. The Constitution, the nation's highest law, became an icon of the civil religion, and courtroom trials, either watched in person in county courthouses or followed in the urban penny press, were familiar rituals affording specific verdicts and judgments as well as larger lessons and meanings. When the French aristocrat Alexis de Tocqueville toured the United States at the request of his government in the 1830s, he was struck by the large roles played by lawyers and courts in Americans' daily lives and also by the way Americans, unlike his fellow Frenchmen, looked at the law with something resembling parental affection. "The spirit of the law, which is produced in the schools and courts of justice," de Tocqueville wrote, "gradually penetrates beyond their walls into the bosom of society, where it descends to the lowest classes, so that the whole people contracts the habits and tastes of the magistrate." Alexis de Tocqueville, *Democracy in America* 207-08 (1835; reprint, 1946).

Given the large role of law, lawyers, and legal institutions in American life, it is hardly surprising that law and legal themes became a part of cultural expression as well. The poet William Cullen Bryant, the essayist Richard Henry Dana, and the popular storyteller Washington Irving had early in their lives been lawyers before turning to literary pursuits. Legal themes found a place in selected pieces of their work, as did a bit of resentment regarding the authors' abandoned profession. *The*

Pioneers (1823), the first of James Fenimore Cooper's Leatherstocking novels, includes a book-long debate between champions of what we would today call natural law and legal positivism. In the decades immediately before the Civil War novels featuring heroic lawyers as well as conniving pettifoggers were common. The former tended to be hardworking Protestants who moved to the city to study and practice law and to fall in love and do good. The pettifoggers, meanwhile, stirred up litigation and duped even their own clients, but at least in most cases they received their just deserts.

Toward the end of the nineteenth century, law-related pop cultural products became staples of the rapidly developing modern culture industry. Committed to selling cultural works and experiences to mass audiences, the culture industry was vertically integrated and employed literally thousands of professional workers. Some have argued that the large number of cultural products made and distributed by the culture industry prefigured the even larger production and distribution of general consumer goods in the 1920s.

At first, the production and distribution of law-related popular culture was most likely to involve works in print and, in particular, law-related cheap fiction. The West Virginia lawyer Melville Davisson Post could have claimed to be the developer of the first law-related pop cultural product line. He was successful but unhappy practicing law in the 1890s in Wheeling and Grafton, and while trying to figure out what to do with his life, he began writing stories about a fictional lawyer named Randolph Mason. G.P. Putman's, a major publishing house, published one collection of the stories and then another as the public rose like fish to the bait.

Post's successes were far surpassed by two other early twentieth-century writers of law-related fiction — Arthur Train and Erle Stanley Gardner. Train, a Harvard Law School graduate and former New York City practitioner, published 87 stories about the fictional lawyer Ephraim Tutt in *The Saturday Evening Post*, the nation's most popular magazine. Beloved by middlebrow readers, the Tutt stories were also collected in volumes such as *Tut, Tut, Mr. Tutt* (1923), and Train even published a mock autobiography of Tutt, which was reviewed in the *Harvard Law Review.* Gardner was a disgruntled California practitioner who published his first two novels about the fictional Perry Mason in 1933. The public never seemed to tire of a lawyer who could dramatically free his innocent client and also identify the true perpetrator, and working on a ranch he called the "fiction factory," Gardner wrote a total of 82 Perry Mason novels.

In later decades, pop fiction about law and lawyers continued to appear, but law-related radio shows, movies, and television series joined published fiction in the pop cultural marketplace. The first national radio networks emerged in the 1920s, and during the so-called "Golden Age of Radio" in the 1930s and early 1940s, as much as forty percent of network radio programming was drama. Radio detectives of the era included not only the venerable Sherlock Holmes but also Nick Carter, Hercule Poirot, Ellery Queen, Sam Spade, and Nero Wolfe. Each episode of *Gangbusters*, a police procedural, started with an especially noisy salvo that spawned the expression "Coming on like Gangbusters." The most popular lawyer program was *Mr. District Attorney*, which aired weekly in thirty-minute episodes on NBC radio from 1939-51.

Law-related films were also immensely successful, especially after the technology for "talkies," which appeared in the late 1920s, enabled filmmakers to show lawyers doing what they sometimes do best — talking. The courtroom setting, meanwhile, was ideal for film. Producers could choose a courtroom for shooting or even build one on the set, and filming could take place with relatively fixed points of sound and light.

However, this does not mean one particular legal genre dominated the 1930s and '40s. Screenwriters adapted several of the Perry Mason novels for the silver screen, and even more popular were films featuring energetic, crime-stopping prosecutors. These films included *State's Attorney* (1932), in which a character played by John Barrymore overcame his reform school youth and prosecuted a leading mobster, and *Manhattan Melodrama* (1934), in which a district attorney played by William Powell is elected governor after successfully prosecuting a boyhood friend played by Clark Gable. John Barrymore won an Oscar for his portrayal of an alcoholic lawyer who defended his daughter's suitor in a murder trial in *A Free Soul* (1931). Barrymore also starred in *Counsellor At Law* (1933), the story of a man who rose from the Lower East Side to a palatial law office in the Empire State Building, only to find his world crashing down around him. The period even concluded with the delightful legal comedy *Adam's Rib* (1949), in which Spencer Tracy and Katharine Hepburn appear as husband-and-wife lawyers representing opposite sides in a trial for attempted murder.

While law-related Hollywood cinema of the 1930s and '40s was fascinating in a scrambled way, it was during the 1950s and early '60s that law-related Hollywood cinema reached its greatest heights. Films from the period included *12 Angry Men* (1957), *Witness for the Prosecution* (1957), *I Want to Live* (1958), *Anatomy of a Murder* (1959), *The Young Philadelphians* (1959), *Compulsion* (1959), *Inherit the Wind* (1960), *Judgment at Nuremberg* (1961), and *To Kill a Mockingbird* (1962). Enriched by superb writing, directing, and acting, most of these films were critical and popular successes, earning a raft of Oscar nominations and qualifying as some of the very best films of their period.

When network television programming began at the end of the 1940s, producers drew more heavily on radio than on the Hollywood movie studios for their stars and types of shows. Also, as was the case with radio, much of the earliest law-related television programming was performed live before a studio audience. The set was customarily a courtroom, and the drama took the form of a trial, usually with actors playing some, but not necessarily all, of the roles. In *They Stand Accused* (1949-52, 1954), for example, actors played defendants and witnesses, but Chicago attorney Charles Johnson was the judge. At the end of each trial, "jurors" chosen from the studio audience were asked to render a verdict. *Famous Jury Trials* (1949-52) reenacted actual trials and then used a jury verdict to reveal to viewers which version of the events suggested at trial was really accurate. These shows and a dozen like them reinforced the American confidence in courtroom trials and also, of course, buoyed the belief that truth and justice were achievable through legal institutions.

This particular type of live programming largely disappeared from prime-time television in the 1950s, as the networks settled instead on a weekly series featuring the exploits of an attractive fictional lawyer practicing on his own or perhaps with a partner. Erle Stanley Gardner, who had guided Perry Mason onto the printed page and disapprovingly watched the production of the Perry Mason films, now brought his hero to television. Portrayed by Raymond Burr, Perry Mason not only became television's first superstar lawyer but also could count dozens of colleagues in the fictional television bar. *The Defenders* (1961-65), starring E.G. Marshall and Robert Reid as father-and-son lawyers, was the most respected series, but lawyer dramas also included *The Law and Mr. Jones, Sam Benedict, The Trials of O'Brien, Judd for the Defense, Harrigan and Son, The Bold Ones, Owen Marshall*, and *Petrocelli*, to name only a handful. Americans found prime-time shows with lawyers tending to innocent clients and a justice system that worked to be soothing, escapist television fare.

In the present, law-related popular culture is a sprawling cultural smorgasbord. New types of stories about law, lawyers, and legal institutions have emerged, but many of the older types have also lived on, compounding into the present in updated formats. *Law & Order* (1990-2010), for example, lionized the work of prosecutors in ways reminiscent of radio shows and films in the 1930s. The series' twenty-year run was extraordinary, and District Attorney Jack McCoy, the series' star played by Sam Waterston, became America's most recognizable pop cultural lawyer.

The publication of fiction in cheap paperbacks and popular magazines such as *The Saturday Evening Post* ended in the post-Vietnam era, but starting in the 1980s lawyers-turned-writers such as John Grisham, Scott Turow, and Lisa Scottolini published dozens of best-selling novels about fictional lawyers and their cases. The covers and publicity for these novels emphasize the authors themselves more than the plots or even titles of individual works. Often lawyers in these novels are not so much heroic as they are flawed and complex human beings — everymen with law degrees.

With the exception of networks of small Christian stations, radio has for the most part stopped broadcasting fictional narratives, but Hollywood continues to produce large numbers of legal films. This body of popular culture is not as stirring as the law-related films of the late 1950s and early 1960s, but recent law-related cinema is nevertheless engaging and delightful. Films such as *A Few Good Men* (1992) and *Philadelphia* (1993) tell familiar tales of heroic defense counsel who win their cases and in the process heal themselves. Hollywood has included a significant number of women in the pop cultural bar in films such as *The Big Easy* (1987), *Suspect* (1987), *The Client* (1994), *I Am Sam* (2001), *High Crimes* (2002), *Two Weeks Notice* (2003), and *The Exorcism of Emily Rose* (2005). Hollywood has also brought fictionalized versions of actual cases to the local cineplex, as in *The Accused* (1988), *A Civil Action* (1999), and *Erin Brockovich* (2000), and legal comedies have included *My Cousin Vinny* (1992), *Jury Duty* (1995), and *Legally Blonde* (2001). Sometimes these comedies ridicule lawyers, as in *Liar Liar* (1997), an extended joke about how difficult it is for lawyers to tell the truth.

Legal shows also continue to roll off television's assembly lines. A show such as *Matlock* (1986-95) was a throwback, albeit a popular one, to the heroic independent lawyer shows of the 1950s, but new types of shows have also appeared. The exemplar for modern-day prime-time evening programming is *L.A. Law* (1986-94).

Each episode included courtroom scenes, but the heroic trial work of a single lawyer was not crucial to the show's success. Instead, a group of lawyers working in a bureaucratic and hierarchical setting were our protagonists, and their personal dilemmas and relationships with one another were as important as their legal cases. *The Practice* (1997-2004) struck some as a grimier, east-coast version of the show, and *The Good Wife* (2009-present) added an interesting twist by featuring a betrayed wife rebuilding her legal career. Other embodiments of the type such as *Ally McBeal* (1997-2002) and *Boston Legal* (2004-08) strove for comedic effect and sometimes displayed large amounts of cynicism. On daytime television of the present viewers can watch syndicated shows featuring resourceful jurists resolving disputes in something resembling small claims courts. *The People's Court* with the grandfatherly Judge Joseph Wapner launched the modern genre in the 1980s, but the biggest star of the present is Judge Judith Sheindlin of *Judge Judy.* Her caustic, insulting manner appeals to millions of viewers and is also the model to which a dozen other ersatz day-time television judges aspire.

For Americans in all walks of life, popular works of fiction, film, and television revolving around law, lawyers, and legal themes have for decades been sources of delight and edification. Those who characterize the United States as the most legalistic nation in the world should to some extent be prepared to base that claim on not only the number of American laws and importance of American legal institutions but also the amount, variety, and popularity of law-related popular culture. This popular culture is not simply a "picture" of American life, but has become a powerful force in the shaping of Americans' understanding of and attitudes about law. It seeps into our consciousnesses. It affects what Americans and even foreign consumers expect from their legal institutions and governments. For law students, lawyers, and judges, law-related American popular culture holds special potential for education and provides a huge and continuing opportunity for critical reflection.

NOTES & QUESTIONS

1.   Innumerable stories about law, lawyers, and legal institutions appear in several of our most important varieties of popular culture — print, film, and television. To what extent does the medium dictate the type of law-related story that can be told and the manner in which it is told? What is the potential for law-related narrative in such other varieties of popular culture as the comics, recorded music, and video games?

2.   Almost from the beginning, the various branches of the culture industry have been interconnected. As the industry's adaptations of the famous Scopes trial from 1925 suggest, a pop cultural narrative that catches the public's eye in one medium is likely to be reproduced in a second and a third. In the actual trial, John Scopes, a science teacher from Dayton, Tennessee, was prosecuted for violating the state's ban on teaching evolutionary theory in the public schools. The American Civil Liberties Union took up Scopes' cause, and the famed litigator Clarence Darrow became his defense counsel. Protestant fundamentalists supported Tennessee's statute, and famous politician and former Secretary of State William Jennings Bryan joined the prosecution. The media cast the trial as the ultimate battle

between science and religion, and hundreds of reporters descended on the small Tennessee courtroom. The trial was the first to be broadcast nationally on radio. Later, in fictionalized form, the trial became *Inherit the Wind*, a highly successful Broadway play of 1955 by Jerome Lawrence and Robert E. Lee. The play, in turn, was adapted in 1960 for the equally successful United Artists film of the same name starring Spencer Tracy, Fredric Marsh, and Gene Kelly. The film was then remade with different casts in 1965, 1988, and 1999.

Some cultural studies scholars use the term "transmogrification" for the conversion of a work from one medium to another. A novel might have the same title as its film adaptation, but the works are not really the same. It might even be unfair to judge transmogrified works against one another. Why does the culture industry routinely reproduce a law-related pop cultural work successful in one medium in other media? What does this process underscore about the nature of popular culture?

3.   The contemporary United States is a polyglot, postmodern nation. It lacks the socio-cultural coherence of a traditional society. To what extent must the existence of different American ethnic, racial, and regional subcultures be taken into consideration in gauging the meaning, reception, and popularity of law-related pop cultural works? Can we speak of one American popular culture or should we recognize a family of popular cultures?

C. GOALS IN THE STUDY OF LAW AND POPULAR CULTURE

As an emerging area of inquiry, the formal study of law and popular culture does not insist or rely on a particular approach. Quite the contrary, the study of law and popular culture is eclectic in the best sense of that term. Those who teach, write, and study in the area have a wide range of styles, methods, and disciplines. Subsequent chapters will exemplify this academic eclecticism, but some of the most common goals in the study of law and popular culture can be underscored at the outset.

1. Points of Law and Practice Skills

The most venerable use of law-related popular culture in legal education is as an illustration of a legal rule or of a practice skill. The obscure rhythms of the Rule against Perpetuities, for example, might be illustrated by screening selected scenes from *Body Heat* (1981), a film in which William Hurt plays a neglectful lawyer overcome by his passions. Or one could use the scene in *The Verdict* (1982) in which a defense attorney played by James Mason prepares an anesthesiologist for testimony as an illustration for pretrial witness preparation. Illustrations from films can be especially effective in an era in which all students and almost all instructors are as comfortable with and engaged by visual presentations as they are with written texts.

In the following excerpt Professor Paul Bergman discusses why he likes to use film clips while teaching Evidence. He also goes on to highlight three scenes from the classic *Anatomy of a Murder* (1959) and points to the ways the scenes may be used to illustrate points of evidence law.

TEACHING EVIDENCE THE "REEL" WAY
Paul Bergman
21 Quinnipiac Law Review 973 (2003)

Rather than analyzing the social meaning of law in film, the discussion below considers the effective classroom use of scenes from law-related films in an Evidence course. Lawyers and courtroom trials have been fodder for countless films, and scenes from such films can serve as excellent texts for illustrating evidentiary doctrine and presenting problems for classroom analysis. Of course, films almost always dramatize or even parody actual legal relationships and proceedings. However, this increases students' engagement with the texts without detracting from the clips' usefulness as teaching devices. . . .

Perhaps the strongest rationale for using film clips is that they are an efficient and involving method of providing context for the application of evidence rules. Teaching Evidence to students who lack understanding of the trial process is like teaching "the crawl" to someone who has no idea what a swimming pool or other body of water looks like. Film clips depict problems and process simultaneously and thus provide a level of understanding that the reading of appellate case opinions does not. Moreover, film clips help train students' ears, as well as their eyes, and thereby promote students' abilities to recognize evidentiary issues as they arrive in the oral courtroom process. . . .

Character Evidence: Impeachment with Prior Acts and Convictions

Background: Character evidence is potentially admissible to attack a witness' credibility. Subject to judicial discretion, a cross-examiner can ask questions about misdeeds that bear on truthfulness but did not result in a conviction, but cannot offer extrinsic evidence of the misdeeds if the witness denies their occurrence. Prior convictions can be admissible to impeach a witness' credibility, and if they involve crimes of dishonesty, they are automatically admissible.

Clip: Anatomy of a Murder — Lt. Manion is charged with murdering Barney Quill. Manion admits killing Quill but claims that he was temporarily insane (acted under an uncontrollable "irresistible impulse") after learning that Quill had raped and beaten Manion's wife. The prosecutor calls a jailhouse snitch, who testifies that Manion had told him that he (Manion) had deceived the lawyer and the jury and intended to beat up his wife after being acquitted of murder. On cross, the defense attorney attacks the snitch's testimony with a variety of misdeeds, including the snitch's having served three prison terms for larceny. The witness had also been in jail on charges of indecent exposure, window peeping, perjury, and disorderly conduct.

Analysis: The prison sentences presumably followed felony convictions. Larceny is a crime involving dishonesty and thus is automatically admissible. Questioning and evidence regarding the other felony convictions is admissible subject to judicial discretion. The snitch's jail time could have been the result either of simple arrest or of conviction of misdemeanors. If the snitch had been convicted of perjury, that too is automatically admissible regardless of whether it constituted a felony or a misdemeanor. The questions referring to arrests or convictions for indecent exposure, window peeping, and disorderly conduct are improper. Arrests may not be inquired into at all, and most of the acts themselves, or evenconvictions, would be improper because the acts do not involve dishonesty. Subject to judicial discretion, however, the defense attorney could cross-examine about the perjury incident even if it did not result in a conviction, since perjury involves dishonesty.

Defense Psychiatrists and the Ultimate Opinion Rule

Background: The Federal Rules of Evidence abolished the common law rule that forbade expert opinion testimony concerning a dispute's "ultimate issue." However, Congress resurrected the limitation with respect to expert witnesses testifying to criminal defendants' mental states. Expert testimony as to a criminal defendant's mental condition that constitutes an element of a crime or a defense is inadmissible.

Clip: Anatomy of a Murder — To support Lt. Manion's claim that he was temporarily insane when he shot and killed Barney Quill, the defense presents an army psychiatrist who examined Manion after the shooting. The psychiatrist testifies that Manion was "temporarily insane" at the time of the shooting. He also testifies that Manion suffered from "dissociative reaction" at the time of the shooting, a popular term for which is "irresistible impulse."

Analysis: Despite the limitation in FRE 704(b), criminal defendants are often able to offer a significant amount of expert testimony concerning their mental states. To some extent, what the rule forbids is crassness, meaning that a defendant cannot offer expert testimony that parrots the exact legal language that constitutes a charge or a defense. Under this interpretation, the rule would probably render improper the psychiatrist's testimony that Manion was temporarily insane. A broader interpretation of the rule might also prevent the doctor from testifying that "Manion was under the influence of dissociative reaction at the moment of the shooting." However, the doctor could testify that Manion suffered from dissociative reaction, because that is a medical diagnosis and not a legal judgment. The doctor could also testify that irresistible impulse is a popular name for dissociative reaction.

The Rape Shield Law

Background: Reversing many years of common law practice, the rape shield rule bars character evidence concerning the prior sexual behavior of a sexual assault victim. The topic obviously must be dealt with sensitively in the classroom. Appellate court opinions, problems, and film clips should be selected with regard to the potential feelings and past experiences of students, and classroom discussions should be thorough but respectful.

Clip: Anatomy of a Murder — The prosecution's factual theory is that the victim, Barney Quill, did not rape Mrs. Manion; rather, they were lovers. Manion found out about the affair and killed Quill in a jealous rage. Testifying on direct examination, Mrs. Manion denies that she had an affair with Quill and insists that Quill raped her.

The scene for analysis depicts part of the prosecutor's cross-examination. He elicits evidence from Mrs. Manion that she had previously been married, that she married Manion three days after her divorce was final (defense counsel volunteers this information) and suggests, therefore, that she must have known Manion before her divorce.

Analysis: The scene offers students an opportunity to consider a number of less-than-obvious rape shield issues. The prosecutor does not refer to any overt sexual behavior by Mrs. Manion; rather, he asks about her divorce and when she began dating Lt. Manion. However, FRE 412 refers broadly to "other sexual behavior," and the context in which the questions are asked suggests that the prosecutor is attacking Mrs. Manion's sexual character. The subtle suggestion is that she cheated on her first husband, and therefore may have been cheating on Manion. Nevertheless, the questions would probably not be barred by FRE 412. By its terms, FRE 412 applies only in proceedings "involving alleged sexual misconduct." As this is a murder trial, it seemingly does not involve sexual misconduct. If it did, however, Mrs. Manion would be protected even though she is not the complaining witness because the rape shield rule protects "any alleged victim." . . .

NOTES & QUESTIONS

1. Bergman acknowledges that law-related films "almost always dramatize or even parody actual legal relationships and proceedings," but he argues that this does not detract from the usefulness of the films as teaching devices. Do you agree? What are the pitfalls in using scenes from dramatic Hollywood films to illustrate either points of law or practice skills?

2. While teaching law and film courses at the University of Connecticut School of Law and at Vermont Law School, Professor Philip N. Meyer was delighted with his students' visual literacy. In an article excerpted in Chapter 10 of this text concerning criminal law and popular culture, Meyer reported, "Participants revealed a heightened and stunning visual sophistication and acuity that I had not anticipated." Philip N. Meyer, *Visual Literacy and the Legal Culture: Reading Film in the Law School Setting*, 17 Legal Studies Forum 73, 92 (1993). However, he also found that detachment, cynicism, and even anger were part of his students' visual literacy. He speculated that this attitude was a product of the students' immersion in a law school culture that devalued narrative and also their leeriness of the visual and aural stories bombarding them in advertising, television, radio, politics, and sound-byte news. "Although extremely thoughtful and perceptive, they were sensitive to manipulation and tended to disbelieve their eyes and ears." *Id.,* 83.

2. Inaccuracies and Misrepresentations of Law and Legal Institutions

In the late 1980s a small group of scholars began to call for more sustained and systematic considerations of the relationships between law and popular culture. In a groundbreaking essay, law professor Anthony Chase provided what he called "a primitive accumulation" of law-related works in fiction television, nonfiction television, advertising, soap operas, and pop music. *See* Anthony Chase, *Toward a*

Legal Theory of Popular Culture, 1986 Wisconsin Law Review 527. In another important article Chase argued forcefully that a contemplation of popular culture could help us develop "a sharper focus on what Americans really think about law and how the system within which they operate really works." *Lawyers and Popular Culture*, 1986 American Bar Foundation Research Journal 281, 300.

For Chase and other early contributors to the study of law and popular culture, the question of popular culture's reliability and accuracy vis-à-vis the law surfaced. Popular culture, of course, does not hold a mirror up to actual law, lawyers, and legal institutions. Those who write novels, direct films, and produce television shows have more on their minds than being precisely faithful to the technicalities of the law and the requirements of legal proceedings. In general, the goal is the creation of engaging drama that will attract and hold readers and viewers. But still, if popular culture is as influential in shaping popular attitudes as many think, one should at least be mindful of the differences between law, legal proceedings, and legal institutions in popular culture and in real life.

In the following excerpt Professor David Ray Papke discusses the ways in which pop cultural courtroom trials differ from actual ones. Papke's observations rely heavily on interviews with a half dozen Indiana trial court judges.

THE AMERICAN COURTROOM TRIAL: POP CULTURE, COURTHOUSE REALITIES, AND THE DREAM WORLD OF JUSTICE
David Ray Papke
40 South Texas Law Review 919 (1999)

Some judges and trial lawyers find it virtually impossible to enjoy pop cultural trials because of their lack of correspondence to what the judges and lawyers experience in actual courtrooms. Their complaints are well taken, and the differences between pop cultural and real-life trials merit underscoring.

For starters, we of course have to acknowledge what most movies, television series, and novels do not mention: the great majority of cases never get to trial. Charges are dropped, sentences are threatened, and pleas are bargained. Defendants, after all, are not necessarily well-heeled or resourceful. In most urban areas, over seventy-five percent of the defendants are indigent.

In the small minority of cases that actually get to trial, we do not encounter the punchy, provocative opening statements so typical of pop culture. On television or in the movies, the opening statement is a powerful prologue or an extended first act, but in the real world lawyers are quite economical. They disdain large civic messages in favor of simply setting out a fact or two and identifying the legal issues.

As for the presentation of evidence and both examination and cross-examination, things are much less dramatic than in the pop cultural courtroom. Real-world attorneys do like visuals when it comes to evidence, and autopsy photos are a favorite in murder trials. But frequently physical evidence is minimal. Defense counsel, most of whom are public defenders, are particularly strapped when it comes to finding or presenting useful evidence. Their caseloads and budgets rarely allow for the large-scale utilization of investigators.

Side-bar conferences among the judge and attorneys are also rare. Usually important evidentiary questions are settled through motions in limine or through pre-trial compromise, and judges in general do not like to slow down their proceedings to sort out evidentiary or procedural matters. Little tête-à-têtes immediately before the bench are difficult because lawyers seem congenitally unable to speak in a soft voice. Excusing the jurors and adjourning to chambers, meanwhile, is risky business. The lawyers can make their way to chambers, but jurors have the distressing habit of disappearing into restrooms, wandering off, and even on occasion going home.

When people take the stand in actual trials, attorneys rarely grill them, and the attorneys also do not pepper the air with objections. Experienced practitioners appreciate that they have only a "limited good will account" with the jury. Jurors do not want lots of interruptions, and if the lawyer keeps objecting, they begin to wonder what he or she is hiding.

While in pop culture almost every witness has a critical piece of the story, real witnesses are often forgetful, boring, or unprepared. People on the stand might cry, but they do not break down, offer dramatic revelations, or confess. The most effective testimony probably comes from police officers, and this is another reason that prosecutors generally have an advantage over defense counsel. Police arrest with an eye to conviction, and in some districts their formal training includes lessons on how to testify.

The majority of defendants do not take the stand. Jurors would like to hear from the defendant, and some defendants would like to get on the stand because they are cocky enough to think they can put one over on people. But defense counsel are justifiably leery. If a defendant takes the stand, a prior record can be revealed, and in addition, defendants tend not to make good witnesses. As noted, most are poor. They also tend to be poorly educated and relatively inarticulate. These factors in turn create "believability" problems.

The roughly contemporaneous rape trials of William Kennedy Smith and Mike Tyson illustrate the point. The former — an atypical defendant — was well groomed and articulate. He took the stand and convinced the jury that he could not possibly rape anyone. Tyson is a different package and, alas, more similar to the typical defendant. When his attorneys made the mistake of putting him on the stand, Tyson's crude, sexist, uneducated world view convinced the jury that he had in fact raped someone.

Closing arguments are important in actual trials, and jurors listen intently to them. Why? It is not because the case is still undecided, as it almost always is at the time of a pop cultural closing. One theory is that even though most jurors have already made up their minds as to guilt or innocence, they are starting to collect their thoughts for the deliberations right around the corner. They are culling the closings for what they think they will need in the jury deliberation room.

In many cases the jurors hear only limited closing arguments. In Indiana, for example, closing arguments have time limits. A lawyer may request more time if he or she wishes, but the maximum time available is presumed to be twenty minutes unless the trial has gone into a second day. The closings, regardless of length, are rarely as stirring as they are on television or in the movies. A surprising number of trial lawyers are at best average speakers, and many cling desperately to their notepads during closing arguments.

As for what happens in the jury room, this is a bit of a mystery. It appears that despite the jadedness and cynicism of contemporary life, Americans still take jury duty very seriously. They may not welcome jury duty, but when they serve on a jury, they are earnest and do their best. In criminal trials the jury's "best" usually takes the form of a conviction. In most urban areas the conviction rate is between eighty-five and ninety percent. One would never guess it from prime-time television, Hollywood movies, or popular novels. Not even a couple of popular prosecutor series on prime time have led to an overall pop cultural conviction rate of any magnitude.

How do the judges perceive the real-life courtroom trial as a whole? While expressing amazement at what they see in their courtrooms, real-life judges also acknowledge that they often have significant managerial responsibilities. Trials do not necessarily have fully shaped story lines. Inconsequential matters surface. We see mistakes in procedure, displays of pettiness, and frequent delays. Sometimes observers feel as if they have walked through the bureaucratic looking glass, hardly the reaction of someone who has just enjoyed a gripping pop cultural courtroom drama. . . .

NOTES

1. Courtroom trials are so ubiquitous in law-related pop culture that the unreflective reader or viewer might erroneously assume that virtually all lawyers are litigators. In fact, less than ten percent of all lawyers routinely litigate.

2. The distinguished cultural studies scholar Fredric Jameson has said of pop songs that you never really hear them for the first time. Instead, you hear them as echoes and variations of countless other similar songs. *See* Fredric Jameson, *Signatures of the Visible* 20 (1990). Viewers of films and television shows with courtroom trials may in a sense never really see the pop cultural courtroom trial for the first time. Viewers may not know the verdict in advance, but they are familiar with the prototypical setting, participants, and process.

3. Ethics and Morality

Many men and women go to law school hoping that a law degree will help them build a better world, but a smaller number graduate with those same dreams. Family obligations begin to develop. Loan indebtedness mounts. And, some would say, simple maturity weans the law student from naïve and idealistic aspirations.

As the second chapter of this text concerning legal education in popular culture indicates, legal education itself may play a role in this transformation. While one might expect questions of what is ethical and moral would surface frequently in law school, this tends not to be the pattern. Individual lessons and even whole courses and seminars focus on ethical and moral concerns, but legal education in general stresses rules posited by courts and legislatures, considers corollaries and exceptions to those rules, and sometimes addresses relevant policy concerns.

Popular culture and especially film afford an opportunity to make the study of ethics and morality a larger part of legal education. Law-related films, after all, are rarely about the laws themselves. More commonly, these films concern individual struggles for justice through, in proximity to, or despite law and legal institutions. These are the narratives that engage consumers of law-related film and law-related popular culture. In the following essay posted on the "Picturing Justice" website, University of San Francisco law professor John Denvir discusses using film to counter legal education's procedural bias, emphasis on craft skills, and general amoral relativism.

WHAT MOVIES TEACH LAW STUDENTS
John Denvir
Picturing Justice (http://www.usfca.edu/pj)

Perhaps it's time to ask exactly what the study of film adds to the student's educational experience that the traditional curriculum lacks. First, I think we have to admit that films about lawyers do not give a very accurate picture of how lawyers spend their days. . . . Movies and television take a great deal of artistic license with procedural rules, thereby diluting any claim that these fictions show students how law actually plays out in a courtroom.

But even if we can't claim verisimilitude for lawyer films and have to confess that lawyer films tend to oversimplify messy reality in their pursuit of a clear battle between good and evil, I think we can still persuasively argue that the study of movies provides an important antidote to the excessively amoral "professional" model of lawyering that infects the rest of the curriculum.

If the typical lawyer movie highlights the human desire for a "just" result with little interest in procedural niceties, the professional model concerns itself primarily with procedures. It assumes that procedural justice will yield substantive justice, but this assumption ignores the fact that when the legal resources needed to work the system are not allocated on a basis even approaching equality, injustice is often the result. Procedural justice might yield justice in a society in which all citizens had equal access to the top-flight lawyers, but this necessary condition is clearly not present in even our most wealthy societies. For instance, in *A Civil Action*, the plaintiffs fail in their suit against two large companies who allegedly have dumped toxins into the town's drinking water not because they had the lesser case in law and fact, but because the defendants had the larger bankroll.

A second element of the professional model is related to this procedural bias; it holds that we must put our faith in the procedures because there are simply no substantively "right" answers in difficult cases, only answers which favor plaintiff or defendant.

Convincing law students of the truth of the "no truth" thesis seems to be one of the major goals of the first year law school curriculum. Students must abandon "fuzzy" thinking and accept that truth and justice are chimeras. Here's how one law student put it: "I made certain naïve emotional and political arguments before law school that I no longer buy into. Part of me feels, well, there are certain things that are just right and wrong and then there's another part of me that says, well, wait a minute, things aren't that simple in the real world and you really can't go around making silly emotional arguments about what's right and wrong."

But the fact that truth is sometimes difficult to determine does not mean that there is no truth. Nor does it mean that all resolutions of a dispute have an equal claim to the adjective "just." The primary goal of a legal system should be to design systems that allow the true facts to emerge in complicated situations.

Worse yet, students are led to believe that their earlier faith in "emotional arguments" is a sign of intellectual immaturity and that adoption of the value-free professional model is a form of personal progress. I would suggest that (again to use the facts in *A Civil Action* as an example) whether or not the defendant corporations polluted the water that the plaintiffs drank is a factual question to which a true answer can be found. And if true, the related question of whether and how much compensation the plaintiffs should receive from the defendant corporations is a question of justice as well as law. And finally, acknowledging an emotional dimension to the assignment of proper legal responsibility to the defendants for their actions is not a sign of intellectual immaturity; instead it is evidence of a richer humanity.

A third element of the professional model is its definition of "good" and "bad" lawyering solely in terms of craft skills. Since law is a series of preset procedures in which plaintiff and defendant wage a form of warfare, and since there is no right answer to the issues they contest, a good lawyer is not a hero who obtains justice, but rather an expert who works the procedures to yield a result favorable to his client. The professional model pictures lawyers operating in a morally flattened universe in which craft values dominate. Once again using *A Civil Action* as an example, the professional model would argue that Jerome Facher (Robert Duvall), who keeps relevant evidence hurtful to his client away from the jury, is the "good" lawyer. Perhaps we need to broaden our definition of the "good."

I don't want to be seen as merely trashing the professional model; it has its virtues. Law students need to learn how to think through problems methodically, not just rushing to embrace emotionally appealing conclusions. But I do think it gives an unduly amoral view of the lawyer's role, one which unnecessarily subverts the idealism that brings many students to choose law as a career in the first place.

The study of lawyer films, even unrealistic lawyer films, therefore can provide an important supplement to the curriculum by teaching some important lessons. The most important lesson is that justice counts. The very quantity of "law" films demonstrates that the human appetite for justice is just as strong as our appetites for power and sex.

Good lawyer films, like *To Kill a Mockingbird* and *A Civil Action*, also teach a second important lesson: the practice of law is fraught with ethical consequence. We can still debate today whether Atticus Finch failed his client in submitting his fate to a racist state court jury instead of seeking the aid of the federal court. So too the ethical dilemmas facing Jan Schlictman, the lawyer who represents the families harmed by toxic water, are worthy of our deepest consideration. Schlictman comes in with a simple goal — to get as large a fee as possible with as little risk as possible. Yet slowly he discovers he wants more; he wants to see justice done even though it's not exactly clear what that concept means in this context. He finds himself in a quandary. If he "takes the money and runs" as he originally planned, he is no more than the "ambulance chaser" the defense lawyers think him. But if he proceeds with the case, he puts his clients, his partners, and himself at financial risk. It's not easy for Schlictman or the viewer to balance these conflicting considerations, especially since they don't calibrate on the same measure, but I think discussion of a movie like *A Civil Action* can teach students that some of the most challenging parts of being a lawyer start just where the professional model leaves off.

NOTES & QUESTIONS

1. How might a defender of traditional legal education argue in favor of the emphasis on procedure and craft that Denvir criticizes? What are the dangers of bringing ethics and morality into legal education?

2. Films can be used in various ways to bring considerations of ethics and morality into the law school discussion. Most obviously, dozens of films raise controversial issues and go on to explore in dramatic form the legal system's response. *Erin Brockovich* (2000), for example, might be used to raise questions of environmental destruction and corporate greed. *Philadelphia* (1993) is a moving critique of homophobia and discrimination because of sexual orientation.

4. Respect for the Rule of Law

Legal education not only exposes students to laws and legal procedures but also encourages them to develop a respect for the rule of law. Neutral laws, the argument goes, can and should be applied fairly to individual controversies in order to achieve justice. Surely such an approach to social ordering is better than any rule by individuals or groups.

Popular culture includes stirring, heroic figures who live by this credo, sometimes with great cost to themselves. *A Man for All Seasons* (1966) cinematically tells the story of Sir Thomas More. Paul Scofield, the film's star, won the Oscar for Best Actor, and the film also won Oscars for Best Picture, Screenplay Director, and Cinematography.

Proud to be both "a lawyer and a lawyer's son," More was the most prominent legal figure of early sixteenth-century England. While presiding in the chancery courts, he succeeded in clearing the docket and also distinguished himself by refusing to accept bribes. Early in the film More's son-in-law argues that the Devil should not be protected by due process, but More's response underscores his belief in a rule of law. "The country's planted thick with laws from coast to coast," More says, "and if you cut them down . . . d'you really think you could stand upright in the winds that would blow then?" Surely, More concludes, we would serve our own interests by giving even the Devil due process.

The later portions of the film portray More's conflict with King Henry VIII. The latter renounced papal authority and declared himself head of the Church of England in part because he wanted to divorce his barren wife and marry Anne Boleyn. More refused to take an oath to the King's authority or to endorse his actions. After a trial for high treason, More was convicted and beheaded. Sham trials, the film invites us to conclude, violate our treasured heritage of achieving justice through a rule of law.

In the following excerpt Professor Kenneth Wagner discusses the way the film explores important jurisprudential issues.

A MAN FOR ALL SEASONS
Kenneth Wagner
Picturing Justice (http://www.usfca.edu/pj)

More's refusal to sign the oath brings up the difference between civil disobedience and conscientious objection as drawn by John Rawls. Civil disobedience for Rawls is a form of debate, a non-violent action aimed at the public and guided by political principles. Change is the central point. Rawls differentiates this from conscientious objection, which is the non-compliance with laws one sees as immoral. Conscientious objection is not meant to change the political sphere; it is just a decision to risk punishment rather than violate one's moral principles. The character of More certainly falls into the category of conscientious objector. He does not use his position to rail against the King's oath; he does not counsel others on the immorality of the oath itself (though certainly this is in part to defend himself through silence). Instead, he refers to himself as a loyal subject to the King who simply will not swear to the oath (he does not even say that by not swearing we should read into his silence disapproval of the oath).

Rawls defends civil disobedience by stating that it acts as a vigilant police on the laws of society, constantly forcing us to examine our laws and measure them by the yardstick of justice. Conscientious objection on the other hand is a personal issue; it is only morally permissible if the harm caused by non-compliance is outweighed by the correctness of the personal principle invoked in conscientious objection. What is the harm that More's refusal could possibly cause? The movie actually hints at such harm when at the beginning Cardinal Woolsey defends his "flexibility" on Church law in granting the King a divorce by pointing to the possible civil strife that could follow an heir-less sovereign. In this context, More's refusal could be a morally impermissible act.

This actually brings up two other issues of legal philosophy thrust upon us by the film. More's refusal to take the oath despite the consequences to himself, his family, and his realm constitutes a form of deontological ethics. According to deontology, some acts are inherently immoral despite the consequences that follow. Thus, the philosopher Immanuel Kant in his famed categorical imperative stated that it was wrong to tell a lie, even in the case of whether one should lie to a murderer who was stalking his victim hidden in a nearby closet. Cardinal Woolsey represents another view, that of the consequentialist. He admonished More to "come down to earth" when More refused to change his position even when warned of the strife that could follow his defiance. In a similar vein, Karl Marx admonished those who clung to an abstract and "neutral" rule of law that had negative consequences on the poor and oppressed.

More's refusal also invokes the debate between positive and natural law. When his soon to be son-in-law, a political radical, argues that law must be made malleable to the interests of justice, More launches into a long defense of the importance of "man's laws." . . . More's speech invokes the theorists of positive law such as John Austin who maintained that man-made law, the order of the sovereign, is all the law there is. Ironically, it is More who is later caught up in the very positive law he defended, and in response he speaks of his duty to his soul. This appeal to God's laws invokes the perpetual counterarguments of natural law theorists who hold that positive law can and should be measured by a "higher" Law of Nature. The King's law has the power to execute More, but does it have the authority?

One of the last striking things about this film may be a much-overlooked feature. Many viewers of the film will likely pessimistically comment on the trumped up [*sic*] nature of the prosecution of More played out brilliantly at the end of the film. However, such pessimism may be unwarranted. More's knowledge of law enables him to conduct a legal strategy based on the precedent that silence on an issue does not necessarily imply disapproval of the King's position (which would then warrant High Treason). In his trial More is given a jury (though one surely bullied by the Crown, as in the scene where the prosecutor declares that surely no break for jury deliberations is necessary and so the verdict is immediately rendered), an account of the charges against him, and the right to defend himself (including cross-examination of witnesses). It is only because of the distortion of evidence (the implication that More took a bribe that he clearly did not) and the testimony of a false witness that More is ultimately convicted. The question of course remains, does this show the advanced state of English rights of the accused at this ancient state, or does it point to the more unsettling conclusion that even abstract legal safeguards cannot protect one when prosecutorial dishonesty rears its ugly head?

NOTES & QUESTIONS

1. *A Man for All Seasons* implies that proceedings more faithful to the rule of law would have been desirable in More's case. To what extent is it ever possible to insulate the rule of law from dishonesty and political bias?

2. An American cinematic hero who embodies a deep respect for the rule of law is Atticus Finch. The novelist Harper Lee modeled the character on A.C. Lee, her father and a lawyer in Monroeville, Alabama. *To Kill a Mockingbird*, her novel featuring Atticus Finch, won the Pulitzer Prize for fiction in 1961, and in the next year Hollywood's adaptation of the novel was honored at Oscar time. Horton Foote won the Academy Award for Best Screenplay, and Gregory Peck won the Academy Award for Best Actor for his portrayal of Atticus Finch. Few scenes in cinematic history are as much praised as those featuring Peck's Atticus Finch defending the unjustly charged African American Tom Robinson in the midst of a racist southern community. Many who came of age in the late 1950s and early 1960s point to Atticus Finch as an inspiration and as a reason they decided to become lawyers.

Does Atticus Finch have any flaws? Might his moral code, professional ethics, and understanding of the rule of law be critiqued? In the following excerpt Professor Monroe H. Freedman refers to both the original novel and the film adaptation. He characterizes Finch's words of wisdom for his children after they face down a lynch mob as fatuous.

ATTICUS FINCH — RIGHT AND WRONG
Monroe H. Freedman
45 Alabama Law Review 404 (1994)

Consider, then, the moral truth that he tells to the children when they experience the lynch mob outside the jail. Walter Cunningham, a leader of the mob, is "basically a good man," he teaches them, "he just has his blind spots along with the rest of us." It just happens that Cunningham's blind spot (along with the rest of us?) is a homicidal hatred of black people. And when Jem replies, with the innocent wisdom of a child, that attempted murder is not just a "blind spot," Finch condescendingly explains to him: "[S]on, you'll understand folks a little better when you're older. A mob's always made of people, no matter what. Mr. Cunningham was part of a mob last night, but he was still a man."

What are we to make of this fatuousness? That a lynch mob is not a lynch mob because it's "made up of people"? That because Cunningham is "still a man," he has no moral responsibility for attempted murder? Who does have moral (and legal) responsibility for a wrongful action if not the person who commits the wrong?

One of the charges I have faced for past criticisms of Atticus Finch is "presentism." This clumsy neologism is meant to express the idea that it is unfair to hold someone in an earlier time to moral standards that we recognize today. Lest anyone miss the point, this contention is derived from cultural relativism. This is a philosophy that rejects the idea that there are any moral values that are absolute (or, at least, prima facie) and eternal. Instead, morality is equated with the notions of right and wrong that are recognized in the culture of a particular time and place. Slavery? Apartheid? Lynching? Sacrificing babies? Well, the cultural relativist says, we might not approve, but who are we to judge the moral standards of people in another time or place?

So let me declare myself. I do believe that there are prima facie principles of right and wrong (which can be called Natural Law), which each of us is capable of recognizing by the use of experience, intellect, and conscience. There may not be many such principles of right and wrong, but . . . the attempted lynching of Tom Robinson, and the apartheid that Atticus Finch practiced every day of his life — those things are wrong today, and they were wrong in Maycomb, Alabama, in the 1930s.

Again, let's take Finch's advice. Let's get inside the skin of the black people of Maycomb and walk around in an ordinary day of their lives. They endure, and their children grow up experiencing minute-by-minute reminders of separateness premised upon their innate inferiority. They are compelled to live in a ghetto near the town garbage dump. They cannot use the white only rest rooms, the white only water fountains, the white only lunch counters, or the white only parks. If their children go to school, their segregated schools, like their churches, have few if any books. They are even segregated in the courtroom in which Finch practices law. The jobs allowed to them are the most menial. And they face the everyday threat of lawless but condoned violence for any real or imagined stepping out of line.

Tom Robinson knows this, and he knows that it will cost him his life. The last thing he says to Atticus before they take him to prison camp is: "Good-bye, Mr.

Finch, there ain't nothin' you can do now, so there ain't no use tryin'." That day, "he just gave up hope." And, of course, Tom Robinson is right. He is shot to death — with seventeen bullets — on the claim that a gentle man with a useless arm, in a prison yard the size of a football field, in plain view of guards with guns, broke into a blind, raving charge in a hopeless attempt to climb over the fence and escape.

You can believe this improbable story, as Finch purports to do. But I believe (and Harper Lee appears to believe) that Tom Robinson was goaded into a desperate, futile run for the fence on the threat of being shot where he stood. Underwood's editorial in *The Maycomb Tribune* calls it a "senseless" killing — not what one would call a killing, with fair warning, of a raving man about to surmount a prison fence and escape. And if Finch averts his eyes from the truth, Scout faces it straight on. "Tom was a dead man," she realizes, "the minute Mayella Ewell opened her mouth and screamed." . . .

The charge of presentism fails also when we consider that other Whites of the time — born, raised, and living in Finch's South — are able to see that the oppression of Blacks is morally wrong. Dill, nine years old, runs out of Robinson's trial, physically sickened by the prosecutor's racist baiting of Robinson. . . .

Maudie Anderson is another who recognizes the injustice against Blacks and, she tells the children, they'd be surprised how many others think the same way. They include prominent and respected members of the community: Judge John Taylor and Sheriff Heck Tate, the landowner Link Deas, and the editor Braxton Underwood. . . . And Jem, in response to Finch's explanation about the "ugly facts of life" and of southern justice, also recognizes right and wrong. "Doesn't make it right," he says, beating his fist softly on his knee.

What, then, do I expect of Atticus Finch *as a lawyer*? First, because there has been some misunderstanding in the past, let's be clear about what I don't expect. I have never suggested that Finch should have dedicated his life to "working on the front lines of the N.A.A.C.P." On the contrary, in rejecting the notion that Atticus Finch is a role model for today's lawyers, here is what I said: "Don't misunderstand. I'm not saying that I would present as role models those truly admirable lawyers who, at great personal sacrifice, have dedicated their entire professional lives to fighting for social justice. That's too easy to preach and too hard to practice."

In fact, part of my commentary is that Finch's adulators inaccurately represent him as a paragon of social activism. . . . Also, it is Finch's adulators who insist on rewriting the book to create a mythologized hero. Typical is a recent piece stating that Finch "decides" to represent an indigent defendant even though he hereby "incurs the obloquy of his friends." This is wrong on two counts. First, Finch does not choose to represent Tom Robinson. He accepts a court appointment, but candidly says, "You know, I'd hoped to get through life without a case of this kind, but John Taylor pointed at me and said, 'You're It.'"

Second, it is inaccurate to say that Finch's friends subject him to obloquy. It is true that many of the townspeople do, but not Finch's friends, not the people whose opinions he values. In fact, those people admire Finch for taking the case and for giving Robinson zealous representation. . . .

I don't say this to disparage Finch, but for the sake of accuracy regarding presentism. Disparagement comes with my next point, which considers what it means that Finch "hoped to get through life without a case of this kind." It means that Atticus Finch never in his professional life voluntarily takes a pro bono case in an effort to ameliorate the evil — which he himself and others recognize — in the apartheid of Maycomb, Alabama. Forget about "working on the front lines for the N.A.A.C.P." Here is a man who does not voluntarily use his legal training and skills — not once, ever — to make the slightest change in the pervasive social injustice of his own town. . . .

But let's assume, for the sake of discussion, that I am guilty of presentism. Assume too that anything Finch tried to do would be futile (which is a familiar justification for being a bystander to evil). Even if those contentions have merit, does that make Finch a role model for today's lawyer? . . .

Finch has an enviable array of admirable qualities and, in one instance, he is truly courageous. He is a loving, patient, and understanding father, successfully coping with the burden of being a single parent. In his personal relations with other people, black and white, he unfailingly treats everyone with respect. Professionally, he is a superb advocate, a wise counselor, and a conscientious legislator. A crack shot, he never touches a gun, except to protect the community from a rabid dog. Even when he heroically waits for and faces down the lynch mob, he arms himself only with a newspaper.

In short, Atticus Finch is both more and less than the mythical figure that has been made of him. He is human — sometimes right and sometimes wrong. And one criticizes Atticus Finch not from a position of superiority, but with respect, like a sports columnist reporting the imperfection in an athlete whose prowess he himself could never match.

NOTES & QUESTIONS

1. Freedman's pointed criticisms notwithstanding, most viewers of *To Kill a Mockingbird* consider Atticus Finch heroic. Indeed, in 2001 the American Film Institute ranked Gregory Peck's Atticus Finch the number-one movie hero of all time.

2. According to Paul Bergman and Michael Asimow, "Atticus Finch sets a standard to which all lawyers should aspire." *Reel Justice: The Courtroom Goes to the Movies* 139 (1996). The large law review literature concerning Atticus Finch and *To Kill a Mockingbird* includes Cynthia L. Fountaine, *In the Shadow of Atticus Finch: Constructing a Heroic Lawyer*, 13 Widener Law Review 123 (2003); John Jay Osborn, Jr., *Atticus Finch — The End of Honor*, 30 University of San Francisco Law Review 1139 (1996); and Teresa Godwin Phelps, *The Margins of Maycomb: A Rereading of* To Kill A Mockingbird, 45 Alabama Law Review 511 (1994).

3. How does Atticus Finch see the law, and what role does he think the law should play in social life?

D.   A CULTURAL JURISPRUDENCE

Law-related popular culture can play a large role in a cultural jurisprudence. The central premise of this way of thinking about law is that law inevitably lives within culture, that is, within a people's values and attitudes, their norms and behaviors. Law draws its content, tones, and aspirations from the culture in which it resides, and law in turn shapes and directs the culture.

In the following excerpt, Stanford University law professor Lawrence Friedman, one of the first scholars to scrutinize the relationship of law and popular culture, contrasts social theories of law with a theory that accords law a pronounced degree of autonomy. Friedman notes that the latter variety of theorizing is particularly common among lawyers, judges, and legal scholars. Why might that be? Or, to put it differently, why might lawyers, judges, and legal educators be hesitant to acknowledge that law lives within culture? Does a cultural jurisprudence challenge the traditional American ideological premise that our nation lives by a rule of law?

LAW, LAWYERS, AND POPULAR CULTURE
Lawrence M. Friedman
98 Yale Law Journal 1579 (1989)

[Popular culture and popular legal culture] are of fundamental importance in constructing *social* theories of law. By social theories, I mean theories of law whose premises deny, altogether or in large part, any notion of legal "autonomy." That is, these theories try to explain legal phenomena by searching for causes and causal factors "outside" the legal system. They treat law as a dependent variable, and assign a leading role in molding the shape of legal institutions and legal arrangements to systems or subsystems that society defines as "non-legal," that is, as economic, social, cultural, or political. Social theories assume some sort of meaningful boundary — conceptual or analytical — between law and not-law; between the legal and the social; but these theories also conceive of this boundary as wholly or largely porous, a kind of network or meshwork through which energy easily flows, rather than as a tough, tight skin.

This cluster of theories firmly rejects the idea that legal systems are sealed and inward-looking; that they respond entirely or primarily to their own logic, traditions, and demands; that they are "self-reproducing," or "self-referential," or the like. A living organism, for example, *is* "autonomous" in an important sense. A horse and a cow have clear boundaries that separate them from each other and from the world. Their skins and shapes are not purely conceptual; rather, they are the real limits of subworlds, each of which develops according to its own internal rules. Both a horse and a cow eat grass, but the digested grass turns into more horse in one case, more cow in the other; never the other way around. The internal program determines exactly how food will be processed; and the organism grows and functions by these "autonomous" rules.

Some theories of law in fact treat legal systems as organisms in the sense discussed in the previous paragraph. Theories that stress the "relative autonomy of law" seem to be enjoying some vogue among legal scholars. The old-fashioned "conceptual jurisprudence" of the nineteenth century, of course, treated law as autonomous with a vengeance. Modern autonomists claim to be different, and are surely more sophisticated. But they do share some points in common with nineteenth-century conceptualists. And they certainly insist that it makes sense to look at legal systems as if they were indeed tight, impermeable, and closed to the outside world; an insular realm controlled by the "mandarins" to a very high degree.

A social theory of law, in contrast, is "social" to the extent that it denies or downgrades the autonomy of law, and insists instead that an analysis of social forces best explains why the legal system is as it is, what shapes and molds it, what makes it ebb and flow, contract and expand; what determines its general structure, and the products that it grinds out day by day. There are, of course, many different social theories of law, real or potential — classical Marxism embodies a social theory of law, for example; so too do some versions of the law and economics movement. But social theories are neither inherently right nor left; they span the spectrum of political views. They may isolate some particular "social force," and assign it the lion's share of responsibility for law and legal institutions; or they may credit some mixture of factors in the outside world. They may focus on politics, on economic organization, or on tradition or culture. It is also perfectly possible to have a "social theory" that explains legal phenomena in terms of more implausible factors — the movements of the tides, or the signs of the zodiac. "New age" social theory may be just around the corner.

Probably no serious scholar clings absolutely to either one of the two polar positions; nobody thinks that the legal system is totally and absolutely autonomous; and nobody (perhaps) seriously puts forward the opposite idea, that every last jot and tittle, every crumb of law, even in the short, short run, can be and must be explained "externally." But most lawyers, and a good many legal scholars and theorists, tend to cluster somewhere toward the autonomous end of the scale. Social scientists interested in law, and legal scholars with a taste for social science, tend to cluster somewhere toward the other end; they prefer external to internal explanations, and are deeply suspicious of the case for autonomy. It is probably true that neither basic view can be "proved" one way or the other. Rather, they are starting points, assumptions, frameworks.

It is precisely in the sense of a methodology, a strategy, that the case for (some version of) a social theory of law is strongest. It seems to me that there is more explanatory power, more richness, more bite, in exploring the manifold connections between the legal system and its surrounding society, than in treating law as an isolated domain. . . .

Social theories, in other words, are mighty tools for grappling with problems of explanation. They are not, as some critics fantasize, infected irremediably with a disease called "behaviorism," which I assume means either a concept of human beings as crude economic robots, or a methodological stance that takes overt, physical "behavior" as the sole social reality (or, in any event, as the only reality we are able to study). Social theories can be, and usually are, deeply aware of emotion, opinion, and in fact of consciousness; and some social theories — the more anthropological ones, for example — are fixated to a fault on culture and consciousness. Nor are social theories necessarily vulnerable to the charge that they (unrealistically) assume a radical distinction between "law" and "society," instead of recognizing that the two are really inseparable, intertwined, faces of the same coin. No doubt the two are inseparable. However, it is possible to separate them analytically, and it may also be sociologically useful to do so since in many societies the two are undoubtedly separated in the minds of their consumers. If anything, it is the believers in the autonomous system who are open to this particular criticism; after all, they and not social theorists are the ones who insist most loudly on the radical separation of law from the social matrix.

But the *idea* of a social theory is a far cry from an actual theory, fully developed, and strong enough to carry on its back a heavy load of explanation. Most attempts at social theory of law are crude and inadequate because they ignore or gloss over what I will call the issue of the *mechanism* or channel. This is nothing more or less than the question of *how* "social forces" actually do their number on the legal system. In what way and through what paths, tubes, hollows, and conduits do the "forces" set up by concrete events, persons, situations, and structures in "society" move, as they deliver their punch to legal institutions, manufacturing or "causing" legal phenomena — statutes, rules, institutions, and cases? A social theory that does not try to answer this question is a blind and almost meaningless abstraction. . . .

NOTES & QUESTIONS

1. Professor Friedman states at the end of the excerpt that a useful social theory of law must indicate mechanisms or channels between society and law. A social theory of law, in his opinion, must point to ways society's values and norms pass into the law. A social theory of law that fails to do this is "a blind and almost meaningless abstraction."

2. Friedman goes on to suggest that law-related popular culture and popular legal culture are important mechanisms or channels for social forces to affect legal phenomena. In his interpretation, law as it appears in stories, in movies, and on television derives at least in part from what average citizens think law is. Law-related popular culture in turn affects what people think about law, and people's thoughts on law influence what law actually is. "To me at least," Friedman concludes in the article excerpted above, "it seems patent that explorations of legal and popular culture, and the way they interact, should be high on the list of scholarly pursuits." Lawrence M. Friedman, *Law, Lawyers, and Popular Culture*, 98 Yale Law Journal 1578, 1606 (1989).

3. In some cases law-related popular culture appears to have had a direct impact on what laymen expect from law and legal institutions. In the 1950s, for example, defense counsel in criminal prosecutions complained that they could never live up to the remarkable exploits of the fictional Perry Mason, America's best-known lawyer of the era. Juries, it was claimed, expected defense counsel not only to demonstrate that a reasonable doubt existed regarding the defendant's conduct but also to actually prove the defendant was innocent. Often, Perry Mason went so far as to identify the true perpetrator, who coincidentally was located in the rear of the courtroom. How could actual defense counsel be expected to do the same? In more recent years, *C.S.I.*, an extremely popular prime-time television series set, has arguably made the work of prosecutors more difficult. Jurors, it seems, expect prosecutors to produce the kind of fingerprints on bullet casings and

DNA test results that the crime scene investigators in *C.S.I.* shows are always able to turn over to their prosecutors. If this evidence is not available — and it rarely is — the defendant must surely be innocent.

4.   The power of law-related popular culture to influence the public's attitudes about law notwithstanding, one need not assume the portrayal of law and legal institutions in pop cultural works will be received by all viewers in the same way. Movies and television series tend to be more didactic than works of fine literature, but pop cultural works still allow for individualized responses by viewers and readers. Hence, law-related movies, television series, and inexpensive fiction do not merely archive meaning. Viewers and readers maintain some degree of freedom to make their own sense of things.

5.   Also, one need not assume that law-related popular culture will necessarily reinforce dominant political beliefs by idealizing images of law and legal institutions. In the following excerpt, Naomi Mezey and Mark C. Niles invoke the insights of the so-called "Birmingham School" and suggest the potential complexities and subtleties of law-related popular culture. Popular culture, in their opinion, need not simply communicate and reproduce the dominant ideology.

SCREENING THE LAW: IDEOLOGY AND LAW IN AMERICAN POPULAR CULTURE
Naomi Mezey and Mark C. Niles
28 Columbia Journal of Law & the Arts 91 (2005)

American popular culture is saturated with legal themes. The "courtroom drama" has been a staple of American commercial cinema for more than 60 years. "Private eye" and "cop" shows, and the "lawyer" shows they spawned, have always been reliable dramatic devices well suited to network television. These shows have proliferated in recent years to the effective exclusion of other dramatic television genres. As Lawrence Friedman has quipped, "television would shrivel up and die without cops, detectives, crimes, judges, prisons, guns, and trials." Furthermore, law and legal issues play a central though sometimes subtler role in the plot development of an impressive percentage of the films and other television shows produced by mainstream Hollywood studios and producers every year.

There are various explanations for the prevalence of legal themes in modern American popular culture, including the profit motives and inertia of popular culture producers. It has never hurt that legally themed shows, and most notably courtroom dramas, are relatively easy and cheap to produce. Yet purely economic accounts of the abundance and appeal of legal themes in popular culture bypass the nature of that appeal.

One focus of this article is the nature of that appeal and the possible cultural and ideological meanings that attach to these pervasive images of law. Millions more people watch trials or oral arguments in *Ally McBeal*, *Law & Order*, *A Few Good Men*, *Liar Liar*, *The Practice*, or even short-lived shows like *First Monday* or *The Court*, than will ever visit a real court, attend an oral argument in the Supreme Court, or even have the faintest idea of what actually goes on there. This is not to suggest that all or even most of the viewers of these shows will assume that the depictions of law they see in popular culture are completely or even essentially accurate. While many will likely make just this assumption, many others will see these images for what they are — fictional stories produced by people much more interested in telling a compelling tale than in providing a documentary of our legal system.

We are decidedly uninterested in whether popular culture gets law "right." As Stanley Fish has rightly argued, images of law in television and film are as much about television and film as they are about law. What we do care about are the uses to which law is put in popular culture. For whatever the level of sophistication the audience brings to these shows, they are nonetheless the dominant images of the law and its institutions that many Americans, within certain demographic categories, will experience. And they are not without their effects on collective expectations, societal myths and the national psyche. So, assuming that we as lawyers and legal scholars ultimately care what the abundant cultural images of our legal system suggest about law and culture, then we need to look closely at the kinds of ideological messages communicated by these pervasive cultural texts.

Since the emergence of the first mass-produced entertainment media, scholars have struggled with similar questions in an effort to make sense of the power of the popular media and to explore their influence on individual consumers and communities. The dominant critical analysis of popular culture, developed by the Frankfurt School in the early twentieth century, has suggested that the primary role of popular culture in our society is to communicate, promote and perpetuate the "dominant ideology," that worldview which provides a conceptual framework and foundation for a particular social order and which tends to serve the interests of the prevailing power structure. This theory follows a Marxist model and views popular culture as a means of convincing the masses that their interests are aligned with the broader capitalist political and economic agenda. According to this theory, the ideology communicated by popular culture encompasses "distinct biases, interests, and embedded values, reproducing the point of view of their producers and often the values of the dominant social groups," and consequently serves to "reproduce social domination, . . . legitimate rule by the prevailing groups over subordinate ones, and help replicate the existing inequalities and hierarchies of power and control."

Applying this traditional conception to an analysis of the depiction of law in American popular culture produces interesting, though somewhat contradictory results. While instructive, this traditional analysis is insufficient, on its own, to explain why law is depicted the way that it is across the full spectrum of contemporary popular culture. While television images of law frequently do serve to reinforce the dominant ideology in a relatively crude way — providing consistently idealized and mythic images of law and government which support the status quo — many images of law in popular film, in contrast, depict law in a way that calls into serious doubt the ability of law to be neutral and just. This more complex and critical view of law, while still essentially "ideological" in its reliance on a legitimate and authoritative legal order and a common and coherent moral order, calls for a more nuanced analysis than that offered by the earliest popular culture critics.

This paper reevaluates Frankfurt School theory, and other cultural critiques, in an effort to bring a more sophisticated analysis to bear on popular culture depictions of law. Specifically, we invoke the cultural critiques of the Birmingham School in order to assess the more subtle ideological content more often found in film. Our focus here is not only on how popular culture functions as a mechanism for communicating and reproducing ideologies, but, based on a theoretical analysis of what this function is, we ask what images of law and legal justice one might expect to see in popular media, and we assess the efficacy of the theoretical frameworks based on an in depth analysis of the kinds of images that are actually out there and the variety of meanings they communicate. Yet for all the interpretive variety, there is a virtual absence of seriously controversial or oppositional images of law, particularly on television. We partially link this insight to recent media consolidations and suggest the ways in which both the theory and practice of popular culture bear on the issue of media regulation and why they matter to democracy.

In one sense our conclusion, stated in its most basic terms, is that for reasons relating to their idiosyncratic profit and aesthetic structures, the dominance of the particular images of law depicted on television — which we refer to as "crudely" ideology-reinforcing, that portray the law as a (if not the) primary vehicle for achieving justice — is best explained by reference to the traditional Frankfurt School culture critiques. In contrast, making sense of the more nuanced ideological content of portrayals of law and justice in popular film requires application of the more recent critical structure of the Birmingham School. This second and more complex version of a legal ideology understands the law as fallible, as either ineffective at reaching justice, or worse, standing in the way of it. But this more complex view still understands the law as fundamentally legitimate and authoritative, situated within a coherent moral universe. However, in another sense, we don't fully subscribe to such a neat alignment of theory and medium. Indeed, the Birmingham School's insistence on the multiple meanings available in cultural texts forces us to modify a pat conclusion about television's uniform content. At the same time, the very differences between television and film readings and the force with which the dominant readings of television shows in fact dominate suggest the limits of our theoretical tools.

NOTES & QUESTIONS

1. In other portions of their article, Professors Mezey and Niles develop further the contrast between law-related movies and television programs. "Due we think to their differences in structuring production, profits and narrative, television more consistently produces quite crude versions of legal ideology while film is more likely to portray more complex images of law and legal institutions. Notwithstanding these differences, a strong ideological message about law's ability to achieve justice in our society is consistently communicated by both media, and neither offers many subversive or counterhegemonic perspectives on law, although film has the greater potential, tantalizingly if rarely realized, to offer truly oppositional messages to at least some viewers." Naomi Mezey & Mark C. Niles, *Screening the Law: Ideology and Law in American Popular Culture*, 28 Columbia Journal of Law and the Arts 91, 184 (2005).

2. Some, of course, remain skeptical that law-related popular culture might have an impact on lawyers' and the lay public's attitudes about law and legal institutions. Professors Victoria S. Salzmann and Philip T. Dunwoody dubbed scholars who work on the relationship of law and popular culture the "pop-culture legal-realist movement," a lumbering moniker highly unlikely to stick. They also surveyed first-year law students at Baylor University School of Law and South Texas College of Law to see if pop cultural portrayals of law had affected the students' expectations and understanding of legal practice and concluded that false perceptions of lawyering had for the most part not been created. *See* Victoria S. Salzmann and Philip T. Dunwoody, *Prime-Time Lies: Do Portrayals of Lawyers Influence How People Think About the Legal Profession?*, 58 Southern Methodist Law Review 411 (2005).

PART II

LEGAL ACTORS AND INSTITUTIONS

Chapter 2

LEGAL EDUCATION

A. FILMOGRAPHY

Legally Blonde (2001)

The Paper Chase (1973)

Rounders (1998)

The Socratic Method (2001)

Soul Man (1986)

B. INTRODUCTION

A handful of Hollywood films portray legal education. The films are neither numerous nor coherent enough to constitute a genre, but they do provide engaging images of law students, law professors, and the overall process of legal education. How do these images compare to the ones you had before you started law school? How does pop cultural legal education compare to what you are actually experiencing? Why does the culture industry portray legal education in the way that it does? How do the pop cultural portrayals call attention to the questionable features of legal education?

C. THE SOCRATIC METHOD

Professor Stromwell: A legal education means you will learn to speak in a new language. You will be taught to achieve insight into the world around you and to sharply question what you know. The seat you have picked will be yours for the next nine months of your life. And those of you in the front row, beware. "The law is reason free from passion." Does anyone know who spoke those immortal words? Yes?

David Kidney: Aristotle.

Professor Stromwell: Are you sure? Would you be willing to stake your life on it?

David: I think so.

Prof. Stromwell: What about his life? (indicating another student)

David: I don't know.

Prof. Stromwell: Well, I recommend knowing before speaking. The law leaves much room for interpretation, but very little for self-doubt. And you were right. It was Aristotle. Good job.

— *Legally Blonde* (2001)

When Elle Woods shows up for her first day of class at Harvard Law School, she is not prepared for class, and Professor Stromwell skewers her in front of the entire class. Elle does not understand the established norms. For example, the faculty expects students to check the assignment board before the semester begins to get assignments and to prepare, even for the first day of class. Law school is not like college. It is not like any experience students have ever had before. It will change them, and their perceptions of the world, forever.

Popular culture emphasizes the Socratic Method as the formative means of education for lawyers. Even if the public knows very little about legal education, it knows about the "Socratic Method" — the ritual professorial harassment of law students. The public might recognize similar harassment in television judges' treatment of the parties in their courtrooms.

Christopher Columbus Langdell, the late nineteenth-century Dean of the Harvard Law School, championed the Socratic Method, based on examination of court opinions with professorial questioning that resembled that of the Greek philosopher Socrates. He believed that such questioning, carefully conducted, would lead students to a series of "aha" moments: an understanding of the reasoning underlying the law. Note that Langdell introduced the method in his Contracts course; do you think the fact that *The Paper Chase's* Professor Kingsfield also teaches Contracts is significant? Or do you think there is just something about Contracts that lends itself to fictional commentary about law and popular culture?

Harvard, as well as other law schools, has now started to abandon the Socratic Method as a primary method of teaching. *See* Orin S. Kerr, *The Decline of the Socratic Method at Harvard*, 78 Nebraska Law Review 113 (1999). The Socratic Method no longer holds sway at most law schools to the extent that it once did. Many law school professors instead combine the Socratic Method with other teaching styles, having adopted the theory that a more diverse student body learns in many different ways. *See* Howard Gardner, Frames of Mind: The Theory of Multiple Intelligences (3d ed., 2011).

However, not all law professors agree; thus law students may still encounter a professor who uses the Socratic Method with Kingsfieldian overtones. Clearly Professor Stromwell is one of these. Consider the reasons for the move away from the Socratic Method and its continued use in the following selections.

YOU CALL THAT EDUCATION?

Morrison Torrey

19 Wisconsin Women's Law Journal 93 (2004)

According to Plato, the essential aspects to Socrates' dialogues were: (1) elenchus, the step in which Socrates leads the responder to understand that he does not know what he thought he knew; (2) aporia, the acknowledgment of ignorance and perplexity; and (3) psychagogia, the construction of a new understanding. Typically, this occurred in small groups and voluntarily. This has been transported to large classrooms where students not only cannot walk away, but will also be graded by their questioner. To a high degree, "legal education has incorporated elements of hostility, competitiveness, and humiliation into what is, essentially, an abuse of the system." The law teacher is in a position of complete authority which can be abused or not.

In reviewing the literature about the Socratic Method, one thing became immediately clear: not only is there no agreement on the value of this pedagogical tool, but there also is no agreement on exactly what it is! I suppose it is not surprising that law professors want to define their own rules for the game; after all, that is what they do in the classroom, including "hiding the ball."

Exactly what is the Socratic Method as embraced by legal education? One professor, Paul Brest, believes that "the terrorist version of the Socratic Method has almost disappeared, and it has been replaced by a mixture of lecture, asking questions of volunteers, and responding to questions from the class at large." Another professor, Steven Childress, characterizes the Socratic Method as "a rigid relationship between teacher and student, immersion of the student in the subject and its analysis, a focus on technical distinctions and massive facts, and large class size," with the negative attributes of potential teacher abuse and covert indoctrination. Professor Gerald Lopez argues that the Socratic Method is currently practiced as "a set of mini-lectures by the teacher interrupted by questions that by now no one really expects to precipitate the kind of critical conversation among students and teacher that many imagine to be the defining strength of legal education." Professor John Cole defines the Method by what it is not; in his view, the Method is neither lecture with occasional questions designed to keep students alert and check their preparation and understanding, nor sharp questions designed to reveal the substance of the law. Rather, he believes Socratic questioning "illuminates the various competing values that inhere in the problem and forces the student to see that it is his [or her] responsibility to order those values in a coherent and defensible way." According to Professor Thomas Eisele, legal education's use of the Socratic Method is premised upon a belief that students have both carefully read assigned materials and have thought about them prior to class. Through Socratic questioning, law teachers "are demonstrating for the edification of our students — and, thus, we are training them in — techniques of thinking, ways of applying (or developing) the thinking skills they already possess." But, in order to accomplish this, the students must first learn that they don't know what they think they know. This process (demonstrating they don't know what they think they know) can be humiliating for students; despair and humiliation "are both natural and necessary" to the process.

Professor Martin Louis defines the Socratic Method as "a dialogue about the subject matter of the class going on almost continuously between the professor and the students." Professor Jennifer Rosato reduces the method to "a dialogue between teacher and student — an 'education by interrogation.' " To her, components of the Socratic Method can include the following: a teacher who knows the answers and challenges the students to win the game by providing the answer the professor wants; students who feel personal humiliation when they cannot find the right answer; competition, not communication, as the dominant classroom atmosphere; mystification and dehumanization of the law; and an atmosphere that thwarts student creativity and silences different perspectives. Professor Pierre Schlag believes that, in the true law school Socratic Method, it does not matter what resolution the student offers: In the true law school Socratic Method, the student is always wrong. The resolution always founders on a new fact scenario, or some previously unnoticed implication, or some unforeseen consequence. And there is always another question, one that is carefully tailored to expose the inadequacy of the student's previous answer. In a perfect display of the Socratic Method the questions would never stop; the class would never end.

Extending Professor Schlag's proposition, Cheryl Herden, writing as a second-year law student, sees the Socratic Method as "socializing students by teaching them the hierarchical notion that the professor knows all but he [or she] need not share his [or her] knowledge."

Professor Ruta Stropus carefully distinguishes Socratic Method from Langdellian Method: "law students read cases and then engage in a question and answer dialogue regarding those cases," learning "how courts reasoned and analyzed," developing "analytical skills to defend a 'position from attack by both faculty and fellow students.' " In sum, this teaching method will "foster analytical skills, encourage independent learning and provide students with the opportunity to practice and refine verbal and rhetorical skills." For Professor Cynthia Hawkins-Leon, the Socratic Method helps students to:

(1) develop analytical skills; (2) think on their feet; (3) engage in intellectual rigor; (4) learn about the legal process; and (5) learn about the lawyer's role. Thus, the Socratic Method appears to be many things to many teachers. And, although a strict and exclusive use of this pedagogy seems to be waning in many law schools, it remains the traditional and most honored legal teaching methodology.

NOTES & QUESTIONS

1. Think about the different definitions of the Socratic Method given by Professor Torrey. How close are they to the teaching methods you have experienced in law school?

2. How do the varieties of the Socratic Method utilized by Professor Kingsfield in *The Paper Chase*, Professor Banks in *Soul Man*, and Professor Stromwell in *Legally Blonde* differ from one another? Which version of the Socratic Method is best suited for a Hollywood film set in a contemporary law school? Why?

3. Hollywood films rarely prioritize precise accuracy with regard to social settings and practices. As noted in the introductory chapter of this text, filmmakers

want instead to touch popular attitudes and to attract admission-paying viewers. How might the portrayal of the Socratic Method as the standard law school form of teaching correspond to popular assumptions about legal education and about the legal profession in general?

   4.   The following excerpt discusses how Professor Kingsfield came to symbolize the Socratic Method and helped fuel opposition to its use. However, Professor Michael Vitiello, the author of the article from which the excerpt is taken, nonetheless vigorously defends the Socratic Method.

PROFESSOR KINGSFIELD: THE MOST MISUNDERSTOOD CHARACTER IN LITERATURE
Michael Vitiello
33 Hofstra Law Review 955 (2005)

Over thirty years have passed since Professor Kingsfield first appeared as a character in *The Paper Chase*. He instantly became a powerful symbol of what many thought was wrong with legal education. For many years, he remained synonymous with a particular form of the Socratic method, so demanding and unkind that it rendered students bitter, unhappy, and cynical. Lest he fade from memory, both the novel and film have been reissued. As a result, Kingsfield is likely to continue to haunt prospective law students and to remain a foil for critics of traditional legal education.

Criticism of the Socratic method and legal education did not begin with the publication of *The Paper Chase*. But beginning in the 1970s, attacks on the Socratic method became more frequent, were often intemperate, and treated Kingsfield as synonymous with the Socratic method and its ills. Among the criticisms leveled at the Socratic method in the hands of Professors like Kingsfield are that it results in poorly trained lawyers; it causes incivility between attorneys; it discriminates against women; and it causes law students to lose their ideals.

Partially in response to such attacks, law schools have become gentler places in a misguided attempt to become kinder to their students. In fact, critics have questioned whether the method ought to be banned or discouraged as a teaching tool. As the cost of legal education has risen, and as law schools are increasingly dependent on alumni giving, institutional pressures have increased to make law schools more student-friendly. As a result, demanding professors like Kingsfield, where they remain in legal education, are on the defensive. While a majority of law professors continue to use some form of Socratic questioning, increasing numbers of professors engage in far less aggressive questioning of their students and adopt an array of techniques to lessen the stress, including allowing students to pass when they are called on or giving advance notice when they will be called on in class. . . .

As a law student, I certainly shared much of the distaste for the Socratic method. I began to rethink my position on my first day as a lawyer. I now believe that the Socratic method needs a vigorous defense. . . . No careful study has determined whether law schools have become gentler places over the past thirty years. One study, acknowledging that it was not statistically valid, concluded that the over-whelming majority of law professors still use the Socratic method. The study did not attempt to define the Socratic method. Beyond that, though, the study made no effort to determine whether law professors use the method in ways that are likely to increase stress. For example, the questionnaire sent to law professors did not ask what sanctions are imposed if students are unprepared or whether they allow students to pass if they do not want to be called on or whether the professor simply accepts volunteers.

Anecdotal evidence seems to cut both ways. Many articles criticizing the Socratic method assert that the method in all of its glory is still in place. But other writers have observed that the atmosphere in law schools has become gentler in recent years. Often, in comments about a retiring colleague, professors state that the honoree is no Kingsfield but instead was a master of a kinder form of the Socratic method. My own observations at four different law schools where I have taught support the latter conclusion.

Institutional pressures dampen enthusiasm for the highly demanding use of the Socratic method. As law schools become more expensive to run and more dependent on alumni giving, deans and others responsible for fundraising may have little enthusiasm for professors who are seen as "infantilizing, demeaning, dehumanizing, sadistic," and "destructive of positive ideological values." Combine institutional pressure with student evaluations that became routine around the time of *The Paper Chase*: in light of the importance that some schools place on student opinion, one doubts that an untenured professor is going to emulate Kingsfield. A quick survey of ads for law schools supports the conclusion that some law schools are no longer hospitable to Kingsfield-style professors. Southern Methodist University, for example, advertises that it has adopted a "kinder, gentler" approach to the first year of law school. Within the recent past, Vermont Law School advertised that "the days of Professor Kingsfield . . . infamy are over." Other schools make similar claims. Concord, the online law school, made much of the fact that it has no "looming" law professors or "quaking" students, while another states that it espouses a culture of civility and respect, "avoiding 'paper chase' or 'cutthroat' law school stereotypes."

At a minimum, the probable decline in the use of the highly demanding Socratic method over the past thirty years in favor of a gentler form of the method should raise doubts about empirical claims that it is a major cause of students' ills. Law schools should hesitate to make sweeping changes in legal instruction without better evidence that the Socratic method is the cause of students' woes. If the Socratic method is a major cause of students' problems, their problems should have diminished over time as the method is employed less vigorously. But the literature lacks careful longitudinal studies of students' problems. . . .

Often ignored by critics of Kingsfield and the Socratic method is that the gentle professor, sensitized not to hurt students' feelings, may create an atmosphere that is not conducive to learning. A student who is poorly prepared will not learn as well as one for whom expectations are high. By comparison, demanding professors set the standard high, forcing students to aim high to meet the professor's expectations.

If this is a problem, it is because such high expectations create a fearful environment that impairs students' learning. Whether Kingsfield-style professors still roam the halls of American law schools is difficult to determine empirically.

Above, I argued that is unlikely. And while professors should aim for a classroom in which students experience enough stress to be motivated to do well, but not too much to paralyze students, the literature today suggests that many law professors are more worried about setting the bar too high, rather than too low. Many well-meaning professors, writing about their teaching, emphasize the need to reach Generation X students, students who have been raised on the media, with shorter attention spans, with less motivation than earlier generations. Those professors often write about making the classroom exchange fun, rather than challenging. . . .

Another question that needs to be explored is whether the goals advanced by advocates of a gentler law school environment necessarily ready students for the practice of law. . . . [A]re we giving our students adequate training to deal with the stress that they will face in practice? In a gentler law school, students who bruise easily will not have training in how to deal with the inevitable frustrations of practice, including the reality that they will face judges and opponents who care little about their feelings and whose conduct will be confrontational.

My point is simply that law schools today run a far greater risk of creating too gentle an environment rather than creating too rigorous an environment. For those legal educators who doubt this assertion, I pose this question: in most American law schools today, are deans more likely to be concerned about professors considered too demanding or not demanding enough? Again, I have no empirical proof. But, based on my own experiences at various law schools, deans give far more attention to trying to soften professors considered demanding than they do trying to get undemanding teachers to increase intensity in the classroom. Indeed, were a not especially demanding teacher confronted by a dean today, the professor might simply rely on the numerous articles attacking the demanding Socratic method as proof that the professor's gentler methods are more effective. . . .

A number of prominent legal educators have based their critique of the Socratic method on learning theory. Some learning theorists recognize that the Socratic method may be effective for many students and may not argue that it should be abandoned. Instead, they contend that law professors should be aware of students' different learning styles and use different methods to reach those students. Their insights are important and influential.

One cannot lightly dismiss their message. Surely, a professor ought to attempt to reach all of her students. In this section, after reviewing the arguments of the learning theorists, I do raise questions about learning theorists' arguments. My concern focuses on a practical question: how will students need to ingest material and to communicate material when they practice law? That is, learning theorists must show that lawyers who lack the ability to learn through reading, listening, and debating their points can be fully effective as practicing lawyers. Learning theorists have not effectively addressed that question.

Educators have argued that students absorb material differently from one another. They identify five kinds of learners. First, verbal learners absorb information through written texts. Second, visual learners absorb information in its entirety. Visual learners may be able to memorize well, but not solve problems well. Third, oral learners absorb information by speaking. Such students need to speak in class to maximize their learning. Fourth, aural learners absorb information by listening. Presumably, like verbal learners, they are well suited for law school because many of the traditional teaching techniques play to their strength. Hence, they benefit from class lectures and discussions. Finally, tactile or kinesthetic learners learn best by doing, e.g., by role-playing or simulation.

Learning theorists have argued that law professors spend too much time using only one or two teaching methods. For example, because so much time in law school is devoted to learning through written materials, verbal learners are more successful than their peers. By comparison, visual learners tend to end up at the bottom of their class. Some critics of current teaching strategies argue that professors can enhance learning of visual learners by using charts and diagrams. Other scholars have suggested a host of strategies to engage more of their students than are able to learn effectively through the use of the Socratic method.

Not all writers agree on the role of the Socratic method in an ideal teaching environment. Some writers have argued that law professors can maintain the academic rigor of the Socratic method and nonetheless help students who are in the bottom half of the class (or who will end up there at the end of the first year). Others have argued explicitly or implicitly that the Socratic method is not a good educational tool. For example, in arguing that their method is superior to the Socratic method, three authors developed an exercise called a Contract Activity Package ("CAP") that allows students to work at their own pace. It also permits learning through different learning styles, unlike the Socratic method.

One can only sound callous if he questions whether we ought to be addressing the learning needs of all of our students. But we must ask whether students need to have a particular learning style in order to succeed in the practice of law. I offer a simple analogy: in my sophomore year in college, I took a basic Art History course. I ended up doing well in the course because I was able to read enough about art to know what I ought to be able to see in the work. Although I did not identify the problem in these terms in 1965, my problem was that I am not a visual learner. I adapted.

Imagine that instead of taking an art course, I was deciding whether to become an art historian or art appraiser. Surely, I chose wisely when I decided not to concentrate in Art History. Had I chosen Art History and sought employment in the field, I would not have been able to compensate for my lack of visual, spatial intelligence. What, for example, if I had been employed as an art critic, to write about modern art? I lacked a skill necessary to work in that field.

Similar examples abound. Social scientists now identify several different kinds of intelligence. But most commentators do not argue that teachers in a given field should compensate for their students' lack of a particularly relevant kind of intelligence by use of different learning styles. Instead, they recognize that individuals should make career choices that call up that individual's strengths.

That point is missed in much of the discussion of learning theory in the law school context. Although learning theorists contend that law students must develop both practical and analytical skills in order to learn how to think like a lawyer, learning theorists do not focus on the particular skills that lawyers need to have. Given the wide variety of kinds of law practice, one might argue that people with different learning styles should find a niche in practice. But the practice of law does have some common denominators.

No doubt, some lawyers are rainmakers, whose interpersonal skills are more important than their analytical skills. Some lawyers have strong oral advocacy skills and weak writing skills. But the overwhelming majority of lawyers must be able to read and analyze statutes, rules, and cases. They must be able to take complex facts and figure out how the various rules and cases apply to those facts. They must be able to draft coherent legal documents whether they are litigators, transactional lawyers, or administrative advocates. They must be able to digest and synthesize large amounts of material.

The literature advocating better accommodation of students with different learning styles misses the latter point. Learning theorists writing about law school fail to ask whether students who are not verbal learners may have difficulty practicing law. Instead, they advocate more diverse teaching techniques to reach those students. Whether that is a sound strategy is debatable.

Not surprisingly, students who lack certain kinds of learning ability end up in the bottom half of the class. Implicit in the literature is that teaching and testing should change to give students without, say, verbal intelligence a better chance of academic success. That makes sense only if I am wrong in my description of what it takes to excel in the practice of law: visual learners may be better architects than lawyers but almost certainly verbal learners are better suited to practicing law than are visual learners.

Given that law schools admit students who may be visual or tactile or aural learners, one might argue that law professors must accommodate them. A similar argument has surfaced in literature that emphasizes the generational gap between law professors, sometimes derisively called "talking heads," and their students, raised on visual stimuli. That is, some commentators argue that law professors must use display technology to accommodate students raised on television.

Here, again, the discussion should begin with the essential skills needed to practice law and the way in which information will be available to practicing lawyers. Yes, lawyers can attend lectures and get some material on tape or CD. But the primary medium of communication remains the printed word. The flood of written material has increased as legislatures pile on new laws, courts publish hundreds of new opinions, and agencies promulgate new regulations. Training law students to read and analyze complex material must remain the primary focus of law school, even though some learners may have more difficulty than their peers. . . .

Law schools today are gentler places than they were when John Osborn [the author of the novel *The Paper Chase*] went to Harvard. Unlike Osborn, I am not confident that his daughter will encounter any, or at least many, Professor Kingsfields at Harvard or anywhere else in the legal academy today. Where they still teach, I suspect they are on the defensive, subject to hostile student evaluations, pressure from their deans to lighten up on their students, and criticism from their younger colleagues, who are armed with "evidence" that the Socratic method, at least the Kingsfield variety, is disabling and discriminatory.

If we listen to the current mythology, the Kingsfields of the academy are responsible for their students' incompetence, incivility, anxiety, alcohol abuse, and cynicism. In addition, Kingsfield's brand of verbal questioning is outmoded in light of a new generation of visual learners raised on television and videogames.

Law schools are heading in the wrong direction. Convinced that Kingsfield's methods lead to unfairness and incompetence, numerous law professors have urged a gentler law school environment. Often a gentler atmosphere deemphasizes the need for thorough class preparation and places students' personal views ahead of understanding the analysis that has moved the courts. Students often mistake the nature of the enterprise: they believe that their views matter, when as practicing lawyers, their views have little relevance to the resolution of legal issues.

Empirically, "gentler" is not necessarily kinder than the methods of Professor Kingsfield. Despite widespread reliance on empirical research, many of the empirical claims do not withstand critical scrutiny. Intuitively, "gentler" may not be kinder. If the goal is comfortable classroom experience, no doubt "gentler" teaching makes sense. But if the goal of a professor is to teach students the skills that they will need to practice law, "gentler" makes little sense. Instead, law professors owe their students a tough intellectual experience; they need to expose them to the pressure of answering hard questions that force them to examine and defend their premises.

Before law schools abandon universally, or water down, the demanding form of the Socratic method, we ought to determine whether the Socratic method is responsible for the parade of ills that its critics claim. We ought to demand far more compelling empirical evidence before we abandon a teaching method that has so many virtues. Further, we ought to explore alternative ways to deal with any negative effects that it may produce. For example, we ought to ask whether more careful psychological screening prior to law school or counseling in law school might help students to adjust. If, instead, we allow students to complete law school without exposure to the demanding form of the Socratic method, we are simply shifting the time when our students come face to face with those demands, in the form of a judge or senior partner or opposing attorney. Surely, our unwillingness to use the demanding Socratic method shifts to others the responsibility of teaching our students.

NOTES & QUESTIONS

1. Professor Charles W. Kingsfield has a solid claim to being the most prominent law professor in American popular culture. He first appeared in *The Paper Chase* (1971), a novel regarding life at the Harvard Law School by John Jay Osborn, Jr. The novel seemed to some a critique of traditional legal education. For a review of the novel and other works of law school fiction, *see* Arthur D. Austin, *The Waste Land of Law School Fiction*, 1989 Duke Law Journal 495. Compare the images of law school and law school faculty in *The Paper Chase* with Michael Graubart Levin's tale of nastiness and intrigue, *The Socratic Method* (1987) (not to be confused with the film of the same name featured in this chapter).

2. Twentieth Century Fox acquired the rights to adapt Osborne's novel for the cinema and used the film to showcase young actors Timothy Bottoms and Lindsay Wagner, casting the former as law student James Hart from Minnesota and the latter as his lover. Veteran actor John Houseman played Professor Kingsfield, and, to the surprise of some, became the film's most memorable character. Bottoms and Wagner failed to receive Oscar nominations, but Houseman won the Oscar for Best Supporting Actor. What made Houseman's performance so noteworthy?

3. As noted in the previous chapter, the culture industry often adapts pop cultural works successful in one medium for other media. Novels become films. Films become television series. *The Paper Chase* itself was developed into a television series. It appeared on CBS for one season (1978-79), and Showtime continued to produce the series for cable for three additional seasons (1983-86). In all, the series lasted longer than it takes most law students to finish law school! Few of the actors from the film appeared in the television series, but the show featured John Houseman once again as crusty Professor Kingsfield. What might have been the challenges in converting *The Paper Chase* into a weekly dramatic series on television? For a discussion of the television series, see Walter A. Effross, *Paper Chase*, in *Prime Time Law: Fictional Television as Legal Narrative* 105-13 (Robert M. Jarvis & Paul R. Joseph eds. 1998).

4. Other less famous television series have featured law professors and law students. These series include *The Nancy Drew Mysteries* (Ned Nickerson was a law student and assistant to Nancy's father); *The Young Lawyers* (law students defend the accused); and *Moon Over Miami* (a law student becomes a private eye). Sometimes law students appear in television series that do not really emphasize law-related themes. In *Spin City* Michael J. Fox's character had a girlfriend who was a law student, and in *How I Met Your Mother* Marshall Erickson, one of the recurring characters, is a Columbia University law student. He eventually graduates over the course of the series and gets a position at Goliath National Bank, even though his dream is to become an environmental lawyer. In the *Cosby Show*, the character of Hilton Lucas, played by Bill Cosby, has a daughter who is a law student and then a lawyer, although she leaves the law to become a chef.

5. Some novels, several of which form the basis for the films in this chapter, also dissect and represent law school life. Amanda Brown based her novel *Legally Blonde* (2003) on her own experiences at Stanford Law School. Are you surprised that Hollywood moved Elle Woods from Stanford to Harvard? Novelist and practitioner Scott Turow writes about his own first year at Harvard Law in the book *One L* (1977). Rick Lax discusses his move from magician to law student in *Lawyer Boy: A Case Study on Growing Up* (2008). Another book in which a law student makes an appearance is Cliff Stoll's *The Cuckoo's Egg: Tracking a Spy through the Maze of Computer Espionage* (1989). Astronomer Stoll's true-life tale is primarily about cornering an East German computer hacker and then convincing the FBI that it needs to take action; his then girlfriend, a law student, is helpful in devising a plan to trap the hacker.

D. LAW FACULTY

While Charles W. Kingsfield is surely the most famous of all pop cultural law professors, the following excerpt discusses how Hollywood films might portray the law professor as a hero, teacher, or sympathetic failure.

CRUSADING HERO, DEVOTED TEACHER, AND SYMPATHETIC FAILURE: THE SELF-IMAGE OF THE LAW PROFESSOR IN HOLLYWOOD CINEMA AND IN REAL LIFE, TOO
David Ray Papke
28 Vermont Law Review 957 (2004)

[M]odern films in which the law professor becomes the hero should be noted. In *Just Cause*, for example, Sean Connery plays law professor Paul Armstrong. His antagonist is . . . , it seems at first, a violent, almost fascistic criminal justice system personified by Laurence Fishburne's Sheriff Tanny Brown. The latter arrested a man for murder and used torture to extract a confession from him. The man now resides on death row in Florida, and his mother pleads with Armstrong for help. In the classic stance of the reluctant hero, Armstrong at first declines. However, Armstrong's wife reminds him, "Every now and then, you have to get a little bloody."

Armstrong leaves his teaching responsibilities and research behind, heads off to Florida, and conducts an investigation. With more than a trace of perceptiveness, a woman whom Armstrong encounters at a cocktail party tells him, "You missed your true calling. You should have been a detective." Armstrong's work frees the man on death row, but unfortunately he turns out to be the murderer. Furthermore, he kidnaps Armstrong's wife and daughter. A dramatic car chase follows, as does a fight to the death in a swamp. In the end, the law professor heroically prevails, and the gators feast on the felon's foul flesh.

A subtler modern tale of the law professor as heroic righter of wrongs is *Reversal of Fortune*. On some level, the film is not fiction. It derives from law Professor Alan Dershowitz's book of the same title, in which Dershowitz recounts his appellate work on behalf of Claus von Bülow, who had been convicted at trial of attempting to murder his millionaire wife, Sunny. Writer Nicholas Kagan and director Barbet Schroeder converted Dershowitz's sometimes whiny account into a classic Hollywood film that Suzanne Shale calls "a tale of heroic odyssey." Veteran actor Ron Silver played the law professor as hero and did so with the ideal combination of arrogance and aplomb.

The Dershowitz character's righteousness does not derive from his representation of Claus von Bülow in and of itself. In the film and, apparently, in real life as well, von Bülow is a rather slippery fellow. We are never certain whether he did in fact try to kill his wealthy wife with injections of insulin. Dershowitz finds his true cause in a more abstracted protection of the right to counsel for criminal defendants. His nobility derives from a commitment to criminal defense work, and this cause, at least according to the filmmakers, does not depend on financial reimbursement. Early in the film, Dershowitz and von Bülow meet in a restaurant to discuss the case, and the latter proposes a retainer. "Not so fast," Dershowitz says. "I'm not a hired gun. I've got to feel there's some moral or constitutional issue at stake." . . .

In one lengthy scene, Dershowitz's student helpers have assembled in his faculty office. A beautiful, imaginary version of the Harvard campus is on display outside the windows, and the office itself is larger than most actual law school seminar rooms. A student in a torn blue-jean jacket named Minnie challenges Dershowitz's representation of someone as obviously guilty as von Bülow. But, before she can steam out of his office, Dershowitz passionately discusses why everyone deserves a lawyer and outlines how the lawyer can be the isolated outcast's only true friend. He also explains the manner in which he approaches his work: "The reason I take cases — and here I'm unlike most other lawyers, who are not professors and therefore have to make a living — I take cases because I get pissed off."

In the end Dershowitz, of course, prevails. He has just dismissed a law school class and is still in the classroom when his student helpers run in to announce that the Rhode Island Supreme Court has unanimously reversed the von Bülow conviction. As did . . . Professor Armstrong, Professor Dershowitz has performed in a heroic fashion. He has fought for a noble cause and won. . . .

Law professors are also eligible for characterization as teachers. The most enduring example of a Hollywood film with a law professor as teacher is *The Paper Chase*, featuring the one and only Professor Charles W. Kingsfield, Jr., Professor of Law. The film is derived from a novel regarding life at the Harvard Law School by John Jay Osborn, Jr. . . .

The filmmakers may have seen the film as a vehicle for promising young actors Timothy Bottoms and Lindsay Wagner, casting the former as a law student from Minnesota and the latter as his on-again, off-again lover. The filmmakers could also have envisioned a "becoming-an-adult" tale. However, scenes with Professor Kingsfield teaching Contracts were numerous and served almost as a pacing motif in the film, and John Houseman in the role of Professor Kingsfield either intentionally or unintentionally "stole" the film. . . .

[W]e learn very little about Kingsfield as a person, but we have ample opportunity to observe him as a teacher. And what a teacher he is. Kingsfield personifies the traditions and culture of the law. He is knowledgeable about issues, concepts, and rules. He is a strict disciplinarian, who expects his students to be prompt, prepared, and able to expound. In the film's most remembered classroom scene, James T. Hart, the law student played by Timothy Bottoms, declines to answer when called on and says he will raise his hand when he wishes to speak. Professor Kingsfield is astounded by the brazen lack of cooperation and asks Hart to come forward to the lectern. Hart complies, and Kingsfield gives him a dime. "Call your mother," Kingsfield says. "Tell her there is serious doubt about your becoming a lawyer."

As the comedy *Legally Blonde* suggests, Hollywood continues to play off the Kingsfieldian version of the law teacher. The film concerns Elle Woods, a California sorority girl, played by Reese Witherspoon, who decides to go to Harvard Law School to prove a point to her ex-boyfriend. He not only attends Harvard himself but also dropped Woods because she was not the right kind of woman for a man with Harvard-sized ambitions. Woods' father thinks little of her law school plans, announcing, "Law school's for people who are boring and ugly and serious." Woods goes anyway, overcomes early difficulties, and becomes a research assistant for one of her professors, a man who seems also to have a rather sizable law firm in Boston. He has sexual designs on Woods, but she eludes his advances. In the final third of the film she takes over a murder case from him and wins an acquittal because she knows one would never wet her hair shortly after getting a perm.

The Kingsfieldian law professor in the film is not Woods' boss but Professor Stromwell, played with appealing verve by Holland Taylor. Professor Stromwell excoriates Woods for not doing the reading for the first class, much as Kingsfield excoriated Hart for the same offense in *The Paper Chase*. Stromwell is a stern, dignified, and learned law teacher, who demands commitment and excellence from her students. She asks one if he would stake his life on his answer, and she smacks another one on top of his head with her pencil. "Be careful of old Stromwell," one can almost hear the student body saying behind her back.

But Stromwell, like Kingsfield, is more than tough and unyielding. She also has what all positively portrayed Hollywood teachers have, namely, a commitment to the interests and future of their students. In one scene, Woods goes to her favorite manicurist. Woods has been devastated by her boss's sexual advances and by how others have misinterpreted her response to those advances. She is about to give up on law school, pick up her Chihuahua, Bruiser, and return to the vapid poolside environment from which she came. Fortunately, Professor Stromwell is also at the manicurist, and she is prepared to teach Woods some of life's fundamental lessons. "If you're going to let one stupid prick ruin your life," Stromwell tells Woods, "you're not the girl I thought you were." Woods snaps back to her senses and renews her resolve as a law student and future lawyer. An able learner, she in the end is the student speaker at the law school graduation ceremony. . . .

[W]e do appreciate Kingsfield and Stromwell as stock Hollywood teachers. They are devoted to their students and teach them both the law and how to live in our society. One hopes Kingsfield and Stromwell delight in their self-images as teachers and continue to rely on those self-images in their future work. . . .

A third and final Hollywood stock character that has proven capable of accommodating the law professor is the personally and morally flawed individual who is sympathetic, bordering on pathetic. . . . [T]he character stumbles through life prompting compassion and pity. Assuming, as is the case, that Hollywood fashions characters who might speak powerfully to potential viewers and in some way or another entice them to spend their dollars, sympathetic failures are viable possibilities. Many of us, after all, recognize ourselves to be flawed and bear the weight of assorted contradictions on our shoulders. We can relate to sympathetic failures. In the present, the sympathetic failure might be a more common character than either the crusading hero or the devoted teacher. . . .

A law professor who might strike us as a sympathetic failure is Professor Thomas Callahan, who is portrayed by actor Sam Shepard in *The Pelican Brief*. The film is derived from John Grisham's third novel, it reached number one on the *New York Times*' bestseller list, and film rights were quickly auctioned off in Hollywood.

The film's hero is Darby Shaw, a brilliant Tulane University School of Law student, who is played by Julia Roberts. In an early scene in Professor Callahan's class in Constitutional Law, Shaw shows both her intelligence and feistiness in a discussion of *Bowers v. Hardwick*. She nicely conceptualizes the right of privacy and explains how it might apply to the facts of the case. When Callahan asks her why the Justices did not agree with her interpretation, she answers, "Because they were wrong." Later in the film Shaw figures out why somebody might have wanted to assassinate two very different Justices, one an arch conservative and the other a wooly liberal. She also finds the proof to back up her discovery, enlists a prominent Washington reporter to help her, and dramatically eludes the villains who try to assassinate her. . . .

Professor Callahan, meanwhile, assumes a more pedestrian form. Immediately after the class on *Bowers v. Hardwick*, we find him leading Shaw not through a discussion of constitutional doctrine but rather into his bedroom. Callahan and Shaw — law professor and law student — are lovers. We learn later from Callahan's old law school friend who works in Washington, D.C. that Shaw is only the most recent of Callahan's student conquests — although this time he seems truly smitten. Unfortunately, Callahan is stalled in his scholarly work and staring down the tunnel of an unsatisfying career. . . . The filmmakers do not invite us to lionize Callahan — he is not a hero, and we have good reason to wonder about his motives and commitments as a teacher. At the same time we are not encouraged to dislike or reject him. Callahan, the law professor, is a sympathetic failure.

Callahan meets his maker less than one-half of the way through the film. He and Shaw are out to dinner in New Orleans, and although the restaurant is elegant and appealing, their evening goes badly. Callahan is self-pitying and obnoxious, telling Shaw that he just wants to stay in bed, drink, and have sex. She reminds him of his book project, but he laughs off the idea, mockingly saying she should write the book instead of him. When Callahan becomes inebriated, she asks him to give her the car keys so that she can drive home, but he refuses to give them to her. She then begins to walk home, while Callahan climbs into the car, rolls down the window, and announces for all the world to hear, "Ms. Shaw, you take my breath away." He then starts the car, which explodes, killing him on the spot. Assassins had hoped to kill Shaw, who had figured out the reason behind the killing of the Supreme Court Justices, but their bomb killed Callahan.

With the body blown to bits, Callahan's funeral was presumably a closed-coffin affair. Those who came to pay their respects no doubt reflected on the tragic end of a morally and personally flawed individual. But couldn't we find flaws in almost all of us? At least Callahan knew his failings and weaknesses. He might even have drawn some energy from this knowledge. A law professor might use one's self-image as a sympathetic failure to at least carry on.

NOTES & QUESTIONS

1. Did you notice that Professor Callahan, who propositions Elle Woods in *Legally Blonde*, is an adjunct, and not actually a tenured (permanent) member of the Harvard Law School faculty? Are you aware of the differences among the faculty who teach you? Some may be tenured or tenure-track faculty, some may be on long-term contracts, and some may be adjuncts, invited to teach one course a semester. Adjuncts are usually judges or practicing attorneys, expert in their area of law, and happy to be associated in this way with a local law school, often their alma mater. Should students' standards and expectations be different for adjuncts?

2. Professor Callahan propositions Elle Woods in *Legally Blonde*, and another fictional Professor Callahan has a clandestine affair with his student Darby Shaw in *The Pelican Brief*. Does your school have any policies against harassment of students by professors and/or relationships between students and faculty? What are the purposes of such policies?

Harvard Law School's Sexual Harassment Policy is available at http://www.law.harvard.edu/academics/handbook/legal/2010-2011-policy-and-guidelines-related-to-sexual-harassment.html. Examine Guideline Number 3. Could Elle Woods have filed a complaint with the Harvard Law School administration under this guideline? Would the professor have had a colorable defense?

3. Perhaps the public's greater awareness and concern with sexual harassment has led to more frequent portrayals of it in the Hollywood cinema, but then, too, Hollywood might simply like sexual harassment scenes because they are lustful and salacious. Why do you think popular culture dramatizes sexual harassment so frequently?

E. LAW SCHOOLS

Think about the number of real law schools that boast fictional graduates. Harvard may lead the pack, with James Hart (*The Paper Chase*), Elle Woods (*Legally Blonde*), Oliver Barrett IV (*Love Story*, 1970), and Mark Watson (*Soul Man*) all attending that school. But Columbia is no slouch: it can claim Marshall Erickson of the television series *How I Met Your Mother*, *Body Heat*'s Edmund Walker (played by Richard Crenna), *Law & Order*'s Jamie Ross (played by Carey Lowell), Matthew Murdock, the everyday persona of the Marvel Comics hero Daredevil, and his law partner Franklin Nelson, *Just Cause*'s Paul Armstrong (played by Sean Connery) and the television series *Raising the Bar*'s Trudy Kessler (played by Jane Kaczmarek). The television series *The West Wing* featured a Yale Law School graduate, Josh Lyman, (played by Bradley Whitford), the President's Deputy Chief of Staff. But other real law schools rate mentions in the movies, although they may not appreciate it. Florida State can claim Ned Levine, the anti-hero of *Body Heat*, who murders Edmund Walker. Darby Shaw (*The Pelican Brief*) attends Tulane. The short-lived television series *The Deep End* (created by David Hemingson, previously a practicing attorney) featured first-year associates who graduated from such prestigious schools as Columbia, Stanford, Cambridge, and that dark horse Case Western Reserve. Why do you think screenwriters and television scriptwriters send their fictional law students to real law schools and graduate their fictional lawyers from real institutions? Why do they repeatedly choose certain schools, and what message does that send to audiences about those particular schools?

When the culture industry wants to send a message about questionable legal education, or questionable lawyering, it sometimes creates fictional law schools, like the one in *The Socratic Method*. The students in that film attend the "Chester A. Arthur School of Law," whose professors swear by the Socratic Method (hence the title of the movie). Notice how the film weaves the most recognizable facet of legal education in with questionable legal tactics to present some very unpalatable behavior on the part of some of its characters. Do you think the movie is just taking potshots at legal education, or do you think some of the criticism is valid? What evidence can you point to in order to justify your opinion?

How does popular culture generally transmit the image of legal education and its effect on law students? Do you think that the way legal education is portrayed (the adversarial method, the necessity to win, the need for competition, and the anxiety for rankings, for example) suggests that law students believe or are taught to believe that the end justifies the means, and that they learn very early in their careers that nice guys finish last? Or does it suggest that law students themselves self-select — that is, people who are naturally ambitious and somewhat ruthless "rise to the top" and triumph over their colleagues who are less ruthless, less ambitious, or nicer?

The film *Shattered Glass* (2003) tells the story of Stephen Glass, a journalist working for the prestigious magazine *The New Republic*, who claims that the pressure of law school classes was partly to blame for the mistakes he made in reporting a story that began to lead to his downfall. Eventually, other reporters and Glass's editor discover that Glass has fabricated a number of stories. Glass resigns, and the film ends with a scene in which he admits only to fabrication of a few stories, although his editor is highly suspicious of other stories he wrote and that the magazine published. Glass later finished his law school education at Georgetown University Law School and wrote a novel, *The Fabulist* (2003), about a reporter who lies constantly.

NOTES & QUESTIONS

1. In 1992, the American Bar Association issued the MacCrate Report, a study of U.S. legal education with recommendations that law schools provide specific skills and values training for law students. Since then the practicing bar has continued to urge law schools to provide such training. Do you feel the MacCrate Report has had an impact at your law school? Is there adequate skills-training? Are there abundant clinical opportunities? Do you think that your law school adequately prepares you to practice law? Most importantly, should preparation for practice be legal education's primary mission? Or should law school prepare you as well for a career — in other words, "to think and behave like a lawyer"?

2. Several of the featured films for this chapter depict law students in search of practical training. For example, Charles Johnson in *The Socratic Method* is so desperate to get a clerkship during law school that he falsifies letters of recommendation. Elle Woods in *Legally Blonde* eagerly seeks work with a practicing attorney (her criminal law professor). Do the films suggest any tensions between "on the job" and classroom learning?

3. Charles Johnson and Elle Woods seek clinical work during their first years of law school. Most law schools discourage law students from working in the first year, for what the law schools consider good reasons. What might those reasons be? Knowing what you know now about the stresses of the first year, do you agree?

4. Is experience in a law school clinic the approximate equivalent of experience one would get as a law clerk? Consider that law clerks get paid, and law students in a clinic do not — they get law school credit. What other differences can you name?

5. In *The Socratic Method*, when Charles Johnson gets a job with Mr. Meffastaffalo, he engages in what can only be described as really underhanded tactics to bring in clients. What do you make of Mr. Meffastaffalo's secretary/paralegal's explanation that Charles, and not her boss, is responsible for the tactics? Is she correct? What image does Charles' subsequent behavior in bringing in clients present to the general public about law students and their training? Does it reinforce stereotypes about lawyers in general, or does Charles' decision to quit (and his stated reasons for quitting) actually bring out heroic images of lawyers in popular culture? (Think about what Charles does to Kenneth Stafford). Do you think that law clinic training is designed to lessen the risk that law students might meet up with a "Mr. Meffastaffalo"? How many "Mr. Meffastaffalos" do you think are really out there?

6. In the film *Reversal of Fortune*, Professor Alan Dershowitz, played by Ron Silver, recruits a number of his current students, as well as a former student, to assist him in preparing an appeal for client Claus von Bülow. One of the students, Minnie, is reluctant to participate because she thinks von Bülow is guilty — after all, a jury has already convicted him. Watch this scene to determine whether you think Dershowitz and the other students manipulate her into going along with the group.

7. In the iconic television show *Perry Mason* (1957-66), Perry (Raymond Burr) takes on a client, law student David Gideon (Karl Held) accused of murder. After he successfully defends Gideon (of course — Mason's clients, with only a couple of exceptions, are never convicted), he hires the law student to clerk for him. Gideon appears in a number of episodes during the 1961-62 season. Another law student, Ken Malansky, appears in the made-for-television movie *Perry Mason: The Case of the Lethal Lesson* (1989) as a student at the school at which Perry is teaching a course. Apparently he so impresses Perry that the legendary lawyer hires him on, and when Ken becomes an attorney, he stays for years (and many made-for-television movies).

F. DIVERSITY

Law schools were at one time filled exclusively (or almost exclusively) with students who were male, white, and (usually) well-to-do. This demographic has changed dramatically in the past 30 to 35 years, but certain kinds of students still face extra hurdles in law school. Thus, this part of the chapter examines the particular pressures faced by law students who are women, members of minority groups, or forced to cope with financial problems. Of course, *Legally Blonde*'s main character Elle Woods is someone who has all the money in the world; still, she encounters a number of problems. She quickly discovers, for example, that money does not buy law school happiness. Use the featured films for this chapter to reflect on how law schools may fail to help some students clear the special hurdles in their lives.

In the next excerpt Professor Jennifer Rosato explores and ultimately rejects the argument that the Socratic Method is especially deleterious for women. She suggests ways legal education can be humanized without being feminized.

THE SOCRATIC METHOD AND WOMEN LAW STUDENTS: HUMANIZE, DON'T FEMINIZE
Jennifer Rosato
7 Southern California Review of Law and Women's Studies 37 (1997)

Complaints have been leveled against the Socratic Method of law teaching for many years. Notwithstanding these complaints, the Socratic Method continues to be the primary pedagogy used by law school teachers. Renewed concerns about the continued use of this teaching method have been raised by recent studies that address its effect on women law students. The results of these studies are overwhelmingly negative: they conclude that the Socratic Method alienates, oppresses, traumatizes and silences women. The study conducted at the University of Pennsylvania Law School (the "Guinier Study") reported that women students perform less well in law school, in large measure because of the teaching methodology employed during their first year. . . .

The studies also have shown that this alienation is exacerbated by the inherent maleness of the law school classroom. The women students complain that they are forced to think in a male-oriented manner: competitively, logically, unemotionally. This type of thinking differs from what has been described as a woman's way of thinking, which includes evincing more concern for the rights of others, and being more sensitive to context. Commenting on the type of analysis required of a law student in the classroom, one author noted that a woman's mind "just does not work that way."

Even more significantly, these studies document how the characteristics of the law school classroom negatively affect women's law school performance. The studies consistently show that women are silenced in the classroom: they volunteer less and ask fewer questions than their male counterparts. They feel isolated and have lost confidence in themselves. A number of women students also report that, even when "playing the game" as effectively as their male counterparts, they feel like they have unwillingly acquired a different (and less desirable) identity. Several women described it as having their voices "stolen." Overall, these studies reflect the women's alienation from the law school experience.

Furthermore, the Guinier study concluded that a significant number of female students do not play the game effectively because they fail to win its coveted prizes with the same frequency as men. The study found that men are three times more likely than women to be in the top ten percent of the first-year class, and that men gain most of the honors in law school such as membership on law reviews and moot court societies. Without extensive follow-up studies, it is unclear whether these results are representative of other law schools or unique to the University of Pennsylvania. The recent Law School Admission Council (LSAC) study, which compared results at ninety law schools, suggests similar disparities in academic performance. Although women performed overall as well as men during the first year, they performed less well than men when matched against the grade distribution, and performed less well than their undergraduate grade point averages would suggest.

Even if women students perform academically as well as their male counterparts, their performance is impaired through silencing, isolation and loss of self-esteem. This disparate impact should concern teachers and students alike. So how should we address this concern effectively? The Guinier Study strongly suggested that the law school classroom should be changed to accommodate women's different learning styles. Such a change would include limiting the use of the Socratic Method and replacing it with more "feminine" teaching methods. Although unintended, this suggestion seems to imply that methods less rigorous than the Socratic Method should be used.

As a legal educator and feminist who regularly uses the Socratic Method, I think that radically changing its use at this time would be a mistake. It would ignore other more important causes of these problems, and would fail to recognize the virtues of this method for all students — even women. Therefore, I urge retention of the Socratic Method as the principal form of pedagogy, particularly in the first year of law school when the foundations of legal analysis are being developed.

One of the primary complaints voiced by the women in these studies is of harassing and inappropriate conduct by certain male professors and fellow students. The professors make sexist jokes or ignore the valuable contributions of women students. More generally, these professors engage in "negative emotional techniques" that have the effect of intimidating women more than men, such as acting aggressively or actively insulting students.

This conduct is unacceptable to men and women students and should cease. But getting rid of the Socratic Method will not necessarily make it happen. Humiliation and harassment are not inherent to the Socratic Method. The true Socratic teacher encourages students to think critically and does not disparage them if they fail to fulfill the teacher's expectations. The true Socratic teacher also assures the students, in one way or another, that they are not expected to "win" the "contest" because it is stacked against them. . . .

The second complaint, that of requiring a woman to think in a male-oriented manner — competitively, logically, and unemotionally — is not so much a complaint about the Socratic Method itself as it is about the adversarial nature of our current adjudicatory system. A number of feminist scholars have made the case for a less male-dominated, less adversarial system of justice, and I agree that this is a long-term goal that we should seek to attain. I also agree that law school teachers have some responsibility for reducing hierarchy in the classroom to the extent necessary to create an atmosphere of openness and to encourage students to present a variety of perspectives.

On the other hand, the primary obligation that I have to my students is to prepare them with the skills and values necessary to enter the practice of law in the 1990s — where jobs are scarce and mentoring is limited. For the most part, I am not preparing my students for jobs in academia and I am not teaching them to be graduate students in the humanities. They have entered law school with the expectation that they would be prepared to become effective practicing lawyers. Therefore, I must assist them in understanding the adversarial system and in playing the role of lawyers within that system. This means that all of my students must learn the fundamentals of legal analysis, which include articulating "neutral" principles of law to decisionmakers who may not agree with them, and determining how these principles apply to problems that clients might present to them. The Socratic Method is an excellent way to help them do that. If we abandon the Socratic Method, it probably will have little impact on the adversarial system as a whole, but will result in students being ill-prepared to work within it because they will not have gained the foundational knowledge they need. Our long-term goal of a less adversarial system should not be achieved at the expense of our students' ability to become competent lawyers. . . .

The third complaint that I hear emanating from the women law students in these studies is a general lack of support in the law school, not just in the law school classroom. The traditional teaching methods would be less threatening to women if they were made to feel as if they belonged in law school. Institutional support for women law students could take various forms: for example, providing women law students with more role models by hiring more women law professors and by placing greater value in the reappointment and tenure process on a professor's contributions to women students; creating and implementing effective sexual harassment policies; providing support (financial and otherwise) for women's groups within the law school and for educational programs that are of particular interest to women students; and making more counselors available that are sensitive to the problems of women law students. None of these changes would require abandonment of the Socratic Method and they would go a long way toward making women feel as though they are an integral part of the institution. . . .

Recognizing the danger of indulging in the gender stereotypes that I eschew, I posit a few reasons why the Socratic Method might affect some women more negatively than men. First, the Socratic Method may discourage women students more easily because the method, by its nature, requires the students to recognize the limits of their knowledge. Although women and men both may feel badly when these limits are revealed publicly, women may be more likely to censor their future participation as a result. Similarly, the requirement of testing out newly formed ideas in front of a hundred peers may be considered a more significant imposition on women students because they may feel more self-conscious "sharing their thoughts" in the classroom discussion, particularly if they are not sure what they are talking about. The inherent competitiveness in attempting to garner the professor's attention may be a game that women students are less willing to play. Finally, women may not be accustomed to the male-oriented thinking required by the Socratic dialogue in the modern law school classroom.

Even if it could be shown that women are more negatively affected by the Socratic Method in these ways or others, it does not mean that the use of the Socratic Method should be circumscribed for their benefit. The Socratic Method provides valuable benefits to women students. It ensures that women students are as comfortable and experienced as men in "thinking like a lawyer." In addition, adapting the law school classroom to fit a woman's learning style (whatever that means) would send the dangerous message that women students cannot withstand the rigors of the Socratic Method or, worse yet, law school in general. . . .

Instead of feminizing the Socratic Method, we should focus on humanizing it to make it an effective teaching method for all law students, not just women. Some male students feel just as anxious about and alienated by the Socratic Method as women. Although I am not the first author to suggest that the Socratic Method be humanized, my suggestions are designed to address directly some of the complaints voiced by women law students in recent studies. Three suggestions can be implemented easily: fostering an ethic of care in the classroom, using the Socratic Method meaningfully, and demystifying the learning process. These are all lessons taken from educational psychology and are used effectively in classrooms outside of the law school.

A. Fostering an Ethic of Care

Fostering an ethic of care in the classroom is necessary to counter the unnecessary competition and alienation that may take place in the law school classroom. This ethic can be fostered by the law school teacher in a variety of ways. Most importantly, the teacher should provide positive reinforcement to students whenever possible. There are various ways to do this during class without digressing from the dialogue. First and foremost, the effective law teacher always should strive to treat students and their ideas with respect. The way in which the teacher poses questions and answers should demonstrate that disagreement about ideas is possible without disrespect for the person. Ideally, modeling that behavior will encourage students to treat each other in a more respectful manner and enable them to engage in critical dialogue with one another.

Specifically, teachers should tell students they have good answers and questions (when they actually do) and refer to their insightful answers and questions in later discussions. Students enjoy having their thoughts recognized by the large group, especially if the teacher is able to credit the student by name.

Students who are struggling with the material or who become nervous when called on also need to be assured that they are valued in the classroom. If the student is initially less than responsive to questions, try to remember to come back to the student later in the discussion: by then the student may have regained composure or focused on the relevant material. The student also may be called into the teacher's office so that the teacher can discuss her approach to class participation and can encourage the student to become more involved in class discussion.

In addition, cooperation among students should be encouraged in the Socratic dialogue by asking them to assist each other with responses — just as they might do in the "real world" of lawyering. When a student has exhausted his ability to participate in the inquiry, or even when alternative views are sought, other students may be asked to assist as "colleagues" or "co-counsel." It is difficult to alleviate the inherently competitive aspects of the dialogue, so efforts to enhance cooperation should be made wherever possible.

B. Using the Socratic Method Meaningfully

Sometimes it seems that law teachers use the Socratic Method because it is the teaching method they are most comfortable with or — worse yet — because it is the only method that they know. As with any teaching method, this one should be used to accomplish educational objectives carefully developed by the teacher. I have made the case for the continued use of the Socratic Method, but I do not advocate its exclusive use. If the teacher cannot articulate why the Socratic Method is being used, it may not be the appropriate pedagogy or the teacher's educational objectives may not be sufficiently defined. The teacher then should consider using other teaching methods such as lecture, problems, role plays, games, or a less structured discussion. Because many fundamental analytical skills are learned during the first year of law school, the Socratic Method probably should be used less frequently in the second and third years of law school. However, it should not be abandoned for other techniques that seem less rigorous and appear the easiest way to contend with the apathy and boredom upper-class students often possess.

C. Demystifying the Learning Process

There are a number of legitimate reasons why a teacher utilizing the Socratic Method might choose to withhold the answers to the questions posed in class. The teacher, like Socrates, may not know the answer. Or perhaps the educational objective is for the students to learn how to derive the answer for themselves, with the teacher providing feedback on the student's proficiency. Once the inquiry is completed, however, the teacher should feel free to discuss the objectives of the questioning with the students and how the objectives were (or were not) achieved during the dialogue. For example, tell the students why you asked particular questions and explain what types of answers you sought and why. As law teachers, we seem to think that debriefing would expose us as impostors, like the Wizard of Oz!

Debriefing has been used effectively in other educational contexts. It can be used in the law school classroom after an exercise or a dialogue without sacrificing the rigors of the Socratic Method. If debriefing is not appropriate or time does not permit it, a teacher can debrief individually with student participants after class to talk to them about the classroom dialogue that the student just experienced. I have talked to numerous students in my office about my goals for our dialogue, and have provided them with supportive and critical comments about their individual participation.

At a minimum, debriefing benefits students by reducing anxiety and isolation. Maybe this tool will help students learn to understand that the Socratic Method does not exist simply to humiliate them unnecessarily. Eventually, students may understand that there is a method to the teacher's madness. It actually may be the way students learn best, regardless of gender. . . .

NOTES & QUESTIONS

1. Do you agree with Professor Rosato that criticisms of the Socratic Method should not be understood as a woman's issue? Does a female law student like Elle Woods in *Legally Blonde* experience the Socratic Method differently from a male law student like James Hart in *The Paper Chase*? What, generally, are the relationships of gender and Socratic teaching?

2. A professor who rejects the distancing inherent in the Socratic Method might encounter different kinds of problems. In *Rounders*, Mike McDermott develops a close relationship with his professor, Abe Petrovsky — so close, in fact, that the good professor loans him money. Is this a good idea?

3. After taking the loan, McDermott returns to gambling, his former life and what he knows best — to raise the cash that he and his friend need to get out of trouble. Money is a dominant theme in many law school films. It is a driving force for many of the characters in the films suggested for this chapter. The desire for it pushes them to study law. The lack of it forces them to do things they would not otherwise do in order to go to or stay in school. Once again, law and money seem to be intertwined. Consider that in the real world, whether a client can pay for an attorney may well determine whether the attorney will take the case. How realistic therefore is the constant link between law school and money in these films? Or do most movies about people in school necessarily discuss financing?

4. Raising money to stay in law school and pay for living expenses is a dilemma discussed in many films and television shows, not just in the ones discussed in this chapter. The television series *The Paper Chase* follows the law students' personal lives, and in some episodes, dramatizes the problems they have in making ends meet. The second season episode "Cinderella" (first aired July 15, 1983), for example, features a single mother who has problems finding day care.

In the docudrama *Conviction* (2010), the main character Betty Anne Waters goes to Roger Williams University School of Law and works as a waitress to pay the bills. At one point her two sons tell her they want to live with their father, her ex-husband, both because law school takes up so much of her time and because she is so obsessed with exonerating her brother Kenny who is in prison for life. Betty Anne also feels somewhat like a fish out of water because of her age and social status; as her friend Abra (played by Minnie Driver) tells her, they are the only two old ladies in the class. Most law students do not have to make difficult choices about work and child care; law students are primarily young and unmarried, and usually white. They also may have debt but do not have to work inordinate hours; indeed, law schools often put limits on the number of hours first-year students may work per week. In the Indian film *Jaalsaaz* (1999), a law student becomes the mistress of a wealthy man rather than marry a young lawyer she doesn't love.

In the film *The Great Buck Howard* (2008), law student Troy Gable (Colin Hanks) abandons law school not just because he wants to join a mentalist (John Malkovich) on the road (that opportunity actually comes later), but because he doesn't see the law as a profession that is likely to satisfy him intellectually and emotionally. His father (played by Tom Hanks) eventually suggests that he consider a compromise — practice entertainment law. Would that be such a terrible fate? What doesn't his father understand about Troy's decision? Notice that Buck Howard ultimately makes the same decision as Troy — he gives up the bright lights of Las Vegas, and the opportunity to be a headliner, for life on the road. What is important in life? Money or happiness? Or does one need enough of both to get by? What should you compromise, if anything, to get them?

5.   The following excerpt discusses the ways Elle Woods in *Legally Blonde* overcomes the obstacles placed in front of her and, in the end, can be seen as heroic.

"WE DON'T WANT ADVANTAGES": THE WOMAN LAWYER HERO AND HER QUEST FOR POWER IN POPULAR CULTURE

Christine Alice Corcos
53 Syracuse Law Review 1225 (2003)

Legally Blonde presents us with a comic view of the law but makes some important points about the nature of success and the nature of integrity. Elle Woods, a pretty, popular "Valley girl," a more grown up Cher, the protagonist of *Clueless*, is expecting a marriage proposal from her longtime boyfriend Warner, a wealthy East Coast preppy with political ambitions. But Warner tells her that his future does not include her. He needs to marry "Jacqueline Kennedy, not Marilyn Monroe." Elle is crushed. Her initial reaction is to try to compete with the woman he is likely to meet in law school. Only later does she begin to see herself as a real law student, and eventually as a real lawyer. At the beginning of the film, she sees herself not as the heroine of her own life, but as Snow White, or at least Cinderella. At the end, no fairy tale character corresponds to her new persona.

Elle decides to apply to Harvard Law School to maintain contact with Warner. As she tells the career services officer, she has no "back-up school." "I'm going to Harvard," she says brightly. The counselor points out that she has a 4.0, but her major in fashion merchandising is not exactly the traditional pre-law curriculum. Elle, like Amanda Bonner and Kathryn Murphy, decides to re-write the rules of the game by emphasizing the transferable skills that her major and her sorority experience have given her. Her application video, professionally prepared, is a model of persuasion. The Harvard Law School admissions committee members are awed (though it must be admitted, they all seem to be men. Still, we must give Elle credit. She knows how to talk to men).

Elle's arrival at Harvard indicates the extent to which she is not willing to give up what makes her an individual. She brings along her Chihuahua, her wardrobe, and her "Valley girl" approach to life, finding solace in getting her hair and nails done. She refuses to compromise by adopting the feminist, anti-male stance of some of the other women students, nor does she abandon her mode of dress, even when faced with Warner's fiancée, a woman who dresses in tweeds, wears her hair in a Hillary Clinton-like page boy [style] and makes her disdain for Elle very clear.

Elle's first few weeks at Harvard are rocky. She shows up unprepared for her first class, is verbally skewered by the female professor, and leaves in embarrassment and anger, planning to quit. Then she takes up the challenge, takes the advice of a young man she meets on campus, whom she mistakes for another student, but who is actually Emmett, a practicing attorney assisting her criminal law professor. She begins to compete successfully with Warner and more particularly with his fiancée Vivian.

Elle makes friends with a local manicurist, who is depressed because her abusive ex-lover has kept her beloved dog Rufus. Elle confronts the man, spouting legalese and figuratively pushing him aside in order to take possession of Rufus. It is her first legal success. She obtains a coveted internship with her criminal law professor and begins work on a murder case. Her particularized knowledge of the client's history and profession, based on her "Valley girl" background, allows her to bond with the client in a way that escapes the other members of the defense team. At the same time, she faces a crisis of conscience when she discovers that the professor who offered her the internship is interested only in an affair with her. She decides to resign her internship, but the female professor who had humiliated her on her first day, and who has changed her mind about Elle's abilities, dissuades her by pointing out that if Elle resigns, she is allowing the man to set both the agenda and the tone of her future career. At the same time, the client's trust in Elle allows her (unbelievably) to take over the lead in the defense case. The client fires the evil male professor, and hires Elle instead (under Emmett's supervision). Elle wins the case, based again on her particularized knowledge of fashion and of the kinds of people who are likely to understand and appreciate fashion and design. She demonstrates that the primary witness against the client is lying about his affair with her, and that the victim's daughter is the real culprit. The daughter has testified that she did not hear the gunshot that killed the victim because she was in the shower washing her hair. As Elle points out, this is unlikely because the girl has just gotten an expensive permanent. No one with a new permanent washes her hair for at least a day; it deactivates the chemicals that curl the hair. Elle's triumph is complete when she graduates first in the class, giving a suitably "Valley girl" address. She and Vivian become best friends. Vivian abandons Warner, who finds himself without a job offer, without a girlfriend, and without honors. Emmett decides to propose to Elle. While *Legally Blonde* is a fantasy, it presents us with the image of a woman who refuses to abandon her interests, her beliefs, her friends, or her dreams, especially the dream she has recently acquired. She imagines herself as a lawyer, then becomes a lawyer. Unlike Alex Owens, the protagonist of *Flashdance*, she actually does the work necessary to achieve her goals. Yet she maintains her interest in makeup, hair styles, clothes, and good design. She calls a sexual harasser by his name, but finds the courage (aided by the female professor who terrorized her in her first year) to continue toward her goal. She finds ways to express her personality within the confines of the law school while still producing the kind of work that legal academia expects. She integrates all of these into the practice of law. Within the limits of this cinematic fantasy, Elle is heroic.

NOTES & QUESTIONS

1. To what extent do Elle Woods' problems in law school derive from the fact she is a woman? What messages does *Legally Blonde* send about female law students and their ability to compete in a male-dominated world? Compare the message that you derive from *Legally Blonde* with the messages sent by other films in which a character (major or minor) is a female law student. Think also about fictional female law students on television such as Sondra Huxtable (played by Sabrina LeBeauf) on *The Cosby Show* (1984-92).

2. Is Elle Woods' main problem not her gender but rather her unusually feminine style of womanhood? Does *Legally Blonde* suggest there are right and wrong ways to be a woman?

3. Compare Elle Woods with other female law students in the films suggested for this chapter, e.g., Sarah Walker in *Soul Man*, who is a single parent, a member of a minority group, and a young woman who has to work during her first year of law school because someone else has deprived her of the scholarship she should have had. Susan Walsh in *The Socratic Method* is a fairly typical contemporary example of the female law student — she goes straight from college to law school. Her father is a successful lawyer, her fiancé is an attorney at her father's law firm, and, as her law school friends point out, she does not have to worry about getting a job offer. One is waiting for her once she passes the bar. One could argue that all three of these characters represent stereotypes of women, not just of lawyers. To what extent do you think that these stereotypes represent the truth about women's roles in our society?

4. Attractive, feminine women may encounter difficulties in legal roles other than that of the law student. Contemplate the obstacles faced by the paralegal Erin Brockovich (played by Julia Roberts) in the film *Erin Brockovich* (2000). To what extent is her inability to get the respect she thinks she deserves the result of her own attitudes and actions, and to what extent is it the result, again, of stereotyping?

5. In the film *Soul Man*, Mark Watson "passes" as a black man, even though he knows nothing about African Americans or African American culture (as he demonstrates by showing up at a Black Law Students Association study meeting dressed as a Black Panther). "Passing is a deception that enables a person to adopt certain roles or identities from which he would be barred by prevailing social standards in the absence of his misleading conduct. The classic racial passer in the United States has been the 'white Negro': the individual whose physical appearance allows him to present himself as 'white' but whose 'black' lineage (typically only a very partial black lineage) makes him a Negro according to dominant racial rules. A passer is distinguishable from the person who is merely mistaken — the person who, having been told that he is white, thinks of himself as white, and holds himself out to be white (though he and everyone else in the locale would deem him to be 'black' were the facts of his ancestry known)." Randall Kennedy, *Racial Passing*, 62 Ohio State Law Journal 1145, 1145 (2001). Mark's conduct is certainly misleading, and the disciplinary committee finds it fraudulent. Is it more fraudulent than it would have been if he had not been a law student? Another film that explores racial/ethnic passing is *The Human Stain* (2003), with Anthony Hopkins and Nicole Kidman, based on a novel by Philip Roth. On that and other films and the issue of racial identity in popular culture, see Bridget K. Smith, *Race as Fiction: How Film and Literary Fictions of "Mulatto" Identity Have Both Fostered and Challenged Social and Legal Fictions Regarding Race In America*, 16 Seton Hall Journal of Sports & Entertainment Law 44 (2006).

6. To what extent are gay and lesbian students "othered" by the law school experience? Sketch the screenplay of a Hollywood film about a gay or lesbian

student. Could such a film attract a mass audience?

G. LAW STUDENTS, ETHICS, AND PERSONAL CHOICES

As part of their professional education nearly all law students learn about (and most adhere to) a code of responsibility known as an "honor code" or a "code of ethics" promulgated by their law school. The code sets out the types of conduct deemed inappropriate for law students. A student reported to the administrative officer responsible for enforcing the code may find herself before a disciplinary board convened for the purpose of deciding whether she should be reprimanded privately or publicly, suspended for a time from attending school, or expelled. A sanction may be recorded on the student's transcript; if sufficiently grave, it may mean that the student might be prevented from taking the bar exam and ultimately from ever practicing law.

The following excerpt provides the most important provisions in one law school's code for its students.

CODE OF STUDENT PROFESSIONAL RESPONSIBILITY
Louisiana State University Law Center 2011

Introduction

Law School is the first step toward becoming a member of the legal profession. Members of the legal profession are subject to the highest standards of professional conduct. The Law Center, therefore, expects its students to adhere to high standards of conduct during their legal education and to avoid even the appearance of impropriety during that process.

Just as lawyer behavior reflects on the bar and the courts even when they are not in Court, student behavior can reflect on the Law Center away from the physical facility. When students represent the Law Center, or when their behavior might closely affect the Law Center or its relationships with other institutions in Louisiana or abroad, students are expected to abide by the professional obligations of the Code of Student Professional Responsibility. It is the obligation of every student to report to the Office of the Vice Chancellor or to a member of the Ethics Committee of the Student Bar Association any violation of this Code of Student Professional Responsibility. Students are expected to live up to the standards set forth in this Code and to assist in its enforcement.

The Code

Lying, cheating, plagiarism, theft, and other forms of student misconduct are prohibited.

1.   Lying includes, but is not limited to, the following:

      a.   Knowingly furnishing false or misleading information to the administrators, faculty, or other personnel of the Law Center.

    b.   Forging, altering, or misusing Law Center documents, records, or identification cards.

    c.   Knowingly furnishing false information in any proceedings undertaken pursuant to this Code.

    d.   Failing to acknowledge one's presence in class when present and requested by the instructor to recite materials or otherwise participate in class.

    e.   Falsifying information on a class roll sheet in any manner, such as by signing or initialing for another student who is not present, by procuring another student to sign or initial for a student not present, or by signing or initialing a roll sheet indicating that the student was present when the student was not actually present in the classroom or was so late that this student missed a substantial portion of the class.

2. Cheating includes, but is not limited to, the following:

    a.   Copying from or looking upon another student's examination paper during an examination with intent to give or obtain information relevant to the examination.

    b.   Using material during an examination not authorized by the person administering the examination.

    c.   Collaborating during an examination with any other person by giving or receiving information without authority.

    d.   Stealing, bribing, otherwise obtaining, selling, giving away, or bribing another person to obtain all or part of an unadministered examination or information about an unadminstered examination.

    e.   Substituting for another student, or permitting any other person to substitute for oneself, to take an examination.

    f.   Submitting as one's own, in fulfillment of academic requirements, a report, term paper, memorandum, brief, or any other written work prepared totally or in part by another person.

    g.   Taking time beyond that allowed other students for the completion of an examination, without the expressed permission of the person administering the examination.

    h.   Selling, giving, or otherwise supplying to another student for submission in fulfilling academic requirements any report, term paper, memorandum, brief, or any other written work.

    i.   Consulting any attorney regarding the specifics of any written or oral presentation, unless authorized by the instructor.

3. Plagiarism is the unacknowledged incorporation of another person's work in one's own work submitted for credit or publication (such material need not be copyrighted).

4. Theft includes, but is not limited to, the following:

a. The taking or unauthorized use of Law Center property, including any materials from the Law Library.

b. The taking or unauthorized use of the funds of the Law Center of any student organization.

c. The taking or unauthorized use of any property of other students while on campus, or of material related to the Law Center while off campus.

5. Student misconduct includes, but is not limited to, the following:

a. Attempting to commit, or being an accessory to the commission of any of the foregoing offenses.

b. Committing any misdemeanor on the premises of the Law Center, or on the premises of student residences associated with the Law Center or its programs, or at an official Law Center function, or committing any felony.

c. Knowingly interfering with any proceedings undertaken pursuant to this Code, including threats directed to students, faculty, or other persons initiating or participating in such proceedings.

d. Repeatedly attending class without adequately preparing the material assigned by the instructor, unless special arrangements are made with the instructor prior to class.

e. Refusing to participate in class discussion when requested to do so by the instructor.

f. Using any other person's work or assistance in the preparation of work to be submitted for credit, unless authorized by the instructor.

g. Committing any act of vandalism or destruction with respect to Law Center property, the property of a Law Center partner institution, the property of student residences associated with the Law Center or its programs, or the property where a Law Center function is being held.

h. Intentionally disrupting a class.

i. Violating any rules established to govern student use of conduct in the Law Library.

j. Talking with another student during an examination with intent to give or obtain information relevant to the examination.

k. Utilizing materials submitted in fulfillment of the requirements of a course to fulfill the requirements of another course or courses without first obtaining consent of all faculty members affected.

Rules of Procedure for Disposition of Complaints

1. Any person having knowledge of a violation of this Code shall report the incident to the Vice Chancellor of the Law Center designated by the Chancellor to receive such reports, or to a member of the Ethics Committee of the Student Bar Association. If a report is made to a member of the Ethics Committee, that member shall promptly report the matter to the designated Vice Chancellor.

2. For Law Center programs and activities away from the physical facility, egregious conduct may be the grounds for expelling a student from the program or activity, in the discretion of the Program Director or Law Center representative.

3. The Vice Chancellor shall investigate the complaint. He may appoint a member of the faculty and of the Ethics Committee of the Student Bar Association to assist him. The Vice Chancellor shall determine whether there are reasonable grounds to initiate a proceeding to determine the merits of the complaint. If reasonable grounds are found to exist, the Vice Chancellor shall appoint a committee to determine the merits of the complaint.

4. The committee shall consist of five members: three members from the faculty and two law student members to be appointed by the Chairman of the Student Ethics Committee and the President of the Student Bar Association.

5. The Vice Chancellor shall set forth in writing the grounds of the complaint against the student and shall furnish a copy of the written complaint to the chairman of the committee.

6. The chairman shall designate the time and place for a hearing to determine the merits of the complaint.

7. The Chairman shall provide the student with a copy of the written complaint. The chairman shall prepare a notice containing the following information: (a) the time and place of the hearing; and (b) the date for furnishing the information described in the paragraphs 7, 8, and 9. The notice shall be furnished to the student and to the Vice Chancellor.

8. The Vice Chancellor and the student shall furnish to each other and to the chairman (a) a list of the names and addresses of witnesses whose testimony should be heard by the committee; and (b) a brief statement describing the substance of the testimony of each witness.

9. The Vice Chancellor and the student shall furnish to each other and to the chairman any documentary evidence which should be considered at the hearing.

10. The Vice Chancellor and the student shall furnish to each other and to the chairman the name of any person designated to assist him or her during the hearing.

11. The following may be present at the hearing: members of the committee, the student, the Vice Chancellor, persons designated to assist during the hearing, the witness under examination, and any person authorized by the committee to record the proceedings.

12. At the request of the student, the committee may permit such other persons as the committee deems appropriate to be present during the hearing.

13. All witnesses whose names have been submitted and who are available will be asked to testify unless the committee determines that their testimony would not assist in finding relevant facts or in making a recommendation as to the proper disposition of the case. The committee may also ask witnesses to testify whose names have not been submitted by the Vice Chancellor or the student. When practicable, notice of such witnesses shall be given to the student. The chairman shall notify all witnesses of the time and place of the hearing.

14. The chairman shall determine whether there are any facts which may be agreed upon and the order in which the witnesses shall be heard.

15. Prior to hearing the testimony of a witness, the chairman shall ask the witness whether he or she will truthfully respond to all questions.

16. The chairman will first examine the witness. The members of the committee will next examine the witness. The chairman may then permit the Vice Chancellor (or the person designated to assist him) and the student (or the person designated to assist him) to examine the witness. The order of examination may be varied by the chairman in order to effectively present the testimony of the witness.

17. The committee may receive any documentary evidence which the committee deems helpful in fairly performing its duty. The committee may receive affidavits based upon personal knowledge addressing relevant facts upon a finding that the witness cannot conveniently attend the hearing. If the committee feels that hearing the witness's testimony is necessary to achieve a fair result and disposition, the committee may ask the witness to appear to testify or, if the witness is unavailable, take whatever alternative steps it deems appropriate.

18. The committee may consider any reliable evidence which it deems helpful in fairly performing its duty. The chairman shall decide whether particular evidence should be heard and considered. His or her decision may be overruled upon motion of a committee member by a majority of the committee. A second to the motion to overrule is not required.

19. At the close of the hearing, the committee shall allow the student (or person designated to assist him or her) and the Vice Chancellor (or person designated to assist him) the opportunity to make a closing statement.

20. The student or the Vice Chancellor may request that the committee vary its procedures or grant a continuance and, upon a showing of good cause for such, the committee shall grant the request.

21. At the time of the hearing, the committee shall deliberate privately. The committee will, by majority vote, make and deliver to the Chancellor of the Law Center (a) written findings of fact and conclusions concerning the complaint; and (b) written recommendations concerning the proper disposition of the case. Any concurring or dissenting views of a committee member, including the chairman, shall be included at the member's request.

22. If the committee finds that the student committed a violation included in the complaint, the committee may recommend any appropriate sanction or combination of sanctions, including recommending that the student be:

   a. expelled from the Law Center indefinitely;

   b. expelled from the Law Center with a right to apply for readmission no sooner than a fixed date;

   c. suspended from the Law Center for a fixed period;

   d. publicly reprimanded by the Chancellor, with a copy of the public reprimand sent the Louisiana State Bar Association;

   e. denied course credit or assigned a grade of .7 in a course if the violation involved the student's conduct in a course.

23. The Chancellor shall advise the student of the recommendations of the committee and allow him or her a reasonable opportunity to respond in writing before imposing a sanction.

24. Determination of the sanction shall be at the discretion of the Chancellor. In arriving at the sanction, the Chancellor shall consult with the committee. Modification of a sanction shall be done only after consultation with the committee.

25. Upon the imposition of a sanction by the Chancellor, an announcement shall be placed on the bulletin boards of the Law Center to the effect that: "A student has been found guilty of a violation of (name the section) of the Code of Student Professional Responsibility in that he or she committed (name the offense), defined by that section as (quote the applicable section). The student has been (name the sanction)." The student's name shall be withheld unless the Chancellor determines that a public reprimand is in order.

26. The Chancellor, with or without a recommendation of the committee, may communicate the results of the proceedings to witnesses, faculty, or other interested parties if he determines it is in the best interests of the Law Center or the legal profession. . . .

NOTES & QUESTIONS

1. As the excerpt suggests, Louisiana State University Law Center has rules regarding the conduct of law students that are different and more refined than the rules for other students at the same university. This practice is common for law schools. Why might administrators and faculty members think different or additional ethical rules are necessary for law students?

2.   Several of the films discussed in this chapter feature conduct that would, if reported, require at minimum a disciplinary hearing. In *The Socratic Method*, Charles Johnson accepts his employer's offer of a "cheat sheet" with the answers to a forthcoming law school exam. What else does he do that would violate a law school's disciplinary code? What does he do that violates the law and would, if reported, disqualify him as a candidate for the bar? Should his friends report him? Does the fact that they do not report him mean that they should be reported to the appropriate law school disciplinary board? Why or why not? Are they fit candidates to practice law? Note that Johnson eventually ends up as a judge, and he hears the case against Kenneth Stafford. Should he have recused himself? What about the accusation Susan Walsh levels at Kenneth Stafford that he razored out an article put on reserve in the law library? The students take matters into their own hands after the library clerk reveals who had the book checked out last, but what do you think they should have done once they discovered the pages they needed to read were missing? Law library personnel have procedures for dealing with missing reserve items. Ask your own law library public services staff what it will do for you if you find yourself in such a predicament, and what sanctions it has in place for dealing with offenders.

3.   In *Soul Man*, Mark Watson accepts a scholarship under false pretenses. Some people might think he gets off extremely lightly — he agrees to pay the money to the person to whom the scholarship should have been paid in the first place, and who, it appears by the end of the film, is likely to turn out to be Mrs. Watson. However, he does learn some important lessons about what it means to be judged on appearances alone. Everyone judges him — blacks and whites alike. Do you think Mark Watson's fraud disqualifies him to be an attorney? If you had been on the panel that heard the complaint against him, how would you have decided his case? Why?

4.   James Hart in *The Paper Chase* and Elle Woods in *Legally Blonde* make the mistake of attending their first law school classes without completing the assigned reading first. Could they be disciplined under the Louisiana State University Law Center's Code of Student Professional Responsibility? Later in *The Paper Chase*, Hart defiantly tells Professor Kingsfield that he will participate in class only when he wishes. Is this a violation of 5.c. of the LSU Law Center Code of Student Professional Responsibility? If not, should it be?

5.   The amount of alcohol consumed in law school films is truly stupendous. In *The Socratic Method*, one of the law students (James Rodgers) seems to live at a bar named the "Frolic and Detour," yet he graduates at the top of his class, gets a great job offer, and eventually purchases the bar. Drinking goes merrily along in *The Paper Chase* and *Soul Man*. To what extent might excessive drinking and drunken conduct subject one to law school disciplinary proceedings?

Should law students be free to drink as much as they wish as long as they are not in their law school buildings or in facilities associated with their law schools? What if the school itself provides the alcohol, for example, at a law school function, or at an event sponsored by a law school organization?

6. While very little has been written about alcoholism as a disability in law school, a 1994 Association of American Law Schools report found that more than 30 percent of law students admitted to abusing alcohol while in school. *See Report of the AALS Special Committee on Problems of Substance Abuse in the Law Schools*, 44 Journal of Legal Education 35 (1994). At a day-long meeting in New York in 2003, several commentators told the assembled law school administrators that things had not really improved. *See* Thomas Adcock, *Despite '93 Report, Substance Abuse Persists in Law Schools*, New York Law Journal, June 27, 2003, at 16. The Washington College of Law, American University, created a video in 2009 that it has distributed to law schools and Lawyer Assistance Programs (LAPs) across the country in an attempt to assist them in dealing with law student addiction. "Getting Healthy, Staying Healthy" is a "significant new tool in our efforts to support the health and future of law students," according to David Jaffe, Associate Dean of Students at American University's Law School. For more information, *see* http://www.wcl.american.edu/news/gettinghealthyvideo.cfm.

Do you think popular culture glorifies drinking? Have you noticed how much drinking goes on at your law school? Do you think alcohol abuse is a problem at your school or among your friends? What, if anything, do you think you or others, including the law school administration, faculty, or student organizations, can or should do about it?

7. Gambling is a major problem in *Rounders*: Mike McDermott, played by Matt Damon, is a recovering gambler who attends law school. Poker is a pastime for the students in *The Socratic Method*, and Susan Walsh turns out to be quite a player, to the extent that Terry King worries that she will win all his scholarship money. While not much has been written about gambling addictions and law students, the lawyer with a gambling addiction is a recognized danger to his or her client. *See* Carol P. Waldhauser, *Identifying the Addiction: Part I (Lawyers Helping Lawyers: Part of the Solution* series) 28 Montana Lawyer 23 (January 2003), and Paul R. Ashe, *Attorneys and the Addiction of Gambling (Lawyers Helping Lawyers: Part of the Solution series)*, 28 Montana Lawyer 30 (February 2003).

8. Prescription drugs can also be a problem. In the season three episode of the television series *The Paper Chase* titled "Laura's Struggle," first aired July 6, 1985, a law student becomes addicted to medication in order to deal with the pressures of law school. Today, some law students use Adderall to stay awake so they can study and deal with law school, not because they have ADHD. Do you think use of a prescription drug in this way gives these students an unfair advantage, or are they simply being "smart consumers" who know what to ask of their physicians? Do you think the use of Adderall is likely to become a new addiction along the lines of what we have seen with the consumption of alcohol? *See* Jennifer Schiffner, *Harder, Better, Faster, Stronger: Regulating Illicit Adderall Use Among Law Students and Law Schools*, available at http://works.bepress.com/cgi/viewcontent.cgi?article=1000&context=jennifer_schiffner.

9. In some cases, law students, who are after all human, just take things too far. *Compulsion* (1959) dramatizes the story of two law students, played by Bradford Dillman and Dean Stockwell, who decide to commit the "perfect murder." They kidnap and kill a young boy simply because they can. Their families hire lawyer

Jonathan Wilk (played by Orson Welles), an attorney modeled on Clarence Darrow. The film is based on Meyer Levin's novel of the same name, which in turn is based on the real-life crime committed by Nathan Leopold and Richard Loeb. After a string of lesser crimes, Leopold and Loeb had decided to kill young Bobby Franks because they believed their superior intelligence entitled them to do so. Their families hired the famed Clarence Darrow to protect them not from conviction but from the death penalty. The Patrick Hamilton play *Rope* (1929) is another work based on the Franks murder. Alfred Hitchcock filmed it in 1948 on a single set, using a number of long unedited shots. The movie stars James Stewart, John Dall, and Farley Granger. For more about the Leopold and Loeb case, see Professor Douglas Linder's Leopold and Loeb trial page at http://law2.umkc.edu/faculty/projects/ftrials/leoploeb/leopold.htm. Another movie with a similar theme is *Columbo Goes to College* (1990); two students, one hoping to go to law school, murder a professor who plans to report them to the dean for ethical violations. When asked why they did it, one responds, "Because we could."

10.   Do you think law schools regiment student behavior, perhaps with honor codes, with rules concerning outside work, or by prescribing acceptable modes of dress? If so, do you think they have a reason for doing so?

H.   THE LAST HURDLE: THE BAR EXAM

Non-lawyers recognize the bar examination, like the Socratic Method, as an obstacle in the path to success for a future lawyer. Thus, references to "the bar exam" or "the bar" are common in popular culture, as are puns on the word "bar." A 2011 advertising campaign for Coors Light beer showed a law graduate entering a bar and looking for the "bar exam study group"; the writers of the commercial are obviously playing on the double meaning of the word "bar." The romcom (romantic comedy) *The Seat Filler* (2004) focuses on a young law grad who spends his days prepping for the bar and his nights earning his living as a "seat filler," someone who occupies celebrity seats at televised events while they are elsewhere (in the bathroom, for example). The documentary *A Lawyer Walks into a Bar* (2004) follows the lives of six California law school grads who prepare for that state's notoriously difficult bar. One of them has failed it more than forty times at the time of the movie's filming. Is the film an argument for fewer law schools? More stringent requirements to be admitted to law school?

In the popular 1992 legal comedy *My Cousin Vinny*, we learn that newly minted lawyer Vinny Gambini (Joe Pesci) has taken the New York bar exam numerous times, finally passing it just before his frantic cousin Bill (Ralph Macchio) calls him from an Alabama jail. Why has Vinny had so much trouble? Is it because he is a graduate of the "Brooklyn Academy of Law," which sounds like a dubious place to get one's law degree? Is it because his law school hasn't prepared him to take the bar, and he doesn't sound as though he has taken a bar review course, or studied much on his own (or clerked for a law firm)? In one funny scene, Vinny explains the weaknesses of the law school curriculum to his girlfriend Lisa:

> Lisa: [I]t didn't look like you knew what you were doin' in that courtroom today. Why is that?

Vinny: Well . . . it's all procedural crap. I'm gonna have to learn it as I go.

Lisa: "Learn as you go"? You didn't learn it in law school?

Vinny: (dismissively) Nah . . . they teach precedents, contracts, interpretations. You're supposed to learn procedure from the firm that hires you, or else you go to court and watch.

NOTES & QUESTIONS

1.   Consider the curricula in the pop cultural law schools mentioned in this chapter. Which ones seem to "teach to the bar exam," thus improving bar passage rates for their graduates? Do you think that is one of the functions of a law school? When you plan your schedule, do you cram as many bar courses into your semester as you can, or do you try to take some courses that will assist you in whatever kind of law you think you would like to practice? What about assisting you in your intellectual development? Since you are using this textbook, we'll assume you are in favor of intellectual development!

2.   In *Conviction* and *How I Met Your Mother*, we see the results of bar exam stress. In *Conviction*, Abra hides Betty Anne's ID as a prank right before they are ready to begin taking the bar. In the *How I Met Your Mother* episode "Spoiler Alert," first aired November 12, 2007, Marshall waits for his bar exam results and discovers that he has lost the password he needs to get access to the results. Do you think a lot of bar exam stress is exaggerated? After all, other professions are just as competitive, if not more so.

3.   Should law schools "teach to the bar"? Or should they prepare students to be good legal citizens and legal thinkers? This debate is taking place right now, both in the halls of academe and in law firms and in judges' chambers, partly because of the faltering economy. Is bar preparation part of a law school education, or the responsibility of the law school graduate?

4.   Ultimately, do you think that many of the less than flattering images of pop cultural legal education, "true-ish" though they might be, stem from some faults in the system that are now more obvious because educational costs are increasing, the economy is lagging, more law schools are opening up, and many more people are popping out of law schools and passing the bar with the right to practice and ready to compete for clients? Or, as you consider the unappetizing image of lawyers throughout the centuries, do you think non-lawyers have always made a sport of disliking lawyers, so it is only natural that they would dislike that lawyer breeding ground — the law school — and tend to portray it as unappealing?

Chapter 3

LAWYERS

A. FILMOGRAPHY

The Devil's Advocate (1997)

Jagged Edge (1985)

Liar Liar (1997)

Michael Clayton (2007)

Two Weeks Notice (2003)

B. IMAGES OF LAWYERS: GOOD OR EVIL?

Virtually all treatments of law in popular culture present their images of the law through the actions of people involved in the legal system, including lawyers, clients, witnesses, judges, jurors, police officers, legislators, government officials, and ordinary citizens. Most of the chapters of this book will deal with depictions of lawyers in popular culture in both general and specialized practices as "embodiments" of the different ways law can be seen and experienced. Although many depictions of the law are offered through the common genres of mysteries, crimes, and thrillers that most often involve criminal law enforcement, detection, and "bad men" in the Holmesian sense, most people who decide to come to law school have come with an image of "lawyer" imprinted on them by some exposure to a lawyer (usually, unrepresentatively, a trial lawyer) from movies, television, or literature (except for that minority of law students who have family members who are lawyers). Depending on the era in which you came of age, your image of lawyers might vary from a crusading justice-seeking do-gooder, to an involuntary hero like Atticus Finch in *To Kill a Mockingbird* (1962), to a greedy profit-maximizer, to sanctimonious prosecutors like those in *Law & Order* (1990-2010), to a sleazy divorce lawyer like Arnie Becker in *L.A. Law* (1986-94), to crafty and brilliant defense lawyers on *Perry Mason* (1957-66), *The Defenders* (1961-65), or *The Practice* (1997-2004), to a victimized prosecutor like Rusty Sabitch in *Presumed Innocent* (1990) and *Innocent* (2011) (this is a recent film of Scott Turow's recent novel), to a flighty Gen-X lawyer like *Ally McBeal* (1997-2002). Though the images of criminal trial lawyers (as prosecutors and defense attorneys) abound, in fact most lawyers are civil lawyers, and most today do not set foot in the courtroom.

Over the last five decades depictions of lawyers from the "Golden Age" of the 1950s of brilliant trial lawyers, seeking truth and justice, have evolved into more complex characters who sometimes violate ethical rules. For example, lawyers sleep with their clients in *Jagged Edge* (1985) and with jurors in *Suspect* (1987), and Frank Galvin in *The Verdict* (1982) rejects a settlement offer without discussing it with a client. Lawyers on screen have also diversified almost, but not quite as much, as the legal profession itself. For example, while in 1951 only 3% of lawyers were women, in 2010 31% of the bar was female, with 47% of the law student population being female. *See* ABA Commission on Women in the Profession, *A Current Glance at Women in the Law 2011*, January 2011. *But see* Timothy O'Brian, "Up the Down Staircase: Why Do So Few Women Reach the Top of Big Law Firms?" *The New York Times*, 19 Mar. 2006, 3-1 (reporting that partnership rates in major law firms for women still do not match their demographic representation in the profession). Demographic minority representation in the bar has also grown, but not at the same rate. *See* Richard Abel, *American Lawyers* (1989); David Wilkins, *From "Separate is Inherently Unequal" to "Diversity is Good for Business": The Rise of Market Based Diversity Arguments and the Fate of the Black Corporate Bar*, 117 Harvard Law Review 1548 (2004). In 2000 there were 40,000 black lawyers, a twenty-fold increase from 1960. *See* David Wilkins, *A Systematic Response to Systemic Disadvantage*, 57 Stanford Law Review 1915 (2005); *see also* Alex M. Johnson, Jr., *The Underrepresentation of Minorities in the Legal Profession: A Critical Race Theorist Perspective*, 95 Michigan Law Review 1005 (1997); Clay Smith, Jr., *Emancipation: The Making of the Black Lawyer* (1993); David Wilkins, *Two Paths to the Mountaintop: The Role of Legal Education in Shaping Values of Black Corporate Lawyers*, 45 Stanford Law Review 1981 (1993). For discussions of different kinds of lawyers in modern television depictions, see Christine Alice Corcos, *Women Lawyers*, and Michael Epstein, *Young Lawyers*, both appearing in *Prime Time Law: Fictional Television as Legal Narrative* (Robert M. Jarvis & Paul R. Joseph eds. 1998).

Images of lawyers in popular culture have veered dramatically over the years from extremes of lawyers as heroes to lawyers as villains, with debates among legal and film scholars about whether lawyers are more likely to be considered forces for social good or evil. *See, e.g.*, Michael Asimow, *Embodiment of Evil: Law Firms in the Movies*, 48 UCLA Law Review 1339 (2001); Michael Asimow, *Bad Lawyers in the Movies*, 24 Nova Law Review 531 (2000); Michael Asimow, *When Lawyers Were Heroes*, 30 University of San Francisco Law Review 1131 (1996); Paul Bergman, *The Movie Lawyers' Guide to Redemptive Legal Practice*, 48 UCLA Law Review 1393 (2001); Anthony Chase, *Lawyers and Popular Culture: a Review of Mass Media Portrayals of American Attorneys*, 1986 American Bar Foundation Research Journal 281; Steve Greenfield & Guy Osborn, *The Double Meaning of Law: Does it Matter if Film Lawyers are Unethical?*, in *Law and Popular Culture* (Michael Freeman ed. 2005); Carrie Menkel-Meadow, *The Sense and Sensibilities of Lawyers: Lawyering in Literature, Narratives, Film and Television, and Ethical Choices Regarding Career and Craft*, 31 McGeorge Law Review 1 (1999); Marvin Mindes & Alan C. Acock, *Trickster, Hero, Helper: A Report on the Lawyer Image*, 1982 American Bar Foundation Research Journal 177; Robert C. Post, *On the Popular Image of the Lawyer: Reflections in a Dark Glass*, 75 California Law Review 379 (1987). Several scholars have compared the practice of law and the practice of magic. *See* Peter D. Baird, *Corpus Juris Hocus Pocus*, Arizona Attorney, October 1989, at 23, and *Law and Magic: A Collection of Essays* (Christine Alice Corcos ed. 2010). Lawyers, of course, have been subject to ridicule and humor from time immemorial, with a compendium of lawyer jokes now collected in Marc Galanter, *Lowering the Bar: Legal Jokes and Legal Culture* (2005). Yet at the same time that lawyers consistently do poorly on polls of sociologists studying who is to be trusted in our society, it is also true that a majority of parents would love to see their children become lawyers. *See* Harris Poll, Feb. 3, 1999. And while you may have heard or read that famous Shakespearean line, "First thing we do, let's kill all the lawyers" (from Henry VI, Part II, Act 4, Scene 2), the reason the lawyers were to be killed was that they were considered guardians of justice and freedom (or at least the controllers of tyrants, through the rule of law), not evil, in that important work of literature.

This chapter will explore some of the many depictions of lawyers as forces for good or evil (or more recently, as complicated human beings who may have mixed motives and complex and morally mixed matters to work on). We will consider how we are to judge lawyers — based on their professional roles, individual acts, or "character." Real lawyers are governed by formal rules of professional conduct (the ABA Model Rules of Professional Conduct, which become law when they are formally approved by a state legislature or state Supreme Court, depending on your state), and as a law student, you are now required to learn these rules in Professional Responsibility. These rules are intended to guide some of the choices lawyers make in doing their work, but often the rules may be ambiguous or even contradictory. Lawyers, like all human beings, have to decide how to act, based on their own personal (and professional) moral codes.

This chapter will ask you to think about how lawyers make choices in their professional and personal lives, how they learn from their experiences, and how they form and create their own character(s) from the decisions and choices they make. By watching pop cultural depictions of lawyer activity, we can see how professional work is conducted, make relatively costless moral judgments (by watching others), and learn to construct our own conceptions and values of what it means to be a good lawyer. Philosopher Martha Nussbaum, among others, has argued that by studying the moral lives of fictional characters we can enrich our own understandings of moral and legal activity. *See* Martha Nussbaum, *Poetic Justice: The Literary Imagination and Public Life* (1995). *See also* Robert Coles, *The Call of Stories: Teaching and the Moral Imagination* (1989); Richard Weisberg, *The Failure of the Word: The Protagonist as Lawyer in Modern Fiction* (1984); John Gardner, *On Moral Fiction* (1978); Lionel Trilling, *Manners, Morals, and the Novel in The Liberal Imagination* (1976).

As the following excerpts suggest, you might profitably consider the source of your first image of lawyers.

CAN THEY DO THAT? LEGAL ETHICS IN POPULAR CULTURE: OF CHARACTER AND ACTS
Carrie Menkel-Meadow
48 UCLA Law Review 1305 (2001)

Consider these two thought experiments: First, what was your first image of a lawyer and where did it come from? Was the lawyer a "good" lawyer? A "good" person? Did the lawyer do good deeds or commit bad acts? Did your first image of a lawyer come from real life or from a movie, a television show, a popular novel, or literature?

Second, what popular, cinematic, or literary image would you select as being "exemplary" of the good lawyer? Do you imagine a person of good character or one who does good deeds? Who seeks justice, possibly at great personal or professional risk to self, or who is "good or helpful" to other people, including clients and third parties? Is a "good" lawyer a person who performs his or her craft well or a person who is fair, kind, and just? Do you see a courtroom trial advocate, ready with razor sharp questions and pithy — but moving — closing arguments? Do you see a skillful draftsperson or law office counselor advising people to do the right thing or create new and interesting entities?

Many critics of lawyers in popular culture have argued about whether recent images of lawyers in movies, popular novels, legal thrillers, and even more complex "high" literature reveal a declining ethicality, or faith and trust in lawyers. Some separate the heroes from the villains, and see a decline in the heroism of lawyers. Others see a more complicated alternation of good and bad images of lawyers in American history as different periods of American cultural representations reflect the vagaries of historical appreciation or deprecation of lawyers, beginning with the period immediately after the American Revolution, and — most agree — culminating in the zenith or "golden age" of lawyer appreciation in the films of the late 1950s and early 1960s. From a period of virtual or actual canonization of such figures as Atticus Finch, Sir Thomas More, and television's *The Defenders*, we are now in a period that not only creates its own more morally and ethically ambiguous lawyers, but also seems to be engaged in some revisionist re-readings of even such heroes as Atticus Finch. With the vast increase in novels, mysteries, thrillers, movies, and television shows about lawyers, images of lawyers — good, bad, indifferent, complicated, and nuanced — are proliferating. These recent depictions present a greater variety of lawyer images to choose from, which, while perhaps still not "representative" (in a socially scientific way) of all lawyers, present a more accurate choice of complex lawyer images to analyze than ever before. . . .

[T]he greater variety of genres and increasing numbers of lawyers in popular literature and culture present an excellent opportunity for students of legal ethics to examine the work of lawyers in both their "macro" (choice of career, choice of client, role in legal institutions) and "micro" (choice of particular actions and behaviors) contexts, and allow us to examine the many different criteria we might apply to evaluate whether a lawyer is a good or bad actor, or a good or bad person. It is also interesting to ask why lawyers have so frequently been depicted as the repositories of professional morality, and used in critiques of morality in American culture, compared to other professionals with ethical dilemmas such as doctors, architects, police officers, and business managers, not to mention other kinds of workers (such as British butlers or French executioners), and ordinary human beings.

The variations of genre allow different aspects of the lawyer's persona to be developed. Long novels and television series allow "character" to be more fully developed. Movies and superficial thrillers or mysteries tend to focus more on acts and discrete plot turns rather than on character. Thus, the multiplicity of ways in which lawyers are represented allow us to create a sociologist's "fourfold table." We can examine and map examples of expressions of legal ethics or morality demonstrated in popular culture, considering lawyers' characters and acts in positive and negative columns, representing both professional and personal choices. I supply some examples in the following chart:

Lawyer's:	+	−
Act - Professional	Taking Unpopular Client	Lying, Deception
Act - Personal	Caring for Someone	Lying, Cruelty, Adultery
Character - Professional	Mentoring, Integrity	Manipulation, Greed
Character - Personal	Kindness, Commitment	Selfishness, Deceit

Longer treatments of lawyers' actions in serialized television shows and longer novels allow more panoramic, less "snapshotted" pictures of lawyers to be painted than in movies or short stories, which, in turn, can be used effectively to highlight particular decisions. Depictions of lawyers' actions in novels, movies, and television shows allow us to view (from multiple "sight-lines") the beginning of the action (what led up to a particular choice point), the action itself, and the consequences of such actions. Thus we are provided multiple ways of seeing (backward, sideways, and forward) the consequences of a lawyer's action, which are often missing from an appellate case as read in the conventional professional responsibility class. . . .

BAD LAWYERS IN THE MOVIES
Michael Asimow
24 Nova Law Review 531 (2000)

I. Introduction

Seen any lawyer films recently? Chances are, most of the lawyers in those films were bad. They were unpleasant or unhappy human beings you wouldn't want as friends. And they were bad professionals you wouldn't admire or want as your lawyer. In the majority of films involving law, lawyers, and the legal system since the 1970s, the lawyer characters and their law firms were pretty bad. This generalization holds whether the film fits the standard lawyer/courtroom genre, whether it involves legal issues, whether the film is a comedy (black or otherwise) or a drama, or whether it falls into other genres such as romances, mystery stories, or thrillers that just happen to have lawyer roles. . . .

This article examines two phenomena. First, it documents the precipitous drop in the public's perception of the character, prestige, and ethics of lawyers that began during the 1980s and continues to the present. Second, it traces the history of lawyer portrayals in film, concentrating on the sharp turn toward the negative during the 1970s and 1980s that continues to the present.

The article asks whether there is any connection between these phenomena. It asserts that one connection is clear and obvious: the trend in filmed portrayals of lawyers accurately reflects public opinion. But the article also speculates that negative filmed images can lead public opinion as well as follow it. My hope is that this article will cause its readers to treat lawyer portrayals in film seriously and critically, both because such portrayals are an important social datum and because they have real world consequences.

II. The Popular Perception of Lawyers

Polling data demonstrates clearly that the popular perception of the character and the ethics of American lawyers, and the prestige of the profession, have plunged precipitously since the 1970s. Granted, the image of lawyers never approached that of pharmacists, the clergy, or algebra teachers. Lawyers will always be distrusted, in part because their assigned task is to play whatever role and manipulate whatever law a client's interest demands. Lawyers tend to represent the rich and powerful; naturally everyone else who can't afford lawyers resents that.

Even more significant, lawyers are doomed to be unloved because criminal practice is their most public function. As lawyers see it, justice requires that an accused person have the benefit of appropriate process, such as the reasonable doubt rule or the privilege against self-incrimination. This perspective is not shared by most members of the public, especially when it comes to criminal law. Most people think that justice means finding the truth regardless of the adversarial system, procedural technicalities, statutory loopholes, police or prosecutorial misconduct, or lawyers' tricks.

The general public will always associate lawyers with some of life's worst moments. We don't fondly recall our divorce or divorces, the probate of our parents' estates, our dispute with the IRS, our credit problems or bankruptcy, or our brush with the juvenile court. Dwelling on the time we got sued by somebody who slipped on the sidewalk or we needed an attorney to sue an insurance company doesn't evoke warm and fuzzy memories. Lawyers were present at those events. Probably, we resented the opposing lawyer. While we may have liked and trusted our own lawyer, we resented being involved in a situation where lawyers were needed and we were probably shocked at the size of the bill. In all likelihood, whether we won or lost, we weren't really pleased by the outcome.

Thus, our profession has never been loved, but in years past it was at least respected and sometimes admired. Today lawyers are more despised than they have ever been before. This is something we probably knew already from the prevalence of nasty lawyer jokes or talk shows, or from social and professional interactions with laypersons. The polling data proves that this dismal intuition is all too accurate.

In its introduction to polling data released in 1997, the Harris Poll wrote:

Recent Harris Polls have found that public attitudes to lawyers and law firms, which were already low, continue to get worse. Lawyers have seen a dramatic decline in their prestige which has fallen faster than that of any other occupation, over the last twenty years. Fewer people have confidence in law firms than in any of the major institutions measured by Harris including the Congress, organized labor, or the federal government. It is not a pretty picture.

In 1977 over a third of the public (36%) believed that lawyers had very great prestige. Today, twenty years later, that has fallen to 19%. In other words, almost half of the people who accorded lawyers great prestige then do not do so today. No other occupation has fallen so sharply. . . .

For the last thirty years Harris has been tracking the confidence people have in the leaders of various institutions. In the most recent survey, only 7% of the public said they had a great deal of confidence in the people running law firms. This places law firms at the bottom of the institutions on the list. The 7% figure is not only the lowest number recorded for law firms over thirty years, it is actually the lowest number recorded for any institution over thirty years.

In the early 1990s, the American Bar Association commissioned a public opinion poll from the Peter D. Hart Research Organization. It indicated that overall, respondents gave lawyers a 40% favorability rating, while 34% of respondents gave them an unfavorable rating. This placed lawyers far below other professions, since the favorability rating for teachers was 84%, pharmacists 81%, police officers 79%, doctors 71%, and bankers 56%. Only stockbrokers at 28%, and politicians at 21% were lower.

In 1999, the ABA published results of a follow-up poll from M/A/R/C Research. It revealed that while 30% of respondents were extremely or very confident of the United States justice system, only 14% were extremely or very confident of lawyers. In contrast, 27% had slight or no confidence in the justice system but 42% had little or no confidence in lawyers. Lawyers were soundly beaten by state legislatures, prison systems, and the United States Congress; only the media came in behind lawyers. Thus, the public seems to have moderate confidence in its justice system but almost none in the lawyers who make that system function. The same survey also asked about public satisfaction with particular lawyer services they had purchased in the last five years. The satisfaction levels with transactional attorneys (real estate, contracts, or estate planning) were much higher than the satisfaction levels with litigating attorneys (family law, civil, or criminal disputes).

According to the Gallup Poll, high percentages of respondents give pharmacists, clergy, dentists, and doctors high or very high ratings for honesty and ethics. Between 1976 and 1985, 25-27% of respondents gave lawyers high or very high ratings. Then the figure started to slide, falling to 18% in 1988. After a bump upwards in 1989-1991, it fell back to 18% in 1992, 16% in 1993-1995, and 14% in 1998. The public opinion of lawyers is inversely proportional to education; the more education people have, the more unethical they think lawyers are. A study by the Media Studies Center of the University of Connecticut asked whether the respondent trusts members of various professions to tell the truth. As to lawyers, 24% of respondents trusted a lawyer "to tell the truth all or most of the time"; this came close to the bottom of the list behind newspaper reporters (30%), your Congressional representative (30%), and network television news anchors (42%). Only the president (21%) and radio talk show hosts (14%) came in below lawyers.

To go out on a limb: I think lawyers are getting a bad rap. I believe that most lawyers (not all of them, of course) are decent, socially responsible people who work hard for their clients, successfully check government overreaching, take a lot of undeserved abuse, are pretty ethical most of the time, and do not earn inordinate amounts of money. Instead, they hew out a living in an extremely tough, competitive environment.

In general, I believe (although I cannot prove) that most legal services, whether oriented to transactions, personal planning, or dispute-settlement, add value and that most of the things lawyers do are good for society. It may be unfashionable to say so, but I think the ABA was right when it concocted the slogan "[f]reedom, justice, equality — without lawyers, they're just words." So, if a normative position is needed from which to criticize popular legal culture over the last twenty years, my position is that film should treat lawyers in a fair and balanced manner.

As to the negative public opinion polls, your attitude may be — who cares? Life for lawyers, judges and law professors goes on regardless of what the public thinks of the profession. Lawyers are accustomed to people not liking them much. It's easy for lawyers to write off the polling data as misguided or inconsequential. However, I think we should care a lot about the venomously negative public perceptions of the profession. . . .

NOTES & QUESTIONS

1. Do you recall your first image of a lawyer? From where did it come? A book, television show, movie, or real person, such as a parent or other relative?

2. What was your thinking about the lawyer you first encountered? Was the lawyer a "good" lawyer, a "bad" lawyer, or a lawyer of mixed qualities (like most human beings)? On what basis and with which factors do you come to these judgments?

3. Professor Asimow reports that people have some moderate confidence in the legal system, but less in the particular professionals who inhabit it — the lawyers. Is it possible to think that the legal system is basically fair, legitimate, or to be trusted when you think that most lawyers are not honest (as the polling data seems to indicate)? Remember that Jack Cade in Shakespeare's *Henry VI* wanted to kill all the lawyers because they represented the rule of law and control of tyrants. See Steve Greenfield, *Hero or Villain? Cinematic Lawyers and the Delivery of Justice, in Law and Film* (Stefan Machura & Peter Robson eds. 2002), suggesting that lawyers uphold the rule of law but just as often "stand outside the law" by protecting and standing with those outside the system (such as unpopular clients like Tom Robinson in the classic 1962 film *To Kill a Mockingbird*), thus encouraging *ambivalent* reactions to professionals who actually play multiple roles within the legal system. What do you think about the tension in the role of the lawyer to represent a client and at the same time to protect the legal system? Can one always do both at the same time? Think about how many depictions of lawyers in popular culture build on this dramatic role tension, what sociologists of the legal profession call "role conflict." Frank Galvin, for example, in *The Verdict*, ultimately achieves "justice" for his client in a medical malpractice trial by committing several ethical violations in case preparation (stealing documents, violating federal postal laws) and witness manipulation. Both the father and daughter Jedediah and Maggie Ward, on opposite sides of a products liability case in *Class Action* (1991), engage in ethical breaches (document destruction, witness harassment, and cruelty) in order to fight for their respective clients. Eventually, in order to achieve "justice," Maggie commits the ultimate act of "role conflict" — she switches sides in a way which clearly violates rules of professional conduct. *See* Model Rules of Professional Conduct, Rules 1.8-1.12 (conflicts of interest). And in *Jagged Edge*, Teddy Barnes, the successful criminal defense lawyer of guilty John Forrester, takes "justice" into her own hands when she kills her client (in self-defense, but also because she knows the formal justice system has not punished him for the crimes he has committed), while she stays faithful to the ethical principle that she cannot reveal client confidences or "secrets" (his guilt). More recently, Michael Clayton, played by George Clooney in the 2007 film of the same name, is a lawyer "fixer" who engages in many shady activities (and clear ethical rule violations), as well as personal transgressions (addiction to gambling) but in the end uses blackmail to achieve justice in a class action case about toxic chemicals in agriculture.

4.   How do we measure what a good lawyer is? Is there a difference between what you would want from a lawyer and what you would want from a friend? Professor Charles Fried suggested quite famously several decades ago that the lawyer should act as a "special-purpose friend." See Charles Fried, *The Lawyer as Friend: The Moral Foundations of the Lawyer-Client Relation*, 85 Yale Law Journal 1060 (1976), arguing that lawyers do things for their clients, legitimately, that might hurt others — the relationship of lawyer-client "friendship" and the loyalty and service it is built on is intrinsically morally valuable. Do you agree? Do you want your friends to "do anything" for you? Lie? Cheat? Steal? Do you want them to give you good, yet honest, advice, or always tell you that you are right?

5.   In a genre he helped create, Louis Auchincloss (practicing lawyer and author of over 60 novels and collections of short stories) has explored the relationship of lawyers giving advice to clients (usually in non-litigational settings, like corporate or probate law), often when they share the same social circles and class but might have conflicting professional or personal moralities. *See, e.g., Diary of a Yuppie* (1986); *The Atonement and Other Stories* (1997); *The Partners* (1973); and *Powers of Attorney* (1987). *See also* William Domnarski, *Trouble in Paradise: Wall Street Lawyers and the Fiction of Louis Auchincloss*, 12 Journal of Contemporary Law 243 (1987). For another dramatic representation in popular fiction of just how hard it is to "do the right thing" when your client is your friend, business associate, or just plain old long-term client who pays you lots of money, see Arthur Solmssen, *The Comfort Letter* (1975) (chronicling a lawyer's decision to disclose corporate fraud in a public offering). Consider whether Anthony Judson Lawrence in *The Young Philadelphians* (1959) is a good lawyer and a good friend, when he advises Mrs. Allen, a very wealthy woman, on how to "avoid" or at least minimize tax payments, and then takes on the criminal defense of his oldest friend Chet (even

when he has no criminal experience at all). What do we mean by talking about a "good" lawyer as friend? Loyalty? Use of skill or craft? Good advice even if it is painful to hear? Objectivity? Promotion of client interests?

6.   With which particular lawyer roles are you most familiar? The most classic genre of lawyer movies is the trial or courtroom movie, but increasingly fewer and fewer lawyers actually try cases. Less than 2% of all civil cases filed in federal courts are actually tried, and the rates of trial are similar for criminal cases in the federal system. *See* Marc Galanter, *The Vanishing Trial: An Examination of Trials and Related Matters in Federal and State Courts*, 1 Journal of Empirical Legal Studies 459 (2004); Carrie Menkel-Meadow, *Is the Adversary System Really Dead? Dilemmas of Legal Ethics as Legal Institutions and Rules Evolve, in Current Legal Problems* (Jane Holder, Colm O'Cinneide & Michael Freeman eds. 2004). Criminal trials are more common in state jurisdictions, like California, where "three strikes" legislation forces incarceration after three convictions and there is now less plea bargaining. Why is the trial lawyer the most common depiction of the lawyer, even as the role becomes rarer and rarer in real life? Is it the drama of confrontation in the courtroom? Our need for sports-like winners and losers when we watch movies or television or read mysteries and thrillers? Is real life really so cut-and-dried? Is it easier for us to perceive "good" (skillful) lawyering in the courtroom setting (the classic cross-examinations of *Perry Mason*; the pithy opening and closing statements of the lawyers on *L.A. Law, The Practice, and Law & Order*) than in the law office consultations, advice, and drafting of transactional work? Must a lawyer have to defeat someone to be a good lawyer? What about the role of lawyers as peacemakers, mediators, or, as Louis Brandeis made famous, being a "lawyer for the situation" in solving problems for clients, even those in conflict with each other? *See* Clyde Spillenger, *Elusive Advocate: Reconsidering Brandeis as People's Lawyer*, 105 Yale Law Journal 1445 (1996). Consider Michael Clayton's complicated role as "fixer," both for the clients of his large law firm, and as he tries to "fix" his own partner Arthur Edens, played by Tom Wilkinson. Edens had been made "unstable" by his realization that his client was very guilty of mass torts and serious harm. Edens is the classic "trial lawyer" but becomes unhinged at depositions when he has to cross-examine plaintiffs he knows are telling the truth and defend corporate executives who are not.

7.   Is the good lawyer kind? A true "helping professional"? Or is he more likely mean or rude? Consider the depiction in *Liar Liar* of Fletcher Reede, who is selfish and rude with his family, lies in his practice, and flatters (falsely) his law firm colleagues until he is forced to tell the truth, becoming more honest and even ruder when he tells people (and judges and courts) what he really thinks. In *The Devil's Advocate* Kevin Lomax is a smug and selfish lawyer who wins cases and ignores his wife. His boss, John Milton (named for the seventeenth-century poet who created the enduring portrayal of Satan in Paradise Lost), is evil incarnate and has come to be the iconic representation of the evil big firm lawyer. John Grisham's many lawyer protagonists are greedy cheats, fronts for the mob, and even vicious killers. *See, e.g., The Firm* (1993). Have you encountered any lawyers who are really this bad in real life?

8.   To what extent do you agree with polling data on the untrustworthiness of lawyers? If you think lawyers are evil or not to be trusted, why did you come to law

school? If lawyers are so bad, why do we continue to make and see movies and television shows about them? Shows like *Law & Order* have been proliferating, and lawyer shows vastly outnumber doctor shows. Only police and detective shows are greater in number than lawyer shows, and these shows are also about "law." Professor Asimow suggests in the article excerpted above that lawyers are depicted more favorably on television than in the movies. Do you agree? Why might this be?

9.   Are lawyers more likely to be repositories of dramatic moral decisions than other professionals? Doctors must treat all and do no harm, but they triage medical seriousness and make life and death decisions every day. Engineers and architects design products and buildings that have the power to harm millions. Business managers and accountants, as we have learned all too recently, can bilk employees, suppliers, vendors, and the general public out of millions of dollars. Politicians lie and send innocent people to fight wars. Car mechanics and assembly line workers would never get away with some of the things more educated "professionals" do. (Is there more formal or market discipline in less "revered" or "learned" professions?)

10.   To return to the "good" lawyer for a moment, why were lawyers so much more likely to be depicted as heroes in times past? Some commentators have suggested that the "golden years" of lawyer movies in Hollywood accompanied important political and social changes — the McCarthy Era, the Cold War, the Civil Rights movement, the early days of the feminist, anti-poverty, and antiwar movements — times filled with demands for justice and clarity of positions and the need for Americans to exalt their way of life in contrast to others. *See* David Ray Papke, *Law, Cinema and Ideology: Hollywood Legal Films of the 1950s*, 48 UCLA Law Review 1473 (2001), and Francis Nevins, *Law, Lawyers and Justice in Popular Fiction and Film*, 1 Humanities Education 3 (1984). This period also made law quite salient for the general public as the Supreme Court ushered in such important decisions as *Brown v. Board of Education* (1954), ruled in important cases on school prayer and the First Amendment, and revolutionized criminal law with such decisions as *Miranda v. Arizona* (1966) and *Gideon v. Wainwright* (1963), radically changing the legal and social landscape and impressing upon a post-war generation that to get things done or changed, law was at least one of the most efficacious means. What does it say about our times that lawyers who do "heroic" things may also be violating ethical rules or transgressing other moral lines (like lawyer Edens in *Michael Clayton* who clearly crosses the ethical lines to befriend an injured plaintiff and plots with her to expose his own guilty corporate defendant client)? Can the good lawyer do good while using wrong or prohibited means?

11.   Ask almost any lawyer who came of age in the 1950s and 1960s (and still some today), and you will find images of Clarence Darrow, a real lawyer, despite the depiction in *Inherit the Wind* (1960), and Atticus Finch as inspirational sources of career choice. Milner Ball has written eloquently about the many modern public interest lawyers who saw their inspiration to fight for justice in these few heroic lawyers. *See* Milner Ball, *The Word and the Law* (1993). Younger lawyers might base their decisions to be "cause" lawyers on Jonathan Harr's nonfictional description of Jan Schlictmann as environmental crusader (and plaintiff's lawyer) in *A Civil Action* (1995) or on Gerald Stern's own description of his representation of a damaged West Virginia community after coal-mining caused a dam break in *The Buffalo Creek Disaster* (1976). (Both of these books are widely used in modern civil

procedure courses to give students a taste of "real lawyers and law" behind the Rules of Civil Procedure.) A more recent possibility is the movie depiction of a class action sexual harassment suit in upper Minnesota in *North Country* (2005), based on the real case described in Clara Bingham and Laura Leedy Gansler's *Class Action: The Story of Lois Jenson and the Landmark Case That Changed Sexual Harassment Law* (the 2003 book, not the 1991 movie of the same name). Do you think there are enough models of "good" cause or public interest-minded lawyers in media depictions? Should there be more? The public interest-minded lawyer Lucy Kelsen (ironically named for noted legal philosopher Hans Kelsen, the author of *The General Theory of Law and the State* (1946), who argued for "pure" positive law?) says in *Two Weeks Notice* that her heroes are Clarence Darrow, Thurgood Marshall, and Ruth Bader Ginsburg. What do these lawyers have in common? What effects on law school enrollment do you think media depictions (good, bad, or more complex) of lawyers have?

12.   As we will explore below, when we focus on what lawyers learn from their lives and cases, some modern lawyers could easily be characterized as redeemed "heroes" as well. Michael Brock in Grisham's *The Street Lawyer* (a 1998 novel and never filmed!) goes from being a conventionally ambitious, partnership-seeking, big-firm associate to being a lawyer for the homeless. Joe Miller (Denzel Washington) becomes a reluctant civil rights gladiator for AIDS-stricken and discriminated-against lawyer Andrew Beckett (Tom Hanks) in *Philadelphia* (1992), and Rita Harrison (Michelle Pfeiffer) in *I Am Sam* (2001) learns the true meaning of family when she focuses on her mentally challenged client's desires to be a parent when it takes more than a village and a binary legal system to care for a child. Is Michael Clayton "redeemed" at the end of the movie by producing justice, by having the "guilty" corporate lawyer (Karen Crowder, played by Tilda Swinton, who won an Academy Award for her performance) arrested in conjunction with a murder? Clayton accomplishes this by secretly taping a manipulative extortion conversation. Is he using his old tricks to do "good" or to extract his own vengeance?

13.   Increasingly, memoirs and descriptions of real lawyers portray the complexity of modern lawyers' choices and lives — their job choices, their decisions in practice, and their personal lives. From Melissa Fay Greene's moving portrayal of real legal services lawyers for the poor in Georgia in *Praying for Sheetrock* (1991), to Abbe Smith's expressed concerns about criminal lawyers, both prosecutors and defense lawyers, in *Can You Be a Good Person and a Good Prosecutor?* 14 Georgetown Journal of Legal Ethics 355 (2001), to the reported stories of class action lawyers in asbestos, Dalkon Shield, and other products liability cases, in Paul Brodeur, *Outrageous Misconduct* (1985), Richard Sobol, *Bending the Law* (1991), and Dan Zegart, *Civil Warriors: The Legal Siege on the Tobacco Industry* (2000), we have many portraits of good lawyers seeking justice and personal fulfillment in hard times. If Professor Asimow is right that depictions of movie lawyers have gotten worse and more evil over time, why do you think we have such a paucity of movies and other popular culture depictions of these more courageous "cause lawyers"? *See* Austin Sarat & Stuart Scheingold, *Cause Lawyers: Political Commitments and Professional Responsibilities* (1998). Do other media portray the complexity of modern lawyers' professional and personal lives more realistically? Consider the richness and depth of Scott Turow's lawyers in *Presumed Innocent* (1989), *The*

Laws of Our Fathers (1997), and *Reversible Errors* (2002). All of the major lawyers are dedicated to justice but humanly flawed.

14.   Carrie Menkel-Meadow has called the new genre of writing by (mostly) young lawyers about their unpleasant experiences in various forms of practice the "bill and tell" memoir or journalistic account. *See* Carrie Menkel-Meadow, *Telling Stories in School: Using Case Studies and Stories to Teach Legal Ethics*, 69 Fordham Law Review 787, 790, n.6 (2000). Examples of the genre include Paul M. Barrett, *The Good Black: A True Story of Race in America* (1999); Lincoln Kaplan, *Skadden: Power, Money and the Rise of a Legal Empire* (1993) (evidencing a new genre of law firm histories, often written by professional historians); William R. Keates, *Proceed With Caution: A Diary of the First Year at One of America's Largest, Most Prestigious Law Firms* (1997); Cameron Stracher, *Double Billing* (1998); David Heilbroner, *Rough Justice: Days and Nights of a Young DA* (1990); James Kunen, *How Can You Defend Those Guilty People? The Making of a Criminal Lawyer* (1983); and Stephen Phillips, *No Heroes, No Villains: The Story of a Murder Trial* (1977).

15.   As you proceed through the readings and viewings suggested in this book, consider how you are making judgments about whether the lawyers depicted and described are "good" lawyers or not. *See The Good Lawyer: Lawyers' Roles and Lawyers' Ethics* (David Luban ed. 1983); Stephen L. Pepper, *The Lawyer's Amoral Ethical Role: A Defense, A Problem and Some Possibilities*, 1986 American Bar Foundation Research Journal 613; and Gerald J. Postema, *Moral Responsibility in Professional Ethics*, 55 New York University Law Review 63 (1980).

16.   Do you look at lawyers in their professional roles, with all the specialized duties and responsibilities that those roles entail? Or do you judge lawyers by the particular acts they perform (or fail to perform)? Anthony Judson Lawrence, the lawyer played by Paul Newman in *The Young Philadelphians*, tells us those acts sum up to form the "character" of a lawyer: "A man's life is the sum of all his actions."

C. LAWYERS' ACTS

Many depictions of lawyers turn on difficult decisions or actions (or non-actions) that lawyers may take. Some of these "acts" are designed to illuminate the character of the individual (explored more fully in section D below), others are designed to explore the difficult ethical choices that professional roles require of those specially trained, and still others are used to move the plot along or crystallize some statement about the law and legal institutions. Moral and legal philosophers have long debated whether the morality of a professional is to be judged by that person's "role morality" (different standards permitted for differently performed and needed societal functions), the acts he commits (or does not), or a more general assessment of the person's character. Society's need for some division of labor has long justified the separate morality of soldiers who can kill; politicians who can "dissemble"; lawyers, doctors, and clergy who do not have to reveal certain private information; and employees who are expected to be "loyal" (within increasingly diminishing limits) to their bosses or institutions. One commentator has eloquently explored the "professional role morality" of Charles Henri-Sanson who was so good at his craft (that of executioner of Paris) that he was able to survive all of the changes in regime during the French Revolution and keep his job. *See* Arthur Isak Applbaum, *Ethics for Adversaries: The Morality of Roles in Public and Professional Life* (1999). The legal profession, as well as many others, has drafted ethical rules and standards that are supposed to guide a professional to do the "right" thing. But many acts that lawyers take are not well-regulated or specified in the formal Rules. How does one choose a client or refuse a case? How does one treat another human being when interviewing a potential client about very private and possibly unlawful behavior? How close (socially and physically) can a lawyer and client become? Modern filmic depictions of lawyer activity allow us to take a closer look (even if only in fictional settings) at the choices that lawyers make about what they do. Consider the "chronology" of lawyer acts described below.

CAN THEY DO THAT? LEGAL ETHICS IN POPULAR CULTURE: OF CHARACTER AND ACTS
Carrie Menkel-Meadow
48 UCLA Law Review 1305 (2001)

It is possible to construct a temporal template of ethical issues depicted in the popular media from the beginning of the lawyer-client relationship to the end of an appeal or transaction (or to a murder for those relationships that end really badly). Russell Banks's *The Sweet Hereafter* (1991) tells the fictionalized story of an actual bus accident that killed a number of children and had a great impact on many lives. The story is told from the point of view of many different participants in the story, but from Mitchell Stephens, Esq., we learn how clients are involuntarily solicited, because lawyers are angry and are able to harness their anger to compensate other people. For Mitchell Stephens, "[t]here are no accidents" — someone is always responsible for things that go wrong, and it is the plaintiff's lawyer's job to find someone (with deep pockets) to blame and to pay up so the injured can be compensated. This is class justice and the lawyer must orchestrate it: "I wanted a mean lean team, a troop of vengeful parents willing to go the route with me and not come home without some serious trophies on our spears." As Stephens describes himself, he lives for these "disaster negligence suits. . . . Nothing else provides me with the rush that I get from cases like this. . . . It's almost like a drug. It's probably close to what professional soldiers feel, or bullfighters." Stephens tells us how he ropes in mourning parents and what he does when one of them, Billy Ansel (who has lost two children), resists him, and how he lies to make his case. We also learn how Stephens appears to his clients (from their point of view), as one of the injured children, Nicole Burnell, takes his measure when she is interviewed and prepped for a deposition (which she later deliberately ruins by telling her own truth and seeking justice against another wrongdoer, her own abusive father, rather than against any of the actors in the accident). Although Nicole likes Mr. Stephens, he makes her feel greedy and dishonest by preparing for a deposition to get the money her parents want from her injury. Nicole over-hears a conversation Billy Ansel has with her father about how the lawyers are all suing each other because some plaintiffs have signed up with more than one lawyer, and the reader feels the pain of grieving parents trying to make sense of what has happened and what could happen to them, while the lawyers fight to profit from their misery.

In contrast, Jan Schlichtmann's [in *A Civil Action*] real-life, initially unwilling plaintiffs grow slowly from distrust of a legal system that will not do anything for a widening group of injured people (never big enough for the class action numbers that would have been possible in the Buffalo Creek disaster) to become increasingly committed to their lawsuit, and to see their lawyer as a mixed bag of altruistic and selfish motives.

Atticus Finch is actually pressed into service in representing Tom Robinson [in *To Kill A Mockingbird*] by the judge handling the case, but he tells a good story to his daughter about the responsibility of lawyers to take unpopular clients and cases (the "n" word is used in both the book and the movie, circa 1960-1962). In so doing, he has given us all a model and argument for the importance of *pro bono publico* and even court-appointed work, especially in criminal law. Representing unpopular clients and taking court appointments has continued on *The Practice*, while in past years, paying clients have been more the rule on *L.A. Law* and on the short-lived *Murder One* (a show inspired by the public's hunger for criminal celebrity trials following the coverage of the O.J. Simpson trial). *A Civil Action* made the economics of contingent-fee lawyers clear to the viewing public, and began to address the inevitable conflicts of interest that accompany virtually any payment scheme for lawyers.

From client acquisition, modern films and movies depict a variety of ethical dilemmas in representation (still mostly restricted to the more dramatic world of litigation and courtrooms, rather than transactional lawyering). For example, *The Practice* has several times, in different settings, explored issues of confidentiality — when must or can a lawyer reveal private, confidential information to others? And, when Bobby and Helen were dating, the show explored difficult, but I suspect increasingly common, professional dilemmas when lawyers on opposite sides of cases date or live with each other, hear confidential information in phone conversations, and see messages and papers left lying around the house. The lawyers on *The Practice* have grappled with what to do with physical evidence, when they can "rat" on their own client, and many thorny witness preparation issues. In a modern replay of the now classic client "coaching" scene of *Anatomy of a Murder*, lawyers tell their clients what the law is before learning the facts. A guilty-feeling Helen, as prosecutor, actually testifies against one of her colleagues whom she believes wrongfully suggested testimony to a material witness. Ellenor Frut commits one of the most egregious, but clever, unethical acts (can you think of what ethical rules she violates?) when she advises a client who has been in an accident and has been drinking, to finish the open bottle at the scene of the accident "to calm his nerves" — and thereby destroy the accuracy of any Breathalyzer test. The lawyers of *The Practice* have conflicts of interest galore — they sleep with each other and the judge, they work both sides of a case, they take on civil matters beyond their competence, but at least they have explicit ethical conversations about what they are doing. There is not only talk about the law, possible ethical violations, and consequences to their firm and their clients, but they do in fact get called on some of their questionable behavior.

Competence is questioned in popular culture, whether by the satire of Joe Pesci's performance in *My Cousin Vinny*, by the too-young and inexperienced colleague in Grisham's *The Rainmaker*, by the all-too-common substance abuse of Frank Galvin in *The Verdict*, by the actual Rule 11 motion filed against Jan Schlichtmann for not adequately investigating and supporting his complaint filing, or by the impression-ability of a lawyer who believed she was zealously representing her client, but who may in fact have been subject to a "con job" that cost her freedom and her law license. Scott Turow counters these images of incompetence by providing perhaps the most detailed and accurate accounts of the hard work that both prosecutors and defense counsel put into their jobs — in investigation, case preparation, courtroom strategy, and court-room execution — even if some of the lawyers and judges turn out to be corrupt or worse.

As most popular culture continues to explore the drama of the courtroom, I am personally interested in recent turns to more typical locales of lawyers' work — the bargaining table. Still located mostly in litigation contexts, the ethics and practices of lawyers in settlement conferences present serious ethical dilemmas, hardly responded to by the rules. While *The Practice* lawyers engage in plea-bargaining and tense settlement negotiations every time they take on a medical malpractice or products liability case, the settlement conference is becoming a more common staple of legal drama. My personal favorite is the blatant ethical violation in *The Verdict*, the premise of which is needed to fuel the rest of the film. Frank Galvin turns down a large, and certainly likely to be accepted by his client, settlement offer from the Catholic Church (which controls the hospital which mistreated his comatose client) without even talking to his client (the family of the comatose woman). In direct violation of Rules 1.2, 1.3, and 1.4 (and all of their predecessors that were in effect in Massachusetts at the time of the film), Galvin turns down the offer. Thus, the case (and the film) can proceed to the more dramatic confrontation in the courtroom, where Galvin, overcoming his alcoholism and violating some laws by stealing mail to get information, triumphs over a major and well-staffed law firm.

Michael Brock's lawsuit against the developer who wrongfully evicted his homeless clients [in *The Street Lawyer*] is completed in a settlement conference, this one in a judge's chambers with Brock's own ethical transgressions (deception used to get evidence and confidentiality violations) as part of the negotiation agenda. Similarly, while nothing overtly in violation of the rules transpires, Jonathan Harr's descriptions (from one side only) of the various settlement negotiations (meetings at the Ritz Carlton in Boston and W.R. Grace headquarters in New York) in *A Civil Action* provide us with some entry into the world of lawyer impression management, guarded information exchange, and normal "deception."

Modern treatments of lawyers demonstrate good acts as well — not all is sex, lies, and videotape. Lawyers like Frank Galvin and Jan Schlichtmann, as well as paralegal Erin Brockovich, demonstrate the power of persistence and the necessity of hard, long, and detailed fact investigation. Although in trial movies and television shows it sometimes looks like victory goes to the clever and the articulate, in truth we seldom see anymore the contrived final question of a devastating and surprising Perry Mason-like cross-examination. As discovery has replaced surprise in trial, popular culture is slowly catching up with what makes good lawyers in real life — hard work! Hard work and long hours get their share of criticism, ruining marriages in *The Firm* and *The Street Lawyer*, not to mention adultery on the job with coworkers. No one could accuse modern lawyers depicted in the media as a lazy bunch — even the "you can have it all" glamour pusses of *L.A. Law*. Good lawyering (as well as realistic lawyering) takes hard work, as the "bill and tell" books painfully recount, and virtually all of these modern tales, both fact and fiction, do want us to consider the consequences of hard professional labor on personal lives.

Changes in the practice of law, both in the work done, and in the demographic composition of the legal profession, are beginning to seep into modern depictions of discrimination issues (partnerships, power, decision-making authority for minority and women attorneys, and sexual harassment). In this, *L.A. Law* showed us other kinds of lawyer work, including Arnie Becker's divorce work, tax, and corporate work. Leland McKenzie even served as an arbitrator in what has to be the first depiction of ADR on screen. As creators of popular culture begin to realize that lawyers do many things besides trying cases, I look forward to depictions of some of the equally difficult and dramatic ethical issues that are encountered in other forms of legal work: conflicts of interest in alternative dispute resolution involving repeat players, corporate deal making, disclosure obligations in transactional negotiations and public offerings, lawyers paid with stock options in dotcoms, and now the fall-out from "dot-gones." . . .

EMBODIMENT OF EVIL: LAW FIRMS IN THE MOVIES
Michael Asimow
48 UCLA Law Review 1339 (2001)

The life of lawyers in big firms is grueling and unglamorous, but what of the moral claims made by the movies? Do lawyers working for big firms lie, cheat, and steal?

1. Ethical Problems of Small Firms

Small firms are more prone to certain kinds of ethical violations than are large ones. The kinds of misbehavior that cause lawyers to be disbarred mostly involve thefts from client trust funds, neglecting or ignoring clients, severe forms of malpractice, or gross forms of ambulance chasing. In many cases, these lapses are traceable to drug or alcohol addiction. At big firms, however, colleagues are likely to realize that a lawyer has a substance abuse problem and take steps to remedy the problem and protect clients. In contrast, a solo practice or very small firm may lack such internal checking mechanisms. Small firms are also more likely to run into cash flow problems that might cause lawyers to raid the trust funds.

Big firms have a great deal at stake in maintaining their hard-won reputations for quality work and ethical behavior. They are less likely than small firms to engage in blatant ambulance chasing or gross forms of malpractice that could cause an attorney to be disbarred. Big firms maintain elaborate computer checking systems to protect themselves against becoming accidentally enmeshed in conflicts of interest, to detect billing irregularities, or to prevent lawyers from missing deadlines. Many have ethics committees to which lawyers can confidentially refer thorny ethics problems. Big firms have the luxury of being choosy about accepting new business; they can afford to decline marginal matters or sleazy clients. Given the surplus of lawyers, however, many small firms or solos are desperate for business; they are more likely to take marginal cases or dubious clients and may feel they have to cheat to survive financially.

2. Ethical Problems of Big Firms

Using the movies as our text, we would assume that big firms cheat big time. In *The Verdict* we find a big firm engaging in numerous forms of creative cheating such as bribing the opponent's expert witness to disappear or planting a sexual spy in the opposition's camp. In *Class Action*, a big defense firm first conceals, then destroys, a critical document. In *The Rainmaker*, the firm plants a bug in its opponent's office and colludes with the client in causing witnesses to disappear; perhaps it also knows that the client has testified falsely and fraudulently altered evidence. In *Regarding Henry* the firm suppressed critical evidence and engaged in discovery fraud. In *Philadelphia*, the firm engaged in various forms of illegal chicanery to get rid of an associate with AIDS and to cover it up afterwards, including perjury. All of these are clear-cut ethical violations that would surely trigger severe professional discipline if detected; some of them are criminal violations.

How much does this sort of thing actually happen in the big firm environment? The answer is elusive. Lawyers who commit major ethical violations keep quiet about it and pray that nobody will ever find out. In my informal Greedy Associate survey, the vast majority of the respondents said that they had never seen anything of the sort and some were offended that I even asked the question. Some remarked that solo lawyers or small firms, desperate to keep business or to keep a contingent fee case going, are more likely to engage in such cheating. Others remarked that clients frequently try to conceal bad documents but that lawyers insist on disclosing them if the client's fraud is detected. For example, an associate who is thoroughly miserable about his own big firm lifestyle responded to my question about gross ethical violations:

> No way, no-how. We chastise clients who ask us to hide bad facts in my practice. Our litigators that I know are good and aggressive but would never cheat or bend rules to suit them. We are way too busy to work with clients who want us to cheat on their behalf and the exposure is far too great. That shit is for desperate lawyers.

A few Greedy Associates did observe gross ethical violations, either in their own firms or in other firms. Some comments:

> — Yes, I lie to the judges, we all do. . . .

> — I have seen lawyers asking staff to sign a proof of service for an incorrect date and I have seen lawyers lying to clients about why work did not get done or about what a judge said.

> — I've heard stories from friends of opposing well-known firms that have destroyed documents or other evidence.

> — In terms of blatant violations, they do happen. I can't go into specifics, this is fairly serious stuff and I can't screw with the confidence of any colleagues or clients.

— An associate left the firm because she had been told to destroy a document.

Serious ethical lapses do occur, and both big and small firms occasionally get caught engaging in them. No doubt, for every one of these publicized incidents, countless others have gone undetected or were quietly dealt with by the parties involved. Still, random publicized incidents involving big firms do not prove or even suggest that big firms are prone to bad ethics nor that they are more morally culpable than small firms or solos. Of course, there is no way for an outsider to know the answer. I am inclined to accept the repeated responses to the Greedy Associate survey that big firms have little need to commit clear-cut ethical violations and far too much to lose from taking such chances. Thus, the repeated depiction in big-firm movies appears to convey an erroneous impression that such violations are widespread.

3. The Harsh Realities of Big-Firm Litigation Practice

Numerous films involving law firms have depicted all-out hardball litigation. In these films, big firms seek to exhaust their opponents with overwhelming discovery demands, resist justified discovery demands, file motions with little merit, and engage in other delaying tactics. Lawyers act uncivilly toward one another and treat deponents harshly.

In this respect, the movies accurately portray the realities of contemporary big firm litigation practice — and a great deal of small firm litigation practice as well. Hardball litigation tactics may or may not lie just on the ethical side of the lines laid out in the Model Rules. They do not, however, contribute to the search for truth or justice in the litigation process. While the great majority of the respondents to my Greedy Associates survey stated that gross ethical improprieties were unthinkable in their firms, they were far more ambivalent about other firm conduct. Numerous responses spoke of behavior that most non-lawyers would think was unethical and immoral. This consists of action designed to conceal the truth or to trick or exhaust the opposing side, but by means that seem to fall just short of ethical violations or which violate unenforced ethical standards. One very prevalent hardball tactic is incivility — that is, rude, bullying behavior that is designed to intimidate other lawyers or witnesses. For the most part, the respondents distinguished hardball litigation tactics from serious ethical improprieties. They do not like to behave this way, but regard such tactics as all in a day's work. One cannot survive in the big firm environment without engaging in them.

> I think the small ethical breaches which are most common contribute most to making the practice of law slimy.

> I have been asked to play dumb by partners ("if the other side calls asking where the new draft is, tell them our system crashed or the paralegal made all the wrong changes last night").

> Less obvious ethical breaches occur — e.g., suggestions that associates lie about who they are ("I'm a college student doing research for a report") or who they represent.

Big firms . . . may flood smaller firms with paper knowing that the first-year grunts and temps they put on the deal will probably miss something . . .

The most common ethical violations I see are: (1) the contortions some firms/partners go through to determine that there is no conflict of interest in taking a case; (2) lawyers who don't consult their clients; (3) fast and loose arguments; and (4) discovery games.

When the imbalance between superior game playing and a fair result is stark, then the system is certainly slimy, and if not slimy themselves, the lawyers who participated at least become slimed in the public's eye.

There are all sorts of sharp litigation practices out there:

— producing documents during a deposition, or late the night before, that were requested and/or subpoenaed many months ago. . . .

— misrepresenting the substance of telephone conversations with opposing counsel

— coaching of witnesses before and during depositions

— excessive and sometimes frivolous motion practice, or unduly burdensome discovery

— obstructionist tactics in "answering" interrogatories, requests to admit, and other legitimate discovery requests;

— egregious mischaracterizations of the facts and law in briefs or in oral arguments before the Court.

[D]elaying production of documents until after a motion to compel has been opposed and lost and, sometimes, appealed and lost, all for the purposes of delay and driving up the other side's costs, is immoral.

But that is the game. Make things as difficult as possible for the other side within the bounds of the law.

Do some documents get put on a privileged list that may not be privileged? Sure, but the other side has an opportunity to challenge that.

There's a lot of unconscious violations — just making blanket exceptions in discovery when you know you will have to disclose, just making trouble for the other side. Lawyers spend time arguing bullshit stuff but they may or may not think it's bad faith.

But I can tell you that we have occasionally buried a document in with others in the hope that it, or its significance, is overlooked.

I think people are obnoxious, and it's true that they spend unbelievable amounts of time writing letters accusing the other side of withholding documents and so forth, but I haven't seen anyone violate the Rules. I do know that lawyers frequently "shade" the facts or law to courts and administrative bodies, so much so that I would consider it deceitful, but again, they are not doing it because they intend to lie; instead they are overzealous in their advocacy.

I think sometimes answers to interrogatories and responses to document production requests place too much emphasis on semantics. An artificially narrow reading of requests allows an attorney to avoid stating or producing something in response to a question . . . that is perfectly understandable in the context of litigation. I sometimes wonder how stupid an attorney can play without going over the ethical line. Playing dumb is pretty common practice.

In their depiction of slippery or hardball litigation practices by big firms, the filmmakers are right on the money.

4. Billing Improprieties

Several movies describe law firm behavior that appears to be aimed at inflating the client's bill. In *The Verdict*, for example, Ed Concannon clearly overstaffs the case. More than a dozen associates sit around a table listening to Concannon prepare a witness. In *The Firm*, a mentor partner tells Mitch McDeere to bill everything, even when he is thinking about client matters in the shower.

Numerous accounts of real-life law firm billing improprieties have appeared. According to Deborah Rhode:

Audits of "legal expenses" have revealed massages during litigation, dry cleaning for a toupee, running shoes labeled "ground transportation," Victoria's Secret lingerie, and men's suits for an out-of-state trial that took longer than expected. Days in which lawyers bill more than twenty-four hours are no longer rare. . . . When heiress Doris Duke died, leaving over a billion dollars to charity, two dozen law firms embarked on what one attorney candidly described as "a feeding frenzy." Some of the nation's leading practitioners, staying at leading hotels, charging at premium rates, managed to duplicate each other's work and keep each other employed, which diverted an estimated $20 million from charitable causes. Deborah Rhode, *In the Interests of Justice: Reforming the Legal Profession* 168-69 (2000).

About half of the Greedy Associates said that their firms never overbilled clients; indeed, they thought that under billing was more likely than overbilling. But the other half of the respondents reported that bill padding occurs at their firms. According to these respondents, both associates and partners inflate the number of their billable hours. Billable hours are often used to compute bonuses and lawyers must bill minimum number of hours to advance in the firm. As a result, lawyers inflate their hours on time sheets, either because they cannot physically work that many hours, or because there is not enough work to do. Indeed, it is difficult to understand how associates can consistently bill 2400 hours a year or more without cheating on their time sheets if they want any sort of life outside the office.

A number of respondents observed that basing everything on billable hours is perverse. It punishes lawyers who are more efficient and it keeps them working past the point of exhaustion. Others pointed to the assignment of unnecessary or even useless work to "churn" the number of hours billed to a particular matter. A sampling of some of the comments:

> . . . overbilling is very troubling. It occurs in many forms. One of the most common forms is the billing of attorney time for work that clearly should be performed by a staff person, whether by a paralegal, at a lower billing rate, or by a secretary or word processor, at no cost to the client. . . . Unnecessary work often is performed and billed to the client, sometimes even when the client expressly has said that it does not want the work performed. . . . multiple people, even multiple partners, read and revise the same drafts of documents, even when a client directs that this should not occur. Duplication of work also is a problem. This can occur from client to client, as in when the same research assignment is performed for two or more clients from scratch, rather than using the first project as a basis for updating and billing the subsequent clients only for the work necessary to update. It also can occur in the context of only one client, where a partner simultaneously assigns multiple associates to research the same thing, or assigns one associate to "double check" the entire work product of another associate.

> The quality of time billed also can be a problem. If an associate works more than 250, more than 300, more than 400 hours in a month, going without sleep for days at a time, what kind of efficiency and accuracy level is the client being billed for by the end of the month?

> Institutionally, it is difficult for partners to "write off" time from the bill. . . . Seasoned lawyers encourage junior lawyers to bill "loosely." Although none would openly condone overbilling or padding, many tacitly accept and reward padding. Senior associates who are known not to fill out timesheets for weeks at a time, to leave the office frequently to work out or attend to personal errands, and who mysteriously come up with 250 hour months, are held out as role models and rewarded with partnership. . . .

> Unnecessary work is rampant (where I work). It's a combination of the desire to bill and the incompetence of higher-ups. I have spent many hours doing things that are totally pointless. This is often referred to as "churning the file."

> Yes, I pad hours, we all do.

> The reality is that if hours determine bonus and especially salary — you have to bill 2400 hours to get the big bonus — people have to cheat and pad. You know who they are, though they never admit it. It's an open secret though not discussed. . . . If you add on an extra.25 here and there, it is a lot of hours.

> People say if I am going to be there 14 hours I'm going to bill all 14 hours despite personal phone calls; they just bill all the time they are there at the office. . . . If client insists on cut in hourly rate, you just stick them with more hours.

Overbilling? You bet. Unnecessary work? Absolutely. Overbilling is the dirty little secret that no one wants to talk about. It happens, and the billable hours model along with hours-based bonuses encourage it. Anyone who says differently still thinks the world is flat. But because it's almost impossible to prove, no one (at least in my experience) mentions it. . . .

NOTES & QUESTIONS

1. Many films about lawyers depend on the drama of particularly egregious acts — the lies of Fletcher Reede in *Liar Liar*; the sexual improprieties of Teddy Barnes in *Jagged Edge* and Katherine Riley in *Suspect*; the discovery abuse on both sides in *Class Action*; the ruthlessness of Kevin Lomax and John Milton in *The Devil's Advocate* (1997); Frank Galvin's drinking problem in *The Verdict*; the fraud, tax evasion, and other outright criminal activities in *The Firm*; and the murders committed by lawyers in *Jagged Edge, Cape Fear* (original 1962; remake 1991), and *Michael Clayton* (corporate lawyer Karen Crowder indirectly orders the killing of her company's own lawyer, Arthur Edens, when she learns he is planning to expose her guilty and liable client). But how common is it for lawyers to commit these evil acts? Professor Asimow contrasts the ethical practices of small-firm and big-firm lawyers and suggests that small-firm lawyers are more likely to be discovered doing incompetent or worse things and to be disciplined for such activity. But at least one scholar has questioned whether small-firm lawyers are actually more likely to commit unethical or disciplinable acts. *See* Manuel Ramos, *Legal Malpractice: The Profession's Dirty Legal Secret*, 47 Vanderbilt Law Review 1657 (1994); Manuel Ramos, *Legal Malpractice: No Lawyer or Client is Safe*, 47 Florida Law Review 1 (1995). *See also* Richard L. Abel, *Lawyers in the Dock* (2008).

2. Some of the "bad acts" described above do occur in real life. The satirical treatment of Fletcher Reede's lying in *Liar Liar* is both a major trope of pop cultural treatments and one of the things most commonly thought about lawyers — that they are liars. A joke is often made by using a Southern accent to say the word lawyer. *See* Rob Atkinson, *Lucifer's Fiasco: Lawyers, Liars and L'Affaire Lewinsky*, 68 Fordham Law Review 567 (1999). The proper dividing line between "zealous representation," making good arguments, and being honest is not very clear, even in the formal ethical rules. For example, Rule 4.1 of the Model Rules of Professional Conduct categorically states:

Rule 4.1 Truthfulness in Statements to Others

In the course of representing a client a lawyer shall not knowingly:

a.   make a false statement of material fact or law to a third person; or

b.   fail to disclose a material fact or law to a third person when disclosure is necessary to avoid assisting a criminal or fraudulent act by a client, unless disclosure is prohibited by Rule 1.6 [confidentiality of lawyer-client communications].

Yet, what the black letter rule giveth, the commentary taketh away. Note the following exceptions to the demands for truth above, stated in the commentary to Rule 4.1:

Comment

Misrepresentation

[1]   A lawyer is required to be truthful when dealing with others on a client's behalf, but generally has no affirmative duty to inform an opposing party of relevant facts. . . .

Statements of Fact

[2]   This rule refers to statements of fact. Whether a particular statement should be regarded as one of fact can depend on the circumstances. Under generally accepted conventions in negotiation, certain types of statements ordinarily are not taken as statements of material fact. Estimates of price or value placed on the subject of a transaction and a party's intentions as to an acceptable settlement of a claim are in this category, and so is the existence of an undisclosed principal except where nondisclosure of the principal would constitute fraud.

Given these rules, lawyers often exaggerate, "puff," or manipulate their words, especially in lawyer-to-lawyer negotiations, where such "generally accepted conventions" are thought to apply. *See* Carrie Menkel-Meadow, *Ethics, Morality and Professional Responsibility in Negotiation, in Dispute Resolution Ethics* (Phyllis Bernard & Bryant Garth eds. 2002); Carrie Menkel-Meadow, *Legal Negotiation in Popular Culture: What Are We Bargaining For, in Law and Popular Culture* (Michael Freeman ed. 2005). Consider what happens in the legal system when everyone "generally accepts" that not everyone will be telling the truth.

The Model Rules do seem to expect a slightly higher standard of candor when matters are formally in litigation before the court:

Rule 3.3 Candor Toward the Tribunal

(a)   A lawyer shall not knowingly:

(1)   make a false statement of material fact or law to a tribunal;

(2)   fail to disclose a material fact to a tribunal when disclosure is necessary to avoid assisting a criminal or fraudulent act by the client;

(3)   fail to disclose to the tribunal legal authority in the controlling jurisdiction known to the lawyer to be directly adverse to the position of the client and not disclosed by opposing counsel; or

(4)   offer evidence that the lawyer knows to be false. If a lawyer has offered material evidence and comes to know of its falsity, the lawyer shall take reasonable remedial measures.

(b)   The duties stated in paragraph (a) continue to the conclusion of the proceeding, and apply even if compliance requires disclosure of information otherwise protected by Rule 1.6.

(c)   A lawyer may refuse to offer evidence that the lawyer reasonably believes is false.

(d)   In an ex parte proceeding, a lawyer shall inform the tribunal of all material facts known to the lawyer which will enable the tribunal to make an informed decision, whether or not the facts are adverse.

Whether a matter is "before a tribunal" or not can itself be quite complicated. Is discovery formally before a tribunal? Is a mediation or arbitration before a tribunal? Is a judge or magistrate-assisted settlement conference before a tribunal? (Hint: See the definitions, e.g., 1(m), in the Terminology accompanying the Preface to the Model Rules.) Consider whether depictions of lawyer activity in the movies clarify or obscure the different rules of candor in different settings. At least one critic of lawyers in popular culture (and a trial advocacy teacher) argues that trial lawyers cannot and should not have to tell the "technical" truth, precisely because, like the auteurs of film, lawyers must create persuasive narratives to convince juries and judges and adequately represent their clients. "[L]awyers often use the techniques of narrative construction to enhance the truth, not to hide it. A fully developed and well conceived "trial story" may result in an account that is actually "truer" in many respects than the client's uncounseled version of events, even though the narrative was adroitly structured with courtroom victory in mind." Steven Lubet, *Nothing But the Truth: Why Trial Lawyers Don't, Can't and Shouldn't Have to Tell the Whole Truth* 1 (2001).

Though it is rare, occasionally lawyers are caught in their misrepresentations or failure to be honest enough to satisfy the ABA Model Rules (both of ethics and of procedure). Consider the divorce lawyer in *Stare v. Tate*, 21 Cal. App. 3d 432, 98 Cal. Rptr. 264 (1971), who knew that the wife's lawyer had made two computational errors in calculating the value of some community property to be divided in the divorce settlement and failed to disclose the error in order to advantage his own client in the property division. The court was so appalled at this behavior (when it was revealed by the stupidly vindictive husband who called his ex-wife to tell her what he and his lawyer had done) that it did more than rescind the divorce settlement as contract law would have suggested (due to unilateral mistake). The court reformed the contract to reflect the correct values, rather than sending the parties back to renegotiate. Rather than "blame" the wife's lawyer for malpractice or incompetence in doing the computation, the husband's lawyer was publicly exposed for his "exquisite" desire to take advantage of the other side and, in effect, misrepresent the property values.

You may recall the national humor (and serious impeachment proceedings) that developed around President Clinton's lawyer-like attempt to get around acknowledging his sexual indiscretions by claiming, in his deposition, "It all depends on what the meaning of 'is' is," and his lawyer-like definitional dance around whether oral sex was, in fact, "sexual relations." *See* Nan Hunter, *The Power of Procedure: The Litigation of* Jones v. Clinton (2002).

Lawyers are famous for bending words, and Jim Carrey may perhaps have been chosen to play Fletcher Reede in *Liar Liar* because of his uncanny ability to literally bend his face and mouth in so many different directions. Consider the word manipulation that occurred in the famous case of *Washington State Physicians Insurance Exchange & Association v. Fisons Corporation*, 858 P. 2d 1054, 122 Wash. 2d 299 (1993). The Washington state law firm of Bogle & Gates (yes, that is

Bill Gates' father's firm) was sanctioned, under the state's civil procedure rule 26 (g), for failing to turn over documents in a serious medical malpractice action because of the way it twisted words in responding to a document discovery request. The plaintiffs requested production of any documents having to do with the drug "Somophyllin Oral liquid" as well as theophylline — the drug's more technical name — and were told such documents did not exist. Several years after the injury (serious brain damage to a young child) and ensuing lawsuit, an anonymous person sent the plaintiffs (both the treating doctor who claimed to have been lied to by the drug company and the child's parents) a copy of a letter which indicated the drug company had in fact warned doctors of the danger of the drug theophylline. The drug company did not produce the "smoking gun" document which revealed how dangerous the drug actually was because they claimed the plaintiffs' lawyers had failed to ask for documents relating to the exact drug compound and that these documents were actually filed elsewhere (in a file having to do with a competitive drug). The court found that the drug company's lawyers twisted every word in discovery requests so as not to produce the incriminating letters, and the lawyers were ordered to pay hundreds of thousands of dollars in sanctions, even though they claimed they were dutifully representing a client zealously in an adversarial system (and even though they were supported in this claim by at least one leading law professor who claimed aggressively resisting discovery requests was an ethical norm of discovery).

3.   At least two of the bad acts described above, after portrayals in movies (and reports on the front pages of many newspapers), have now been more formally dealt with by ethical rules (and empirical study). The billing improprieties described above have now been documented by Professor Lisa Lerman and have led to more disciplinary hearings in these cases. *See* Lisa Lerman, *Blue-Chip Bilking: Regulation of Billing and Expense Fraud by Lawyers*, 12 Georgetown Journal of Legal Ethics 205 (1999); Lisa Lerman, *The Slippery Slope from Ambition to Greed to Dishonesty: Lawyers, Money and Professional Integrity*, 30 Hofstra Law Review 878 (2002). And the American Bar Association has at least attempted to regulate information about billing, if not to provide substantive prohibitions on particular practices. Rule 1.5 of the ABA Model Rules of Professional Conduct states that a lawyer's fee must be reasonable. It offers suggestions for putting fee arrangements in writing and for setting contingency fees.

In the last two decades (coinciding with many depictions of lawyer-client, lawyer-judge, or lawyer-juror personal and sexual relationships in the movies, and also in real life), more and more states have passed formal statutes or regulations prohibiting sexual relations between lawyers and those with whom the lawyer might have a conflict of interest (including clients, jurors, and judges), but the particular formulation of the rule and who is included or excluded may still leave lots of opportunity for such "abuses" of relationships. And where, in some cases, consensual relations are still permitted, how are we to know what is really consensual when the power relations may be unequal (and can run in all sorts of different directions)? Many jurisdictions have passed statutes which attempt to regulate sexual or romantic relations between lawyers and clients by prohibiting sex unless the relationship predates the lawyer-client relationship. Does this solve the problem? *See* William Grady, "Legal World Starts to Build Case Against Sex With Clients,"

Chicago Tribune, 27 June 1993, C1; Lynda Crowly-Cyr & Carol Caple, *Sex With Clients and the Ethical Lawyer*, 8 James Cook Law Review 67 (2001); Caroline Forell, *Lawyers, Clients and Sex: Breaking the Silence on the Ethics*, 22 Golden Gate University Law Review 611 (1992).

4.   Is it ever appropriate to consider acts committed outside of the professional role when evaluating lawyer or professional behavior? Consider the following examples of conduct by lawyers or legal officials:

— John Tower's rejection as Secretary of Defense because of alleged drinking and "womanizing";

— Gary Hart's loss of the Presidential nomination due to dishonesty and deceit about his adulterous affairs;

— President Bill Clinton's impeachment for perjury and obstruction of justice in one sexual harassment case linked to his behavior in a consensual sexual liaison with a White House intern;

— Senator Packwood's forced resignation from office due to many claims of sexual harassment;

— Mayor Giuliani's televised announcement of his plans to divorce his wife while she was recuperating from cancer and spend his future with a partner from an adulterous liaison;

— Posthumous disclosure (widely believed during his lifetime) of President Thomas Jefferson's unmarried sexual (and perhaps loving) relationship with slave Sally Hemings;

— Judge Sol Wachtler's removal from office and incarceration for criminal harassment following termination of an adulterous relationship and for threats made to his former lover and her family;

— Withdrawal of nomination of General Ralston for Joint Chief of Staff following disclosure of an earlier adulterous affair;

— Resignations by members of Congress Livingston and Gingrich and public "apology" of Dan Burton, following disclosures of affairs, children born out of wedlock and "hypocrisy," exposed by *Penthouse* publisher Larry Flynt, following Clinton sex scandals;

— Resignation from Congress of Joseph Kennedy, following a scandal involving his pursuit of an annulment of his marriage of twelve years;

— Disclosure of a variety of sexual liaisons between President John F. Kennedy and a number of paramours;

— The now common knowledge that President Franklin Roosevelt had an ongoing adulterous and loving relationship with his wife's social secretary, both before and after entering the White House;

— Disclosure of President George W. Bush's arrest and conviction for driving while under the influence of alcohol some years before his candidacy;

— The forced resignation of British Secretary of State for War John Profumo, following the disclosure of his adulterous liaison with "model" Christine Keeler (who was rumored to be consorting with Russian spies);

— The failed Cabinet appointments of several appointees, mostly women, such as Zoe Baird and Kimba Wood, for failing to pay social security taxes for childcare workers (otherwise known as "Nannygate").

What are we to make of the relationship of personal lives to professional work, responsibility, and morality? What is relevant to the consideration of what makes a good lawyer, both for purposes of admitting a new member to the bar and for purposes of disciplining, sanctioning, or removing a member of the legal profession? To what extent must legal professionals be judged by different standards than those applied to other professionals or from those applied to them in their capacity as ordinary human beings? The scope of inquiry into a lawyer's private life has had an accordion-like existence in American history, opening and closing in relation to larger political and social forces. *See* Carrie Menkel-Meadow, *Private Lives and Professional Responsibilities: The Relationship of Personal Morality to Lawyering and Professional Ethics*, 21 Pace Law Review 365 (2001). Consider whether Michael Clayton's compulsive gambling should put him at risk for loss of legal license. What about the lawyer who drinks too much off the job but still manages to put in a full day of work? And, if one were to do a systematic study of the sexual indiscretions of public officials (from Presidents to Congressmen and local officials), would ethics discipline, voluntary resignation, or forced removal from office turn on whether the officials were lawyers or not?

The ethical rule which attempts to define professional misconduct for a lawyer states:

Rule 8.3 Misconduct

It is professional misconduct for a lawyer to:

(a)   violate or attempt to violate the Rules of Professional Conduct, knowingly assist or induce another to do so, or do so through acts of another;

(b)   commit a criminal act that reflects adversely on the lawyer's honesty, trustworthiness or fitness as a lawyer in other respects;

(c)   engage in conduct involving dishonesty, fraud, deceit or misrepresentation;

(d)   engage in conduct that is prejudicial to the administration of justice. . . .

How many of the acts described above or viewed in the movies you have seen about lawyers violate this rule? The murders committed by Teddy Barnes in *Jagged Edge*, Sam Bowden in *Cape Fear*, and Karen Crowder in *Michael Clayton*, are clear violations, as is the widespread criminal conduct depicted in *The Firm* (unless you do not think these criminal acts "reflect adversely on the lawyer's honesty, trustworthiness, or fitness as a lawyer"). Thus, even this "criminal acts" standard seems to require some nexus to lawyering to constitute an ethical (not criminal) violation. What about all the sexual indiscretions described above or depicted in the movies? Does it matter if the parties are married or in particular legal relationships? Should anyone care about people's private lives if they perform their "professional" duties appropriately? When are private lives and private acts relevant to assessing professional quality or character?

What about the demonstrations and protests Lucy Kelsen engages in to prevent the demolition of her beloved community center and other properties in New York (for which she is arrested)? Do lawyers have First Amendment rights too? Can a lawyer be disciplined for arrests or even criminal convictions if they have no bearing on the quality of her work as a lawyer? What if, as Lucy would probably argue, her arrests are actually *part* of and integral to her work as a politically active lawyer? What could have happened to Arthur Edens in *Michael Clayton* if he had exposed his guilty corporate client? Does it matter if he used lawyer-client privileged information or public information? Does he have to remain "loyal" to a client he knows has done wrong? (see ABA Model Rule 1.6, which varies in each state).

5.   Do lawyers who advise their clients to "avoid" or "evade" (do you know the legal difference?) taxes, or who advise about or predict the likelihood of enforcement of the law (when they know clients will use the information to commit unlawful acts) violate this rule? Is Fletcher Reede's habitual lying professional misconduct?

6.   Was it misconduct for Anthony Judson Lawrence in *The Young Philadelphians* to intentionally violate ABA Model Rule 1.1 (A lawyer shall provide competent representation to a client) when he took on the criminal defense of his friend Chet, knowing that he had no expertise as a criminal trial lawyer? Can you pinpoint when in *The Devil's Advocate* Kevin Lomax's zealous advocacy turns into misconduct? Does John Milton commit any acts of lawyer ethical misconduct?

7.   Many legal scholars and critics have argued that the use of the lawyer's technical skill to develop "technocratic" interpretations of the ethical rules is precisely what leads lawyers down the "slippery slope" to John Milton's legal hell. From "simple" exaggerations of a few minutes in billing, to "puffing" in negotiations, to "misplacing" a few key documents, to asking a secretary or assistant to lie about your whereabouts, to lying to your spouse and family about your activities or whereabouts, soon the lawyer may not know what is true or good or right in either personal or professional life. *See* Patrick J. Schiltz, *On Being a Happy, Healthy, and Ethical Member of an Unhappy, Unhealthy, and Unethical Profession*, 52 Vanderbilt Law Review 871 (1999); Heidi Li Feldman, *Codes and Virtues: Can Good Lawyers be Good Ethical Deliberators?* 69 Southern California Law Review 885 (1996).

8.   What "good" or inspiring acts do you see taken by lawyers in popular culture? Perhaps the most common theme is the representation of an unpopular (but usually wrongly accused) defendant like Tom Robinson in *To Kill a Mockingbird*. But think of some more modern examples. Lucy Kelsen goes to work for the Trump-like real estate developer George Wade in order to preserve the Coney Island community center and encourage her boss to make many important charitable and public interest contributions. Michael Brock in John Grisham's novel *The Street Lawyer* becomes a lawyer for the homeless after he is held hostage by a homeless person in his swank law firm. Anthony Judson Lawrence demonstrates

one of the few examples of good craft lawyering outside of the courtroom by giving helpful corporate and tax advice, although there might be some unethical activity in his giving advice to an already represented client. *See* ABA Model Rule 4.2. Scott Turow's lawyers often have trouble in their personal lives, but more often than not they work hard and eventually "do the right thing" with their cases (even disgorging harmful information when they have to). Scott Turow knows first-hand about potential ethical improprieties, having been complained against and acquitted of "assertive" prosecutorial practices. *See* Carrie Menkel-Meadow, *Scott Turow, in Yale Biographical Dictionary of American Law* (Roger Newman ed. 2009).

9.   And what do you make of those more complex or "mixed" acts like Atticus Finch's lie at the end of *To Kill a Mockingbird* to cover the murder committed by Boo Radley to save Finch's children, or the "wired" extortion of Michael Clayton or the murders by Teddy Barnes in *Jagged Edge* and Sam Bowden in *Cape Fear*? Lawyers (in the movies and probably in real life too) often commit what look like unlawful or "bad" acts to achieve a higher, if not fully "legal," justice. Professor William Simon calls this "moral pluck" when the lawyer commits an act of "transgression and resourcefulness in the vindication of justice." William Simon, *Moral Pluck: Legal Ethics in Popular Culture*, 101 Columbia Law Review 421, 422 (2001). He suggests that depictions of more complex lawyering (and personal) acts reveal the need for less authoritarian rules and the recognition that we must exercise moral and discretionary judgment when choosing our own acts, as well as judging others'. Ambiguous, ambivalent, or "mixed" motive acts of not-so-clear good or bad, in popular culture as well as in real life, demonstrate that good lawyers need to exercise individual initiative, respond sensitively to different contexts, and be flexible, smart, and morally accountable practical problem solvers. We must be careful not to judge too quickly those single acts, that when accumulated, may form a lawyer's more complex "character."

D.   LAWYERS' CHARACTER(S)

Although the dramatic moments in films about lawyers tend to turn on particular acts (the incisive cross-examination question, the discovery of a hidden document, the investigation of an unknown fact, the brilliant closing argument, the suffered-over refusal of a settlement offer, the ruthlessly negotiated contract or divorce settlement, the delivery of brilliant tax advice or good P.R. material, and — most dramatically — the return of a verdict), after the film is over we are more likely to remember the "gestalt" of the character of the lawyer. John Milton (*The Devil's Advocate*) is evil incarnate, and the fictional Atticus Finch (like the real Clarence Darrow) has become an iconic folk-hero of good lawyering, even though anyone who has seen the movie knows Atticus Finch is actually more complicated as a character. Gregory Peck, who is linked in our mind's eye forever with Atticus, is even more complicated in the other role he played in the same year (1962) — Sam Bowden in the first version of *Cape Fear*. In both films the southern lawyer of white suits and professional, legal, and moral "purity" takes justice into his own hands (by lying in *To Kill A Mockingbird* and killing in *Cape Fear*). These acts are morally justified, perhaps, but they are not subjected to the scrutiny of the legal process and the ultimate trial scene on which so many films depend. Less caricatured lawyer characters and those who learn, grow, and are often "redeemed" in films or books about lawyers offer more nuanced and perhaps more accurate reflections of what it actually means to be a lawyer, confronted with complicated and difficult professional, personal, and moral decisions.

At least one commentator has suggested that popular and populist treatments of these more complex characters offer a corrective to overly rigid conceptions of good/moral and bad/unethical lawyering:

MORAL PLUCK: LEGAL ETHICS IN POPULAR CULTURE
William H. Simon
101 Columbia Law Review 421 (2001)

A study of legal ethics in popular culture has two possible payoffs. First, popular culture is a source of evidence about popular moral understanding. The Conformist Moralism of the Bar and the impeachment proponents is based in part on factual premises about popular morality. The Conformists justify their precepts partly as responsive to categorical and authoritarian tendencies in the moral thinking of ordinary people. The evidence to be examined here suggests that these assumptions are mistaken. At least in some moments, popular morality is disposed to a style of moral judgment considerably different from the one Conformist Moralism attributes to it. Second, Moral Pluck is a substantive challenge to Conformist doctrine. The challenge is made, not through an explicit argument, but through dramatic representations of a type of ethical predicament and of styles of response to it. To be sure, these works romanticize lawyering, just as "lawyer jokes" demonize it, but their distortions are no greater than those of established professional responsibility doctrine. While popular culture is utopian about the possibilities of individual initiative, established doctrine is utopian about the reliability of official institutions. . . .

I. The Conformist Perspective

Elite moralism in general and professional responsibility doctrine in particular is strongly categorical and authoritarian. Ethics is categorical when it insists on appraising conduct in terms of rigid rules, with few if any exceptions and excuses. To take the most famous and extreme example, Kant insisted that lying is always wrong, even when necessary to save an innocent life. In the impeachment crisis, the President's prosecutors denied that either the private nature of the conduct involved or its marginal relevance to the Paula Jones case excused or even mitigated his perjury. They insisted that excusing any kind of perjury would threaten the "rule of law."

Professional responsibility doctrine is categorical in its proclivity for rules insensitive to the contingencies of particular situations. Such rules tend to require mechanical judgment or literal application. They frequently mandate that the decision maker take actions that she correctly sees as unjust or contrary to important public values. Notoriously, for example, the confidentiality rules require that the lawyer keep secrets even in some situations where disclosure might save an innocent life and the client's interests are trivial.

Ethics is authoritarian when it conflates moral authority with the explicit commands or enactments of government institutions. For the impeachment propo-nents, it was sufficient that the President had violated a judge's order and the terms of a federal statute. Even if they had been convinced that the judge's order was wrong or that the statute, as applied, would subvert fundamental privacy values, they would not have deemed these considerations relevant. The President's lawyers seemed to concede this authoritarian view by focusing their arguments, not on appeals to the privacy values that were threatened by an inquisition into consensual sex, but on casuistic claims that the President's deceptive answers did not amount to perjury.

The authoritarian disposition appears in professional responsibility doctrine in the tendency to define law and legal authority in terms of the state. The Model Code distinguishes legal authority from moral, economic, social, and political factors that, though sometimes important, must take a back seat. Lawyers are obliged to press for their clients' interests subject only to the constraints of formally-enacted commands. At the same time, lawyers are obliged to respect any norm that qualifies as law by formal enactment, even where such respect contributes to injustice. There is no tolerance, for example, for civil disobedience — principled noncompliance with unjust positive law. The Bar's norms condemn "even minor violations of law by a lawyer." They insist that the only appropriate response to unjust law is to petition institutions with formal legislative authority to enact revisions.

All these themes contribute to a pervasive hostility to independent judgment in professional responsibility rhetoric. This hostility is transparent in the Multistate Professional Responsibility Examination, which in most states is the only testing of legal ethics in connection with admission to the bar. The examination is preoccupied with black-letter disciplinary rules. Since it is multiple-choice and machine-graded, it focuses on situations that lend themselves to glib black-and-white responses. Bar review instructors commonly advise applicants: "What they are testing is your ability to memorize."

In informal legal ethics discussions, a variety of rhetorical tropes are routinely deployed to penalize independent judgment. When lawyers appeal to informal norms of justice to explain either violations of enacted law or refusals to push client interests to the limits of enacted law, they are charged with self-righteousness and self-aggrandizement: "playing God," "arrogating power to herself," "imposing her own values," "undermining the established process." In the academic literature, frequent disapproval of discretionary norms is linked to concerns about "account-ability." Although it is not always clear to whom accountability is sought, it usually appears that the authors contemplate control by the state.

The moral premises of popular fictional portrayals of lawyering are often quite different from this Conformist tradition. Popular fiction is anti-categorical and anti-authoritarian. Categorical norms require us to disregard all but a narrow range of the particularities of the situation. But fiction is committed to particularity. These works tend to evoke situations in which general norms are at war with more powerful particularistic intuitions. The authoritarianism of Conformist Moralism implies a consistently benign and reliable state. But popular culture warns that the state is often incompetent or corrupt and draws attention to the frightening and unjust consequences of its failings. . . .

V. Lessons from Popular Culture

This material from popular culture has two potential contributions to ethics: first as a source of evidence about popular moral thinking, and second as a substantive contribution to ethical understanding. . . .

These entertainments usefully remind us that there is a moral orientation with broad popular appeal that is neither categorical and authoritarian on the one hand, nor relativistic on the other. They raise doubts about the view that has influenced both the Bar and the Congressional leadership that moral precepts framed in categorical and authoritarian terms are most likely to be compatible with ordinary moral thinking. For the appeal of these works seems to depend on a capacity for contextual judgment and a principled skepticism toward authority.

The second potential contribution of these works is substantive. They offer an ethical perspective that competes with Conformist Moralism as a source of moral guidance. The tone of this perspective is Emersonian. It is an ethic of self-assertion that encourages us to think of morality as an occasion for creativity. By contrast, the tone of Conformist Moralism is Puritanical and Kantian. It is an ethic of self-restraint that emphasizes the need to curb our more aggressive and destructive impulses through deference to external authority. Moral Pluck insists that ethics is not simply a matter of duties to society, but rather of character and personal integrity. While philosophers have argued for this perspective abstractly, popular culture teaches it by urging us to identify imaginatively with an attractive figure and then confronting us with the damage to the character's commitments and self-conception that deference to authority sometimes would require.

At the same time, these works insist that we take account of situations in which norms of authority are in tension with substantive justice. They remind us incessantly of the widespread ineptitude and corruption of official institutions. At one extreme — in the darker Grisham novels — these institutions are integral parts of a vast criminal conspiracy. The works also remind us of the limitations of categorical norms that arise from their unresponsiveness to vital dimensions of some morally urgent situations. The confidentiality norm is the most prominent example. Many of these works try to demonstrate that the Bar's established norms are potentially incompatible with morally plausible responses to situations with high stakes. These are important lessons, and Conformist Moralism is deficient for ignoring them. Its view of the good lawyer is unattractive in its passivity and complacency.

Nevertheless, the type of popular works we are considering have undeniable limitations as a form of ethical reflection. One familiar complaint is that popular culture oversimplifies. Instead of promoting reflection, it gratifies unconscious desires for self-assertion by abstracting away the most important moral and strategic difficulties of real world ethical dilemmas. Some of us get visceral satisfaction watching Clint Eastwood or Sylvester Stallone blow away bad guys unconstrained by due process or physical limitations, but on reflection we do not regard their characters as role models. These fantasies grossly understate the dangers of transgressive self-assertion and underestimate the importance of institutional authority.

The works considered here are more self-conscious and thoughtful about ethics than the typical Hollywood "action" movie. Still, it has to be conceded that, as ethical discourse, they are unambitious. To begin with, the dilemmas they portray tend to take a Manichean form with implausible frequency. The works mislead by suggesting that, in the situations where lawyers perceive a tension between the dictates of established authority and their conceptions of substantive justice, defiance of authority would usually meet with the approval of most ordinary people (at least if they knew the facts). In fact, popular moral values are strongly divided across a broad range of situations. There are many situations in which many people would find unattractive the substantive values lawyers would assert in good faith defiance of constituted authority. . . .

The attitude expressed in these works toward institutions is also fanciful. The problem is not that they exaggerate the ineptitude and corruption of official institutions, though they probably do. More importantly, they portray Moral Pluck exclusively as an individual matter. The protagonists accomplish their heroic feats by themselves, or with the informal help of a few close friends. And their own transgressive initiatives leave no institutional traces. They do not contribute to new, more satisfactory institutions or alter the basic contours of established ones. . . .

NOTES & QUESTIONS

1.   Professor Simon's article explores the "transgressive" ethical choices made by lawyers in John Grisham's novels and the lawyers on television shows such as *L.A. Law* and *The Practice.* He says that these works show lawyers who are more "self-conscious" and "thoughtful about ethics" than those in "the typical Hollywood action movie." Recall that Professor Asimow suggested above that lawyers are depicted in a more positive light on television programs than in the movies. Why might this be so? How do the different media show-case or develop different aspects of professional behavior? Does the movie format require dramatic action in individual acts where novels and ongoing television programs allow a longer observation of the development of character over time?

Consider that when professional disciplinary committees have to decide how to punish ethical violations they have to consider "acts" (in determining if there is an ethical violation) and then look to a whole career ("character") in meting out punishments or other remedies.

How do you judge professionals? Based on single acts or ongoing behavior? How do you make judgments about other people in your life? Relatives and family members? Friends? Classmates? Teachers? How much "data" do we need to have about a person or the context in which they act to understand whether what they are doing is worthy or not?

2.   While praising the "moral pluck" of some lawyers in popular culture, Professor Simon is also worried that the messages suggested by popular culture overemphasize the romantic power of the individual. Lawyers are seen making "heroic" or brave decisions on their own and are less often shown changing the corrupt or problematic institutions in which they must operate (such as the American legal system, legislative lobbying, corporate decisionmaking). Other

commentators have suggested that individual lawyers of exceptional professional character can positively affect not only their own profession, but the polity at large. See Robert Gordon, *The Independence of Lawyers*, 68 Boston University Law Review 11 (1988), and Anthony T. Kronman, *The Lost Lawyer: Failing Ideals of the Legal Profession* (1993), discussing the lawyer as "statesman."

Can you think of any popular depictions of institutional or collective law reform? (The 1979 film *Norma Rae* dramatized a union organizing campaign.) Lucy Kelsen, in *Two Weeks Notice*, is presented as both an individual and collective law reformer and protester (the daughter of a law professor mother and a civil liberties-seeking father) for anti-poverty, community, environmental, and other legal causes. The lawyers on *The Practice* at least band together as a group to put the state to its proof in the criminal justice system. The prosecutors in all the *Law & Order* shows (even with cast changes) act as if they share an institutional commitment, both to the workplace and to criminal justice. Do lawyers for the state, as depicted in both movies and films, ever make "brave" ethical choices that demonstrate their commitment, not just to convictions, but to justice? ABA Model Rule 3.8 requires more of prosecutors; they must not only represent their clients (the "people" or the State) but also seek justice. Rule 3.8 Comment says a prosecutor has the responsibility of a minister of justice and not simply that of an advocate.

3.   How much "control" do you think individuals have over their own moral development in their careers? To what extent does the particular law office or context of practice influence or socialize a lawyer's character? Consider the different law firm cultures depicted on *L.A. Law* (glamorous and diverse, mostly civil, practice), *The Practice* (chummy, committed, diverse criminal defense practice, with many ethical discussions and debates), *Law & Order* (committed long-term colleagues with explicit supervisory and political meetings with bosses, seniors, and juniors), and the large law firms in *Philadelphia, The Young Philadelphians, The Verdict, Class Action, Erin Brockovich* (2000), *The Devil's Advocate* and *Michael Clayton*. How often do films about lawyers depict the full complexity of character development in the crucible of law practice settings, including the economics and personal stress of partnership decisions and economic pressures? *See* Marc Galanter & Thomas Palay, *Tournament of Lawyers: The Transformation of the Big Law Firm* (1991); Milton C. Regan, *Eat What You Kill: Fall of a Wall St. Lawyer* (2005). Does size of law practice make a difference? The modern films about lawyers seem to "blame" the structure of big law firms, as much as the individuals. See Lance McMillian, *Tortured Souls: Unhappy Lawyers Viewed Through the Medium of Film*, 19 Seton Hall Journal of Sports and Entertainment Law 31 (2009), which suggests that the re-assignment of Michael Clayton away from his passion of litigation to "fixer" led to his downfall; *see also* John Denvir, *Being Bogart: Professional Identity after* Michael Clayton (2011), available at http://ssrn.com/abstract=1777210.

4.   How are characters formed or influenced by mentors or supervisors in the media? Consider how the classic lawyer and doctor programs of the Golden Era had Dr. Massey advising Dr. Kildare, Dr. Zorba advising Ben Casey, and Lawrence Preston using his senior authority to morally instruct his son and junior partner Kenneth Preston on *The Defenders*. *See* David Ray Papke, *The Defenders, in Prime Time Law: Fictional Television as Legal Narrative* (Robert M. Jarvis & Paul R.

Joseph eds. 1998); Harris Dienstfrey, *Doctors, Lawyers and Other TV Heroes, in* 35(6) Commentary 519 (June 1963), *reprinted in Television: The Critical View* (Horace Newcombe ed. 1976). Contrast the depiction of the parental role models of John Milton in *The Devil's Advocate* and Jedediah Ward in *Class Action*. How often do we see senior and junior lawyers grappling with generational differences in ethics, as depicted in Auchincloss' *Diary of a Yuppie* (1986)? The ABA Model Rules recognize a complex structure of hierarchy and deference to seniors, but they still require reporting of ethical violations. *See* Model Rule 5.1, Responsibilities of a Partner or Supervisory Lawyer and Model Rule 5.2, Responsibilities of a Subordinate Lawyer).

5.   Is character framed, in part, by who the individual is demographically and personally? To what extent do you think your character was framed in your family, in your religious training (*see* Howard Lesnick, *Religion in Legal Thought and Practice* (2010)), in your peer cultures, or by who you "are" (male, female, black, white, Hispanic or Latino, Asian, European, mixed race or nationality, Christian, Jew, Muslim, Buddhist)?

In a debate that has raged for several decades now, many scholars have argued that women may bring a different moral sensibility to the practice of law, "by seeking to do less harm, solve more problems, be more concerned with human relationships of both clients and of those who interact with clients, and to deal with others more honestly and fairly." Carrie Menkel-Meadow, *Can They Do That?, supra*, at 1323; Carrie Menkel-Meadow, *Portia in a Different Voice: Speculations on a Women's Lawyering Process*, 1 Berkeley Women's Law Journal 39 (1985); Carrie Menkel-Meadow, *Portia Redux: Another Look at Gender, Feminism and Legal Ethics*, 2 Virginia Journal of Social Policy & Law 75 (1995); Carrie Menkel-Meadow, *The Feminization of the Legal Profession: The Comparative Sociology of Women Lawyers, in Lawyers in Society: Comparative Theories* (Richard Abel & Philip Lewis eds. 1989). See the source for this argument in Carol Gilligan, *In a Different Voice* (1982).

Consider how this debate was humorously depicted in *All of Me* (1984), a classic "transposed bodies" film. In this film, which uses a now-standard plot of bump-on-the-head transformation into someone else, Steve Martin, playing a stereotypically aggressive and dishonest lawyer, becomes literally embodied with the soul of Lily Tomlin, a deceased, do-gooding woman. In what has to be one of the funniest and most serious critiques of the character of lawyers, Lily Tomlin and Steve Martin literally, figuratively, and linguistically fight over the control of both body and soul of a lawyer who, in Steve Martin's body, makes a dishonest closing argument, as Lily Tomlin struggles to push the truth out of Steve Martin's mouth. Of course, this scene can be read not only as a gender critique of lying male lawyers but also as the "layperson as moral, lawyer as good professional but bad person" critique found in much moral philosophy. Carrie Menkel-Meadow, *Can They Do That?, supra*, at 1323.

Do you think women lawyers are depicted differently than men in popular culture? Are Lucy Kelsen and Teddy Barnes more "moral" or sensitive than Frank Galvin, Kevin Lomax, and Atticus Finch? Consider how tough the female prosecutors in *Law & Order* are or how much more complex the female lawyers of *L.A. Law* and *The Practice* were (Ann Kelsey, Grace Van Owen, Helen Gambel, Ellenor Frutt, Lindsay Dole, and Rebecca Washington). And consider the ethical improprieties committed by Teddy Barnes in *Jagged Edge*, Kathleen Riley in *Suspect*, Karen Crowder in *Michael Clayton*, and Maggie Ward in *Class Action*. Do you think there is anything to the argument that women lawyers are more likely to use "caring" or "morally connected" approaches to practicing law? Why or why not? What might be the reasons for differences in styles, approaches, or philosophies of the practice of law by gender? Do women judges act differently than male judges? *See, e.g.*, Carrie Menkel-Meadow, *Asylum in a Different Voice? Judging Immigration Claims and Gender, in Refugee Roulette* (Jaya Ramji-Nogales, Andrew Schoenholtz, & Philip Schrag eds. 2009). Consider the women judges that now appear regularly on *Law & Order* and other legal television programs — are they any different?

There are also occasionally depictions of minority lawyers confronted with issues about their racial, national, or minority identity and how that interacts with the way they make decisions or practice law. Consider Joe Miller, the character played by Denzel Washington in *Philadelphia*, who is not particularly sympathetic to gay rights and initially turns down the representation of Andrew Beckett, a gay white lawyer discriminatorily dismissed from his law firm because he has AIDS. Miller, a black lawyer, clearly understands what discrimination is all about, and the film uses his race to "double" track the discrimination story. And consider how *L.A. Law* used (and made the career of) Jimmy Smits as the Hispanic Victor Sifuentes, who initially refused to join the firm because he did not want to become "the Mexican gardener picking up the snails." John Brigham, *L.A. Law, in Prime Time Law, supra*, at 29.

Consider the poignancy with which the black lawyer on *The Practice*, Eugene Young, was depicted as struggling for his parental custody rights after his son was arrested for drug possession. His wife tried to take his son away from him because of the son's exposure to criminals in his father's practice. Young courageously underscored important lawyer character issues (commitment to justice and equal treatment) and coupled them with sensitivity to the added social dimension of race. His defense of his profession and its purpose is one of the most eloquent vindications of the criminal defense lawyer's calling and commitment to justice that has been seen in the popular media in decades. *See* episodes *Cross-Fire*, broadcast ABC, March 4, 1999, and *Target Practice*, broadcast ABC, March 7, 1999. *See also* Carrie Menkel-Meadow, *Can They Do That?, supra*, 1323-24.

Perhaps the most troubling of lawyer character issues depicted in the popular media, which replicates the debates among legal philosophers and ethicists, is the tension between commitment to law and commitment to justice in a lawyer of good character. As Americans and lawyers, we argue throughout the world for the sanctity, as well as the instrumental fairness, of the rule of law. Some legal ethicists seek clarity and conformity in the "law of lawyering." Writers of popular fiction, movies, and television mirror the challenge that William Simon and others have posed to the law of legal ethics.

Is lawyer character constituted from ordinary human mettle? Strength of character? Commitment? Loyalty? Honesty? Selflessness and protection of others? Good judgment? Leadership? Or, is good lawyerly character supposed to be faithful to the rules of law, ethics, and procedure? Literary and popular depictions of lawyers dramatize these tensions, as legal philosophers debate the differences between morality and positive law.

In the movies and on television, the good lawyer character just as often demonstrates a departure from the rules of law in the name of a greater justice as it does conformity to it. We may want to question why this is so; do these fictional depictions help us develop role models committed to justice, or is there also a danger that good and strong characters might allow us to take justice and law (as long as we are "worthy" and morally justified) into our own hands"? Carrie Menkel-Meadow, *Can They Do That?*, *supra*, 1324-25.

How do we feel when we watch Teddy Barnes and Sam Bowden, both lawyers, commit murder to achieve some form of human "justice"?

E.   LAWYERS' CHOICES AND LEARNING: REDEMPTION OF THE LEGAL PROFESSIONAL

Good drama is intended to illuminate our human condition — both the actors in the play and the viewers in the audience should learn something (and, in many forms of drama, "change" as a result of that learning) during the action. The more sophisticated films, novels, and television shows about lawyers demonstrate how lawyers have learned from the actions they have taken and how they can be better, both professionally and personally, as a result of what they have learned. Kevin Lomax (*The Devil's Advocate*) wakes from his Hollywood-provided dream to realize he does not have to work for his devilish father and represent the guilty; he can withdraw from that representation and seek the truth, as well as the just. Fletcher Reede (*Liar Liar*) learns to speak the truth about the love of his son (how this will affect his legal career is not clear at the end of the movie). Lucy Kelsen (*Two Weeks Notice*) finds true love outside her legal aid office when her former boss, George Wade, gives up his ill-gotten fortune to be with her, just as Teddy Barnes (*Jagged Edge*) loses (kills) her ill-gotten romance with her client, while recognizing her own gullibility and lost faith in the criminal justice system. Anthony Judson Lawrence (by narrating his own story in *The Young Philadelphians*) tells us at the beginning of the movie that we will have to wait until the end to judge his full character; he has been an ambitious social climber, but he has been a good lawyer. When he defends his college friend out of loyalty, he is rewarded with the love of a good (and very rich!) woman. Maggie Ward (*Class Action*) sees the error of her big-firm ambitions and joins her father by switching sides in a products liability (car design) case to seek justice for the injured. Michael Clayton's tale unfolds in flashbacks and present time, but he too is a changed man (or is he still just a "fixer" by the end of the film?). And, in what is likely to go down in the annals of lawyer films as the ultimate redemption movie, Frank Galvin (*The Verdict*), a dissipated, lazy, and drunken solo practitioner, learns to sober up and do some hard work, both in investigation and trial, and triumphs over the cocky Boston Brahmin law firm representing the Catholic Church's hospital.

These filmic depictions of learning by lawyers offer viewers an opportunity to see acts change characters. By stumbling through law practice or life, these lawyers learn that they can be better than they seem — often after they come to realize that the legal system may not be all that it seems to be.

THE MOVIE LAWYERS' GUIDE TO REDEMPTIVE LEGAL PRACTICE

Paul Bergman

48 UCLA Law Review 1393 (2001)

The Chinese use two brush strokes to write the word "crisis." One brush stroke stands for danger; the other for opportunity. In crisis, be aware of the danger — but recognize the opportunity.

An enduring film image is the "moment of crisis" that produces the "moment of truth." Ships about to sink or brakeless cars plummeting down steep mountain roads often provide the impetus for dramatic revelations. In such settings, and in line with the policy behind the "dying declaration" exception to the hearsay rule, characters are prone to revealing long-hidden truths. In Filmland, crises can also be very good medicine. Characters who are fortunate enough to survive moments of crisis often emerge with improved happiness and moral values. Forced by crises to confront suppressed realities, movie characters may choose to redeem their lives by committing their futures to performing what audiences are likely to perceive as good works. Thus, filmmakers may use crises as a tool for sending powerful normative messages about what constitutes a morally good and personally satisfying life.

This Essay examines films in which movie lawyers are redeemed by moments of crisis. Just as crises may serve as tools for sending normative messages about what constitutes a morally good and satisfying personal life, so too may crises lead movie lawyers to "redemptive lawyering," or morally good and personally satisfying professional lifestyles. The Essay examines images of redemptive lawyering for reel lawyers and compares those images to the attitudes of real lawyers.

I. Redemption for Reel Lawyers

Redemptive lawyering in films occurs when sudden, dramatic, or even catastrophic events jolt movie lawyers into adopting morally good and personally satisfying professional lifestyles. Images of redemptive lawyering can convey powerful normative images of lawyering ideals, and of what lawyers can be and can do to emerge from frustrating, unsatisfying, and even unethical careers. The subsections below describe three forms of redemptive lawyering that movie lawyers have adopted in response to crises.

A. Problem-Centered Lawyering

"Problem-centered lawyering" is one form of redemptive lawyering. Redemption occurs when a crisis enables a lawyer to realize that ultimate professional satisfaction consists of using legal knowledge and legal experience to craft satisfactory solutions to clients' problems. The idea is that a life devoted to problem solving is personally satisfying. Moreover, because most of us tend to believe that helping people in need is a socially valuable activity, audiences are likely to perceive devotion to clients' problems as morally good.

Counsellor at Law [1933] presents an archetypal example of a movie lawyer who finds redemption in problem-centered lawyering. George Simon (John Barrymore) is an up-from-the-gutter Jew who has become one of New York City's most successful lawyers. Simon's office, where the entire movie takes place, is a jumble of frantic activity. Simon is in his element, juggling a stream of legal and personal problems brought to him by clients, his mother, his partner, his wife, an investigator, various office employees, and others. However, what matters most to Simon is not his law practice, but his non-Jewish trophy wife Cora (Doris Kenyon). He brags about Cora constantly, and is so concerned with preserving Cora's social status that he turns down a case that would have produced a lucrative fee, but that Cora felt would embarrass her in the eyes of her friends. Thus, when Simon finds out that Cora has been unfaithful, the moment of crisis is at hand. For Simon, because law practice was but a means to acceptance by what he considered the social elite, Cora's unfaithfulness robs his practice of its meaning. Simon opens the window of his suddenly dark, quiet office and prepares to jump to his death. But like many a prizefighter, Simon is saved by the bell — in this case, the bell of his telephone. Simon's adoring secretary Regina Gordon (Bebe Daniels) was supposed to have left for the day, but she returned to the office because she was worried about him. Regina answers the phone and tells Simon that the caller is the president of a steel company whose son is in serious trouble. At first, Simon remains in suicide mode; he orders Regina to hang up. In moments, however, Simon reverts to the confident, energetic lawyer we have seen throughout the movie. He excitedly grabs the phone, shouts instructions to the president, and rushes out of the office with Regina to his client's aid.

The moment of crisis enables Simon to achieve redemption by becoming a problem-centered lawyer. In crisis, Simon recognizes that chasing after Cora and her elite society friends is unimportant compared to the personal satisfaction and even the exhilaration of confronting and overcoming challenging legal problems. Moreover, Simon's commitment to problem solving is morally good, as he places himself in the immediate service of a client who, although the president of a steel company, is at bottom a father worried about his son. The film's final scene symbolizes Simon's redemption. As he leaves his office for the first time in the film, so he sheds his old self and what he had falsely valued in law practice. *Counsellor at Law* conjures a strong image of commitment to problem solving as a lawyerly ideal, and suggests that devotion to problem solving is both professionally satisfying and morally good without regard to the status of the client.

B. Client-Centered Lawyering

"Client-centered lawyering" is a second form of redemptive lawyering. Redemption occurs when crisis enables a lawyer to realize that the ultimate source of a satisfactory professional career is bonding with clients. This image depicts clients as weak and in desperate need of protection. It suggests the need for lawyers to empathize with clients in order to provide them with the legal help they deserve. An empathic lawyer is both professionally happy and morally good.

Lawyer Man [1933] is an early and somewhat general example of client-centered redemption. Anton Adam (William Powell) has a small but successful practice serving the largely immigrant population on New York's lower east side. Olga Michaels (Joan Blondell) is Adam's standard-issue adoring secretary. After a significant courtroom victory, Adam closes his store-front office and joins a powerful uptown practice, where he prospers. To Olga's disgust, Adam seems to have turned his back on his former clients. Economic success for Adam comes with a price, however — the mob wants him to do its bidding. When Adam refuses, the mob sets him up and the ensuing criminal charges ruin his lucrative career. Adam's specific moment of crisis emerges when the mob boss offers Adam a judgeship. While this probably would not be a crisis for most lawyers, it is for Adam because he understands that the offer was made with the idea that, because he has been publicly disgraced and has nowhere to turn, the mob will expect to dictate Adam's decisions. Adam does have a place to turn, however — the lower-east-side practice where he started his career. Arm in arm, Adam and Olga happily walk through streets teeming with the politically powerless population to which Adam will devote the remainder of his career.

Adam's bond is not with a specific client, but with a population with which he shares common roots. More typically, personal redemption for movie lawyers comes from the plight of a specific client. In *The Verdict*, Frank Galvin (Paul Newman) is a boozed-out personal injury lawyer who tries to scratch out a living by soliciting clients in funeral parlors. Galvin has one case of real value, a medical malpractice case against two anesthesiologists and the hospital that employed them. The complaint, which had been filed by Galvin's mentor, Mickey Morrissey (Jack Warden), alleged that the doctors administered an improper anesthetic to a young woman who entered the hospital's emergency room to have a baby. The improper anesthetic left the young woman comatose. Unfortunately for his clients, the comatose woman's guardians, Galvin has done nothing on the case. It's hard to prepare for trial when you're dead drunk most of the time.

Galvin's moment of redemption occurs when he decides to visit the comatose woman in the hospital. As he takes photographs of her lying helplessly in a hospital bed, kept alive by a respirator and feeding tube, he bonds with her though she cannot speak, hear, see, or offer him a drink. For the first time, Galvin realizes the woman's helplessness and his responsibility to bring to justice the doctors who ruined her life. Significantly, Galvin tells the nurses who want to know why he is in the hospital room, "I'm her lawyer." Thereafter, Galvin works relentlessly for his client. Further evidence of Galvin's redemption occurs when he engages in pretrial settlement negotiations with defense lawyer Ed Concannon (James Mason) in the chambers of Judge Hoyle (Milo O'Shea). Judge Hoyle chides Galvin for turning down a large settlement offer, commenting, "your client could walk out of here with a lot of money." "She can't walk," is Galvin's reply. Galvin is so personally connected to his client that he takes the judge's figurative comment as a personal slight. The film's conclusion further signifies Galvin's redemptive transformation. Though the jurors have no legal basis for doing so, they return a huge verdict in favor of the comatose woman. Galvin later receives a phone call from Laura Fischer (Charlotte Rampling) whom Concannon had employed as a spy to report on Galvin's trial strategy. Galvin's refusal to answer the phone suggests that he has renounced his former habits and will devote himself to his clients.

Joe Miller (Denzel Washington) in *Philadelphia* becomes a client-centered lawyer when he connects discrimination against homosexual AIDS sufferer Andrew Beckett (Tom Hanks) to discrimination against African Americans. Miller is an African American lawyer with a small but successful neighborhood personal injury practice. At the start of the film, Beckett is an up-and-coming star attorney with one of Philadelphia's largest and most prestigious law firms. However, by the time he asks Miller to represent him in an employment discrimination lawsuit against the law firm, Beckett is deathly ill with AIDS. Beckett claims that he was illegally fired because of his illness. Miller initially refuses to take the case, partly because he thinks it unwinnable, but primarily because he wants nothing to do with the AIDS virus or homosexuals.

Some weeks later, Miller and Beckett are doing legal research at adjacent tables in a public law library. Miller's moment of crisis emerges when he notices a white patron staring at him. The patron's disdainful look suggests that as an African American, Miller could only be a client and therefore should not be in a section of the library reserved for lawyers. Miller then observes a librarian rudely trying to convince a noticeably ill Beckett to move to a private research room. At this redemptive moment, Miller recognizes that both he and Beckett are targets of discrimination. After Beckett holds his ground, Miller asks him about the status of his employment discrimination claim. Beckett calls Miller's attention to a portion of a case establishing that Beckett's claim is legally valid. Miller reads the last portion, in which the court refers to discrimination against AIDS sufferers as the equivalent of "social death," and comparable to any form of illegal discrimination in which prejudice is based on the presumed characteristics of a group rather than individual merit. The language cements the personal bond between Miller and Beckett as targets of discrimination. In the next scene Miller is representing Beckett; he serves the senior partner of Beckett's ex-law firm with a complaint for employment discrimination.

The film suggests the redemptive power of client-centered lawyering. Miller had been anti-gay, and his practice seemingly consisted of going through the motions on behalf of clients in whom he had no personal interest in order to earn a good, steady income. After taking on Beckett's case, Miller becomes aware that homosexual relationships are much like his own, and he views gay rights as an important civil rights issue. He tries the case with a zeal that demonstrates that he has a personal, as well as an economic, stake in its outcome. Thus, *Philadelphia* suggests that lawyers can redeem themselves by personally bonding with clients.

The Accused offers a final example of client-centered redemption. Sarah Tobias (Jodie Foster), who scrapes out a meager living as a waitress, is raped by three men in a bar. Numerous barflies cheer the rapists on. Prosecutor Kathryn Murphy (Kelly McGillis) initially seeks the maximum punishment. However, she soon finds out that Tobias has a spotty past and that just before the rape, Tobias had been drinking heavily and dancing provocatively. Fearful of losing, Murphy agrees to guilty pleas to a lesser, nonsexual charge.

As it did for Frank Galvin in *The Verdict*, Murphy's moment of redemption occurs bedside in a hospital. Shortly after Murphy has plea-bargained away her case,

Tobias is in a parking lot when she is taunted by one of the barflies. She furiously rams her car into his truck, and sustains serious injuries which result in her being hospitalized. Murphy's moment of crisis arrives when she visits Tobias in the hospital. Tobias accuses Murphy of treating her no better than did the barflies — both, Tobias says, treated her "like a piece of shit." Recognition of the truth of Tobias's statement produces Murphy's moment of redemption. Murphy insists on prosecuting the barflies for contributing to the rape, over the vehement objections of her boss, the district attorney. Murphy identifies with Tobias personally and tells him, "I owe her." The case goes to trial. Tobias describes what happened, a key witness comes forward to support her story, and the barflies are convicted.

The Accused suggests how easily what may be "business as usual" for lawyers can appear contemptuous to the outside world. After all, Murphy's conduct prior to her redemptive moment is in no way unusual or improper. Prosecutors routinely offer plea bargains when they face weaknesses in proof. From Tobias's perspective, however, Murphy abandoned her and implicitly denied Tobias's worth as a human being. By personally bonding with Tobias, Murphy derives personal satisfaction and punishes immoral behavior.

C. Justice-Centered Lawyering

"Justice-centered lawyering" is a third form of redemptive lawyering. Redemption occurs when crisis enables a lawyer to realize that ultimate professional satisfaction consists of pursuing justice. Like client-centered lawyers, justice-centered lawyers typically represent politically powerless clients. For the latter group of lawyers, however, personal satisfaction and moral goodness result from the positions they advocate rather than personal attachments to individuals.

In *An Act of Murder* [1948], Calvin Cooke (Fredric March) is a strict, letter-of-the-law judge known in the community as "Old Man Maximum" for his harsh sentencing policies. Off the bench, Judge Cooke is devoted to his wife Cathy (Florence Eldridge). Judge Cooke's moment of crisis occurs when he learns that Cathy has a terminal illness. Judge Cooke crashes his car with the intention of killing Cathy in order to spare her a long and painful death. Although the authorities are prepared to assume that Cathy's death was the result of an accident, Judge Cooke confesses that he intentionally killed her. He is charged with murder, and insists on pleading guilty. Over Judge Cooke's objection, the trial court judge appoints defense attorney David Douglas (Edmond O'Brien) to represent Judge Cooke so as to ensure that a factual basis for the plea exists. Douglas asks for an autopsy, which produces surprising evidence: Cathy was dead from lethal poison before the crash occurred. Additional evidence shows that Cathy also knew of her illness, and that she ingested poison before taking the fatal car ride. After hearing this evidence, the judge dismisses the case. The experience redeems Judge Cooke. Acknowledging his moral guilt, Judge Cooke states that if he is allowed to remain a judge, he will have an enlightened view of justice. To do justice, he must look not only at a person's behavior, but also the person's circumstances and the reasons for that behavior. Henceforth, in his court, "a man shall be judged not only by the law, but by the heart as well." Thus, Judge Cooke's personal crisis allows him to recognize that a uniform application of black-letter rules will not necessarily produce justice. Moral application of rules demands that judges holistically evaluate people's backgrounds and circumstances.

A yearning to do justice also characterizes the redemption of Maggie Ward (Mary Elizabeth Mastrantonio) in *Class Action.* Maggie is an associate in a large civil defense firm, hungry for partnership. As second chair to Michael Grazier (Colin Friels), Maggie defends Argo Motors against a lawsuit filed by her father Jedediah Ward (Gene Hackman), a crusading plaintiff 's personal injury lawyer. Jedediah's complaint alleges that design defects in a car manufactured by Argo, the Meridian, caused numerous deaths and injuries. Maggie learns of a "smoking gun": Dr. Pavel (Jan Rubes), an Argo engineer, had submitted a report stating that the Meridian's design would cause it to explode under certain conditions. Argo disregarded the report, figuring that defending a few wrongful death cases would be cheaper in the long run than retrofitting thousands of cars. Rather than turn the report over to Jedediah in response to his legitimate discovery request, Maggie accedes to her firm's plan to mislabel the report and bury it in a truckload of Argo documents given to Jedediah. Her moment of crisis emerges when she realizes that the law firm duped her. The report was not turned over to Jedediah at all, and even the copy that Maggie had in her desk was removed. Maggie redeems herself by responding to her law firm's deceitful conduct with some trickery of her own. She tells Jedediah about the report, tricks Grazier into denying under oath that the report existed, and provides an Argo witness who testifies to having seen the report. Argo's defense collapses and it has to settle Jedediah's claims for millions of dollars. Maggie then joins Jedediah's law firm, happily dancing and reuniting with her father.

An Act of Murder and *Class Action* manifest markedly different conceptions of justice. For Judge Cooke, justice is a process, a method of evaluating individual responsibility. For Maggie, justice requires choosing sides. Automobile manufacturers and the corporate law firms that represent them are evil; individual consumers and the solo and small firm practitioners who represent them are good. Nevertheless, both Judge Cooke and Maggie experience crisis, and both react by committing to justice. . . .

NOTES & QUESTIONS

1.   Can you think of other film or fictional depictions of lawyers who are changed or redeemed by particular events or choices they make? Can you think of examples in real life? Bernadine Dohrn, now a clinical law professor at Northwestern Law School, was in her youth a political radical and member of several leftist organizations which advocated revolutionary ideals (The Weather Underground) and committed some violent crimes. She lived underground for many years in the 1960s and 1970s and was on the FBI's Most Wanted List, until the government dropped charges against her. As a result of her activities, several states (New York and Illinois) refused to grant her a license to practice law (she is a graduate of the University of Chicago Law School); she appealed these decisions. *See* John J. Goldman, "Ex-Radical Fights for Bar Status," *L.A. Times,* 11 Nov. 1985, 1-4. She is the founder of Sidley & Austin's pro bono program (where she worked as a paralegal in the 1980s) and has been appointed to many lawyer taskforces and committees (including those at the ABA) on juvenile justice. She remains an

advocate for many progressive causes. If you were a member of the Bar Admissions Committee, would you refuse to admit to the Bar a very productive lawyer who advocated revolutionary change in her youth? Why or why not? What is the relationship of morally committed civil (or even criminal) disobedience by a lawyer for principled reasons to the practice or "rule of law?" *See* Judith McMorrow, *Civil Disobedience and the Lawyer's Obligation to the Law*, 48 Washington & Lee Law Review 139 (1991).

2. What if a person seeking bar admission killed someone? One individual who committed murder (unrelated to political activities), served his time, was paroled, was then admitted to study law in Arizona (and graduated from a fully accredited law school), and passed the bar examination has never been admitted to the Arizona bar. The bar says that anyone who is on probation for a serious crime cannot be admitted to the bar. What would you do if you were on the committee deciding this admissions issue? Does such a ruling say someone can never be redeemed from a past bad act? Does it make a difference that someone is asking to be a lawyer (who should not violate the law)? Consider that two Presidents have been disbarred (Richard Nixon for his actions in Watergate and William Clinton for his acts of perjury during the Paula Jones litigation). Given the "good acts" of these men, should they have been readmitted to the bar? What does redemption mean in these contexts? Should Teddy Barnes or Sam Bowden be disbarred for the murders they commit? Should they have to prove justified self-defense in a trial or lawyer disciplinary hearing?

3. Stories about lawyers also use the device of coming-of-age stories or *Bildungsroman* (novels of education or formation) to show developments in social and professional character. *To Kill a Mockingbird* tells the story of Atticus Finch and the role of law through the eyes of his daughter Scout (a slightly fictionalized version of the author, Harper Lee), who comes to understand the complexity of community and justice at several junctures in the novel. Professor Simon says that "Most of Grisham's books are coming-of-age novels that chronicle the moral growth of a new lawyer. The hero learns two lessons through participation in a series of adventures. First, you cannot possibly understand legal or professional responsibility norms as the categorical injunctions they purport on their surface to be. To apply them in a manner that would make them worthy of respect requires a flexible, dialectical judgment. Second, to the extent the social order functions, it is not because of a system of promulgated rules more or less routinely enforced by a self-propelling governmental system of checks and balances, but through creative, transgressive moral entrepreneurialism on the part of individuals in crisis." Simon, *Moral Pluck, supra*, at 426. Consider how the young lawyers in Grisham's novels *The Firm* (1991), *The Pelican Brief* (1992), *The Chamber* (1994), and *The Rainmaker* (1995) learn about the legal system from both their elders and their "adventures." What does Kevin Lomax learn from John Milton in *The Devil's Advocate?*

4. Learning about choices in lawyering, law, and legal institutions from acts, adventures, and mentors is also a common theme where there are "learning communities," as one scholar has named them. Carrie Menkel-Meadow, *Can They Do That?, supra*, at 1320. Another element of modern character development is significant to note — the recognition of small worlds of professional communities.

Many of the earlier depictions of modern heroes focus on the strength, courage, redemption, or recovery of the individual lawyer. But there are also interesting depictions of some of the lawyers' commitments to each other and to the professional communities they create. Over thirty years ago, one commentator noted the creation of "professional communities" on a variety of the early lawyer and doctor television programs, in which lawyers help and succor each other while performing difficult, but important, public service. Many of the dramatizations of professionals on television in the Golden Era of the 1950s and 1960s involved character development in the training and mentoring of a younger professional by an older and wiser professional — the senior Lawrence Preston (*The Defenders*) guiding his son Kenneth, Dr. Gillespie and Dr. Kildare, Dr. Zorba and Ben Casey. In more recent times, Leland McKenzie sometimes guided the younger lawyers in *L.A. Law*, and an only slightly older, but clearly more experienced Bobby Donnell was a mentor on *The Practice*. Jedediah Ward, as father figure, encourages his daughter, big-firm defender of corporate interests, to become a lawyer also seeking social justice in *Class Action*. These "learning communities" of lawyers (and other professionals) demonstrate that being a professional does require good character (loyalty, ongoing learning, honesty — at least with one's colleagues, if not the system — and devotion to the larger public and to social good). Note what one television critic has said of the television professionals of the 1960s and consider how much of it is still true:

> [T]hey know that without such work the quality of everyday life would plummet, society would flounder. Their jobs, in short, are the best of all possible jobs: they offer both inner meaning and public worth. Television's city-dwelling professionals thus serve as living proof that work in the modern world can be beautiful. . . . The professionals of these programs are not only public servants; they are also spokesmen of society, and their behavior reveals the way society operates to take care of its own. . . . The professionals themselves are tireless, selfless, and profoundly equitable. . . . In the presumably cold, dead heart of contemporary life and society, television's professional dramas have managed to find nothing less than the pulse of the good community. The living there may have its difficulties, admittedly, but in the end the problems are only superficial ones. For this is a place that offers meaningful work, a public devotion to the common good, and secure, vital values.

Harris Dientsfrey, *Doctors, Lawyers and Other TV Heroes, supra*, at 83-85.

More recent professional series demonstrate an even more equalitarian sense of community. Although Leland McKenzie presided over highly fictionalized daily firm meetings, the lawyers of *L.A. Law* and *The Practice*, like their compatriots on *ER*, mostly soldier on together in relative equality and with unrepresentatively little concern about partnerships and hierarchy. Occasionally there are treatments of partnership and income, but these modern-day professionals mostly help each other through their difficult cases. They seem to be more likely to help and to fall in love with each other (which involves all kinds of conflicts of interest that the shows do not portray with much ethical accuracy) than to engage in the kind of ruthless competition with each other that is the presumed culture and frequent depiction of legal education. *See* Carrie Menkel-Meadow, *Can They Do That?, supra*, at 1320-21.

Do you think that the movies are accurate in their depictions of how much lawyers do or do not help each other through difficult choices or decisions? What do you think happens in real life?

5.   Some of the learning or redemption stories show lawyers changing their types of practices (returns to where they "came from," service to the legally needy, commitments to new kinds of cases or new causes). How common is it for lawyers to change fields or specialties within a career? Do you think that you will change what kind of practice you have at different points in your career?

6.   What does it take to change your mind about what is right or wrong? About what kind of a law practice you think you would want? About what kind of a person you think you would want to be? What are the "dramatic events" in real life that change the choices we make or that cause us to seek some form of "redemption" by doing something different or better?

7.   What have you learned about lawyers in general and what kind of a lawyer you want to be specifically by studying the depictions of lawyers in popular culture? If you were to write a modern script about lawyering, what would it look like?

Chapter 4

CLIENTS

A. FILMOGRAPHY

The Client (1994)

Nuts (1987)

The Social Network (2010)

The Sweet Hereafter (1997)

A Time to Kill (1996)

B. CLIENT-CENTERED LAWYERING: THE MODEL

Popular culture does not always accurately reflect the "real world." One commentator described the dialogue of the Harvard students who became clients in *The Social Network* as crafted for "an as-yet-not-evolved species of humans — ordinary people, here students, who talk perpetually with the wit and brilliance of George Bernard Shaw or Bertrand Russell." Lawrence Lessig, *Sorkin vs. Zuckerberg: 'The Social Network' Is Wonderful Entertainment, But Its Message Is Actually Kind of Evil*, The New Republic, available at http://www.tnr.com (posted 1 Oct. 2010). Yet despite the differences between pop cultural portrayals and social reality, the study of pop cultural clients interacting with their lawyers certainly enhances our understanding of the various ways that lawyers can and should work with clients. Viewers who are reflective and critically minded when watching clients in the movies can learn a lot about the lawyer-client relationship.

Admittedly, few movies show clients working closely with their lawyers. Although lawyers are very visible actors in movies about law, clients are largely invisible. Law school mirrors popular culture; clients are similarly invisible, or at most constructed, rather than real, in much of legal education. Ann Shalleck, *Constructions of the Client within Legal Education*, 45 Stanford Law Journal 1731 (1992-1993). Scholarship about law and popular culture follows suit. Many law review articles have been written about lawyers in the movies, but clients and the relationship between lawyers and clients have received little attention. In contrast, clients are quite visible in newspaper accounts and online discussions of actual cases, although they are often portrayed in stereotypical ways. Consider the media frenzy around the O.J. Simpson case, or more recently, Casey Anthony, the mother who was acquitted of murdering her daughter Caylee.

This chapter seeks to counter the prevailing pop cultural image of clients as passive and largely invisible by highlighting five movies in which clients are key actors in the stories these movies tell about law. The roles these clients play are explored through the lens of the lawyer-client relationship. These relationships develop not only in the courtroom, where most movies about law are situated, but also outside the courtroom, in a wide variety of interactions: in lawyers' offices, in jail cells, in psychiatric hospitals, and at home.

The contexts are different — three of the films involve criminal cases (*The Client* (1994), *Nuts* (1987), and *A Time to Kill* (1996)), while two (*The Social Network* (2010) and *The Sweet Hereafter* (1997)) feature civil litigation. All but one (*The Sweet Hereafter*) involve individual representation, although *The Social Network* briefly shows lawyers for the Facebook partnership. *The Sweet Hereafter* is set in Canada; the other films are set in the United States in locales ranging from Mississippi to Los Angeles to New York City. With the exception of Mark Zuckerberg (played by Jesse Eisenberg), the Internet entrepreneur and creator of Facebook, and the other litigants in *The Social Network*, the clients are not wealthy, or powerful in any conventional sense. In *The Client*, Mark Sway (played by Brad Renfro) is an eleven-year-old boy from a single-parent family who pays his lawyer one dollar to represent him. In *Nuts*, Claudia Draper (played by Barbara Streisand) is a prostitute represented by a public defender appointed by the judge. In *The Sweet Hereafter*, the parents of the children killed in the school bus accident are small-town working-class people whose lawyer represents them on a contingency fee basis. In *A Time to Kill*, Carl Lee Hailey (played by Samuel L. Jackson), an African-American man who works a blue-collar job, barely scrapes together enough money to hire a lawyer.

The fact that all of these films are set in litigation settings, which is typical of law-related films, shows how popular culture views lawyers and clients, and in turn influences the perceptions of the consumers of popular culture (all of us). Clients engaged with lawyers in transactional, lobbying, or other interactions are rarely portrayed in film, although *The Social Network* contains a marvelous scene showing lawyers discussing a contract with Eduardo Saverin (played by Andrew Garfield), Mark Zuckerberg's original partner in the Facebook enterprise.

This chapter examines these lawyer-client relationships in the context of a theory of lawyering known as client-centeredness. Client-centeredness is an approach to lawyering that puts clients — not lawyers — at the center of legal representation; it stands in sharp contrast to the more traditional lawyer-focused approach.

The following two excerpts explain the difference between these approaches to lawyering. The first excerpt sets out the traditional lawyering approach in the context of legal counseling, which is one of the most important activities that a lawyer undertakes on behalf of a client. Counseling is defined as "the process by which you help clients decide what courses of action to adopt in order to resolve problems." David A. Binder, Paul Bergman, Susan C. Price & Paul R. Tremblay, *Lawyers As Counselors: A Client-Centered Approach* 271 (2d ed. 2004). The second excerpt describes the client-centered model of lawyering. As you read the excerpts, compare the two approaches. Does the portrayal of clients in the featured films influence your understanding of the client-lawyer relationship?

CLIENT-CENTERED COUNSELING: REAPPRAISAL AND REFINEMENT
Robert D. Dinerstein
32 Arizona Law Review 501 (1990)

Traditional legal counseling reflects an absence of meaningful interchange between lawyer and client. The client comes to the lawyer with some idea about his problem. The lawyer asks questions designed to adduce the information necessary to place the client's problem within the appropriate conceptual box. At the proper time, he counsels the client by essentially conducting a monologue: the lawyer tells the client something of the nature of his actions on the client's behalf and then advises the client about the course of action he recommends. The lawyer may go into great detail about the rationale for his advice. Alternatively, she may provide a relatively terse recitation of technical advice and let the client decide how to proceed. The lawyer is concerned with the client's reaction to his advice but tends not to value client input, for he believes that the client has little of value to contribute to the resolution of his legal problem. Lawyer and client are likely to talk at, rather than with, each other. Any assurance that the lawyer provides to the client — and it could be substantial — is likely to be based on the client's perception that the lawyer is "taking care of matters" rather than on a belief that the lawyer truly tried to understand the client as a whole, complex person.

In general, the traditional legal counseling model assumes that clients should be passive and delegate decision-making responsibility to their lawyers; that ineffective professional service is relatively rare; that professionals give disinterested service and maintain high professional standards; that effective professional services are available to all who can pay; and that professional problems tend to call for technical solutions beyond the ken of laypersons. . . .

FORTRESS IN THE SAND: THE PLURAL VALUES OF CLIENT-CENTERED REPRESENTATION
Katherine R. Kruse
12 Clinical Law Review 369 (2006)

As a theory of lawyering, client-centered representation has enjoyed unparalleled success. . . . Indeed, the client-centered approach has so thoroughly permeated skills training and clinical legal education, it is not an exaggeration to say that client-centered representation is one of the most influential doctrines in legal education today.

Despite its popularity and influence — or perhaps because of it — there is a growing lack of consensus about what it means to be a client-centered lawyer. As the client-centered approach has grown from its earliest articulation . . . to its current status as well-established bedrock of clinical legal education, it has evolved naturally into what might be called a plurality of approaches, which expand aspects of the original client-centered approach in different directions. Client-centered representation has been perhaps most commonly associated with an approach to legal counseling that seeks to minimize lawyer influence on client decision-making, relying on strategies of lawyer neutrality. However, some proponents of client-centered representation seek to increase client participation in the legal representation, and thus value lawyer-client collaboration over lawyer neutrality. Some client-centered theorists have made connections between client-centered representation, client voice, and narrative theory, placing central value on the importance of preserving or translating a client's story into legal terms. Other proponents of a client-centered approach view it as primarily concerned with effective problem-solving, and favor holistic lawyering approaches that reach beyond the boundaries of the client's legal case to address a broader range of connected issues in the client's life. Still others focus on the notion of client empowerment, and favor approaches that facilitate a client's ability to make decisions by creating a more equal relationship between the client and the lawyer. Finally, some claim a traditional zealous advocacy model as the essence of client-centered representation, equating it with the unmitigated advancement of a client's legal interests. . . . Taken together [these approaches] define a richly elaborated philosophy of lawyering that strives at once to be client-directed, holistic, respectful of client narrative, client-empowering, and partisan. . . .

[These] five client-centered lawyering approaches [are] built around the core values of client-centered representation. Each approach — holistic representation, narrative integrity, client empowerment, partisan advocacy, and client-directed lawyering — begins with a representational value and supposes an approach to lawyering that would pursue that value exclusively. Each approach is "client-centered" in that it puts the client at the center of the representation instead of something else: the client's legal issues, the lawyer's construction of the client, the client's stated wishes, the interests of third parties, and the client's best interests. Each model is also "client-centered" in that it is supported by a reasonable conception of what it means to respect client autonomy. They are intended not as full-blown alternative models of lawyering, but as component parts of a well-rounded client-centered practice. Indeed, adopting or pursuing any one of these approaches to the exclusion of the others would create a caricature of client-centered lawyering.

When faced with a difficult case in the context of actual practice, this value pluralist approach to client-centered representation would change the kinds of questions that lawyers ask themselves. The question "What would a client-centered lawyer do?" is replaced by a series of questions: What would a holistic lawyer do?; What does narrative integrity require?; What would a client-empowering lawyer do?; What would a partisan advocate do?; and What does client-directed lawyering require? . . .

The plural approaches of client-centered representation that I propose are laid out in the following table . . . .

Plural Approaches To Client-Centered Representation

Client is at the center of the representation

LAWYERING APPROACH	*instead of:*	*to prevent:*	Autonomy Concern
HOLISTIC	Client's Legal Issues	Lawyer misdiagnosis or narrow legal framing of client's problem	Removal of external constraints to self-actualization caused by lack of options in the world
NARRATIVE INTEGRITY	Lawyer's Construction of the Client	Lawyer distortion of client narrative in legal story telling	Preservation of client's project of self-authorship
CLIENT-EMPOWERMENT	Client's Stated Wishes	Client misdiagnosis of what the client "really wants"	Removal of internal constraints to client self-actualization caused by client's attitudes, beliefs or unrealistic expectations
PARTISAN	Third Parties	Loss of client's legal rights and interests	Preservation of freedom for the client's "future self"
CLIENT-DIRECTED	Client's Best Interests	Lawyer paternalism	Negative liberty—client's right to be "left alone"

1. Holistic approach

The Holistic Approach to client-centered lawyering places the client as [the] "whole person" at the center of the representation, in place of the client's legal issues. . . . The primary concern of the Holistic Approach is to avoid the sometimes distorting effects caused by lawyers who, viewing the client's legal issues as the center of the client's problem, fail to take into account the importance of the non-legal considerations with which the client's legal issues are intertwined. Such lawyers, as the client-centered approach points out, are in danger of misdiagnosing the client's problems by imposing the structure of legal doctrine on the problem without understanding the full scope of the client's situation.

Taking a Holistic Approach, a lawyer will combat the tendencies to view a client's problems too narrowly by attending to the interconnected set of legal and non-legal concerns that the client's situation presents, rather than just the client's legal issues. Hence, a lawyer operating under a Holistic Approach will seek to work outside and around the law to achieve the client's goals by non-legal means. Holistic lawyering may sometimes occur through a lawyer representing a client on multiple and interconnected legal problems. For example, representing a client in a child custody dispute may require a lawyer to address other legal issues, such as getting the client immigration status or resolving a landlord-tenant dispute so that the client has an adequate home for the children. Holistic lawyering may also occur outside the parameters of purely legal strategies — such as helping a client find a job or qualify for assistance — and may sometimes be achieved best through coordinated efforts with other professionals like social workers. . . .

2. Narrative integrity approach

The Narrative Integrity Approach to client-centered lawyering places the client at the center of the representation instead of the lawyer's construction of the client. It focuses on preserving the integrity of the client's own narrative or voice, and seeks to structure the representation as much as possible around the way the client views the world. The primary concern of the Narrative Integrity Approach is to prevent the lawyer from distorting the legal representation by recreating the client's narrative within legal doctrinal categories that fail to capture the client's perspective. . . .

[R]espect for a client's Narrative Integrity may impel a lawyer past neutrality into a more interactive and collaborative process of legal representation. Legal storytelling is formed by an interaction between the client's story, stories that are embedded in legal doctrine, and "stock stories" that express basic conditions of justice. To maintain the client's voice in the legal representation may require the client to participate more actively in decisions and processes that are traditionally thought of as distinctively legal and strategic in nature, such as the formulation of case theory. . . .

3. Client-empowerment approach

The Client-Empowerment Approach of client-centered lawyering is based on the idea that the legal representation needs to move the client in the direction of self-sufficiency and self-actualization. Its primary concern is that a client's stated wishes may not accurately reflect the client's true desires, and that lawyers who too quickly accept the client's stated wishes as "marching orders" will end up working in ways that are at odds with the client's real needs and interests. Hence it puts the client's real, true, or more fully realized interests and values at the center of legal representation, in place of what the client may initially say (or think) that he or she wants.

The idea of client empowerment has been particularly attractive to lawyers working with communities of poor clients or with battered women, where the experience of political or social subordination is seen as having created passive or accommodating patterns of thinking and behaving, which may need to be confronted or changed before a client has the capacity to make truly autonomous choices. The strategies for assisting clients in such situations go beyond the lawyer merely spelling out the alternatives and consequences of different courses of action, and include facilitating the client's connection and solidarity with others, and helping the client sort through the multiple and conflicting narratives that may describe her situation. . . .

The pull of the Client-Empowerment Approach is thus the strongest when the client's autonomy is constrained by internal obstacles arising out of his own attitudes, perspectives or beliefs. But the concern for paternalism is also the strongest in these kinds of situations, placing limits on the strategies that it is appropriate to employ.

4. Partisan approach

The Partisan Approach puts the client in the center of the representation in place of the interests and needs of third parties. It privileges the client's legal rights and interests, and emphasizes the protection of those rights over the rights of others. The primary concern in the Partisan Approach is that the client may give up a legal entitlement: waive a right, forego an available remedy, miss a deadline, or enter into an agreement that will limit actions the client may want to take in the future. . . .

[I]t comes as no surprise that many of the proponents of strong intervention to protect a client's future freedom would come from the realm of criminal defense, where the freedom at stake — freedom from incarceration — is particularly acute. However, intervention to protect future freedom may also be particularly appropriate to situations like divorce, where the client is undergoing a transition between phases of life, and may be either undervaluing or overvaluing interests that will take on different importance as the transition becomes complete. It is in these kinds of situations where extreme deprivation of future freedom is at stake, or where a client is making irrevocable choices at a time of life transition, that protection of future freedom has a strong pull against a client's current desire to give up a legal right or interest.

5. Client-directed approach

The Client-Directed Approach picks up on the concern about lawyer domination inherent in more traditional visions of lawyering. Rather than concerning itself strictly with the distortions that arise from interpreting the client's problem through legal doctrinal categories, the Client-Directed Approach is concerned more broadly about the ways in which a lawyer may influence a client's decision based on what the lawyer believes is best for the client. The problem that the Client-Directed Approach addresses is less that the lawyer will be narrow-mindedly legal in his approach; and more that the lawyer will develop his own view of what would be prudent or wise for the client to do — either legally or in non-legal matters — and impermissibly interject that view into the client's decision-making. . . .

The Client-Directed Approach is evident in the client-centered approach's skepticism about lawyer expertise on the non-legal matters that are most vitally important to the client. . . .

NOTES & QUESTIONS

1.   Professor Kruse outlines the five cornerstones of client-centered representation: holistic representation, narrative integrity, client empowerment, partisan advocacy, and client-directed lawyering. Which of these cornerstones is most appealing to you? Why? Which of these cornerstones is least appealing to you?

Why? In what situations would you employ one approach over the other? Another theory of client-centered representation is less categorical, and offers the idea of engaged client-centeredness across a variety of interactions. *See* Stephen Ellmann, Robert D. Dinerstein, Isabel R. Gunning, Katherine R. Kruse & Ann C. Shalleck, *Lawyers and Clients: Critical Issues in Interviewing and Counseling* (2010).

2. Compare these client-centered approaches to the traditional lawyer-centered approach. Does the traditional approach have any advantages over the client-centered approach? What are the biggest disadvantages of the lawyer-centered approach? Think of your own experience as a law student in a clinic, externship, or other professional legal setting. Which of these approaches have you observed lawyers using in these environments? Should a client's role in the case matter? For example, Mark Sway in *The Client* is a witness, not a party in the case. For an excellent discussion about representing a victim in a criminal case, see Abbe Smith, *On Representing a Victim of Crime, in Law Stories* 155 (Gary Bellow and Martha Minow eds. 1996), in which she describes representing Claudia Brenner, the surviving victim of a hate-crime murder motivated by homophobia. Ms. Brenner's account is equally riveting. *See* Claudia Brenner, *Eight Bullets: One Woman's Story of Surviving Anti-Gay Violence* (1995).

3. The rules of professional responsibility provide some guidance on the allocation of decision-making authority between lawyers and clients. Some decisions, such as the decision about whether to settle a case, or in a criminal case, whether to plead guilty, waive a jury trial, or testify, are clearly reserved for clients. *See* Rule 1.2 of the ABA Model Rules of Professional Conduct. However, the ethical rules do not provide clear directions regarding the role of clients in making other decisions. Instead, Rule 1.2 simply states: "a lawyer shall abide by a client's decisions concerning the objectives of representation [and] shall consult with the client as to the means by which they are to be pursued." How would you interpret this rule in light of the traditional lawyer-centered approach? Which client-centered approach is most consistent with the letter and spirit of the rule? How should a lawyer proceed if she is convinced that the client is making a really bad decision?

4. Since client-centered lawyering is context-specific, is it appropriate for all types of clients? How applicable is the client-centered approach for lawyers representing wealthy and powerful clients? Professor Carle argues that "lawyers for more powerful clients should resolve close ethical questions with an eye toward protecting the interests of the less powerful adversary." Susan D. Carle, *Power as a Factor in Lawyers' Ethical Deliberation*, 35 Hofstra Law Review 115, 153 (2006). How should we go about determining which clients deserve a client-centered lawyer and which do not? What version of client-centeredness is appropriate for the clients in the featured films? Should clients' personal backgrounds make a difference in how the model is applied?

5. The line between a client-centered approach and a traditional approach to lawyering is not always so clear. In *The Sweet Hereafter*, Mrs. Otto, an angry parent of a child killed in the bus accident, confronts Mitchell Stephens (played by Ian Holm), the lawyer who is soliciting her business: "So you're just the thing we need? Isn't that what you want us to believe? That we're completely defenseless? That you know what's best?" When Stephens responds: "Listen to me, Mrs. Otto. Listen very

carefully. I do know what's best," is he behaving as a traditional lawyer, or as a partisan advocate? Could he be viewed not only as paternalistic but also as fighting hard to protect her future interests in the way that a partisan advocate would by making sure that she does not waive an important legal right?

6.   As Professor Kruse explains, the line between the various client-centered approaches is also fluid:

> [These] core values of client-centered representation can sometimes come into conflict in situations of actual practice, posing dilemmas for client-centered lawyers about whether — or how forcefully — to intervene into client decision-making. For example, in representing a battered woman who is poised on the brink of leaving an abusive relationship, the goals of client empowerment may push a lawyer into deeper connection with the client or broader involvement in her life than neutral methods of client-directed lawyering would sanction. When representing an immigrant seeking legal status in the United States, the partisan protection of a client's legal interests may conflict with the goal of gaining full information that would help the lawyer engage in holistic problem-solving, because knowing too much may impair the lawyer's ability to act ethically as an advocate. The desire to give voice to a client's narrative may confound a lawyer's partisan advocacy if the client's story undermines rather than supports a client's goals.

Kruse, *supra*, at 372. Do you see similar conflicts in the featured films?

7.   Not only do the various approaches to client-centeredness sometimes overlap, but so do the roles of lawyer and client. The film *Presumed Innocent* (1990) offers a fascinating look at a situation in which prosecutor Rusty Sabich (played by Harrison Ford) becomes a client who faces prosecution as a criminal defendant in a murder case. Although his criminal defense attorney requires him to play a passive role in his case in the courtroom, Sabich rejects that role in other venues and conducts an independent investigation into the circumstances of the crime that he is charged with committing. How was Sabich better positioned to take charge of certain aspects of his case by virtue of the knowledge of the system which he gained as a prosecutor?

8.   A familiar criticism of class action lawyers is that they often substitute their own agendas for the agenda of their clients. For example, lawyers involved in school desegregation litigation have been criticized for taking strong pro-busing positions when their African-American clients wanted more resources to be given to schools in their neighborhoods. *See* Derrick Bell, *Serving Two Masters: Integration Ideals and Client Interests in School Desegregation Litigation*, 85 Yale Law Journal 470, 471-72 (1976). Think about the challenge that a client-centered class action lawyer would face in determining which goals should take precedence in a situation like the one in *The Sweet Hereafter* in which the clients themselves have conflicting goals:

> The film reminds us of the different ways that loss and suffering become part of the life stories of different people, with some people accepting their fate and others insisting that causes be identified, blame be assigned, and compensation be provided.

Austin Sarat, *Exploring the Hidden Domains of Civil Justice: "Naming, Blaming, and Claiming" in Popular Culture*, 50 DePaul Law Review 425, 430 (2000). Describe how each of the plaintiffs (or potential plaintiffs) viewed the lawsuit and its role in their lives. Would you characterize their goals as primarily legal or non-legal? How did the goals of these clients change as the result of interactions with their lawyer?

9. An astute client whose goals and values differ from her lawyer can undermine the lawyer's agenda in sometimes unexpected ways, as the film *The Sweet Hereafter* demonstrates. Nicole Burnell (played by Sarah Polley), a teenager who survived the bus accident, testifies in a way that undermines the lawsuit:

> Because her testimony, which the viewer knows to be a lie, places blame on the person with the shallowest pocket, it effectively ends the suit. It serves not only both (for us if not for Nicole) as a satisfying act of revenge against Sam [her father], depriving him of the money he so desperately wants, but also as a way of exposing the vulnerability of law. . . . [A]ll of Stephens's legal acumen, all of his work, is defeated and derailed by a teenaged girl. . . .

Austin Sarat, *Imagining the Law of the Father: Loss, Dread, and Mourning in The Sweet Hereafter*, 34 Law & Society Review 3, 34 (2000).

What motivated Nicole to change her story? Was it only revenge, or was it something else? Do you think that her role as a member of the community of townspeople had any impact on her decision, or was she purely motivated by individual concerns? Should Stephens have anticipated the possibility that Nicole would change her story, or was it completely unexpected? If he had anticipated this possibility, what difference might it have made? How could the lawyer have employed a client-centered approach before the deposition in order to learn the "alternative" story?

Professor Lucie White describes a similar incident with a client she represented at a welfare hearing, who "came to the hearing well-rehearsed in the lawyer's strategy. But in the hearing, she did not play. When she was cued to perform, without any signal to her lawyer she abandoned their script." Lucie E. White, *Subordination, Rhetorical Survival Skills, and Sunday Shoes: Notes on the Hearing of Mrs. G.*, 38 Buffalo Law Review 1, 46 (1990). Was Nicole well-rehearsed in her lawyer's strategy? Should she have been? How can lawyers in these kinds of situations determine what really happened?

C. PUTTING CLIENTS AT THE CENTER OF THE REPRESENTATION: THE CLIENT-CENTERED APPROACHES IN CONTEXT

Pop cultural portrayals of clients allow us to view all five client-centered approaches in context. These portrayals allow us to reflect on the myriad ways that clients interact with their lawyers, which affect our expectations and our behaviors, both as lawyers interacting with clients and clients interacting with lawyers. Because the selected films show clients who are not mere bystanders in their cases, they are in fact atypical examples of client portrayals in popular culture, where most clients are mere props to the shows in which their lawyers star. Thus, these films are offered not as representative portrayals of law and popular culture, but rather as a lens through which to examine the relationship between lawyers and clients.

A central tenet of client-centeredness holds that clients do not share the same concerns or approach problems in identical ways. Client values are paramount in all of the client-centered approaches — client-directed, narrative integrity, holistic, client empowerment, and (to a lesser extent) partisan. Consider the $65 million settlement in *The Social Network* in a case in which the plaintiffs' allegations seem to have had little legal merit. Mark Zuckerberg could have settled the case for any number of reasons — a payoff to avoid future expensive litigation, remorse for some of his actions, or a sense of responsibility for his former friend Eduardo Saverin. The film does not explore which reason (or reasons) motivated Zuckerberg — his lawyers take a lawyer-centered approach and do not even tell him that they are negotiating a settlement offer on his behalf. Nonetheless, the film allows us to reflect on the complexity of the relationships and values that underlie clients' actions and decisions.

The story of who owns Facebook and has a right to share in its profits is told through the frame of depositions taken in two lawsuits, with flashbacks to the parties' relationships before the lawsuits and the setting that allowed Facebook to flourish. Thus, *The Social Network* can also be seen as a place where law, film, and the Internet — itself a form of popular culture — intersect. According to one commentator, the film succeeds as a compelling drama, but fails as a story about the Internet, "the most important social and economic platform for innovation in our history." Lessig, *supra*, at 2. The director Aaron Sorkin "simply hasn't a clue to the real secret sauce in the story he is trying to tell." *Id.* at 1.

1. The Client-Directed Approach

Among the client-centered approaches, the client-directed approach, which warns against lawyer domination of client choices, provides the starkest alternative to the traditional approach. In the following excerpt, Professor Nancy Polikoff describes the classic justification for client-directed lawyering and then describes her effort to implement this model with a client arrested following a civil disobedience action. Consider whether there are limits on the ability of clients to be the decision-makers in their cases. Should age matter, as in the case of a very young client (*The Client*)? Does it make a difference if a client is experiencing extreme emotional distress, as in *Nuts*?

AM I MY CLIENT?: THE ROLE
CONFUSION OF A LAWYER ACTIVIST
Nancy D. Polikoff
31 Harvard Civil Rights-Civil Liberties Law Review 443 (1996)

[Client-directed lawyering] rests upon the conviction that clients bear the consequences of their decisions and are in the best position to understand the full non-legal as well as legal significance of their choices. Accordingly, lawyers counsel clients best by helping them to explore all of the possible consequences of their actions so that the clients can make decisions that best suit their needs. . . .

After the initial paperwork was completed, we learned the name of the protestor whose case would be called first. It was "Jenifer," a friend of mine. As we stood together in the cell block, she and her fellow demonstrators (including my lover and other close friends) behind the bars and me outside of them, she tried every way imaginable to have me make a decision for her. First, she asked directly what I thought she should do. Then she asked what I would do if I were she. Resolutely, I maintained my role as client-centered counselor. I explained consequences and helped her articulate her goals. I engaged in active listening and reflected back what I heard.

My responses were somewhat frustrating to Jenifer. We had common personal and political bonds, but our relationship in this situation was really no different from that of any client trying to get her lawyer to make a decision and any lawyer resisting with the knowledge that it is the client, not the lawyer, who must live with the consequences of that decision. . . .

NOTES & QUESTIONS

1. Professor Dinerstein suggests that one goal of client-centered lawyering is "to provide opportunities for clients to make decisions themselves." Dinerstein, *supra*, at 507. Should the lawyer in the preceding excerpt from Professor Polikoff have resisted her client's effort to get the lawyer to make the decision? Or is it client-centered for a lawyer to make a decision for a client when that client has decided she wants the lawyer to be the decision-maker? Is part of client-centered lawyering giving a client what she wants, not forcing a process on the client that she does not want? Professor Simon notes the dilemma that lawyers face when they "must either acquiesce in the client's choice to put her fate in the lawyer's hands or force her to be free by denying her the advice that she considers most valuable." William H. Simon, *Lawyer Advice and Client Autonomy: Mrs. Jones's Case*, 50 Maryland Law Review 213, 217 (1991). Does a decision to accede to the client's wishes enhance or undermine her autonomy?

2. Consider this example from a medical setting:

   I recall our pediatrician advising my wife and me as to whether we should have our then two-month-old son vaccinated against whooping cough, several cases of which had occurred in our area. There was a specified small probability of an adverse reaction to the vaccine, and given an adverse reaction, a specified small probability of death, and specified small probabilities of less extreme bad outcomes. Without the shot, there was a specified small probability of contracting the disease, a specified small probability given contraction of death, and specified small probabilities of various bad results short of death. I found this explanation, which went on for several minutes, overwhelmingly oppressive, and I felt a sense of deliverance when she concluded by saying, "In the case of my own child, I decided to give him the shot." I felt, and still do, that that sentence was all that I needed or wanted to know.

Simon, *supra*, at 216-17.

In what respects is medical advice different than legal advice? Compare the role of statistics and probabilities in the context of patients making medical decisions to their role for clients making legal decisions. Do clients in legal situations have a stake in the meaning of the story that is different than the kind of stake medical patients have in their care? Should doctors and lawyers respond in different ways to these kinds of questions? Why?

3.   If the client-directed approach is premised on lawyer neutrality, how realistic is it? Consider the following:

Even where they think of themselves as merely providing information for clients to integrate into their own decisions, lawyers influence clients by myriad judgments, conscious or not, about what information to present, how to order it, what to emphasize, and what style and phrasing to adopt.

Simon, *supra*, at 217.

4.   Should every client be given the same decisionmaking ability? The ethical rules provide:

When a client's capacity to make adequately considered decisions in connection with a representation is diminished, whether because of minority, mental impairment or for some other reason, the lawyer shall, as far as reasonably possible, maintain a normal client-lawyer relationship with the client.

ABA Model Rule of Professional Conduct 1.14.

Given the limited guidance this rule provides, how should lawyers go about negotiating these relationships with clients? Should the role afforded the client depend on the extent of the client's capacity, the nature of the decision, the consequences to the client, or something else?

5.   Claudia Draper in *Nuts* goes to great lengths to seize control of her case from her lawyer, beginning with her effort to speak on her own behalf in court when represented by her first attorney, who ignores and patronizes her, to her later efforts, both inside and outside the courtroom, when represented by Aaron Levinsky (played by Richard Dreyfuss), a public defender. While her first attorney is clearly not client-directed, how client-directed is her public defender? How might his actions have been more client-directed?

6.   Despite his age, Mark Sway in *The Client* clearly views himself as the decision-maker in his case, ignoring the advice of Reggie Love (played by Susan

Sarandon) that he should talk to the FBI, and admonishing her: "You're my lawyer and you have to do what I tell you." Two commentators see Mark as playing a major role in the representation, arguing that while Reggie Love "outsmarts all manner of wicked adversaries," she succeeds only because her client guides her. Michael Asimow & Shannon Mader, *Law and Popular Culture* 186 (2004). Do you agree? Why? How realistic is Mark's character?

7. The classic legal film *To Kill a Mockingbird* (1962) presents the lawyer as a heroic actor while relegating the client to a passive role. Can this juxtaposition be explained solely by the fact that the client was African American, as two commentators argue? Asimow & Mader, *supra*, at 37-38. Or are there other factors at play? Why do you think Carl Lee Hailey, the African-American client in *A Time to Kill*, was an active client?

8. Given that Mark Zuckerberg in *The Social Network* is in the conventional sense a more powerful person than the clients in the other films featured in this chapter, is his lack of involvement in his case surprising? Why or why not? At times he seems almost detached from the legal process, despite sparring with opposing counsel in the deposition. Why do you think his interaction with his lawyers is limited to a few conversations with the second-year associate who is observing the deposition? Some commentators have argued that expert clients, including business clients, are more likely to tell their lawyers their goals and let the lawyers figure out how to achieve the goals. Stefan H. Krieger & Richard K. Neumann, Jr., *Essential Lawyering Skills: Interviewing, Counseling, Negotiation, and Persuasive Fact Analysis* 278-79 (4th ed. 2011). Why might this be the case? Here, can we even know what Zuckerberg's goals are? At the end of the film, when the associate tells Zuckerberg to pay the $65 million settlement because "in the scheme of things it's a speeding ticket," Zuckerberg seems to agree. Does his attitude that the case is just about money seem realistic, given how strongly he feels about the idea that he was the creator of Facebook?

2. The Narrative Integrity Approach

As Professor Kruse notes, the question of narrative integrity arises most acutely in the context of case theory and storytelling. Indeed, the constructing of case theory is an aspect of lawyering in which lawyers often take very different approaches to questions of client-centeredness. Binny Miller, *Give Them Back Their Lives: Recognizing Client Narrative in Case Theory*, 93 Michigan Law Review 485 (1994). Case theory is the short version of the story that the lawyer tells on behalf of her client. It is not the whole story, but rather the storyline that captures the facts, the law, and all of the surrounding circumstances of the client and her case. The question of who controls case theory, the story that emerges, and how that story is told is a question of ethics and professionalism.

Three of the featured films for this chapter (*Nuts*, *The Social Network*, and *A Time to Kill*) explicitly raise questions about the content of case theory and the role of clients in constructing a case theory. These pop cultural portrayals present vivid and compelling case theories and often show clients actively involved in trial strategy and tactics. While these films may or may not reflect the "real" world of lawyer-client relations, they provide a model of engaged clients that lawyers seeking a more participatory relationship with their clients can emulate.

The next two excerpts relate to case theory. The first excerpt explains the idea of case theory and argues that movies are an especially good vehicle for conveying story-based case theories. The second, in describing an actual case handled by a student in a law school clinic, provides a good example of case theory in action and the role that clients might play in developing a case theory.

TEACHING CASE THEORY
Binny Miller
9 Clinical Law Review 293 (2002)

As the key means of framing a case, case theory is *the* central problem that lawyers confront in putting a case together. Case theory drives much of the work in representing clients, from interviewing the client, to fact-gathering and investigation, and finally to negotiation, trial, or some other resolution of the case. Many of the decisions made during the life of a case are decisions that rest on case theory, including the question of which witnesses to call at trial, the content of their testimony, and indeed, the shape of the trial itself. . . .

I teach a concept of case theory that I have developed over years of litigating, clinical teaching, and writing about case theory, in which case theory can best be described as "storyline." A "storyline" is the short version of the lawyer's story of the case that takes into account the context in which it will be told. The case theory is a snapshot, a framework, the essence of the story or what the case is about. It is not the whole story that a video camera filming the event would tell, but rather the coherent meaning that the elements create. Yet it is in stories that storylines are found. . . .

The view of case theory as storyline places law in a narrative rather than an analytic modality. Facts do not serve law in an element-by-element categorical analysis, but rather work side-by-side with law in the story. Case theory provides an explanation for what happened, and in doing so, shapes what happened. Law plays an important role in some explanations, a lesser role in other explanations, and at times, no role at all.

For example, in a case theory that incorporates the idea of self-defense, who did what first, and with what force, matters because the law says that it does. But in some self-defense cases, the credibility of the complaining witnesses might be the key, and the legal definition of self-defense hardly matters. Context, however, always matters, even in cases that might seem to be about legal categories. . . .

[I]t is the tendency of movies about lawyering to simplify antagonists' competing versions of a story that makes case theory stand out so clearly. Detailed, legalistic accounts of real-life drama are not what sells movies. Colorful accounts of interesting characters do. It is the relative factual richness of movie portrayals of cases, and the rather limited role of law, that makes case theory so vivid. In a medium that "dumbs down" law, story elements become much more powerful.

LEGAL FICTIONS: CLINICAL EXPERIENCES, LACE COLLARS, AND BOUNDLESS STORIES

Nancy Cook

1 Clinical Law Review 41 (1994)

Last summer, the summer of 1992, a woman was arrested in Albuquerque for disorderly conduct. The statute she was alleged to have violated prohibits ". . . engaging in violent, abusive, indecent, profane, boisterous, unreasonably loud, or otherwise disorderly conduct which tends to disturb the peace." Through connections with the local Public Defender's office, our law school clinic, which provides supervised student representation to a limited number of individuals, acquired the case. I read through the police report, which was virtually all there was to the file we received from the Public Defender, and assigned the case to one of my eight students, Rachel Kolman.

In the beginning, this is all we knew about the case: The police responded to a call "in reference to a male and female fighting" in a motel room on Central Avenue. Central Avenue is the old Route 66, and this particular section is known for having more than its fair share of drug-related activities and prostitution. On arrival, the two responding Anglo male police officers encountered several people in the parking lot, one of whom advised them that "a crazy woman" had come to his room and wouldn't leave.

As the men were conversing, this woman came around the corner. When she saw the police and the man they were interviewing — the man from the motel room — she began screaming at them. The officers attempted to calm her, but she "just got louder and more uncooperative." First the officers merely asked the woman to leave, but when she continued to yell, they advised her that she was under arrest for disorderly conduct. She then went to her car and locked herself in. At this point, under the threat of being forcibly removed from her vehicle, the woman got out and was handcuffed and transported to the detention center.

This information was contained in the police report that served as the basis for the criminal information filed against the woman. Buried in the middle of the report was this sentence: "We couldn't find anyone or find any reason to support her claim of rape."

Subsequent conversations with the police revealed that the man who spoke to them about the "crazy woman" was calm and articulate. The woman had asked him for money which he would not give her. Asked if they had seen any animals around, a fact that was significant to the defendant's version of events, the officers said that they had not. The defendant appeared to be intoxicated, but the officers' main concern was that she had been creating such a disturbance that many of the motel residents were coming outside and shouting back at her.

Rachel arranged to meet with the defendant, Debra, who was out on bond. Briefly, what Rachel learned in the interview was that Debra, a twenty-six-year-old, single, black woman, had recently arrived in New Mexico from the east coast. She and her boyfriend, with whom she was living, had moved to Albuquerque because they had heard that it was a tolerant place. At the time of the interview, Debra was unemployed, having lost her job because of her several days' absence while she sat in the Bernalillo County Detention Center trying to make bail on this charge.

On the day of her arrest, Debra had gone to a bar with a female friend and there flirted with a man whom she thought was very good looking. She had three or four drinks, after which she left, voluntarily accompanying the man to his nearby motel room.

When she left the bar, Debra wasn't sure whether she was "interested" in the man. It was after they were in his room for a while and he started getting "aggressive" that she decided to cut the evening short. She tried to leave, but was stopped by a pit bull that was positioned in front of the door. The man tore off her clothes and raped her. She was yelling, which brought the motel manager to the room. Her assailant opened the door to speak to the manager, and when he did, Debra screamed out that she was being raped. The manager left, but after that, the man backed off. She was able to grab her clothes and run from the room.

Debra called the police from a pay phone around the corner, unaware of the fact that the motel manager had already done so. When she returned to the motel, she was surprised to see that a patrol car was already there. She immediately went up to the officers, who were standing with the man who had raped her, to tell them what happened. They wouldn't listen to her, which made her very angry. In the end, they arrested her and let the rapist go. She spent the weekend in jail, during which time she received no medical attention.

This was the point in the semester when we were dealing in the classroom with case planning and investigation. I thought this case provided an excellent opportunity for working through case theory and investigative plans. In class, Rachel presented the "facts" as we knew them, and I then divided students into two groups, four representing the prosecution and four representing the defense. As anticipated, the two teams came up with widely different perspectives on the case, both of which were potentially credible to a fact finder, factually supportable, and predictable. The prosecution theory was, she's a prostitute on the run, possibly a drug addict, she didn't get paid for her services, so she cried rape to get back at the john who stiffed her; she had been "violent, abusive . . . , unreasonably loud" and "otherwise disorderly" in the motel parking lot, drawing a crowd and disturbing the other residents at the motel. The defense theory was, two racist, sexist, white cops saw a poor black woman and immediately thought junkie whore and couldn't be bothered to listen to her; under the circumstances (she had just been raped), any disturbance she caused was more than justifiable. . . .

When Rachel spoke to Debra, client, defendant, victim, with our "theory" of the case in mind, Debra, unique, whole, independent individual, balked. She didn't see racism. She didn't see sexism. She didn't see a great social structure built to disadvantage the poor, women, people of color, or poor women of color. What did she see? Her own innocence. A rapist's guilt. Simple injustice. She expected simple justice to prevail in the courtroom. She expected vindication. If we tell the truth, she maintained, motives, class, and race differences won't matter. All that feminist cow dung doesn't mean anything when the truth is so simple.

Was that all she saw? We don't know. After their first several conversations, in which Debra expressed to Rachel her heartfelt thanks that Rachel had been assigned to the case because finally, *finally* someone was listening to her, Debra changed her mind about having student representation. She had described Rachel as "a godsend," but as the investigation proceeded, she grew distant, she avoided Rachel, and spoke of her boyfriend wanting her to hire private counsel. Privately, Rachel sought to understand why. Had she alienated her with her whiteJewish-middleclassfeminist "theories"? Was Debra's boyfriend exerting pressure because *he* didn't trust a woman, a white woman, a student? Had Rachel been naïve? Was the boyfriend Debra's pimp and the whole rape story a scam? . . .

Rachel's dilemma was, what to do in light of the client's unwillingness to make race, class, or gender an issue? She was uncomfortable about pursuing a theory of discrimination in the courtroom if Debra opposed it. From Rachel's perspective, "part of being an advocate" was allowing Debra's voice to come through, since, as Rachel put it, "it's *her* story." At the same time, she did not share Debra's faith that simple truth would win out. Having come to law school believing, as Debra apparently did, in "the myth that courts give fairness," and having quickly been disabused of that notion as a first-year law student, Rachel searched in vain for a satisfactory way to explain to Debra what she might reasonably expect in a courtroom. "How was I going to tell her story," Rachel asked, "in a way a judge would understand, a jury would believe?"

NOTES & QUESTIONS

1. Professor Miller asserts that viewing case theory as story "has meant a move away from case theory as doctrine towards a view of case theory as persuasive storytelling." Miller, *Teaching Case Theory, supra*, at 295. What are the disadvantages of this move? Does this approach to case theory mean that law simply disappears? Consider this question in the context of Debra's case. In what respect do the various case theories take the law of disorderly conduct into account? In what other instances can you imagine that storytelling would be effective in clarifying the law?

2. Does the balance between storytelling and categorical analysis vary depending on the decision-maker? Is one type of analysis more appropriate for juries, another more appropriate where the trier of fact is a judge? Why?

3. Consider the idea of lawyer as translator proposed by Professor James Boyd White. Professor Milner Ball explains, "One of White's central points is that the practice of law is the practice of translation. The lawyer constantly moves between languages, mediating between them, between the stories of clients and the arguments of law. . . ." Milner Ball, *Just Stories*, 12 Cardozo Studies in Law and Literature 37, 40-41 (2000). How does this idea fit with the idea of client-centered case theory?

4. Consider the following examples of different story-based case theories developed by students in a law school class after watching *Miracle on 34th Street* (1947):

> The movie tells the story of Kris Kringle, the white-bearded elderly gentleman hired by Macy's department store as the store Santa Claus at Christmas. When the store manager discovers that Kris thinks that he is

Santa Claus, a series of events unfold in which the store psychologist seeks to have Kris committed to a mental institution. In a scene that takes place at a mental hospital to which Kris has been sent for examination pending a commitment hearing, Kris meets with a lawyer (who also happens to be a friend) to plot strategy. From this interaction, students quickly identify a number of theories, from the solidly basic to the sublime. These include theories that Kringle is joking or pretending to be Santa Claus, that although he believes himself to be Santa Claus, he's not dangerous to himself or others, that he doesn't really believe that he's Santa Claus, but that he comes to so closely resemble the role that he identifies as Santa Claus. This last theory has two variations, the first is that helping others is so much a matter of principle to Kris that he is a Santa-like character, the second is that in playing the role at Macy's he has become the fictional character that he cares so much about. Embedded in this last theory is the idea that if someone knows a character is fictional, that person can't really believe himself to be that character. Kris is sincere in telling the world that he's Santa Claus, while at the same time he doesn't believe in reindeer coming down the chimney on Christmas Eve. The claim that "I am Santa Claus" can also be seen as a metaphor representing goodness, generosity, and love of children.

Miller, *Teaching Case Theory, supra,* at 311-12. How could Kris Kringle's lawyer work with him to select a case theory from among these many variations? Which of these theories would Kris Kringle prefer? Can you think of other theories that are not included in the excerpt?

5. During his deposition in *The Social Network,* Mark Zuckerberg tells the attorneys deposing him: "a guy who builds a nice chair doesn't owe money to everyone who ever has built a chair." He tells the Winklevoss twins that "if you guys were the inventors of Facebook . . . you'd have invented Facebook" and accuses Eduardo Saverin, "You're going to blame me because you were the business head of the company, and you made a bad business deal with your own company?" The viewer can't tell whether these story-based legal theories originated with Zuckerberg or his lawyers. If you were a lawyer for Mark Zuckerberg, what kind of conversation would you have in order to elicit these types of theories? The discussion at the end of the film about the settlement agreement and why Zuckerberg will need to pay more for a nondisclosure agreement is reflective of case theory in a different context — negotiation. The associate explains to Zuckerberg that the "likeability" factor, and the fact that he said stupid things when he was drunk and angry (comparing women students at Harvard to farm animals) is a factor in the settlement amount.

6. Professor Kruse suggests a framework for determining when keeping the legal narrative consistent with the client's own story matters most:

[T]he value of Narrative Integrity in legal representation may be most important in situations in which the client's legal story is integrally connected with the client's sense of self. . . . For example, a client who has been charged with drunk driving may simply want to get his driver's license back so that he can keep his job. Likewise, in some cases, the client's sense of self might be better preserved by keeping the client's own story private, rather than submitting it to public scrutiny. But sometimes legal representation is itself an avenue for a client's self-expression in ways that connect the client's project of self-authorship with the telling of her legal story, such as a client who is challenging discriminatory treatment in the workplace. In such cases, the pull of Narrative Integrity is especially strong.

Kruse, *supra*, at 555.

Discuss how the clients in *Nuts* and *A Time to Kill* wished to be portrayed and the impact of that portrayal on case theory. What are the various storylines suggested by the clients' situations in these movies? In which of these situations is narrative integrity most important? Least important? How client-centered are the lawyers in allocating decisionmaking authority to their clients when it comes to choice of case theory? How do these case theories evolve as the relationships between the clients and the lawyers deepen?

7. Professor Cook portrays Debra as a client at odds with her student attorney's portrayal of her case. According to Cook, Rachel viewed what happened to Debra in terms of race, class, and gender discrimination, while Debra saw "[h]er own innocence. A rapist's guilt. Simple injustice." Cook, *supra*, at 50. Do you agree with Cook that the views of Debra and Rachel are necessarily so far apart? From this excerpt, we do not have much sense of the conversation between Rachel and Debra. How might Rachel have discussed a case theory based on gender without evoking a reaction from Debra that framing the case in these terms was just so much "feminist cow dung"? Rachel clearly respects her client's narrative integrity, but is there another client-centered approach that might have been helpful in understanding her client's goals?

8. In *A Time to Kill*, race as a component of the case theory is embraced by the client, but initially rejected by the lawyer — the reverse of the situation in Debra's case. In representing Carl Lee Hailey, an African-American man who killed the two white men who brutally raped and almost killed his ten-year-old daughter, Jake Brigance (played by Matthew McConaughey), a white lawyer, initially defends the case on a fatherhood revenge theme, but by the time Jake delivers his closing argument, race is an explicit theme. How does Jake come to see the case in this way? Compare the use of a racial perspective for a case in rural Mississippi, where the events in *A Time to Kill* occurred, to the use of this perspective in city like Albuquerque, New Mexico, where Debra's case arose. What difference might these two locales make to the choice of a case theory? Does it matter that the racial animus of the men who raped Carl Lee Hailey's daughter is palpable, while the motivations of the police in Debra's case were unclear?

9. What are the ethics of choosing among different case theories in the featured films? For example, in *A Time to Kill*, the lawyer does not incorporate a racial perspective in the case until after the psychiatrist called as an expert to prove the insanity defense implodes on the witness stand; at that point the lawyer feels that he has "run out of legal arguments." In selecting from among multiple theories does it seem "as if case theories are 'made up' or make-believe, either pulled out of thin air, or fictions conceived by lawyers"? Miller, *Teaching Case Theory*, *supra*, at 303. Would it be more ethical for the lawyer to determine "what really happened" and go with that theory? Is it possible to determine what really happened when it comes to questions of race? Or in any situation? In writing about the novel *The Sweet Hereafter* (1991), on which the film is based, one commentator argues: "[T]his powerful novel is really about the unknowability of 'truth' and 'facts' and what really happened." Carrie Menkel-Meadow, *The Sense and Sensibilities of Lawyers: Lawyering in Literature, Narratives, Film and Television, and Ethical Choices Regarding Career and Craft*, 31 McGeorge Law Review 1, 21 (1999). Do you agree with this characterization?

10.   Professor Miller notes that connecting case theory more closely with client experience has "meant a greater focus on the respective rights and responsibilities of the lawyer and the client for the story that is ultimately told." Miller, *Teaching Case Theory, supra,* at 295. In moving beyond case theory, clients can play an explicit role in other aspects of their cases, including matters such as witness examinations, which are typically relegated to lawyers as questions of strategy and tactics. One commentator argues that clients should decide whether to call particular witnesses and whether to cross-examine the opposing party's witnesses. Mark Spiegel, *Lawyering and Client Decisionmaking: Informed Consent and the Legal Profession,* 128 University of Pennsylvania Law Review 41, 123-26 (1979). What is your view about whether clients ought to participate in questions of case tactics and strategy, or even "call the shots" when the lawyer and client disagree?

11.   *A Time to Kill* and *Nuts* both offer examples of clients playing a fairly significant role in trial strategy and tactics. In *A Time to Kill*, Carl Lee Hailey urges his lawyer to ask a prosecution witness a question that his lawyer considers the "one question too many" that lawyers are taught not to ask, and his lawyer resists. Why does the lawyer eventually ask the question? Is he simply following the client's marching orders? Does the witness's answer vindicate the client? What lessons can we draw from this example about the types of expertise clients possess in matters that are traditionally considered within the purview of lawyers? In *Nuts*, Claudia Draper has strong feelings about whether her mother should be called as a witness in the case and what questions her father should be asked on cross-examination. How does Aaron Levinsky, the public defender appointed by the judge to represent Draper, respond to her? What do you think of his choice to reveal her secret in the courtroom in the interest of winning the case? Can Levinsky's behavior be seen as a clash between the competing values of narrative integrity (staying true to the client's story) and partisan advocacy (preserving the client's freedom from legal harm)? What do you make of his later apology ("I'm so sorry; I got so wrapped up in being a goddamn lawyer.")? What does Levinsky's response to the judge's request at the hearing the next day that his client consent to an independent psychiatric examination reveal?

12.   In *A Time to Kill*, Lucien Wilbanks (played by Donald Sutherland), a wise older lawyer who has fallen on hard times, advises Jake Brigance that his client "is as guilty as sin under all legal systems. [The law] does not permit vigilante violence, and he took the law into his own hands. He murdered two people." Later, during a strategy session on jury selection, Brigance announces, "Now to win this case we need a sympathetic jury, a jury willing to acquit, and a jury that can use the insanity plea as an excuse to do so." Is Brigance talking about jury nullification, a means for juries to ignore the law and instead rely on their emotions or sense of justice, or is he talking about a law-based case theory? What types of client pictures should lawyers paint to persuade juries to acquit under these circumstances? Consider Professor Paul Butler's argument for jury nullification:

> I argue that the race of a black defendant is sometimes a legally and morally appropriate factor for [black] jurors to consider in reaching a verdict of not guilty or for an individual juror to consider in refusing to vote for conviction.

> My thesis is that, for pragmatic and political reasons, the black community is better off when some nonviolent lawbreakers remain in the community rather than go to prison. The decision as to what kind of conduct by African-Americans ought to be punished is better made by African-Americans themselves, based on the costs and benefits to their community, than by the traditional criminal justice process, which is controlled by white lawmakers and white law enforcers.

Paul Butler, *Racially Based Jury Nullification: Black Power in the Criminal Justice System*, 105 Yale Law Journal 677 (1995).

Professor Butler makes a similar argument in his book, *A Hip-Hop Theory of Justice* (2010). What notion of community is embedded in this argument for jury nullification? Can the thesis be extended to other communities besides the African-American community? Does law have any role to play in this type of analysis?

3. Holistic Approach

The holistic approach emphasizes the importance of nonlegal considerations and encourages lawyers to use nonlegal means to address clients' legal problems and to assist clients with problems that may not be strictly "legal." These holistic lawyers also look beyond the initial legal problem that the client presents to see other legal issues. Consider the scene in *The Client* in which Reggie Love brings food and clothes to her client's mother in the hospital, or the scene in *A Time to Kill* in which Jake Brigance helps his client collect money at church to buy food for his family. Friendship, jealousy, loneliness, and hurt feelings all play a role in the relationships in *The Social Network*, debunking the myth that clients with business disputes do not have nonlegal concerns because they are more rational and less emotional than the typical legal services client.

The next excerpt describes the holistic approach taken by a clinical professor who represents domestic violence survivors.

REPRESENTATION OF DOMESTIC VIOLENCE SURVIVORS AS A NEW PARADIGM OF POVERTY LAW: IN SEARCH OF ACCESS, CONNECTION, AND VOICE

Peter Margulies

63 George Washington Law Review 1071 (1995)

Connection invokes the affective style of lawyering — an approach which stresses mutuality, care, and empathy between lawyer and client. Connection also requires spanning disciplinary boundaries, such as the boundaries between law, social work, and psychology. . . .

Connection also breaks down barriers between disciplines. . . . [L]egal services should be available alongside other services such as medicine or education sought by survivors of domestic violence. In addition to the physical location of services, a multidisciplinary approach involves an integration of both knowledge and action on the lawyer's part.

Knowledge of the psychology of domestic violence is important not only to establish connection with a client, but also to assist her in making sound decisions. Discerning "the interplay between emotion and reason" reveals "connections between knowledge and power." Without an understanding of power in abusive relationships and in gender roles, lawyers cannot hope to represent a domestic violence survivor effectively. . . .

Lawyers for domestic violence survivors also move from interdisciplinary knowledge to action. This action may collapse the wall between "law" and "social work." For example, I, on occasion, provide transportation for clients, and people from my office have gone with clients to seek jobs and housing. This also is a part of connection. It may be distinct from lawyering, in the narrow sense, and encroach into the domain of "social work," but often the lawyer is the only person in a position to provide this service. In a contextual vision of lawyering, lawyers help clients as much through getting a job and housing as they do with legal work. . . .

NOTES & QUESTIONS

1. Although Professor Margulies does not label his approach "holistic," what aspects of holistic lawyering are reflected in this excerpt? How can lawyers become experts in all of the areas identified by Margulies, or would it be preferable, as some have suggested, to work closely with other professionals, such as social workers, in a multi-disciplinary practice? *See* David Dominguez, *Getting Beyond Yes to Collaborative Justice: The Role of Negotiation in Community Lawyering*, 12 Georgetown Journal of Poverty Law & Policy 55, 77 n.73 (2005). Is the "go it alone" approach suggested in this excerpt justified only in situations where limited resources mean that clients do not have access to other experts? For holistic lawyers who seek to collaborate with other professionals, such as social workers or psychologists, what barriers might those lawyers face? Does working with an expert in another field absolve the lawyer of responsibility for understanding the non-legal aspects of the client's problem? Why or why not? For another example of "collaps[ing] the wall between 'law' and 'social work,'" as Margulies puts it, see Jane Aiken and Stephen

Wizner, *Law As Social Work*, 11 Washington University Journal of Law and Policy 63 (2003).

2. Professor Margulies describes holistic lawyering in the context of representing clients seeking civil protection orders in domestic violence cases. In what other areas of practice would knowledge of the "psychology" of the client or her situation be important? Does this effort to categorize clients (domestic violence survivors) run the risk of stereotyping those clients and thus failing to recognize and value their unique experiences?

3. In the case of Debra, described in the earlier excerpt from Professor Cook's article, Debra's student attorney and the supervising attorney considered other options beyond her immediate case, involving both litigation and other avenues of reform:

> We considered alternatives other than trial that might result in reforms of police procedures as well as in dismissal of the charges against Debra. The Police Department was already under scrutiny for its handling of several investigatory stops that had resulted in the deaths of two young men the previous spring, and this increased the likelihood that, if approached, the press would take an interest in the department's handling of rape complaints. Media pressure might have some desirable effects. There was also the option of filing a civil suit against the police department in either state or federal court. One thing that was appealing about these alternatives was that they focused attention on a problem that was much larger than the charge pending against Debra; they gave Rachel (and Debra) the opportunity to make a difference on a grander scale.

> Debra, however, was not interested in discussing these options. She wanted the charges to go away, yes, and she wanted the police to conduct themselves differently, but she did not want to be involved in a major law reform effort. As far as she was concerned, the sooner this mess got cleaned up, the better; she had been inconvenienced enough.

Cook, *supra*, at 52.

Is the client's reaction somewhat expected? How many clients would have the time and energy to be involved in pursuing options beyond those options that address their immediate needs?

4. When Reggie Love in *The Client* and Jake Brigance in *A Time to Kill* helped ensure that their clients and their families did not go hungry, did these lawyers step outside of an appropriate lawyer role? How do these actions affect our view of the kinds of services that lawyers provide clients? What impact does Reggie Love's experience as a woman and a mother have on her ability to practice law holistically? Notice how Reggie first refers to Mark in court as "the child," and only later refers to him as "my client." What is the relevance of these word choices? Is it easier for women to practice law holistically than it is for men to practice law this way? Does the lawyer's gender make a difference in how his or her actions are viewed?

5. Consider these examples of nonlegal concerns from *The Social Network*. In one scene, one of the Winklevoss twins says, "We're not suing [Zuckerberg] . . .

because we're gentlemen of Harvard." He only later agrees to pursue litigation ("screw it, let's gut the frickin' nerd") after his crew team loses to a team from Cambridge, England, where they learn that Facebook is all the rage at English universities. Can this aversion to litigation stem from the idea that lawsuits are messy and disputes are best worked out informally among "gentlemen"? Or, is Zuckerberg right when he describes the twins as motivated to sue because, for the first time in their lives, they didn't get what they wanted?

The relationship between Zuckerberg and Saverin is more complex. Zuckerberg describes Saverin as his "best friend" during the deposition in which an attorney wryly notes, "Your best friend is suing you for 600 million dollars." Saverin is visibly affected when he learns that Zuckerberg is not the source of embarrassing deposition questions about whether Saverin abused a chicken as part of a bizarre Harvard hazing incident, and at other times, both men's facial expressions indicate that they feel some remorse for their choices. Do you think this focus on relationships is typical of business practice in the United States? Is the entrepreneurial business setting in Facebook fundamentally different than the more traditional corporation? Why or why not?

4.   Client-Empowerment Approach

This approach encourages lawyers to work with clients so that they have an expansive view of their options — the first thing that a client wants may not be what she ultimately wants, especially when a client sees her options as limited — and to encourage clients to be proactive, either working alone or with others in their community. In *The Client*, Reggie Love practices the arguably paternalistic "individualist" form of client empowerment when she chases after Mark after he tries to fire her as his attorney, an action which she sees as not being in his best interests. The clients in three of the films — *A Time to Kill*, *The Social Network*, and *The Sweet Hereafter* — are situated in close-knit communities, although not all of the communities are disempowered.

The community-building aspect of client empowerment is described in the context of a case study from South Africa.

TO LEARN AND TEACH: LESSONS FROM DRIEFONTEIN ON LAWYERING AND POWER
Lucie E. White
1988 Wisconsin Law Review 699

On August 26, 1985, the South African government announced that it would not force the residents — all of them Black — of a small farming community called Driefontein to relocate to resettlement camps in remote rural areas. Rather, the government acceded to the villagers' demands that they be allowed to continue living, farming, and owning land in a region of the country that had been officially designated as the exclusive domain of whites. The reprieve for Driefontein came just a month after the government had placed a large part of the country under a "state of emergency," tantamount to martial law, in an aggressive effort to quell anti-apartheid activism in Black communities. In the context of these emergency regulations and the heightened repression that they signaled, the government's backing down on the Driefontein removal was hard to comprehend. It did not fit within the overall pattern of events in South Africa at the time. What could have compelled the government to give in, at that time, to a few isolated Blacks on an issue as central to the logic of apartheid as Black ownership and occupancy of land?

This Article explores that question by reconstructing the story of Driefontein's opposition to the South African government. It is a case study of the community's resistance, with a focus on how a lawyer and an organizer worked with the community to enable and support that effort. To work effectively with a community which had few clear-cut legal rights, the outsiders — the lawyer and the organizer — had to depart sharply from traditional notions of their proper professional roles. Instead of following established norms for serving clients, the lawyer collaborated with the organizer and the villagers in a joint project of challenging structures of domination that disabled the community, and of creating sources of their own power. . . .

The villagers' victory may not have ended the era of forced removals, but the work they did to achieve their reprieve undermined apartheid in another way. The villagers did not hand their problem over to a lawyer, who then acted for them. Rather, the lawyer and organizer worked with the villagers to help them gain power. With the help of these outsiders, the villagers educated themselves about the removals. They spread that knowledge among themselves and to others. They set up their own facilities when the government withdrew services. They compelled the government to pay the public benefits that they were due. They analyzed the government's position on the removal and devised strategies for responding to it. They negotiated with government and homeland officials. . . .

The lawyer and the organizer took on distinct tasks as the case developed. The lawyer worked primarily with the negotiating committee and the government, devising strategies to block the removal. The organizer worked primarily with villagers, educating them about the removal threat and helping them build independent community institutions. These two efforts were not isolated from one another. Rather, the tasks of the lawyer and the organizer complemented each other in a single advocacy strategy. As the villagers gained confidence in themselves and consolidated their community, the problem of implementing the removal became more difficult for the government. It became more likely that the villagers would move only if direct physical force was used. Similarly, as the lawyer and the organizing committee gained information and got concessions from the government, the villagers' motivation to build their community increased. Thus, the two efforts — of negotiation and community work — built upon one another. They were two aspects of a "lawyering" effort, in which no single actor occupied the "lawyer" role. . . .

The villagers used public support for two purposes. First, active villagers used the events generated by the public interest in the removal — the visits of outside journalists, the press clippings, the play that they produced about the removal — as occasions to motivate their neighbors to get involved in the community building activities. Second, public opinion, both within South Africa and throughout the world, was a central source of leverage that the villagers had against the government. Ultimately, they were able to pressure the government to agree to the land deal because those officials were unwilling to risk the international outcry that might follow a violent removal.

Public opinion — the audience — became a significant source of power to the villagers only because it was cultivated, consciously, through the lawyering effort. The outsiders — the lawyer and the organizer — were indispensable to this effort; they had the connections to the internal and international press, and they knew the psychology of the white world. Yet the villagers themselves gave the accounts that resonated so deeply in the conscience of the "outside" world and even in some parts of the white community inside South Africa. . . .

[Other community] activities include[d] the informal conversations between the organizer and the villagers, the development of the health clinic and the legal clinic, and the strategizing work that the lawyer did jointly with the villagers and the negotiating committee. All of these activities helped the villagers understand the full measure of their own power. . . . Through those activities, villagers found themselves working together effectively and successfully in their own community and against the government. As a result, the community coalesced and resolved that it would not cooperate in another "voluntary" removal.

NOTES & QUESTIONS

1. In the article excerpted earlier in this chapter, Professor Kruse describes the client-empowerment approach as encouraging individual clients to think outside the box of their own world view so that they can make better decisions, an approach in which lawyers use strategies that "facilitat[e] the client's connection and solidarity with others." Kruse, *supra*, at 423. It is this community aspect of client-centeredness that is reflected in the Driefontein case study from South Africa. What aspects of the case study demonstrate a client-empowerment approach to the problem of forced removal? What other lawyering approaches might be implicated?

2. Does a client-empowerment approach apply to all cultural settings, or was there something unique about the cultural setting of South Africa at that time? What impact did friendship and community have on the relationships that the clients in *A Time to Kill* and *The Sweet Hereafter* developed? Are some clients and communities more deserving of a lawyer who facilitates empowerment? Why or why not? Are all clients to some extent disempowered when dealing with their lawyers? Note Zuckerberg's passive role in the litigation, and the fact that Saverin signed a document provided by the Facebook lawyers without even reading it, a document that diluted the value of his stock in the company.

3. The connections that are forged among members of a community — a hallmark of empowerment — may facilitate a holistic approach to problem-solving. In *The Social Network*, the Winklevoss twins pursued multiple strategies — some more "legal" than others — to achieve their goals, and their Harvard buddies helped them formulate some of these strategies. The twins contacted their father's lawyer to send a cease and desist letter to Zuckerberg, while at the same time pursuing an action under the student honor code. When that failed, they met with Larry Summers, the president of Harvard, portrayed in a marvelous scene in which he

shows as much disdain for Harvard students as the Winklevoss twins show for everyone else. Mark Zuckerberg in *The Social Network* can be seen as a creative genius rather than as a business entrepreneur who relied on associates with business acumen to make Facebook a billion dollar enterprise.

4.   What are the dangers in assuming that clients' articulated desires are not their real desires? Reggie Love's refusal to allow Mark to fire her in *The Client* may present an easy case for client-empowerment since otherwise Mark would have been without legal counsel, but what about harder cases? What might these be?

5.   In *Nuts*, Aaron Levinsky, Claudia Draper's lawyer, tells her, "If we win the hearing, you get a trial [on manslaughter charges]. If you lose, you could go to jail for twenty-five years." She replies, "I'll take the risk. If I don't, I could end up wearing this nightie until I collect Social Security." What might a client-empowering type of lawyer have said or done next to help Claudia consider her options?

5. Partisan Approach

Pop culture is replete with portrayals of attorneys engaging in partisan advocacy, and this advocacy is sometimes close to the ethical line. The lawyers in the featured films for this chapter (with the possible exception of *The Social Network*) at times act as partisan advocates with less concern for the niceties of legal rules than the interests of their clients. In *The Client*, the lawyer puts the interests of her client above everyone else, jeopardizing a federal investigation through actions that could constitute obstruction of justice. In *Nuts*, the lawyer cross-examines witnesses by going for the jugular with a no-holds-barred cross-examination style. In *The Sweet Hereafter*, the lawyer promises potential clients, "I shall sue for negligence until they bleed." In *A Time to Kill*, the lawyer makes a plea for acquittal that arguably has no basis in law.

In making the case for zealous and partisan advocacy in the context of criminal defense lawyering, the next author discusses the views of legal ethicist and criminal defense attorney Monroe Freedman. An excerpt from Freedman's controversial critique appears in Chapter 1 of this textbook.

THE DIFFERENCE IN CRIMINAL DEFENSE AND THE DIFFERENCE IT MAKES
Abbe Smith
11 Washington University Journal of Law & Policy 83 (2003)

[Monroe] Freedman argues that an essential function of the adversary system is to "maintain a free society in which individual rights are central." As Freedman notes, the rights that comprise the adversary system include the right to personal autonomy, the right to counsel, the right to equal protection of the laws, the right to trial by jury, the right to call and confront witnesses, the right to be free from compelled self-incrimination, and the right to a presumption of innocence. Freedman further notes that the government must bear the burden of proof, and must prove its case beyond a reasonable doubt.

Freedman regards the right to counsel as the most important of all rights because it is inextricably connected to the "client's ability to assert all other rights." Through adversarial advocacy the lawyer functions to uphold the client's rights, and protects the client's autonomy, dignity, and freedom. Thus, to Freedman, an ethical and professionally responsible lawyer is an ardent civil libertarian who, in zealously representing individual clients, also upholds the political philosophy underlying the American system of justice.

In Freedman's view, the central concern of a system of lawyers' ethics is to strengthen and protect the role of the lawyer in enhancing individual dignity and autonomy through advocacy. This is a constant theme throughout Freedman's considerable body of work. To use the phrase currently in vogue, which he himself may have coined, Freedman is an eloquent champion of "client-centered" lawyering. Thus, to Freedman, lawyers do justice when they pursue their clients' interests with devotion and zeal.

My own view of criminal defense lawyering owes much to Monroe Freedman. I agree with his "traditionalist view" of criminal defense ethics as a lawyering paradigm in which zealous advocacy and the maintenance of client confidence and trust are paramount. Simply put, zeal and confidentiality trump most other rules, principles, or values. When there is tension between these "fundamental principles" and other ethical rules, criminal defense lawyers must uphold the principles, even in the face of public or professional outcry. Although a defender must act within the bounds of the law, he or she should engage in advocacy that is as close to the line as possible, and, indeed, should test the line, if it is in the client's interest in doing so. . . .

NOTES & QUESTIONS

1. Professor Smith argues that criminal defense attorneys should "engage in advocacy that is as close to the line as possible, and, indeed, should test the line, if it is in the client's interest in doing so." What personal and professional risks does this approach pose for attorneys who practice in this way? Consider this example:

> My client Norman, and his co-respondent, Steve Thomas, were charged with receiving stolen property. The police happened upon Norman and Steve in an alley transferring a stereo and TV from a junked car into the back seat of a white Pontiac.

> The case hinged on whether our clients knew (or should have known) that the property was stolen. . . .

> When Norman borrowed his cousin's Pontiac, he told us, he was given only the ignition key, not the trunk key. But when all the evidence was in, no mention had been made of that fact. At Steve Thomas's lawyer's suggestion, we made what was to me, at that time, a novel and shocking argument: obviously Steve and Norman had no idea that the property was stolen, else why would they have been loading it into the Pontiac's back seat, instead of concealing it in the trunk?

James S. Kunen, *"How Can You Defend Those People?": The Making of a Criminal Lawyer* 117 (1983), *quoted in* William H. Simon, *The Ethics of Criminal Defense*, 91

Michigan Law Review 1703, 1704 (1993).

Would you be comfortable trying to gain an advantage in a case by arguing that the evidence supports an inference that you know is untrue?

2. Professor Smith argues that in the criminal defense context "[s]ometimes even lawyers who see themselves as their clients' friends will scold clients, gang up on them, twist their arms, brow-beat them to do the right thing." Abbe Smith, *Too Much Heart and Not Enough Heat: The Short Life and Fractured Ego of the Empathic, Heroic Public Defender*, 37 U.C. Davis Law Review 1203, 1231 (2004). Are lawyers who practice the partisan advocacy brand of client-centered lawyering more likely than other client-centered lawyers to ignore their clients' stated interests, bullying their clients to "do the right thing" until they give in? Does this behavior respect clients and their viewpoints? What special expertise do lawyers have in helping clients weigh complicated choices which have both legal and non-legal consequences for their lives? Consider the clients in *A Time to Kill* and *Nuts*. While a plea would have helped Carl Lee Hailey serve a shorter prison term than if he had been found guilty of murder, and a finding of incompetency would have allowed Claudia Draper to sidestep a possible murder conviction, neither client was willing to consider these options. Why? What were their life circumstances that made these options unappealing?

3. In your view, are the aggressive actions of the lawyers described in the introduction to this section justified? Would you have done the same thing if you had been the lawyer for these clients? Given that a partisan advocate will fight like hell for a client, all the while twisting the client's arm, would you want a partisan advocate as your lawyer? How do you think most clients would react to a partisan advocate-type lawyer?

4. While the reliance on racial themes is appropriate in the context of circumstances like those found in *A Time to Kill*, the use of racial case theories has been criticized when those theories rely on negative racial stereotypes, as in a case involving a highly publicized assault on Reginald Denny, a white truck driver in Los Angeles:

> To win acquittals, the Williams-Watson defense attorneys challenged and ultimately refuted substantial evidence of intent and voluntary conduct available to prove criminal liability for attempted murder and aggravated mayhem in the beating of Reginald Denny and others. Their main defense rested on a "group contagion" theory of mob-incited diminished capacity. Marshaled as a partially exculpatory defense, the theory holds that young black males as a group, and the black community as a whole, share a pathological tendency to commit acts of violence in collective situations. Both Williams and Watson are young, male, and black. Among the victims, Denny is white, and the others are of mixed ethnic and racial backgrounds.

Anthony V. Alfieri, *(Er)Race-ing An Ethic of Justice*, 51 Stanford Law Review 935, 942 (1999). Do you agree that the use of these types of racial themes is inappropriate? Why? Does partisan advocacy require using any and all themes, regardless of the impact on particular groups?

5. In Professor Smith's view, partisan advocacy means adversarial advocacy, which brings to mind aggressive, competitive behavior. As a client, Mark Zuckerberg verbally spars with the lawyers taking his deposition, telling one lawyer who asks Zuckerberg if he has his full attention: "No. . . . You have part of my attention. . . . The rest of my attention is back at the offices of Facebook, where my colleagues and I are doing things that no one in this room, including and especially your clients, are intellectually or creatively capable of doing. Did I accurately answer your condescending question?" When another lawyer asks him if someone is lying, he sarcastically replies, "I guess that would be the first time somebody's lied under oath." This behavior might be viewed as haughty, arrogant and obnoxious, or alternatively as fair turnabout for the lawyers. If Zuckerberg were acting as a lawyer, would his behavior be considered partisan advocacy? Or is there a different way to be partisan, without resorting to the kind of one-upmanship that Zuckerberg demonstrates?

6. Is the focus on partisan advocacy in criminal defense practice warranted? Are there other contexts where clients face losses as severe as the potential loss of freedom resulting from incarceration in a criminal case? What might those losses be? And consider that even in the context of public defender practice, the actual practice of client-centered lawyering varies widely among offices, as demonstrated by a study of five public defender offices. *See* Rodney J. Uphoff, *Strategic Decisions in the Criminal Case: Who's Really Calling the Shots?*, Criminal Justice 4-10 (Fall 1999).

D.   ESTABLISHING THE RELATIONSHIP: TRUST, EMPATHY, AND SHARED LIFE EXPERIENCES

All lawyers, no matter their approach to lawyering, must be able to gain the trust of their clients, and in turn be able to empathize with clients in difficult situations. They meet clients who have preconceived notions about lawyers, and these perspectives in turn affect the ability of their lawyers to establish a personal connection. The films featured in this chapter present an array of clients who are complex human beings, and we learn more about them as the movie plots unfold. Mark Sway, the child client in *The Client*, and Carl Lee Hailey, the avenging father in *A Time to Kill*, gain our empathy immediately. The clients and potential clients in *The Sweet Hereafter* run the gamut of human character, from greedy and abusive to generous and kind. Mark Zuckerberg in *The Social Network* is rich and at times arrogant, but he seems hurt by the experience of being socially rejected at Harvard. Claudia Draper in *Nuts* seems out of control until we understand her circumstances.

The next excerpt was written with public defenders in mind, but it applies to many other types of lawyering as well.

BEYOND JUSTIFICATIONS: SEEKING MOTIVATIONS TO SUSTAIN PUBLIC DEFENDERS
Charles Ogletree
106 Harvard Law Review 1239 (1993)

Although the term "empathy" has been used in numerous contexts, with various meanings, it is a seriously undervalued element of legal practice. Empathy has been broadly defined as "understanding the experiences, behavior, and feelings of others as they experience them. It means that [lawyers] must to the best of their abilities put aside their own biases, prejudices, and points of view in order to understand as clearly as possible the points of view of their clients." Gerard Egan, *The Skilled Helper* 87 (3rd ed. 1986), *quoted in* David Binder, Paul Bergman, & Susan Price, *Lawyers as Counselors: A Client-Centered Approach* 40 (1991). I use the term to capture two different concepts: first, to require the listener not simply to hear her clients, but to understand their problems, and, second, to have compassion for her clients. This dual concept of empathy is frequently invoked in feminist jurisprudence and in clinical legal scholarship. In both areas, empathy plays a central role in the development of the theory and practice of client-centered lawyering.

My view of empathy has significant implications for the character of the lawyer-client relationship. My relationships with clients were rarely limited to the provision of conventional legal services. I did not draw rigid lines between my professional practice and my private life. My relationship with my clients approximated a true friendship. I did for my clients *all* that I would do for a friend. I took phone calls at all hours, helped clients find jobs, and even interceded in domestic conflicts. I attended my clients' weddings and their funerals. When clients were sent to prison, I maintained contact with their families. Because I viewed my clients as friends, I did not merely feel justified in doing all I could for them; I felt a strong desire to do so. . . .

I want to emphasize that the quality of a lawyer's representation often will improve when she takes an empathic view of her client. Empathizing with a client necessarily means caring more deeply for the client. The attorney with a deeper understanding of and sensitivity to the client wants to help him, and this desire directly affects both her will to represent the client and the form that the representation itself takes. When she cares about the client as an individual, not only does she want to assist him through the complex maze of our legal system, but she also wants him to succeed; as a result, her defense is zealous.

Additionally, empathy provides defenders with the ability to hear "complex, multivocal conversations." As a result, empathy enhances a lawyer's ability to interview and counsel clients, to negotiate with opposing counsel, and to engage in the numerous other types of communication that are demanded of lawyers. Empathy also improves a lawyer's problem-solving skills, for she is better able to assess the client's goals and to integrate them into an evaluation of potential solutions. This client contact may in turn have positive effects on one's motivation to do the work, for when an attorney sees her success rate in terms of improvements in the overall quality of her clients' lives, she may come to realize that she does much more good on a daily basis than the record of her "wins" and "losses" might indicate.

NOTES & QUESTIONS

1.　How is it possible for anyone to "understand the experiences, behavior, and feelings of others as they experience them," as Professor Ogletree urges lawyers do with clients? Or is Dolores, the bus driver in *The Sweet Hereafter*, right when she angrily asks Stephens, "How do you know what I've been feeling?" Are you troubled by Professor Ogletree's statement that "my relationship with my clients approximated a true friendship"? When Mark refers to Reggie Love as a "friend" in *The Client*, what do you think he means?

2.　One aspect of empathy is the emphasis on the client as a whole person, not just a person with legal needs. What role does this emphasis on the life experiences of clients play in the various conceptions of client-centeredness: narrative integrity, client empowerment, partisan, holistic and client-directed? The lawyers in the featured films recognize the importance of the totality of their clients' life circumstances in different ways. In *Nuts*, Aaron Levinsky visits his client's apartment, rifles through her dresser drawers, and looks at her photographs. While ostensibly he may be viewed simply as visiting the murder scene, his behavior suggests something more. What do you think he is looking for? How does the client react to his trip to her apartment? In contrast, Mitchell Stephens, the lawyer in *The Sweet Hereafter*, seeks information about the lives of potential clients by talking to their neighbors.

3.　What difficulties might a lawyer encounter in seeking the type of close relationship Professor Ogletree sought with his clients? Consider the barriers that the economics of law practice present to spending enough time with a client to really get to know him. Even where money is not an issue, professional roles can create barriers. In *The Social Network*, the lawyers for Mark Zuckerberg do not seem to really know him or care about getting to know him, with the possible exception of the associate who talks to him during deposition breaks and suggests that the deposition must have been difficult for him. When she refuses his request to have dinner with him, is this an example of a lawyer trying to maintain a professional boundary with a client, or something else?

4.　In forging relationships with their clients, lawyers often face clients with preconceived notions about lawyers, and in some cases negative experiences with lawyers. For example, when Aaron Levinsky met his client in *Nuts*, she had just punched her previous attorney in the courtroom, and she greets Levinsky with hostility, sarcasm, and disdain. In *The Client*, when Mark first visits Reggie Love's office, he quizzes her about her experience, her fees, and whether she will actually keep his secrets. How do these clients' views and experiences affect the relationship that is ultimately forged with their lawyers?

5.　In *Treme* (2010–present), the HBO television series about post-Katrina New Orleans, lawyer Toni Bernette (played by Melissa Leo) represents Ladonna Batiste-Williams (played by Khandi Alexander) in an effort to find her brother, who was arrested during the hurricane and then lost in the jail bureaucracy. After Bernette runs into several dead ends in her investigation, Batiste-Williams takes matters into her own hands by contacting her brother-in-law, a well-connected New Orleans judge, to see if he can help. Later, Batiste-Williams sheepishly tells Bernette about these efforts (*Treme*, Season 1, episode 3). Does this behavior show that Batiste-Williams does not trust her lawyer to reach out the judge? Or that she does not want her lawyer to know that she wants to use her family influence to get an answer to her brother's whereabouts? Bernette is white, and Batiste-Williams is black. What impact might race have had on this situation? What are the risks for clients who make these kinds of strategic decisions without discussing them with their lawyers?

6.   Are there any downsides to focusing on the personal lives of clients? When Mitchell Stephens, the lawyer in *The Sweet Hereafter*, discusses the case with the Ottos, he stresses the importance of having "upstanding citizens" as clients, "folks like you who won't come back to haunt us." Is he acting appropriately? Can lawyers screen out clients with poor reputations or a lot of personal baggage? Are these individuals any less deserving of compensation as personal injury plaintiffs because they have committed minor crimes or personal indiscretions?

7.   Distinguish the strategic use of empathy with clients from true empathy. For example, Mitchell Stephens in *The Sweet Hereafter* can be viewed as a manipulative and completely non-empathic lawyer, akin to the ambulance-chasing paralegal that Danny DeVito plays in the John Grisham film *The Rainmaker* (1997). As one commentator describes Stephens:

> He is a seducer of the weak, preying on human vulnerabilities and needs that his finely tuned legal sensibilities can sniff out in a minute. To some of the town's parents he offers dignity and status, treating them as the embodiment of the community's values, its respectability, even as he invites them to gossip about their neighbors' debts, their defects, their criminal records. To other people he holds out different hope and he promises different benefits. To the Ottos, the hippie parents of an adopted child, he promises to give voice to their anger.

Sarat, *Imagining the Law of the Father, supra*, at 24.

Is Stephens' character more complex than described by this commentator? Is he out for money for himself, or something else? Is it possible that he feels a duty to get money for individuals who have suffered losses? When he solicits the Ottos as clients, telling them "I'm here to give your anger a voice," is this just a manipulative ploy for business, or is he sincere in feeling their grief, loss, and anger? If his motives are purely strategic, is there anything wrong with that? Are his actions any different than the actions of Reggie Love in *The Client*, who sought a bond with her client through her familiarity with the band Led Zeppelin?

————————

In telling the story of Ms. Parsons, a foster mother who had lost custody of the three foster children she was seeking to adopt, the next excerpt reveals how a lawyer's relationships with a client can change based on the lawyer's own life experience.

REFLECTIONS ON A CASE (OF MOTHERHOOD)

Jane M. Spinak

95 Columbia Law Review 1990 (1995)

Twelve years of lawyering in the foster care system organized Ms. Parsons's story into a case file. This was not a case that [a] lawyer wanted. At another time I would have redoubled my efforts to find her counsel, given her some advice, and told her that the office couldn't undertake such a massive job as the end of the semester approached. I was going to have to do that with other prospective clients. But I couldn't say no that day. Her anguish as a mother overwhelmed me: her terror became mine. Her boys became my girl. My shoulders and chest ached under my dress as I listened to her loss. I let myself listen to the client for the first time as a mother and I couldn't say no. . . .

I had thought, when contemplating motherhood, that the central impact on my work would be balancing my need to be a mother to a child with my need to be a teacher to students and a lawyer to clients. Even though I have always urged students to draw on their life experiences for their lawyering, I never considered that becoming a mother would change the way I considered the process of my work. . . .

Ms. Parsons became a foster mother when she was in her early forties. Her goal was to adopt children and taking foster children appeared to be the most effective route. She wanted to be a "pre-adoptive" foster parent, one who accepts foster children already freed or likely to be freed for adoption. The foster care agency knew she preferred two boys, toilet trained but not much older. She anticipated some of the difficulties of being a single mother and had elaborately organized her life, nursing schedule, and home to minimize the chaos of suddenly being thrust into this new role. After more than a year of waiting, three small boys — Juan, Mati, and Michael — appeared at her door one night, aged seven, four and two. One more than expected and one needing a crib and diapers: the first step away from control over chaos. Her joy at beginning her life as a mother was tempered by her fear that her plans were altered. As she recounted the story, I felt that fear. At the time my daughter was born, when I was in my late thirties, I knew the fear of losing the control built over years of professional adult life. Early in my daughter's life, the fluidity of our days unnerved me: What would I have done if our plans had been altered? If I had not had the support of a sharing husband, a maternity leave, financial stability, years of working with children and parents? Ms. Parsons's fear was mine confirmed. She nevertheless plunged into motherhood.

Ms. Parsons is a proud and contained woman. She does not easily share her feelings and rarely finds humor in life's vagaries. When she first told us what had happened, she circled around her despair. The disjointed narrative, her flashes of anger at "the system," her constant vigilance toward our ability to take her side were intended to keep us at a distance from her pain. She wasn't looking for sympathy or compassion. I don't think she cared what I thought of her as long as I could help her reclaim her motherhood. I have helped other mothers who have been separated from their children. With some of them I have developed an easygoing rapport. We like each other, we try to develop a mutual trust, and we share fairly easily in the struggle to reunite their families despite enormous differences in our backgrounds and experiences. Maybe they are better at hiding their pain. Maybe I shut my eyes to it so that I can do this work. Maybe I distance myself from them intellectually so that I can distance myself emotionally. Maybe they take similar actions. Maybe they just act the way they think I want them to. I certainly would not like to feel about all my clients and cases the way I feel about Ms. Parsons. . . .

Here's what I think my clients think about me. I am privileged. I am a white woman lawyer who always has some money for emergency cabs or lunches for them, who wears a gold wedding ring and who doesn't look or act like I have or will ever experience motherhood in the way they do. I have the perquisites which keep poverty, homelessness, dislocation, unemployment, maltreatment, and thus the state from my and my child's door. I know no one will keep the shop locked against me after the briefest look at my skin. I will not live with fear that my sexual orientation could strip me of my parental rights. I do not have to protect myself or my child from domestic violence. I work for pleasure as well as money. The inequality of this existence is so profound that I wonder whether most of my clients realize its true power.

These differences have usually existed between my clients (or, when I represented children, my clients' parents) and me. I treated them as divisions between us which could be intellectualized as much as felt. They were societal injustices which my lawyering skill was supposed to be able to abstract and thus help alleviate. When I became a mother, and returned to practice as a lawyer, something changed. In assuming the responsibility for another life, I had shed something of my insularity. Love and care for another adult — husband, parent, friend — has required various amounts of time, commitment and adjustments. They are part of but do not permeate my entire existence. I do not feel their responsibility incessantly. Whatever kind of mother I am, mother I am. This is what I felt when Lucy first came to my office. We shared — with our differences — this incessant, maddening pull. I hate its strength, its ability to arouse guilt, jealousy, and fear, especially fear. Random harm is a constant part of my consciousness; deliberate or unintentional cruelty a subconscious menace. As I listened to this client — and later to others — her exposure to me became more personal. Her otherness defined and intensified but did not destroy this shared existence. . . .

I do not expect that most of this story's readers are mothers or lawyers for mothers nor, even if they were, that their experience of these conditions mirrors mine or my client's. The particulars of our lives remain ours. Something about motherhood, nevertheless, came to center the way in which I worked with this client and its power began to infect the way I thought about lawyering. . . .

NOTES & QUESTIONS

1. Professor Spinak's story about Ms. Parsons shows that lawyer-client relationships are not static. Lawyers have different relationships with each client, and, indeed, their relationships with particular clients change over time. How did the fact that Professor Spinak and her client each had the experience of being mothers affect their relationship? At the same time they were separated by differences in race and class. What are the risks inherent in the assumption of a shared experience? Does the shared experience of motherhood matter more in the lawyer-client relationship than differences in race and class?

2. In describing how her view of lawyering changed once she became a mother, Professor Spinak also explains how her view of empathy changed:

> This did not feel like the lawyerly empathy that enabled me to listen "actively" to a client, both following and conducting the client through her tale. That respectful empathy was a learned construction with clear benefits: the client would provide more relevant information in a shorter time period if the lawyer confirmed her understanding of the client's tale during the client's telling. Empathy's thoughtfulness does not deconstruct the tale or the teller. It does not offer an alternative vision. It does not require the listener to abandon learned knowing. It is polite but not political.

Spinak, *supra*, at 2052.

How does Professor Spinak's view of "lawyerly" empathy comport with the view presented by Professor Ogletree in the article excerpted earlier? How does her "political view" of empathy comport with his view? In his article, Professor Ogletree describes how in the aftermath of his sister's murder he relied on qualities of empathy and heroism to represent criminal defendants charged with murder. Ogletree, *supra*, at 1260-81. How do you think a tragedy of this sort would affect your lawyering?

3. Like his client, Jake Brigance, the lawyer in *A Time to Kill*, is also the father of a young daughter, and thus could understand (at least to some extent) the anger and pain that motivated Carl Lee Hailey to shoot the men who raped his daughter. How did the shared experience of fatherhood affect Brigance's relationship with Hailey?

4. At first glance, Mitchell Stephens, the lawyer in *The Sweet Hereafter*, appears to have little in common with the parents whose children were killed in the bus accident. He is a high-profile lawyer from a big city; they are working-class residents of a small, remote town in British Columbia. The town is vividly described as "populated by 1960s leftovers, hippies, families built around interracial adoptions, disabled people, and Vietnam veterans turned into single fathers and Allman Brothers 'wanna-bes'." Sarat, *Imagining the Law of the Father, supra*, at 23. The parents are members of a tight-knit community; the lawyer is an outsider. But viewers come to learn that he also is a grieving parent, grieving not for the death of his daughter, but for her descent into the world of drug addiction and the loss of her childhood innocence. As one commentator notes, "Running alongside the story of [the lawyer's] efforts to generate a lawsuit on behalf of the victims of the bus accident is his own troubled relationship to his drug-addicted daughter, Zoe." *Id.* at 20. Thus, "it is hard to tell where Mitchell Stephens the lawyer ends and where Mitchell Stephens the father begins, and whether it is possible to separate the lawyer's public duty, his 'job,' the law itself, from that private agony that marks his life as a father." *Id.* at 22-23.

5. The identity issues in *The Client* concern a lawyer whose experience in losing custody of her own children affects her relationship with her young client.

According to one commentator, "Reggie's motivation to practice family law clearly seems to be a replacement. She misses her biological children and uses her clients as substitutes." Carrie S. Coffman, *Gingerbread Women: Stereotypical Female Attorneys in the Novels of John Grisham*, 8 Southern California Review of Law and Women's Studies 73, 94 (1988). Another commentator notes that the lawyer's "last name, 'Love,' also signifies the mothering she is able to give to Mark — mothering she cannot give to her own children but can now dole out to Mark under the cover of her astute command of the law." Judith Grant, *Lawyers as Superheroes: The Firm, The Client, and The Pelican Brief*, 30 University of San Francisco Law Review 1111, 1117 (1996). Do you agree with these assessments? What are the dangers for Reggie Love in confusing her role as a lawyer for her client with a mothering role? Another commentator notes that Love, "largely by supplementing her legal judgment with maternal impulses, achieves both a legal advantage for her client and a large measure of personal gratification." Stacy Caplow, *Still in the Dark: Disappointing Images of Women Lawyers in the Movies*, 20 Women's Rights Law Reporter 55, 57 (1988-99). In what respect do Love's parental impulses help her client legally? Are legal judgment and parental impulses mutually exclusive? Is she a better lawyer for having been a mother? For having lost a custody battle to her former husband?

6. Identities related to race, ethnicity, gender, and sexual orientation are important in contemporary life. In Mark Zuckerberg's deposition in *The Social Network*, he was asked about a comment he made to Eduardo Saverin that Saverin's acceptance into an exclusive Harvard club was "probably just a diversity thing, so what?" Can both Zuckerberg and Saverin be considered "outsiders" at Harvard, Zuckerberg because of his social awkwardness and Saverin because he is Latino in a predominantly white environment? Consider the various identity groups to which you belong and your own life experiences. How do you think your identity and your experiences will affect your relationship with clients? Are there certain types of clients you would find easiest to represent? Most difficult to represent? Why?

E.   UNBRIDGEABLE GAPS?

Despite the promise of the client-centered approaches to lawyering, and the important role that empathy, trust, and shared life experiences can play in bringing clients together with their lawyers, the worlds of lawyers and clients often diverge. As one commentator notes in writing about *The Sweet Hereafter*:

> When viewers see Delores [the bus driver] giving a deposition, recounting the horror of the accident, stating that the bus was "like a huge wave about to break over us," we are reminded of the gap between her world and the world of law. Delores sobs as she particularizes the "us," by naming every child on the bus. The panning of the camera from Delores to Stephens,who sits impassively toying with a ring on his finger, ignoring her distress as he asks matter-of-factly, "and then what happened," suggests that the gap is truly unbridgeable.

Sarat, *Exploring the Hidden Domains of Civil Justice, supra*, at 444.

In the following excerpt, the author interviews a 72-year-old sharecropper in North Carolina as part of the author's research about the Head Start program. The interviewee was the great-grandmother and legal guardian of a child participating in the program. The results of the interview — which the author was not conducting as lawyer for the grandmother — reveal the tension between connection and distance.

SEEKING ". . . THE FACES OF OTHERNESS . . .": A RESPONSE TO PROFESSORS SARAT, FELSTINER, AND CAHN
Lucie E. White
77 Cornell Law Review 1499 (1992)

In the interview, she gave me a brief account of the highlights of her life. She told me of her father's defiance in sending his daughter to school when the white plantation bosses expected her to be working in the fields. She told of receiving a scholarship to an elite women's college, but turning it down because she could not afford a bus ticket to get there. She told of graduating from an African-American teacher's college and of teaching for fifty years in the public schools. She told me what it was like to teach before the schools were integrated, when her students were given text-books handed down from whites. She also told me what it was like to teach after integration, when white children asked, and were allowed, to transfer out of her class. She referred only in passing to the civil rights movement. I learned from others that she had been one of the movement's many local leaders in the rural counties of the south.

As I contemplated this story, comparing it to what others had told me about the record of racial violence in the county and the courage this woman had shown in combating it, two features stood out. First, throughout the story, she expressed inexhaustible patience, and indeed love, for the white people she had dealt with over the years. Second, although she recounted many injustices, her narrative carefully excluded the details of the violence she had endured. I had noted similar themes in interviews with other African-American Head Start parents.

After the formal interview was completed and the tape recorder turned off, I casually inquired about the woman's older great-grandchild, who, like my own daughter, had recently started kindergarten. When I asked this question, my informant became visibly sad. She told me that when she had dropped this child off at school earlier that morning, a young white child had run up to take her hand. Just as her great-granddaughter reached back, however, a second white child came up to the first and yanked her hand away, explaining that white girls should not touch people who were black.

Then the woman looked hard at me, and said, "The white people will go to any lengths to keep us down, even if it means keeping themselves down as well. They're making Frankensteins of us all."

This encounter could be examined through a Foucaultian lens. Such an examination would reveal an important reality. It would reveal this woman's skillful maneuvers, designed to ensure that our mutual reality was negotiated on her terms.

This lens would show a woman who was artful in controlling the pace and extent of her revelations, and in determining how the injuries she had suffered would be named. This lens would reveal a woman negotiating the power between us to shape an account that she wanted me to hear.

Yet this is lens reveals only a partial reality. For when this woman told me of her child's morning at school, she was not merely controlling how that event would be interpreted, and thereby trumping my own power to do the same. She was also speaking to me as another person. Through her brief story, I "felt," for a moment, something of the impossible sadness that eluded our language game. At the same time, I picked up her astute reminder that as one of those whites, I dare not claim to have "felt" her pain. . . .

NOTES & QUESTIONS

1. In this eloquent essay, Professor White suggests that true understanding may be difficult to achieve between people from different backgrounds. How can we reconcile the grandmother's "love for the white people she had dealt with over the years," despite many injustices, with her statement that "the white people will go to any lengths to keep us down"? Is it possible to understand the meaning of her story without sharing her experience of racism? Given the limitations of shared experiences and common backgrounds, how, other than through life experience, can lawyers and law students become more culturally competent? How would you design a cultural competence plan for yourself? For an excellent approach to learning cross-cultural concepts and skills, see Susan Bryant, *The Five Habits: Building Cross-Cultural Competence in Lawyers*, 8 Clinical Law Review 33 (2001).

2. Can lawyers' revelations about their own personal lives help establish connections with clients? When a lawyer has (or thinks she has) experiences in common with a client, how much of her personal life should she reveal to her client? When Professor Ogletree represented a client charged with rape and murder soon after his sister's death, he disclosed the fact of his sister's murder to his client so that his client could assess whether he wanted Ogletree to represent him. The client accepted Ogletree as his lawyer. *Id.* at 1264. Is this the kind of personal detail you would be comfortable sharing with a client? Does the motivation for the disclosure or its timing make a difference in whether disclosure is appropriate? In *The Client*, Reggie Love reveals that she is a recovering alcoholic. In *The Sweet Hereafter*, Mitchell Stephens reveals his daughter's drug addiction to Billy Ansel, a hostile parent who did not join the lawsuit. Why do you think Mitchell revealed this information, and did he act appropriately? Would his actions be more or less appropriate if Billy were a client?

3. Professor Nancy Cook describes a lower level criminal court:

The scene is this: In the basement of the Metropolitan courthouse is a small, locked-in, white room where arraignments take place every weekday. In the morning, when court is in full swing, the pews in the center of the room are filled with men and women in scruffy, faded, jailhouse blue serge. These people have slept poorly, if at all; they have not bathed. Some are shoeless, some are hung over, some are bloodied. Some are half asleep, while others are frightened and edgy. They are not permitted to speak, and certainly not to move from their seats.

Around the perimeters of the half dozen or so benches are the professional people, the lawyers, sheriffs, and court personnel whose livelihoods all depend, to a greater or lesser degree, on those individuals whose arrests have brought them into arraignment court. They are mostly standing — except for the judge who looks down from her high bench and the clerk beside her — and they are actively engaged in whispered discussions, only some of which are of a professional nature. With rare exceptions, these people moving around at the edges are well dressed, well rested, and comfortable. The contrast between the standers and the sitters is ludicrously obvious, like a lace collar on a used, blue serge jumpsuit.

I am reminded of an important truism: Law is for Lawyers.

Cook, *supra*, at 58.

How does this description of legal institutions and processes compare to the experiences of the clients in *The Social Network*, who are, if anything, more privileged than their lawyers?

4.   Does a relationship between a lawyer and a client that predates their professional relationship affect the ability of the lawyer to bridge these gaps? In *A Time to Kill*, Carl Lee Hailey knew Jake Brigance because Brigance had represented Hailey's brother on a drug charge. What difference did that make in terms of their lawyer-client relationship? Another example is provided by *Miracle on 34th Street*, in which Fred Gailey, Kris Kringle's lawyer, first knew Kris as a friend. Although Gailey and Kris had little in common in terms of their personal backgrounds, Gailey was committed to zealously representing Kris.

5.   *The Social Network* presents a multi-faceted clash between different cultures: old-style corporate and legal on the one hand and entrepreneurs grounded in the Internet on the other. The film demonstrates how the difference between these cultures can impact lawyer-client relationships. In the deposition scene in which Zuckerberg spars with the lawyers about whether he is paying attention, he responds with a comment that shows his belief that Internet entrepreneurs are doing important, creative and innovative things, while the lawyers are stuck in the tired, plodding question-and-answer format of a deposition. How would you describe these cultures, their similarities and their differences? Do the big-firm lawyers seem stodgy compared to the edgy, younger Internet entrepreneur? Do cultural differences explain the disdain that Zuckerberg shows for the lawyers in the deposition, or is his reaction typical of a client facing a lawsuit with little merit?

Parenthetically, some have argued that Hollywood itself has a stodgy side. In describing the production process for a Hollywood feature film, Lawrence Lessig notes: "No field of innovation is more burdened by the judgments of idiots in the middle than film. Scores of directors have watched in horror as their creativity gets maimed by suits-carrying-focus-groups." Lessig, *supra*, at 2.

6. In a review of empirical research about lawyer-client relationships, one commentator argues:

> What lawyers consider to be important, proper, and moral may be considerably different from their clients. These differences are likely to cause a gap in understanding, even a difference in morality, which could cause lawyers to be perceived negatively as cold, dispassionate, uncaring, overly logical, fact-driven, aggressive, competitive, ruthless, and even amoral. Lawyers do appear to be more competitive and aggressive, need more dominance, and be driven to succeed more than most adults. Clients may perceive lawyers as cold, uncaring, uncommunicative, disinterested in anything but the "relevant facts," overly rule-oriented, aggressive, competitive, and hard-driving because they actually are more that way than the norm.

Susan Daicoff, *Lawyer, Know Thy Self: A Review of Empirical Research on Attorney Attributes Bearing on Professionalism*, 46 American University Law Review 1337, 1411 (1997).

If the author is correct in her characterization of lawyers, how can lawyers understand clients whose values and personal traits are so different from their own? Narrative accounts of actual clients abound. *See* Binny Miller, *Telling Stories about Cases and Clients: The Ethics of Narrative*, 14 Georgetown Journal of Legal Ethics 1 (2000). However, empirical studies of lawyer-client relationships are relatively scarce. One notable exception is Austin Sarat & William L. F. Felstiner, *Divorce Lawyers and Their Clients: Power and Meaning in the Legal Process* (1995). More empirical studies could help us determine what the gaps are and help lawyers address these gaps.

Chapter 5

WITNESSES

A. FILMOGRAPHY

The Accused (1988)

The Crucible (1996)

My Cousin Vinny (1992)

Witness for the Prosecution (1957)

The Wrong Man (1956)

B. WITNESSING WITCHCRAFT — PAST AND PRESENT

In spite of its reliance on technology and science, the legal system still relies on witnesses of all kinds to power it and to assist fact-finders to come to conclusions and deliver verdicts. Even though experts like Elizabeth Loftus have brought eyewitness testimony into question because human memory can be so undependable, it is still quite persuasive, especially for jurors. Popular culture often depicts the appearance of the eyewitness as crucial to a court case and the time spent to persuade a reluctant witness to appear as absolutely necessary to a party's "win" at trial.

Most of this chapter will focus on the pop cultural portrayal of witnesses in the context of the American adversary system, but witnesses played important roles in adjudicatory systems long before the emergence of the current system. One might be inclined to dismiss the earlier uses of witnesses as irrational, superstitious, and — fortunately — just part of the past. However, the past continues to echo in the present.

The most notorious example of pre-modern witnessing to occur in what is today the United States involved the Salem witchcraft trials of 1692. As a result of proceedings between June and September of that year, the Salem courts hanged nineteen supposed witches, and one man, Giles Corey, was pressed to death with heavy stones because he would not concede the court's jurisdiction.

The Salem witchcraft trials have captured the imagination of not only historians but also artists, most notably the renowned American playwright Arthur Miller. His play *The Crucible* (1953) employed the Salem witchcraft trials as a backdrop and was much acclaimed for its emotional and intellectual power. *The Crucible* was a success on the New York stage and remains popular for community and high school productions.

On the surface, Arthur Miller's *The Crucible* is about accusers and defendants in the Salem witchcraft trials, but on a deeper level it concerns the dangers and excesses of McCarthyism. Between about 1947 and 1954, aggressive anti-Communists, including but not limited to Senator Joseph McCarthy of Wisconsin, identified, berated, and otherwise harmed thousands of Americans.

Indeed, when other citizens who were not Communists refused to "name names" for Congressional committee members and others, these citizens were often humiliated, censored, and jailed. In Hollywood, Communists and Communist sympathizers were "blacklisted" and soon found themselves unable to find work. Later, in an ironic turnaround, some of those who "named names," e.g., director Elia Kazan, were shunned by members of the Hollywood community.

Arthur Miller himself adapted *The Crucible* for the cinema in 1996. The film features Winona Ryder in the role of Abigail Williams, a young woman infatuated with a married man named John Proctor, played by Daniel Day-Lewis. Does the film seem a metaphor for a modern society in crisis? What aspects of the Salem witchcraft trials were emphasized in the cinematic version?

In the following excerpt Professor Jane Campbell Moriarty describes the witnesses and types of evidence in the Salem witchcraft trials and offers summaries of the cases against two of the witches.

WONDERS OF THE INVISIBLE WORLD: PROSECUTORIAL SYNDROME AND PROFILE EVIDENCE IN THE SALEM WITCHCRAFT TRIALS
Jane Campbell Moriarty
26 Vermont Law Review 43 (2001)

III. The Trial Evidence

We may never fully uncover the reason that the Salem witchcraft trials escalated so dramatically, but one explanation for the growth of the accusations was the discovery by several accused witches that confession and accusation of others was a likely way to avoid the gallows. Indeed, there was much approval of confessions as the surest evidence of guilt. Cotton Mather himself wrote of the importance of confessions in assuring proper convictions, and the renowned witchcraft expert William Perkins had also ordained their utility. The benefit of false confession and false accusation was apparent after the initial wave of convictions and hangings, since those who clung to claims of innocence were executed.

During the trials, witnesses began piecing together historical memories of strange events that occurred after an unpleasant interaction with the accused which, as Perkins had instructed, was evidence of witchcraft. For example, while the victims would come into court and identify the defendant as the specter bewitching them, other witnesses would provide historical evidence of the defendant's witchcraft acts as well. Robert Calef, who wrote scathingly about the trials after their conclusion, summed up the evidence as follows:

> In the Tryals, when any were Indicted for Afflicting, Pining, and wasting the Bodies of particular persons by Witchcraft; it was usual to hear Evidence of matter foreign, and of perhaps Twenty or Thirty years standing, about over-setting Carts, the death of Cattle, unkindness to Relations, or unexpected Accidents befalling after some quarrel.

Robert Calef, "More Wonders of the Invisible World" (1700), *reprinted in Narratives of the Witchcraft Cases, 1648-1706* 373-74 (George L. Burr ed. 1914).

A. Categories of Evidence

Much of the trial evidence seems to break into a number of discrete categories, although arguably some evidence seems to fit into more than one. These categories are: (1) confessions; (2) reputation evidence; (3) physical evidence; (4) spectral evidence; (5) syndrome evidence; and (6) profile evidence. The first three are discussed as a group; the remaining three are considered separately. . . .

1. Confessions, Physical Evidence, and Reputation

Confessions played a curious role in the Salem witchcraft trials. Some defendants admitted their complicity with the devil — often testifying about "signing the devil's book" — while others steadfastly maintained their innocence. Cotton Mather was firmly convinced that confession was the strongest evidence to support a proper conviction as was Perkins. While many have written about the reasons for these confessions, as well as their importance, it is indeed a curious and much-studied part of the trials that so many people confessed to something most of us do not believe was true.

To determine whether one was a witch, factfinders could also rely on reputation or character evidence of the accused. For example, Cotton Mather wrote that the defendant in the Glover trial, which pre-dated the Salem trials, possessed a poor reputation. Experts such as Perkins opined on the importance of reputation, noting that if a person was defamed as a witch, that yielded a strong suspicion. In certain trials, such as Bridget Bishop's and Sarah Good's, reputation likely added to the reasons for conviction.

Although it most likely played a minor role, physical evidence was apparently also introduced into the trials. This type of evidence would include "poppets" or dolls made for diabolical purposes, along with pins, nails, and other physical evidence of witchcraft.

2. Spectral Evidence

Spectral evidence, of course, is the most vilified and most difficult evidence to comprehend. According to some sources, it was of dubious value for many in 1692 as well. The definition of spectral evidence is somewhat elusive, and it is difficult to imagine this type of evidence ever being admissible in court.

One scholar provides a useful description: *"Spectral evidence refers to the* common belief that, when a person had made covenant with the devil, he was given permission to assume that person's appearance in spectral form in order to recruit others, and to otherwise carry out his nefarious deeds." Wendel D. Craker, *Spectral Evidence, Non-Spectral Acts of Witchcraft, and Confession at Salem in 1692*, 40 Historical Journal 331, 332 (1997). Alleged witchcraft victims testified that the specter of a witch would appear to them — often at night in their bedrooms — and urge them to cast their lot with the devil and his followers. For example, in the trial of George Burroughs, Mercy Lewis testified that she witnessed "the apparition of Mr. George Burroughs, whom I knew very well, which did grievously torture me, and urged me to write in his book." There were also claims that these specters would not only attempt to lure the victims into joining the devil's band of followers, but they would also threaten to inflict very real injury on the victims if the victims did not.

Only those self-selected victims with special sight could see specters, although it would be fair to say that many believed it. Spectral evidence was consistently admitted in the Salem trials, as a review of the trial documents establishes. Generally, it was admitted into trials in three different ways: testimony by observers about witnessing victims afflicted by specters; observations in the court of victims apparently being afflicted; and testimony by victims about spectral torment that occurred outside of the court.

In the first type of spectral evidence, there was testimony from observers about fits and strange behaviors of the girls believed to be afflicted by witches. For example, in the trial of George Burroughs, Thomas and Edward Putnam supplied affidavits stating that they heard Mercy Lewis declare that the defendants had appeared to her in a spectral form and that they "also beheld her tortures which we cannot express, for sometimes we were ready to fear that every joint of her body was ready to be displaced."

In the second category were in-court demonstrations of spectrally-caused discomfort, as occurred in the proceedings against Martha Corey and the others accused. Observer Deodat Lawson recorded one scene:

> It was observed several times, that if she [Goodwife Corey] did but bite her Under lip in time of Examination the persons afflicted were bitten on their armes and wrists and produced the Marks before the Magistrates, Ministers and others. And being watched for that, if she did but Pinch her Fingers, or Graspe one hand hard in another, they were Pinched and produced the Marks before the Magistrates, and Spectators. After that, it was observed, that if she did but lean her Breast against the Seat, in the Meeting House, (being the Barr at which she stood,) they were afflicted.

The third type of spectral evidence admitted was testimony by victims about events that they experienced in places other than the courtroom. They testified about their visions (specters as well as ghosts) and what these visions said or did to them. In George Burroughs' trial, for example, Ann Putnam testified that she was visited by the apparitions of two women who claimed to be Burroughs' [deceased] wives. They told Putnam that Burroughs had murdered them. Mercy Lewis testified that Burroughs had appeared to her and carried her off to a very high mountain, offering to give her his Kingdom, if only she would sign his book. She testified that when she refused Burroughs' offer, he tormented her dreadfully.

Wendel D. Craker argues compellingly that no defendants were tried or hanged on spectral evidence alone, but opines that the trials relied upon more traditional types of witchcraft evidence, what he terms "non-spectral acts of malefic witchcraft." Craker, *supra*, at 332. Many of these "non-spectral acts of malefic witchcraft" fit within the definition of syndrome evidence.

3. Syndrome Evidence

There are two categories within the type of evidence here termed "witchcraft syndrome" evidence. In the first, witnesses told stories about cattle dying after the accused had cursed them ("bewitched cattle syndrome"), or children becoming sick and dying after an unpleasant interaction with the accused ("bewitched child syndrome"). In this category the victims truly were afflicted physically, but the causative factor was deemed demonic, not biological; what Craker termed "acts of malefic witchcraft."

The second type of syndrome evidence consisted of observations of the alleged fits and bizarre symptomology of the victims ("spectral syndrome"). These behaviors may have been feigned, or they may have been real (or some of both); there is still no agreement about their cause. Nevertheless, these behaviors are within my definition of witchcraft syndrome evidence. Thus, the claims of "biting, pricking, burning, and poking" along with the writhing, strange movements, and the like, are also collected under this category of witchcraft syndrome evidence.

4. Profile Evidence

The category of evidence that this Article refers to as "witchcraft profile" includes (1) unusual physiological marks known to be characteristic of witches, such as a "witch's mark"; and (2) inexplicable attributes believed to be of demonic origin, such as unnatural strength or the inability to say the Lord's Prayer. As is true in contemporary cases, the use of profile evidence was far more limited than syndrome evidence in the Salem trials. . . .

Sarah Good

Sarah Good, one of the first three women accused of witchcraft by the affected girls, was indicted for acts committed upon Sarah Vibber, Elizabeth Hubbard, and Ann Putnam. The indictment accused Good of practicing "wicked arts" upon Vibber, by which Vibber "was and is tortured, afflicted, pined, consumed, wasted and tormented, and also alleged sundry other acts of witchcraft."

Like Bridget Bishop, Sarah Good lived on the fringes of Salem society, apparently panhandling and moving from household to household performing whatever tasks were provided. Samuel and Mary Abbey testified that they had let Sarah Good live with them, but had to turn her out, since "Sarah Good was so turbulent a spirit." Sarah's own husband had called her a witch and claimed "with tears that shee is an enimy to all good." Sarah Good's four-year-old daughter, Dorcas, confessed to witchcraft, going so far as to claim she had suckled a familiar, from a spot on her hand. Examiners observed a "deep red spot, about the bigness of a flea bite." Thus, the accusations of witchcraft against Sarah Good surprised few and likely upset even fewer.

When Sarah Good was examined in the court, the accusing girls were asked to "look upon her, and see, if this were the person that had hurt them." According to the transcribed testimony, as soon as the girls looked at Good and identified her as one who had harmed them "they were all tormented." Testimony was taken from a variety of witnesses who claimed to see the apparition of Sarah Good, whose torment included biting, pricking, and pinching the victim, as well as choking. In addition, Tituba had confessed to witchcraft and had inculpated Sarah Good, as did Dorcas Good (Sarah Good's daughter), Deliverance Hobbs, and Abigail Hobbs.

Samuel and Mary Abbey testified against Sarah Good. They first informed the court that they had permitted the Good family to live in their house, since the Goods were destitute. However, after they "could not suffer her to live in their howse any Longer," they "began to Lose Cattle, and Lost severall after an unusall Manner, in drupeing Condition and yett they would Eate: and your Deponenets have Lost after that manner 17 head of Cattle within two years, besides Sheep, and Hoggs: and both doe believe they Dyed by witchcraft."

Another witness, Sarah Gadge, told a similar story. After refusing Sarah Good entry into her house, Good began muttering and scolding. The very next morning, one of Gadge's cows died in "A Sudden, terible & Strange, unusuall maner soe that some of the neighbors & said Deponent did think it to be done by witchcraft." Despite their "opening" the cow after its death, Thomas Gadge, Sarah Gadge's husband, said they could find no natural cause for the cow's demise.

Two young men also testified that Good had bewitched their cattle. Henry Harrick testified that after his father sent Sarah Good away from his barn for fear that she would light the barn on fire with her pipe smoking, she replied that it would cost him one or two of his best cows. According to another young witness, fourteen year old Jonathon Batchelor, cattle were removed from their places and several had been set loose in a strange manner.

Sarah Vibber testified about being visited by the spectre of Sarah Good. Vibber claimed that Good had tormented her and her four-year old child. She claimed that her child had had a great fit and was almost impossible to hold. Vibber also testified that she had witnessed the spectre of Sarah Good tormenting Mercy Lewis.

Sarah Good's husband, William, testified that the night before his wife was examined on witchcraft charges, "he saw a wart or tett a little belowe her Right shoulder which he never saw before." Nevertheless, a physical examination of Good by a group of women failed to discover any unnatural findings. Sarah Good was found guilty, the death warrant was signed on July 12, and she was hanged on July 19, 1692. . . .

Rebecca Nurse

Rebecca Nurse and Martha Corey were named by the girls in the second wave of witchcraft accusations. Both Corey and Nurse were older women in good standing in the Salem community. Neither woman was prepared for the accusations, and even "Corey's sarcastic dismissal and Nurse's earnest bewilderment at the charges did not deter the growing number of unofficial witchfinders." Like Bishop and Good, Nurse was indicted for witchcraft as a result of the claims that she had "tortured afflicted consumed Pined wasted & tormented" the four complaining witnesses, Ann Putnam, Abigail Williams, Mary Walcott and Elizabeth Hubbard.

During her initial examination before the court, Rebecca Nurse was accused of tormenting the girls, which was graphically displayed by the complaining witnesses: "Ann Putnam in a grievous fit cryed out that she hurt her." When Nurse exclaimed "Oh Lord help me, & spread out her hands," the "afflicted were greviously vexed." When Nurse turned her head to the side, "so were the afflicted taken."

After the indictments were returned, dozens of residents signed a petition on behalf of Rebecca Nurse, claiming they never had any grounds to suspect her of anything for which she stood accused. Other residents were not of a similar mind. In addition to the standard allegations consisting of visionary spectral evidence, there were several instances of syndrome evidence.

The Reverend Samuel Parris, Nathaniel Ingersol, and Thomas Putnam provided testimony that they had witnessed the torture of Ann Putnam senior, her daughter Ann, Mary Walcott, and Abigail Williams during the examination of Rebecca Nurse. Thomas and Edward Putnam testified that they had witnessed Ann Putnam during and after her fits and saw her "much afflicted, being bitten, pinched, her limbs distorted, & pins thrust into her flesh, which she charged on Rebekah Nurse that she was the Acter thereof & that she saw her do it." They also claimed they observed, during the examination, that when Nurse "did clinch her hands, bite her lips, or hold her head aside the said Putnam Hubbard & Williams was set in the same posture to her great torture & affliction."

John and Hannah Putnam related a particularly upsetting incident about the death of their infant, although he had been thriving in the first eight weeks of life. Hannah Putnam testified that after she had "reported" information about Nurse, she was "taken with strange kinds of fits," but recovered quickly. Her child, however, did not fare as well. She stated that quickly after her recovery, "our poor young child was taken about midnight with strange and violent fits which did most grievously affright us, acting much like to the poor bewitched persons, when we thought they would indeed have died." The child's grandmother (also a Putnam), said that she "feared an evil hand upon it." The child's "strange and violent fits" continued on for two days, until he succumbed to "a cruel and violent death."

Sarah Houlton testified about another incident linking death to Nurse's alleged witchcraft. She claimed that one Saturday morning, Rebecca Nurse yelled at Sarah's husband, Benjamin, because his pigs had gotten into her field. Nurse would not be placated, but continued "railing and scolding a great while together." Within a short time, Benjamin Houlton was "taken with a strange fit in the entry, being struck blind and struck down two or three times." He continued to languish through the summer, suffering stomach pains and attacks of blindness. Two weeks before he died, however, he was "taken with strange and violent fits." The implication of this testimony was that Nurse had bewitched him.

As with Bridget Bishop, the examining women found evidence on Rebecca Nurse of a "preternatural excrescence of flesh between the pudendum and anus, much like teats, and not usual in women." However, upon later examination, "instead of that excrescence within mentioned, it appears only as a dry skin without sense [i.e. without sensation]." Nurse was found guilty and she was hanged on July 19, 1692. . . .

NOTES & QUESTIONS

1.   In the fall of 1692 — less than a year after the Salem witchcraft trials began — several Puritans publicly criticized the proceedings. Increase Mather, a prominent minister, singled out spectral evidence as a problem. He did not condemn the judges or deny the existence of witches, but he condemned convictions based on witnesses' assertions that the Devil had appeared in the spectral form of the accused. The merchant and scientist Thomas Brattle seconded Mather's indictment of spectral evidence, and he also complained about the use of a "touching test" in court.

On October 12, 1692, Governor William Phips stopped the trials. He was probably influenced not only by Mather and Brattle but also by allegations that his own wife was a witch. At the time of the Governor's decree 52 accused men and women were awaiting trial. The great majority of them had confessed, no doubt in hopes of saving their lives. All but two of the accused were acquitted, and the Governor granted reprieves to those two.

2.   The secondary literature on the Salem witchcraft trials is immense, but one useful volume focusing on just the legal aspects of the controversy is Peter Charles Hoffer's *The Salem Witchcraft Trials — A Legal History* (1997).

3.   While Arthur Miller's *The Crucible* and the film of the same name invite reflection on McCarthyism, other important films portray the McCarthy Period directly. Woody Allen's *The Front* (1976) presents a picture of the era and features formerly blacklisted actors Herschel Bernardi and Zero Mostel. More recently, George Clooney directed, co-wrote, and starred in another film about the period, *Good Night, and Good Luck* (2005), in which David Strathairn played veteran broadcaster Edward R. Murrow, who took a stand against Senator McCarthy. Clooney played producer Fred Friendly. The film received six 2006 Oscar nominations, including for Best Picture, Best Director, and Best Actor.

4.   Senator McCarthy's eventual downfall was due in part to a confrontation with attorney Joseph Welch in a televised Congressional hearing. In one of Hollywood's most intriguing casting decisions, director Otto Preminger put Welch into the role of Judge Harlan Weaver in *Anatomy of a Murder* (1959). Welch had no acting credits, but his careful, restrained portrayal of the judge proved quite effective.

5.   Suppose that the witnesses had accused the defendants not of witchcraft but rather of child abuse. Would your reaction to them be different? In fact, a number of child abuse prosecutions have been initiated by nothing more than the say-so of witnesses whose stories collapsed when carefully examined. *See, e.g., The McMartin Preschool Abuse Trials: 1987-90*, at http://www.law.umkc. edu/faculty/projects/

ftrials/mcmartin.html. In 1995, James Woods, Mercedes Ruehl, Lolita Davidovich, and other gifted actors starred in Abby and Myra Mann's *Indictment: The McMartin Trial.* You may remember that Abby Mann won a 1962 Academy Award for his screenplay adaptation for *Judgment at Nuremberg* (1961). He and Myra Mann received an Edgar nomination for the *Indictment* script. For more information about the actual trial, see Professor Douglas Linder's *Famous Trials* page, *The McMartin Preschool Abuse Trials*, at http://law2.umkc.edu/faculty/projects/ftrials/mcmartin/mcmartin.html.

6. Do you see issues or events today that could be transformed into "witch hunting" episodes? Do you think that the call to place patriotism above loyalty to family and friends, especially if citizens have no real knowledge of someone's terrorist affiliations, might become a weapon for "witch hunters"?

Consider, for example, the actions of many governments after the events of 9/11, in wishing to find members of terrorist groups and in asking citizens, in effect, to inform on neighbors, friends, or even family members if they thought those people might be dangerous. In the United States, the Department of Justice launched Operation TIPS (Terrorism Information and Prevention System) to "involve" the "millions of American workers who, in the daily course of their work, are in a unique position to see potentially unusual or suspicious activity in public places."

See http://www.dojgov.net/tips_main_page.pdf. The Department also expanded the existing Neighborhood Watch program, to provide community residents "with information which will enable them to recognize signs of potential terrorist activity, and to know how to report that activity. . . ." *See* http://www.dojgov.net/tips_neighborhood_watch_program.pdf. The American Civil Liberties Union opposed the program. (http://www.aclu.org/stop-government-turning-neighbor-against-neighbor) and Business Week suggested that the DOJ's idea was "un-American." Jane Black, *Some TIPS For John Ashcroft*, July 25, 2002, at http://www.businessweek.com/bwdaily/dnflash/jul2002/nf20020725_8083.htm.

C.   FINDING, EMPLOYING, AND CAJOLING WITNESSES

Witnesses are taken to be crucial in the contemporary adjudicatory system. Law enforcement begins looking for witnesses as soon as a crime is reported. Lawyers on both sides of a case interview witnesses and might call them to the stand, presumably to influence neutral adjudicators. Lawyers might also present documents and forensic evidence, but human beings speaking about what they saw, heard, and even smelled is central in the quest for fair and just decisions.

Not surprisingly, popular culture frequently depicts the finding, use, and treatment of witnesses as central to a case. Witnesses themselves can be important characters in films, television series, plays, and novels. An especially poignant story might be told about a witness who is needed to win a case but who, for one of many reasons, is reluctant to testify. In the film *Witness* (1985), for example, Detective John Book, played by Harrison Ford, must work hard to win the trust of cautious, frightened members of an Amish community including Rachel Lapp, played by Kelly McGillis, and her son. The testimony of the latter will make or break Book's effort to demonstrate that high-level police corruption has occurred. Likewise, in

Conviction (2010), Betty Anne Waters and her colleagues spend days trying to convince a reluctant former girlfriend of Kenny's to recant her testimony.

Sometimes a judge is asked to order a witness to testify. In the film *My Cousin Vinny*, for example, attorney Vinny Gambini has a difficult time with a number of witnesses, but he perseveres after realizing that the only way to save his clients is to discredit the testimony of the prosecution witnesses. One of his own witnesses, his fiancée Mona Lisa Vito, played by Marisa Tomei, is in fact a hostile witness, and he must resort to asking the trial judge to order Vito to answer his questions.

One problem with witnesses is the so-called "bystander effect." In some cases, people are reluctant to try to halt a crime in progress, or to assist a victim, even by calling the police, because they "don't want to get involved." They even refuse when they face no repercussions — that is, they can report the crime absolutely anonymously. Some psychologists say they have traced this reluctance to the horrific attack on Catherine (Kitty) Genovese, a young New Yorker, who was raped and stabbed to death at her apartment building on March 13, 1964, reportedly while 38 of her neighbors heard her lengthy cries for help and did nothing to intervene. *The New York Times* published an angry article that presented this view of her death, which has become the popularly accepted version. *See* Martin Gansberg, "37 Who Saw Murder Didn't Call the Police," *The New York Times*, 27 Mar. 1964, 1, 38.

THE PHYSIOGNOMIC TURN
Carrie A. Rentschler
4 International Journal of Communication 231 (2010)

The story of Kitty Genovese's murder was that 38 of her neighbors watched or heard Winston Moseley, an African-American business machine operator and family man, assault and kill Genovese, a lesbian barkeep, but did not call the police. The story of her witnesses was used to transform criminal justice practice, urban crime prevention, and psychological research on bystanders up to the present. Among other things, it serves as the founding myth on which the social psychological theory of mass society "bystander effects" is based. The story of the 38 witnesses is taught in every introduction to psychology textbook in the United States and Britain, and in many other countries as well, and has been made popularly known through television programs and books, such as Alan Moore's, Dave Gibbons' and John Higgins' 1986 graphic novel *Watchmen* and Malcolm Gladwell's 2000 bestseller *The Tipping Point*. . . .

As a tale of public inaction and white anomie, the Genovese murder was at once both specific to middle-class Kew Gardens and argued to indicate a national epidemic of urban apathy. Its story created "a peculiar physiognomy of the subject," a subject who was neither the killer nor the victim, but the "made up subjects" of urban witnessing. The place of the crime and the face of the victim became facial markers for a national imagination of street crime, proxies for the mental life of the metropolis. The murder site sat at the confluence of commercial, communication, and transportation infrastructures connecting Kew Gardens to Manhattan. A host of urban/suburban encounters were enabled by these infrastructures and their classed, raced, and sexed mobilities. The physiognomy of witness to Genovese's murder reveals this network of encounters. It also reveals the attempts the city and its neighborhoods made to manage encounters and meanings across social differ-ence, especially white fear of black crime and white distrust of African Americans.

NOTES AND QUESTIONS

1.   Later research has shown that Ms. Genovese's wounds, to her thoracic cavity and lungs, meant that she could not have screamed for help for half an hour. Further, her attacker actually left, then returned. None of her neighbors is likely to have seen all of the attack, or to have understood that it was as serious as it later turned out to be. And two of them actually did phone police for assistance. Yet the story of the seemingly indifferent neighbors is now a staple of popular culture. Songwriter Phil Ochs (1940-1976) is famous for "Outside Of a Small Circle of Friends," inspired by the accounts of Genovese's death. Abe Rosenthal's book *Thirty-Eight Witnesses: The Kitty Genovese Case* (1964), which the University of California Press reprinted in 1999, presents as a kind of morality play and commentary on the alienation of American society. A 1975 television movie, *Death Scream*, dramatized the events, and a *Law & Order* episode, "Remand" (aired January 10, 1996), used the story as a basis for its plot.

2.   Why do we seem to find "witness in danger" movies so interesting? Think about movies like *Witness*, *Narrow Margin* (1990), *GoodFellas* (1990), *My Blue Heaven* (1990), *Sister Act* (1992), *The Client* (1994), *Did You Hear About the Morgans?* (2009), the television movie *Mystery Woman: Oh Baby* (2006), and yes, even *Our Lips Are Sealed* (2000) with the unforgettable Mary Kate and Ashley Olsen, as well as the television series *In Plain Sight* (2008 — present). What do these movies, and the novels on which some of them are based, say about the reluctance of witnesses to come forward and the ability of law enforcement to protect them? What about the reasons witnesses resist testifying? What mecha-nisms and inducements do society and the legal system use to persuade or force them to testify? How does popular culture present these mechanisms and induce-ments? If these witnesses die, does this sad end send a real message to potential witnesses that the legal system cannot protect them? (That is, do you think viewers take stories about the Federal Witness Protection Program, for example, seriously?)

3.   If you want to read the entire "trial transcript" from *My Cousin Vinny*, consult this link, provided by a professor at Indiana University School of Law (Bloomington)   (http://www.law.indiana.edu/instruction/tanford/web/movies/My CousinVinny.htm).

4.   In the next excerpt, Professor Russell Dean Covey discusses some of the reasons a witness might refuse to testify and how that decision might affect the outcome of the trial.

BEATING THE PRISONER AT PRISONER'S DILEMMA: THE EVIDENTIARY VALUE OF A WITNESS'S REFUSAL TO TESTIFY

Russell Dean Covey

47 American University Law Review 105 (1997)

The reasons for non-cooperation might be as numerous as there are witnesses, but reasons powerful enough to compel a witness to suffer the heavy sanctions resulting from citation for civil contempt and criminal contempt or both are more limited. In most cases when a witness refuses to testify despite lacking a legitimate fear of self-incrimination, non-cooperation is likely to stem from one of four main reasons.

First, a witness might refuse to testify in fear of the defendant. Although understandable, such refusal is not legally cognizable, and the witness will still be subject to civil or criminal contempt charges. If a witness's fear of a defendant is sufficient to compel that witness to violate a court order and place himself in contempt of court, an adverse inference would seem especially warranted. It would be perverse for a defendant's coercive threats to allow the defendant to escape punishment while the victim of that coercion, the witness, goes to jail. The Federal Rules of Evidence already provide for admission of hearsay statements where the unavailability of a witness results from the coercive or obstructive efforts by the defendant. Thus, where a legitimate fear of violent retaliation motivates the witness's refusal to testify, there seems to be ample justification for drawing adverse inferences based on the witness's behavior.

Second, a witness may refuse to testify out of a desire to adhere to a code of silence. The force of the code of silence, or omerta, may spring from internal assimilation of a set of values adverse to the duties imposed by the criminal justice system. It also may be enforced from without by other members of the criminal organization seeking to quiet "squealers," perhaps with extreme threats of force and violence. If the fear stems from other members of the criminal organization, an agency theory subjecting each member of the conspiracy to liability for all the other members justifies a finding that the defendant is at least derivatively responsible for suborning the contemptuous act of the witness. As argued below, it is reasonable and consistent with the evidentiary rules to allow inferences adverse to the defendant to be derived from the witness's own internalized refusal in this context.

The fact that the refusal springs not from a realistic threat of retaliation, but rather from the witness's own internalized acceptance of the code against cooperation, does not significantly alter the logic of the argument. Fear that the testimony may diminish the esteem in which a witness is held in his or her community, or may affect the witness's status, is not a legally cognizable basis to withhold testimony. If the witness and defendant both mutually participate in a shared "culture of conspiracy" that valorizes criminal behavior and demonizes cooperation with the legal authorities, the defendant should share responsibility for the creation and maintenance of the ethic against cooperation. While punishing a defendant for participation in a particular culture goes against the grain of a criminal justice system constructed to punish individual culpability, it does not eliminate altogether the doctrine of individual autonomy. In a multicultural society such as urban

America, the choice to join and strengthen the culture of conspiracy reflects the autonomous decision of the organization's participants.

Third, a witness may refuse to testify out of fear that he or she may at a later date be prosecuted for perjury. Although the witness has no immediate fear of self-incrimination, he or she could be subjected to criminal prosecution for lying on the stand. The witness might therefore argue that the Fifth Amendment privilege should prevent him or her from providing the grounds for incrimination. Although this argument is made frequently in criminal contempt proceedings, it obviously does not withstand scrutiny.

First, no witness has a right to invent testimony with impunity. Second, because the witness has been immunized, truthful testimony cannot provide any basis for incrimination, and the witness cannot be prosecuted for prior perjured testimony based on contradictory testimony later given under oath. Any remaining incentive to lie must spring, therefore, not from the witness's own fear of self-incrimination, but from reluctance to implicate a conspirator. If that reluctance fuels the defendant's desire to avoid testifying, the adverse influence is again justified.

Finally, the witness simply may have a powerful desire not to incriminate the defendant. It is, of course, this last reason that provides the strongest basis both for allowing the witness's refusal to testify to occur before the jury, and for an adverse inference to be drawn against the defendant. If the witness has no real fear of self-incrimination, the willingness to suffer what appears to be the comparatively minor penalty of criminal contempt in hopes of preventing a coconspirator from receiving a long criminal sentence is rational as an organizational or conspiratorial strategy. The tactic of making the witness refuse to testify in front of the jury should be permitted in order to undermine this strategy.

In short, although the ambiguous evidentiary value of a witness's rightful invocation of the privilege makes that evidence less probative of the defendant's culpability, the problem of ambiguity is substantially reduced when the witness no longer possesses the right to refuse to testify. While giving testimony that implicates the witness in criminal activity may be embarrassing to the witness, the refusal to testify in the face of a court order is unlikely to be motivated by mere embarrassment. The removal of this fundamental ambiguity dramatically transforms the underlying context and restructures the logical interferences that naturally flow from the act of non-cooperation.

Some courts, in sorting out the circumstances under which the forced invocation of the privilege can be sanctioned, have distinguished between the "ordinary witness" and those witnesses who are "so closely connected with the defendant by the facts of the case, the pleadings, or relationship, that the inferences of the witness's guilt would likely be imputed to the defendant." While forcing witnesses who fall into the latter category to invoke their privilege before the jury might unavoidably prejudice the defendant, "it may well be proper in some cases to have the proceeding in the presence of the jury where the government is dealing with" witnesses of the more ordinary variety. This approach seems logical when the witness invokes a Fifth Amendment privilege, because the very certainty that accompanies the invocation is likely to taint the defendant. If the witness has the right to invoke a privilege, the logic is reversed. When a defendant has no justifiable fear of self-incrimination, the close relationship with the defendant creates a powerful inference that the witness is refusing to testify in order to protect the defendant. An adverse inference therefore becomes much more appropriate. In contrast, "ordinary witnesses" who lack such a relationship with the defendant, yet refuse to testify, are much more likely to have other reasons for refusing to cooperate aside from protecting the defendant.

NOTES & QUESTIONS

1. Do you find a law enforcement animus in Professor Covey's comments? Would his reasoning be less persuasive if one did not have the prosecution of organized crime participants in mind?

2. What dramatic potential exists in each of the types of refusal to testify discussed by Covey? How might each type be used in a film or other pop cultural work?

D.   EYEWITNESSES

The verdicts in many actual and pop cultural cases depend on the availability of eyewitness testimony. However, as the following excerpt from an article by Robert Hallisey indicates, social and scientific researchers have serious concerns about how eyewitness testimony is received and the extent to which eyewitness testimony can be trusted. Hallisey also discusses the extent to which expert testimony regarding the formation and reliability of the memories of eyewitnesses might be helpful in a trial.

EXPERTS ON EYEWITNESS TESTIMONY IN COURT — A SHORT HISTORICAL PERSPECTIVE
Robert Hallisey
39 Howard Law Journal 237 (1995)

II. Eyewitness Reliability

A. The Concern

At the root of our criminal justice system is the premise that "[i]t is far worse to convict an innocent man than let a guilty man go free." Thus, we presume defendants not guilty. They need not testify; and the jury may not draw negative inferences from the defendant's choice not to testify. The prosecution bears the burden of convincing all the jurors beyond a reasonable doubt that an identification is correct.

Yet, "[t]he annals of criminal law are rife with instances of misidentifications." For example, the *Newsmagazine of the Center for Responsive Psychology* describes eight cases in which witnesses confused people who resembled each other with the real subject. Wagenaar and Loftus, Bedau and Radelet, and Rattner all provide samples of recent miscarriages of justice, with erroneous eyewitness testimony playing a central role in most examples. Kassin and Wrightsman describe a typical miscarriage where seven restaurant employees, all white, identified the defendant as the robber, even though he was six feet tall and they had said the robber was five feet, six inches. The defendant had no criminal record, and nine of his co-workers testified that he was at work, fifty miles away, at the time of the robbery. He was nevertheless convicted. The prosecution dropped the charges, after the defendant had already served one year in jail, when four of the original witnesses changed their minds and identified another person.

Although it appears that eyewitness identification provides an especially knotty problem for jury fact-finders, it is nearly impossible to discern how jurors actually analyze witnesses' testimony because of the confidentiality of jury deliberations. Many judges advise jurors not to discuss their deliberations with anyone. Occasionally, however, the course of their deliberations can be pieced together from individual juror's reports concerning a verdict. For example, some reports suggest that jurors often attempt to reenact key events involved in the case. But such juror reports are always incomplete and of uncertain reliability. Consequently, social research involving experiments and statistical analysis of results, usually based on mock juries rather than on actual juries, is the major source of information about jury deliberation.

B. Milestones in Research

Most scholars would cite the research by Professor Hugo Munsterberg at the turn of the century as the first major application of behavioral science methods and theories to eyewitness evidence in this country. In his book, *On the Witness Stand* [1908], Professor Munsterberg notes that common beliefs, even among judges, have been proven invalid by psychological experiments. "[C]ases . . . show that the psychological inspirations of the bench are often directly the opposite of demonstrable facts." Honest witnesses often give contrary testimony, but judges refuse to accept evidence from psychologists that could help fact-finders sort out the truth.

Munsterberg found that associations, suggestions, and expectations played a large role in witnesses' recollection and reported observations. He also claimed that psychology could point out the unreliability of some types of testimony such as the sources of sounds (front or back), tastes from different parts of the tongue, estimated distances, and reports of tactile sensation (for example, something wet is often confused with something smooth, cold, and metal).

Munsterberg believed that, without psychological assistance, fact-finders could go astray in many instances. "[C]onfidence in the reliability of memory is so general that the suspicion of memory illusions evidently plays a small role in the mind of the juryman. . . . Justice would less often miscarry if all who are to weigh evidence were more conscious of the treachery of human memory." For example, classic studies of perception and memory, conducted beginning in the 1940s, show that individual experience is not recorded on a clean slate; rather, it is immediately interpreted against the background of the observer's experience, biases, prejudices, and preconceptions. In a famous experiment by Professor Gordon Allport at Harvard University, a photograph was shown to students in which a white man, holding a straight razor, was threatening a black man. Social stereotypes led students to report that the black man held the razor.

Robert Buckhout, a professor at Brooklyn College Center for Responsive Psychology who testified extensively as an expert in cases involving eyewitness evidence, has criticized judges who exclude expert testimony on the grounds that it is an invasion on the province of the jury, and has encouraged experts to continue their efforts to testify. He has also criticized form jury instructions on evaluation of identification testimony. "For the most part, the recommended instructions for judges to give to juries are relatively simplistic, very contradictory and totally devoid of any reference to scientific findings." Referring to *U.S. v. Telfaire*, he somewhat grudgingly describes the recommended instructions as "[n]ot bad on the vagaries of initial perception, but they neglect the problems of testing recognition such as in line-ups and contain no reference to date." He thus suggests that "in any trial, a judge who is not close-minded or threatened may allow a psychologist to testify on the problems of eyewitness identification providing that the psychologist is qualified and that the testimony is relevant." But he expresses some pessimism about the widespread use of this " 'new' type of expert testimony since it carries with it the threat of reform; [and] reform in the criminal justice system will always be resisted."

Professor Buckhout buttressed his opinions by conducting research involving sixteen factors in three areas that were shown to affect the unreliability of eyewitnesses: (1) with reference to the *original situation*: significance of the event, shortness of period of observation, and observation conditions; (2) with reference to the *witness*: stress, physical condition, prior conditioning and experience, personal biases, needs and motives, and desire to be part of history; and (3) with reference to the situation in which the eyewitness's *memory is tested*: length of time from event to test, filling in details that were not there, suggestions from the test procedure (line-up, photo array), suggestions from test giver, conformity, relation to authority figures, and passing on a theory ("the self-fulfilling prophecy").

Other research has also fortified the attack on the reliability of eyewitness testimony. For example, there exists a common belief that deception can best be discovered by watching the faces and bodies of witnesses, but studies have shown that the most accurate detection occurs when only the witness's words are heard. In addition, research findings show that, frequently, eyewitnesses are simply inaccurate. In "staged" crime events, witness reports varied markedly from the facts, and over half of the relevant details were not reported. Other studies show great disparity in reports of suspect height and duration of an incident. They also reveal that cross-racial identifications are less reliable than same-race identifications, and, furthermore, witnesses are often influenced in what they believe they observe by their subjective expectations. Stereotyping and prejudice also seem to affect reports. These findings, coupled with the effects of memory loss over time, have caused many, including Buckhout, to conclude that research psychologists should be used as expert witnesses in trials.

Elizabeth Loftus is the most publicly visible expert in this country on the strengths and weaknesses of eyewitness testimony. She is best known for studies demonstrating that the presentation of conflicting (and sometimes deliberately misleading) information about a scene or a narrative — for instance, a slide show depicting a traffic accident — can dramatically interfere with peoples' ability to report what they originally observed. Elizabeth F. Loftus, David G. Miller, & Helen J. Burns, *Semantic Integration of Verbal Information into a Visual Memory*, 4 Journal of Experimental Psychology: Human Learning and Memory 19 (1978). For example, asking subjects misleading questions about the presence of traffic signs at an intersection was shown to reduce accuracy on a subsequent memory test from seventy-five percent to forty-one percent.

In another representative study, Loftus and her colleagues questioned thirty-two preschool children after they viewed four short films. Philip S. Dale, Elizabeth F. Loftus, & Linda Rathbun, *The Influence of the Form of the Question on the Eyewitness Testimony of Preschool Children*, 7 Journal of Psycholinguistic Research 269 (1978). The results showed that the children's recollections concerning entities actually present in the films were quite accurate. "Leading" questions involving entities not in the film, however, were mostly answered in the affirmative. The experiment thus confirmed the hypothesis that children are susceptible to suggestion, are affected by leading questions, and are prone to answer in accord with the suggestion.

In [her 1979 book] *Eyewitness Testimony*, Loftus acknowledges that she developed her consuming interest in the subject by learning of cases where defendants were falsely identified, particularly the case of Edmond D. Jackson. Jackson was incarcerated for eight years before the Second Circuit in 1978 set aside his conviction as fatally flawed by suggestive police investigative procedures.

Loftus challenges, as wholly incorrect, the commonly held belief that information once acquired by the memory system is unchangeable. To the contrary, Loftus asserts that evidence supports her conclusion "[t]hat once memory for some event is distorted by interweaving events, the information acquired during perception of the original event may never be accurately re-acquired." Yet Loftus also contends that, in terms of persuasiveness, "[a]n eyewitness identification and the victim's memory of the incident . . . are far more important than any other characteristics a witness possesses, such as age, race, or level of income." Additionally, the degree of confidence expressed by such witnesses and ability to speak in a forceful tone combined to lend considerable credibility to their testimony.

Loftus also conducted experiments to evaluate the validity of laypersons' beliefs about eyewitness testimony. Overall she found that 45% of the subjects asked to evaluate factors affecting eyewitness testimony were wrong. Thirteen percent thought white persons could identify a black man more easily than they could a white man. Although 90% understood the effects of leading questions on eyewitness accuracy, one-third failed to give correct answers about the effects of extreme stress on reliability. Finally, Loftus' studies revealed that only 40% appreciated the effects of "weapon focus" on reliability and only 18% correctly indicated the effects of the violence of an event on reliability.

In her 1980 book, *Memory*, Loftus wrote that people can come to believe they saw and heard things that never really happened. She also found that memory is malleable and that people use "refabrication" to "[s]upply bits and pieces, largely unconsciously, to fill out fairly incomplete knowledge." In addition, she found that people "[t]end to rewrite history more in line with what they think they ought to have done than with what they actually did." She cites instances where suggestions from third persons became part of and were incorporated into the listener's memory.

Addressing memory in the courtroom context, she concluded: "According to the cliché — memory fades. In fact, however, it grows! . . . Every time we recall an event, we must reconstruct the memory, and so each time it is changed, colored by succeeding events, increased understanding, a new context, suggestion by others, other people's recollections."

The conclusions from a large chorus of behavioral science researchers reinforce doubts about the reliability of eyewitness testimony, and most conclude that expert testimony can be useful. A staunch cadre of scientific researchers, however, is much more skeptical about the utility of conclusions concerning eyewitness memory that are based almost exclusively on laboratory testing.

C. Can Experts Help? The Public Debate Among Psychologists over the Utility of Expert Testimony

Taking a strong opposing view concerning the utility of expert testimony on eyewitness reliability, Johns Hopkins University Professors Michael McCloskey and Howard Egeth asserted in May, 1983, that "it is by no means clear that expert psychological testimony about eyewitnesses would improve jurors' ability to evaluate eyewitness testimony." They suggested that such testimony could "[i]n fact have detrimental effects." Michael McCloskey & Howard Egeth, *Eyewitness Identification: What Can a Psychologist Tell a Jury?* 38 American Psychologist 550, 550 (May 1983). Furthermore, they argued there was no empirical evidence that people in general are ignorant of the problems with eyewitness testimony; and, moreover, recent studies cast doubt on the conclusions reached by Loftus in her 1974 and 1979 studies.

They cite instances in which eyewitness testimony was apparently disbelieved and point out a number of situations in which jurors believed that the defendant was probably guilty, but concluded that the evidence was insufficient for conviction. They showed that the ratio of convictions in cases where there was at least one eyewitness identification of the defendant to convictions in cases without such identification was only 1.1 to 1. They conceded, however, that jurors cannot readily discriminate accurate from inaccurate eyewitnesses.

McCloskey and Egeth also cited a study which found that where witness viewing conditions varied principally by duration from poor to moderate to good, jurors were able to ascribe credibility to the better viewing conditions, indicating that they had taken at least that factor correctly into account. In the study, identifications were 33%, 50%, and 74% accurate; the juror belief rates for each of these identifications was 62%, 66%, and 77%, respectively. McCloskey and Egeth conceded that, while these figures make it "[c]lear that jurors' ability to discriminate accurate from inaccurate witnesses is far from perfect," jurors do take relevant factors into account when evaluating witness accuracy.

Turning to the possible effect of expert psychological testimony on jurors' ability to discriminate accurate from inaccurate eyewitnesses, the authors found only one relevant study that provided a direct comparison between results in a case where jurors received expert advice and a case where they did not. McCloskey and Egeth asserted that this study showed that expert testimony had "absolutely no effect on jurors' ability to *discriminate* accurate from inaccurate witnesses." The expert testimony only appeared to reduce jurors' overall willingness to believe eyewitnesses.

McCloskey and Egeth then challenged the conventional wisdom that cross-race identifications are more error-prone than intra-racial identifications, as based on overly complex questions. As to "weapon focus" (witnesses' tendency to selectively direct their attention to threatening objects, rather than to the perpetrator) and stress experienced during the course of a crime event, they pointed to research showing that, while ten studies found decreases in eyewitness accuracy under stress, nine studies found that stress increased accuracy or had no effect on accuracy.

Elizabeth Loftus replied to McCloskey and Egeth, re-asserting her argument that the well-documented cases of innocent people wrongly convicted based on faulty eyewitness accounts require experts to educate the jury. Loftus also criticized McCloskey and Egeth for "us[ing] experimental evidence to support their views and yet attack[ing] those very same studies when they run counter to their prevailing view."

Loftus reiterated her firm conviction that post-event information can modify a person's recollection and stated that hundreds of experiments demonstrate this phenomenon. She also defended the "battle of experts" that plays out in many courtrooms by arguing that use of experts can often avoid tragic effects — for example, as in the case of the drug thalidomide in the 1950s. She claimed that science need not be perfect to be useful in the courtroom. . . .

D. Impact of Erroneous Eyewitness Testimony on the Jury

Many American trial and appellate courts have acted as though unreliable eyewitness testimony is not a major threat to the validity of the legal fact-finding process. In comparison to European authorities, American practice includes fewer proscriptions and safeguards concerning eyewitness evidence.

It is not surprising that the roles of professionals involved in the justice system reflect their attitudes toward eyewitness testimony and its "handling" in jury trials. One survey of Florida defense and prosecuting attorneys, county sheriffs, and police departments about eyewitness testimony revealed that prosecuting attorneys and law enforcement officers regard eyewitness identification as generally accurate and believed that judges and juries appropriately emphasized its importance. In contrast, defense attorneys surveyed felt that such identifications are often inaccurate and overemphasized by jurors and judges, and that over-reliance on such evidence is a serious problem. Defense attorneys also were likely to endorse the admission of testimony by psychologists and other researchers as expert witnesses.

Deffenbacher and Loftus contended that "[t]he American judiciary have traditionally viewed knowledge of variables affecting eyewitness performance as part of common understanding." Kenneth A. Deffenbacher & Elizabeht F. Loftus, *Do*

Jurors Share a Common Understanding Concerning Eyewitness Behavior? 6 Law and Human Behavior 15, 15 (1982). They also point out inconsistencies in judicial treatment of expert testimony, with many judges excluding such testimony as invading the province of the jury. *Id.*, at 16.

A. Daniel Yarmey and Hazel P. Tressillian Jones also addressed this question, stating that "[j]urors have been deliberating about questions regarding perception and memory for over 200 years and there is nothing new a psychologist can tell us about these processes." A. Daniel Yarmey & Hazel P. Tressillian Jones, "Is the Psychology of Eyewitness Identification a Matter of Common Sense?" *in Evaluating Witness Evidence: Research and New Perspectives* 13 (Sally M. Lloyd-Bostock & Brian R. Clifford eds. 1983). Yet, in a survey they conducted among judges, lawyers, law students, potential jurors, and experimental psychologists to test this hypothesis, they found ninety percent of the experts agreed that extreme stress reduces the ability to notice and remember details of an event, whereas few potential jurors thought so. Also, ninety-five percent of the experts agreed that witnesses generally overestimate the duration of crimes, whereas fewer than half of the potential jurors did so. Yarmey and Jones concluded that "[t]he findings of this study strongly support our contention that knowledge about the psychological variables that influence eyewitness identification and testimony does not fall within the province of common knowledge." *Id.*, at 33. Furthermore, "[t]his study suggests that the adversary system, in and of itself, is not necessarily sufficient to safeguard against miscarriages of justice when the question of the reliability of the eyewitness arises." *Id.*, at 39.

In 1980 Reid Hastie wrote: "Granted that there is scientific evidence concerning the reliability of eyewitness testimony, there is no evidence that eyewitness unreliability introduces important errors into the trial fact-finding process." In reviewing the extent of literature on eyewitness testimony, he found the prevailing view was "[t]hat men perceive visually like a videotape, and remember auditorially like a tape recorder." Reid Hastie, *From Eyewitness Testimony to Beyond Reasonable Doubt*, unpublished paper presented at the Annual Meeting of the Law and Society Association and the Research Committee on Sociology of Law of the International Sociological Association (1980).

Hastie, in conjunction with the author, conducted a study regarding jury evaluations of eyewitness testimony that found seven aspects of eyewitness testimony that were neglected in jury deliberations: (1) selective attention during encoding; (2) the possibility of directly suggestive police behavior (that is, communication of bias through nonverbal or subtle verbal cues); (3) the possibility of the non-independence of two witness identifications (for example, influence of a confident, high status witness on a second witness); (4) the possibility of distortion, elaboration, or additions to witnesses' memories during the retention interval; (5) the significance of witnesses' non-responses to "distractors" or "lures" (non-target individuals) during identification procedures; (6) witnesses' consistent selection of the same individual across identification procedures; and (7) discussion of the characteristics of "lure" individuals presented as "distractors" in identification procedures.

More important, there were two persistent errors of "commission" concerning human memory that appeared repeatedly in jury deliberations. First, a substantial number of jurors argued that high levels of stress and emotionality would create a "flashbulb effect" such that memories from a threatening or violent crime scene would be especially strong, vivid, and accurate. Second, jurors appeared to rely heavily on witnesses who expressed confidence in their testimony, although research has shown that confidence is a relatively poor index of eyewitness identification accuracy.

Hastie concluded that these results provide the "missing link" identified by Wigmore and demonstrate that potentially unreliable eyewitness testimony combined with erroneous beliefs about eyewitness accuracy threaten the validity of jury decisions based primarily on eyewitness testimony. He further argued that the evidence of juror errors in the evaluation of eyewitness testimony supports the claim that expert testimony can aid the factfinder (jury) in such cases.

William M. O'Barr, in his book *Linguistic Evidence*, concluded that the credibility ascribed to a witness often was not based on factors that judges thought important but was influenced by the language used by witnesses and their manner of delivery. William M. O'Barr, *Linguistic Evidence* 27 (1992). He concluded that narrative answers by calm witnesses using familiar words without long hesitations and exaggerations or qualifications had the most impact. In addition, the use of powerful, active words and analogies carried more credibility. Hyper-correct language also seemed to carry less credibility (for example, "transport" instead of "carry"; "not cognizant" instead of "unaware"). Like Loftus and others cited above, O'Barr was sharply critical of the courts' reliance on experts on blood and handwriting while neglecting to examine the memory report of a witness.

John C. Brigham and Robert K. Bothwell also were concerned with the ability of prospective jurors to estimate the accuracy of eyewitness identification. John C. Brigham and Robert K. Bothwell, *The Ability of Prospective Jurors to Estimate the Accuracy of Eyewitness Identification*, 7 Law and Human Behavior 19 (1983). Using actual empirical studies on eyewitness identification involving "target-present" line-ups, the researchers presented the prospective jurors with scenarios derived from the previously conducted studies and asked the prospective jurors to estimate the eyewitnesses' "hit" rates. They found that respondents overestimated witness accuracy by an average of 83.7%. They concluded that "[a]wareness of the unreliability of eyewitness evidence does not appear to be part of the 'common knowledge' of prospective jury members," and that the data can be interpreted as refuting the claim made by some courts that expert testimony about eyewitness evidence does not "tell the jury members anything they do not already know."

Earlier researchers found approximately two-thirds of the citizen jurors were unaware that eyewitnesses tend to overestimate the length of time involved in a crime; two-thirds of the citizen jurors believed that the police would be superior to civilians as eyewitnesses; and 15% thought that eyewitness memory of faces would be 90-95% accurate several months after seeing the face. Over half were unaware that an eyewitness identification of someone from a set of photographs is likely to later produce an identification of the same person in a lineup (regardless of whether the identified person is guilty or not) and two-thirds of the respondents indicated they "believed in the existence of a positive relationship between eyewitness accuracy and eyewitness confidence." The final conclusion was that "the present data indicate that the testimony of an expert on these matters would not invade the province of the jury. Rather, such testimony would aid the jury in its evaluation of evidence and would thereby further the cause of justice."

Even the U.S. Supreme Court seems to have been in error when, in *Neil v. Biggers*, it recommended that jurors evaluating identification evidence consider, among other factors, the degree of certainty expressed by the witness. Many social research studies following that decision showed it to be in apparent error. For example, a comprehensive review by Wells and Murray of more than thirty studies of the confidence-accuracy relationship found that there were some statistically significant relationships between confidence and accuracy, but that these relationships were practically useless.

Other reports are more negative. For example, Wells, Leippe, and Ostrom found that while degree of certainty was not related to accuracy, the perceived seriousness of the crime and consequent higher degree of attention were. Lindsay, Wells and Rumpel found that witnesses' confidence was unrelated to accuracy and that persons in the position of jurors could not detect the errors on cross-examination. Smith, Kassin, and Ellsworth concurred, finding that "[c]onfidence is neither a useful predictor of the accuracy of a particular witness or of the accuracy of particular statements made by the same witness."

E. Post-1986 Research

Following the painful self-examination and heated debate of the early 1980s, researchers responded by returning to more careful empirical explorations of some of the earlier conclusions in ways that made them more readily applicable to the courtroom context. For example, in 1986, *The British Journal of Psychology* published an article exploring different ways in which people encode faces.

Gary Wells and John W. Turtle observed that it was time to move beyond the simple questions that were central in the debate over expert testimony: "We now know, of course, that eyewitness testimony depends on a great number of factors and that it is sometimes quite reliable and that it is sometimes not. Attention should now be given to the question of under what conditions is eyewitness testimony reliable and when is it unreliable?" They explored identification from lineups and photospreads, pointing out that the wording of instructions can influence whether the witnesses chose anyone, even if the actual offender is present — a conclusion reached in other studies as well. They also discussed prior studies by Wells that demonstrated that some eyewitnesses make false identifications when presented with a "lure" lineup (in which no to-be-identified target is present) and that knowing this helps screen out some witnesses. They discussed a 1986 study by Lindsay and Wells in which suspects were presented sequentially rather than simultaneously, producing fewer false identifications. The *Journal of Experimental Psychology* reported research on misleading post-event information showing that post-event misinformation either impaired the original memory or led to confusion about what had occurred during the original event. While memory test results and confidence ratings supported an interference or inaccessibility interpretation, the results could not rule out "overwriting" of the original information in some cases. The results also supported the conclusion that subjects who were misled might not have known what they saw, but they *did know what they did not see.* Furthermore, they found that subjects are more confident when they are correct than when they are not.

Loftus and Hunter G. Hoffman maintained that "misleading information presented after an event can lead people to erroneous reports of that misinformation." Elizabeth F. Loftus & Hunter G. Hoffman, *Misinformation and Memory: The Creation of New Memories,* 118 Journal of Experimental Psychology: General 100, 100 (1989). They argued that "erroneous reporting will depend on the conditions of acquisition, retention and retrieval of information" and that "misinformation acceptance plays a major role, memory impairment plays some role, and pure guessing plays little or no role" in the creation of erroneous eyewitness reports. *Id.* Yet acceptance of misinformation by witnesses, as a phenomenon worthy of sustained scientific investigation, does not receive the attention that it deserves. . . .

NOTES & QUESTIONS

1. Eyewitnesses and challenges to them can be used effectively in pop cultural drama. In Alfred Hitchcock's *The Wrong Man,* several eyewitnesses accuse jazz musician Manny Balestrero, played by Henry Fonda, of being a hold-up man. Although he is innocent, the evidence of guilt appears overwhelming. Yet all of it has been obtained through police work that is at best shockingly sloppy and at worst deliberately deceitful. In one scene, for example, the cops have him write out a note used by the robber. In another, they put him in a line-up with several other men, none of whom look particularly like him, and ask two eyewitnesses to identify the perpetrator (both pick out Balestrero). In a third, they send him into a delicatessen to walk up and down to see if an eyewitness can identify him. The store owner asks Balestrero if he is the man the precinct "sent over."

2. Consider the many ways in which *The Wrong Man* telegraphs the injustice being done to Balestrero, from the limited and focused lighting used in the police station (indicating the intense interest the police have in Manny, their only suspect) to the repeated images of bars (which represent both symbolic and actual imprisonment). How does the film, to use a phrase well-suited for the concerns at hand, bear witness to the reality of false accusations brought against the innocent? Also think about the number of times that a reference to Manny's religion (Catholicism) appears in the movie (such as the rosary the desk sergeant tells him he can keep and the woman who asks if he has thought about praying for assistance). Do these also represent a type of "witnessing," albeit not the kind we usually think of in connection with the law?

3. The eyewitnesses in *The Wrong Man* are sure of their identifications, partly because of the way the police arrange the line-ups. Though commonly used, line-ups have come under fire as inherently unreliable. *See, e.g.,* Richard Willing, "Police Lineups Encourage Wrong Picks, Experts Say," *USA Today,* 26 Nov. 2002, 1A. Should they therefore be discontinued, or perhaps used only to exclude suspects? Consider the physical resemblance between Manny and the perpetrator. How much do they look alike? In the actual case that inspired the film, the similarities were significant. *See* Jay Maeder, "The Stork Club's Most Famous Bull Fiddle Man,

1953," *N.Y. Daily News*, 14 Nov. 2005, 34.

4. Alfred Hitchcock always made a cameo appearance in his films. In *The Wrong Man*, however, he deviated from his practice (so as not to trivialize Balestrero's plight) and instead walked onto a sound stage at the beginning of the film and addressed the audience. What effect does this have on the message he is trying to relay?

5. In its own way, the film *My Cousin Vinny* also casts doubt on the validity of eyewitness testimony. During the trial, Vinny Gambini convinces us that all of the prosecution's eyewitnesses are mistaken. As usual, he makes us laugh along the way. On a more serious note, we might wonder if the prosecution intentionally or unintentionally suggested to Mr. Tipton, Mr. Crane, and Mrs. Reilly what they should say on the witness stand.

6. One of the jury's problems is reconciling contradictory testimony on the part of eyewitnesses. Consider that problem in the light of films such as *The Wrong Man* or *Witness for the Prosecution*, or films such as the Japanese classic *Rashomon* (1950) in which the conflict among eyewitnesses is the entire point of the film. How do the eyewitnesses ultimately reconcile their versions of what happened with the real story? Whom does the audience believe? Does it matter? Is the filmmaker telling us that in film, like in the courtroom, the purpose of the exercise is to resolve the conflict and come to a conclusion rather than to arrive at the truth?

Note that *Rashomon* has influenced episodes in a number of television series, including *CSI, Leverage, All in the Family, Star Trek: The Next Generation, King of the Hill, Magnum, P.I.*, and *Two and a Half Men*. When you next see the device of multiple characters telling their stories to an independent third party, and their stories diverge violently, you will recognize *Rashomon*'s influence.

7. Witnesses can also be important in legal novels. Henry Cecil's novel *Independent Witness* (1963) makes entertaining use of the roles that witnesses play in a trial. Cecil (Henry Cecil Leon) was a British judge who wrote prolifically, churning out clever mysteries in which lawyers and judges figure prominently. He also wrote a number of nonfiction works about the legal system in the United Kingdom.

E.   CROSS-EXAMINATION

The aggressive cross-examination of a witness is a mainstay in law-related popular culture. Sometimes this cross-examination seems stylized and phony, as in the *Perry Mason* television series from the late 1950s and early 1960s. The resourceful Mason has the uncanny ability to detect who is lying and to subject liars to blistering cross-examination. Sometimes the witness turns out to be the perpetrator of the crime and admits his or her guilt right on the stand. In other pop cultural works, meanwhile, the cross-examination provides the best, most engaging drama. For example, the tense cross-examination of Colonel Nathan Jessup by Lieutenant Daniel Kaffee provides the most powerful scene in *A Few Good Men* (1992).

The next two excerpts critique the cross-examination of Christine Vole, played by the incomparable Marlene Dietrich, in the classic film *Witness for the Prosecution.*

CHARLES LAUGHTON, MARLENE DIETRICH, AND THE PRIOR INCONSISTENT STATEMENT
James Carey
36 Loyola University Chicago Law Journal 433 (2005)

In the movie *Witness for the Prosecution*, Charles Laughton plays a defense barrister in a murder case. On cross-examination, he confronts Marlene Dietrich, a key prosecution witness, with her own letters contradicting her direct testimony. The letters destroy her credibility. The confrontation is the denouement of the trial, but not of the movie. We learn after the trial that Dietrich contrived the letters herself, enabling Laughton to destroy her in front of the jury, thereby gaining an acquittal for the defendant, Tyrone Power, her lover. In a climactic twist, Dietrich kills Power when she discovers that he no longer loves her — before ultimately being represented by Laughton in her own murder trial.

There comes a point in a trial when advocacy skill, knowledge of the law, and professional responsibility uniquely come together. This is also the time when the adversarial nature of our system is clearest. This point occurs when a witness is impeached with a prior inconsistent statement, as portrayed dramatically in the Laughton-Dietrich confrontation. This essay supports the assertion that witness impeachment is an indispensable part of the common law justice system, returning from time to time to the movie, *Witness for the Prosecution.* . . .

Before discussing this technique in detail, I make three preliminary points. First, the rationale for the three-step approach is that jurors are limited in the ways they can learn the facts of the case. Typically jurors learn by listening, which is one-dimensional and is made more difficult by their general inability to ask questions. They must therefore listen and hear correctly the first time that the words are spoken, which emphasizes the obvious importance of repetition, diagrams, and photographs. When the examiner impeaches with a prior statement, she expects the jurors to understand an abstraction, or "inconsistency," between the two statements. If the contradiction is "yes" versus "no," or "red" versus "green," it is relatively easy for the jurors to "see" the contradiction. In the world of real trials, however, the contradiction is embedded in phrases and paragraphs and is difficult to "see" just by listening. Thus, the three-step prescription of commit, build up, and confront addresses this problem by building up to and setting off the contradiction.

Second, the approach creates the opportunity for dramatics. Specifically, when the cross examiner confronts the witness with the prior inconsistent statement, she has the chance to "ring the changes" for emphasis. She can raise her voice; she can lower her voice to a stage whisper. The examiner can also slow down the delivery and labor over each word of contradiction (as Charles Laughton does inimitably in confronting Marlene Dietrich), or can pause for dramatic effect. Here then is the high drama of a real trial: making the witness agree to the examiner's damning words.

Third, a skillful examiner will then emphatically confront the witness, because once the witness answers, the impeachment is complete. There is no room for follow-up along the lines of "[w]ere you lying then or are you lying now?" Such a question only gives the witness a chance to explain the inconsistency, thereby taking the clear edge off of the effect of the inconsistent statements. . . .

Charles Laughton's use of Marlene Dietrich's contrived letters is a delightful and realistic practice in staging. Laughton asks Dietrich questions about letters he alleges she wrote to a certain "Max." As he asks these questions, he holds a piece of paper, apparently the letter to which he refers. This paper in fact has nothing to do with the letter, but instead is a mere piece of scrap paper that he had retrieved from his briefcase. The real letters that Laughton intended to use to impeach were placed underneath a book on his desk. Dietrich's answers become shrill denials of his assertions. As he waves the paper in front of her, she blurts out, "[w]hy that is not even my stationery. Mine is light blue with my initials on it." At this point, Laughton pauses and slowly lifts from the pages of his book the actual letters, in blue with initials on them. He then asked sonorously, laboriously, "[l]ike . . . this?"

Thus, Laughton holds back the writing, induces the vehement denial, and then proceeds to produce the writing with a vengeance. Dietrich is reduced to shrieking insults at Laughton ("Damn you!"). In reality — this technique, if not her reaction — is wholly plausible.

One loose evidentiary end remains untied: does it make any difference whether the prior statement is admissible not only for impeachment, but "substantively" as well — that is, as a true statement?

Today many jurisdictions permit some kinds of prior inconsistent statements to be admitted as true statements. Typically, rules which permit such a use require that the person who made the statement be on the witness stand and be subject to cross-examination on the statement, and that the statement be under oath, or be made under equivalent circumstances supporting the conclusion that it was reliable, such as tape recording.

It is up to the examiner whether she wants the jury to accept the statement as true. The statement's admissibility as a true statement does not necessarily mean that it must be used as true. Its use is determined by the examiner's theory of the case. The examiner offers the prior inconsistent statement as true only if the statement helps support her theory. Yet, even if the examiner intends the statement to be taken as true as well as to be used to impeach, she follows the same technique as she would were the statement being used solely for impeachment purposes. This technique provides the best means of emphasizing the making of the statement. To effectively accomplish impeachment with a prior inconsistent statement in a dramatic fashion, the advocate must know the evidence rules related to impeach-ment and the procedural rules governing cross-examination and impeachment. She must also possess the advocacy skill to isolate and emphasize the contradiction.

So where does professional responsibility come into play? The advocate needs a good faith basis to assert a fact on cross-examination. This good faith requirement is an aspect of the general obligation that the advocate has to be honest with the court, and to not "perpetrate a fraud upon the court." But what does "good faith basis" mean, concretely?

There are two versions of good faith: one strict and one relaxed. A strict view of good faith requires that the examiner have admissible evidence showing that the impeaching fact is true. Under this view, good faith would require that in order to assert to a witness, "you said before that the light was green," the examiner must have admissible evidence that the witness said the light was green. If the examiner has only some indication that the statement had been made, but has no admissible proof, the statement is not in good faith.

The second good faith view treats it as a rule of reasonableness; specifically, as long as the examiner has a reasonable basis for believing the impeaching fact is true (for example, that the previous inconsistent statement was made) he is operating in good faith. Thus, if the examiner's basis for impeachment is a hearsay report, made by someone other than the witness, and the report nevertheless seems authentic and reliable, she may assert the impeaching fact contained in the report.

Which view of good faith to apply depends upon the law of the jurisdiction. In *Witness for the Prosecution*, Laughton possesses letters that contradict Dietrich's earlier testimony. Laughton has a good faith basis to confront Dietrich with the statements, both because of the circumstances of the letters coming into his possession, as developed in the movie, and his expectation that he can authenticate them, through handwriting analysis, and introduce them, if necessary. Thus, he both acts reasonably and possesses admissible evidence. Of course it is the penultimate twist in the movie that the letters are false, created by Dietrich to enable Laughton to discredit her. . . .

Mirjan Damaska, the Sterling Professor at Yale Law School, is a prominent Comparative Law scholar who has compared the differences between the accusatorial and inquisitorial systems. One of his focuses is on the relative degree to which each system is designed to get at the "truth of what happened":

> It is openly stated by some common law lawyers that the aim of criminal procedure is not so much the ascertainment of the real truth as the just settlement of a dispute. . . . In talking about ends of the criminal process continental lawyers place a primary emphasis on the discovery of the truth as a prerequisite to a just decision.

Mirjan Damaska, *Evidentiary Barriers to Conviction and Two Models of Criminal Procedure: A Comparative Study*, 121 University of Pennsylvania Law Review 506, 581 (1973).

Accepting the distinction Damaska describes for argument's sake, how does impeachment with a prior inconsistent statement quintessentially assist a "just settlement?"

It can be argued that impeachment does so in two ways. First, impeachment balances the witness's assertions with his contradictory words, thereby giving the jurors a balanced view of what the witness has said. Ultimately, a judgment based on these balanced assessments is itself more balanced, fair, and thus a "just settlement."

Second, impeachment assists a just settlement in a criminal case by enforcing the burden of proof beyond a reasonable doubt. This strict burden is itself illustrative of Damaska's characterization of the common law system, as "not so much [concerned with] the ascertainment of the real truth." The burden of proof expresses "a fundamental value determination of our society that it is far worse to convict an innocent man than to let a guilty man go free." Impeachment can itself create reasonable doubt. A judgment based solely upon a witness who has been substantially impeached is not beyond a reasonable doubt, and is not a just settlement.

Impeachment is an effective tool in our adversarial system. Specifically, impeachment may be so effective as to create a reason to believe the very opposite of what the witness has asserted. This is the strategy behind Dietrich's set up of Laughton to impeach her on the stand. Although the trial outcome is a false one, we only know that because we are watching the movie. On its face, the trial outcome appears to be a "just settlement."

LEGAL FICTIONS: IRONY, STORYTELLING, TRUTH, AND JUSTICE IN THE MODERN COURTROOM DRAMA
Christine Alice Corcos
25 University of Arkansas at Little Rock Law Review 503 (2003)

In *Witness for the Prosecution*, Robards overlooks the evidence and truths spoken which would explain much of the mystery of Christine's testimony ("She's an actress, and a good one," Leonard has already told him) in favor of speculation. "It's too easy, something's wrong," he tells Brogan-Moore after the acquittal. His own experience tells him that his abilities in the courtroom do not extend to the kind of miraculous outcome the "hopeless" Vole case presents. He prefers to believe in what seems to him to be an ordinary motive carried out through an extravagant plan (that she is in love with another man and frames Leonard) to an equally mundane motive carried out by an even more elaborate plan (that she loves her husband and frames herself).

Christine taunts Robards with the words "the great Sir Wilfred Robards has done it again," and then goes on to explain how her actions were part of a grand design to obtain Leonard's acquittal. Robards's subtlety and chauvinism forced him to seek a motive beyond Christine's love for Leonard in what she has done. He is therefore amazed to discover that a foreign woman untrained in the law, but an astute observer of human behavior, can manipulate the system far more successfully than he. Christine piles irony upon irony in this scene, since both Christine and the observer clearly believe that they have an accurate understanding of the outcome of the trial, although Christine knows more than the observer, while Robards mistrusts the surface but fails to comprehend the reality. Christine's initial story, that she loves her husband, does not convince Robards because she overplays the part intentionally to raise questions about her veracity. Her next story, that she loves another man, seems more likely to him, yet he is still unconvinced. Robards does not re-exert his natural dominance until, in the courtroom, the truth becomes known and the full extent of Christine's plot and Leonard's duplicity is revealed.

As it is revealed, the defendant, Vole, and the primary witness against him, Christine, concocted a defense together. They manipulated the experienced defense lawyer into unwittingly helping them. Christine tells the defense counsel, "the great

Sir Wilfred Robards," that her knowledge of English law ("a wife cannot testify against her husband") gave her the idea for the winning defense. Since Christine is not Vole's wife, although initially no one knows this, and because she will not be believed if she appears as an alibi witness, Christine decides to reveal the truth on the stand, knowing that Robards will characterize it as a lie and that the jury will believe that it is a lie. Ironically, the truth does set Leonard Vole (temporarily) free. When he tells Christine the truth at the end of the drama, that he is leaving her for another woman, she stabs him with the knife that earlier he used to kill Mrs. French. Christine becomes an ironist who unconsciously ironizes herself, what Muecke calls the "irony of self-betrayal."

Christine succeeds in misleading Robards because his experience and prior success in the courtroom have made him cocky and over-confident, although his recent heart attack has reminded him of his mortality. Throughout the film he firmly believes that he is fooling the doctors and nurses at the hospital and continues to fool his nurse by concealing cigars in his cane, replacing the hot cocoa in his thermos with brandy, and cadging smoking materials from colleagues and clients. He tests Leonard Vole's veracity with his "monocle test" in which he focuses the sun's light on Vole's eyes via the monocle lens to see Vole's reaction — extreme nervousness that would indicate guilt, or calmness, which would indicate innocence. When his associate Brogan-Moore asks him the result of the test, he admits that Vole did not react to the light (he passed, a circumstance which baffles him, since he suspects that Vole is guilty). Christine, however, refuses to play the game. She and Robards spar over what he considers her rather too cool attitude toward her husband's very real danger of conviction. "I want to help Leonard," she responds, "and I want to help *you*, Sir Wilfred." As the light reflected from the monocle continues to bother her, she gets up and adjusts the curtains, saying as she does so, "Now, isn't that better?" The dual meaning of the phrase may escape him, as it initially escapes the observer. Vole's reaction represents his ability to take circumstances and rules as they are in life and change his own behavior to manipulate the reaction of the observer. Christine's action in closing the draperies shows her willingness to manipulate perceptions to prevail. Leonard initially and repeatedly lies to Robards. Christine tests the waters, and when she finds that the truth disguised as a lie will be more convincing than a real lie which follows the lines Robards expects, she tells the truth-as-lie. As Robards points out, the danger to his client lies in the fact that the jury does not like Christine, but they believe her. They like Leonard, but they do not believe him. The failure of Robards's previously surefire "monocle test" is the first intimation to the observer that truth will be an elusive creature in this story.

NOTES & QUESTIONS

1. Is Carey correct that an attorney bent on impeaching a witness will never follow up with questions such as "Were you lying then, or are you lying now?" Does such a question open the door to an objection by opposing counsel? If so, what objection and with what result? Notice also that Christine Vole is a hostile witness, is not married to the accused, and has (arguably) already perjured herself.

2. What does Robards' monocle test represent to him? When both Christine and Leonard pass it, what do those events symbolize? Are Christine and Leonard even aware that they have passed the test?

3. A recurring motif in many films is that of the attorney who browbeats a witness as opposing counsel ineffectually tries to object. Often the witness spills the beans right on the spot. The motif is so familiar that its disruption or alteration of it can be used to garner laughs, as in Woody Allen's hilarious *Bananas* (1971). In the film, Fielding Melish, played by Woody Allen himself, calls himself to the stand and delightfully runs back and forth from the defense counsel's table while conducting an aggressive examination.

4. Regardless of how the judge rules, the loud-mouthed lawyer examining a witness routinely seems to score points with the jury. However, aggressively cross-examining certain kinds of witnesses (such as a child) is tricky. In the movie *The Accused*, the defense must be careful in how it approaches the complainant and rape victim Sarah Tobias (Jodie Foster). If its questions are too confrontational, Tobias will gain extra sympathy from the jury.

5. Compare the television series *Perry Mason* (played by Raymond Burr) with the film *Perry Mason* (often played by Warren William, once by Ricardo Cortez), and the Perry Mason as described in the novels by Erle Stanley Gardner. (A 1973/1974 television series also starred Monte Markham as Perry Mason). How do the various Masons differ in terms of their courtroom behaviors, examining witnesses, and dealing with evidence? With regard to direct and cross-examination of witnesses, compare the courtroom behaviors of pop cultural attorneys with real-life attorneys that you know and have observed. How do they differ and why? Are they at all similar? Can you learn anything at all (valuable or not) in this regard from actors who play lawyers, and from the scripts that tell them what to do? If so, what?

6. In the film *Find Me Guilty* (2006), Joe diNorscio, who appears *pro se*, demolishes the prosecution's witnesses in various ways. The movie, which is based on a true story, emphasizes both the defendant's lack of education and his common sense, as well as his ability to triumph over seasoned prosecutors. What message do you take away from the movie's depiction of diNorscio's cross-examination of the prosecution's witnesses, particularly of the FBI agents? That they are badly prepared? That they profile Italians? That the case against the defendants is a weak one? Or something else? Are you offended by the film's depiction of the defendants as "family" and "family men" and of the federal prosecutors as somewhat nasty and ambitious, and by the fact that the defendants are acquitted? Remember that under the Hayes Code, "bad" people had to be shown to be convicted. In a film that depicts a real trial, a filmmaker cannot (or should not) alter the ending.

F. QUESTIONS ABOUT THE WITNESS'S CHARACTER

Sometimes attorneys attempt to expose not inconsistencies in a witness's testimony but rather personal flaws in the witness. However, there are limits on how the examining attorney might proceed and what he or she might reveal. The most discussed limitation involves the prior conduct and sexual promiscuity of a rape victim. State statutes are not uniform, but in different ways the states have attempted to "shield" the rape victim's sexual history.

The following statutes represent California's attempt to prevent the rape victim's past sexual conduct and arguably flawed character from being presented in court.

CALIFORNIA EVIDENCE CODE
Divisions 6 and 9 (2005)

§ 782. Evidence of sexual conduct of complaining witness; Offer of proof; Affidavit; Procedure

(a) In any prosecution under Section 261, 262, 264.1, 286, 288, 288a, 288.5, or 289 of the Penal Code, or for assault with intent to commit, attempt to commit, or conspiracy to commit any crime defined in any of those sections, except where the crime is alleged to have occurred in a local detention facility, as defined in Section 6031.4, or in a state prison, as defined in Section 4504, if evidence of sexual conduct of the complaining witness is offered to attack the credibility of the complaining witness under Section 780, the following procedure shall be followed:

(1) A written motion shall be made by the defendant to the court and prosecutor stating that the defense has an offer of proof of the relevancy of evidence of the sexual conduct of the complaining witness proposed to be presented and its relevancy in attacking the credibility of the complaining witness.

(2) The written motion shall be accompanied by an affidavit in which the offer of proof shall be stated. The affidavit shall be filed under seal and only unsealed by the court to determine if the offer of proof is sufficient to order a hearing pursuant to paragraph (3). After that determination, the affidavit shall be resealed by the court.

(3) If the court finds that the offer of proof is sufficient, the court shall order a hearing out of the presence of the jury, if any, and at the hearing allow the questioning of the complaining witness regarding the offer of proof made by the defendant.

(4) At the conclusion of the hearing, if the court finds that evidence proposed to be offered by the defendant regarding the sexual conduct of the complaining witness is relevant pursuant to Section 780, and is not inadmissible pursuant to Section 352 of this code, the court may make an order stating what evidence may be introduced by the defendant, and the nature of the questions to be permitted. The defendant may then offer evidence pursuant to the order of the court.

(5) An affidavit resealed by the court pursuant to paragraph (2) shall remain sealed, unless the defendant raises an issue on appeal or collateral review relating to the offer of proof contained in the sealed document. If the defendant raises that issue on appeal, the court shall allow the Attorney General and appellate counsel for the defendant access to the sealed affidavit. If the issue is raised on collateral review, the court shall allow the district attorney and defendant's counsel access to the sealed affidavit. The

use of the information contained in the affidavit shall be limited solely to the pending proceeding.

(b) As used in this section, "complaining witness" means the alleged victim of the crime charged, the prosecution of which is subject to this section.

§ 1103. Evidence of character of victim of crime

(a) In a criminal action, evidence of the character or a trait of character (in the form of an opinion, evidence of reputation, or evidence of specific instances of conduct) of the victim of the crime for which the defendant is being prosecuted is not made inadmissible by Section 1101 if the evidence is:

(1)   Offered by the defendant to prove conduct of the victim in conformity with the character or trait of character

(2)   Offered by the prosecution to rebut evidence adduced by the defendant under paragraph (3).

(b) In a criminal action, evidence of the defendant's character for violence or trait of character for violence (in the form of an opinion, evidence of reputation, or evidence of specific instances of conduct) is not made inadmissible by Section 1101 if the evidence is offered by the prosecution to prove conduct of the defendant in conformity with the character or trait of character and is offered after evidence that the victim had a character for violence or a trait of character tending to show violence has been adduced by the defendant under paragraph (1) of subdivision (a).

(c) (1)   Notwithstanding any other provision of this code to the contrary, and except as provided in this subdivision, in any prosecution under Section 261, 262, or 264.1 of the Penal Code, or under Section 286, 288a, or 289 of the Penal Code, or for assault with intent to commit, attempt to commit, or conspiracy to commit a crime defined in any of those sections, except where the crime is alleged to have occurred in a local detention facility, as defined in Section 6031.4, or in a state prison, as defined in Section 4504, opinion evidence, reputation evidence, and evidence of specific instances of the complaining witness' sexual conduct, or any of that evidence, is not admissible by the defendant in order to prove consent by the complaining witness.

(2)   Notwithstanding paragraph (3), evidence of the manner in which the victim was dressed at the time the commission of the offense shall not be admissible when offered by either party on the issue of consent in any prosecution for an offense specified in paragraph (1), unless the evidence is determined by the court to be relevant and admissible in the interests of justice. The proponent of the evidence shall make an offer of proof outside the hearing of the jury. The court shall then make its determination and at that time, state the reasons for its ruling on the record. For the purposes of this paragraph, "manner of dress" does not include the condition of the victim's clothing before, during, or after the commission of the offense.

(3)   Paragraph (1) shall not be applicable to evidence of the complaining witness' sexual conduct with the defendant.

(4)   If the prosecutor introduces evidence, including testimony of a witness, or the complaining witness as a witness gives testimony, and that evidence or testimony relates to the complaining witness' sexual conduct, the defendant may cross-examine the witness who gives the testimony and offer relevant evidence limited specifically to the rebuttal of the evidence introduced by the prosecutor or given by the complaining witness.

(5)   Nothing in this subdivision shall be construed to make inadmissible any evidence offered to attack the credibility of the complaining witness as provided in Section 782.

(6)   As used in this section, "complaining witness" means the alleged victim of the crime charged, the prosecution of which is subject to this subdivision.

NOTES & QUESTIONS

1.   Why do you think the California lawmakers used the phrase "complaining witness" in the statutes? Is the rape victim best understood as a witness? If we understand the rape survivor as a witness, should we have the same skepticism regarding her eyewitness testimony as the materials in section D of this chapter suggest we should have for eyewitness testimony in general?

2.   *The Accused*, starring Oscar-winner Jodie Foster as Sarah Tobias, nicely dramatizes the rape survivor's dilemma. Tobias's promiscuous past initially turns even the prosecutor Kathryn Murphy, played by Kelly McGinnis, against Tobias. However, through the course of the film Murphy comes to appreciate Tobias's victimization and also develops a degree of "sisterhood" with Tobias. To what extent can sisterhood truly bridge socioeconomic gaps? To what extent does Hollywood want us to think sisterhood can bridge socioeconomic gaps?

3.   *The Accused* is based on an actual case from New Bedford, Massachusetts. In 1983, a 22-year-old mother of two was raped by three young Portuguese-American men on a pool table in Big Dan's Bar. Other bar patrons cheered on the rapists. The defendants and defense witnesses testified that the victim was drunk and had "come on" to the perpetrators. The Portuguese community in the area strongly supported the defendants and held rallies on their behalf. Why might the filmmakers have left this ethnic dimension of the actual case out of the film version?

4.   In the "Big Dan" trial the three rapists were convicted and sentenced to nine to twelve years in prison. Two onlookers who had cheered on the rapists during the rape were acquitted. After the trial the complaining witness moved to Florida, where she died a few years later in a car crash. How do the lessons that might be taken from the actual case differ from those viewers are invited to take from the film? What do these differences suggest about the goals of the typical Hollywood filmmaker who retells, and transforms, the story of an actual case in a film intended for a mass audience?

Chapter 6

JUDGES

A. FILMOGRAPHY

Judge Dredd (1995)

Judge Judy: Second to None (2008)

Judgment at Nuremberg (1961)

The Life and Times of Judge Roy Bean (1972)

The Star Chamber (1983)

B. THE ROLE OF THE JUDGE

What do we want in a judge? When it comes to judicial images in film, audiences seem schizophrenic. We want a profoundly thoughtful, moral judge like Spencer Tracy's character in *Judgment at Nuremberg*, but we also enjoy a good old rascal like Paul Newman's Judge Roy Bean. We want a judge who is deeply principled and committed to following the letter of the law, like Michael Douglas's character early on in *The Star Chamber*, but we can sympathize with that same character's subsequent compulsion to take the law into his own hands when he believes justice has not been done.

Perhaps our ambivalence concerning judges has a very down-to-earth explanation: judges are only human, but we place them in a superhuman role. To judge another human being is a god-like act. All the trappings of power that surround a judge in a courtroom (the somber black robes, the physical layout of the courtroom, the formalities of address) support the judge's role as majestic law-giver. A judge embodies the law in his or her own person — small wonder, then, that so many judicial characters, from the real-life Wild West Judge Roy Bean to comic book characters such as Judge Dredd, intone the fateful words, "I am the Law!"

In movies centering on judges, a central theme often is the tension between the judge's allegiance to the system versus his or her desire for justice. How do real-life judges balance doing justice with the daily pressures of getting through the docket? Read the following two excerpts by judges for a glimpse into the different perspectives judges themselves have on their changing institutional roles.

WHAT IS THE ROLE OF THE JUDGE IN OUR LITIGIOUS SOCIETY?

Hon. Marjorie O. Rendell
(United States District Judge, Eastern District of Pennsylvania)
40 Villanova Law Review 1115 (1995)

The inquiry which is the subject of this discussion, namely, "What Is the Role of the Judge in Our Litigious Society?," can be interpreted in as many ways as there are listeners. To one, it may be perceived as asking whether Judge Ito did a good job; to another it may be viewed as inquiring about judicial activism or "legislation" by judges; yet to others, it may echo the cry for help of a harried, overworked benchsitter — not unlike the question, and I quote: "What's a mother to do?" These differing interpretations of the question illuminate the immense difficulty of divining an answer. The role of the judge as one who presides over trials and assists the jury in understanding legal issues is of course the most popular and usual depiction. While sometimes donning a wig (as in the British courts) or a southern accent (as in *My Cousin Vinny*), but always donning the robe, the universal view of judge as trial over-seer is as a character larger than life, above the fray, exuding dignity and dispensing justice for all.

The statue of Justice — regal, impartial, literally blind to any outside influence on her measured judgment — is a familiar symbol of judicial demeanor. Professor Judith Resnik has described how this personification of Justice represents the traditional view of the neutral judiciary:

> The goddess herself — aloof and stoic — represents the physical and psychological distance between the judge and the litigants. . . . Justice is unapproachable and incorruptible. The scales reflect evenhandedness and absolutism. The sword is a symbol of power, and like the scales, executes decisions without sympathy or compromise. Finally, the blindfold protects Justice from distractions and from information that could bias or corrupt her. Masked, Justice is immune from sights that could evoke sympathy in an ordinary spectator.

Judith Resnik, *Managerial Judges*, 96 Harvard Law Review 374, 383 (1982).

Federal judges, seen in the light of this image of justice, have traditionally been presumed to play their most important role at trial. The judge is overseer and umpire. However, the traditional role of the federal judge was never limited to that of a mere umpire. Instead, the judge has always been "the governor of the trial for assuring its proper conduct." In the exercise of this power, the trial judge has the prerogative and, at times, the duty of eliciting facts necessary to the clear presentation of issues. To this end, she may examine witnesses who testify, as long as she preserves an attitude of impartiality and guards against giving the jury the impression that the court believes that one side or the other should prevail. The blindfold on the statute of Justice symbolizes this impartiality, a necessary element in an adversarial system. The integrity and independence of the judiciary is mandated and assured, its separateness from the executive and legislative branches a hallmark of our system. This was thought important by the framers of the Constitution as a safeguard against government tyranny over people, their rights, and their property. Justice's blindfold represents not only an attitude of impartiality in the case at hand, but also an institutionalized blindness to outside influences from other branches and other sectors.

The perception of the judge as isolated and removed has historically carried over into the reality of what a judge does, day to day, in connection with the matters before her. Traditionally, judges have remained above and removed from the more unseemly aspects of litigation — the filing of papers, trial preparation and discovery, settlement negotiations, and other attempts to resolve cases amicably or short of a full-blown trial by jury. The traditional judge was aloof and isolated, holding the scales at arm's length. Due to the adversarial nature of our system, the parties controlled the pace and shape of litigation. They defined the case or controversy; the judge merely acted as listener, observer and occasional inquisitor. The macro aspects of the system — the number of cases filed or the progress of cases before them — were not the judge's concern. It was in most chambers anathema to urge a resolution of disputes other than by a constitutionally-guaranteed trial by a jury of one's peers.

All that has changed. To say that the discrete role of judges in 1995 is to preside over trials is like saying that the role of women in the 1990s is to care for the home. Surely, we do that, but we do so much more. Analogies can easily be made between the expansion of the roles of judges and of women, especially those with children, in these fast-moving, no-holds-barred times. The complexity of society, the awakening of individuals to ever-increasing needs, rights, and desires, the advent of technological advances, to say nothing of the countervailing pressures of time and money, make the role of a judge, and that of a parent today, challenging indeed. The teenager was content to wear sneakers until someone called them Nikes, said you had to have them and slapped a $130 price tag on them. Counsel were content to correspond and informally exchange information in preparation for trial with little or no judicial involvement until someone enacted the Federal Rules of Civil Procedure and discovered you could charge fees not only for trial but for hours spent in pretrial discovery. Judges and parents must moderate these influences. I belittle neither of these callings by the foregoing remarks, just note the reality of life in our times.

With the advent of the Federal Rules of Civil Procedure, the judge joined the fray. Justice no longer merely holds the sword as a symbol of power, but wields it actively through involvement at every turn. She monitors not only the trial, but all aspects of litigation — especially the discovery phase and pretrial proceedings.

At the same time as the procedures have been expanded, the basic rights of individuals for which there are remedies, and citizens' awareness of these rights and readiness to seek recourse in the courts, have increased greatly. The number of civil cases has doubled in the last twenty years, with 239,000 civil cases filed in 1995. This reflects an increase of 15% in the last four years alone. Criminal cases in the federal courts have increased as well — filings in 1994 were 58% higher than in 1980. The average district court judge's caseload in 1994 consisted of 396 civil and 58 criminal cases. . . .

While shepherding the cases along, careful that none stray from the fold, the judge must make room for the determination of motions in her copious free time.

The roles of speed reader and juggler are thus added, as well as that of interpreter of foreign tongues. Summary judgment is now in favor, and summary judgment motions of six inches or more in thickness predominate. The court's ruling on an issue rarely depends upon a clear legal principle, but rather upon whether defendant's mound of evidence will meet plaintiff's mound of evidence, and raise it one. In fact, I find it curious that summary judgment motions are thought to be an economical way of avoiding trial when they, in and of themselves, are costly undertakings indeed: costly to litigants in terms of attorney hours devoted to their preparation, and costly in terms of the expenditure of judicial time and effort. Once the motion, the answer, the reply, and the surreply have been filed, the judge then examines the four corners of the 1500 pages of deposition testimony and determines whether there are genuine issues of material fact — any one of which would thwart the entire motion — and whether movant is entitled to judgment as a matter of law. You might scoff at this and suggest that this is law clerk's work (and sometimes it is, but usually because of the press of other matters, not because the judge prefers it this way). Pennsylvania Superior Court Judge Spaeth commented on his modus operandi in addressing appellate cases before him:

> I have four clerks. That is too many to permit proper supervision. I ask each clerk to draft at least six opinions a month. That asks more than is wise; only the ablest and most diligent clerk can meet such a norm and still do good work. I rarely read the entire record of the trial testimony and documents, usually reading only those parts that seem from the briefs or my clerk's draft opinion likely to be critical. In reviewing a draft opinion, I often accept the clerk's exposition, so that my revisions are mostly stylistic. Sometimes I do not read the record at all. In deciding whether to join the opinion of another judge, I often accept the judge's statement of the record, on my clerk's assurance that the statement is accurate. In ruling on motions, I usually rely on summaries and recommendations prepared by the staff attorneys and my clerks. . . . I assent to every criticism that may be made of this breakneck way of doing things. I am sure that I should have decided some cases differently had I proceeded in a more deliberate and thorough way. But what else can I, or any judge like me, do? The cases keep piling up. They must be decided.

A. Leo Levin & Michael E. Kunz, *Thinking About Judgeships*, 44 American University Law Review 1627, 1640-41 (quoting Edmund B. Spaeth, Jr., *Achieving a Just Legal System: The Role of State Intermediate Appellate Courts*, in 462 The Annals of the American Academy of Political and Social Science 48, 55 (A. Leo Levin & Russell R. Wheeler eds. 1982).

NOTES & QUESTIONS

1. "Speed reader," "juggler," and "interpreter" are not perhaps the first qualities we might think of as essential for a judge. Yet, as Judge Spaeth notes, "The cases keep piling up." Are the daily pressures of the litigation docket realistically reflected in popular culture? Do judges in popular culture have plenty of time to ruminate thoughtfully over the finer points of a case? As various methods of Alternative Dispute Resolution (mediation, arbitration, mini-trials, etc.) become

more and more common, will judges no longer be necessary? Could a computer program do what a judge does?

2. Can any judge ever be as impartial and aloof as the blindfolded symbol of Justice seems to require? Do we hope a judge will rule fairly, but fear he or she will rule based on political ties?

3. What kind of assumptions do we make about the nature of the ideal judge? How do race, gender, ethnicity, religion, and sexual orientation come into play in our image of the "ideal" judge? Many lawyer films and television series now feature minority or women judges in the courtroom scenes. Does this visibly changing face of the judge in popular culture reflect real progress toward social justice, or is it just window dressing?

4. In the next article, Judge Richard Posner (a renowned Law and Economics scholar) suggests an economic explanation for the role of the judge. He argues that although economic incentives for a judge to rule a particular way are largely non-existent (because of such factors as set salaries and lifetime tenure), there are other deeper, less tangible incentives that can help us understand how a judge decides cases and how he or she plays the judge's role.

WHAT DO JUDGES AND JUSTICES MAXIMIZE? (THE SAME THING EVERYBODY ELSE DOES)
Richard A. Posner
3 Supreme Court Economic Review 1 (1993)

A difficult question remains — that of the judge's motivation, when all monetary punishments and rewards have been stripped away and a choice between work and leisure is not in the offing, to vote for one side rather than another, or to vote for one interpretation of a statute or legal doctrine rather than another, or to adopt one judicial philosophy (such as "conservative," "liberal," "activist," or "restrained") rather than another. The traditional objection to the secret ballot — that it promotes, or at least protects, irresponsible voting — has carried the day with respect to voting by judges. Every judicial vote is public, although sometimes a judge will tell his friends that he joined an opinion with which he disagreed because he didn't think the issue important enough to warrant a dissenting opinion. The public character of judicial voting facilitates criticism, which can be expected to have a greater effect on behavior when ordinarily more powerful incentives, such as money, are not in play. Yet most judges in fact are relatively insensitive to criticism other than by other judges, believing conveniently that most of it is motivated by political disagreement, envy, ignorance (willful or otherwise) of the conditions under which judges work, and self-promotion. Moreover, public comment on judicial decisions other than by the Supreme Court is rare. Only a tiny fraction of the tens of thousands of other appellate opinions published each year receive any sort of critical attention that might get back to the judge and alter his future behavior.

Choices of the kind that face a judge who must vote in a case — choices that cannot be made on the basis of wanting to increase one's pecuniary income, leisure, fame, or other forms of utility — are common in other areas of living. They are for example the choices we make when watching dramatic or cinematic performances.

Athletic contests are different, mainly because of the built-in "bias" in favor, normally, of the "home" team, a bias that makes the judicial analogy strained. The bias is highly relevant to state court adjudication, however, and can help explain not only the federal diversity jurisdiction but also the exclusive federal jurisdiction over many types of cases that pit a state resident against federal taxpayers.

The audience for a play or movie is detached, having no tangible stake in the outcome of whatever struggle is being depicted on stage or screen. Yet ordinarily it is induced to "choose" one side or the other. Usually the choice is manipulated by the author — he "tells" us as it were to side with the hero against the villain. But in dramatic works of deep ambiguity, which often are highly popular among intellectuals on that account, such as *Hamlet*, or *Measure for Measure*, or *Pygmalion*, the choice offered to the spectator is a real one, because the author either has not resolved in his own mind the central tension in the situation dramatized or has not been able (or desired) to communicate the resolution clearly. This explains the popularity of revisionist interpretations of literature, such as arguing that the real hero of *Paradise Lost* is Satan. The spectator, or, in the last example, the reader (but a "live" performance provides a closer analogy to the judicial process, though today many cases are submitted for decision without any oral argument or other hearing — much as when a play is read rather than performed), has to weigh the evidence and come to a decision. The position of the judge is similar. If spectators get consumption value out of such choices, it is not surprising that judges do.

Spectators make choices about the meaning of a play or movie by bringing to bear their personal experiences and any specialized cultural competence that they may have by virtue of study of or immersion in the type of drama that they are watching, and often by discussing their reactions with friends who may have a similar competence. The judge brings to bear on his spectatorial function not only a range of personal and political preferences, but also a specialized cultural competence — his knowledge of and experience in "the law." And if he is an appellate judge he will often discuss with his professional colleagues the proper outcome of the contest before making up his mind.

Of course not every case has the rich ambiguities of *Hamlet*. Many cases involve puzzles soluble with the technical tools of legal analysis — here the judge is like the reader of a detective story. The jury as fact-finder performs a similar function. It is a different kind of spectatorship from the one I am stressing here, that of the appellate judge asked to decide not where truth lies but which party has the better case. But in either case the choice, like that of the theater audience, is a disinterested one; the judge's or jury's income is not affected by it. A further point is that the less informed the tribunal is, the more "dramatic" the trial must be to hold the "audience's" attention. It is not surprising that Anglo-American trials, historically dominated by juries, are far more dramatic than Continental trials, historically dominated by professional judges.

The voting and spectatorship analogies to judicial decision-making are similar. This is most easily seen by comparing applause to voting — for in a large audience the clapping of a single spectator contributes little more to the overall decibel level than a single vote in an election contributes to the outcome. The voter is the spectator in a contest between candidates, much as the reader or viewer of *Antigone* is the spectator of a contest between Antigone and Creon. It is no surprise that voter turnout is higher, the more publicized and the closer an election is, just as the audience for a heavily advertised, highly dramatic play is likely to be larger than the audience for a meagerly advertised, undramatic play.

Why has the spectatorship analogy to judging been overlooked? One reason is the piety in which the public discussion of judges is usually clothed. The analogy seems to give judging a frivolous air. But serious engagement with the arts as reader or viewer is not a frivolous activity; nor is "play" (contrasted with work) incompatible with adherence to rules. A chess player would reduce rather than enhance the pleasure he received from playing the game if he violated its rules, and so would the theatergoer who refused to enter into the lives of the characters on the stage, on the ground that they were not real people; and likewise the judge who violates the rules of the judicial game. Sports fans, theater fans, movie fans, and opera fans often develop a degree of connoisseurship which enhances their pleasure. In other words, they learn the rules (broadly understood) of the game they are watching, and respond in accordance with those rules. It is the same with judges, but with the important difference that some of the rules of the judicial game are uncertain and contested.

A second reason why the spectatorship analogy to judging has been overlooked is the domination of analyses of judicial behavior by legal academics. The academic is a spectator too, but he is a spectator not of the little drama that the judge witnesses — the trial or other contest that the judge resolves — but of the judge's opinion. He usually does not attend oral argument or even read the briefs in the cases that he discusses. Naturally, therefore, he tends to ascribe more importance to the opinion, to its reasoning, its rhetoric, etc. than to the decision itself. Yet these are secondary factors for most judges. For the judge, as for Hamlet, "the play's the thing." When judges got busy, the first thing to be delegated was opinion-writing; yet even today it would be considered a scandal if judges delegated the hearing of testimony or argument (though there is in fact some delegation of these functions to magistrates and masters).

The analogy to spectatorship can help us see how judicial outcomes reflect both the judges' preferences going in *and* the quality of the briefing and argument in particular cases. It can also help us understand the function of confirmation hearings in enabling legislators to ascertain a judicial candidate's policy preferences, since those preferences can be expected to guide or at least influence a judge's decisions. We might also expect that "ideologues" would be appointed to judgeships at an earlier age on average than other candidates. Not only may it be difficult to determine the trajectory of the non-ideologue's views save by a process of inference from behavior over a long career, but to the extent that an ideologue is inherently more predictable there is less worry that if appointed young he will have a long time to change his views.

Contrary to appearances, this analysis does not justify complacency about judicial performance. To eliminate by means of rules governing conflicts of interest all personal stakes from the judge's decision-making increases the weight (by reducing the cost) of ethical consideration, including the ethical duty to follow legal rules, but at the same time, as with the nonprofit enterprise, it reduces the penalty for careless, erratic, inattentive, or willful decision-making. The problem is deeper. We can see it by returning to the analogy between political and judicial voting, and by examining more critically than before the analogy between judicial and theatrical spectatorship. Most political campaigners appeal primarily, though not exclusively, to the voter's self-interest. The judge, in contrast, like the theatrical spectator, is asked to cast a disinterested vote. It is easy to see why the spectator's vote is likely to be disinterested; what has he — being powerless — to gain by refusing to play the spectator's game? But a judge has some power. Supposing that the conflict of interest rules are effective in insulating his decision from any consequences for his personal or family wealth, one can still imagine a host of inappropriate considerations that might enter into his utility function: personal dislike of a lawyer or litigant in the case, gratitude to the appointing authorities, desire for advancement, irritation with or even a desire to undermine a judicial colleague or subordinate, willingness to trade votes, desire to be on good terms with colleagues, not wanting to disagree with people one likes or respects, fear for personal safety, fear of ridicule, reluctance to offend one's spouse or close friends, and racial or class solidarity. These are common factors in the decisions of everyday life — why not in the decisions of judges, unless we ascribe to them a utility function different from that of the ordinary person, which would be inconsistent with treating them as ordinary persons?

Such factors do influence judicial decisions, but less often than the suspicious layman might suppose. The reason is not that judges have different utility functions from other people but that the utility they derive from judging would be reduced by more than they would gain from giving way to the temptations that I have listed. It is the same reason that many people do not cheat at games even when they are sure they can get away with cheating. The pleasure of judging is bound up with compliance with certain self-limiting rules that define the "game" of judging. It is a source of satisfaction to a judge to vote for the litigant who irritates him, the lawyer who fails to exhibit proper deference to him, the side that represents a different social class from his own; for it is by doing such things that you know that you are playing the judge role, not some other role, and judges for the most part are people who want to be — judges. This is consistent with most judges' not wanting to work too hard, for working as hard as a lawyer in private practice is not one of the rules of the judicial game. It is also consistent with judges' often voting their policy preferences and strong personal convictions. For in our system the line between law and policy, the judging game and the legislating game, is blurred. Many cases cannot be decided by reasoning from conventional legal materials. Such cases require the judge to exercise a legislative judgment, although a more confined one than a "real" legislator would be authorized to exercise.

The analogy to playing games is worth pursuing a bit. Rules are not always irksome restraints. They are often constitutive. It is difficult to write a sonnet, because the sonnet is a genre with rigid rules; but without the rules, there would be no sonnets, and this would be a loss not only for the reader but for the sonneteer. And similarly with a game, for example chess. If you decided that your bishops should be allowed to make the same moves as your queen, or that some of your pieces should be allowed to make moves off the chessboard, you would no longer be playing the game of chess. It is true that people sometimes cheat at games when they think they can get away with it. But that is because the pleasure of the game is not the only argument in their utility function. A person might cheat at tennis (this is very common in fact) because he saw an advantage from winning, but if at all reflective he would realize that his pleasure from playing the game itself was diminished, that he was trading off that pleasure against another source of utility. The judicial "game" has rules that lawyers learn in law school and then in practice or teaching, and both self-selection and the careful screening of federal judicial candidates help to assure that most lawyers who become federal judges will be lawyers who enjoy this particular game. They are therefore likely to adhere, more or less, to the rules limiting the materials and considerations that enter into their decisions. The rules, it should be noted, are not the rules of substantive law, to which the community is subject but to which judges in their judicial capacity relate differently, as law givers and law appliers; they are the institutional rules of judging, to which only judges are subject. These rules, as I have said, are not altogether clear or uniform, especially in application; they are probably less clear and uniform, at least in the United States, than the substantive law. Some judges play by "activist" rules, more by rules of "restraint" because those rules are more congenial to the legal profession's self-image; and judges, like game players, sometimes bend or break the rules for the sake of other values, such violations being in fact rather common because detection and sanctioning are difficult. Nevertheless most judicial decisions do have a "ruled" quality, and the analogy to games helps to show how this property of decisions is consistent with utility maximization and how therefore it does not presuppose — what would be contrary to the assumptions of my analysis — heroic self-abnegation on the part of the judges.

Another aspect of rules makes it reasonable to expect most judges to abide by the rules of the judicial game. In creating games, as in creating art, people create a reality in which they can find temporary refuge from, by imaginative transformation of, the sinister realities of ordinary life, the realities of hatred, disease, crime, betrayal, war, and so forth. The judicial game has aspects of this refuge and transformation. Its raw materials are the ugly realities of life, but they are transformed in the judicial game to intellectual disputes over rights and duties, claims and proofs, presumptions and rebuttals, jurisdiction and competencies. And that is a comfort; it spares the judge who inflicts or upholds the death penalty from having to think of himself as a killer. But to get to this comfort the judge must play by the rules of the judicial game, because the rules constitute the game.

Elected judges play the judge game too, and legislators play a related game called statesmanship or public service. But unlike life-tenured federal judges, these players face higher costs (and obtain no greater benefits) from abiding by the rules of the game and therefore break them more often. Not always, which is why many and indeed most decisions by non-elected judges have a ruled quality and why much legislation has a genuine public-spirited character — not necessarily because the voters are public-spirited but because legislators derive satisfactions from acting in the public interest that may outweigh the costs when those costs are small.

NOTES & QUESTIONS

1. If judges are largely insulated from most economic incentives, what other incentives do they have to rule one way or the other? Moral righteousness? Intellectual satisfaction? Aesthetic satisfaction? Do you agree with Judge Posner's judge-as-spectator and judge-as-gamester models? What are the pleasures of judging?

2. Judges (like many of us) may have too lofty of a notion of their social and cultural position. Should every judge periodically visit the courthouse in disguise, to see how ordinary people are treated? The next reading shares insights from feminist criticism on the power structure of the judicial role.

ON THE BIAS: FEMINIST RECONSIDERATIONS OF THE ASPIRATIONS FOR OUR JUDGES
Judith Resnik
61 Southern California Law Review 1877 (1988)

After [Malcolm Lucas] completed his statement, Lucas was asked [by the Commission on Judicial Appointments] only one question — whether he had preconceived ideas about any issue that might go before him. He said he had none. [Thereafter, Lucas was sworn in as an Associate Justice on the California Supreme Court.]

> As reported by Dan Morain, "Lucas Sworn in as High Court Justice," *Los Angeles Times*, April 7, 1984, Part 2, at 1, Col. 1.

Question No. 4: "Do you think women judges will make a difference in the administration of justice?" . . .

Well, I answer honestly. "What does my being a woman specially bring to the bench?" It brings me and my special background. All my life experiences — including being a woman — affect me and influence me. . . .

My point is that nobody is just a woman or a man. Each of us is a person with diverse experiences. Each of us brings to the bench experiences that affect our view of law and life and decision-making. . . ."

> The Honorable Shirley S. Abrahamson, *The Woman Has Robes: Four Questions*, 14 Golden Gate University Law Review 489, 492-94 (1984). . . .

IV. A. The Voices of Women

In addition to quoting comments by Malcolm Lucas, of the California Supreme Court, I began this essay by quoting Shirley Abrahamson, a Wisconsin Supreme Court Justice, who has written a good deal about the act of judging. "What does my being a woman specially bring to the bench? It brings me and my special background. All my life experiences — including being a woman — affect me and influence me. . . ." Notice that her comments are "in a different voice," for, unlike the tradition of distance, Shirley Abrahamson accepts her history and rejoices that her life informs her work. But, just as Carol Gilligan has been accused of a selection bias, so can I be challenged. A few phrases out of context. Those of one woman, compared to those of one man.

But listen to more from Justice Abrahamson. In an address to the National Association of Women Judges (NAWJ), Abrahamson urged judges to visit — essentially incognito — courtrooms in other cities. She described her experience in one courtroom, where she arrived, "dressed in my t-shirt, wrap-around jean skirt, and sandals." The clerk was abrasive and "unfriendly," the lawyers condescending, the legal activity taking place in chambers, outside the public purview. Justice Abrahamson's request that judges enter into the world of litigants and the public was, in essence, a plea that judges attempt not only to understand the perspective of another, but to be an other (when possible), to experience the meaning of being a person in a courtroom who lacks the first name "Judge." By going to the courtroom unrobed, and therefore temporarily powerless, Shirley Abrahamson was able to understand more clearly how much her position of power affects her own construction of courtroom reality.

Justice Abrahamson also exhorted her sibling jurists to speak to the public and to participate in community organizations. Contrast this view with the Code of Judicial Conduct, which worries about extrajudicial activities that will "detract from the dignity" of the judicial office. The judicial canons have been used as the basis for criticism of judges who have participated in too many public activities. Felix Frankfurter made statements about judicial distance from the fray, all the while engaging in backroom politicking. Unlike Frankfurter, Shirley Abrahamson's views unify theory and practice and provide a very different conception of the judicial role.

Listen also to Judge Patricia Wald, now Chief Judge of the United States Court of Appeals for the District of Columbia. Judge Wald joined Justice Abrahamson and Deans John Ely and Jesse Choper on a panel entitled "Judicial Review and Constitutional Limitations." Judge Wald commented on the academic vogue of considering the question of judging in the context of constitutional jurisprudence. "I am not at all sure that the debate among the judicial review jurisprudentialists is really aimed at affecting the behavior of ordinary judges at all. . . . The point is simple: constitutional cases for most federal judges are a rarity — gourmet fare, definitely not the bread and butter of our everyday worklives." Her criticism was deeper than the problem of irrelevance. Judge Wald argued that the academics failed to take into account the experienced reality of judging:

> [F]ew judges I know reach out for or even want to decide constitutional issues. Such reticence does not stem from innate humility alone; but from a weary recognition that anytime you reverse some governmental action on constitutional grounds, it almost inevitably means en banc review, or certiorari granted and probable reversal. The prognosis, of course, is quite different if you decide that challenged action is constitutional. I suggest there is institutionally and experientially a very strong built-in bias in the lower courts against holding laws or actions violative of the federal constitution.

Nina Totenberg, moderator, *Panel Discussion: Judicial Review and Constitutional Limitations*, 14 Golden Gate University Law Review 645, 650 (1984).

In short, Judge Wald argued that the "big " academic questions — the creation of new rights and the judicial usurpation of legislative and executive roles — are uninformed by, and irrelevant to, the reality of judging. Judge Wald argued for an appreciation of the daily experiences of judging and for a jurisprudence of judging built upon the experience of judges, rather than imposed from theory.

Compare Judge Wald's voice to that of Antonin Scalia, Associate Justice of the United States Supreme Court. Like Judge Wald, Justice Scalia has commented on the everyday work of judges. In a recent speech, he deplored the drudgery of a federal judge, "processing many . . . less significant cases," such as "many routine tort and employment disputes." Justice Scalia spoke of his understanding, in 1960, when he graduated from law school, of the task of federal judges. "When I had the unrealistic ambition of being a federal judge, back in 1960, I did not want to dispose of predominantly routine cases. . . ." Justice Scalia suggested that "trivial cases" — explicitly defined as many Social Security claims and implicitly defined as those of little dollar value — be removed from the federal courts. Note that the commentary of Judge Wald and Justice Scalia have a similar basis — the experience of being a judge. Both Wald and Scalia remark on the distance between the reality of judges and the rhetoric of judging. Judge Wald seeks to have the reality inform the rhetoric, while Justice Scalia wants to change the reality to conform to his view of what judges "should" do; important men do not engage in routine tasks.

In addition to individual voices, there is a bit of information about how women judges speak in the aggregate. The National Association of Women Judges (NAWJ) provides some data. "As a large national organization, we can speak out on those issues — often controversial ones such as discriminatory clubs or federal judicial appointments — that individual judges, with all their ethical restrictions, do not feel they can appropriately address." The NAWJ addressed the issue of discriminatory clubs because of a perceived link between behavior in the world at large and the task of judging; the NAWJ opposes membership by judges in clubs that practice invidious discrimination. The NAWJ argues for an appreciation of the connection between what a judge does "on the bench from 9:00 a.m. to 12:30 p.m. supposedly making decisions without regard to race or sex" and what the judge does at lunch "at a social club which excludes women and blacks from its dining room."

I do not want to overstate the distance between female judges and the NAWJ, on the one hand, and male judges and the canons of judicial ethics, on the other. Like the NAWJ, the American Bar Association's Code of Judicial Conduct acknowledges that a relationship exists between the person on the bench and the person off the bench. The Code is replete with prohibitions on certain kinds of "extrajudicial activities" and with acknowledgments that, while a judge can engage in civic activities, a judge must not do so in a manner that "detracts from the dignity" of the judicial office. Moreover, the American Bar Association recently adopted a change in the commentary to the Code to recognize that membership in discriminatory clubs was problematic, insisting that individuals withdraw from such institutions. And, unlike Justice Shirley Abrahamson, the Code does not embrace the obligations of judges to leave their protected role and attempt to experience the judicial systems as do those without robes.

I also do not want to leave the impression that the few female voices on the bench all exemplify what could be seen as the "upside" of feminism. Another bit of collective information, provided by a statistical analysis of decisions made by federal judges, reminds us that some traditions of women — subservience and deference to a patriarchal culture — may also come with women to the bench. Thomas Walker and Deborah Barrow wanted to learn whether black and female federal judges appointed by the Carter administration decided cases differently from their white, male colleagues. Using a "pairing" device, the researchers compared opinions of twelve female/male pairs and ten black/white pairs. One of the study's findings was that "female judges were . . . more prone to rule in favor of the government in federal regulatory disputes. . . . Female judges exhibit a much greater tendency to defer to positions taken by government than do male judges."

How are we to interpret this information? Putting aside possible methodological complaints such as sample size, a first problem is that the researchers' analysis assumed that appropriate behavior was displayed by the male judges. Women were compared to men, and women were found wanting — found to be more deferential than were men. Perhaps the women's behavior was appropriate and the male judges were simply displaying male arrogance and a lack of humility. Alternatively, if the women were, in Sara Ruddick's terms, engaging in a learned but undesirable behavior, obedience to the "actual control and preferences of dominant people," then how do we explain the women judges who rise above such obedience? The real difficulty is thinking about how, over time, a person could hold the position of judge, retain humility and yet be able, when necessary, to challenge the powers of government. Responses to this problem must come in part from learning how judges experience their power and whether those experiences of power change over time. Learning from the practice of judging will teach us lessons about ourselves, as well as lessons about how we might transform our understanding of judging. . . .

NOTES & QUESTIONS

Does gender affect the way a judge experiences and administers power? How does popular culture answer this question? Consider images of women judges in film such as *First Monday in October* (1981) and in television series such as *Judging Amy* (1999–2005), *Ally McBeal* (1997–2002), and *Judge Judy* (1996–present). In *First Monday in October*, Jill Clayburgh plays the first woman Justice of the Supreme Court. At her confirmation hearing, she addresses the issue of her childlessness (something we would not expect to hear a male nominee discuss about himself): "The FBI is wrong in reporting I have no children. I have hundreds. . . . We are the parents of our ideas. My children [are] my opinions." This little exchange highlights her intelligence, but the scene also suggests a personal lack. It seems that if a woman is successful in her professional life, she has to be lacking in her personal life. In this regard the film seems a bit double-edged, exhibiting a progressive veneer (the first woman Supreme Court Justice), but also a reactionary underpinning (she's lacking a fulfilling family life).

Interestingly, the film does pick up on one very influential aspect of feminist theory — the idea that because of the material conditions of their lives, men and women may "see" the world differently. Walter Matthau's long-suffering wife leaves him after asking him to describe the wallpaper in the house he has lived in for years. He cannot do it because, as she tells him, "you can't memorize what you don't even see." Later, Matthau's character tests Jill Clayburgh at a Chinese restaurant by covering her eyes and asking her, "What's on the wall?" She describes in great detail the wallpaper, which she has seen only once. The positive spin on these scenes is that perhaps our life experiences help us see the world in different ways, and that men and women can learn from each other. The negative spin is that women notice "trivial" details while men pay attention to the "important" things in life. But who decides what counts as trivial?

Television shows have been a mixed bag as far as presenting women judges as well-rounded human beings. *Judging Amy*'s Judge Amy Grant has an interesting family life (a young daughter, an ex-husband, a strong-willed mother) as well as challenging cases in juvenile court. But *Ally McBeal*'s Judge "Whipper" Cone seems like yet another stereotypical example of a strong professional woman who is unfulfilled in her personal life. (The main character in the show also has this same problem.) And then there's Judge Judy.

C.   THE SEMIOTICS OF JUDGMENT

1.   Reality TV — "Real cases! Real people! Judge Judy!"

What do judges symbolize? Semiotics, or the study of signs and sign systems, would remind us that is important to pay close attention to the production of meaning in the sign that is "the judge." As a cultural symbol, "the judge" is not only the image of the person in the black robes (the signifier) but also the idea of a judge (the signified). How we decode the meaning of such cultural symbols as "Judge Judy" can have an effect on how we understand the meaning of other juridical signs in other "real" courtrooms.

In the next excerpt Professor Kimberlianne Podlas comments on a study of 241 individuals reporting for jury duty in Manhattan; Washington, D.C.; and Hackensack, New Jersey. She reports that regular watching of reality-based courtroom television shows such as *Judge Judy* encourages viewers to take as the norm behavior that in real life would constitute gross judicial misconduct. As you read, consider how popular culture shapes our perceptions of "proper" judicial behavior.

BLAME JUDGE JUDY: THE EFFECTS OF SYNDICATED TELEVISION COURTROOMS ON JURORS
Kimberlianne Podlas
25 American Journal of Trial Advocacy 557 (2002)

Findings suggest that syndi-court [syndicated television courtrooms] "teaches" the public about the law, but that its teachings may be flawed. A significant portion of frequent viewers believe that judges should be active, ask questions during the proceedings, hold opinions regarding the outcome, and make these opinions known. Frequent viewers, unlike non-viewers, stated a desire to look for clues to a judge's opinion and interpreted judicial silence as indicating a clear belief in one of the litigants. Moreover, the prior personal experience of viewers and non-viewers with the justice system exhibited no discernible effect on these measures.

When these frequent viewers become jurors, the ramifications are profound. Not only might these individuals enter the courtroom with a diminished respect for judges and a perverted sense of the trial process, but they may also actively search for clues to a judge's opinion, impute opinions where they do not exist, and draw mistaken inferences from judicial behavior or silence. Consequently, trial advocates should craft strategies to address these potential biases and misunderstandings. Some mechanisms include juror orientation, voir dire on the issue, and requests for instructions upon impaneling the jury and as part of the main charge.

I. Television's Influence on Public Opinion About the Law

In the last decade, networks have added the "reality programming" of the syndicated television courtroom, or syndi-court, to their repertoire. As of this writing, there are eleven syndicated courtroom shows airing, including *Judge Judy*, *Judge Mathis*, and *The People's Court*. These courts add to the stream of information feeding "law" to the American populace. Although individuals within the legal profession may disregard these forums as aberrational or embarrassing, they are a key source of information about judges and the law for many citizens.

In contrast to other televised, reality law, syndi-court's ratings demonstrate that the public systematically tunes into these shows: One year after the show's 1996 debut, *Judge Judy* boasted the nation's top syndicated ratings and continues to enjoy significant popularity. Additionally, this slate of television programming follows a remarkably similar format. Hence, syndi-courts exude the consistency and repetition required for cultivation and social learning. Their metaphors and images are repeated both within each individual show and among the slate of syndi-court programs. What one sees on *Judge Judy* is confirmed by what is seen on *Judge Mathis*. And, because these are broadcast daily instead of sporadically (as the trial arises), they create a unified body of information. One criticism of the typically televised trials, including those on Court TV, is that they are too unique to actually educate the public. High-profile trials may excite interest, but viewers tend to fixate on the political lure of the trial and not the legal issues. This is not true of syndi-court.

Furthermore, syndi-court is accessible to the average person in a way and to a degree that other televised legal proceedings are not. In terms of availability — how easy it is to find a syndi-court on the dial — anyone with a television set can find at least one syndi-court telecast on any weekday. Cable is not a pre-requisite. Finally, the production style of these shows ensures that their stories are easily digestible, their conflicts clear, and their resolutions swift. The end of the program always brings closure. Whereas real trials may confuse viewers with procedural and strategic issues and can drag on for a number of days, syndi-courts are intellectually accessible. At five hours per week, fifty-two weeks per year, viewers of only one show are exposed to 260 hours of syndi-court programming. Consequently, these shows possess a tremendous potential for impacting mass public opinion regarding the justice system. Even New York's Chief Judge has posited that knowledge and direct experience with the court system, even if that experience is "sitting in front of a television, watching *Judge Judy* . . . play(s) a huge role in public perceptions of the justice system." . . .

The Primacy of the Judge in Law and Syndi-Court

A primary symbol of law is the judge. Judges are the most important figures in our legal system in light of the responsibility and discretion they are given to orchestrate the proceedings before them. In fact, empirical evidence suggests that a judge can direct a jury to a verdict, even one the jury feels is unjust, as long as the jury believes the decision is legally correct. This prominence also makes judges important figures to society in general, carrying "multiple resonating meanings and associations, under-and-over-tones of mystic power."

The primary focus in syndi-court is also the judge: Judy, Gerry, Joe, and Mathis. Not only are most shows named after the judge (rather than the types of disputes or the venue), but the judge monopolizes much of the airtime. Yet, the role and authority of the syndi-court judge is one of the most significant points at which the line between law as pop culture and law as a means of regulating human affairs becomes blurred. Many individuals are not aware that syndi-court is not a real court of some type, that television brethren are not acting in the role of true judges, and in fact, that these "moral judges" are not real judges at all. To illustrate: One member of the California Commission on Judicial Performance has reported that "the public regularly submits complaints about Judge Judy and other TV judges," not "understand[ing] that Judge Judy and most of her cohorts are not present members of any judiciary." This confusion among the viewing public is hardly surprising, given that the tag-line of many of these shows intones that these are "real people, real cases." Thus, both types of judges play a critical role in the public's perception of justice. . . .

III. Discussion: The Influence of Syndi-Court

. . . The study's results demonstrate that syndi-court cultivates in frequent viewers beliefs that judges: are (and should be) an aggressive, expressive, opinionated, inquisitive lot; should indicate their opinion about the evidence or witnesses obviously and often; and are doing so even when silent. This may impact the public and potential jurors in a number of ways. First, the behavior of television judges may "diminish the brand" in the eyes of the public. Negative opinions about television judges may be extended to a negative view of the bench generally, the outcomes with which they are associated, and the justice system that they represent. Second, the television bench may alter the public's expectations of the justice system regarding what its functions are and how its successes are measured. Third, syndi-court may alter the behavior of viewers in response to the law. They may become prone to litigation, act out television litigant behavior when they appear in court, or seek to represent themselves pro se believing they know the law. Finally, the actual behaviors exhibited by the television bench may imply to the public the appropriate behavior of the true bench and the meaning of certain behaviors. Thus, judicial syndi-court behavior becomes an unintentional interpretive guide to be (mis)used by jurors in real-life trials. Jurors may actively look for clues, misinterpret behavior, or weigh innocuous behavior in real courtrooms.

Ironically, while syndi-court viewing seems to have a significant impact on viewers' perceptions of judges, study results also suggest that actual, personal experiences seem to have little impact. . . .

NOTES & QUESTIONS

1.   Popular court "reality" shows can be misleading because they overemphasize the judge's role and simplify procedural issues. But is there any benefit from the popularity of such shows? Does popular culture make us smarter about the legal system?

2.   What impact does Judge Judy's gender have on her persona as a television judge? Does her often harsh behavior seem more surprising because she is a woman? Traditionally, assertive women have been viewed as "unfeminine" or "bitchy." Is Judge Judy playing into that stereotype, or playing with that stereotype? Compare Judge Judy with some of her male counterparts. What kind of judicial personae do you see in Judge Joe Brown, Judge Mathis, or other male judges on daytime courtroom shows?

3.   How do real-life judges cultivate their own personae for the public eye? What is the most common persona among federal judges? How do elected state and local judges present themselves in their campaigns?

2. Judges as Cultural Symbols in Popular Culture and Senate Confirmation Hearings (is there any difference?)

Traditionally, the character of the judge in popular culture often seemed more like a cardboard caricature than a flesh and blood human being. But are judicial candidates at confirmation hearings any more "realistic?" Candidates for judgeships seem to do everything in their power to be perceived as bland, noncontroversial, and boring. Are portrayals of judges changing? As you read the next two articles, consider the judge as a character in popular culture.

FROM FLAT TO ROUND: CHANGING PORTRAYALS OF THE JUDGE IN AMERICAN POPULAR CULTURE
David Ray Papke
31 Journal of the Legal Profession 127 (2007)

American judges are not only important governmental functionaries but also familiar cultural symbols. For much of our history they have symbolized the vaunted rule of law, a system in which officials can resolve disputes and end controversies fairly and without bias by referring to a neutral, accessible body of laws. The concomitant notion that in the United States, law rules man rather than vice versa is at the very center of this nation's dominant ideology.

However, in recent decades new and different portrayals of judges in American popular culture suggest a change is occurring. Many pop cultural judges have slipped off their pedestal and joined the ranks of routine pop cultural characters. By accepting this new type of judicial characterization, consumers of American movies, television shows, and inexpensive fiction may be demonstrating that the rule of law itself is no longer particularly important in the way they understand their lives and nation. . . .

II. The Traditional Portrayal of the Judge in American Popular Culture

Portrayals of judges are hardly new in American popular culture. Melville Davisson Post was an immensely popular writer at the turn of the twentieth century, and many of his early stories concerned the mysterious lawyer Randolph Mason. Often, Mason won victory for his client at trial, and judges of course presided in the fictional courtroom. One of America's earliest law films was the legendary D.W. Griffith's *Falsely Accused.* The film built to a dramatic courtroom proceeding in which a devoted boyfriend screened a film in court in order to protect his true love from murder charges. Without batting an eye, the presiding judge sorted out which, if any, evidentiary rules might be relevant in these pop cultural proceedings.

Yet while judges were important and common in these and many other early pop cultural works, the judge generally was a simple, banal, even trivial character. Conventional literary theory would have described these judges as "flat" rather than "round" characters. E.M. Forster said that flat characters in their purest form "are constructed around a single idea or quality: when there is more than one factor in them, we get the beginning of the curve towards the round." Forster's goal was not to deplore or dismiss flat characters. He thought they "are easily recognized whenever they come in." Flat characters are useful "since they never need reintroducing, never run away, have not to be watched for development, and provide their own atmosphere — little luminous disks of a pre-arranged size pushed hither and thither like counters across the void or between the stars." E. M. Forster, *Aspects of the Novel and Related Writings* 103-105 (1927).

With hardly a bat of the eye, the culture industry routinely used judges in this way. When developing judicial characters, writers, actors, and producers rarely developed them fully. The judge himself — and traditionally the judge was always male — showed little emotion or passion. We learned little about his motivation and goals, his personal history and politics. The judge lacked individualizing detail and was also static, that is, he did not develop or change in the course of the film, short story, or television show. The judicial character was like a table top or a linoleum floor. He was flatter than flat.

As flat characters, pop cultural judges not surprisingly played limited roles in the plot. They made important decisions and rulings, especially in the courtroom and sometimes in chambers. However, we rarely saw them with their families and their lovers or anywhere but in the courthouse. They seldom interacted with the other characters in significant ways or altered the central course of events. In general, pop cultural judges were supposed to rule on objections, maintain order in the courtrooms, and sit sagely on high wearing a judicial robe. The film scholar David A. Black argues that even in the courtroom film genre the judge has "no causative relation." While one might refer to a western as a cowboy film, one never hears a courtroom film referred to "as a 'judge film.'"

Judicial characters do what they are supposed to do. Showing a taste for double-entendre, Black speaks of the judicial character's "narrative determination." On the one hand, Black points out, the judge is an agent of determination, that is, he rules on objections, resolves courtroom disputes, and even renders verdicts. Judges "have the privilege of determining the narrative, steering it, constraining it to take certain forms to the exclusion of others." On the other hand, judges are themselves determined by the narratives which have in fact been written and produced by others. "For all their decision-making and narrative-steering power, judges in film tend to be, in a word, predictable — specifically, predictable on the basis of narrative likelihood, antecedent, and idiom." David A. Black, "Narrative Determination and the Figure of the Judge," in *Law and Popular Culture* 680, 678 (Michael Freeman ed. 2005).

A particularly interesting but also fully representative flat judicial character appears in *Anatomy of a Murder*, a distinguished addition to the so-called "golden age" of the law film in the late 1950s and early 1960s. Many of the features of the pop cultural courtroom proceeding came to be standardized as a result of these films, and the films as a group constituted a formidable endorsement of the rule of law in the United States in the midst of the Cold War. . . .

III. Round Judges

When did the portrayal of the judge in American popular culture change? The question itself is potentially misleading. Intertwined with culture as a whole, popular culture does not shift overnight. The culture industry does not seal one package tightly and then immediately rip open a new one. The culture industry develops new conventions and genres, but it also readapts and rediscovers older ones. It combines older types of narratives into one, and it varies older types of narratives in ways that produce new types of narratives.

Perhaps the best that can be said is that during the 1970s changes in the pop cultural portrayal of judges became detectable. This did not happen with a single work or in a single year. An occasional rounded judicial character surely can be found before the 1970s, and numerous flat judicial characters still preside in our films, novels, and television shows thirty years later. But still, as the 1970s drew to an end, pop cultural judges were less likely to be undeveloped, flat characters. Instead of being simple symbols for the rule of law, pop cultural judges increasingly took the form of villains, sympathetic souls and egomaniacs.

It is tempting to link this kind of development to larger political developments of the decade. As his lies and dirty tricks came to light, Richard Nixon, the thirty-seventh President of the United States and second in the Duke University Law School Class of '34, resigned the Presidency in 1974. His successor, Gerald Ford, Yale Law School Class of '41, pardoned many of the Watergate conspirators, survived assassination attempts, and kept stumbling and bumping his head on doorways. Ford's successor, Jimmy Carter, the only man without a law degree to serve as President during the 1970s, came to Washington as an outsider, never established a working rapport with the Congress, and — much worse — could not find a way to extract the American hostages from their Iranian captors.

But as sorry as the major political events of the 1970s look in retrospect, it is difficult to argue any one of them caused a change in the way judges were portrayed in the popular culture. The change might instead derive from the more general "crisis of confidence" regarding the legal system and its major institutions that had begun in the 1960s and then settled more fully into place in the 1970s. Commentators were aware of the phenomenon in the 1970s, and major works appeared bemoaning the legal system's political biases, undue reliance on technicalities and detectable separation from morality and righteousness.

NOTES & QUESTIONS

1. Professor Papke goes on to point out a number of "round" (albeit very flawed) judge characters in films, including: *And Justice for All* (one judge in the film is a rapist, while another is crazy); *The Verdict* (the judge is corrupt); and *Suspect* (the judge is a murderer). Additionally, in the realm of television, the judge in the television series *Judging Amy* is a complex, multi-dimensional character. What images of judges in films, television, or novels can you think of that show the judge as a believable human being? Why do we still see flat judicial characters in popular culture? Is it easier to portray a round character in a weekly television series rather than in a film?

2. As a society, who do we select to be judges? Do we look for a "flat" character or a "round" character? Is there a particular backstory that plays well in judicial confirmation hearings? As you read the next article, think about the latest judicial confirmation hearings in the news, and the type of persona each candidate presents.

JUDICIAL CONFIRMATION WARS: IDEOLOGY AND THE BATTLE FOR THE FEDERAL COURTS
Sheldon Goldman
39 University of Richmond Law Review 871 (2005)

I. Why the Focus on Ideology?

Ordinarily, with the exception of the nomination of U.S. Supreme Court Justices, the nomination and confirmation of federal judges is not a subject of extensive media attention and consequently not on the minds of most Americans. During recent presidential election campaigns, including the most recent one in 2004, the opposing sides have raised the issue of the appointment of federal judges. The major party platforms adopted by each party's national convention mention judicial selection, and it is clear that the party division over judicial selection is profound. The 2004 Democratic Party platform is succinct in what it has to say about the selection of judges: "We support the appointment of judges who will uphold our laws and constitutional rights, not their own narrow agendas."

The 2004 Republican Party platform is more expansive in what it has to say about judges and judicial selection. In a special section of the ninety-two page platform, titled "Supporting Judges Who Uphold the Law," the platform states in part:

> In the federal courts, scores of judges with activist backgrounds in the hard-left now have lifetime tenure. Recent events have made it clear that

these judges threaten America's dearest institutions and our very way of life. In some states, activist judges are redefining the institution of marriage. The Pledge of Allegiance has already been invalidated by the courts once, and the Supreme Court's ruling has left the Pledge in danger of being struck down again — not because the American people have rejected it and the values that it embodies, but because a handful of activist judges threaten to overturn common sense and tradition. And while the vast majority of Americans support a ban on partial birth abortion, this brutal and violent practice will likely continue by judicial fiat. . . . President Bush has established a solid record of nominating only judges who have demonstrated respect for the Constitution and the democratic processes of our republic, and Republicans in the Senate have strongly supported those nominees. We call upon obstructionist Democrats in the Senate to abandon their unprecedented and highly irresponsible filibuster of President Bush's highly qualified judicial nominees, and to allow the Republican Party to restore respect for the law to America's courts.

In another section of the platform there is a clear statement of the use of ideological litmus tests for the appointment of judges: "We support the appointment of judges who respect traditional family values and the sanctity of innocent human life."

The core constituencies of both parties, as well as scholars of law and courts, understand that judging is an art and not a science. It is a process of applying the provisions of statutes or constitutions — which may be vaguely worded — to a specific set of facts. The judge must figure out for herself what the words of the Constitution, the statute, or the precedent mean as applied to the case at hand. The study of the use of discretion by judges and how that judicial discretion impacts the claims of the parties is the study of judicial behavior, a major facet of the public law subfield within the Political Science discipline.

Studies of judicial behavior have identified judges who are judicially liberal in their willingness to give a generous interpretation to those asserting their civil rights, political liberties, or due process rights. Other judges have been identified as judicially conservative in their willingness to support government's claims that regulation of rights and liberties is in the greater public interest. And there are judicial moderates who by definition fall somewhere in between the judicially liberal and the judicially conservative. . . .

Federal judges can and do rule on almost every facet of life in the United States. Indeed, it matters who sits on the Supreme Court of the United States and on the lower federal courts. And Justices and judges are not fungible, something very well understood by advocacy groups on the right and left who have mobilized their forces and resources in the judicial confirmation wars seeking to influence presidents and senators.

NOTES & QUESTIONS

1. Lately, judges have been cast as troublemakers. Republicans complain of liberal "activist judges," and Democrats bemoan the narrow agendas of judges who must pass conservative ideological "litmus tests." What role should ideology play in judicial confirmations?

2. Is being a judge dangerous? If you are a judge, are you in physical and spiritual peril? In popular culture, judges frequently are portrayed as powerless victims in dire peril from the profaning world of politics and money. In *The Pelican Brief*, a hit man kills two Supreme Court Justices who were going to rule against a developer.

3. Death is not the only peril for those involved in the power plays of judicial selection. Moral and spiritual corruption are possibilities, too. In *The Seduction of Joe Tynan* (1979), Alan Alda plays a Senator (Joe Tynan) who becomes embroiled in the political machinations surrounding the nomination of a Supreme Court Justice. The judicial nominee made a racist speech some twenty years ago, and a film of that speech has recently come to light. Civil rights lobbyist Karen Traynor, played by Meryl Streep, seductively tells Tynan, "Senator, I think you are the most exciting political figure in this country today, and when I think of the splash you could make if you had this film, I get weak in the knees." She adds belatedly, "And, of course, it's the right thing to do." But is it in fact the right thing to do? The problem is that Tynan's friend and mentor, an elderly Senator, has asked Tynan to support this nominee because the elderly Senator does not want the nominee running against him in the next election. The question of who is the best nominee for the Supreme Court quickly becomes subsumed in back-room deals and the exchange of political favors or political threats (if you don't go along with my nominee, that favorite bill of yours will be stuck in committee forever, etc.). Ultimately, Tynan betrays his old friend and abandons his family. Tynan convinces himself he is doing everything for an ultimate greater good, but he fails to recognize his own corruption.

Is the judicial selection process inherently political? Is that necessarily a bad thing? What is the best method of choosing judges — periodic elections, political appointments, rotation of candidates, or other methods?

3. Where Does Justice Dwell? The Courthouse as the Judge's Domain

Judges are powerful not just because of who they are, but because of what they represent. But what signs and symbols surround the figure of the judge? The next reading makes the important point that the physical space and design of a courtroom or courthouse actually manifest and reinforce certain ideologies about judicial power in our legal system.

Courthouses and courtrooms act as sign systems, signifying justice through their architectural details and use of space. If you take a drive through any old city center, chances are that you can tell which building is the courthouse. But how do you know this? Imposing pillars, images of scales of justice, lots of steps, cathedral-like facades — how does the structure of a building send a message about power? What do we "naturally" expect to see in a building that houses Justice itself?

How does the sign system that is a courtroom signify messages about justice and power? Every litigant (and every attorney, for that matter) has had the experience of entering a courtroom for the first time and being overawed or intimidated or even exhilarated by the physical trappings of justice. The space of the courtroom sends a number of subtle messages about power. For example, the judge's bench often is elevated so that he or she literally is above everyone else in the courtroom. The next reading suggests that courtrooms are designed to signify that a judge is independent, separate, in control, and neutral.

SOCIAL IDEOLOGY AS SEEN THROUGH COURTROOM AND COURTHOUSE ARCHITECTURE
Jonathan D. Rosenbloom
22 Columbia-VLA Journal of Law & the Arts 463 (1998)

2. The Judge's Space

. . . The architecture creating the judge's position embodies an ideology based in independence, separation, and authority. By isolating the judge's seat and designing it to be the highest in the courtroom, the architecture implies that the judge is independent from anyone or anything in the courtroom. He is elevated above the bickering between the attorneys below him and the jury off to the side of him. His position implies detachment from the proceedings and that he is an impartial referee.

The location of the judge's bench underscores his control over the proceedings. Positioned at the end of the courtroom, the judge is able to maintain a watchful eye over everyone in the courtroom and over the proceedings. The only corner that would have been out of the judge's perspective is cut short by three extended triangles, giving the judge the maximum opportunity to view the entire courtroom.

Because the architecture symbolizes the judge's role as an unbiased arbitrator separate and independent from the proceedings, the architecture is consistent with the ideology invested in the judge's position in the actual application of the law. During a criminal trial the judge is "the chief member of a court" and is in "control of proceedings and the decision (maker) of questions of law or discretion." Moreover, unlike the adversarial attorneys, the judge is required to play a passive and unbiased role as "the citadel of the public justice and the public security." Further, the Supreme Court has held that the Due Process clauses of the Fifth and Fourteenth Amendments entitle a criminal defendant to a trial before an "unbiased judge."

From the moment the judge enters the courtroom, his stature as "the citadel" of justice is recognized. The judge enters from his private entrance in area two. He is the only courtroom inhabitant to use this entrance. [Figure Deleted] This separate entrance implies that the judge is apart and independent from the proceedings, attorneys, jurors, and public — consistent with the constitutional principles cited above.

When a witness is called to testify, the architecture further exemplifies the judge's position as an unbiased arbitrator. After being called, a witness assumes her designated position and all attention is directed toward the corridor of conversation in Figure 14. [Figure Deleted] The judge becomes secondary and his appearance is only acknowledged when opposing counsel makes an objection. Upon objection, the focus shifts from the corridor in Figure 14 [deleted] to the adversarial set-up in Figure 9. [Figure Deleted] Once the judge rules on the objection, focus moves back to the attorney-witness corridor and again secondary importance is placed on the judge. The architecture forces the judge to play a much more passive role by having the judge fall into the background, emphasizing the importance of conducting the proceeding in a manner that allows the attorneys to tell their story.

Designing the judge's space to reflect her passive role during witness examination is critical to the architecture of the American courtroom. For example, this type of architecture would be inadequate to serve the Chinese criminal court system, which permits active questioning of a witness by the judge. In the 1984 criminal trial in China of the "Gang of Four," while a witness was being examined, the judge stopped the proceedings and stated:

> "[The defendant's] denial absolutely cannot stand up. Today the court's investigation has made it clear that [defendant] schemed with [another defendant] to conduct illegal searches and to persecute close acquaintances from the literary and art world of the 1930s, and this had a goal she would not disclose. What must be especially pointed out here is that his crime had extremely serious consequences. The five literary and art figures mentioned above, after having had their homes illegally searched, all met vicious physical persecution. . . .

> [Defendant] cannot evade her criminal responsibility. It must also be pointed out that the illegal searches of those people's homes, and the physical maltreatment of them, were crimes committed jointly by [the defendants].

> Call [the next witness]."

This colloquy during an American trial would not only raise serious constitutional issues about the judge's bias but also would not function in the architecture of the American courtroom, where a judge's position is designed to be unbiased and passive during witness examination. Designing the judge's position to be secondary during witness examination implies a position of passivity and neutrality — ideals embraced by our society's view of the judge's role.

The architecture defining the judge's space emphasizes his position as defined by the constitutional principles. Those principles warrant a design that embodies a judge's role of independence, separation, control, and neutrality in the actual application of the law. . . .

IV. The Courthouse — A Perspective on Society's Perception of the Law

If dissecting the interior design gives us a glimpse of how the law is actually practiced from an internal perspective, dissecting the exterior design of the courthouse should provide us with a glimpse of how the public at large views law from the outside.

A necessary starting point to unearth this perception is a brief review of architectural courthouse history to unveil the initial social perceptions of law and the architecture those perceptions embodied. If, as in courtroom architecture, there are no architectural changes in courthouse design, then the perception unearthed from the original architecture should be the same as today's perception of the law. However, as we will see, this is not the case and courthouse architecture has evolved taking on a new shape — implying a changing external perception of the law.

A. A Brief History of Courthouse Architecture

Courthouse architecture is partially responsible for creating one of the most prolific public architectural periods in America — the Greek Revival. The Greek Revival period was introduced to American public architecture during the early 19th century. The birth of the Greek Revival period was a product of several significant historical events both architecturally and politically. In 1738 at Herculaneum and then in 1748 at Pompeii, both in southern Italy, major ancient Roman cities were excavated. These excavations attracted many scholars who produced numerous books, sketches, and discussions analyzing the rediscovered architectural style of the Roman cities.

Thirty years later in 1776, America declared its independence from England and began searching for an independent identity. Part of that search included breaking away from England's Georgian architectural style popular in the 18th century. Georgian architecture became a symbol of the English monarchy, and adopting a new architectural style would symbolize the new-born country's freeing itself from England. Intrigued by the newly rediscovered classical architecture of Herculaneum and Pompeii and searching for a new architectural style, the new United States began to adopt classical architecture as its defining architectural style. . . .

Although America had begun to adopt the classical style, it was not until the War of 1812 with the destruction of Washington D.C. and the beginning of a new era of presidents, James Monroe (1817-1825) and Andrew Jackson (1829-1837), that Greek Revival began to flourish. Architects such as Robert Mills (1781-1855), William Strickland (1799-1854), and Thomas U. Walter (1804-1887) proposed numerous public buildings all designed in the Greek Revival style to maintain the national ideology of independence, worldliness, and liberty adopted by Jefferson and Clerisseau. While holding the official government position of Architect of Public Buildings, Mills stated, "we have the same principles and materials to work upon that the ancients had, and we should adapt these materials to the habits and customs of our people as they did theirs."

By the mid-1800's all public buildings and most large residential buildings were being built in the Greek Revival style. Greek Revival had become the adopted symbol of democratic America and produced some of the most symbolic and celebrated early American buildings that would influence generations of architects to come.

One of those architects was Cass W. Gilbert (1859-1934). Architect of the United States Supreme Court in Washington D.C. and the old United States District Court, Southern District of New York ("Old Courthouse"), Gilbert embraced and maintained the architectural ideals of democracy, independence, worldliness and stability presented by Jefferson, Mills, Strickland, and Walter into the 20th century. To Gilbert, it was above all else that public architecture:

> should inspire "just pride in the state, and [be] an education to oncoming generations to see these things, imponderable elements of life and character, set before the people for their enjoyment and betterment. The educational value above is worth to the state far more than it cost — it supplements the education furnished by the public schools and university [and] is a symbol of the civilization, culture and ideals of our country.' "

Lois Craig et. al., *The Federal Presence* (1977) at 234 (quoting Gilbert).

Gilbert believed, like the architects for some 100 years before him, that Greek Revival architecture had embodied a perception of "civilization, culture and ideals of our country" essential to a courthouse and the external perception of what occurs within it. He and other architects of government buildings created a government style based on Greek Revival, known as Beaux-Arts, to symbolize the stability and strength of the government. . . .

B. Modern Courthouse Architecture — The New United States District Court, Southern District of New York

The days of the classical courthouse are over. In the past five years, architects have proposed designs for new federal courthouses in Alexandria (Virginia), Boston, Charleston (South Carolina), Kansas City (Missouri), Minneapolis, St. Louis, and Tampa. These designs abandon Greek Revival architecture for new modern designs.

One example of the new design is the new Federal District Court, Southern District of New York ("New Courthouse"). Completed in 1995, the New Courthouse is the nation's largest federal district courthouse. Rising twenty-seven stories with a nine story wing, the New Courthouse stands less than 100 feet away from the Old Courthouse but could not be more different. It completely abandons the classical style and employs an entirely different architectural style. While the Old Courthouse is symmetrical, unified in color, and classically structured with columns and capitals, the New Courthouse is asymmetrical, multicolored, and structured with curves and modern exterior facing. . . .

Before actually entering the New Courthouse, it is impossible to know what type of activity occurs within it. . . .

C. Inconsistency of Exterior Courthouse Architecture

The exterior courthouse architecture has stylistically changed in recent years. The new style abandons the classical vocabulary used for courthouse architecture for 200 years. Since the founding of the nation, architects employed the classical style of architecture because it created an external perception that the law and the country were based on an ideology founded in democracy, independence, and stability. The exterior façade embodied this perception by physically structuring society's perception of the law without while harnessing the legal activity within. It influenced society's perception of the law and imputed stability. Stability has been one of the keystones of the American criminal justice system and has been embodied by the use of classical architecture. The classical architecture provided faith and an expectation of justice in law. However, the classical style of architecture has been abandoned by the new courthouse design. If the exterior courthouse architecture is society's perception of the law and that architecture has experienced a change, it follows that society's perception of the law has changed as well.

V. Unchanged Courtroom Architecture Versus Changed Courthouse Architecture

We can only speculate as to what this change in society's perception of the law as experienced through courthouse architecture means. There are, however, two fundamental components of that change: first, there is the rejection of the classical architecture and the ideology it sustains; and second, there is the adoption of a new style and the corresponding ideology the new style sustains.

As a starting point, rejecting the old classical style may be interpreted as an expression of society's increased discontent with the law and its growing uncertainty regarding the system's ability to administer justice.

However, what replaces that style? A quick comparison of architectural styles reveals that the new architectural style is one commonly recognized as the style used for corporate architecture. . . .

What does housing the system of justice in a style recognized for its association with corporate structures say about society's external perception of law? Does it mean law's role in society is to be read as couched in corporate values?

Disguising the internal functions of the law behind a corporate façade could be interpreted as an attempt to impute corporate order and to overcome uncertainty by embracing corporate values such as efficiency, order, and predictability. It proceeds on the perception that the internal functions of the building are anchored in something perceived to be secure, or at least more secure than the current perception of the legal system. The corporate structure symbolizes what today's society considers or recognizes to be stable, and the need to house the internal application of the law in that stability.

In this way, the exterior façade functions as corporate advertising that masks prevalent, negative views about the law's state of efficiency and legitimacy. The façade advertises to the public a perception of the law as efficient, predictable, and stable. The corporate façade represents that stability and is tacked onto the courtroom functions, so as to create an almost parasitic relationship, where the wounded reputation of the legal system aligns itself with the power, wealth, and largeness of the corporate structure and society's perception of it on the outside. Once seen as the symbol of monumentality, power, and stability, classical architecture has given way to society's new perception of monumentality, power, and stability — the corporate structure.

Aligning the courthouse with the private corporate sector also has the effect of rejecting the independence commonly associated with the justice system. The exterior façade blurs the line separating the independent public functions in the courtroom and the private realm by linking the legal system to the corporate sector. It implies a connection with the corporate structure or an external perception that only the corporate world can get justice. In other words, the system of justice housed within operates only within the confines of the corporate structure without. . . .

Conclusion

I began this article as an investigation of courtroom and courthouse architecture and the extent to which it embodies societal ideology. The investigation quickly revealed an internal strife between the interior courtroom design and the exterior courthouse design. A dissection of the interior, where the law is actually practiced, revealed that the design is consistent with ideology invested in the actual application of law. It also revealed that just as the ideology in law has remained substantially consistent, so too has the interior architecture. A dissection of the exterior courthouse, however, revealed that there is a changing societal perception of the law that was reflected in a changing architectural style of the exterior. The external perception of the law is no longer viewed as the stable vestige of justice as perceived through the classical architecture. The new courthouse architecture raises questions of stability and performance by breaking with the classical style of the past and adopting a corporate architectural style. To the extent that a dominant societal ideology exists, it is manifested in courthouse architecture and an analysis of that architecture indicates a postmodern ideology.

What this discovery and the existence of this internal/external clash mean is open to speculation. It is, however, a significant indication that something is changing in the way the public perceives law's role in contemporary society. It is a perception that sharply contrasts with the impression of continuity within the building's interior.

NOTES & QUESTIONS

1. Has the classical, Greek Revival style of courthouse been replaced in your city with the more corporate-style building? Does it matter if today's courthouse looks like another office building or insurance company? Do you agree that this suggests law's social role is becoming more business-oriented and less focused on intangibles such as democracy or justice?

2. Are there any positive benefits to the more corporate and less Greek temple style? Are lay people more comfortable in a business-like setting than in a Greek temple? Are courthouses with the "business" look less intimidating? Or do they seem more bureaucratic and less idealistic? Which style do you prefer? Does your answer depend on whether you think law is more of a down-to-earth, practical business, or something concerned with loftier goals?

3. According to Rosenbloom, while the exteriors of modern courthouses may have changed, the layout of courtrooms has remained remarkably consistent over time. What signs and symbols still operate within the courtroom to signify the power of the judge? Consider not only the layout of the court, but also such signs as judicial robes; the bailiff's announcement that all must rise when the judge

enters; the manner in which attorneys address the judge; the judge's gavel; and other accoutrements of power. If you were a visitor from another country sitting in an American courtroom, how would you know which person is the judge?

4. The Outlaw Judge

Judges who break the law are an unsettling group in popular culture. Some, like Paul Newman's Judge Roy Bean, blithely and unconcernedly break laws left and right. Others act only after a deep moral struggle and extensive soul searching. Does the disturbing figure of the Judge-as-Lawbreaker reflect our societal anxiety that those we "allow" to have legal power over us through our societal institutions may not have the requisite moral authority? The following excerpt describes the real Judge Roy Bean.

LAW IN TEXAS LITERATURE: TEXAS JUSTICE — JUDGE ROY BEAN STYLE
Shawn E. Tuma
21 Review of Litigation 551 (2002)

"Hear ye! Hear ye! This honorable court is now in session, and if anybody wants a snort before we start, step up to the bar and name your poison, hod-ziggity dog."

— Judge Roy Bean

I. Introduction

The mention of the name Judge Roy Bean causes most people to think of "the Hangin' Judge." Roy Bean is one of Texas's most infamous jurists. He gained his reputation by dispensing "law, of a sort, in the dusty country west of the Pecos River." It was this reputation that gave rise to his becoming known as "The Law West of the Pecos."

Roy Bean had no legal training, but he played a judge in real life; using his saloon for a courtroom, he dispensed justice while serving and consuming beer. Judge Bean, whose real name was Phantly Bean, was technically a justice of the peace who, according to some, appointed himself to office. Bean relied on one law book — a copy of the 1879 Revised Statutes of the State of Texas — and a six-shooter for the basis of his judicial decisions.

Bean's decisions were "witty, unorthodox, prejudiced, but sometimes wise decisions, defying higher courts and scandalizing jurisprudence." Frequently, he would fine culprits a round of drinks for the crowd and require lawyers to "cover" beers for Bruno — the beer-guzzling black bear he kept in his saloon.

Although Bean is a legitimate historical figure, his reputation has made him mythical to such a degree that it is often impossible to distinguish between what is fact and what is fiction. According to Jack Skiles, one of the few biographers of Roy Bean:

Numerous stories have been told about Roy Bean and many were true, or at least based on truth, but just as many were tall tales. It was only natural that the truth would be stretched, for he was a colorful character and many of the genuine stories about the old judge were strange and interesting enough to be fiction.

His colorful character is what makes Judge Roy Bean suitable for studying in the context of law and literature. Judge Bean was such a notorious jurist that many of the stories associated with him, be they fact or fiction, are widely recognized in contemporary culture. The legendary stories surrounding Bean serve as good indicators of what is on many people's social conscience. Moreover, the many character traits exemplified by stories about Judge Bean serve as good examples for the people with whom lawyers come into contact. . . .

IV. Judge Roy Bean — What a Character!

A. Bean's Respect for the Law

The legend of Judge Roy Bean has had a profound impact on giving the Old West the image with which it is saddled. Modern day authors continue to make analogies to Roy Bean to convey to their readers a rough and rowdy image or one lacking fairness and basic procedure.

Bean cared very little for the substantive law. Early in his career, he decided cases based upon the "law" as he thought it should be as he had no legal training and no law books. However, to make his decisions seem more dignified, he had a blank book in which he had written his own "staoots" in addition to his poker rules: "Cheating and horse theft," he recorded, "is hanging offenses if ketched." On another page he wrote, "A full beats a straight unless the one holding the full is not straight or is himself too full." Bean later obtained a law book, but little changed.

As Bean's career progressed, it became clear that his authority rested squarely on his one law book — though only when it supported his decision — and his six-shooter, with the latter carrying more weight. He didn't pay much attention to technicalities and ran his court on common sense principles; he simply did not see the need to keep up with the current laws. In his words, "They sent me a new book every year or so . . . but I used them to light fires with."

Even when confronted with a valid law, Bean wouldn't let it sway his decision. In one story, Bean and an attorney were debating whether there was a statute governing the attorney's case. The attorney requested to see Bean's Revised Statutes and, upon finding the statute for which he was looking, replied to Bean: "Here it is — you may start reading, Section F, Article 48." Bean looked it over carefully and ripped the page out. "It's a bad law — it's been repealed — you're still a thief."

Bean didn't always ignore laws; sometimes he would just "interpret" them to support the result that he desired. In what is perhaps Bean's most famous decision, he once ruled that he could find no Texas law prohibiting killing a "Chinaman." "I find the law very explicit on murdering your fellow man, but there's nothing here about killing a Chinaman. Case dismissed." Bean's inaccurate construction of the law may be attributed to the fact that an Irish rail-hand killed the Chinese worker and the Irishman was accompanied in court by a large group of fellow Irishmen there to ensure that their countryman was treated fairly. It was only after Bean surveyed the "tough crowd" that he made his decision.

In addition to ignoring laws, Bean was not opposed to making up laws when it suited his purposes. In another of Bean's better-known cases, he held an inquest over the body of a man who had fallen to his death while working. Bean searched the man's body and found a six-shooter and what is believed to be approximately forty dollars, and then he said, "I will have to fine this man $40 for carrying concealed weapons and that's my rulin'." There remains little doubt that the fine influenced Bean's decision more than the law. Bean's respect for procedure was no different than his respect for substantive law — he wasn't going to let technicalities interfere with the business of his court.

Bean is said to have "considered it a personal affront if a defendant hired a lawyer, and he chose to use jurors only on rare occasions — then selecting them from his best customers." Bean's court usually resembled an inquest, but it has been said that on occasions he actually heard evidence and decided serious cases.

The rough and rowdy way that Bean implemented his own justice demonstrates that a "system of justice" need not follow even its own rules. This system has been called "a legal system only in the Pickwickian sense that a void contract is one kind of contract." For example, one of Bean's more famous literary quotes is, "I always give 'em a fair trial before I hang 'em." In literature he was understood to be a strong proponent of stern and swift justice — justice as he saw it: "He sentenced a number of supposed horse thieves and cattle rustlers to death, sometimes on the flimsiest evidence, and these sentences were carried out. 'Give him a drink and tie him to the nearest limb! Well, what'll you have feller?' And that was all."

NOTES & QUESTIONS

1.   What is appealing about a character such as Judge Roy Bean? What is subversive about an outlaw judge? Most practitioners know at least one hard-nosed, "hanging" judge. Apocryphal stories circulate about such judges, and newly minted practitioners quake in their shoes if they must make an appearance before the hanging judge. Do modern-day judges ever attempt to play into the "cowboy justice" style of judging? Is this a judicial persona that is limited to white males?

2.   In his portrayal of Judge Roy Bean in *The Life and Times of Judge Roy Bean*, Paul Newman embodies the law, even draping himself in the American flag. He puts up a sign on a former brothel — "Law West of the Pecos" — and tells the itinerant preacher played by Anthony Perkins, "I am the new law in this area." However, his law is very much grounded in his perception of individual justice, and when he comes to a law he does not like, he simply rips it out of the statute book. (When a lawyer points to a statute, the Judge says, "That's a bad law. I just repealed it." He then threatens to feed the lawyer to a pet bear.) Ironically, he says, "I know the law, since I have spent my entire life in its flagrant disregard." In one of his final battles, when the Judge comes to fight by the side of the daughter he has

abandoned, he clarifies that his role as a judge is to pursue justice. "Who are you?" asks a puzzled ruffian during the fight. "Justice, you sons of bitches!" the judge replies from horseback, before beginning one last rampage.

3. In *The Star Chamber*, Judge Stephen Hardin, played by Michael Douglas, feels all too keenly the disjuncture between law and justice and agonizes when he lets two alleged child molesters go on a technicality. The murdered child's father confronts Hardin in the hallway and tries to get him to look at his son's school photo. The father says, "Look at the photo. That was my boy, not a plaintiff or a statute!" Hardin protests, "I can only deal with law." The father responds, "What about justice? Do you ever deal with that?"

Near the breaking point, Hardin confesses his doubts about the system to his wife: "First day of law school, looking at law books in the library, it was like I was looking at the truth . . . in all those rows . . . . The truth. The law. Nothing is right or wrong. It's either the law or it's not the law. Turns out that right and wrong count. See, the bad guys, they get hold of one of those books, they find something and I give them the prize. Doesn't matter that it wasn't put there for them, it was put there for that little kid and the five women, it doesn't matter. What happened to right and wrong? It's gotta be somewhere in one of those books."

After yet another child is murdered, Hardin contacts Judge Benjamin Caulfield, a mentor played by Hal Holbrook, who convinces Douglas to join a secret group of vigilante judges who hire hit men to kill defendants they believe to be guilty. As Caulfield says, "We're the goddamned law. . . . We are accountable, we are the judges, for Christ's sake. We are the law. . . . Someone has kidnapped Justice and hidden it in the law. Now who's better qualified than we are to find it, you tell me that?"

A revenge fantasy fuels the thirst for justice we feel as an audience, but those emotions dissolve once we learn, along with Judge Hardin, that the wrong men are going to be executed. Does the film "cheat" by making the defendants actually innocent? Would *The Star Chamber* have been a better, more honest film if the guilt of the defendants was never in doubt?

4. Can we split off our professional lives from our personal lives? What are the costs of doing so? Many of us know judges or lawyers who, like the lawyer Wemmick in Dickens' *Great Expectations* (1860), are coldly professional at work and warm and loving at home. Wemmick takes this trait so far that if you ask him the same question at work and then again at home (where he cares lovingly for his aged father), he will give two completely different answers.

Similarly, Fredric March's Judge Cooke in *An Act of Murder* (1948) is a loving husband and father at home, but his daughter, who is a first-year law student, complains that Dad stops being a human being and becomes "a talking law book" in the courtroom. (The Judge's first name is "Calvin," a name resonant with a sacred and uncompromising belief system.) When he learns his wife is terminally ill, Judge Cooke struggles with the relentless overlap between the world of law and the world of the home. He lies to his wife about her condition, the first breach of his moral code. "It's only a lie of omission," says the doctor. The Judge wretchedly responds, "[T]he thing that has always made our life so good is the truth between us." His wife's condition dramatically worsens, and Judge Cooke purposely crashes the car in which they are riding, unaware that his wife has already taken an overdose of pills. The Judge then asks the District Attorney to issue an indictment for murder, although he doesn't want a lawyer: "I've committed an act of murder, and I must be tried for it." His rigidly rule-oriented solution is that he must be punished for his actions. However, his refusal to consider the nuances of judgment shows him as a judge who may know the letter of the law, but lacks an understanding of the spirit of the law. After his trial, Judge Cooke has been educated into being a better judge. He has learned that the law is not simply the letter, but also the spirit. As he says, "A man's heart must be considered."

5.   Like the prior reading on Judge Roy Bean, the next reading also centers on an unorthodox type of judge. While Judge Roy Bean brings his own brand of justice to the Wild West, the futuristic Judge Dredd is a street judge authorized to carry out instant punishment in a dystopian future society. However, where Judge Roy Bean plays fast and loose with the law (tearing out pages of a statute he does not like), Judge Dredd is ultra-committed to the law — at least until he himself is wrongfully accused. Consider the differences and similarities between the two judges as you read the next section.

5.   The Judge as Action Hero: Comics, Science Fiction, and Heavy Metal

The great legal scholar Robert Cover noted that legal interpretation takes place "in a field of pain and death." This is particularly true in the violent, dystopian world of *Judge Dredd*. The character of Judge Dredd began life in a popular British comic book and has continued to be the reigning action hero judge in several videogames, a science fiction feature film, and even heavy metal lyrics ("I am the Law" proved an irresistible line for the group Anthrax). Some of the appeal of the character surely lies in the power and immediacy of justice delivered on the streets. What is lost in due process is gained in visceral satisfaction at the spectacle of righteous punishment. Consider what else is lost (or gained) when the courtroom disappears and judging is done on the wicked streets.

FILM, LAW AND THE DELIVERY OF JUSTICE: THE CASE OF JUDGE DREDD AND THE DISAPPEARING COURTROOM

Steve Greenfield and Guy Osborn

6(2) Journal of Criminal Justice and Popular Culture 35 (1999)

IN THE THIRD MILLENNIUM, THE WORLD CHANGED, CLIMATE, NATIONS, ALL WERE IN UPHEAVAL . . . THE EARTH TRANSFORMED INTO A POISONOUS SCORCHED DESERT, KNOWN AS "THE CURSED EARTH."

MILLIONS OF PEOPLE CROWDED INTO A FEW MEGA CITIES, CITIES WHERE ROVING BANDS OF STREET SAVAGES CREATED VIOLENCE THE JUSTICE SYSTEM COULD NOT CONTROL. LAW AS WE KNOW IT COLLAPSED. FROM THE DECAY ROSE A NEW

ORDER. A SOCIETY RULED BY A NEW ELITE FORCE. . . . A FORCE WITH THE POWER TO DISPENSE BOTH JUSTICE AND PUNISHMENT. . . . THEY WERE THE POLICE, JURY AND EXECUTIONER ALL IN ONE.

THEY WERE THE JUDGES.

James Olmeyer III, History of the Megacities, Chapter II "Justice," *in Dredd in the Future: One Man is Law* (N. Barrett, 1995).

. . . The focus of this essay is the law film outside of the courtroom and more particularly the notion of justice delivered on the street. In many ways this phenomena has its roots in vigilante films that have witnessed both civilian (the *Deathwish* series) and "flesh and blood" police (*Dirty Harry*), examples of direct justice. This "procession" is completed by *Judge Dredd* in which formal judicial power is taken from the court to the streets of Mega City by judges who convict and sentence offenders instantaneously with due process replaced by a blast from Dredd's Lawgiver. Whilst Judge Dredd would not obviously appear to be a law film in terms of our traditional expectations of what that denotes, it does share common themes with more conventional law films with central issues of right and wrong, justice and injustice, law and lawlessness. This essay seeks to explore the cinematic view of informal justice and will show that the development of such films indicate that the issue within postmodern filmic justice is not the question of "*what* is a legal film?"; rather a less spatially defined notion of "*where* is justice delivered?" Once outside of the traditional courtroom and without the formal legal procedures, law has been portrayed as subjective reductionism; any suggestion of an objective impartial process is removed. However there may still be rules and procedures that need to be followed and it is this particular element of *Judge Dredd* that draws it back within the more traditional law film boundaries. . . .

The film, *Judge Dredd*, was based on the very successful comic of the same name. Dredd is a clone who, having excelled at the Academy, becomes a full judge in 2079. He has some of the physical attributes of Robocop; although he is totally human, he has an automaton and dogmatic approach to law enforcement; Robocop is almost the alternative; an automaton with added humanity. In an early scene, Dredd announces his presence to a group of squatters with the aphorism; "I am the Law". This is a neat encapsulation of his perceived role and duty; to arrest, sentence, and if necessary execute:

"All right!" Purple Ears raised his hands. "I gives up. You bes takin' me in!"

"Niner-eight-zero-four. Assault on a Judge with a deadly weapon . . ."

Purple Ears forced a weak grin through his bloody teeth. "Don't tell me. Life, right?"

"No," Dredd said. "Death."

He squeezed the trigger of his weapon. Squeezed it and didn't stop. Purple Ears began to sizzle like bacon in a pan. (Barrett, 1995).

While Dredd operates as a judge empowered to dispense justice on the street, he is simultaneously bound to the strict formality of the Mega City law book. This is neatly exemplified by his speech to student judges at the Academy:

> Helmet and body armour. Yours, *when* you graduate. Lawgiver 2, 25 rounds side arm with mission variable voice programmed ammunition. Yours, *if* you graduate. Mark 4 Law Master. Improved model, with dual arm based lazer cannon, vertical take-off and landing capabilities, range 500 km. Yours if you can get it to work. All of these things you see here are toys. At the end of the day, when you're all alone in the dark, the only thing that counts is this. . . . **The Law.** And you will be alone when you swear to uphold these ideals. For most of us it's only death in the streets, with a few of us that survive to old age, the proud loneliness of the long walk. A walk that every judge must take outside these city walls into the unknown of the cursed earth and there spend your last remaining days taking law to the lawless. This is what it means to be a Judge and this is the commitment I expect. Class Dismissed. (From Screenplay)

Dredd's adherence to the letter of the law is seen early on in the film when he arrests Herman Ferguson following a block riot in Megacity One. Dredd's suggestion that Ferguson should have jumped from the window of the block to protect himself rather than commandeer a food unit (and hence commit a legal violation) is met with Ferguson's reply that as it was 40 floors up it would have been a suicidal move. Dredd's riposte is merely that it may well have been fatal, but at least it would have been legal. This formality perhaps best described as an overly literal and black letter approach to the law is relaxed as Dredd himself relaxes. He becomes more at ease with his own humanity as a result of his growing relationship with one of his female colleagues, Judge Hershey. As Dredd is searching for companionship outside of the law, the strict letter of the law becomes less important and justice dominates. Dredd even kills guards, albeit they are trying to kill him, in his pursuit of the truth. Law is given a vestige of humanity, as is Dredd, when it is shown that errors can be made, a concept that Dredd doesn't at first accept. That Dredd himself is framed and wrongly convicted forces him to confront his belief in the infallibility of the law.

As noted above, Dredd is located in a hinterland between the formalism of the law and a quest for (higher) justice. Judge Dredd switches the "action" from the courtroom to the sidewalk but unlike the vigilantism of police or civilians, his sidewalk justice is given with the full backing of the law — the sidewalk becomes Dredd's own legitimized courtroom. However, unlike many of the legal films based within the courtroom, Dredd's obedience to the law and belief in the sanctity of the law is absolute — law being more important than justice. Effectively, Judge Dredd operates within a contradiction of informalism (of arena) and formalism (of law), although he is finally forced to confront his black letter approach to the law when he is wrongly convicted.

Conclusion

Initially, the major difference between the techno enforcement law films and the more traditional film appears to be the manner in which justice is delivered. . . . Dredd is far more rule-bound than many of the attorneys whose duty to the court is overlooked in the pursuit of justice. Law is revered in the Mega City that Judge

Dredd inhabits. Senior Judges must eventually take the "long walk to the cursed earth" to take law to the lawless, a task of high honour showing the importance of upholding the law — those who will not uphold such law are excluded from the city boundaries. Dredd's heritage is in fact not so much *Dirty Harry* as *Young Mr. Lincoln*. At times, this mythical Lincoln is portrayed as superhuman, seemingly a god with the power of life and death and marrying physical strength with cerebral agility. Even Henry Fonda, the actor who played Lincoln in Ford's film, baulked initially at taking on such a figure with the historical and mythical baggage that it carried. Indeed, Fonda felt that playing Lincoln was tantamount to playing God.

Whilst *Judge Dredd* might, at first sight, appear to signal a departure from the courtroom drama, it can in fact be seen as part of that very tradition while simultaneously perhaps developing a subgenre of techno-law films. Dredd is as much the master of his "courtroom" as any previous cinema judge, the change is the arena not the authority, his judicial robes are signposted as clearly as those historically trimmed with ermine. When Dredd indicates his judicial supremacy by declaring "I am the Law" he is still acknowledging the legal process albeit it one vested within him, only that the parameters of the courtroom are no longer fixed. What then of the effect of such depiction. Whilst historical portrayals mined many of the themes covered in the techno-law films, the depiction was far removed in terms of decorum and ceremony. Dredd, and to a lesser extent Robocop, show judicial pronouncements disrobed of such ceremony and stripped bare of deference or reverence. This may have one of two effects, both to demystify the law and show its upshot without its inherent disguise, or place the law and legal process in disrepute, with a loss of respect for the law that might have been engendered by contact with more traditional law films.

NOTES & QUESTIONS

1. Librarians everywhere rejoiced when the character of Rupert Giles in television's *Buffy the Vampire Slayer* (1997–2003) showed that librarians can be action heroes. Is it a good thing or a bad thing to have a judge as an action hero?

2. The authors suggest that films such as *Judge Dredd* can have a positive effect by demystifying the law, or a negative effect by causing a loss of respect for the law. What do you think is the effect of such a film on cultural attitudes towards the law? Judge Dredd says, "at the end of the day, when you're all alone in the dark, the only thing that counts is this. . . . The Law!" Is this fascism? Is it the Rule of Law? Is it just another postapocalyptic revenge fantasy? Or is it something else?

3. The character of Judge Dredd began life as a popular comic book. Lawyers sometimes turn up as comic book heroes (*see, e.g.*, "She Hulk"). But while the Judge Dredd universe does include other action hero judges (such as Psi-Judge Cassandra Anderson), judges in general are not frequently portrayed as action heroes. Is this because a judge's job is mostly about thinking and writing and hence not visually dramatic enough for action hero status? But judges deal (literally) with matters of life and death. Should there be more action hero judges?

4. Several video games feature Judge Dredd. These games tend to be "first person shooters" (where the player is the main character and sees and acts from the

perspective of Judge Dredd). Some of the games give the player the choice to execute or arrest criminals. (Which choice do you think is more popular?) Could you design a video game that had a positive message regarding judges? Could you design it so that teenagers would actually want to play it? What reward systems or storyline might you include to achieve this?

5. The next reading gives us a contrast to the action hero judge by showing us a judge who spends almost the entire film thinking (and agonizing) over the right thing to do. Who is more heroic — Sylvester Stallone's Judge Dredd, or Spencer Tracy's Judge Haywood? Which one is more of a flat character versus a round character? Which one would you rather watch in a film? Why?

D. WHO JUDGES THE JUDGE?

Perhaps we expect more of judges because we have given them power over us and we desperately hope they will use it wisely. We want them to be more fair, more humane, more righteous than we ever could be. But judges, like the rest of us, are only human.

Law or justice — where does a judge's highest duty reside? And who decides when a judge oversteps his or her prescribed boundaries and strays too far into one realm to the neglect of the other? At one extreme we have the image of a secret vigilante Star Chamber lawlessly meting out punishments according to its own private notion of justice. At the other extreme we have the horrors of the Nazi judges in the Nuremberg trials, who followed the letter of the law and sent innocents to extermination.

The film *Judgment at Nuremberg* invites reflection on how people, even judges, come to do evil. Dan Haywood, played by Spencer Tracy, is a judge at the Nuremberg tribunals who desperately wants to understand how a seemingly moral judge such as Ernst Janning, played by Burt Lancaster, could have become so inhumane. The answer seems to lie with the distinction between law and justice. One of the defendants makes the following statement in his own defense: "I followed the concept that I believe to be the highest in my profession. The concept that says to sacrifice one's own sense of justice to the authoritative legal [oath]. To ask only what the law is, and not to ask whether or not it is also justice. As a judge, I could do no other." As a judge sitting in judgment on other judges, Haywood says, "The real complaining party at the bar in this courtroom is civilization," and he condemns those "men who sat in black robes in judgment on other men, men who took part in the enactment of laws and decrees the purpose of which was the extermination of human beings."

As the next excerpt makes clear, although the Nazi judges literally are on trial, Judge Haywood also will be tried during the course of the hearings. How does one acquire the moral authority to judge the judges? Which is the higher good, law or justice? And how does a storyteller best encapsulate such wrenching real-life dilemmas in a fictionalized form?

THE CONFLICTS OF LAW AND THE CHARACTER OF MEN: WRITING *REVERSAL OF FORTUNE* AND *JUDGMENT AT NUREMBERG*

Suzanne Shale

30 University of San Francisco Law Review 991 (1996)

This essay is about the collision of two worlds, the world of the law and the world of drama in the form of cinema. In it, I consider the process of writing a trial movie based on real life events. Tracing the creation of the feature film from legal and life facts helps us to understand a little of how knowledge of law moves from the legal to the popular domain, how the dramaturgy of the law itself influences popular culture, and, further, how the conventions of popular culture form the structure of popular legal knowledge. What message, to recall Marshall McLuhan, is the medium of film? I will discuss the writing of two films, *Reversal of Fortune* and *Judgment at Nuremberg*, to show how the demands of film as a narrative medium affect the stories that films tell about law. I shall argue that some movies represent far more of the nature of law than we acknowledge. But I shall also argue that Hollywood movies are bound to represent law in what might best be described as an epic form. . . .

Judgment at Nuremberg was originally a television play written by Abby Mann, who adapted his own work into an Academy-Award-winning screenplay. Directed by Stanley Kramer, and acerbically described by one critic as an "all-star concentration-camp drama with special guest victim appearances," *Judgment at Nuremberg* is based upon the trial of a group of German judges and legal officials by the United States Military Tribunal in Nuremberg in 1947. The judges (ten in Nuremberg, but only four by the time they got to Hollywood) were charged with various offenses, including crimes against humanity, complicity in the degradation of the German legal system, and denial of due process of law to defendants. All were convicted of one or more offenses and were imprisoned by the American occupying forces. Along with many other minor war criminals, they were subsequently released by the Americans only a few years after the trial ended. . . .

In preparing the screenplay of *Judgment at Nuremberg*, Abby Mann read thousands of pages of trial transcript, corresponded with the legal principals, consulted other legal authorities with knowledge of the Nuremberg war crimes tribunals, and visited Germany, where he conducted research into the Nuremberg trials. The screenplay quotes verbatim from American law and jurisprudence, and some of the characters' speeches bear traces of the Nuremberg pleadings.

To understand fully the processes by which . . . the Nuremberg trial [was] transmogrified into a satisfying feature film, we need to look on three levels at how film narratives are constructed. First, we must consider the narrative conventions that structure the paradigmatic Hollywood movie, shaping it into a tale of heroic odyssey. Second, we must look at the way in which a screen-writer creates a story from the life-stuff of events. In asking how a story emerges, I am asking how the writer creates a meaningful, thematic narrative rather than an inconsequential, flat recitation of occurrences. Third, we need to turn our minds to the problem of plot — that is, how the meaningful story is presented to the audience as a series of discrete events. Having a meaningful story in the life events, the screenwriter must still establish a satisfying way of telling it.

II. The Foundations of Form

Hollywood requires stories to embrace a distinctive principle of causality and to be plotted according to certain conventions. Hollywood stories are ones in which the leading characters are propelled into some personal odyssey, in pursuit of something they desire. By the journey's end, their experiences will have changed them in a significant way. As David Bordwell has summarized it:

> The classical Hollywood film presents psychologically defined individuals who struggle to solve a clear-cut problem or to attain specific goals. In the course of this struggle, the characters enter into conflict with others or with external circumstances. The story ends with a decisive victory or defeat, a resolution of the problem and a clear achievement or non-achievement of the goals. The principal causal agency is thus the character, a discriminated individual endowed with a consistent batch of evident traits, qualities, and behaviors.

David Bordwell, *Narration in the Fiction Film* 157 (1985).

Bordwell argues that the principles of the conventional Hollywood narrative are not unique to the cinematic medium, but are, rather, the specific application of a "canonic" story form in American filmmaking. Research into story comprehension has identified a story structure widely used in western culture. This "canonical" story format embraces six elements: introduction of setting and characters, explanation of a state of affairs, complicating action, ensuing events, outcome, and ending. This is not so different from the three-part narrative structure embraced by Hollywood: the set up, complication, and resolution. This principle is most graphically articulated in Root's advice to "get your man up a tree," "throw stones at him," and "get him down out of the tree." Wells Root, *Writing the Script: A Practical Guide for Films and Television* 2 (1979). If we compare the European cinematic narrative with the Hollywood product, however, it would appear that while the canonic story is widespread, it is most markedly in Hollywood that these principles of narration have been refined, exaggerated, and elevated to a hegemonic position.

Hollywood movies are stories about "character" and how character determines the outcome of life events. "Character" is the sum of a human being's personhood: biography, memory, virtues and vice, reactions, capabilities, potentiality, and weakness. In movies, we learn about such character when it is expressed in the actions which emerge from human conflict: conflicts between people, conflicts within a person, and conflicts between persons and their environments. Human lives and, perhaps even more so, movie lives, are littered with incompatible goals and incommensurate values. In the movies, it is the task of "character" to resolve the human conflicts that our goals and values create. It is always a character who takes steps, a character who makes choices, a character's responses that drive the story forward or spin it around in new directions. It is a character who overcomes, a character who changes or learns. . . .

In *Judgment at Nuremberg*, Abby Mann emphasizes the importance of character early in the film. In *Judgment* [*at Nuremberg*], the protagonist is Judge Haywood, a man who is possessed, we learn early-on, with all of the down-home, plain-speaking, salt-of-the-earth, and man-of-the-people American virtues. His antagonist — and in many respects his antithesis — is the German judge Ernst Janning: a repressed Teutonic archetype — intellectual, aristocratic, austere. Herr Rolfe, Janning's defense counsel, bespeaks the crux of the matter at the very outset of the case. (Note that it is Ernst Janning's *character* that is on trial at Nuremberg. Hence, for the movie audience, it is Judge Haywood's character that will be tried in the film.) Rolfe stated:

> The avowed purpose of this Tribunal is broader than the visiting of retribution on a few men. It is dedicated to the reconsecration of the Temple of Justice. It is dedicated to finding a code of justice the whole world will be responsible to. How will this code be established? It will be established in a clear, honest evaluation of the responsibility for the crimes in the indictment stated by the prosecution. In the words of the great American jurist, Oliver Wendell Holmes, "This responsibility will not be found only in documents that no one contests or denies. It will be found in consideration of a political or social nature. It will be found most of all in the character of men."

> What is the character of Ernst Janning? Let us examine his life for a moment.

> He was born in 1875. Received the degree of Doctor of Law in 1907. Became a Judge of East Prussia in 1914. Following World War One, he became one of the leaders of the Weimar Republic and was one of the framers of its democratic constitution. In subsequent years, he achieved international fame. Not only for his work as a great jurist but also as the author of legal text books which are still used in universities all over the world. He became Minister of Justice in Germany in 1935.

In Ernst Janning, Abby Mann has rendered the real defendant Schlegelberger a much more sympathetic character. The real Schlegelberger played a significant role in executing the savage "Nacht und Nebel" ("Night and Fog") plan, whereby the civilians of occupied countries involved in resistance activities would be dispatched to face summary justice in secret trials in Germany. Schlegelberger was also responsible for drafting laws for the occupied territories which imposed the death sentence on Jewish and Polish citizens for nothing more than speaking out against Nazi occupation. Ironically, the Schlegelberger that the Law Reports portray, a man who acted with unmitigated inhumanity, would have been a character for cinematic purposes too stark, too villainous, and too quaintly melodramatic. The fictitious Janning, on the other hand, a smoldering amalgam of shame, pride, and repression, is the far more plausible character.

Whether hero or anti-hero, if the movie is to succeed, the audience must find itself able to identify with the protagonist. How? The most compelling invitation to identify oneself with the screen character is offered when the protagonist is forced by the narrative to make hard choices and difficult decisions. This is the moment when the audience recalls the agony of minds we would rather not make up, and are generous with our sympathy for characters who cannot avoid doing so. In the courtroom, the advocates and the judges, who must decide from moment to moment how to conduct the case, are the decision-makers. In courtroom drama, therefore, the protagonist is frequently an advocate, and if not an advocate, a judge. . . .

III. The Search for Story

Within the opportunities and constraints of the canonic structure, there is still an infinity of story choices to be made.

I want to move on now to consider the creation of story from life events. E. M. Forster illustrated the difference between flat narration and meaningful story as the difference between recounting "the king died, and then the queen died" and "the king died, and then the queen died of grief." E. M. Forster, *Aspects of the Novel* 93-94 (1962). The difference between story and a simple series of events is a principle of causality that permits us to ascribe some meaning to what happened. Story is therefore the outcome of a writer's point of view and the events with which she is concerned. Events are given story meaning by a writer's beliefs and values, and her own ethical sense of the material with which she is working.

It is the power of both law and drama that they operate analogically. In the telling of one story, we can be commanded or encouraged to bring to mind another. In some courtroom movies, as in *Reversal of Fortune*, the trial we see fought on the screen invites us to reflect only upon itself and its own meaning. In others, the trial in the movie may also argue, by implication, a quite different case. In *Judgment at Nuremberg*, the trial is ostensibly a tale about the evils of the Nazi legal system. But Mann wrote it in such a way that in the conflicts between moral right and logic and between justice and political expediency, the movie recalls not only Nazism and the Nuremberg trials, but also McCarthyism and Hollywood's complicity in it.

Many stories could have been written about the Nuremberg trials, and the story Mann told reflected his own beliefs. He constructed the courtroom scenes so that they would lead the audience toward his own views about Nazi law, rather than point ineluctably toward the Tribunal's stated conclusions. Mann felt that the judgment of the Nuremberg tribunal over-emphasized the importance of denial of due process and under-emphasized the depravity of the substantive laws under which the victims of Nazi racial ideology were tried. In his movie courtroom, Mann chose to emphasize the intrinsic inhumanity of Nazi laws. In one scene, Petersen, a confused and not very clever laborer, testifies about the proceedings that led to his sexual sterilization. When Petersen is cross-examined, Herr Rolfe has no difficulty in establishing that Petersen is indeed mentally incompetent and could legitimately have been sterilized under the eugenic laws. But Rolfe's legal "victory" brings him little satisfaction, and the audience is left with no doubt that Mann believes such laws to have been morally wrong in and of themselves, however correct the procedure by which they were enforced.

But Abby Mann also wanted to write a screenplay that reflected his concern for the state of America, as well as his compassion for the victims of the Holocaust:

> It was very much on my mind [that] there were writers like Dalton Trumbo
> and John Howard Lawson, writers who had been blacklisted. . . . I came
> after that and I tried to help them, I tried to get them jobs. And so the fact
> that this could happen, could have taken more steps . . . that was very

important. And the big thing that was bugging me too was . . . I wanted to pierce the lie; the big lie [in Germany] was, "we didn't know about it." . . . There were certain emotional feelings that I had, I don't think that I violated the basis of the trial . . . but these things were very much on my mind.

Shale, interview with Abby Mann, screenwriter, in Los Angeles, Cal. (Oct. 5, 1995).

Judgment at Nuremberg is a serious attempt to explore the significance of the Nuremberg trials, but Mann's initial outline of the film suggests a depth and sophistication diluted in the process of preparing the commercial presentation. It is this author's opinion that it was Kramer who was responsible for injecting into the movie the sentimental liberalism of which some commentators were so critical. The first outline Mann submitted to Kramer was an exploration of many more of the moral conundra of the war crimes trials than are discussed in the resulting film. Straightforwardly, there was more law in Mann's outline: more explanation of the difference between the German and American legal systems and their conceptual-izations of the role of the judge; more discussion of the nature of the charges being brought against the defendants; more concern with the legitimacy of the military tribunals. The figure of Judge Haywood, too, was drawn more complex and ambivalent, an exploration of the character of a man of modest esteem as he rises, unexpectedly, to the occasion of judgment. Judge Haywood appeared in Mann's outline with a wife and daughter who served the narrative by drawing it into the sexual and material chaos of Nuremberg, in images of defeat which were to be juxtaposed against the sanitized order of the trials. The novelistic complexities that these characters introduced appear to have been sacrificed in pursuit of the entrenchment of Judge Haywood in the role of the lone protagonist, an approach that was perhaps more appropriate to the condensed cinematic form. . . .

IV. Presentation and Plot

Both Abby Mann and Nicholas Kazan [the writer of the screenplay for *Reversal of Fortune*] had as their first creative task to discover what was, for them, the true story of the events about which they wrote. Only then could they organize events from the months and months of trial and pre-trial work into a plot capable of illustrating the aesthetic and factual truths in which they believed.

How is it possible to compress the human action of twelve months into two hours? The writer must make a highly restricted selection from factual material. He may choose to adapt the strict reality of facts to suit the needs of the emerging screenplay, or he may invent entirely new, fictitious material. . . .

[I]t seems that Abby Mann had to be persuaded to create a conventional romantic drama around the figure of his Nuremberg judge. The character of Madame Bertholt, Judge Haywood's "love interest," was born quite late. She came into existence sometime between the outline Mann initially submitted to Kramer and his first draft of the screenplay. While the love interest seems a harmless enough element in the film, it elicited vigorous complaint from the film's legal advisors. They objected that if the story was a true one, Judge Haywood's liaison would have been highly unethical. In their view, the fictional romantic subplot was defamatory to the real Nuremberg judge upon whom Haywood was based. . . .

In the earlier discussion of *Twelve Angry Men*, I touched upon that distinction, so central to art, between factual truth and dramatic truth. Plot, no less than story, may embrace the same distinction. In an early scene in *Judgment at Nuremberg*, Ernst Janning refuses to concede the jurisdiction of the tribunal:

> *Haywood* (addressing Janning): How do you plead to the charges and specifications set forth in the indictment against you — guilty or not guilty?
>
> [Janning refuses to speak]
>
> *Rolfe*: Your Honor. May I address the court?
>
> *Haywood:* Yes.
>
> *Rolfe*: The defendant does not recognize the authority of this tribunal and wishes to lodge a formal protest in lieu of pleading.
>
> *Haywood*: A plea of not guilty will be entered. The prosecution will make its opening statement.

While Schlegelberger himself did not challenge the jurisdiction of the tribunal, many of the war criminals did refuse to acknowledge it. The issue of jurisdiction was discussed in the *Alstötter* trial, and legal scholarship was cited in judicial opinion. One member of the tribunal, Judge Blair, entered a dissenting opinion regarding the extent of the jurisdiction that the military tribunals claimed for themselves. Haywood's response, to formulate a legal answer from a refusal to speak, acknowledges an important truth about the obduracy and inescapability of trial procedures. There was, therefore, much legal truth in that fictional exchange, although Mann maintains that he wrote the scene for purely dramatic reasons. . . .

NOTES & QUESTIONS

The fall of a judge is particularly tragic (per Aristotle's classic definition of tragedy), for it implicates a person of great social significance, and by extension, the judge's fall from grace implicates the fall of an entire society. Spencer Tracy's character in effect judges the whole of German society during the Nuremberg trials. (That is why Marlene Dietrich's Madame Bertholt is so eager to show him the art, music, and architecture of Germany — she desperately hopes he will weigh such things in the balance.)

Chapter 7

JURIES

A. FILMOGRAPHY

12 Angry Men (1957)

The Juror (1996)

Jury Duty (1995)

Runaway Jury (2003)

Trial by Jury (1994)

B. WHAT THE JURY MEANS TO US

A juror's lot is a hapless one in most popular films. Everything starts innocently enough, with a naïve citizen dutifully responding to a summons for jury duty. The situation, however, degenerates speedily, with the juror being threatened, harassed, and assaulted by Mafia hit men and various and sundry criminals. Soon, the hapless juror is forced to sway the deliberations in the defendant's favor or else her child will be killed by the defendant's goons. Finally, unable to trust anyone, our beleaguered juror has to single-handedly kill the villain with an ice pick in an isolated mansion while she is seductively dressed like Rita Hayworth in a glamorous evening gown. (See *Trial By Jury* and *The Juror* for suitable examples.) Alternatively, in *The Devil and Daniel Webster*, a classic film from 1941, the jury actually consists of a group of damned souls — evildoers called up from their sufferings in hell to sit on a trial for the soul of a New Hampshire farmer. (It must have been a toss-up as to which was worse — jury duty or hell.) In perhaps the most unspeakable option, the juror can suffer the indignity of being Pauly Shore (*Jury Duty*). No wonder we look forward to jury duty with all the eager anticipation we give to a root canal.

In real life, even if you respond to a jury summons, dutifully sit through a lengthy trial, and work hard in deliberations to reach a verdict, there is always the chance the media will reduce the whole complex trial to a 30-second sound bite and talking heads will gleefully ask, "What were the jurors thinking?"

It is all about power. The jury is a powerful, profoundly democratic institution at the heart of our system of jurisprudence. Perhaps the imperiled juror in popular culture reflects a cultural anxiety not that jurors are powerless, but that they in fact can be extremely powerful. (A juror in *Runaway Jury* brings the entire gun industry to its knees.) The type of power is deceptively ordinary — it is the power of talk. "I just want to talk about it," says Henry Fonda as the lone juror holding out against a guilty verdict in a murder case (*12 Angry Men*). That talking, that idea of the give and take of discourse among a group of citizens, resonates strongly as an American ideal. In the next readings, consider what the jury stands for in contemporary American culture.

INTRODUCTION TO THE JURY AT A CROSSROAD: THE AMERICAN EXPERIENCE
Nancy S. Marder
78 Chicago-Kent Law Review 909 (2003)

Introduction: Popular Portrayals of the Jury

The American jury is an institution that has proven resilient in the past and yet remains vulnerable in the future. Although national polls show that the American populace continues to think highly of juries, that citizens who actually have served on juries give high marks to their experience, and that judges, for the most part, agree with decisions rendered by juries, the jury remains under attack in the popular press and many legislatures.

Over the past few years, press coverage of jury trials has been somewhat critical, at least in several high-profile cases. In press coverage, criminal juries have been faulted for reaching erroneous verdicts and civil juries have been chastised for awarding excessive damages. The press typically has attributed the erroneous verdicts to juror bias or sympathy and the excessive damages to juror incompetence or sentiment.

Just a few of the high-profile jury trials that garnered headlines in recent years serve to illustrate the press's generally critical portrayal of these juries. For example, the juries in the state criminal trial of police officers Stacey Koon and Laurence Powell for the beating of motorist Rodney King and the state criminal trial of O.J. Simpson for the murders of Nicole Brown Simpson and Ronald Goldman received largely negative treatment in much of the press. Both juries failed to convict the defendants. In both cases, much of the press portrayed the jurors as having reached the wrong verdict out of prejudice against the victim or sympathy for the defendant.

Civil juries have been portrayed in an unflattering light as well. One of the best-known civil cases in which the jury came under blistering attack was the McDonald's coffee cup case. In that case, the jury awarded Stella Liebeck, the elderly woman who scalded herself on McDonald's coffee, punitive damages of $2.7 million. The jury was lambasted for this award in almost every newspaper account of the case. What received little attention in the press, however, were the facts of the case including the following: McDonald's served coffee that was significantly hotter than that of other eateries; it previously received hundreds of complaints by people who had been burned, but nevertheless, McDonald's chose not to lower the temperature of its coffee or to warn customers; Ms. Liebeck, who had been severely burned, required skin grafts, yet McDonald's had refused to pay her medical expenses, which was all that she initially had sought; and the damage award was likely to be reduced by the trial judge through remittitur, which it eventually was.

Although the McDonald's jury became emblematic in the press for much that was wrong with the civil jury system, this jury was not alone in receiving condemnation for its damage award. Numerous other cases in which the jury awarded damages that the press depicted as excessive contributed to this view of the civil jury as having gone awry. Indeed, if one were to read only newspaper accounts of civil jury trials, one would conclude that most juries award excessive damages, and that they do so because they sympathize with the plaintiffs at the expense of corporations. Coverage of cases involving tobacco, asbestos, and other types of product liability paint this picture. Yet, empirical studies indicate otherwise.

Legislatures, both at the state and national levels, are intent upon responding to the so-called crisis in jury behavior. A number of state legislatures have limited the types of cases that civil juries can hear and have capped the damages that civil juries can award, at least for pain and suffering. Recently, the U.S. House of Representatives passed a bill that would cap at $250,000 the damages that civil juries could award for pain and suffering in medical malpractice suits, although the Senate refused to consider the bill. . . .

The press's portrayal of the jury as an institution in need of fixing, and the interest of the executive and legislature in fixing it quickly, should raise concerns for those who care about and study the jury. Although press coverage of the jury is certainly not monolithic and not every article is a critique, many articles, particularly in high-profile cases, paint a picture of an institution that is unreliable and erratic at best, and biased and extreme at worst. Legislatures, too, have shown a deep distrust of the jury and have responded with mechanisms that would further limit the power of the jury, such as capping civil jury awards, or would further limit the power of the individual juror, such as abandoning the unanimity requirement in criminal jury verdicts. Although press depictions of and legislative reactions to the jury are not the only sources of popular images of the jury, they certainly contribute to some of the more powerful portrayals.

I. Possible Explanations for Unflattering Portrayals of the Jury

Why do the press and legislatures view the jury as an institution in need of repair? The press could be reporting, and legislatures responding to, problems that actually exist. There is no doubt, for example, that high medical malpractice insurance premiums for doctors are real and driving some doctors to re-examine whether they can afford to remain in practice. Whether jury awards are responsible for the high insurance premiums or whether other factors, such as insurance practices, are at work, is still unknown, though many [members of Congress] have concluded that the jury is to blame.

Another explanation for the critical press coverage is that a more sensational view of the jury will sell newspapers, and so the press focuses on that story. After all, a jury gone awry makes for a more interesting, dramatic story than a jury that is functioning properly and doing its job. The press's emphasis on what is wrong with the jury helps to persuade legislators and the public that the jury needs to be "fixed."

Yet another explanation for the critical view of juries expressed by the press and legislatures alike is that the jury is a convenient scapegoat. Juries consist of laypersons who are summoned for jury duty and who serve for one trial and then return to their private lives. They have no particular stake in defending the institution. Thus, the jury can be criticized, and there is no repeat player to come to its defense. Individual jurors might speak out after a trial and defend their verdict, if it has been criticized, but then they return to their private lives and any further criticism goes unchallenged. Judges cannot comment on cases that might go up on appeal, and in any event, they usually are quite restrained in making statements outside of their judicial opinions. Lawyers, especially those on the winning side, could speak out in the jury's defense, but their views would be seen as those of self-serving advocates, not disinterested observers.

Finally, another explanation might be that the press and legislatures, consisting of professional journalists and politicians respectively, distrust an institution consisting entirely of laypersons. Although, on one level, the fact that the jury is an institution of ordinary citizens temporarily summoned to serve is a source of national pride, on another level, jury composition is a source of national distrust. How can laypersons perform the tasks with which they are charged in this increasingly specialized world in which we usually depend on professionals or experts?

II. Potential Harms from Such Portrayals

Critical press coverage and legislative distrust of the jury can lead to a number of harms to the jury. One harm is that press and legislative focus on perceived weaknesses of the jury may deflect attention from weaknesses of other institutions. For example, the high medical malpractice premiums, currently attributed to excessive jury awards, actually may be the result of insurance practices. The jury may simply be a convenient target. However, there is no one to defend the institution of the jury on an on-going basis, or to look after its interests as lobbyists are paid to do for other institutions and interest groups, such as the insurance industry.

Moreover, the press's and legislatures' focus on some perceived weaknesses of the jury system may obscure more serious shortcomings of the jury that are worthy of attention, but are not receiving it. Unfortunately, the jury weaknesses that both the press and legislatures focus on are likely to be driven by vocal or influential constituencies rather than by the needs of jurors, or even parties to litigation.

A third harm is that legislatures, at least with respect to the jury, tend to look for quick-fix solutions. Such reforms are not finely calibrated to intrude as little as possible into the workings of the jury, nor are they developed from the jury's perspective. Rather, these remedies tend to take power away from the jury. Legislators do not seem to consider a less blunt approach, such as providing jurors with the tools they need to perform their tasks more effectively. For example, in the debate over whether juries have the expertise to decide certain kinds of cases, the legislative response in some states has been to take the cases away from the jury, rather than to consider whether juries should be permitted to take notes, to ask questions, and to take written copies of the jury instructions into the deliberation room. Although these practices would help juries in all cases, they would be particularly beneficial in complex or highly technical areas of the law.

A fourth harm in focusing solely on what juries are doing wrong is that it distracts both the press and legislatures from considering what juries are doing well. Perhaps this is an unfair criticism because it is not the press's job to provide "good news" or the legislature's job to commend institutions for good performance, but to fix institutions that fall short. One consequence, however, is that critical coverage and debate dominate and obscure the virtues of the jury. What is lost from public consideration is the way in which the jury works properly in the myriad jury trials that never find their way into press stories. What is lost in the legislative debate is the way in which the jury can be made into an even stronger institution by giving jurors the tools they need to do their job more effectively.

Finally, another harm is that the press and legislatures, in framing the debate about the jury, focus on very narrow functional roles for the jury. Neither the press nor legislature has the luxury of exploring the aspirational goals for the jury, of articulating a vision of the jury; rather, this is the province of academics. . . .

NOTES & QUESTIONS

1. Mark Twain wryly commented, "We have a criminal jury system which is superior to any in the world; and its efficiency is only marred by the difficulty of finding twelve men every day who don't know anything and can't read." Mark Twain, *After-Dinner Speech: Meeting of Americans, London, July 4, 1873, in Mark Twain Speaking* 75 (Paul Fatout ed. 1976). Is a verdict too important to be left up to, as the old saw goes, twelve people who weren't smart enough to get out of jury duty?

2. Why are there so many negative portrayals of juries in the media? Is it simply a case of the media ignoring the vast majority of cases in which juries do a good job? Or have juries (particularly civil juries) become obsolete and ineffective in this age of complex litigation and highly specialized cases? If the jury at one point in history served a vital democratic purpose, is that function still necessary? Consider the following reading.

ECHOES OF THE FOUNDING: THE JURY IN CIVIL CASES AS CONFERRER OF LEGITIMACY
Victoria A. Farrar-Myers & Jason B. Myers
54 Southern Methodist University Law Review 1857 (2001)

I. THE JURY AS A POLITICAL INSTITUTION

The Framers of the United States Constitution developed a political system to protect American citizens against tyranny. To guard against tyranny by a minority, the Framers adopted a system of majority rule. To protect against tyranny of the majority, they developed an elaborate system of checks and balances in which political power and authority were split among various political institutions. This framework, coupled with the Bill of Rights added to the Constitution during the first session of Congress, created a limited government that flows from the popular sovereignty of the American citizenry and at the same time protects that sovereignty.

After Alexis de Tocqueville traveled throughout America, he compiled his insights on the still-new American political system in the classic *Democracy in America*. At the end of his discussion of "what tempers the tyranny of the majority," Tocqueville distinguished the jury system as a political institution as compared to a judicial one. In terms of the jury's role in "facilitating the good administration of justice," he acknowledged, "its usefulness can be contested." But in terms of the jury as a political institution, he insisted that it "should be regarded as one form of the sovereignty of the people." The jury system provided a means by which the American citizenry could participate in and make decisions regarding the political system: "There is always a republican character in it, inasmuch as it puts the real control of affairs into the hands of the ruled, or some of them, rather than into those of the rulers." For Tocqueville, the jury's role represented as important an expression of popular sovereignty as voting.

Tocqueville also noted that the use of the jury system is "bound to have a great influence on national character" and that such "influence is immeasurably increased the more [juries] are used in civil cases." Among the ways in which Tocqueville saw the jury system enhancing the national character:

> "Juries, especially civil juries, instill some of the habits of the judicial mind into every citizen, and just those habits are the very best way of preparing people to be free."

> "It spreads respect for the courts' decisions and for the idea of right throughout all classes."

> "Juries teach men equity in practice. Each man, when judging his neighbor, thinks that he may be judged himself."

> "Juries teach each individual not to shirk responsibility for his own acts, and without that manly characteristic no political virtue is possible."

> "Juries invest each citizen with a sort of magisterial office; they make all men feel that they have duties toward society and that they take a share in its government."

> "Juries are wonderfully effective in shaping a nation's judgment and increasing its natural lights. That, in my view, is its greatest advantage."

> "I regard it as one of the most effective means of popular education at society's disposal."

For Tocqueville, jurors were more than just participants in the legal process. They served as a vital component of the American political system.

Let us now fast-forward approximately two centuries from the framing of the Constitution and Tocqueville's travels. The American experiment in guarding against tyranny has proved successful, and the country has grown up from the youthful nation that Tocqueville experienced. One change that has accompanied America's growth is that the jury system's role as a political institution seems to have receded into the background. Instead of the positive benefits that the jury system provides, news stories on juries focus more on their excesses and the ways in which jurors pervert the legal process. Most Americans probably are familiar with the jury that awarded $2.7 million to an elderly woman who, after spilling coffee on herself, sued McDonald's for serving the drink too hot; or with the jury in Florida that arguably ignored the judge's instructions in awarding $145 billion in a suit brought against tobacco companies. Juries are often seen as out of control and in need of being reined in.

As hinted at by the reference to the McDonald's and tobacco litigation, this criticism is levied largely against the use of juries in civil proceedings. But it is not a recent development. Tocqueville's words of praise aside, ever since the days of America's Founding and continuing today, many have questioned the need for juries in civil cases. If the jury system does help educate the citizenry and "gives them added confidence in democracy," as Judge Jerome Frank asked, "can that contention be proved? Do not many jurors become cynical about the court-house aspects of government? And should education in government be obtained at the expense of litigants?" For critics of the jury system, one of the best ways to rein in juries would be to limit the role of the jury in resolving civil disputes. . . .

NOTES & QUESTIONS

1.   Is the political role of the jury still a viable goal? Or is the potential for a miscarriage of justice too steep a price to pay for the benefits of civic education?

2.   Does the jury system still retain a moral authority in popular culture? The next reading suggests that we must neither unduly romanticize the jury system as a democratic institution nor unduly demonize it in popular culture. Rather, the significance of the jury is in its very ordinariness. Both good and bad, jury verdicts are among the most visible workings of democracy in our justice system.

"THE IMAGE WE SEE IS OUR OWN": DEFENDING THE JURY'S TERRITORY AT THE HEART OF THE DEMOCRATIC PROCESS
Lisa Kern Griffin
75 Nebraska Law Review 332 (1996)

I. INTRODUCTION: THE JURY IN THE SPOTLIGHT

Public disenchantment with the criminal justice system increasingly centers on the jury. Sensational stories, like the Simpson, King, and Menendez trials, undermine the legitimacy of jury verdicts and call into question the compatibility of the institution with the ideal of the rule of law. Such controversial verdicts have prompted reforms to limit the jury's power and to restructure the jury system. While the parade of celebrity trials attracts the spotlight, 1.2 million people participate in jury deliberations each year, and they generally reach a verdict that the presiding judge considers correct. Moreover, rather than subverting legality, the jury nurtures it by allowing for community input within the framework of the rule of law, and by linking the public to the institution of the courts.

The jury system operates under a complex mandate: Jurors must affirm that laws appear legitimate to the community, protect the interests of individual defendants, and strive for an accurate verdict. The jury, like the rule of law, negotiates the "tolerable accommodation of the conflicting interests of society." Where the jury sacrifices degrees of certainty, it also enhances flexibility and individualized justice; when public condemnation of an individual influences a verdict, the individual suffers, but there is a corresponding gain in community cohesion and the perceived legitimacy of the system. Many verdicts generate criticism about the balance the jury strikes between these competing interests. To those most concerned about the harm to the community, a jury that fails to convict an unpopular defendant appears unjust. Because the jury's consideration of the evidence is mediated through an adversarial process, fairness to the individual does not always produce the result the public expects. The jury represents the public's interests, but the deliberative process also tempers the anger and fear of the community and protects individual defendants from hasty judgments.

The language used by both critics and defenders of the jury system reveals tensions between democratic values and countermajoritarian fears of tyranny by the people. William Blackstone called the jury "the palladium of liberty," Thomas Jefferson deemed it the touchstone of our peace and safety, and Patrick Devlin praised it as "the lamp that shows that freedom lives." But critics of the jury emphasize its tensions with founding principles like the rule of law rather than its compatibility with democratic foundations like liberty and equality. Judge Jerome Frank considered the jury incompetent, prejudiced, and lawless. He cited jurors as obstacles to legal certainty because they apply "laws they don't understand to facts they can't get straight." Judge Frank responded to the champions of the jury system's democratic origins that what "was apparently a bulwark against an arbitrary tyrannical executive, is today the quintessence of governmental arbitrariness. . . . If anywhere we have a 'government of men,' in the worst sense of that phrase, it is in the operations of the jury system." Jerome Frank, *Courts on Trial: Myth and Reality in American Justice* 132 (1949).

Although some of our romantic ideals about jury service are mythical, many popular criticisms of the jury are also misguided. Jury verdicts give effect to beliefs held by a substantial portion of the public. When those beliefs are deemed illegitimate, efforts at change should focus not on the jury system, but on the underlying sources of the disjunction. Moreover, when the jury appears to falter, forces beyond its control often cause the failure. It is only the most visible component of a complex system, and criticisms of the jury reflect failings in other workings of the court as well. The public, however, takes a results-oriented view of the law, and "clues to the legitimacy of courts are not to be found in the structure of doctrine, or in the formal texts of jurists, but in the broad messages traveling back and forth between the public and the organs of popular culture." Lawrence M. Friedman, *Law, Lawyers, and Popular Culture*, 98 Yale Law Journal 1579, 1605 (1989). Popular culture portrays the criminal justice system as an obstacle course of legal rules that prevent police and prosecutors from doing their jobs. Because of both fictional depictions and the increasing coverage of real cases, many believe that all defendants have the opportunity to go to court and that high profile jury trials constitute typical cases.

The jury system lies at the heart of our democratic system, but it has lost much of its moral authority in the popular legal culture. . . .

II. DEMOCRATIC IDEALS

The direct and raw character of jury democracy makes it our most honest mirror, reflecting both the good and the bad that ordinary people are capable of when called upon to do justice. The reflection sometimes attracts us, and it sometimes repels us. But we are the jury, and the image we see is our own.

Jeffrey Abramson, *We, The Jury: The Jury System and the Ideal of Democracy* 250 (1994). . . .

NOTES & QUESTIONS

1. What is your response to Judge Jerome Frank's suggestion in the preceding excerpt that jurors apply "laws they don't understand to facts they can't get straight"? Are jurors too incompetent to handle the complexities of a trial? Should we hand the trial process over to professionals? Or are these the wrong questions to ask, because a jury's purpose is not efficiency of judgment? How might we re-think the jury for the twenty-first century?

2. Does popular culture suggest it is too easy to manipulate jurors? Or is the reverse true? Do the great lengths to which characters go to ensure a favorable jury vote suggest that it is tough to manipulate jurors?

"Trials are too important to be left up to juries," says Rankin Fitch, the unscrupulous jury consultant played by Gene Hackman in *Runaway Jury*. Fitch is an expensive and thoroughly venal jury consultant, a cunning mastermind hired to help a group of gun manufacturers ensure that no victim of gun violence ever wins a suit against them. He has thoroughly researched the prospective jurors (even putting them under surveillance), finding or creating blackmail material to bring pressure to bear on the jurors. One juror has had an abortion, one is HIV positive, and Fitch has entrapped one juror's husband with a shady real estate deal.

Fitch's disdain for the jury process is apparent. He tells Wendell Rohr, the plaintiff's attorney played by Dustin Hoffman, "You think your average juror is King Solomon? No, he's a roofer with a mortgage, he wants to go home and sit in his Barcalounger and let the cable TV wash over him, and this man doesn't give a single solitary droplet of shit about truth, justice, or your American way."

3. Can we scientifically predict whether certain jurors will be pro-plaintiff or pro-defendant? (There is a whole jury consulting industry built around a "yes" answer to this question.) If we can make such predictions, should we? Do attorneys who use jury consultants skew the very spirit of the jury system? Is this "cheating"? Of course, every attorney tries to pick a favorable jury panel during voir dire. At the

very least, attorneys try to eliminate prospective jurors who seem to have pre-judged a case or a defendant. But not every client can pay the fee for consultants. The whole topic of jury consultants raises key questions about human nature (how predictable are people?) and issues of equity (because of the vastly different resources clients can afford to spend on jury selection).

RETHINKING THE JURY
Phoebe A. Haddon
3 William & Mary Bill of Rights Journal 29 (1994)

III. THE CASE FOR JURY DECISION-MAKING

What are the distinctive values of civil jury decision-making? Often "[e]nthusiasts of the jury have tended to lapse into sentimentality and to equate literally the jury with democracy," without more clearly delineating what are decision-making qualities and distinguishing truth-determining features which justify its use. Litigators, even when supportive of the jury guarantee, often cast jurors as pawns in a litigation game. Conscious that prejudice in their communities runs high, citizens, when asked, express serious doubt about whether the jury promotes socially just results in civil trials; yet they also respond that they want juries to decide their cases.

There is much disagreement about whether and how the jury serves the interests of social justice in civil litigation. Legal commentators who favor its use emphasize the importance of the community's presence in legal decision-making and the significance of the collective's expression of popular will. Critics who are more skeptical of the community's decision-making role disparage the capacity of the jury to grasp the legal issues or move beyond individual self-interest, often questioning whether there should be any policy-making or law-making function for the jury. Many critics argue that the jury is expensive, unpredictable, and inefficient as well as incompetent.

Essentially the competing arguments concerning the civil jury trial guarantee suggest that there are differing conceptions of social organization and its impact on law. One view stresses the importance of community and shared values and beliefs, conceiving the community as potentially greater than the number of its constituents and treating positive law as but one of the ways to find expression of community values. An alternative view emphasizes the more formal process of law making; law becomes not so much a reflection of shared social values as the product of procedures adopted by the individual or group in control of law-making.

Preferring the first conception, I seek to identify what is significant about jury decision-making as distinguished from decision-making by judges and legislators. This significance historically was located in the capacity of members of the jury to provide local knowledge from experience and community connection, knowledge unavailable to the judge or other expert. It can be argued that the significance of jury decision-making today can be drawn from an understanding that truth is socially constructed and that the interchange of views of members of diverse communities not only meaningfully contributes to the derivation of truth, but that the interchange can be important for the many communities to feel a part of the larger lawful enterprise.

In our multicultural society of often estranged individuals and communities, jury duty can be a useful opportunity for citizens to come together in a public setting which promotes exchange. Jury deliberation can be a time for the exercise of authentic self-government by ordinary citizens who, through conversations, expose their differences and provide opportunities for others to understand them. Jury decision-making need not pale against either a model of political majority rule or expert decision-making by judges. Rather, the jury can be distinguished by its small-group, collective capacity to explore competing or emerging normative understandings and to achieve consensus through deliberation. Consensus reached by the group of individual jurors representing diverse communities who have engaged in dialogue is important since through their deliberation these participants can learn from and about each other. In short, jury deliberation can help individuals through their resolution of public controversies to realize the meaning of citizenship, thereby claiming a role in government.

A. The Value of Juries

Debate about the jury has centered on five principal areas of disagreement about its strengths: (1) its law-legitimating features; (2) its role as "little parliament"; (3) its truth-determining and decision-making competency; (4) its ability to foster good citizenship; and (5) its educational value. In the following sections, I will present competing arguments concerning the benefits of jury decision-making related to these areas and suggest how a model which emphasizes the representative and deliberative, participatory potential for juries strengthens the case for the jury.

1. Legitimacy

The jury has been said to forge public acceptance of court decisions by legitimizing them. This legitimacy feature holds great promise, particularly if the jury can reflect the social makeup of society in light of the explosion of common law and statutory rights in the late twentieth century. Traditionally, the legitimizing function has had two aspects. First, the fact of popular participation through the jury makes tolerable certain decisions which the litigants or the public would otherwise find unacceptable, because the jury verdict is seen as the product of the group, and thus the legitimacy of the result is supported in a manner that might not be attainable if one person, the judge, decides. Second, the transitory nature of the jury, though often characterized as a weakness of the jury system, can also protect the court: the jury can serve "as a sort of lightning rod for animosity and suspicion which might otherwise be directed on the judge."

This account, emphasizing two legitimizing features of the jury, however, minimizes the creative, deliberative possibilities of decision-making by the collective. Historically, proponents of this account have made use of the no-name, "black-box" quality of jury decision-making which implies that no one need assume responsibility for decisions. Perhaps as a consequence of this responsibility, to protect the independence of the jury but limit its abuse, we developed procedures to circumscribe the areas where the jury's impact could be felt.

The transient, informal nature of the jury could be looked upon as an extraordinary opportunity for individuals who are normally preoccupied with the mundane, private affairs to "redefine as private citizens, our collective identity," while recognizing that no citizen can live a wholly public political life.

In support of that conception of the community's role, we could, in fact, explore ways of making the jury more accountable for its decisions. One means, one which is connected with the desirable objective of having the decision-making be a product of the diverse views of the citizenry, is to permit those with minority views to feel confident to challenge the assumptions and perspectives of the majority.

2. Little Parliament

The jury is often characterized as "a little parliament," protecting the public against tyranny, or, in modern times, abuse of government. That characterization suggests that the jury device is useful to ensure that we are governed by the spirit of the law and not merely its letter; but it also implies that, like the legislature or other politically motivated institution, in the jury lies the propensity for self-interested decision-making. This view minimizes the fact that the jury's peculiar value lies in its capacity for dialogue and deliberation. The capacity to arrive at socially acceptable resolution of disputes is enhanced by the presence of multiple perspectives. But I also stress the importance of fostering accountability through exchange between jurors and other participants in the litigation process. Thus, rather than limit the jury function, we should seek ways to expand its contribution, by giving it more of an interactive, participatory role in legal decision-making. The fact that the jury is not electorally accountable should not be a reason for marginal treatment, or for its decision-making to be viewed as effectuating "justice beyond law." The resolution of factual controversy and application of law supported by knowledge communicated by jurors in the exchange of life experiences and reflections of jurors is law making.

3. Truth-Determining and Decision-Making Competency

Much of the criticism about jury participation concerns issues of competency. Critics focus on the superior intelligence of the judge, her training, discipline, and social experience in handling other cases, and conclude that the jury is superfluous or, by comparison with other expert decision-makers, incompetent. Earlier this century, some legal realists depicted jury decision-making as irrational and manipulable, sometimes reflecting shifts in norms while often not consciously appreciating such normative turns. A reconceived jury model not only must more fully underscore the peculiar deliberative function of the jury, it must also respond to charges of unpredictability.

In addition to disagreeing with the view held by legal realists, that the jury is an irrational group with limited potential for contribution, I question the importance placed on predictability which generated the critique of juries and which led to a preference for other expert decision-makers. Laypersons are able to view the context of the controversy with freshness lost to the experts and with insight built on cultural and social knowledge. There is a significant role for the community both in the interpretation of law and in delineating the application to a controversy of generally recognized legal standards. A focus on scientific — professional — expertise ignores the reality that bias arises out of any human's personal experience and can accumulate over the course of time. Through dialogue among diverse community members, bias can be exposed and checked. A focus on lay decision-making potential reaffirms the value of the personal perspective which, when offered through dialogue with other community representatives, can blunt bias. Deliberation by a representative jury drawn from a cross-section of the community provides special meaning and insight. Of course, this conclusion contests the legal realists' premise of scientifically derivable and objective truth, instead viewing the resolution of disputes as social and the claim of neutrality in law as contestable.

4. Citizenship

Among the recognized advantages of jury participation is that it provides an important civic experience for citizens. For many citizens, jury duty may be their only experience with the law and government beyond the exercise of a local or federal vote. Thus the opportunity for citizens through jury participation to come together and "enter into the heart of a public matter" should not be lost. Ideally the jury institution can afford diverse citizens the chance to join other citizens in a common enterprise that can be transformative. In my view, that enterprise is concerned with achieving an approximation of truth through the exchange of ideas by diverse people, thereby meting social justice.

The reality is, however, that exposure to jury duty at present is often disenchanting and causes citizens to lose confidence in the administration of justice and to be cynical about their role. The disenchantment experienced by citizens may in part be the result of the failure of the other principal participants to communicate with the community's representatives with civility and in an engaging way. It can stem from a sense of alienation — of not meaningfully being a part of the system of administering justice. Through orienting instructions given by the judge, and other information made available by the judge at the outset of trial, including efforts to educate jurors about the function of all the actors and reasons for procedures which may be unfamiliar to laypersons, this feeling can be allayed. These steps, which some but not all judges perform, can engage the jury and communicate to the other participants the value of the jury's work. Similar to the judge's ability to enlighten and explain matters to the jury through instructions, the attorneys in their arguments and case presentation can enlighten the jury.

Disenchantment among jurors may also be a product of diminished expectations about the quality of the administration of justice, pertinently, the level of representation and case management. Moreover, jurors' images of trials may be largely drawn from fictionalized court-room drama portrayed in movies and television programs. The development of rules and procedures which emphasize the value of active citizen participation in adjudication can both contribute to a more productive role for jurors and can result in a better educated pool of participants. The one-day, one-trial movement, responsive to overburdened caseload conditions, can also meet these objectives. Note-taking, question-asking, and even interviewing of witnesses are other reform efforts which promote active participation and interest.

Jurors have complained of the passive role that they play in litigation as a principal reason for viewing the experience as tedious and ultimately unappealing. Critics of assertive juror activity like taking notes, asking questions, and interviewing witnesses, however, argue that these steps transform the trial process from an adversarial one to one of inquisition, where the fact investigator becomes combined with the fact-finder. This conclusion preempts an assessment of the benefits which could flow from a power-sharing emphasis on community participation. It promotes the image of the trial process as combative and the jury as a group of strangers confronting the judge and litigants in an alien and alienating environment.

Reform measures which emphasize decentralizing control by the judge and power-sharing with the jury build upon the understanding that dialogue and decision-making by lay participants have distinctive value important in adjudication. The citizenship building quality is meaningful if full representation of communities and opportunity for meaningful participation in deliberation by community representatives is promoted.

A focus on nourishing citizenship through jury participation might be said to reflect an instrumental conception of jury participation which does not properly focus on the kind of decision-making that directly benefits the individual litigants. Emphasizing this individualistic posture, some critics have also argued that jury service imposes an unfair tax and social cost on those forced to serve.

My reconceived model assumes that the citizen has a stake in resolving public controversies. It begins with the proposition that any dispute worth pursuing in court and thus utilizing the resources of the state has a significant public dimension, and that the use of courts for the resolution of disputes is an aspect of self-government which has transformative potential for the citizen and, ultimately, for the law. The jury's civic responsibility, however, extends beyond its principal duty of resolving the dispute for individuals in a particular case. The jury role can be seen as providing the citizen with opportunities to develop a relationship with other citizens and with the state. The significance of adjudication also lies in defining public values and in identifying the interests of the political community in defining rights and obligations of citizens that has effects beyond the boundaries of an individual dispute. This conception reflects the general democratic principle "that people should be represented in institutions that have power over their lives."

Moreover, the citizens' participation does directly benefit litigants involved in the trial process. The justice-seeking goals of adjudication in a diverse society can be served by recognizing the distinctive capacity of the community's representatives to bring their perspectives to bear on the legal stories presented in court. The value of the jury's participation in terms of enhanced administration of justice lies in the jury's size, limited life, and deliberative quality. Finally, the jury's truth-defining function should be understood in terms of its members' distinctive capacity to engage in the social construction of truth.

5. Education about Differences

The jury's coming together can have an impact on the ability of its members and other participants in the trial — including the judge — to perceive differences among themselves and to reflect upon whether those differences have social significance affecting judgment. My construction of the arguments favoring jury participation has emphasized that the involvement of citizens with different perspectives in resolving public disputes, including their opportunity to converse and to deliberate, has educational potential both in and beyond the particular trial. That educational potential arises from evaluating the stories of the parties and their witnesses, from voir dire, and from evaluating the other jurors by reflecting on their capacity for judgment.

The jury has the potential, moreover, for causing the judge to reflect upon whether his responses are drawn from a too narrowly situated perspective and to benefit from the alternative social experiences offered by the jury-participants. Another aspect of the jury's role has to do with exposing the judge and other professionals to their insulation and to the effects of repetition experienced by these experts. This proposition reflects the view that "[w]e come to know who we are — our authentic selves, what sort of person we want to be, and what we should want — only through deliberation and dialogue with others." A civic objective of reconceiving the jury, emphasizing its representative potential, can be cultural exchange benefiting traditional dispute resolution objectives but also contributing to the fertilization and growth of normative understandings affecting other participants. . . .

NOTES & QUESTIONS

If you agree that the jury system has value (because of its citizenship-building qualities, its community-based conception of social justice, or other reasons), how can it be improved? Should jurors have a more active role during trial? Should they be allowed to take notes? Should they be allowed to ask questions? Should jurors be paid more for jury service? Are there any other incentives (child care, perhaps?) that the system should offer potential jurors?

C. AVOIDING JURY DUTY

If we believe that the jury is crucial to our system of justice, why do we try so hard to get out of jury duty? In the next reading, Judge Patricia D. Marks comments on real-life excuses made by potential jurors and intersperses these with her analysis of pop cultural images of jurors. Truth still proves itself stranger than fiction, but popular culture definitely appears to influence jurors' understanding of their roles.

MAGIC IN THE MOVIES — DO COURTROOM SCENES HAVE REAL-LIFE PARALLELS?

Hon. Patricia D. Marks

New York State Bar Journal, Vol. 73, No. 5, 40 (2001)

As the 100 prospective jurors walked into my courtroom for the next trial, my mind wandered: Does real life imitate film? Are there jurors anxious to find the excuse that will get them off of jury duty as Dennis Quaid did in *Suspect* (that was, until he learned the defense attorney was Cher)? Will a single mom like Valerie Alston in *Trial by Jury* come into the courthouse worried about the danger to her and her son if she serves on a jury? Is there a Pauly Shore in *Jury Duty* angling to escape jury duty on a short trial in favor of a notorious case where the jury is sequestered throughout the trial? Is there someone looking for romance, like Dennis Morgan and Ginger Rogers found in *Perfect Strangers*? Is there a Henry Fonda here about to re-enact *Twelve Angry Men* and turn the tide of jury deliberations?

The entertainment industry has long had a fascination with the law and courtroom drama. A search on the internet readily discloses hundreds of movies with courtroom themes. The growth of television shows depicting courtroom scenes is extraordinary — *Judge Judy, Judge Joe Brown* and *The People's Court* are flanked by *The Practice, Law & Order* and *Ally McBeal* to name a few. Those depictions, of course, include jurors from time to time, but this article looks at juries and jurors as they are depicted in the movies and suggests that in some way the fictional portrayals may or may not influence the way real jurors look at their role in the system. . . .

A Place to Sleep

Pauly Shore was truly amusing in *Jury Duty* as he went from trial to trial seeking the one that would provide him with a place to sleep. He pulled a fake prosthesis from his arm in jury selection for a medical malpractice case involving an orthopedic surgeon. He feigned recognition of a defendant during an embezzlement trial, and finally he posed as the perfect juror in the trial of a homicidal maniac so he could be selected and sequestered for a lengthy period of time.

Pauly Shore is not unique in his clever excuses to be disqualified from jury duty. Throughout New York State there are reports of the tactics employed by jurors to get excused. A news anchor arrived for jury duty in New York City wearing a NYPD t-shirt and carrying a beach chair and portable radio. Another juror reported that he could not come to court because "my summons was taken by aliens." Excuses vary, from "my cat just had kittens and I have to stay home with them for six weeks" to the man in the process of becoming a woman who wanted to know whether he should dress for court as a man or as a woman. In another case involving a defendant charged with driving while intoxicated, a mistrial was called during jury selection when a juror told the court that he and the accused used to drink together.

Valerie Alston portrays a juror in *Trial by Jury*. She endures the rigors of voir dire and is retained as a juror in a murder trial even though she describes the defendant as Mafia-related and known as "the Big Spaghetti-o." In an assault trial in upstate new York, a juror who described the defendant as a "Mafia hit man" but assured the court that she would try to set aside her preconceived notions and be fair, did not fare as well. She was not selected as a juror. The case was ultimately reversed because the trial court denied an application for a challenge for cause.

Character Development

I have saved the best for last. Who can forget Henry Fonda's memorable portrayal of a juror in *Twelve Angry Men*? Of course, the accuracy and completeness of the evidence are subject to some challenge, but who would quibble with a jury being told to "separate facts from fancy" or with the simplified reasonable doubt charge: "If there is a reasonable doubt of guilt you must acquit the defendant. If there is no reasonable doubt you must find the defendant guilty." In fact there are jurisdictions that recommend such a simplified charge.

What is unique in *Twelve Angry Men* is the way the characters of each of the 12 jurors — all male — are developed and their approaches to the deliberations. The accountant was quite reluctant to give an opinion and preferred the comfort of his numbers. The successful businessman, on the surface, was a self-assured juror who made reasonable and logical arguments, but as time went on he began to unravel and show signs of instability. The juror who openly voted guilty because of the defendant's background was the most troublesome. The immigrant watchmaker was provoked to anger by the indifference of another juror. It is remarkable that this film can succeed in providing an intelligent plot and developing 12 distinct and interesting characters. It succeeds in reminding us of the uniqueness of each juror in a real trial and how each personality contributes to the ultimate verdict.

The initial vote is 11 to one to convict but as the discussion progresses it is apparent that the reasons for the votes are not what they should be. One juror votes to convict because his anger toward his son gets in the way of an objective view of the guilt of the defendant, who is charged in the death of his father.

An experiment in the jury room influences some votes. The unique knife is not so unique after all when juror Henry Fonda produces a knife similar to the murder weapon and displays the angle of the death-producing wound. He finds the knife when he goes for a walk in the neighborhood where the defendant lives and where the crime occurred.

While experimentation is not permitted, the books are full of cases where such experimentation has occurred. During the overnight sequestration in one trial, a juror adjusted the lighting conditions and opened the curtains in her hotel room to simulate what she believed to be the conditions of the crime scene, based on the victim's testimony. She then asked another juror to walk in and out of the room, wearing clothing similar in color to that worn by the attacker, so that she could determine whether the victim would have been able to make a reliable identification. The contrived experimentation was not approved by the courts and the conviction was reversed.

Application of everyday experience is acceptable. When the defense counsel suggested that the jurors place the gun in the pocket of their shorts during their deliberations, the court held that jurors are not precluded from applying their everyday experiences and common sense to the issues presented in a trial. Was it contrived experimentation, an application of everyday experience, or a little of both? I'll leave that to you.

As the 100 members of the group before me were reduced to 14 jurors and they prepared for deliberations, I had satisfied myself that jurors would not be influenced by the movies or television. And then I saw on the Internet an entry by a juror who was summoned to jury duty in California and immediately did his "homework" by watching the following videos: *Jury Duty, Trial by Jury,* and *Twelve Angry Men.*

NOTES & QUESTIONS

1. Can popular culture serve an educational function for jurors? What are the benefits and the dangers of relying on popular culture to educate citizens about juries? Should prospective jurors be required to watch a movie such as *12 Angry Men* before serving on a jury? Many jurors are puzzled about how to go about their task of deliberating. (While they do receive instructions about the law, instructions about the mechanics of how they actually are supposed to deliberate are sparse to non-existent.) Is the proper spirit for deliberations best taught through entertainment? *12 Angry Men* definitely gets the spirit of the process right, but some aspects of the film (such as Henry Fonda going out to purchase a knife similar to the murder weapon) are beyond the pale as juror experimentation.

In *Jury Duty,* Pauly Shore plays a slacker who, needing a free place to live, maneuvers to be a juror on a lengthy murder trial. (Jurors get put up at a hotel and also get the princely sum of five dollars a day.) After listening to a fellow juror and new citizen describe how, in his former country, no one had the right to a trial by jury, Shore has a change of heart and decides to take the trial seriously. Shore prepares himself for serious deliberations by renting and watching a number of classic law-related videos, including *12 Angry Men, Judgment at Nuremberg* (1961), *And Justice for All* (1979), and *Witness for the Prosecution* (1957). (He also reads the Cliffs Notes of *Law for Beginners.*)

2. Jury duty is serious business. Yet movies about jury duty, such as Peter Bogdanovich's *Illegally Yours* (1988), and *Jury Duty,* the Pauly Shore vehicle, are broadly farcical comedies. The next excerpt suggests that comedy is a good fit for stories about law because (1) comedy has a strong truth-seeking potential (laughter can be subversive) and (2) comedy helps make the law accessible to laypersons. As you read, consider whether you agree with these propositions.

TRIAL AND ERRORS: COMEDY'S QUEST FOR THE TRUTH
Rajani Gupta
9 UCLA Entertainment Law Review 113 (2001)

Comedy is a social phenomenon, a reflection, if not critique of the prevailing (or narrow-minded) beliefs of a given culture. It develops as a community outgrowth, a moment of light attack on the existing norms of a given population. Comedy finds its way into the smallest forms of human communication and expression, extending from tiny witticisms or ill-mannered jokes to the full-blown parodies or comprehensive satires of human existence often found long-form in the mediums of novels or films, or, in other words, through the outlets of pop culture itself.

Comedy defines itself in relation to social categories; directed as an often derisive attack on the status quo, it situates itself as a disrespectful observer of a given situation, society, culture, or even a particular human behavior. While comedy consists of universal components attributable to many facets of human interaction and activity, its true thrust (and intended goal) depends on its ability to delve into a communal understanding of its intended comedic "victim" as a sort of foil for its alternative proposition. This alternative is a model of possibilities, a substitute to the current approach that could potentially replace the generally accepted proto- type. In a manner of speaking, comedy presents a playful challenge to traditionally held notions of social behavior by way of a light approach to the serious; it pokes fun at current conduct through parody or exaggeration while always depicting the existence of a different manner of acting in that particular situation.

The legal system itself is a social construction, the epitome of social categoriza- tion of acceptable behavioral norms. Varied from culture to culture, law represents the classification of proper moral values according to the body politic (depending on the particular political structure) along with its complementary enforcement mechanism. Through and within its malleable structure, an aggregation of laws creates a hierarchy of social values that attempts to define proper human deeds in relation to an overarching ideology. The courtroom has come to represent the battleground of these values. It presents a forum for conflicting notions of proper social behavior. Borrowing from a Rousseauian theory of the social compact, the courtroom can be seen as the constant renegotiation of the terms of the communal contract. In this theoretical analysis of the ideal, the lawyers represent opposing approaches to the same situations, testing their philosophies of justice against the sounding board of the community — a jury composed of twelve members who, in the ideal, represent a cross-section of the community and its component values.

Now the question that arises here is: Where do the two intersect? What are the possibilities when law merges with comedy and exposes a connection through the medium of popular culture?

The links between comedy and the law are endless. Both depend upon a categorization of social norms; however, whereas law defines these customs, comedy exists as a foil of them, creating an alternative community with different possibili- ties that could work within the existing community. Where law is the epitome of social structure, comedy functions as the anti-structure, the breakdown of hierarchy and order and the comic subversion of dominant ideas. Comedy presents breaks in traditional logic, demonstrating a play upon form that produces humor through its unconventional pattern. In addition, both comedy and the law depend on a sort of community consensus to attain their ends. One seeks order through the creation of social parameters; the other seeks laughter and social critique through the destruction of constraints. Both are, however, the construction of worlds that encapsulate a certain notion of behavior while attacking that which is outside of it, "the other."

Together, comedy and the law present great possibilities of truth-seeking. Comedy has been often considered a truth-seeking mechanism with its constant consideration of that which challenges the status quo. Of all social creations, the law requires such a challenge in order to evolve towards a stronger understanding of truth and the proper means that should be exercised in order to attain those ends. Since popular culture has come to define and characterize the general public's understanding of justice and the legal process, a comic portrayal of the law can become a strong vehicle for social criticism (and eventual change) of the legal process. . . .

III. Law and Comedy: How Do They Work Together? . . .

A. Comedy That Makes the Law More Accessible

Comedy, being a medium that is accessible to a broad spectrum of the population, has the unique ability to make the subjects it covers more accessible to its target audience. In the legal context, this is especially clear. In the first instance, legal comedies are almost always delivered through inherently comedic actors. While this observation seems brutally obvious, it is important in the context of the law because these actors generally appear to be more approachable and closer to "real" people. Comedic actors have an already established comic persona and a pattern of humorous gestures which the audience then recognizes. The comic personality of the character is then laid on top of this persona. When the movie star glamour of an actor can be more easily separated from the character he is portraying, the situation and the subject becomes more lucid and authentic to the viewer.

Aside from the actor, the characters themselves are notably accessible to the public and often intentionally created to pattern real people. . . .

Yet another perspective of the legal system is shown in the utterly awful movie *Jury Duty*, starring Pauly Shore as Tommy Collins, an unemployed trailer park resident who seeks jury duty as a source of income and guaranteed room and board. Throughout the entire film, Collins seeks to delay the trial, using every tactic possible to turn around a guilty verdict by eleven of his twelve fellow jurors. Despite his own abuse of the system, even Collins seeks out the truth and finds it, resulting in the release of a man falsely accused of murder. Eventually Collins discovers the mastermind behind the whole plot to frame Carl Wayne Bishop (Sean Whalen), and justice prevails. Although the casting alone makes the film's message accessible (who does not feel superior to Pauly Shore?), the fact that the truth was secured through an unskilled and seemingly unintelligent man such as Collins places a certain responsibility upon the average person in their search for truth from the jury box. In addition, if Pauly Shore can discover the truth and have it be recognized in a court of law, then the court system is certainly accessible to the average person. . . .

NOTES & QUESTIONS

1.   What connections do you see between law and comedy? Literary scholar Northrop Frye notes that law in comedy serves as a blocking force which must be overcome before the lovers can be united in a happy ending. The paternal (legalistic) figures in charge of society at the beginning of a comedy must give way to the young

lovers who will represent a new, freer social order. Frye succinctly notes, "The action of comedy in moving from one social center to another is not unlike the action of a lawsuit, in which plaintiff and defendant construct different versions of the same situation, one finally being judged as real and the other as illusory." Northrop Frye, *Anatomy of Criticism* 166 (1957).

2.   Why must juror-heroes so frequently break the law in films? *Runaway Jury, The Juror, Illegally Yours* (1988), *Jury Duty*, and *Trial by Jury*, among others, all feature juror protagonists who lie, cheat, steal, or even kill. Of course, in comedy most lawbreaking is played for laughs, but what kind of message does a film send about our legal system when the one sure-fire way to achieve justice is through breaking the law?

Illegally Yours and *Jury Duty* feature plenty of law-breaking by jurors. The films are romantic comedies of the so-bad-they're-good variety. Director Peter Bog-danovich seems to be channeling a Zen version of *What's Up, Doc?* (1972) in the genuinely weird *Illegally Yours*, in which a very young Rob Lowe plays a character named Richard Dice who rolls a pair of dice to help him make big decisions. *Jury Duty* features Shelley Winters, Tia Carrere, and Pauly Shore, plus a cute miniature dog. (How could anyone resist?) Both films center on a hapless juror-hero who saves the defendant and finds love.

Both Rob Lowe's and Pauly Shore's characters break the law left and right. Dice is a dorky guy who lies during voir dire when he denies knowing the defendant in a murder trial. (In fact, he has been in love with her since first grade.) Convinced she is innocent, Dice's law-breaking investigations escalate to include breaking and entering, impersonating a judge's wife, stealing, assault, etc. (The only thing that really troubles his mom is when he tells her he is considering law school. "Richard," she tells him, "We've done a lot of stupid things over the years, but we've never been boring people.") Dice muses to himself that he is the only one who can save Molly (the defendant), "and yet everything I was doing was completely against the law. . . . Still, there were the laws of love to consider."

The laws of love seem as inexplicable and chancy as the laws of the legal system, but fortunately for Dice, he lives in a romantic comedy. He gambles on love, and the legal system be damned! As Johnny Cash sings "Love is a gambler" on the soundtrack, Dice kisses Molly, while the police read them their Miranda rights.

Pauly Shore's juror character, of course, breaks or bends the law every few minutes in *Jury Duty*. This includes such visual gems as dressing up as the defendant's "girlfriend" to visit him in jail to investigate the case. However, unlike Dice in *Illegally Yours*, Shore's character has a genuine change of heart about the legal system, fueled in part by his education in pop culture. He uses actual dialogue from *12 Angry Men* in his arguments with other jurors. Ultimately, with the help of Peanut, his trusty dog, he saves the innocent defendant. (Of course, since the film is a Pauly Shore vehicle, the movie ends with Peanut competing on *Jeopardy.*)

D. THE WORK OF A JURY

1. Jurors and Storytelling — "I guess we talk"

How does a jury use evidence to reach its collective determination? In a key scene in *12 Angry Men*, the jurors take a preliminary vote, and it is 11-1 for a guilty verdict. A juror asks, "What do we do now?" and Henry Fonda's character responds, in his classic laconic style, "I guess we talk." What kind of talk is jury talk? Is jury talk always purely and coldly rational? How do emotions affect the process of jurors working toward a decision? And what about the internal talk, the cognitive process inside a juror's head as he or she listens to and tries to understand the evidence at trial? Most commentators today believe that jurors use a story model in the way they decide. Consider the following excerpts from an article by Reid Hastie, one of the preeminent researchers into juror decision-making.

EMOTIONS IN JURORS' DECISIONS
Reid Hastie
66 Brooklyn Law Review 991 (2001)

I. THE JUROR'S DECISION-MAKING PROCESS

Most conceptions of the juror's decision assume that the process is primarily cognitive, even rational in character. Descriptive psychological theories all focus on cognitive information processing functions, and none of the currently popular models include an explicit account of the role of sentiments, moods, emotions, and passions in the process.

Normative theories also assert that legal decisions should be predominantly rational. For example, the Advisory Committee's note on Federal Rule of Evidence 403 comments that one consideration in deciding whether to exclude evidence should be to avoid "unfair prejudice," defined as "an undue tendency to suggest decision on an improper basis, commonly, though not necessarily, an emotional one."

There is an apparent contradiction between the conception of the ideal juror as a logical reasoning machine and also as a source of community attitudes, sentiments, and moral precepts. Robert Solomon noted this discrepancy when he commented that "[t]he idea that justice requires emotional detachment, a kind of purity suited ultimately to angels, ideal observers, and the original founders of society, has blinded us to the fact that justice arises from and requires such feelings as resentment." This apparent contradiction may be resolved by distinguishing between the several functions required of the jury, some of which (for example, fact-finding) demand cold rational assessments, while others (for example, determining the moral egregiousness of a defendant's conduct) require a more passionate evaluation. Nonetheless, psychologists know of no satisfactory normative analysis of the relationship between cognitive and emotional functions in the decision-making process.

Theoretical analyses provide extremely cognitive versions of the jurors' decision-making processes, but any realistic assessment concludes that jurors experience varied emotions and that these emotions sometimes influence their decisions. First person reports of jury service invariably mention emotional experiences: anxiety or irritation produced by jury service, reactions of anger, fear, and sympathy evoked by the events that led to the trial or by participants in those events or the trial, and sometimes dramatic evidence exhibits that evoke strong emotions. It is also likely that emotions caused by events outside the trial may be carried into the jury box and that even these irrelevant events may influence a juror's decision. . . .

This Essay starts with an overview of the three major cognitive theories of juror decision making.

Many scholars claim that jurors' judgments are best described by algebraic models of mental processes like those proposed by philosophers and mathematicians as rational belief revision principles. A popular choice is Bayes Theorem, which describes the judgment process as starting from a prior probability of guilt and then adjusting from that initial point by multiplicatively integrating the implications of new evidence according to the laws of mathematical probability theory. The other popular algebraic process model supposes that jurors form their initial beliefs about guilt (analogous to the Bayesian prior probability) and then adjust using an averaging, rather than multiplying, information integration process. Empirical studies favor the statistically robust linear, averaging model over the Bayesian model as a description of jurors' decision-making processes.

A second, more complicated theoretical description comes from research on cognitive judgment heuristics. The reigning metaphor is that the juror carries a "cognitive toolbox" of useful inference heuristics in long-term memory, and selects relevant judgment tools, algorithms, or strategies to solve the problem of making a legal decision. . . .

The third theoretical description is of the juror as a "naïve reporter" who constructs a narrative summary to explain the evidence, concluding with the verdict that is most consistent with that story. The primary cognitive activities in the decision-making process are inferences made to serve the goal of creating a coherent, comprehensive story to summarize the situation implied by credible evidence. The final stage of the decision-making process involves classifying the constructed story into one of the legal criminal verdict concepts or relying on the story for premises to infer causation and responsibility to decide many civil cases.

None of these approaches is a unique winner in the competition for "best theory" status, although the Story Model provides the most valid description of a typical juror's decision-making process. It includes many of the heuristic judgment strategies as sub-components, and it is intended to describe cognitive processes that could, at a general level, be captured by the parameters of an algebraic equation. This Essay will review what is known about the influence of emotions on juror decisions and conclude with an interpretation of those effects, in terms of the Story Model, as it provides the most systematic, detailed, and empirically-supported account of the juror decision-making process. First, this Essay will further describe the Story Model.

II. THE STORY MODEL OF THE JUROR'S DECISION PROCESS

The Story Model proposes that the central cognitive process in juror decision making is *story construction* — the creation of a narrative summary of the events under dispute. Applications of the Story Model to criminal jury judgments have identified three component processes: (1) evidence evaluation through story construction, (2) representation of the decision alternatives (verdicts) by learning their attributes or elements, and (3) reaching a decision through the classification of the story into the best-fitting verdict category. . . .

The distinctive claim is that the story the juror constructs determines the juror's verdict. More generally, the approach proposes that causal "situation models" play a central role in many explanation-based decisions in legal, medical, engineering, financial, and everyday circumstances . . . .

IV. EMOTIONS IN JURORS' DECISIONS

. . . Three important categories of emotional experience most relevant to the decision act are "incidental emotions," "decision process emotions," and "anticipated emotions." What is known about the effects of these emotional phenomena on the outcomes of decisions? There is no scientific research on "decision process emotions" in legal contexts, but there are a few studies demonstrating the effects of incidental emotions and anticipated emotions on jurors' decisions.

The extant empirical research literature does not provide us with a comprehensive list of emotional phenomena that occur in jury decisions. The most important examples include: reactions to jury service, primarily anxiety and irritation; reactions to the events that led to the trial, primarily anger; reactions to participants involved in the trial, primarily anger, sympathy, and fear; and reactions to evidentiary exhibits, primarily disgust and horror.

If a juror's general decision-making strategy follows the stages described by the Story Model, we can locate the various effects of emotions within that framework. Since, according to the Story Model, the story is the central determinant of the decision, this Essay suggests that most of the effects of emotions will be manifested in characteristics of the juror's story.

Where do jurors' stories come from? The initial stages of story retrieval and creation can be biased by simple associative or appraisal processes. Sometimes, while trying to comprehend the evidence, the juror is reminded of another story, and that story is used as a template for comprehension of the current case. The original story may come from a television show, a movie, a novel, the news, or everyday conversations. Or perhaps the juror knows of a generic story schema or story skeleton such as a "script" for a kidnapping, an oil spill, or a traffic accident. Under these conditions, the jurors' emotional states will influence the reminding process and bias the selection of a relevant story from memory.

In other cases, no related story comes to mind, and the juror constructs a story from background knowledge. We liken this process to deduction from a database of facts and inference rules. Again, it is likely that associative or appraisal-based influences of incidental and anticipated emotions will affect the nature of the "premises" that are salient, those that come to mind when a juror attempts to construct a story de novo. For example, if a juror is in an angry emotional state, he or she is likely to attend to, or retrieve from memory, information that is negative, perhaps exaggerating the egregiousness of the defendant's alleged conduct or the severity of the injury to a plaintiff or victim or constructing a story for the instant case from another story that produced an angry reaction. . . .

NOTES & QUESTIONS

1.   What role should emotion play in a jury trial? Hastie is right to point out that Federal Rule of Evidence 403 frowns on the use of unfairly prejudicial, i.e., overly emotional, evidence. But the key is "unfair" prejudice. Jurors expect emotional testimony at trial (in accord with what they see in popular culture), and jurors themselves experience a great many emotions during trial (boredom, anger, sympathy, sadness, etc.). Anecdotal evidence abounds suggesting that jury duty is so emotionally stressful it is actually bad for your health. One study found mixed results, but concluded that serving on a traumatic trial can have a negative health effect in the area of depression. *See* Daniel W. Shuman, et al., *The Health Effects of Jury Service*, 18 Law & Psychology Review 267 (1994).

2.   It is common to speak of lawyers as storytellers. However, we forget that jurors, too, are storytellers. They use stories as cognitive tools to help process, sort, balance, and understand the evidentiary story they hear at trial. Additionally, as they talk to each other during deliberations, they consider the alternative possible stories presented at trial and must decide which story makes the most sense. How might the stories that circulate in popular culture affect jurors' processing of a trial story? Consider the following excerpt.

"DESPERATE FOR LOVE II": FURTHER REFLECTIONS ON THE INTERPENETRATION OF LEGAL AND POPULAR STORYTELLING IN CLOSING ARGUMENTS TO A JURY IN A COMPLEX CRIMINAL CASE
Philip N. Meyer
30 University of San Francisco Law Review 931 (1996)

During 1990 and 1991, I attended criminal trials in the state and federal courts of Connecticut. It had been many years since I had attended trials as a young attorney specializing in litigation. Over the course of observing several high-profile criminal trials I noticed several developments.

To begin with, I observed that the nature of lawyering practice and storytelling at trial is changing rapidly. Many of these changes are the result of new technologies, especially the use of aural and visual "paratexts" at trial. These new technologies include computer simulation, visual aids, and other "storytelling" devices. The impact of this new storytelling technology at trial is profound. The use of these paratexts has permitted reinvention of the ways that stories are now told, and often the types of stories that are told. Evidence is often presented aurally and visually. These are "present-tense" simulations of voices and images, rather than past-tense testimonial evidence. This adjustment enables, and perhaps compels, a radical reinvention of the types of stories told at trial.

Secondly, the law is increasingly complex. Evidentiary details accumulate over weeks and even months. This legal and factual "complexification" of the trial provides additional room for narrative invention and ultimately severs the trial from the events that the storytellers purport to describe. Furthermore, the storytelling at trial often "slows down" some events that led up to the trial, as the past is re-imagined and reconfigured from multiple perspectives. Consequently, the story-telling at trial takes far longer than the events themselves. Crucial moments in the dramatic action of the trial can be examined through multiple media and from multiple perspectives (audio and visual tapes, witness testimony, inventive storytelling). At other times, the storytellers can skip over vast spaces of time, especially in the back story that frames the action, and choose to focus on crucial moments of criminality or drama.

Additionally, lawyers' work has become popularized and narrativized in the popular imagination through the media, including television and film. These stories incorporate artistic and aesthetic patterns embedded in the cultural imagination.

As a result of these changes, a phenomenon has occurred that is notable in the high-profile and complex criminal trials I observed: jurors seem to make sense out of increasingly complex situations through references to other imagistic stories. The new media world at trial evokes other cinematic stories of popular culture. There is an apparent interpenetration between popular stories and the stories that lawyers tell at trial. No longer does popular culture merely reflect the stories told by lawyers at trial — popular culture creates these stories. . . .

NOTES & QUESTIONS

1.   What are the implications of Philip Meyer's comment that popular culture creates the stories lawyers tell at trial? Should every law school require a course in popular culture? If jurors have certain expectations about trial stories based on popular culture, the wise lawyer will be familiar with popular culture.

2.   A great deal of debate recently has centered on the question of whether jurors are influenced by something called "the CSI Effect." The New England Law Review even devoted a symposium issue to the subject in 2007. *See Symposium: The CSI Efect: The True Effect of Crime Scene Television on the Justice System*, 41 New England Law Review 435 (2007). According to this theory, the popularity of television shows such as *CSI* makes it harder for prosecutors to win cases, since jurors now are conditioned by popular culture to expect overwhelming scientific proof in criminal cases. Does such a theory mask our cultural anxieties about the competence of juries? The relationship between art and life has been debated for literally thousands of years. Is art the mirror or the lamp? Aristotle argued that art is mimetic, an imitation of life (art as mirror), while others would say art can actually affect life (art as lamp). The literary scholar M.H. Abrams discussed this at length in his important book, *The Mirror or the Lamp: Romantic Theory and the Critical Tradition* (1953). Whether or not "the CSI Effect" is real (and some empirical studies cast cold water on the theory, or at least suggest there is no simple cause and effect), television shows are part of the common lexicon of jurors. The

first rule of storytelling is to know your audience.

3.   Professor Meyer suggests in the above excerpt that new technologies (such as computer simulations) have changed the very nature of storytelling at trial. As you read the next excerpt, consider the changing nature of the twenty-first century jury as an audience for legal storytelling.

REALITY PROGRAMMING LESSONS FOR TWENTY-FIRST CENTURY TRIAL LAWYERING
Gary S. Gildin
31 Stetson Law Review 61 (2001)

[T]wo interrelated changes are occurring as we enter the new millennium that must affect the way trial lawyers present their cases to the jury — the evolution in the demographics of the jury pool and the revolution in technology that has transformed how our new breed of juror receives and is presented out-of-court information.

A spate of recent articles has documented that Generation X has arrived not only to populate, but to dominate, the jury pool. Jury consultants Elizabeth Foley and Adrienne LeFevre offer that, in the year 2000, thirty percent of all jury panels will be composed of representatives of the 78.2 million Americans born between 1966 and 1976. Projecting that Generation X will make up forty-one percent of the jury pool in the year 2000, Sonya Hamlin updated her seminal work *What Makes Juries Listen* — newly minted as *What Makes Juries Listen Today* — on account of "[t]he fundamental changes in the jury and how people get information." Michael Maggiano, in his article *Motivating the Modern Juror*, cites data predicting that, in the next five years, fully half of the jurors will be members of Generation X. All who have recognized Generation X's invasion of the venire agree that trial lawyers must adapt both the substance and manner of their presentations to the contemporary juror. For members of Generation X, life experiences have not only given rise to a unique set of values and biases, but also have imbued these jurors with ways of receiving and evaluating information that differ vastly from preceding epochs.

Invariably, the assessment of new strategies for shaping trial presentations to Generation X jurors is accompanied by acknowledgment of the second galvanizing change in society — the rapid rise of new technologies to accumulate and convey knowledge. Indeed, most commentators cite an interrelationship between the technology that may have been instrumental in affecting the thought processes of Generation X and the metamorphosis that the ascension of that generation has mandated in trial advocacy. Hence, while the ultimate object of the trial has remained constant, the twenty-first century lawyer must adapt his or her advocacy to accommodate the new audience, as well as to employ new means of information delivery.

While consultants and trial lawyers are in the nascent stages of pondering how to adjust to the new jurors and technologies, other disciplines have already changed the way they go about the business of informing and persuading. This Article proposes that television is the medium that currently serves as the most useful guide for informing and persuading the new generation of jurors about the truth of past events — more particularly, its two species of reality programming.

II. How Television Can Help Us Learn Modern Trial Techniques. . . .

Like examining movies and theater, studying television may lend insight into precisely how jurors will process information offered at trial. In his recent, fascinating book, *When Law Goes Pop: The Vanishing Line Between Law and Popular Culture*, Professor Richard K. Sherwin cautioned how the media affects the manner in which jurors will interpret reality:

> Popular culture, especially through its chief agency, the visual mass media, also contributes to law by helping to shape the very processes of thought and perception by which jurors judge. . . . Each generation learns a new set of skills for making sense of experience. These meaning-making skills make up what may be called a "communal tool kit." . . .

> For most people the source [of the tool kit] is not difficult to ascertain. It is the visual mass media: film, video, television, and to an increasing degree computerized imaging. This vast electronic archive provides us with the knowledge and interpretation skills we need to make sense of ordinary reality. . . . In a sense, we "see" ' reality the way we have been trained to watch film and TV. The camera is in our heads. . . .

Sherwin, Richard K. *When Law Goes Pop: The Vanishing Line Between Law and Popular Culture* 18, 21 (2000).

NOTES & QUESTIONS

How would the type of Gen X juror Gary Gildin describes compare to a Baby Boomer juror raised on images of Raymond Burr as Perry Mason and Henry Fonda in *12 Angry Men*? If television is the key medium for Gen X jurors, is the Internet the key medium for Gen Y? How does the internet affect jurors' storytelling expectations at trial?

2. Doing the Work of Community Justice

A jury's work has a both a microcosmic impact (on the particular litigants) and a macrocosmic impact (on society). The work done by jurors not only decides individual cases but also helps constitute the type of community in which we live. How does jury work help answer the questions of who we are and who we want to be? The next reading, by Professor Milner S. Ball, suggests that a jury's work is the communal work of telling stories to create something, finally, like justice.

JUST STORIES
Milner Ball
12 Cardozo Studies in Law & Literature 37 (2000)

"For [Paul] Ricoeur, the justice that sought to be the aim of responsible politics is one that is always in the making. It calls for an ongoing conversation about justice itself, a conversation that always calls upon and contests both convictions and the criticisms of them."

— Bernard Dauenhauer, *Paul Ricoeur*

"A juror's decision between competing narratives is, moreover, a definition of public identity. Because he is taking public action through public institutions, his judgment is inevitably determination, in a strong sense, of the nature of his community."

— Robert Burns, *A Theory of the Trial*

Richard Weisberg says public discourse is in disarray, and he is clearly right. But I imagine a possibility within it. I imagine an accessible public discourse about justice whose central activity is telling and contesting stories. Narrative is the primary medium for talking together about who we are — and would be — as a people, and this is the talk in which conversation about justice chiefly subsists. Notwithstanding disarray and continued academic belief in theories rather than stories of justice and a lingering assumption that justice is — or should be — practically separated from law, the American story is regularly performed in law. The current version invites the critique of other stories and therefore a public discourse richly arrayed.

I. Justice, Story, and the People

There are various ways to approach these things. Augustine, for example, urged that justice is a less adequate gauge of a people than are the objects of their love. A people is greater or lesser, he thought, depending on the greatness of what they love, and he therefore took up the conversation as one about love. I would not divide the terms, for to talk about justice is to talk about love. As Paul Lehmann said, "justice is the political form of love." Paul Lehmann, *Ethics in a Christian Context* 255 (1963). But, primarily as a matter of rhetorical strategy for the time being, I judge that dialogue about justice has a better chance of making headway than disciplined public discussion about the politics of love.

What is true of love is true also of righteousness: It is companion to justice as a measure of a people, but it is generally unfamiliar in contemporary discourse about political fundamentals. The alignment of justice with righteousness is embodied in the Hebrew Bible's employment of *mishpat* and *tzedaka* as synonyms and in the use of "justice" and "righteousness" as alternative translation for both *mishpat* and the Greek *diakaiosyne* in Christian scripture. Notwithstanding the efforts of people like Aviam Soifer and Stephen Wizner to re-familiarize us with the valid relation of justice and righteousness and the need for righteous acts by lawyers and judges,

Justice Antonin Scalia employed "righteousness" as a term of disparagement in his dissent from the Court's opinion in *Romer v. Evans* [1996]. He dismissively accused the majority of placing "heavy reliance upon principles of righteousness rather than judicial holdings." I think that the Justice on righteousness reflects a general attitude, for although fidelity in constitutional interpretation is familiar enough at least to academics, I have seen no symposia on righteousness. "Righteousness" must wait until public discourse has been better prepared for its return. For present purposes, then, I turn primarily to "justice" rather than to "love" or "righteousness."

As a rule, when we talk to each other about who we are and would be, as the American people that is, when we talk about justice, we tell stories — about pilgrims, about July the Fourth, about the frontier, about wars we have fought, about struggles for rights, about our own political experiences. It may be that there is an inherent connection between narrative and justice. Melvyn Hill, for example, proposes that storytelling in general "must be understood not just as the primary form of thinking about experience, but also as the primary form of communicating with each other about experience. . . . Stories tell us how each one finds or loses his just place in relation to others in the world. And the communication of the story is confirmed when justice has been recognized." Melvyn Hill, *The Fictions of Mankind and the Stories of Men, in Hannah Arendt: The Recovery of the Public World* 290 (Melvyn Hill ed. 1979); *quoted in* Robert Burns, *A Theory of the Trial* 173 (1999).

Certainly stories of origin orient us in the world and in justice, but, like all stories, they are forgotten unless they are retold. In the retelling, the story continues to constitute a living community of remembrance. Consider, for example, the gathering effect, then and now, of the story that begins: "We were Pharaoh's slaves in Egypt and the Lord brought us out of Egypt with a mighty hand . . . that he might bring us in and give us the land which he swore to give to our fathers."

Ricoeur observes that "the identity of a group, culture, people, or nation is not that of an immutable substance, nor that of a fixed structure, but that, rather, of a recounted story." Paul Ricoeur, *Reflections on a New Ethos for Europe*, Philosophy and Social Criticism 21:5/6 (Sep./Nov. 1995) 7; *quoted in* Bernard Dauenhauer, *Paul Ricoeur* 128 (1998). A fresh, multi-layered experience of narrative communal identity was offered by a version of the mystery play *The Nativity* recently produced by the Royal National Theater in London in its small, experimental Cottesloe theater. The primary subject of the production was the biblical story of Jesus's birth and the gathering of shepherds and wise men at the manger. Another was the telling of the story by the community of tradesmen, as acted, who had originally performed the play and whose lives in England had been shaped by the biblical stories. But the present actors and audience, too, became a community, a fact uniquely underscored by the absence of seats and separate stage and by the continuous movement of the action through the playgoers. I found it deeply affecting to be drawn thereby into a community of witnesses with the present actors, the medieval tradesmen, and the ancient shepherds and wise men. The community that a story constitutes is not limited by divisions between past and present.

Arendt noted that the incessant talk that saves deeds and experiences and their stories from futility will itself remain "futile unless certain concepts, certain guideposts for future remembrance, and even for sheer reference, arise out of it." And she noted that a loss of bearings has accompanied "the 'American' aversion from conceptual thought." Hannah Arendt, *On Revolution* 222 (1965). Concepts do play necessary, valuable roles as prompts for memory or as analytical tools for testing stories, but their end lies in service to the underlying story. It is the story that counts.

Of course narrative has limits and defects. It does not create the conditions for its realization and interpretation. It is not immune to monopolization or aggressive use. And it may bear no helpful relation to the story-less, those whose world is consumed by pain or oppression. Memory, too, has limits and defects. Aviam Soifer points out that, while forgetting what happened can have grievous consequences, "too much remembering may also be dangerous," as the grim, revengeful violence of ethnic conflicts in Rwanda and the former Yugoslavia exemplify. And in conjunction with a reflection on legal responses to unspeakable horror, Martha Minow reminds us of the complex need for remembering what to forget.

More and other stories do not cure narrative — it cannot save itself — but they do compose a corrective response. The story of the founding of America is (would be) improved by different versions, especially the versions of those excluded from, or harmed by it. By bringing alive the story of slaves, Toni Morrison's *Beloved* offers readers a contesting experience of the story of American origins. "Recounting differently," Ricoeur observes, "is not inimical to a certain historical reverence to the extent that the inexhaustible richness of the event is honored by the diversity of stories which are made out of it, and by the competition to which that diversity gives rise." Paul Ricoeur, *Fallible Man* 61 (Charles Kelbey trans. 1986). Moreover, as Bernard Dauenhauer says, even if it is only symbolic, participation in the founding stories of other nations as well as our own and in the stories or origin of various ethnic minorities and religious confessions "not only teaches us about one another's cultures but also [helps to free] capabilities for renewal . . . trapped within our own dead traditions." Dauenhauer, *supra*, at 130, 276-277.

The telling and hearing of stories — the participation, the giving and receiving, the performance — "is really a matter of living with the other in order to take that other to one's home as a guest." In this way and for this reason, the process enacts something like what Richard Weisberg refers to as "poethics," and what James Boyd White calls "justice as translation": "Good translation . . . proceeds not by the motives of dominance or acquisition, but by respect. It is a word for a set of practices by which we learn to live with difference, with the fluidity of culture and with the instability of the self. It is not simply an operation of mind on material, but a way of being oneself in relation to another human being." James Boyd White, *Justice as Translation* 257 (1990).

One of White's central points is that the practice of law is the practice of translation. The lawyer constantly moves between languages, mediating between them, between the stories of clients and the arguments of law, and, crucially for the democratic character of law, she makes "the ultimate translation [of law] into the ordinary language of the citizen." Lawyers come to public discourse about justice already engaged in it.

II. Justice, Story, and the Law

Some decisive national occasions precipitate community willingness "to reassess fundamental beliefs and commitments as few events in political life do." "Constitutional moments" are an example of the phenomenon, and one seems to be in progress in Britain just now. Another is show trials in transitions from administrative massacre to democracy as may be illustrated by the prosecution of military juntas in Argentina. Such singular occasions concentrate the mind of the polis on fundamentals.

The civil rights movement may have precipitated an American constitutional moment. An obituary for Federal Judge Frank Johnson of Alabama celebrated his opinions during that time and described him as one of the "courageous men and women asking Americans to decide what kind of people they wanted to be." His courtroom joined the streets of Birmingham and Montgomery as a site for raising the issue of justice.

The question of who Americans would be, however, is not reserved for such extraordinary times. It is regularly before us, and answers to it are routinely in formulation in law. A photographic study of courthouses, those landmark centers of community life, makes a successful visual argument that "they are our history" and that the study of them is a "way of reconstructing the American people's story." The structured telling and contesting of stories that takes place in trials and to some extent in appeals and that lies at the heart of law is an ongoing performance of our story of justice. As White says, law is "a way in which the community defines itself, not once and for all, but over and over, and in the process it educates itself about its own character and the nature of the world." The participants are working out our story.

Robert Burns helpfully observes that the trial structure of competing stories "assures that the jury will not act on the basis of One Big Story authorized by a state official. . . . It reflects a distinctly Anglo-American approach that the inability to agree on one story to be told is precisely what brings the parties to trial." There is no "metanarrative that resolves the differences." Burns, *supra*, at 165-166. The jury's decision in that tension between competing stories "decisively shapes what the community is becoming." *Id.*, at 173. Trials are one of the ways in which we determine and perform our story of justice. . . .

NOTES & QUESTIONS

1. Why is it important that stories of justice be "performed"? Other countries do not have a jury system. What kind of national values does having a jury system suggest?

2. Does the jury's work in performing justice differ in civil and criminal trials? What norms do civil juries evaluate when deciding whether to rule for or against an injured plaintiff? Can you pinpoint any normative themes about work, reward, blame, or responsibility in popular culture stories about civil jury trials? In the following excerpt, Jeffrey Abramson suggests there are at least four narratives surrounding the work of the civil jury in popular culture. They are: (1) the populist narrative (think David and Goliath, a deserving "little guy" plaintiff and a corrupt big corporation as in *The Runaway Jury*); (2) the Hamiltonian narrative (the reverse of populist — think devious plaintiffs suckering naïve or incompetent jurors into rendering obscenely huge awards); (3) the Wilsonian narrative (law and jury trials as a force for reconstituting norms); and (4) the narrative of Alexis de Tocqueville (the civil jury as the ultimate in democratic discourse).

THE JURY AND POPULAR CULTURE
Jeffrey Abramson
50 DePaul Law Review 497 (2000)

Ours has not been a culture that likes to tell stories about juries out-of-school. Whether from respect for the sanctity of juries, the awe of their oracular mystery, or just plain fear of what lay inside Pandora's box, the law regards the jury room as virtually off limits to journalists and outside observers. Even screenplay writers and novelists rarely make jury deliberation central to the drama. There are exceptions of course, John Grisham's *The Runaway Jury* being the most famous contemporary example, the teleplay *Twelve Angry Men* is an older exhibit. However, deliberation is still largely a subject waiting for its dramatist. In fiction, as in real trials, the jury remains on the sidelines, an audience rather than an actor, passive rather than active.

In contrast, we have vast popular literature about jury selection, devoted to all types of lore about the cunning of lawyers and the strategies of that already legendary figure, the paid scientific jury consultant. A familiar feature of trial coverage is the running tally that reporters offer about how many accountants versus social workers, women versus men, whites versus Hispanics have been selected to date. This box score is updated daily and repeated throughout trial coverage, resonating with the prevailing view that the real drama in jury trials is played out during jury selection.

Legal thrillers offer rich and nuanced portraits of victims (the heroes and the fakes), lawyers (the crusaders and the parasites), communities (their prejudices and their sufferings), Whistleblowers (their fates and their fortunes), witnesses (their fears and their foibles), the cop (the crooked and the honest), and the reporter (the insider and the outsider). However, jurors appear mostly in stock and supporting roles such as the bribed or intimidated juror in a Mafia trial, the planted juror in a big tobacco lawsuit, the juror in mid-vendetta or love affair, and the juror out of his league or over his head.

If we look behind the stock-in-trade jury characters, however, popular portrayals of civil jury trials do capture great public debates about injury and claiming in America, as well as debates about blame and responsibility. "I'm having a hard time understanding why we're supposed to make this woman a multimillionaire," a Grisham juror says of a smoker suing the tobacco companies. The remark resonates with the struggle jurors frequently go through to reconcile the deep cultural norms about work and reward with the legal norms about liability and compensation. Jury work is about constituting and reconstituting those norms, and the best of the courtroom dramas at least place us, the audience, in the position of the jury. . . .

Populists tell stories from the bottom up, victims recouping their honor by taking on the giant corporations destroying their communities. Lawyers are rarely the driving forces in populist narrative, they are more likely to be saved and uplifted by the company of ordinary people than the other way around.

Hamiltonians tell a mirror-image story, about victimized corporations and fraudulent plaintiffs served by the big industry of trial lawyers. The undeserving poor in popular welfare legends easily translate into the undeserving plaintiffs in popular jury lore. "Popular justice" is an oxymoron for Hamiltonians. Lawyers are no better than are pickpockets who like their pockets deep.

Wilsonians believe that law, lawyers, and trials can force and direct social change by pushing for new norms. Law never floats free of public opinion and cultural practices, but trials and juries can reconstitute norms in ways that energize social forces ready to apply the norms in practice.

There used to be a fourth narrative about juries and civil litigation. It was the story Alexis de Tocqueville told about the American jury, a more robustly democratic story than is told by any of the three surviving narratives. I close by recounting Tocqueville's democratic discourse on the civil jury, as a way to show the limits of contemporary aspirations for the civil jury.

Tocqueville purposely refrains from defending the jury, whether civil or criminal, as a way of deciding cases. "If it were a question of deciding how far the jury, especially the jury in civil cases, facilitates the good administration of justice, I admit that its usefulness can be contested." Indeed, already in the 1830s, the French visitor had heard arguments that the complexity of modern lawsuits outstripped the competence of jurors as fact finders. The jury arose "in the infancy of society, at a time when only simple questions of fact were submitted to the courts." Adapting the jury "to the needs of a highly civilized nation, where the relations between men have multiplied exceedingly," is "no easy task."

However, "arguments based on the incompetence of jurors in civil suits carry little weight with me," Tocqueville continued. Partly he thought the concern with "the enlightenment and capacities" of jurors was misplaced, as if the jury were merely a "judicial" institution to be judged narrowly by its use to litigants. More crucially, Tocqueville saw the assessment of juror qualifications as too static, unmindful of the moral uplift and civic education that comes from investing citizens with responsibility for justice. This is the part of the Tocquevillian narrative that has wholly dropped out of contemporary conversation about the civil jury. Ultimately, the jury for Tocqueville was rightly as much a political as a legal institution. The jury was as characteristic of democracy as universal suffrage. Juries took an abstract ideal such as "popular sovereignty" and "really puts control of society into the hands of the people."

Applied to the criminal jury, Tocqueville's emphasis on the jury as a political institution is familiar. Even today, we continue to value the criminal jury as a forum for popular input into the law. However, descriptions of the civil jury as a "political body" are far more jarring to the contemporary ear. Nevertheless, Tocqueville believed the civil jury was more important than the criminal jury as a way of empowering and educating citizens for self-government. The civil jury of the 1830s was "one of the most effective means of popular education at society's disposal." The jury was "a free school which is always open," a place where ordinary citizens rub elbows with the "best-educated" and gain "practical lessons in the law." Service on civil juries was the principal reason a broad segment of the American public came into "political good sense."

Criminal trials involve the people only "in a particular context," but civil litigation "impinges on all interests" and "infiltrates into the business of life." Few people can imagine themselves a defendant in a criminal trial. However, "anybody may have a lawsuit." Therefore, "[e]ach man, when judging his neighbor, thinks that he may be judged himself." In this way, civil juries "teach men equity in practice."

Far from fomenting class divisions and rich versus poor adversary relations, civil juries moderate popular passions by establishing the judge as legal tutor for jurors. Law is the only aristocratic force left in America, Tocqueville thought, and via the jury, it extends its empire over the common person. "[T]he legal spirit penetrate[s] right down into the lowest ranks of society."

Tocqueville's republican narrative of the civil jury as a crucible of democratic learning is fairly unspoken in America. Hamiltonians scoff at the idea that ordinary people can be brought up to speed by some ritualistic recital of legal instructions. Wilsonians agree that law is a matter for professional elites, not amateurs. Only populists remain enticed by the ideal of participatory democracy. Ultimately, populists lack patience to practice the ideal; they would rather stay home and are aroused to wrest control back from elites only when betrayed. Therefore, the populist tells great stories about muscular juries delivering an occasional blow for the people. However, they do not tell Tocqueville's kind of story, the republican story about the daily, undramatic work of juries and the slow ways jury duty inculcates habits of persuasion and deliberation, the civic virtues of collective argument upon which self-government depends. For all the popularity of the courtroom drama, there remains no drama since *Twelve Angry Men* that centrally portrays the dynamics of jury deliberation.

NOTES & QUESTIONS

Can you think of any popular culture examples of Professor Abramson's fourth type of jury narrative — Alexis de Tocqueville's idea of the civil jury as ideal democratic institution? Is this notion too old-fashioned or too undramatic to make a good film? *12 Angry Men* seems to fit the bill best, except for the fact that it is a criminal rather than a civil trial. How would you tell this kind of story?

3.   Jurors Behaving Badly

The jury has a major role in what Milner Ball calls the performance of our story of justice. But what happens to justice when jurors fail to perform correctly? And how would we even know, given the general secrecy surrounding deliberations? The next excerpt discusses some of the myriad ways jurors can misbehave.

CONTAMINATING THE VERDICT: THE PROBLEM OF JUROR MISCONDUCT

Bennett L. Gershman

50 South Dakota Law Review 322 (2005)

Bias and misconduct by jurors have been demonstrated in several different ways. Instances of jurors violating their oath and engaging in improper conduct have produced a significant body of case law analyzing the juror's conduct, the nature and seriousness of the impropriety, the extent to which the conduct may have prejudiced the trial, and the appropriate methods available to the trial judge to remedy the problem. The kinds of misconduct include the following: contacts by third parties with jurors; exposure by jurors to extra-judicial non-evidentiary materials; efforts by jurors to conduct experiments and reenactments to test the evidence; untruthful statements by jurors during the voir dire; conduct by jurors that evinces bias and prejudgment; physical and mental impairment of jurors; pre-deliberation discussion by jurors; and efforts by jurors to repudiate the trial court's instructions on the law.

A. Third-Party Contacts

It is fundamental that "the 'evidence developed' against a defendant shall come from the witness stand in a public courtroom where there is full judicial protection of the defendant's right of confrontation, of cross-examination, and of counsel." Violations of these protections occur when third parties engage in private contacts or communications with jurors concerning matters pending before the jury. The leading case involving juror exposure to external influences is *Remmer v. United States* [1954]. There, the jury foreman was contacted by an unknown caller and offered a bribe to acquit the defendant. Without advising the defense, the judge asked the FBI to investigate the matter and concluded that the approach was harmless. The Supreme Court remanded for a hearing, holding that a "presumption of prejudice" should apply to any extra-judicial contact with a juror about the case. The Court stated:

> In a criminal case, any private communication, contact, or tampering directly or indirectly, with a juror . . . about the matter pending before the jury is, for obvious reasons, deemed presumptively prejudicial, if not made in pursuance of known rules of the court and the instructions and directions of the court made during the trial, with full knowledge of the parties. The presumption is not conclusive, but the burden rests heavily upon the Government to establish, after notice to and hearing of the defendant, that such contact with the juror was harmless to the defendant. . . .

B. Exposure to Extra-Judicial Materials

A jury's exposure to extraneous information not presented as evidence in the courtroom can contaminate a verdict as readily as third-party contacts. When such extrinsic information relates to a material issue in the trial, it can seriously impair a defendant's right to a fair trial and an impartial jury. Such information may reveal a defendant's guilt, prior criminal record, prior misconduct, reputation for violence, or a co-defendant's guilty plea. Extrinsic information may come from a juror's personal knowledge, the jury's exposure to mid-trial publicity, or from official documents and records made available to the jury. The distinction between intrusions from extra-judicial contacts by third parties and exposure to extra-judicial information ordinarily has no bearing in determining whether the verdict was tainted by the event. The nature of extra-judicial information to which jurors have been exposed ranges from the very prejudicial to the insignificant. Exposures to external information that required a new trial included knowledge by one juror that was imparted to other jurors that the federal defendant had been convicted in state court for the same conduct; jurors' pre-existing knowledge of specific facts surrounding the crime and defendant's connection to it; an opinion by two jurors who had professional expertise in medicine on whether defendant's explanation for blood loss was credible; and the trial court's acceding to the jury's request, after the close of the evidence and during deliberations, to return to the courtroom to observe the defendant's ears, which were covered during the trial for Spanish translation through headphones.

Jurors also may acquire extraneous information relating to the facts of the case or the meaning of certain legal principles by engaging in extra-judicial research. A juror's acquisition of extra-judicial, non-evidentiary knowledge, particularly when the juror disseminates the information to the other jurors, may produce sufficient prejudice to require reversal. Moreover, the ready accessibility of the Internet makes such research not only easy, quick, and extremely informative, but also potentially highly prejudicial. Examples of jurors engaging in extrinsic research include consulting an encyclopedia to confirm that a blood type is rare, researching law treatises to ascertain the meaning of legal concepts such as "malice," or the possible penalties for first and second degree murder, and gaining access to a dictionary to define prominent terms associated with the case, such as "enterprise" in a RICO prosecution, or "callous" and "wanton" in a homicide trial. *People v. Wadle* [2004] is a recent example of a jury verdict being tainted by a juror's unauthorized use of the Internet to acquire information relevant to the case. The defendant was charged with the shaking death of her 4-month-old step-grandchild. The prosecution presented evidence that the defendant was taking the anti-depressant Paxil for stress and holiday season depression. During deliberations, a juror who had training as an emergency medical technician told the other jurors that Paxil was a "very strong drug" that was "used for people who are antisocial, violent, or suicidal." Despite the trial judge's denial of the jury's request to consult a pharmacological reference, a juror downloaded from the Internet a description of Paxil and the next day read the description to the jury. The description stated that the drug is used to treat "mental depression, obsessive-compulsive disorder, panic disorder, and social anxiety disorder."

Following a conviction, and learning of the jury's action, the trial court conducted an evidentiary hearing and concluded that the juror's use of the Internet constituted misconduct, but denied the defendant's motion for a new trial on the ground that there was no reasonable possibility that the extraneous information affected the verdict. The appellate court reversed, finding that the juror's use of the Internet, in direct violation of the trial judge's order, tainted the verdict. The court noted that given the sharp conflict in the testimony, the jury may have used the specialized and complex terminology from the Internet to assess the defendant's motive, state of mind, and credibility as a witness. The fact that the defendant was taking an anti-depressant, anti-anxiety medication for panic attacks may have been a determining factor in the jury's verdict. Recognizing the problems created by the availability and widespread use of the Internet, the court instructed trial judges to emphasize to jurors that they "should not consult the Internet or any other extraneous materials" during the trial and deliberations. . . .

C. Experiments and Reenactments

Jurors do not live in capsules. It is not expected that jurors should leave their common sense and cognitive functions at the door before entering the jury room. Nor is it expected that jurors should not apply their own knowledge, experience, and perceptions acquired in the everyday affairs of life to reach a verdict. However, a juror's procurement of new knowledge gained through extra-judicial means may contaminate the deliberations and upset the verdict. The line between the two sources of information, needless to say, is not easily drawn.

Courts are much more likely to recognize as appropriate a juror's knowledge gained from ordinary life experiences. For example, there is no impediment to a juror's knowledge gained from personal experience that a particular neighborhood is busy all night, drawing a map to show the location of buildings in a certain area, or describing a person's ability to make an accurate identification from a moving automobile. These mental processes involve no more than the application of everyday observations and common sense to the factual issues in the trial. By the same token, the application by a juror, trained as a professional engineer, of his technical knowledge of physics to refute an opinion offered by a defense witness also was permissible.

By contrast, a juror's deliberately contrived investigation or experiment that relates to a material issue in the trial ordinarily undermines the integrity of the verdict. Acquiring relevant factual information in this manner puts the jury in possession of evidence not presented at the trial and not subjected to confrontation and cross-examination. Examples of improper juror experimentation include a juror who placed a heavy load in the trunk of his car as a conscious way to determine whether such weight in a trunk would have imparted knowledge to the defendant of the presence of drugs, a juror's experiment in attempting to fire a weapon while holding it in a position consistent with the defendant's account, clocking how long it would take to drive a certain distance, and simulating a witness's use of binoculars to determine whether the witness could possibly have seen what he claimed he saw. The same principle that forbids jurors from acquiring specialized knowledge through extra-judicial means also accounts for the prohibition against jurors making unauthorized visits to locations described in the trial testimony. . . .

Reenactments in the jury room based on the jury's recollection of the testimony are usually allowed as an application of the jury's common sense and deductive reasoning to determine the truth of the facts in dispute. The reenactments by jurors portrayed in the classic film *Twelve Angry Men* illustrate the use of critical analysis by jurors of the evidence based on their knowledge and experience. One of the reenactments in the film involved a juror who, based on his experience as an adolescent familiar with the use of a switchblade knife, described the manner in which a switchblade knife ordinarily would be opened and thrust outward, thereby contradicting a key theory of the prosecution. Another reenactment in the film portrayed a juror simulating the time it would take for an elderly, crippled witness to go from his bedroom to the door of his apartment in order to determine whether the witness's estimate of the time it took to travel the distance — a critical issue in the trial — was accurate and believable.

However, if the reenactment is not merely a more critical analysis of the evidence but puts the jury in possession of extraneous information that might be based on flawed and irrelevant conclusions, the reenactment may be found improper. For example, a juror engaged in improper conduct by biting another juror to observe the resulting bruises. Also improper was a reenactment by a juror with machinery that had been admitted into evidence but was operated under conditions wholly unlike the conditions relevant to the charges.

D. Untruthful Statements During Voir Dire

The Sixth Amendment and the Due Process Clause guarantee a defendant the right to an unbiased jury. The voir dire of prospective jurors serves to protect a defendant's right to an impartial jury "by exposing possible biases, both known and unknown, on the part of potential jurors." Bias of prospective jurors may be actual or implied. Actual bias is a bias in fact; implied bias is a bias that is presumed as a matter of law. Actual bias may be established by showing that a juror failed to respond honestly to questions during voir dire and that a truthful response "would have provided a valid basis for a challenge for cause." As the Supreme Court observed, "[t]he necessity of truthful answers by prospective jurors if this process is to serve its purpose is obvious." Bias also may be presumed or imputed to a juror by establishing from the circumstances that the juror is unable to exercise independent and impartial judgment. Proof of juror bias necessitates a new trial.

There is a presumption that prospective jurors answer the voir dire questions truthfully. There is also a presumption that a juror's failure to respond honestly during voir dire is indicative of bias. Prospective jurors for various reasons may give deliberately untruthful answers. Deliberate concealment or misleading responses also may impair a party's right to meaningfully exercise challenges to the juror's ability to serve and ordinarily provide a basis for relief. However, only intentionally dishonest or misleading responses provide a basis for relief. Forgetfulness or honest mistakes, by contrast, do not establish dishonesty and are not grounds for a new trial. As the Supreme Court noted, "[t]he motives for concealing information may vary, but only those reasons that affect a juror's impartiality can truly be said to affect the fairness of a trial.". . .

E. Bias and Prejudgment

Apart from showing that a juror gave dishonest or misleading answers during voir dire, a party still may be entitled to relief by demonstrating that a juror harbors an actual bias or that a bias may be imputed to the juror based on the juror's conduct and the surrounding context and circumstances. As noted above, the ability to substantiate a claim of bias may be hampered by the rule against impeaching a juror's verdict, which would probably disallow testimony by jurors concerning negative or inappropriate comments made by a juror during deliberations. In *Smith v. Phillips* [1982], the Supreme Court suggested that only proof of actual bias could be the basis for a new trial. The Court stated: "This Court has long held that the remedy for allegations of juror partiality is a hearing in which the defendant has the opportunity to prove actual bias." In *Smith*, a juror submitted during the trial an application for employment as an investigator with the same district attorney's office that was prosecuting the case. At a post-trial hearing on whether to grant a new trial for juror bias, the trial court found that the letter "was indeed an indiscretion" but that the letter did not demonstrate bias or prejudgment. Thereafter, on a petition for habeas corpus, the federal district court granted the writ by imputing bias to the juror as a matter of due process, finding that "the average man in [the juror's] position would believe that the verdict of the jury would directly affect the evaluation of his job application." The Court of Appeals for the Second Circuit affirmed. However, the Supreme Court rejected the conclusion that bias should be imputed to this juror and made the following observation:

> [D]ue process does not require a new trial every time a juror has been placed in a potentially compromising situation. Were that the rule, few trials would be constitutionally acceptable. The safeguards of juror impartiality, such as voir dire and protective instruction from the trial judge, are not infallible; it is virtually impossible to shield jurors from every contact or influence that might theoretically affect their vote. Due process means a jury capable and willing to decide the case solely on the evidence before it, and a trial judge ever watchful to prevent prejudicial occurrences and to determine the effect of such occurrences when they happen. . . .

F. Physical and Mental Incompetence

A necessary corollary of the right to an impartial jury is the right to a jury in which all of its members are physically and mentally competent. Proof that a juror was mentally impaired, intoxicated, or unconscious would appear to cast grave doubt on the integrity of the verdict. When such claims are raised during the trial, the judge is in a position to correct the problem and permit the trial to continue. When such claims are raised after the verdict, attempts to take corrective action become much more difficult. As noted earlier, the courts are reluctant to allow a post-verdict inquiry into a juror's mental state. The rule against admitting juror testimony to impeach a verdict is based on several policy considerations: the need for finality of the proceess, the interest in encouraging "full and frank discussion in the jury room," the interest in encouraging jurors to return an unpopular verdict without fear of community resentment, and the interest in inspiring the "community's trust in a system that relies on the decisions of laypeople." These interests routinely prevent jurors from giving testimony to invalidate a verdict based on allegations that jurors considered prejudicial and irrelevant matters, may have engaged in bizarre behavior during trial, were inattentive during the testimony, did not understand the judge's instructions, or disregarded those instructions. These policy reasons are often strong enough to overcome post-verdict proof that a juror was mentally impaired and to justify a court's refusal to conduct any formal investigation into her condition.

The same policy considerations supported the Supreme Court's decision in *Tanner v. United States* [1987], upholding the trial judge's refusal to conduct an investigation into broad allegations that a jury "was on one big party" and numerous claims alleging jurors' excessive use of alcohol and drugs. The Court rejected the defendant's contention that substance abuse constituted an improper external influence. According to the Court, "drugs or alcohol voluntarily ingested by a juror seems no more an "outside influence" than a virus, poorly prepared food, or lack of sleep." As an internal matter, ingestion of drugs and alcohol was within the rule prohibiting juror testimony to upset a verdict.

G. Pre-Deliberation Discussions

Whereas some courts and commentators have argued that it should be permissible for jurors to have intra-jury discussions about the case during the trial, it is well-settled that jurors are forbidden to discuss the case before they have heard all of the evidence, closing arguments, and the court's legal instructions, and have begun formally deliberating as a collective body. Judges routinely admonish juries at the outset and throughout the trial to not discuss the case among themselves prior to deliberations. There are several reasons for this admonition. Premature discussions are likely to be unfavorable to a defendant, incline jurors who expressed opinions prematurely to adhere to those opinions, impair the value of collective decision-making, lack the context of the court's legal instructions, prejudice a defendant who may not have had the opportunity to present evidence, and benefit the prosecution by reducing the burden of proof. . . .

H. Nullification

Jury nullification is understood as a refusal by a jury to apply the law as instructed by the court. Nullification has been condemned as "lawless," an "aberration," and a "denial of due process." As one court observed,

> [a] jury has no more "right" to find a "guilty" defendant "not guilty" than it has to find a "not guilty" defendant "guilty," and the fact that the former cannot be corrected by a court, while the latter can be, does not create a right out of the power to misapply the law.

The dangers of nullification were described by Judge Simon Sobeloff in an oft-quoted statement:

> To encourage individuals to make their own determinations as to which laws they will obey and which they will permit themselves as a matter of conscience to disobey is to invite chaos. No legal system could long survive if it gave every individual the option of disregarding with impunity any law which by his personal standard was judged morally untenable. Toleration of such conduct would not be democratic, as appellants claim, but inevitably anarchic.

It is commonly recognized that juries have the power to nullify the law, although they do not have the right to do so. It has thus been the settled rule in federal courts and virtually all state courts for over a century that the jury's function is to accept the law that is given to it by the court and to apply that law to the facts, and that no instruction should be given to a jury that it has the power to nullify. Counsel's invitation to a jury during summation to disregard the law is misconduct and subject to contempt. Jurors who engage in the practice may be removed.

A trial judge has the power to remove jurors who become incapacitated or otherwise become unavailable during the course of deliberations. Whether a court has the power to remove a juror who refuses to follow the law has received much less attention. However, the few cases that have addressed the question emphatically support the judge's power of removal. The major difficulty in administering this power is being able to conduct an appropriate investigation into the allegation of misconduct without jeopardizing the traditional rule of secrecy in jury deliberations. . . .

NOTES & QUESTIONS

1. What examples of juror misconduct can you pinpoint from popular culture? Dennis Quaid plays a juror who has an affair with defense counsel, played by Cher, in *Suspect* (1987). (Bias, anyone?) Pauly Shore's character lies during voir dire in order to get on the jury in *Jury Duty*, as do Richard Dice, played by Rob Lowe in *Illegally Yours*, and Nick Easter, played by John Cusack in *Runaway Jury*. There are outside threats and violence against jurors in *Trial by Jury* and *The Juror*. It is surprisingly easy to find examples of juror misconduct in popular culture. Why is this? Surely the films had legal consultants. Are these incidents just inserted for dramatic effect, to tell a good story? Or is there something more insidious at work? Does popular culture exhibit a certain cynicism or distrust toward the jury system, suggesting jurors are generally corrupt or capable of corruption?

2. Nullification is the great mortal sin of jury misconduct, in the eyes of many. Why is this so? Consider the heated debates about nullification that occurred after the O.J. Simpson criminal trial.

In popular culture, however, jury nullification is often the "happy ending" to courtroom dramas. For example, think of *The Verdict*. Paul Newman's closing argument to the jury is an eloquent appeal for justice, but he has no case left (the judge has instructed the jury to disregard the key evidence). Perhaps the greatest moment in the film is when the jury returns a verdict in favor of Newman's clients, and the foreman inquires whether they are limited by what plaintiff has requested in damages or whether they can award higher damages. Why do we experience this as a profoundly exhilarating moment? Was it an example of jury nullification?

E. IMAGES OF THE JURY IN POPULAR CULTURE: THE GOOD, THE BAD AND THE INVISIBLE

What kind of stories does popular culture tell about juries? Which juror characters are good, and which are bad? It depends, of course, on what we mean by "good" and "bad." Surely Henry Fonda's Juror #8 in *12 Angry Men* would fulfill almost everyone's idea of a good juror. His character is firm but fair, strong enough to make a stand against the majority, and quietly heroic in insisting on a full deliberation. Fonda's juror character exhibits integrity and courage. On the other hand, he also engages in juror misconduct by conducting an unsupervised experiment (he buys a knife in a pawn shop, to determine whether the murder weapon was unique). Is the jury as a whole a good jury? Do they deliberate fully and freely? Do they reach the right result?

At least Fonda's Juror #8 engages in straightforward deliberation, not the manipulative trickery of Nicholas Easter, John Cusack's character in *Runaway Jury*. Easter is portrayed as the hero, but he is heroic only in contrast with the deeply evil and venal jury consultant played by Gene Hackman and the greedy and immoral corporate defendants. Easter out-manipulates the other manipulators. Easter's character uses manipulation and mind games to influence other members of the jury and direct the course of deliberations. Is he a "good" juror?

And what are we to make of the popular character of the imperiled female juror caught in the clutches of evil men and forced to "throw" the jury deliberations in order to protect herself and her family (as played by Joanne Whalley-Kilmer in *Trial by Jury* and Demi Moore in *The Juror*)? Are these "good jurors?" Not until the end of each film do these characters take on power, and they do so at the expense of personal integrity (for example, by committing murder) and the integrity of the system.

Jurors and juries in popular culture can be complex characters, with both good and bad qualities. Sometimes, as the following articles suggests, the very process of being on a jury and deliberating can prove transformative.

INTRODUCTION TO THE 50TH ANNIVERSARY OF *12 ANGRY MEN*
Nancy S. Marder
82 Chicago-Kent Law Review 557 (2007)

II. The Transformative Power of Jury Deliberations

One way to understand *12 Angry Men* is to see it as a movie about the transformative power of jury deliberations. Twelve men have been summoned to serve as jurors and have been placed together in a cramped, uncomfortable jury room in New York City on the hottest day of the year. They have sat through six days of a murder trial and they want to complete their deliberations as quickly as possible and return to their private lives.

The jurors have not been given much guidance as to how to conduct their deliberations. The foreman (Martin Balsam) suggests that they can proceed in one of two ways. Either they can vote, and then discuss the case if necessary, or they can discuss the case first. They choose to vote immediately with the hope that the vote will be unanimous and that there will be no need for further discussion. Their decision to take an initial vote produces what several social scientists have described as "verdict-driven" deliberations. Verdict-driven deliberations are characterized by an early public vote, the formation of coalitions, and potentially a more adversarial atmosphere as each side offers evidence in support of its position and stifles dissenting points of view. Social scientists have contrasted this style of group deliberation with "evidence-driven" deliberations, in which there is greater emphasis on story construction, each individual's view is sought, and a vote is not taken until later in the process.

When the initial vote results in eleven guilty votes and one not-guilty vote, with Juror #8 (Henry Fonda) casting the lone, dissenting vote, the jurors are not quite sure what to do. Fonda, who plays a critical role in helping the men learn how to be jurors, suggests that they owe the defendant, who is on trial for his life, some "talk." One juror thinks this means telling a story; another juror thinks this means doodling. Fonda corrects these mistaken notions. Eventually, the jurors agree to go around the room and have each juror explain why he voted the way he did in an effort to convince Fonda of the error of his vote. The jurors do manage to engage in a more evidence-driven style of deliberation, but they do not manage to have each juror give his view because they continue to interrupt and insult each other. Fonda cannot change the confrontational tone, but he has managed to slow down the pace of the deliberations so that the jurors begin to talk to each other.

In spite of the tone, the jurors do manage to achieve some of the benefits of an evidence-driven style of deliberation. Eventually, different jurors start contributing their recollections of the facts and evidence, without being concerned, as they had been initially, with whether their recollections support their verdict preferences. For example, Juror #5 (Jack Klugman), who described himself as having grown up in a slum, knows how to hold a switchblade knife and offers his opinion on how the knife would have been held and whether the defendant could have made the wound given that he was shorter than his father. The other jurors do not have this knowledge because they did not grow up in places where such knives were commonplace. Similarly Juror #9 (Joseph Sweeney) pays close attention to the elderly witness and understands how this witness might have exaggerated what he had seen and heard because he is elderly and feels ignored by the world. Juror #9 understands this witness because he, too, is elderly. Fonda has begun to have an effect on the jurors, not only in terms of changing their votes, but also in terms of changing their approach to their role as jurors and their understanding of their responsibility during deliberations.

Fonda does not know whether the defendant is guilty or not guilty, but he hopes that through careful deliberation and full participation of all the jurors that the jury will avoid an erroneous decision. He counts on the recollections and insights of all of the jurors. When Juror #11 (George Voskovec) wants the jury to consider a question that has troubled him, Juror #3 (Lee J. Cobb), a strong proponent for a guilty verdict, chides him for undercutting his earlier guilty vote. Juror #11 explains that he does not have to limit his recollections or questions to one position or another. When Juror #9 focuses on the indentations on the eyewitness's nose, which he surmised could only be made from eyeglasses and which called into question the reliability of this eyewitness because she was not wearing her glasses in court and was unlikely to have been wearing them when she awoke at night and witnessed the murder through a passing elevated train, Juror #3 questioned why the others, including the lawyers, did not notice this earlier. Fonda pointed out that nobody had noticed this earlier, but that all of the jurors were now pooling their recollections and observations together and that Juror #3 should join in this effort.

The group effort to recollect and to evaluate the evidence cannot persuade two of the jurors who are blinded by their own prejudices. They must acknowledge their prejudices and recognize that they have judged the defendant guilty, not based on what they had heard at trial, but based upon their preconceptions about the defendant. Juror #10 cannot be persuaded by the evidence (or lack of evidence) because he sees the defendant as a Puerto Rican and he sees all Puerto Ricans as people who "lie" and who do not value human life. Until Juror #10 is ostracized by the other jurors and made to confront his prejudice against Puerto Ricans, he cannot decide the case based on the evidence nor be open to arguments made by his fellow jurors. Similarly, Juror #3 cannot be persuaded by the evidence or the arguments because he sees the defendant as a young man who is about the same age as his estranged son. Juror #3 wants to punish the defendant just like he wants to punish his son. Only when he is made to see the connection between his guilty vote and his feelings toward his son is he able to be persuaded by the other jurors and to change his vote.

Fonda and the other jurors only know by the end of the deliberations that they have "reasonable doubt" about the defendant's guilt. Fonda had some doubts during the trial. Indeed, he wondered whether any case could really be so open-and-shut as this case was presented at trial. But the deliberative process helps him to reach the conclusion that he has reasonable doubt. The movie leaves open the question whether the defendant was guilty or not guilty. The audience knows no more than the jurors in the end. The open-ended question is just one way in which this movie invites multiple interpretations from the audience.

NOTES & QUESTIONS

Did the jury in *12 Angry Men* get it right? The following article suggests that, despite the film's enshrined status as an exemplar of the workings of the jury system, the jury reached the wrong result.

12 ANGRY MEN: A REVISIONIST VIEW
Michael Asimow
82 Chicago-Kent Law Review 711 (2007)

12 Angry Men is considered the iconic jury film, and it has done more than any movie, television show, or other cultural work to enshrine the jury as the central and indispensable element of the American criminal justice system. For generations of film watchers, Henry Fonda as Juror #8 has exemplified the heroic anti-conformist juror, a common man standing alone against the other eleven, changing an 11-1 vote for conviction into a unanimous and correct verdict of not guilty. I would like to suggest a contrary reading of the film. In my opinion, the defendant should have been found guilty. . . .

I suggest that the jury erred badly. Fonda, of course, never argued that the defendant was innocent, only that the prosecution failed to prove guilt beyond a reasonable doubt. While nobody can say what level of certainty is necessary to surmount the reasonable doubt hurdle, it is probably around 90% and certainly less than 100%. It is in the nature of evidence about a past event that it cannot establish any proposition with absolute certainty. Eyewitnesses can be mistaken or lying. Circumstantial evidence raises an inference, one that could be incorrect. However, despite the objections raised by the jurors to the prosecution's case, I believe that the mass of circumstantial evidence presented against the defendant was overwhelming and the probability that he killed his father is close to 100%. In other words, the prosecution met and far exceeded its burden of proving its case beyond a reasonable doubt.

The circumstantial evidence against the defendant was overwhelming and was easily enough to convict by itself, even if one disregards the testimony of the two eyewitnesses. Let's start with the fact that there was no other known suspect. Who killed the father if it wasn't the defendant? To find the defendant not guilty, we would have to assume that someone unknown (with an unknown motive) sneaked into the upstairs apartment soon after the defendant left for the movies and stabbed the father to death. Yet there was no sign of a forced break-in and no indication of robbery or theft. This account is conceivable, of course, but seems highly implausible.

On the night of the murder, neighbors across the hall from the father's apartment heard the father and son having a fight around 8:00 p.m. and heard the father hit the defendant twice. The defendant was often physically punished by the father. Just before the murder, the landlord testified that he heard the boy say "I'm going to kill you." This item of circumstantial evidence was thrown into some doubt because the words could have been inaudible. An elevated train was passing at the time the father was stabbed, and the words could have been spoken during the ten seconds or so that the train was passing. The fight between father and son and the physical violence accompanying it provided ample demonstration of motive. In addition, the defendant had numerous previous brushes with the law because of violent behavior — generally a pretty good indication that he was prone to violence.

The father was killed with an unusual knife identical to a knife purchased by the defendant on the night of the killing. He claimed he lost it when it fell through a hole in his pocket. This account is highly implausible. The objections to this evidence raised by Fonda and the other jurors are far from convincing. True, the knife was not unique because Fonda found another just like it at the local pawnshop. So what? It was still an unusual knife, and chances that the true killer had one just like it are extremely remote (it is even less likely that the real killer picked up the knife after the defendant lost it and used it to kill the father).

Furthermore, the defendant could not remember anything about the movie he claimed to have just seen. Fonda attempted to cast doubt on this evidence by questioning another juror about a movie he had seen days before. The juror remembered the name and actors of both films in a double feature, but not perfectly. This "demonstration" hardly diminishes the strong inference of guilt raised by the fact that the defendant could remember nothing at all about the movie he claimed to have just seen. And nobody saw him at the theater. His alibi, therefore, is highly suspect.

Another juror claimed that an experienced knife fighter would not have stabbed downward with an overhand motion, especially against a taller victim. But a demonstration quickly dispelled that idea. An overhand, downward stabbing motion was perfectly possible. The juror claimed that a switchblade is used for underhanded, upward jabs. Well, perhaps; but perhaps not. What made the juror such an expert on knife fighting? Regardless of how switchblade knives were usually used in knife fights, the knife could have been used either to stab upwards or downwards. The murder did not occur during a knife fight, so the comparison to knife fighting technique was of little utility. The knife could easily have been used to stab downward when the boy impulsively grabbed it from his pocket and struck out against his father. And, of course, if there were an unknown killer instead of the boy, that person also stabbed downward.

In this view, the testimony of the two eyewitnesses is cumulative and entirely unnecessary. If you believe either or both of the eyewitnesses, the probability moves even closer to 100%; if you disbelieve both of them, it does not reduce the probability below the very high level of certainty already produced by the circumstantial evidence.

NOTES & QUESTIONS

Scenes of a jury deliberating are actually quite rare in trial films, making *12 Angry Men* something of an anomaly, as noted in the next reading. Why do you think so few courtroom films include scenes of juror deliberations?

THE UNSEEN JURY
Bill Nichols
30 University of San Francisco Law Review 1055 (1996)

The films *Twelve Angry Men* and *Inside the Jury Room* both belong to the sub-genre of the courtroom movie that address the theme of the wrong man. What separates these two films from the rest of the sub-genre is their singular focus on the process of jury deliberation. My nomination of these two films stems from the rarity with which jury deliberations receive representation and from the insights the two films offer into the complexities of the process.

The open courtroom trial is the outward and visible sign of legal justice. Many works, from the Perry Mason television series to films like *Inherit the Wind*, *To Kill a Mockingbird*, and *Reversal of Fortune* celebrate the process by which the legal skills, argumentative strategies, and psychological acumen of great lawyers can so arrange evidence that the work of the jury becomes an invisible afterthought, a mere ratification of the truth already discovered or revealed by prosecution or defense. During the careful process of in camera deliberation, the image of guilt or innocence registered in the grain of court-room evidence and argument develops into a clear, decisive verdict. Popular culture often presents jury deliberation as a largely technical and somewhat mechanical process, similar to film developing. Evidence, argument, and verdict should correspond closely with one another, almost in the same spirit of correlation as that between symptom and disease or barometric pressure and weather.

Twelve Angry Men and *Inside the Jury Room* reverse this underlying assumption; the jury's job is not done for it by heroic courtroom lawyers. The deliberation process has an autonomy of its own. It leads to verdicts that seem in flagrant violation of both evidence and law. What strategies both prosecutors and defense lawyers should adopt to take the distinctiveness and autonomy of jury deliberation into account is not pursued in either film, but the two trials of the Los Angeles police officers who beat Rodney King and the O.J. Simpson murder trial are vivid reminders of the importance of doing so.

Twelve Angry Men opens with a judge who can barely keep awake as he delivers his instructions to the jury. The self-evident verdict appears so foregone as to require no effort. We never see the lawyers or hear their arguments. If there is drama to be found here, it will have to come from the jury itself. . . .

Trial by jury may be a legal right, a "buffer between the accused and the power of the state," as the narrator of *Inside the Jury Room* intones, but it also testifies to a philosophical dilemma. Since antiquity, trials have provided a prime example of how to decide the undecidable. What really happened stands in doubt; no scientific procedure exists that can render a conclusive determination. The result is that someone must decide, following one or another set of criteria. Our trial process relies on the jury's verdict to arrive at a sense of an ending — but not at an incontestable conclusion (except by convention). Trial by jury is a social ritual by which we dispel certain forms of uncertainty about the past. We confer on a jury the obligation to put a stop to debates in which accuser and accused can both claim to uphold the truth, based on the terms and assumptions used to make their case. Two different arguments would string the same set of evidence into narrative chains endowing fact with meaning, doubt with certainty. And yet these meanings and truths diverged from, if not contradicted, each other. Guilty or innocent? It all depended on the adopted premises, rhetorical skill, and point of view. Both sides of such debates rely on language; verbal (and sometimes visual) representations. But as Richard Lanham notes:

> [Language has an] imperfect correspondence to the "outside world," whatever one might think that world to be. . . . It is from this accommodation to antithetical structure that Anglo-Saxon jurisprudence descends: we arrange social issues into diametrically opposed questions, arrange a dramatic display of their conflict, and (since the law cannot afford aporia [radical doubt] as a conclusion to social disputes) accept the jury-audience's verdict as a defining truth. . . .

Richard Lanham, *A Handlist of Rhetorical Terms* 58 (2d edition, 1991).

Rather than continue courtroom debate indefinitely, jury deliberation has a different dynamic. As Henry Fonda asserts in *Twelve Angry Men*, "I don't have to be on a side, I'm just asking questions." One of the citizen-jurors in *Inside the Jury Room*, a doctor, shares this view: "I have lots of questions; we need to talk." The social dynamics of consensus building prevails over the public rhetoric of argumentation. What allows consensus to arise? What dynamics come into play? Anna Deveare Smith's play, *Twilight: L.A. Uprising 1992*, gives some insight into how this process involves a mix of psychodrama, personal confession, and the forging of a common resolve through narrative revision — telling yet another story with the same set of evidence. This "final" story puts a stop to argumentation not simply by choosing prosecution or defense as right or true, but by conforming the facts to a somewhat different frame. If the jury were to admit that "what really happened" is undecidable, it could not reach a verdict, but if it reaches a verdict, "what really happened" must be decidable after all. This double bind can be resolved by changing the frame. Consensus arrives not when the jury agrees on a common sense of what truly happened, but rather when it agrees on a common interpretation of what happened. This interpretation escapes the double bind by invoking a higher criterion of truth than the question of what really happened in a literal sense, namely justice.

Twelve Angry Men and *Inside the Jury Room* present complementary views of the process by which jurors base their verdicts on a sense of justice rather than conclusive truth. Common to both films, and abundantly evident in the Rodney King and O.J. Simpson trials, is that juries must undergo a reasoning process of their own, regardless of the argumentative clarity of prosecution or defense. Juries resist wholesale rubber-stamping of others' arguments and conclusions. As one juror from *Inside the Jury Room* puts it, in a highly individualistic version of this sentiment, "I am not a computer. I won't accept everything I'm told just because I'm told it is true. I can't do that as a thinking, breathing human being." This resistance provides the entry point for assumptions and arguments external to the courtroom phase of the trial. Resistance introduces personal predispositions and values, social biases and goals, and cultural differences and ideals acquired long before the trial began. It is between the hammer of cultural ideals and the anvil of ideological practices that consensus must be forged.

Twelve Angry Men dignifies the principle of the jury as buffer and of the arduous process of consensus-building as its central theme. The jury's charge is to determine the guilt or innocence of a teen-age male accused of murdering his father with a knife after an argument. The defendant belongs to a minority group and is probably Puerto Rican. Supporting the charge is the testimony of two eyewitnesses, countered only by an apparently weak alibi. The boy had a similar knife, but he had lost it, and he was at the movies at the time of the crime, but he could not remember the movie's title.

The jury initially votes eleven to one guilty. The sole holdout is our questioning, open-minded hero, Henry Fonda. Reprising his role from *Young Mr. Lincoln*, Fonda's function is to serve as the great unifier, dispelling prejudice, faulty reasoning, and uncommon haste to allow others to discover the truth they would have otherwise never seen. As in *Young Mr. Lincoln*, which pivots on Fonda's performance as a lawyer who discovers that a key witness has lied to hide his own guilt, Fonda again ferrets out the truth others fail to see. In this case, he exposes the vindictive hatred that poisons fellow juror Lee J. Cobb's judgment, driving him to insist intransigently on a guilty verdict against a rising tide of doubt. The penultimate vote is eleven to one not guilty with Cobb the now isolated and ostracized holdout.

In *Twelve Angry Men* Fonda ensures justice by rising above the presumptions and prejudices of his all too susceptible peers. At first the other jurors display astonishment that he is willing to doubt what they regard as settled. To dramatize the point, *Twelve Angry Men* attributes haste to selfish indifference (one juror, Jack Warden, hopes to finish quickly enough to get to a ball game that night) or personal bias (holdout Lee J. Cobb wants to punish the defendant unjustly as a surrogate for his own rebellious son). The jurors begin by almost humoring Fonda's hesitation but gradually come to see that his questioning spirit is right and their own rush to judgment is wrong; their willingness to accept testimony at face value jeopardizes the defendant's right to a fair trial. Another holdout, E.G. Marshall, insists on the use of cold logic. He shares none of Cobb's vitriolic hatred or the glib indifference of Jack Warden's baseball fan. Marshall finally comes around when the group discovers vital flaws in the testimony of the two eyewitnesses. Marshall's flaw was not haste but a failure to scrutinize evidence rigorously enough.

Fonda embodies a spirit of doubt aligned with the higher truth of justice and the spirit, not the letter, of the law. He opposes easy solutions, biased assumptions, prejudicial convictions, and faulty reasoning. To eliminate such limitations does not guarantee guilt so much as make doubt possible. His character's mission bears noticeable hints of a Christlike quality in the mise en scene and iconography of the film through such aspects as leaving him nameless until the very end, setting him physically apart, dressing him in white, and bestowing on him an air of transcendent serenity. Fonda puts a stop to debate, less by arriving at conclusive certainty, than by eliminating the proclivity to easy answers and quick fixes in a complex, divided world.

In *Twelve Angry Men* Henry Fonda works to make a verdict of not guilty serve justice when guilt initially seemed beyond doubt. He instigates a process, resisted by the others, of throwing the evidence back into doubt, dissolving the argumentative cohesiveness of the prosecution's case, and catalyzing the discovery of another story, another point of view, unveiling what haste and bias — in essence, the failure to scrutinize apparent facts with sufficient rigor — had hidden. Consensus emerges. Even though the truth cannot be known, justice can be done. Lumet [the film's director] gives us a close-up shot of the defendant as he hears the not guilty verdict; his look of innocence and vulnerability confirms the triumph of justice. (The film uses its own narrating authority to affirm what Fonda intuited.) Fonda prompts others to conclude that doubt is indeed reasonable, not simply in an absolute or philosophic sense, but in a historical sense, in this specific case. . . .

NOTES & QUESTIONS

1. *12 Angry Men* is perhaps the most well-known of jury films, and Henry Fonda's character is the juror as hero (his all-white suit, his courage, and his deep integrity all operate to code him as a Christ figure). We feel good about the system after watching *12 Angry Men*. Fonda's character has been a powerful juror. But what about another type of juror film, those that tap into our anxieties about the powerlessness of the juror?

In *The Juror*, Demi Moore plays a single mom (Annie Laird) who does not try to get out of jury duty, because she thinks she needs "a little excitement." Her wish is granted; a psychotic hit man known as "Teacher" (played by Alec Baldwin) bugs her home, murders her best friend, threatens to kill her young son, and generally makes her life hell. He insists on the impossible — that she manipulate the jury deliberations to get an acquittal, not just a hung jury. He also makes her wear a necklace containing an eavesdropping device so he can make sure she is doing her best during deliberations. Some kinky mind-games are going on, too. Laird is an artist, a sculptor who makes art in boxes. (You are supposed to feel the art, not see it.) Laird describes the process of viewing her art as "reaching up and feeling her private stuff." Teacher buys some of her art and tells her they are "kindred spirits," both artists in their own fields.

Baldwin's enforcer character makes Laird's helplessness crystal-clear early on in one scene where he takes her for a car ride and threatens to kill her son, who is riding on a bicycle ahead of them. Teacher says, "The grey suits want you to love the law, justice. . . . But can the grey suits shield you from somebody like me?"

But are films with imperiled jurors really about the lack of power of the juror? Or are they perhaps about our cultural anxiety that an individual juror may in fact have too much power and abuse that power? Are these films the flip side of *12 Angry Men*? In *The Juror*, Annie Laird manages to single-handedly sway the other jurors to vote for acquittal. She does whatever it takes to get each juror to vote her way. She flirts with one juror who finds her attractive. She verbally beats down any arguments for guilt with a relentless emphasis on reasonable doubt. She even convinces a grandmother on the jury that letting this killer go free will make children safer. Listen carefully to the irony in this speech, where Moore desperately (and disingenuously) argues for the rule of law in order to save her son's life: "[I]f you twist the law even just a little for the best of reasons, then the law loses whatever power it's got and then my child is in even more danger than before, and so are your grandchildren." The jury votes for acquittal.

Similarly, in *Trial by Jury*, Valerie Alston, the single mom played by Joanne Whalley-Kilmer, is coerced into helping a murderer go free. In this film the mob-enforcer and former cop, Tommy Vesey (played by William Hurt), merely wants her to hang the jury (not get a complete acquittal). After she does the job, Vesey tells her not to fret about the jury's decision. She asks, "And when he kills again?" Vesey replies, "It won't be nobody you'd have to dinner."

Both Annie Laird and Valerie Alston get revenge, of course. They kill the bad guys. Valerie Alston does it most memorably. Dressed up as the glamorous kind of '40's pin-up that the mobster Rusty Pirone (played by Armand Assante) likes, she seduces him and then kills him with an ice pick. But such "happy" endings do not make us eager to sign up for jury duty.

Popular culture seems to suggest that jurors are at one and the same time devoid of power and filled with power, and neither state seems especially desirable. What do you make of this? Why is there this ambivalence? Are juror movies enabling or disabling for an audience that is itself filled with potential jurors?

2. *I, the Jury* (1947) is a wonderfully trashy Mickey Spillane detective novel. It was made into two films of the same name, one in 1953 and another in 1982. In *I, the Jury*, hard-boiled private eye Mike Hammer acts as judge, jury and executioner on a very personal case. *I, the Jury* could also be a potential explanation for why juries are curiously absent in trial films — the film audience is the jury. In the next reading, Carol Clover uses cinematics to help explain the jury's ambiguous role in popular culture. She hypothesizes that, in many trial films, the audience becomes the jury. As you read, consider not only what we see but what we do not see when it comes to the jury in films.

MOVIE JURIES
Carol J. Clover
48 DePaul Law Review 389 (1998)

Let us begin with a simple question: how does the camera look at juries in trial movies? A "trial movie" can provisionally be defined as a plot in which the significant action bears directly or indirectly on a specific trial, in which some important part plays out in a courtroom, and in which the outcome of the trial coincides with the climax of the film. The form is overwhelmingly Anglo-American, and, given its popularity, it is no surprise that academic lawyers have looked to it for an understanding of "popular legal culture." Most discussions of trial movies have been thematic, treating films in the same terms as they might treat novels or stage plays. But what happens if we look at such films, and more particularly their juries, cinematically? What do the cinematics in trial movies tell us that we do not already know about the place of juries in the public imagination?

The some two hundred Anglo-American trial movies that I have reviewed (in connection with an in-progress book on trials and entertainment) are remarkably consistent in their inventory of jury shots. The run-of-the-mill trial movie shows us images of the jury filing in (and/or out), listening attentively, occasionally registering some emotion (disgust, horror), and, in the person of the foreman, rendering a verdict. The "listening attentively" shots are the most common, if only because Hollywood cinematographic protocol calls for establishing shots and reaction shots in certain set-ups, and in the courtroom, the jury is an indicated position and "listening attentively" fits the bill. More telling, perhaps, is what we do not see. We seldom see jurors individually (when the camera does single one out, it is in a reaction shot, and the demeanor of the juror is understood to represent that of the group as a whole). We seldom see them anywhere but in the courtroom — not in hallways, elevators, or jury room. We almost never see them doing anything but being normally attentive; shots of the jury are remarkably contentless (in keeping with their function as reaction and establishing shots). We almost never see the jury close up; on the contrary, it is typically viewed at a distance and even indistinctly (because focus is on a lawyer in the foreground). Finally, and most significantly, we do not see the jury at any length. Most jury shots are held for three or four seconds at most, and in the standard trial movie, they add up to no more than a minute or two. There are some minor exceptions to these rules, but they are remarkably few and far between. The first and most important thing to be said about trial-movie juries, then, is that they barely exist. In the courtroom, juries are seen only briefly, and the work they do, their deliberation, is with very few exceptions avoided altogether. Within the film's universe, the jury is a kind of visual and narrative blank, viewed as so much human furniture when present, but mostly just absent.

This habit of avoiding the jury may seem a little odd in light of our public commitment to the institution and also in light of the ongoing discussion about its value. It seems odd that a culture as manifestly obsessed with jury trials as ours is (that obsession measured by film and television alone) should have so little interest in the actual decision process. It seems no less odd that our trial movies are so often critical of lawyers, judges, and law enforcement generally, but so rarely question the institution of the jury. (On this point, trial movies echo the bias of law jokes; lots about lawyers, almost none about juries.) So odd is the patterned avoidance of the jury as both a narrative issue and a visual subject that it wants an explanation. Is this a new development, or is it an abiding feature of the form?

One very early trial movie, the 1916 film *By Whose Hand?*, suggests an answer. In it, a woman is on trial for murder, but evidence keeps emerging that casts doubt on her guilt, and the film closes with a title exhorting the film audience to determine the truth: "YOU ARE THE JURY! YOU DECIDE!" Question mark endings of one sort or another are not as unusual as one might think in trial movies, and early examples like this one put the lie to the common claim that the unclosed or "contingent" text is somehow postmodern. What interests us here, however, is the apostrophizing of the film viewer as trier of fact. Film scholars distinguish between diegetic and extradiegetic effects, the former located in the fictional world of the film (like the music Sam plays in *Casablanca*) and the latter somewhere beyond it (like the Phillip Glass score in The Thin Blue Line). What the ending of *By Whose Hand?* suggests is that we should extend our search for the missing jury beyond the diegetic out into the realm of the extradiegetic. . . .

[E]ven rule-obedient trial movies have ways of gesturing toward an extradiegetic jury. One such gesture is the empty jury-box topos, dramatically used in recent times by *Presumed Innocent.* The film opens with the shot of the vacant courtroom. Our vision pans ever so slowly to the right until it arrives at the jury box. We pause. Then, at an almost imperceptible rate, we start moving forward. The empty, ornate chairs of the jury loom ever larger in our vision, and as the credits crawl over them, we hear a man's voice intone:

> I am a prosecutor. I am a part of the business of accusing, judging, and punishing. I explore the evidence of a crime and determine who is charged, who is brought to this room and tried before his peers. I present my evidence to the jury, and they deliberate upon it. They must determine what really happened. If they cannot, we will not know whether the accused deserves to be freed or punished. If they cannot find the truth, what is our hope for justice?

What is most striking about the voiceover is its incantatory tone. It is as though we, the spectators, are being ushered into the empty courtroom, directed to the empty chairs, and sworn in. Two hours later, we will revisit this scene — same shot of the empty courtroom and jury seats, voiceover in the same monotone. The time in between we spend not in the courtroom, but following the fortunes of the speaker, District Attorney Rusty Sabich (Harrison Ford) as he investigates the murder of his colleague Carolyn Polhemus (Greta Scacchi) with whom, it emerges, he had been having an affair. In fact, the finger of suspicion begins to point to him: the blood type matches his and a wineglass found in her apartment has his fingerprints on it, as well.

The visualized story roams into Sabich's obsessive relationship with Carolyn, into his home life with wife Barbara (Bonnie Bedelia), a woman angry about her husband's affair with Carolyn and dissatisfied with her role as bedmaker (she is at work on a dissertation but it's slow going), into his relation with his own lawyer, and into the District Attorney's political ambitions and shady connections. Even when we finally arrive in the courtroom, some eighty minutes into the film, our narrative and cinematic focus remains stubbornly on Rusty and his lawyer Stern (Raoul Julia) as we approach the bench with them, go to chambers with them, and so on. When it comes down to it, Sabich's own "work" is pretty much the work of the jury, which is to say pretty much our work — at least until some point in the last third of the film, when something seems to dawn on him that does not dawn on us. At that moment, he splits off from us, leaving us behind with the (unseen) diegetic jury, with whom we "vote," in the end, for a verdict of not guilty — not because we positively know otherwise, but simply because the prosecution did not meet the standard of reasonable doubt. The fact that we subsequently learn who really did it (Sabich's wife) does not mean that we have finally transcended our role as jurors in the rhetorical economy of the film; it only means that we are jurors who learned more after the fact, as jurors sometimes do. (*Presumed Innocent* lets us off easier than films like *Anatomy of a Murder*, in which we realize we are jurors who may have screwed up, or *Witness for the Prosecution*, in which we learn we are jurors who surely *did* screw up.) Our position and our predicament are slammed home in the film's closing scene, which returns us to the scene (same courtroom, same empty jury seats) and the sound (same flat voiceover) of the opening, the only difference being that this time the voice tells us, in effect, that the search for justice sometimes fails. At no time during the film's two hours do we so much as catch a glimpse of the jury actually trying the case — an omission all the more striking in light of the attention lavished on the empty seats in the beginning and again at the end. The point could hardly be clearer: we are it. *Court TV* and CNN viewers will recognize the empty jury-box as an image routinely used to advertise and to introduce coverage of current trials.

But let us turn from Mercedes strategies to Hyundai ones. Most trial movies and trial television dramas neither address us directly nor present us with a yawning jury box. But if we watch closely, we see that even the most run-of-the-mill examples have their own cinematographic strategies for positioning us as an outboard jury. Consider, to pick a couple of examples almost at random, *The Accused* and a trial sequence from the television serial *Law & Order.* Here we see the workaday strategy of trial movies. In both cases, the lawyers, in their closing arguments, look not quite at the camera, but just below it, shifting their gaze methodically between a point very slightly to the right of the camera and a point very slightly to the left of it, and so on, back and forth. In short, they come as close as one can to looking at us, without actually doing it — off just enough to meet the terms of the invisible-camera rule. Lest we miss the point, we see the backs of heads in our foreground — the heads of our fellow jurors in the front row. No one looks at us or calls us jurors, but we are jury-boxed as squarely by this "not quite" strategy as we were by the blunt strategies of *The Trial of Mary Dugan, Free, White, and 21,* and a host of other films, starting in 1906, that reach out directly to put us in our place.

But what, then, are we to make of *12 Angry Men*, a trial movie that not only shows the jury, but shows almost nothing *but*? It should be clear by now that for all of the respect that film enjoys, it is something of an oddball in the tradition. Three facts may bring its difference into focus. The first is that it based on a French original, *Justice est faite*. A film about jurors' overdetermined reactions in a mercy killing case, *Justice est faite* played the U.S. art-cinema circuit first in 1950 and again a couple of years later. (Reginald Rose's teleplay of *12 Angry Men* aired in 1953, and the film version was released in 1957.) A second fact to keep in mind about *12 Angry Men* is that it was hardly a success in its day. Indeed, it was a box office mediocrity, not even close to the top ten grossing films of that year. Reviews were mixed, and not a few venture some version of the opinion that it was not a proper trial movie. Finally, the idea did not start a trend. There have been a few remakes and takeoffs (recognizable as such) but no new subgenre of jury dramas. The fact that it was cloned but never produced offspring attests rather eloquently to its problematic hybridity as far as genre is concerned. As a public, it seems, we prefer trial dramas that do not disturb our role as triers of fact, even if they are less smart and less well acted, and so it is that after this very small blip on a very long horizon, we reverted to the security of the traditional arrangement. In short, *12 Angry Men's* jury-focus was an experiment conducted under the sign of European art cinema, and the film's present reputation is to a considerable extent the creation of academics and intellectuals after the fact. That reputation may be deserved, but I daresay it has somewhat deformed our perception of the place of the jury in cinema.

In the beginning of this presentation I proposed a definition of the trial movie as a plot in which the significant action bears directly or indirectly on a specific trial, in which some important part plays out in a courtroom, and in which the outcome of the trial coincides roughly with the climax of the film. To that definition we can now add that the trial movie is also a plot that both rhetorically and cinematically positions its audience as extradiegetic triers of fact. In his classic work on the rise of the English novel, Ian Watt proposed that the

> novel's mode of imitating reality may be . . . well summarized in terms of the procedures of another group of specialists in epistemology, the jury in a court of law. Their expectations, and those of the novel reader, coincide in many ways. . . . The jury, in fact, takes the "circumstantial view of life," which [may] be the characteristic outlook of the novel."

Ian Watt, *The Rise of the Novel: Studies in Defoe, Richardson, and Fielding* 31 (1957).

As with the novel, so with film, even more obviously so. The jury system has provided Anglo-American popular cinema with a subject matter and with a rhetorical geometry that is fundamental not only to trial movies, but to a variety of genres (notably the detective thriller) that are trial-derived but stand at some remove from the courtroom. When German film director Uli Edel, assigned to a trial movie in Hollywood, tells how he "had to learn to set up the courtroom scenes in such a way that the whole film audience participates as the jury would," he put into words a procedure that is normally just performed as a matter of course. *Magill's Survey of Cinema*, Feb. 2, 1999, *available in DIALOG*, File No. 299. (His remark also acknowledges either a different practice in Europe or, just as tellingly, no experience making trial movies there.) The cinematics of trial movies not only bear him out, but gesture toward a silent contract of sorts between film and audience, an ongoing deal whereby we enter the theater prepared to double as audience and as outboard triers of fact, and, for better or worse, ready to judge the film both as a piece of cinema and as a piece of law.

It must be the film's presumption of an extradiegetic jury that explains why diegetic juries are so little seen and the process of their deliberation so consistently avoided in Anglo-American cinema: we are the jury, and any sustained representation of an opposite number within the diegesis would interfere with our habitual relation to the text. This analysis may also make some sense of the oft-lamented tendency of jurors to perceive real-life courtroom proceedings through the lens of scenarios from popular culture. (One could argue, given how many of those scenarios were born in the courtroom and, more generally, how deeply our most popular narrative forms have been imprinted by adversarial logic, that the chickens are merely coming home to roost. Call it reverse migration.) Finally, this analysis may explain why it is that in the world of law and politics, the jury can be the subject of critical debate, but in the world of popular culture, it remains for the most part serenely untouchable.

NOTES & QUESTIONS

1. Why do juries, as Clover notes, "barely exist" in so many trial movies? Is Clover correct in her point that in many trial movies the film audience is the jury? How could such a cinematic positioning affect popular critiques (or the lack of critiques) of the jury? Does this "*I, the Jury* stance" in which we find ourselves make us reluctant to criticize the portrayals of juries in popular culture?

2. Clover suggests a "reverse migration" effect, whereby jurors in real life expect certain things to happen at trial based on popular culture. Think back to our *Blame Judge Judy* reading in the previous chapter of this text concerning judges. What are the negative ways popular culture affects jurors' perceptions? Are there any positive effects?

Chapter 8

PUNISHMENT

A. FILMOGRAPHY

A Clockwork Orange (1971)

Cool Hand Luke (1967)

Dead Man Walking (1995)

I Want to Live! (1958)

The Shawshank Redemption (1994)

B. INTRODUCTION: GOOD GUYS AND BAD GUYS

Hollywood is ambivalent about crime and punishment. The crime thriller, casting a would-be victim or a valiant police detective as protagonist against an evil, often faceless villain, is a Hollywood mainstay. But when film directly takes on the subject of punishment, the perspective tends to shift. The prisoner becomes the protagonist, pitted against a brutal and corrupt penal system. Even then, Hollywood feels compelled to paint the protagonist as innocent or otherwise undeserving of the harsh punishment meted out. In the films discussed in this chapter, compare and contrast the ways in which the movie portrays the objects of society's punishment with those charged with the responsibility of carrying it out.

Unlike most films discussed in this book, lawyers and judges are all but absent from films set in penal institutions. The courtroom drama has played out, the jury and judge have spoken, and any mention of lawyers is limited to the occasional derisive remark about the public defender, prosecutor or judge who facilitated an unjust conviction. The typical prison film protagonist has been abandoned to the state's punishment machinery, forced to survive in a strange and hostile world with its own complex, unwritten rules of right and wrong that reflect the moral relativity of the cruel prison environment. The law and its accoutrements are noteworthy only for their absence.

The depiction of America's penal system in film conjures up some memorable villains. Warden Samuel Norton in *The Shawshank Redemption* and the authoritarian chain gang captain in *Cool Hand Luke* personify the principle that power corrupts, and absolute power corrupts absolutely. In *Brubaker* (1980), corruption permeates the entire prison system, taking on a life of its own so that even a brave, dedicated, reform-minded warden is virtually helpless to bring about meaningful change. While every Hollywood prison film has its hardened criminals, the focal point is the prisoner's struggle to preserve his human dignity and assert his individuality against his evil oppressors. These films examine the human condition in a way that transcends other forms of conflict presented in legal films.

Criminal punishment films raise questions about human nature and the potential consequences of empowering one group of people forcibly to impose its will on another. Consider the Stanford Prison Experiment, in which researchers attempted to create an artificial prison environment, fill it with people playing the roles of guards and prisoners, and observe their interaction over time. Although the experiment was intended to extend over several weeks, it was terminated after only a few days because the faux "guards" began to physically abuse the pretend "inmates." *See* Craig Haney & Philip Zimbardo, *The Past and Future of U.S. Prison Policy: Twenty-Five Years After the Stanford Prison Experiment*, 53 American Psychologist 709, (1998). Does human nature make this inevitable? What is it about the unnatural prison environment that compounds the corrupting influence of power? When society authorizes people to administer harsh punishment in the name of the State, what kind of person steps up to accept that responsibility? Does society have a responsibility to protect both the administrator and recipient of punishment from excess? How do we define or identify excess, and who polices the line between proper punishment and abuse of power? Hollywood does a great job of raising these questions but is not so good at providing answers.

C. LIFE IN THE BIG HOUSE

The Shawshank Redemption follows the protagonist, Andy Dufresne (played by Tim Robbins) through twenty years of hard time in the Shawshank Penitentiary. Andy is a banker who is wrongly convicted of murdering his wife and her lover. After his arrival at Shawshank, he is befriended by Ellis Boy Redding (played by Morgan Freeman), an institutionalized convict who can get anything for the right price. Like most films, *The Shawshank Redemption* paints a bleak picture of penitentiary conditions, in sharp contrast to political propaganda about country club prisons where criminals are coddled with good food, cable television, and plenty of leisure time. Is there truly a wide gap between perception and reality, or is some other cultural force at work?

"FAILURE TO COMMUNICATE": THE REEL PRISON EXPERIENCE

Melvin Gutterman

55 Southern Methodist University Law Review 1515 (2002)

The signature of "Big House" movies in particular is legend. The camera captures the microcosm of prison life as the massive stone edifices and towering guard posts are contrasted sharply with the small cells that house the inmates. The structured boredom of daily prison life emerges as the groups of convicts are shown circulating in the prison yard. Of course, there is the first appearance of the newly arrived convicts before the "righteous warden," and the ever present brutal, sadistic Captain of the guards, the towering master of arms. These are all the standard trademarks, and *The Shawshank Redemption*, the prototype of the "Big House" cinema, is Hollywood's finest example of the prison film genre. Shawshank's convicts endure prison hardship magnificently. Their triumphs, designed to fire the human spirit, succeed brilliantly. . . .

Bob Gunton portrays one of the most evil wardens in film history. As a self-righteous, Bible-carrying warden, Samuel Norton is a bundle of contradictions as he bellows to the new arrivals that the first rule in his prison is no blasphemy. "I'll not have the Lord's name taken in vain in my prison . . . I believe in two things, discipline and the Bible. Here, you'll receive both. Put your trust in the Lord. Your ass belongs to me." Right in front of the warden, during his pompous introduction, the sadistic Captain of the guards shouts profanities at a disrespectful prisoner, as he forcefully jams his baton into the convict's stomach. And so we are welcomed into the incongruity of Shawshank Prison.

Apart from the Sisters, the convicts in Shawshank appear to have better character than many people we may encounter in the free world. We begin to think of them less like hardened criminals and more like Andy, harmless people caught in a hopeless place. Although Andy is routinely raped and beaten by the Sisters (as Red explains, they are not homosexuals because they are not human), he remains unbowed by the sadism that swirls through the prison. Andy eventually mentors Tommy (Gil Bellows), an exuberant young hood who brings fresh insight into Andy's reformation. Tommy, who has recently married and will soon be a father, solicits Andy's help to earn a high school equivalence diploma. Only after Tommy promises "one-hundred percent — nothing half-assed," does Andy accept him as his "new project." Andy's investment in their relationship pays abundant emotional dividends. He finds it "a thrill to help a youngster crawl off the shit heap," as he helps Tommy to restore his hopes and dreams through education.

Throughout the movie the warden masquerades as a man of the Bible, but in truth he is a corrupt hypocrite who accepts bribes and kickbacks for not using his men as laborers to underbid building contractors. Andy can match the warden in Bible quotes, and in time gains his confidence so fully that the warden profits from Andy's financial skills to help launder payoff money. By having the skill to juggle the warden's various secret skimming operations, Andy is assured a better life at Shawshank, but he is also now much too familiar with the warden's corrupt operation to ever be released. When it is learned that Tommy has information that would exonerate Andy, Warden Norton has Andy placed in solitary for a month for his arrogance, and then has Tommy shot by a tower guard. Only after several months of Andy's apparent subservience and seeming faith in the Bible, does the warden once again puts his trust in him. . . .

The Shawshank Redemption brings a sense of dignity, strength and compassion to the convicts. There are memorable moments of laughter, as well as pain. Overall, the movie, by taking a candid look at the warehouse approach to incarceration, has serious intentions. The reformists had their dream of an enlightened era in prison treatment, but it failed to bloom. The architects of the penitentiary program hoped to create a world from which those that had temporarily faltered would eventually emerge as worthy citizens. But as *Shawshank* reveals, by the 1900s, the concept of reformation had practically disappeared, and for the most part, penitentiaries like

Shawshank served a purely custodial function — as a warehouse for the convicted.

The reform-minded moviegoer remains somewhat disappointed, as the director and script writer, Frank Darabont, fails to provide any suggestions of how we are expected to narrow the gap between our universe and the nightmarish world of Andy Dufresne. At the movie's conclusion we surely feel vindicated by the Warden's suicide, exhilarated at the Captain's arrest, gladdened when Sister Bogs Diamond is severely beaten, and elated at Andy's escape and the eventual reunion with his friend Red. There is redemption to this story — a triumph of Andy's human spirit, which we can admire. The movie stirs our emotions, and it touches our heart: but the basic message eludes us, lost perhaps in our overwhelming sensations. The popularity of the movie cannot be attributed to its disenchantment with the penitentiary system. There still appears to be widespread public endorsement for the massive, fortress-like castles that remain ready to house the next generation of criminals. The basic symbol of Shawshank, as a warehouse for criminal outcasts, is still an acceptable program for most Americans. The real hell of *The Shawshank Redemption* may, in actuality, be its reality.

The movie confirms that prison brings into play many disastrous influences: normal sociability is shown to be severely curtailed and self-assertion is practically forbidden. Additionally, the natural sexual outlet is totally prohibited. In *The Shawshank Redemption*, Andy is sexually assaulted by Bogs Diamond and two other men (the "Sisters", a band of degenerates that sexually prey on the other inmates) who unmercifully taunt and beat him senseless: Red assures us that "prison is no fairytale world." The effects of all these factors are intensified by the regimentation and emotional cruelty practiced in many conventional prison settings. As a consequence of all the physical and psychological debasement, the inmate acquires a conscious resentment toward the prison system and those who put him behind bars. The result is not that a reformed prisoner is released to the community, but rather an emotionally dangerous person is unleashed, ready to avenge himself on society. . . .

The Shawshank Redemption is especially timely for its portrayal of the brutal treatment of convicts in the Big House. To remove all traces of their former identity in the free world (and in part to demean them) the new convicts must undress, be hosed down with high pressure water spray, and dusted with white delousing powder. They are then given a new prison outfit and a Bible, and paraded naked to their individual six-by-eight foot cells; their new residence in the cellblock of a three-story structure of cement and dark steel. The old cons know that somebody always breaks down, sobbing. . . . [Red's narration describes the typical first day at Shawshank]:

> The first night's the toughest, no doubt about it. They march you in naked as the day you were born, skin burning and half blind from that delousing shit they throw on you, and when they put you in that cell, when those bars slam home, that's when you know it's for real. Old life blown away in the blink of an eye. Nothing left but all the time in the world to think about it. Most new fish come close to madness the first night.

As a diversion, the old cons bet on who will break, as they taunt, and "bait the fishes" and "they don't quit till they reel someone in." The one nicknamed "Fat-Ass" is cold-heartedly tormented about being sodomized by "the big ol' bull queers that would just love to make your acquaintance, especially that big white mushy butt of yours." When the squeamish victim bawls and pleads desperately to the Captain of the Guards that he does not belong here, and wants to go home, he is unmercifully whacked with a baton and kicked in the face until he lies still on the floor of the prison catwalk. "Call the trustees. Take that tub of shit down to the infirmary," Captain Hadley tells his subordinates. Left without medical treatment in the infirmary, "Fat-Ass" succumbs to his savage beating. . . .

NOTES & QUESTIONS

1.   According to Professor Gutterman, "The central message of the movie is clear; in Shawshank penitentiary nothing is quite like the outside world would believe." Gutterman, *supra*, at 1523. He provides several examples. The prosecutor calls Andy Dufresne "icy and remorseless," but in prison he cultivates friendships and works to bring meaning and purpose to the lives of his fellow prisoners. While Andy's character is revealed as intrinsically good, we tacitly approve his rule bending and breaking. Red's methods for "getting things" from the outside are never revealed, but of course his success depends on stealth, corruption, and breaking rules. In one particularly satisfying moment in the film, Andy manipulates a prison guard into smuggling beer into the prison for his fellow inmates. In another, he breaks into the prison office and plays music over Shawshank's public address system. And of course in the end the audience learns that his seemingly innocent request that Red acquire a pin-up girl poster and a rock hammer was part of a much more nefarious long-term plan. In contrast to Andy and Red, those charged with running the prison are portrayed as thoroughly corrupt. How does the film move the audience to accept the prisoners' wrongdoing, while simultaneously condemning the warden? How would you articulate the moral difference between the prisoners and the warden?

2.   Human dignity is an abstract concept which is never explicitly discussed in the film, but it plays a prominent role in *The Shawshank Redemption*. A central message is that in the long run human dignity will find a way to assert itself against severe repression. What scenes do you find most effective in communicating this message? How does the film reveal the human dignity of the key figures?

3.   Prison is an important aspect of modern American culture. With approximately 2.3 million people behind bars, America leads the world in the rate at which it incarcerates civilians. The incarceration rate hovered around 109 prisoners per 100,000 in the general population from 1925 until 1980 before skyrocketing to its current rate of more than 600 prisoners per 100,000 in the general population. This explosion in the prison population was not accompanied by an increase in crime rates. "[I]n the United States, we put more people in prison than anyone else in the world by choice; we imprison more than other societies not because we have to, but because we want to." Craig Haney, *Riding the Punishment Wave: On the Origins of Our Devolving Standards of Decency*, 9 Hastings Women's Law Journal 27, 31 (1998). This trend has had disparate impacts upon the poor and ethnic minorities in the United States, and is having an unmistakable influence on American culture. One writer warns:

As hip-hop has roared to an ever increasing apex in connection with its power, influence, and global impact, and as hip-hop artists recognize this influence and impact, it would behoove the traditional majority to sit up and recognize what this global genre is saying about crime, punishment, inequality, and imprisonment in the United States and across the world.

Andre Douglas Pond Cummings, *Thug Life: Hip-Hop's Curious Relationship with Criminal Justice*, 50 Santa Clara Law Review 515, 528 (2010).

Hip-hop artists such as Public Enemy, KRS-One, N.W.A., and Ice-T describe "in stark rhymes and narratives, a United States criminal justice system that was inequitable and unfair, a system that targets and profiles African-Americans and inner city youth, and the descriptions by those artists became, in Chuck D's words, "the Black CNN." *Id.*, at 532. Lil Wayne's lyrics are an example of hip-hop simultaneously protesting U.S. prison policy and educating listeners:

> I was watching T.V. the other day right
> Got this white guy up there talking about black guys
> Talking about how young black guys are targeted
> Targeted by who? America
> You see one in every 100 Americans are locked up
> One in every 9 black Americans are locked up
> And see what the white guy was trying to stress was that
> The money we spend on sending a mothafucka to jail
> A young mothafucka to jail
> Would be less to send his or her young ass to college

Lil Wayne, "Dontgetit" *on Tha Carter III* (2008). Other hip-hop tunes, such as N.W.A.'s "Fuck tha Police" (1988) or Ice-T's "Cop Killer" (1992), glorify law-breakers and vilify police. What effect do you think America's mass incarceration has on the socio-economic groups directly affected? Is America's incarceration rate healthy, necessary, or beneficial for society?

4. When first performed in 1953, Samuel Beckett's play, *Waiting for Godot*, was puzzling to audiences and critics alike. Seemingly devoid of action or plot, the play consists of two men, Vladimir and Estragon, who meet on a country road near a tree and express their existential angst while waiting for Godot, who never comes. They sing, dance, play games, and contemplate suicide to occupy themselves. In 1957, the San Francisco Actor's Workshop performed the play for fourteen hundred convicts in San Quentin penitentiary, who gave it a standing ovation. The play which had so "bewildered the sophisticated audiences of Paris, London, and New York was immediately grasped by an audience of convicts." Martin Esslin, *The Theatre of the Absurd: Revised Updated Edition* 1 (1973). The review in the prison paper the next day explained, "We're still waiting for Godot, and shall continue to wait. When the scenery gets too drab and the action too slow, we'll call each other names and swear to part forever — but then, there's no place to go!" *San Quentin News*, 28 Nov. 1957, *quoted in* Esslin, *supra*, at 2-3. Beckett had managed to articulate the ennui of doing hard time. In 1999, the British Royal National Theater voted *Waiting for Godot* the most significant English language play of the twentieth century. Normand Berlin, *Traffic of our Stage: Why* Waiting for Godot*?* 40 The Massachusetts Review 420, 420 (1999). Why do you think the play resonated with prisoners?

What can you infer about life in prison from *Godot's* success at San Quentin? What conclusions can you draw about the prisoners themselves?

5.   What about the Sisters in *The Shawshank Redemption*? All we know about them is their predatory behavior in prison. We do not hear their story, and Red calls them less than human. It is a fact that such people exist in prison, but they are nevertheless unique human beings, each with his own life story. Why are their characters not fleshed out in the story? What kind of narrative might explain who they are, and how they came to choose this course of behavior?

D.   THE POLITICS OF REFORM

Unlike *The Shawshank Redemption*, which is based on the Stephen King novella *Rita Hayworth and Shawshank Redemption* (1982), *Brubaker* is rooted in fact. It is based on a nonfiction book of 1969 by Tom Murton and Joe Hyams entitled *Accomplices to the Crime: The Arkansas Prison Scandal.* Robert Redford played the title role, a progressive prison warden whose character is based on Tom Murton, one-time warden of the infamous Tucker Penitentiary in Pine Bluff, Arkansas. The events and conditions depicted in the film are very real, and are documented in books, reports of investigative commissions, and class action lawsuits arising from Tucker Penitentiary and the Cummins Prison Farm in Arkansas in the 1960s. Professor Marc L. Miller cautioned, "Like Scottsboro, the full prison reform story is sufficiently disturbing and complex that it should only be read in daytime hours. But it should be read." Marc L. Miller, *Wise Masters*, 51 Stanford Law Review 1751, 1756 (1999).

STRETCHING THE ADJUDICATIVE PARADIGM: ANOTHER LOOK AT JUDICIAL POLICY MAKING AND THE MODERN STATE
Daniel A. Farber
24 Law & Social Inquiry 751 (1999)

Like many southern prisons, the Arkansas prison at Cummins Farm was run on the pre-Civil War plantation model, with the prisoners playing the role of slaves. Prisoners worked in the fields six days a week, under the supervision of "trusties" (other prisoners who were allowed to administer corporal and sometimes even capital punishment). The prisoners' sleeping area was unsupervised, leaving the way open for homosexual rape and other crimes. For safety, "some of the inmates would come to the front of the barracks and cling to the bars all night." The prison lacked any medical facilities. Prisoners had to pay the trusties to obtain medicine or other amenities; they generally could make money only by selling their blood. Thus, to obtain medical care, an ordinary prisoner would have to sell his own blood.

The litigation began with several *pro se* habeas corpus petitions. Judge J. Smith Henley appointed two local lawyers to represent the prisoners. Henley's early decisions in the Arkansas case marked the first time a federal judge had given serious scrutiny to prison conditions. He was appalled by what he found. A prominent early issue involved the use of the "Tucker telephone," a device for administering severe electric shocks to the prisoners' genitals. Judge Henley's rulings on this and other issues broke new ground. But federal intervention into the Arkansas prisons was almost immediately endorsed by the Eighth Circuit, in an opinion by Harry Blackmun banning corporal punishment in the prison system.

The case expanded to cover a broader range of issues, prompted by an investigative report by the state police ordered by Governor Faubus, which documented "institutionalized torture, near starvation diets, rampant violence, and widespread corruption." In the wake of this report, a reform-minded corrections director was appointed, who became the model for the Robert Redford character in the movie *Brubaker.* In the next round of the litigation, the judge held unconstitutional the prison's isolation units and its failure to guard the prisoners from nocturnal attacks. The new commissioner played an important role in this round of the litigation — indeed, he is widely thought to have helped draft the prisoners' complaint.

New lawyers were appointed to represent the prisoners, and they launched a full-scale investigation into the prison. At this point, the judge's intervention became more sweeping. He found conditions in the prison as a whole to violate the Eighth Amendment. "For the ordinary convict," he said, "a sentence to the Arkansas Penitentiary today amounts to a banishment from civilized society to a dark and evil world completely alien to the free world, a world that is administered by criminals under unwritten rules and customs completely foreign to free world culture." . . .

Feeley and Rubin leave little doubt about their assessment of the Arkansas litigation as a success:

> . . . Inmates no longer had to bribe brutal inmate overlords to obtain basic necessities. They no longer had to fear for their lives every time they went to sleep. They no longer were capriciously deprived of food and medical services. They no longer had to worry that their genitals might be taped to electrodes or their knuckles cracked with pliers. They were no longer stripped to the waist and whipped for failure to pick a sufficient amount of cotton or okra. . . . The Arkansas prison system had entered the twentieth century.

Malcolm Feeley & Edward Rubin, *Judicial Policy Making and the Modern State: How the Courts Reformed America's Prisons* 79 (1998).

NOTES & QUESTIONS

1.   Arkansas was not the only state in need of prison reform in modern times, but it drew substantial attention because of public reports generated by formal state and federal investigations, many of which are discussed in Feeley and Rubin's *Judicial Policy Making and the Modern State, supra.* Federal judges played a prominent role in the reform effort, including Arkansas district judges J. Smith Henley and G. Thomas Eisele and then-Chief Judge of the Eighth Circuit Court of Appeals, Harry Blackmun. Arkansas was the only state in the nation that openly sanctioned the corporal punishment of prisoners, which Justice Blackmun declared to be cruel and unusual punishment. *See Jackson v. Bishop,* 404 F.2d 571 (8th Cir. 1968). In declaring some of the practices of Tucker Penitentiary and Cummins

Farm unconstitutional, Judge Henley described the condition, culture, and social order in the Arkansas penal system:

> At both Cummins and Tucker the inmate population is divided into three categories. At the bottom of the list are ordinary laboring convicts known as "rankers." At the top of the list are privileged inmates known as "trusties." Between those two categories is a third class of convicts known as "do pops"; how they came to be so called is not clear. . . .
>
> [M]ost of the inmates at Tucker are young men who are not, in general, a particularly vicious lot, although there are exceptions. The Cummins population is extremely varied. Some are run-of-the-mill non-violent criminals; others are extremely violent and dangerous; many are incorrigibles; some are properly classified as either sociopathic or psychopathic, if not psychotic. A few of them have to be kept in isolation cells for 24 hours a day to protect them from other inmates or to protect other inmates from them.
>
> Certain characteristics of the Arkansas prison system serve to distinguish it from most other penal institutions in this country. First, it has very few paid employees; armed trusties guard rank and file inmates, and trusties perform other tasks usually and more properly performed by civilian or "free world" personnel. Second, convicts not in isolation are confined when not working, and are required to sleep at night in open dormitory type barracks in which rows of beds are arranged side by side; there are large numbers of men in each barracks. Third, there is no meaningful program of rehabilitation whatever at Cummins; while there is a promising and helpful program at Tucker, it is still minimal.

Holt v. Sarver, 309 F. Supp. 362, 366-370 (E.D.Ark. 1970).

Judge Henley meticulously described the lexicon peculiar to the prison and its social order. The "Tucker telephone" was a euphemism for a device used to deliver electrical shocks to a prisoner's genitals. "Long lines" were chain gangs working in the fields. "Long line riders" were trusties on horseback supervising the inmate workers. "High powers" and "shotguns" were trustees with rifles or shotguns assigned to guard other prisoners. "Floor walkers" were inmates allowed to roam free in the housing units at night, ostensibly to notify the guards of disturbances. "Punks" were inmates who passively submitted to homosexual acts; "pressure punks" were compelled to perform homosexual acts. These inmates were generally assigned to "punk row," the two rows of bunks closest to the bars. "Coming to the bars" or "grabbing the bars" was a euphemism for seeking protection. According to Judge Henley, "it is not unusual" for an inmate to "cling to the bars" all night. Evidence before Judge Henley established many abuses, even murder, committed against the rankers at Cummins and Tucker.

Judge Henley could have simply said that inmates were unwisely given control and authority over other inmates, which led to unchecked abuse, including extortion, rape, and murder. Why did he resort to prison vernacular to get these points across? What does the common parlance of the prison say about its culture?

2. Judge Henley concluded that the prevalent conditions and culture in the prison were damaging to both inmates and society:

Living as he must under the conditions that have been described, with no legitimate rewards or incentives, in fear and apprehension, in degrading surroundings, and with no help from the State, an Arkansas convict will hardly be able to reform himself, and his experience in the Penitentiary is apt to do nothing but instill in him a deep or deeper hatred for and alienation from the society that put him there. And the failure of the State to help him become a good citizen will be compounded by the ever present willingness of his fellow inmates to train him to be a worse criminal.

Id. at 379. Is Judge Henley's view consistent with current popular discourse on prison conditions and prisoners' rights? In what ways does it differ? Have American culture and attitudes about prisoners changed since Judge Henley wrote his opinion? To what do you attribute those changes? Do you think Americans today would be outraged by the practices described by Judge Henley?

3. Psychologist Philip Zimbardo in 1971 conducted what has become known as The Stanford Prison Experiment to observe the effects of the prison environment on human interaction. As noted in the introduction to this chapter, subjects were randomly assigned to play the role of inmate or guard and were placed in a mock prison setting. Although the experiment was intended to span several weeks over the summer, it was prematurely terminated after only six days because of the increasingly physical aggression and sadism by the pretend guards. *See* Haney & Zimbardo, *supra*, at 712. Current ethical standards governing human experimental research prevent the study from being replicated, leaving social psychologists to wonder what might have happened were it allowed to continue. "We no longer need to wonder," says Professor J.C. Oleson:

Within the walls of Corcoran Prison, the California Department of Corrections has conducted the forbidden experiment for us. With their supervisors willfully turning a blind eye, Corcoran guards staged gladiator-style fights for years. The fights, between members of rival gangs or ethnic factions, were "staged for the amusement of correctional officers." Inmates fought, even if they did not want to, because they knew that the guards were watching, and that they might be shot if they did not put on a good show. Even a valiant fight was no guarantee that one would not be shot. On April 4, 1994, inmate "Preston Tate was shot dead by a Corcoran guard at close range with a nine-millimeter assault rifle." The shooting was not spontaneous. Moments before the shot was fired, one guard reportedly said, " 'It's going to be duck-hunting season.' " Preston Tate was not the only dead duck to come out of Corcoran, however. Between 1989 and 1995, fifty Corcoran prisoners were shot under a variety of circumstances. Seven were killed.

In Corcoran, correctional officers also coordinated a system of inmate rape. When twenty-three-year-old, 120-pound Eddie Dillard was transferred to Corcoran for kicking a female guard at Calipatria Prison, Corcoran guards decided to teach him a lesson: you don't kick guards and you don't kick women. Dillard was assigned to a cell with Wayne Robertson, even though Robertson was listed in prison records as Dillard's enemy. Robertson, also known as the "Booty Bandit," was well known for beating and raping black prisoners as a favor for Corcoran guards. In return for this service, he was provided with extra food and tennis shoes. Another prisoner from Corcoran described the situation, "the lights went out and Robertson grabbed Dillard. They struggled, Dillard pounded on the cell door, but no one came. Eventually, Robertson overpowered and raped him. Guards walked by two hours later, but just laughed at Dillard. Over the next two days, he was repeatedly raped."

J.C. Oleson, *The Punitive Coma*, 90 California Law Review 829, 854-55 (2002).

There are other well-known recent episodes of prisoner abuse, including those at the military prisons at Abu Ghraib in Iraq and Camp X-Ray at Guantanamo Bay. All of these episodes of violence against prisoners and other human rights abuses post-date the Arkansas prison scandal by three or four decades. Why do human rights abuses continue in U.S. prisons? Do such episodes reflect American culture? Will it require a change in American culture to prevent future abuses? How would you begin to bring about such a change?

4. The human rights abuses that set the stage for the making of *Brubaker* outraged the public and generated genuine reform, at least temporarily. Since the 1970s, the prison population in America has skyrocketed, even though crime rates have not. The California prison system houses twice as many prisoners as its facilities were designed to hold. Justice Kennedy recently wrote that "[n]eedless suffering and death have been the well-documented result" of poor medical care and unsanitary conditions caused by prison overcrowding. *Brown v. Plata*, 179 L. Ed. 2d 969, 982 (2011). He gave examples of suicidal prisoners with serious mental illness being held for prolonged periods in telephone-booth-sized cases without toilets, including one "inmate who had been held in such a cage for nearly 24 hours, standing in a pool of his own urine, unresponsive, and nearly catatonic." *Id.* at 983. Prison officials explained that there was nowhere else to put him. Another prisoner died of testicular cancer after complaining of pain for seventeen months before seeing a doctor, at which time his cancer was beyond treatment. *Id.* at 983-84. Because of inadequate medical care, a "preventable or possibly preventable death occurred once every five or six days" in California prisons during 2006 and 2007. Attempts to remedy the unconstitutional conditions in California prisons have been frustrated by "severe and pervasive overcrowding." *Id.* at 982. Why is it so difficult for public officials to correct these obvious problems? The majority of the Court expressed frustration at the ineffectiveness of previous efforts to remedy the inhumane conditions in California prisons and upheld the drastic remedy of ordering immediate release of prisoners in significant numbers. Would or could California officials implement a solution without being forced by the Court? Why or why not? Does public sentiment have anything to do with it? Would today's public have the same reaction to the Arkansas prison scandal? Justice Kennedy wrote, "Prisoners retain the essence of human dignity inherent in all persons. Respect for that dignity animates the Eighth Amendment prohibition against cruel and unusual punishment." *Id.* at 987. Would the average American agree with that statement? What is it about American culture that could explain the plight of men and women housed in California prisons?

5. Maricopa County Sheriff Joe Arpaio describes himself as "America's toughest sheriff." Arpaio is credited with starting the nation's first female and juvenile

chain gangs. He makes Maricopa County inmates wear pink, and in 2008 made 700 prisoners march to a new county jail in public wearing only chains and pink underwear. He has eliminated virtually every comfort in county jails, including recreation, coffee, salt and pepper, and movies. He prides himself for serving the cheapest prisoner meals in the United States, at fifteen cents each. He installed a large neon "Vacancy" sign on a guard tower at the Maricopa County Jail. To reduce the cost of housing Maricopa County's growing inmate population, which has doubled on his watch, Arpaio houses inmates in tents that commonly reach temperatures of 120 degrees Fahrenheit in the long Arizona summer. He is at the forefront of Arizona's efforts to criminalize, arrest, and incarcerate undocumented foreign nationals. During his tenure, he has cost the taxpayers of Maricopa County more than $43 million in settlement costs and legal fees. In one lawsuit, he was sanctioned by a federal judge for serving prisoners only two meals a day, and for forcing inmates to eat moldy bread and rotten fruit. Although criticized widely for human rights abuses, Arpaio has been re-elected five times by double-digit margins, and over three thousand Facebook users are fans of "Sheriff Joe." *See* Randy James, "Sheriff Joe Arpaio," *Time*, 13 Oct. 2009, available at http://www.time.com/time/nation/article/0,8599,1929920,00.html. What accounts for Arpaio's popularity? What does his popularity say about the values Americans place on human dignity? Does Arpaio's support reflect some Americans' fear and frustration over crime, or are there other attitudes at work? Are these feelings well-grounded? Are there more effective solutions than Arpaio's? On the issue of criminal punishment, are there considerations that are more important than human dignity and respect?

E.   WORKIN' ON THE CHAIN GANG

Hard labor was a common form of punishment in the post-Civil War South, and it flourished during the Great Depression. Chain gangs are memorialized in folk songs, from Woody Guthrie's Depression-era "Worried Man Blues" and "Chain Gang Special" to Sam Cooke's 1960 single "Chain Gang." Georgia was the last state to eliminate chain gangs in 1955. Beginning with Alabama, several states flirted with the reinstatement of chain gangs in the 1990s, including Arizona, Arkansas, California, Florida, Indiana, Iowa, Montana, Nevada, Oklahoma, South Carolina, Tennessee, Washington, West Virginia, Wisconsin and Vermont. Most legislatures rejected bills to resurrect chain gangs. Wendy Imatani Peloso, *Les Miserables: Chain Gangs and the Cruel and Unusual Punishments Clause*, 20 Southern California Law Review 1459, 1460 (1997). The few states that restored chain gangs abolished them within a year, except for Arizona, where inmate hard labor crews can still be seen working in the desert heat. In spite of their near-extinction from civilized society, chain gangs are an important chapter in the history of American culture.

SCREENING THE LAW: IDEOLOGY AND LAW IN AMERICAN POPULAR CULTURE

Naomi Mezey & Mark C. Niles

28 Columbia Journal of Law & the Arts 91 (2005)

Among the most interesting and dense films of this genre . . . is *Cool Hand Luke*, a 1967 film directed by Stuart Rosenberg and staring Paul Newman in the title role. It was written by Donn Pearce, a convicted felon and a former member of a Southern chain-gang. While its moral clarity might suggest ideological complexity, its characterization of law and legal authority as irretrievably illegitimate, evil and soul-killing suggests otherwise — that this a film which positions itself in opposition to any dominant ideology of law.

The first shot is a close-up of the window of an expired parking meter. The red "Violation" indicator fills the screen. In the next shot a drunken Luke is using an odd tool to cut the heads off the meters. He seems completely uninterested in extracting the coins from the meter heads that have dropped to the street, and indeed, he appears not only inebriated but delighted by his own antics. This is an amusing activity for someone with an odd sense of humor; he even affectionately kisses the face of one of the meters before proceeding to cut it off. The police arrive, and we next see Luke being deposited with a prison chain gang. It is immediately clear that the rules of the chain gang are minute and exactingly enforced: the prisoners are obligated to ask permission from the guards to perform the most basic acts — taking off their shirt, wiping their face, taking a drink of water — and are chastised for simply looking a guard in the eye. The prison guards are epitomized by their chief, Godfrey, who never says a word but wields enormous and ferocious power. We never see Godfrey's eyes, which are perpetually shielded behind the lenses of his mirrored sunglasses, but his face is impassive. Justice is blind, but injustice sees all without being seen.

It is not long before we learn that Luke, who has been convicted of "maliciously destroying municipal property while under the influence," is a war hero with the remarkable distinction of having earned four medals for valor in combat while still failing to earn a single promotion during his service. He is an unapologetic rebel, an almost compulsive nonconformist with an innate disdain for authority and power. And it is precisely Luke's refusal to submit to authority that makes him heroic within the film. His heroism is matched and made possible by the cruelty of the guards.

Once in the barracks, Luke and the other new prisoners are taught an extensive set of rules — and the dreaded punishment for their violation — spending a night in the box, a small, dark, poorly ventilated shack barely large enough to hold a grown man. Luke's immediate contempt for the rules leads the floor walker to warn, "I hope you're not gonna be a hard case." At dinner Luke learns another set of rules imposed by the prisoners themselves. There are special seats, special names and other special requirements applicable to all the prisoners and to the new entrants in particular. Luke refers to the apparent leader of the prisoners, who informs the newcomers of these rules, as "Boss," which is the same name used for the prison guards. The way the prisoners imitate and even assist their guards by imposing more rules is not lost on a natural rule-breaker like Luke. Later, when the prisoners play a trick on one of the new inmates, and as a result he is confined to the box for the night, they try to absolve themselves from responsibility for this excessive punishment. One of them says, "He ain't in the box because of the joke played on him. He back-sassed a free man. They got their rules; we ain't got nothing to do with that." Luke's response is sarcastic and disdainful: "Yeah, those poor old bosses need all the help they can get."

The conflict between Luke and the lead prisoner, Dragline, continues to grow, and the two finally meet in an officially sanctioned boxing match in the prison courtyard. Outmatched and battered, Luke refuses to give up and submit to the imposition of Dragline's authority. As the fight begins, the inmates root for Dragline, but their sympathies change as they watch Luke refuse to give up; he takes a horrible beating and keeps coming back for more. They beg Luke to stop, and Dragline tells him, "Stay down, you're beat." But Luke responds, "You're gonna have to kill me." The guards, who had been ignoring the fight, and indeed, probably welcomed the help knocking the cocky new inmate down a few pegs, finally take notice. They understand the danger posed by a prisoner willing to withstand so much to avoid surrendering to authority. What makes Luke a threat to the guards is also what makes him heroic to the other prisoners. Luke's efforts even win over Dragline himself, who stops his assault, picks Luke up and carries him into the barracks.

Luke's inevitable clash with the true authority in the prison comes after he gets word that his mother has died, and the prison warden confines him to the box in order to prevent him from trying to escape to attend her funeral. As one of the sympathetic guards leads him to the tiny cell and locks him in, he apologizes: "Sorry, Luke, I'm just doing my job, you've got to appreciate that." Luke responds, "Calling it your job don't make it right, Boss." The guard himself implicitly acknowledges the inherent injustice of both punishing Luke before he has even escaped and preventing him from attending the funeral of his mother in the first place (a right, the film strongly suggests, even a prison inmate should not be deprived of). And, as with the images of justice that permeate *The Verdict*, this film is encoded so that Luke's own sense of right and wrong is naturalized, making him seem both sympathetic and heroic in his extreme resistance to the injustices of authority. . . .

It is interesting that popular culture's stories of heroic criminals are usually inverted morality tales. In some sense they are a rejection of the dominant legal ideology: they usually make law and its enforcement appear illegitimate or immoral, they valorize rejection of legal authority and social conformity and they applaud rebellion and resistance.

NOTES & QUESTIONS

1. The chain gang as depicted in film and song is an inherently brutal and dehumanizing institution, viewed by some as more brutal than slavery. Southern states leased inmate labor — primarily black convicts — to private contractors. Pointing out that a typical prison labor farm, Parchman, Mississippi, "resembled a slave plantation," Professor Gutterman explains that "unlike the African slave, bought for life, the African American convict lacked any value to the boss at the end

of his contract." Gutterman, *supra*, at 1529. Because he had no resale value, "there was no interest in his well-being, so the bosses worked him like an animal." *Id.* John Spivak described conditions on Georgia's infamous Buzzard's Roost chain gang:

> [T]here were vermin and stench, cursings and beatings and stocks but out of Slatternville seventeen Negroes went into the wilderness of the South Carolina hills in a floating cage, a cage drawn by four mules, a swaying, creaking, rumbling prison of thick wood with no bars or windows for air on nights that choked you, and bunks of steel with rings for master chains to lock you in at night. Bedbugs slept with you in that cage and lice nestled in the hair of your body and you scratched until your skin bled and the sores on your body filled with puss. Meat for the floating kitchen wrapped in burlap bags, stinking meat swarming with maggots and flies, and corn pone soaked by fall rains, slashing rains that beat upon the wooden cage through the barred door upon the straw mattresses until they were soggy.

John L. Spivak, *Georgia Nigger* 186-87 (1932). Would these conditions be tolerated in today's society? Could the government operate chain gangs without risking inhumane treatment of prisoners? In *Cool Hand Luke*, the hearse carrying Luke's body passes under a traffic light which changes from green to red, without flashing the yellow caution light. What is the director saying in that scene?

2. Even though most convicts on chain gangs were black, the protagonists in these films are usually white. Why would Hollywood choose white characters to spotlight human rights abuses? Is the message enhanced by sidestepping the issue of race? In what ways might the message of *Cool Hand Luke* change if a black actor had been cast in Paul Newman's role?

3. One commentator asserts unequivocally that chain gangs are cruel and unusual punishment:

> The Eighth Amendment guarantee against cruel and unusual punishment "is testimony to a belief that the way a society treats those who have transgressed against it is evidence of the essential character of that society." Chain gang proponents state that a chain gang is intended to be "a very strong and powerful symbol." While the truth of this statement is self-evident, the question remains, what are modern chain gangs intended to symbolize? Our intolerance of crime? Our thirst for revenge? Our willingness to treat society's transgressors as less than human?

> For almost 200 years, our nation has struggled to define the boundaries of punishment. Although the path toward enlightenment has twisted and turned, it has always pointed us forward — until today. While states are surely obligated to punish their criminals, if the Cruel and Unusual Punishments Clause is to be infused with any integrity or meaning, courts must find chain gangs unconstitutional per se under the Eighth Amendment. Otherwise, the impoverished character of our nation will be revealed for all the world to see.

Peloso, *supra*, at 1511.

Is American culture responsible for our appetite for harsh punishment? To what extent, if any, does popular culture inform the modern standards of decency embodied in the Eighth Amendment? How would the courts perceive what popular culture tells us about a particular method of punishment? Ms. Peloso notes that the long-term trend is in the direction of more moderate punishment, notwithstanding the temporary resurgence of chain gangs. Does the long-term trend track with popular culture, or are other forces at work? Are punishment trends driven by society's values, or are they largely reactive to politicians' perceptions of popular sentiment?

4.   Luke's dying mother comes to visit him in the labor camp one last time to say good-bye. She tells him, "You know, sometimes, I wish people was like dogs, Luke. Comes a time, a day like, when the bitch just don't recognize the pups no more, so she don't have no hopes, nor love to give her pain. She just don't give a damn. . . ." She wants to forget him, but she is unable to because of their humanity. How does this scene advance the message of the movie? What is disclosed about Luke during this scene that gives some insight into his character?

5.   Luke's non-conformity and disrespect for rules is an integral part of his character. Luke is constantly rebelling, attempting to flee, or otherwise flaunting the rules, for which he is severely punished. At other times, he demonstrates that he is capable of hard work, exceeding the bosses' expectations, but even then it is only to frustrate the system. When the captain gets word that Luke's mother has died, he orders Luke to be placed in the "windowless box" to keep him from trying to escape to attend her funeral. As one of the bosses locks Luke away, he says, "I wanna say a prayer for your Ma, Luke. . . . Sorry Luke. Just doin' my job. You gotta appreciate that." Luke replies, "Aw, callin' it your job don't make it right, Boss." What is Luke rebelling against? The rules, or the enforcers of the rules? What, if anything, is he trying to accomplish through his rebellion?

6.   One analyst observed, "Luke has character. With character he soars and plummets to his death. His thorough-going individuality is his flaw: perhaps mock-heroic, sometimes puerile, always romantic, and eventually fatal." William Haltom, *Laws of God, Laws of Man: Power, Authority, and Influence in* Cool Hand Luke, *in Symposium Issue: Crime and Popular Culture*, 22 Legal Studies Forum 233, 243 (1998). The audience learns early on that Luke is a decorated combat veteran, having earned the Silver Star, Bronze Star, and two Purple Hearts. What can the audience infer about Luke from these tidbits of information? Much of Luke's rebellion seems pointless and self-destructive. Is his behavior an assertion of his individuality, or might something else be driving his defiance? What if he is simply a post-traumatic combat veteran, resenting authority and having difficulty coping with his frustration? Would that change the way his character is perceived?

7.   Luke's nickname, "Cool Hand Luke," comes from his prowess at poker, which he demonstrates by bluffing his way to victory with a worthless hand. Luke says, "Sometimes nothin' can be a pretty cool hand." This sentiment is reminiscent of the line, "Freedom's just another word for nothin' left to lose," made famous by Janis Joplin's posthumous #1 single, "Me & Bobby McGee" by Kris Kristofferson and Fred Foster (1968). Self-destructive individualism is a central theme in other films about punishment imposed for the purpose of enforcing conformity. In the end, did

Luke die for nothing, or did he make a point? How does the film resolve this issue? How does the audience know whether Luke's spirit of individuality accomplished anything?

F. THE DEATH PENALTY

American culture has long had a love-hate relationship with the death penalty. Popular support for capital punishment has been described as a mile wide and an inch deep. Although opinion polls consistently show that a majority of Americans favor the death penalty, they also show that a majority of Americans would reject the death penalty if life without parole were an option. When the questions hypothesize additional factors, such as restitution to the victims or mitigating factors about the defendant, support for the death penalty dwindles even further. The alarming frequency of death row exonerations — 138 innocent prisoners exonerated from death row since 1973 — has been credited with the diminished support for capital punishment. If a popular opinion poll hypothesized capital punishment as practiced in America, complete with its exclusive application to the poor, inhumane confinement on death row during decade-long appeals, inexperienced defense lawyers, and the ever-present risk of error, a majority of the people would most certainly reject it.

The trend in the twentieth and twenty-first centuries has been a sharp reduction in the classes of crimes and offenders punishable by death, a steady decline in new death sentences imposed by juries and in the number of executions, and outright abolition of the death penalty in Illinois, New Jersey, New York, and New Mexico. The American Law Institute has stricken § 210.6, dealing with capital sentencing, from the Model Penal Code "in light of the current intractable institutional and structural obstacles to ensuring a minimally adequate system for administering capital punishment." American Law Institute, *Message from ALI Director Lance Liebman* (23 Oct. 2009), available online at http://www.ali.org/_news/10232009.htm. Yet for now the death penalty remains an integral part of "tough on crime" politics in America.

American films reflect society's ambivalence about capital punishment. In the films that carry an unequivocal abolitionist message, such as *I Want to Live!*, protagonists are frequently innocent of the capital crime. *Dead Man Walking* is one of the few films depicting the offender as clearly guilty of capital crimes, but its message on capital punishment is ambiguous in spite of the staunch abolitionist message of the book on which it is based. Although there are many compelling arguments against the death penalty, filmmakers have yet to rise to the challenge of crafting a compelling abolitionist narrative that humanizes an obviously guilty offender.

I WANT TO LIVE! FEDERAL JUDICIAL VALUES IN DEATH PENALTY CASES: PRESERVATION OF RIGHTS OR PUNCTUALITY OF EXECUTION?

Teree E. Foster

22 Oklahoma City University Law Review 63 (1997)

I Want to Live!, a 1958 film which recounts a few years in the brief life of Barbara Wood Graham, tells an arresting story. The film is a 1950s drama classic, a period piece that reflects the established social mores of that era. Nevertheless, considered from a near-millennium perspective, *I Want to Live!* defines modern systemic paradigms that provide insight into the relationship between the judiciary, the criminal justice system, and the society that these institutions influence and shape. . . .

III. The Federal Judiciary's Role: Buffer or Promoter of Expediency?

Principal among the film's motifs is a compelling reminder that, at least in criminal cases, it is essential that an impartial entity interpose itself as a barrier between the accused and the unfettered force of governmental, prosecutorial power. This buffer role is an integral component of the guarantee that procedures used to gather incriminating information and to build a case "beyond a reasonable doubt" against an accused comport with due process and substantial justice. When Barbara Graham was tried in California in the mid-1950s, the judiciary had not yet assumed this insulating role. Thus, although her conviction was tangibly dependent upon the testimony of the ironically-named Ben Miranda, the undercover police officer who adopted the guise of friendship, and extracted from Barbara a ruinously incriminating — and possibly unreliable — statement, Miranda's testimony evoked little judicial comment.

Barbara Graham's trial occurred almost a decade prior to the assault of the Warren Court on a plethora of egregious police tactics that had become accepted as the sine qua non for vigorous law enforcement. During the 1960s, the Supreme Court breathed vitality into constitutional protections for criminal accuseds found in the Fourth, Fifth, Sixth, and Eighth Amendments. Decisions of the Warren Court during this period revolutionized the substance and focus of criminal procedure. A touchstone of Warren Court jurisprudence was the shielding of suspects from coercive law enforcement tactics; an interposition function was assumed with vigor and alacrity by the federal judiciary and the United States Supreme Court. . . .

Whether or not the imposition of capital punishment is morally defensible or desirable, it is apparent that in reviewing convictions in capital cases, the Supreme Court has abdicated, actively and absolutely, its role as insulator of the individual from the force of governmental, prosecutorial power. The Warren Court's position was that a federal court, in considering a habeas corpus petition from a state prisoner, should independently consider the merits of the constitutional challenge, notwithstanding the previous state court adjudication. State court rulings were entitled to the respect ordinarily afforded to opinions of a court of another jurisdiction, but did not preclude federal review of constitutional claims raised in a habeas corpus application.

A series of recent cases demonstrates that values of efficiency, expediency, and finality predominate over any obligation to consider potentially meritorious claims on behalf of the condemned. No longer is habeas corpus readily available to defendants incarcerated under state authority, even defendants convicted of capital offenses, as a device to challenge the constitutionality of their confinement. Instead, the Court has transmuted habeas corpus into a mechanism by which federal courts are permitted to do little more than ascertain whether state courts properly considered all constitutional challenges raised by the defendant during direct appeal. Above all, the Court, in its current preoccupation with punctuality in the execution of state-condemned capital defendants, has transmogrified its own role from shielding protector to detached timekeeper. . . .

That finality, efficiency, and expediency are legitimate and valuable goals for the criminal justice system cannot be gainsaid. Yet, these concerns must not eviscerate substantive interests in preserving individual liberties. If Barbara Graham was, as portrayed in *I Want to Live!*, an innocent victim of circumstance, the governmental termination of her life is an unspeakable perversion of justice. If Barbara Graham was guilty of Mrs. Monaghan's murder, premising her conviction for that crime upon information acquired by illegal, abusive and reprehensible law enforcement tactics sabotages fundamental principles of respect for the dignity of the individual — even the individual criminal — and for her inviolable constitutional rights.

NOTES & QUESTIONS

1. The movie *I Want to Live!* cinematically adapts real events from a high-profile murder trial that resulted in the conviction and execution of Barbara Graham in the gas chamber in California. Unlike director Errol Morris in the 1988 film *The Thin Blue Line*, the screenwriters and director of *I Want to Live!* readjusted some of the facts to suit the public's taste. *I Want to Live!* is akin to contemporary docudramas developed from real events rather than to, for instance, *The Thin Blue Line*, which is a narrative documentary. In the movie, Susan Hayward's Graham is a feisty, extremely attractive and, in many ways, deeply sympathetic character, and is also apparently innocent. In the "real" case, however, the character of Graham is darker, and there is stronger evidence of her complicity in the murder of Mabel Monahan. Graham was not merely a passive observer; she allegedly asphyxiated the victim — a 64-year-old invalid — by placing a plastic bag over her head. And her jailhouse confession to the police informer included incriminating knowledge of details of the crime that would have been difficult for a non-participant to know. These details, however, are omitted from the movie. Why did the moviemakers find it necessary to tweak crucial facts, especially since the opening to the film specifically states that it is a "real" story based upon the articles of a Pulitzer Prize-winning journalist and Barbara Graham's own letters?

2. Is *I Want to Live!* truly an exploration of capital punishment? Or is the film a reworking of a more traditional Hollywood theme about the wrongful punishment of an innocent defendant? Here, unlike many predecessors, the innocent victim is not released at the end, but instead maintains stoic and "heroic" dignity in the face of injustice. Would a film audience have been interested in the film (or the story) if

Graham was depicted as a less attractive or sympathetic protagonist? If she was guilty rather than innocent?

3. *I Want to Live!* details realistically (or at least as realistically as possible within the constraints and limitations of a two-hour movie format) many of the procedural details of death penalty practice such as the multiple appeals and petitions for stays of execution and requests for clemency. The movie also explores the psychological effects upon the convicted defendant of these protracted proceedings and accurately details the workings of the machinery of death by depicting the physical preparations for, and the execution of, a prisoner in the gas chamber, right up to the moment the cyanide tablets are dropped into the sulfuric acid and the prisoner inhales the fumes and struggles for life. In Graham's case, this execution was a public enactment of the biblical admonition of "an eye for an eye." The type of execution paralleled the form of the murder Graham purportedly committed by asphyxiation of another woman. How, if at all, do these scenes compel you as viewer to respond emotionally? How, if at all, is the film persuasive to you? Does it change or reinforce your attitudes about capital punishment?

4. Does it matter that Barbara Graham is a woman? That is, are the story and the film's cinematic argument against capital punishment made more compelling because of Graham's gender or the fact that she is a mother with a young child? (In fact, Barbara Graham was the mother of three children.) Is there anything more troubling to you about executing a woman convicted of murder than executing a man? Suppose Barbara Graham was unquestionably guilty of the crime. Is there something more unsettling about her crime because she is a woman? Would we be equally troubled if a man engaged in the same behavior?

5. Contrast Barbara Graham with Aileen Wuornos, a woman convicted and executed in Florida for multiple homicides of male victims. Charlize Theron won an academy award for her portrayal of Wuornos in the movie *Monster* (2003). Wuornos was not innocent of her crimes, but there was substantial mitigating evidence. Unfortunately, her story was distorted by both the prosecution and the defense's reliance upon gender stereotypes which "reinforce societal norms that equate the use of violence by women with an impermissible attempt to subvert their subordinate position in a deeply hierarchical, and deeply gendered, social order." Chimene I. Keitner, *Victim or Vamp? Images of Violent Women in the Criminal Justice System*, 11 Columbia Journal of Gender and Law 38, 59 (2002). The prosecution portrayed her as a predatory man-hater with an insatiable appetite for sex in search of "ultimate control," while the defense characterized her as a trapped and helpless victim of circumstance. *Id.* at 60. Neither version has narrative integrity. Her first homicide victim had served ten years for a violent sex offense, which is consistent with Wuornos' claim that she was defending herself against a "customer" who became violent. Psychologists believe this may have started Wuornos' shooting spree. Wuornos herself explained, "I'm supposed to die because I'm a prostitute? No, I don't think so. I was out prostituting. And I was dealing with hundreds and hundreds of guys. You got a jerk that's going to come along and try to rape me? I'm going to fight. I believe that everybody has a right to self-defend themselves." *Id.* at 65-66. Ms. Keitner argues that "[u]nlike men, women who use violence commit the additional transgression of doing something 'unwomanly.'" *Id.* at 54. She further contends that using stereotypes as "courtroom shorthands can be destructive when,

instead of illuminating characters and events, they obscure and even distort them."
Id. at 68. Do you agree? Which side gains an advantage by the use of stereotypes
in a death penalty case? In a society so focused on gender roles, Wournos's gender
is crucial to understanding how her life experiences brought her to the point of
killing several men. How would you craft a narrative that transcends rather than
invokes gender stereotypes?

6.   How do factors such as race, economic circumstance, and the physicality or
attractiveness of convicted defendants affect the probability of imposition of the
death sentence? Is it appropriate to account for such factors in deciding whether to
impose the death penalty? Are there circumstances in which it would be inappropriate to do so? Does it matter if such facts are used to support an argument to
impose the death penalty? How would you create a narrative that would encourage
a decision-maker to account for these factors in an acceptable way when choosing
between life and death?

THE CULTURAL LIFE OF CAPITAL PUNISHMENT: RESPONSIBILITY AND REPRESENTATION IN *DEAD MAN WALKING* AND *LAST DANCE*
Austin Sarat
11 Yale Journal of Law & the Humanities 153 (1999)

Punishment, as Nietzsche reminds us, makes us who we are and constitutes us
as particular kinds of subjects. The subject constituted by punishment is watchful,
on guard, fearful, even if never directly subject to the particular pains of
state-imposed punishment. One of the primary achievements of punishment, to use
Nietzsche's vivid phrase, "is to breed an animal with the right to make promises,"
that is, to induce in us a sense of responsibility, a desire and an ability to properly
discharge our responsibilities. Dutiful individuals, guilt-ridden, morally burdened
— these are the creatures that punishment demands, creatures worthy of being
punished.

Punishment constitutes subjectivity through the complex juridical mechanisms
that put it in motion, as well as the moral tenets and legal doctrines that legitimate
it. Here too, we can see the centrality of responsibility. The state will only punish
responsible agents, persons whose "deviant" acts can be said to be a product of
consciousness and will, persons who "could have done otherwise." As Blackstone put
it, "to constitute a crime against human laws, there must be, first, a vicious will, and,
secondly, an unlawful act consequent upon such vicious will." Thus, the apparatus of
punishment depends upon a modernist subject and a conception of the will that
represses or forgets its "uncertain, divided, and opaque" character.

In addition, because most citizens are not, and will not be, directly subjected to
the state's penal apparatus, punishment creates a challenge for representation that
is deepened to the point of crisis when the punishment is death. Punishment is
inscribed in both our unconscious and our consciousness. It lives in images
conveyed, in lessons taught, in repressed memories, in horrible imaginings. Some of
its horror and controlling power is, in fact, a result of its fearful invisibility.
"Punishment," Foucault reminds us, "[has] become the most hidden part of the
penal process." He argues that:

This has several consequences: [Punishment] leaves the domain of more or less everyday perception and enters that of abstract consciousness; its effectiveness is seen as resulting from its inevitability, not from its visible intensity; it is the certainty of being punished and not the horrifying spectacle of public punishment that must discourage crime. . . . As a result, justice no longer takes public responsibility for the violence that is bound up with its practice.

Michel Foucault, *Discipline and Punish* 9 (Alan Sheridan trans. 1977).

It may very well be, however, that the more punishment is hidden, the less visible it is, the more power it has to colonize our imaginative life. We watch; we seek to conjure an image of punishment; we become particular kinds of spectators, anticipating a glimpse, at least a partial uncovering of the apparatus of state discipline.

What is true of all punishment is particularly true when death is a punishment. That the state takes life and how it takes life insinuates itself into the public imagination, even as the moment of this exercise of power is hidden from view. This particular exercise of power helps us understand who we are and what we as a society are capable of doing. And as Wendy Lesser so skillfully documents, the hidden moment when the state takes the life of one of its citizens precipitates, in an age of the hypervisual, a crisis of representation. *See* Wendy Lesser, *Pictures at an Execution* (1993). This crisis occurs as we confront the boundaries of our representational practices, where we must determine who decides what can and cannot be seen, and whether particular representations of the "reality" of the pain on which the penal apparatus depends are adequate.

The modern execution is carried out behind prison walls. In these semi-private, sacrificial ceremonies a few selected witnesses are gathered in a carefully controlled situation to see, and by seeing to sanctify, the state's taking of the life of one of its citizens. As Richard Johnson suggests:

In the modern period (from 1800 on), ceremony gradually gave way to bureaucratic procedure played out behind prison walls, in isolation from the community. Feelings are absent, or at least suppressed, in bureaucratically administered executions. With bureaucratic procedure, there is a functional routine dominated by hierarchy and task. Officials perform mechanistically before a small, silent gathering of authorized witnesses.

Richard Johnson, *Death Work: A Study of the Modern Execution Process* 5 (1990).

Capital punishment becomes, at best, a hidden reality. It is known, if at all, by indirection. "The relative privacy of executions nowadays (even photographs of the condemned man dying are almost invariably strictly prohibited)," Hugo Bedau notes, "means that the average American literally does not know what is being done when the government, in his name and presumably on his behalf, executes a criminal." Hugo Bedau, *The Death Penalty in America* 13 (1982).

While executions have been removed from the public eye for more than fifty years, in most states capital punishment still must be witnessed by members of the public in order to be legal. It is this linkage between violence and the visual that

Lesser explores when she notes that witnesses are "there not just to ensure that the deed is actually done . . . but to represent and embody the wider public in whose name the execution is being carried out." Lesser, *supra*, at 37. Thus the state's power to kill is linked to the imperatives and privileges of spectatorship. Whatever the means chosen, execution is always a visual event.

NOTES & QUESTIONS

1. Professor Sarat argues that the power of punishment, and its hold over our imaginations, is based upon its secrecy. That is, "punishment is inscribed in both our unconscious and our consciousness. It lives in images conveyed, in lessons taught, in repressed memories, in horrible happenings. Some of its horror and controlling power is, in fact, a result of its fearful invisibility." Further, "what is true of all punishment is particularly true when death is a punishment." Do you agree? If so, how might the televising of executions affect or change public attitudes about how we respond to this punishment? Would it diminish the imaginative power of the punishment? Do you believe that it would cause us to recoil in horror? Or are we already so deadened to the effects of violence that we would not have any response? Or would we find the presentation of ceremonies of death another type of entertaining reality programming?

2. *I Want to Live!* depicts in graphic detail how the death penalty was carried out in California in 1953; the images documenting the externals of an execution in the gas chamber are presented with precision. Yet these images may have little sway or power over the imaginations of some viewers. The story may also seem dated to some viewers. Why is this so? Reflect upon your own responses to *I Want to Live!* in the context of Sarat's observations about punishment.

3. Today, in many jurisdictions, death by injection is a seemingly antiseptic practice without the obviously horrific imaginative external dimensions of other forms of execution, such as firing squad, hanging, the electric chair, or the gas chamber. The vast majority of death penalty jurisdictions execute by lethal injection using a process that sedates the prisoner into unconsciousness, then paralyzes, so that the moment of death is not apparent to the observer. The images of the gurney and of lethal injections do not carry the visual freight of earlier forms of execution. In Sarat's words, it is less of a "visual event." Some of the power of the ritual of the "sacrificial ceremonies" described by Sarat may have been lost — its power to colonize the imagination made less compelling. Does this diminish the effectiveness of the punishment as a deterrent?

4. Hugo Bedau notes, "The relative privacy of executions nowadays (even photographs of the condemned man dying are almost invariably strictly prohibited) means that the average American literally does not know what is being done when the government, in his name and presumably on his behalf, executes a criminal." Do you agree or disagree with Bedau's observation? Explain and reflect upon the reasons for your responses.

THE SOCIAL CONTEXT OF CAPITAL MURDER: SOCIAL HISTORIES AND THE LOGIC OF MITIGATION
Craig Haney

35 Santa Clara Law Review 547 (1995)

Film provides one of the few mediums through which any in-depth study of criminal behavior is even attempted for public consumption. Yet, almost invariably, such films sensationalize the nature of criminality, pander to the worst conceivable popular stereotypes, and are similarly uninformed by any realistic analysis of social context and personal history. Indeed, the American public has learned many of its "deepest" lessons about crime and criminality primarily through watching mythically frightening cinematic figures, figures like Hannibal Lecter — "Hannibal the Cannibal" (the sadistically mad killer, played with Oscar-winning skill by Anthony Hopkins in *Silence of the Lambs*) — they are tricked into believing people who have committed capital murder relish their deadly work, plot brilliantly, diabolically, and joyfully to perform it, would just as easily polish off a meal of their victim's liver with a little Chianti as give you the time of day.

Almost as soon as the lessons of a movie like *Silence of the Lambs* have been lost or forgotten, Hollywood delivers another dose of this abominably bad media criminology. Last year, for example, Oliver Stone taught vast audiences that most capital murderers are "natural born killers." Mickey and Mallory — Stone's gratuitously, mindlessly, unbelievably violent couple — were violent for the sheer aesthetic joy of it, violent as an act of self-expression while they carved up bodies and dispensed flesh-tearing gunshots much as an artist might decorate a canvas. For lack of any better, more serviceable lessons, the public was encouraged to believe that this is what capital punishment is about: People whose evil is so profound that it defies any attempt at rational explanation. Stone was forced at one point to stencil the word "DEMON" across his psychopathic protagonist's chest to make sure he got the point across.

Indeed, these were people whose frenetic addiction to violence was so inhuman that the filmmaker was forced numerous times to resort to animated cartoon figures because no real human being could adequately capture the extraordinary and grotesque distortions of body and soul he wished to convey. Yet, the reason a film like this fails as satire is because its distortions fall far too close to the dominant view. Audiences must have an alternative, competing vision of the truth against which to measure Stone's exaggerations. Too few of them did, in large part because of the extensive media miseducation they had received in the past. . . .

As the mood of the public has swung — and been coaxed, nudged, and shoved — to the right on the issue of violent crime, a conservative criminology has grown up to support mindlessly punitive strategies of control. This pseudo-scientific literature feeds the public's already increasing levels of fear. Indeed, one author claimed that serial murder — easily the very rarest form of homicide — was a disease "that had to be identified and diagnosed before it engulfed all of our social institutions." As one commentator noted, "scholars who continue to investigate social explanations [for crime] are currently on the defensive against new voices calling for a return to a consideration of biology and psychology as the sources of criminal behavior." Academics are still living in the political wake of James Q. Wilson's assertion that "wicked people exist. Nothing avails except to set them apart from innocent people." Increasingly, the "innocent" members of our society have taken to setting their "wicked" brothers and sisters apart from them by attempting to execute them.

The media's obsession with demonizing the causes of crime is not difficult to explain and tells us a great deal about the underlying dynamic that supports the death penalty itself. The slant in coverage is both economic and psychological in nature. For one, the economic mandate of television broadcasting seems to dictate a false clarity in depictions of crime and punishment. Only story lines in which pure good triumphs over pure evil leave audiences comfortably reassured: "Police dramas offered a sense of security to their audiences. In theory that made them better consumers, which from a sponsor's view is the real purpose of all programming. Consequently, the new crime shows and commercial television were a perfect match." In addition to the economic incentive, demonizing the perpetrators of certain kinds of crimes gets the rest of society off the hook for attitudes and practices that are widespread but which implicitly promote and condone violence. For example, as one theorist has argued, "in myriad ways, the culture regularly doublethinks a distance between itself and sexual violence, denying the fundamental normalcy of that violence in a male supremacist culture and trying to paint it as the domain of psychopaths and 'monsters' only." And, because the media presents us with the most distorted and extreme possible versions of violence — individual grotesques that bear so little relationship to the rest of us that no one in the audience can identify with them — we are saved the unpleasant task of confronting the potential for violence that we all share.

In addition, it becomes justifiable "to kill those who are monsters or inhuman because of their abominable acts or traits, or those who are 'mere animals' (coons, pigs, rats, lice, etc.). . . ." because they have been excluded "from the universe of morally protected entities." But locating the causes of capital crime exclusively within the offender — whose evil must be distorted, exaggerated, and mythologized — not only makes it easier to kill them but also to distance ourselves from any sense of responsibility for the roots of the problem itself. If violent crime is the product of monstrous offenders, then our only responsibility is to find and eliminate them. On the other hand, social histories — because they connect individual violent behavior to the violence of social conditions — implicate us all in the crime problem.

Yet, as somebody who has studied capital murder for the last 19 years, and extensively examined the backgrounds and social histories of people accused or convicted of capital crimes, I have a secret to reveal. People like Hannibal Lecter and Mickey and Mallory do not exist. To the extent to which there are persons who manifest even the slightest resemblance to these terrifying figures — and even then only because of what they have done, not who they are — they exist in numbers so utterly insignificant as to be literally irrelevant to any meaningful discussion of the death penalty. To be sure, these sensationalized, demonic images have become so much a part of the public's "knowledge" about crime and punishment that, despite their fictional, socially constructed quality, they wield significant power in actual legal decisions. They have garnered an important hold on matters of life and death. Indeed, these are the images that American citizens bring into many courtrooms and voting booths across the country. Unless they are effectively debunked, there is little hope that we will ever develop an effective strategy of crime control in the

United States or that any significant measure of fairness and justice will be brought to capital case decision-making. . . .

When I began to study the backgrounds and social histories of capital defendants almost 20 years ago, very little was known about the social and psychological forces that helped to shape and influence their life course. It quickly became clear that many capital defendants shared a pattern of early childhood trauma and maltreatment. What was lacking was a theoretical framework with which to understand how the effects of that shared history could be manifested years later. But we now have developed much of that theoretical framework. In part, it reflects a turning away from a century-old bias that located the causes of violent criminality exclusively inside the individuals who engaged in it. There is increased recognition that the roots of violent behavior extend beyond the personality or character structure of those people who perform it, and connect historically to the brutalizing experiences they have commonly shared as well as the immediately precipitating situations in which violence transpires. Capital penalty trials, then, have become unique legal forums in which it is possible to tell the truth about the lives of capital defendants. These are stories that are being told almost nowhere else in the United States. Yet these stories — and what they tell us about the roots of violence — can assist in our understanding of capital murder, provide a framework for comprehending a single, violent social history, and serve as the basis for the development of a responsible social policy of violence prevention in lieu of the mindless punitiveness with which our society has become recently enamored.

NOTES & QUESTIONS

1. Professor Haney's article proceeds to demonstrate how conditions known to affect crime — poverty, racism, mental illness, childhood neglect and maltreatment — can be shown to operate in the lives of individual defendants. Professor Haney concludes:

> [I]f we can identify with their struggles, if we are moved in our heart by the things that made them this way, and realize that they did not choose these formative experiences any more than they chose the emotional consequences of having to grapple with them, then we take the sum of that life, and the terrible turn that it took, into account when deciding how to punish them. The legal, psychological, and moral significance we attach to these lives of trauma, deprivation, abuse, and neglect is often all that stands between a capital defendant and the execution chamber. No, we don't excuse them for their actions, but neither do we kill them.

Supra, at 609.

Do you agree with Professor Haney? Why would giving the jury a narrative account of the defendant's life story make a difference to a jury deciding how to punish him or her for a terrible crime?

2. Well-defended death penalty cases support Professor Haney's conclusion. Jurors specifically selected for their willingness to impose the death penalty have recently spared the lives of defendants in several nationally publicized, highly aggravated murder cases in which multiple innocent people were murdered. These

include Zacharias Moussaoui, charged as a conspirator in the September 11, 2001 terrorist attack that brought down the World Trade Center, Brian Nichols, a criminal defendant who killed four people while escaping from an Atlanta, Georgia, courtroom, Terry Nichols, who conspired with Timothy McVeigh in the Oklahoma City bombing, and Lee Boyd Malvo, the "Beltway Sniper" whose random murders terrorized the Washington, D.C. area for months. In each of these cases, defense lawyers called dozens of witnesses to testify about the defendant's life history. Yet, consistent with Professor Haney's observations, very little of the defense narrative found its way into the mainstream press. Why not? Do you think the story is just too detailed and nuanced to convey in today's instant media formats? What other explanations are there for the relative obscurity of the mitigation stories of these high-profile defendants?

3.   The Supreme Court has been moved by compelling life history narratives to grant habeas corpus relief to defendants who committed capital crimes. The Court summarized portions of Ronald Rompilla's life story:

> Rompilla's parents were both severe alcoholics who drank constantly. His mother drank during her pregnancy with Rompilla, and he and his brothers eventually developed serious drinking problems. His father, who had a vicious temper, frequently beat Rompilla's mother, leaving her bruised and black-eyed, and bragged about his cheating on her. His parents fought violently, and on at least one occasion his mother stabbed his father. He was abused by his father who beat him when he was young with his hands, fists, leather straps, belts and sticks. All of the children lived in terror. There were no expressions of parental love, affection or approval. Instead, he was subjected to yelling and verbal abuse. His father locked Rompilla and his brother Richard in a small wire mesh dog pen that was filthy and excrement filled. He had an isolated background, and was not allowed to visit other children or to speak to anyone on the phone. They had no indoor plumbing in the house, he slept in the attic with no heat, and the children were not given clothes and attended school in rags.

Rompilla v. Beard, 545 U.S. 374, 391-92 (2005). The Court also discussed Rompilla's mental impairments, which included Fetal Alcohol Syndrome, intellectual disability, and schizophrenia. Rompilla was convicted of murdering a local tavern owner by stabbing him multiple times and setting him on fire. In spite of this terrible crime, the Court found that this narrative would have moved one or more jurors to spare Rompilla's life. Do you agree? What is your response to the Court's description of Rompilla's childhood? Would this narrative evoke a sympathetic response? Do you understand why jurors would be moved to spare Rompilla's life based on this information? In court, this narrative would unfold over many days and involve the testimony of dozens of witnesses. Do you think Hollywood would or could tell a story with a protagonist like Ronald Rompilla?

FICTIONAL DOCUMENTARIES AND TRUTHFUL FICTIONS: THE DEATH PENALTY IN RECENT AMERICAN FILM

David R. Dow

17 Constitutional Commentary 511 (2000)

When it comes to death, most Hollywood movies cheat. They cheat by tinkering with the truth, because the truth as it actually is is too complex or too disturbing to confront honestly. (The so-called happy ending is the most famous form of such cheating.) They cheat because people generally prefer happiness and simplicity to darkness and complexity, especially where their entertainment is concerned, and filmmakers tend to give people what they want. . . .

Death penalty movies cheat as well. . . . [T]hey cheat by featuring an innocent inmate: someone who, by nearly anyone's estimation, deserves to be living. This focus is their mode of distraction, their mode of avoiding moral complexity. Death penalty movies that focus on innocence cheat because they allow the viewer to be certain that the protagonist ought not to be killed; such movies permit viewers to oppose a death penalty without opposing the death penalty. In real life, we do not have that indulgence.

When death penalty movies cheat, they obscure the fundamental moral questions that the death penalty involves. One might expect documentaries to be more real and Hollywood productions to be less so, but one would be wrong. Exactly the opposite is true. Documentaries cheat much more than Hollywood movies. Most (though not all) documentaries cheat by focusing almost exclusively on the issue of innocence, whereas many Hollywood movies willingly grapple with moral complexity by featuring at least one guilty inmate. Moreover, although the focus on innocence might seem innocuous, it is in fact rather pernicious, because it contributes to the increasingly widespread view that there is no great harm in violating a person's rights as long as we are certain that the person is guilty. . . .

I am not urging that documentary filmmakers and lawyers and journalists cease their efforts to identify individuals who have been wrongfully convicted; I am suggesting that the recent obsession with claims of innocence has obscured the fact that innocence is a symptom of a larger, systemic corruption.

Thus, *The Thin Blue Line*, a film that led directly to Randall Dale Adams's release from death row, has nothing to do with the philosophical issue of the death penalty's moral legitimacy. Similarly, *Fourteen Days in May*, which details the final two weeks of the life of a death row inmate who suffered nearly every injustice that the capital punishment regime can serve up, ultimately elects to focus on the inmate's claim of innocence, thereby blunting the force of, and even obscuring, all else. . . .

Someone who believes that the death penalty is inherently wrong cheats by focusing solely on innocent inmates. Worse, this cheating tends to legitimate the increasingly entrenched legal doctrine that holds that unless an inmate can prove that he did not actually commit the crime for which he was sentenced, then virtually any constitutional violation can be overlooked. Surely innocence should matter, but it should not be all that matters. Constitutional values and moral norms are not applicable only to the wrongly accused.

NOTES & QUESTIONS

1.   Dow emphasizes that "Hollywood" movies about the death penalty — and non-Hollywood documentaries including *The Thin Blue Line* — "cheat" by focusing upon claims of innocence, rather than challenging the moral legitimacy of the death penalty. Do all narratives "cheat"? That is, as the section on legal storytelling in criminal cases in Chapter 10 of this text notes, narratives convert the complex stuff-of-life into tightly ordered forms. Narratives turn upon clear themes. Events are carefully selected, shaped, and ordered to create purposeful and forward plot-driven stories. Players then become characters (protagonists, antagonists, secondary characters). Surroundings are transformed into settings. Time is modified into "narrative" time that seldom is equivalent to literal clock time or simple chronology. Stylistic choices including perspective and point of view control and shape what is seen and heard, from where the action is viewed, how it is viewed, and how the audience responds to the events that are depicted. Can this shaping that stories undergo be distinguished from the "cheating" Dow describes?

2.   Post-conviction relief practice in death penalty cases is primarily a writing practice, as well as a storytelling practice. Unlike the testimony provided by witness participants in Errol Morris' *The Thin Blue Line*, the convicted inmate's story is usually told by an attorney in a written "brief." The inmate is not entitled automatically to an evidentiary hearing. Instead, the attorney representing a condemned inmate must persuade a judge in writing that she should be afforded an opportunity to represent witnesses and testimony. The brief is, of course, a fact-specific and legally specific story; it is not a theoretical argument against the "moral legitimacy" of the death penalty. That is, the core of the brief is narrative; it must retell the story that has already been certified as truthful in an appellate opinion affirming an inmate's conviction. To do this requires powerfully retelling the story anew, as a different story that requires a new ending. There are, of course, constraints upon this storytelling practice, e.g., the story must be true; certain facts are given; there is an opposing storyteller; parts of the story certified to be true must be changed; the audience is a judge rather than a jury; etc. To change the story, after re-investigating the crime, the attorney sometimes tells stories of an innocent defendant (actual innocence) akin to the story told by Errol Morris in *The Thin Blue Line*. But there are clearly other story themes depending upon the procedural posture and the requirements of the law. For example, stories with a theme of "betrayal" are common in post-conviction relief briefs. Here, the state actors or, perhaps, the convicted inmate's own attorney, have betrayed him and made it impossible to tell his story accurately and completely in a fair initial proceeding. For example, the state has withheld information about a plea agreement with a crucial witness testifying against the defendant. Alternatively the story may be about the law itself. For example, in a petition for certiorari the confused interpretation of a previous case or statute may be characterized as "the trouble," arriving to disturb a peaceful "steady state" in the law. The Supreme Court is then cast in the role of the hero to step in and to resolve the trouble, restoring order in the legal community. The form of the storytelling is akin to the mythology of a popular film about the Wild West. These written stories, as Dow observes about *The Thin Blue Line*, convert or transform legal arguments into thematic and plot-driven stories. Not all issues are given full consideration.

DO OR DIE: DOES *DEAD MAN WALKING* RUN?

Carole Shapiro

30 University of San Francisco Law Review 1143 (1996)

Sister Helen Prejean's book *Dead Man Walking* is passionately anti-capital punishment. When she began spiritually ministering to Louisiana Death Row inmates, she knew little about the issue. But her immersion in the efforts to save their lives made her an anti-death penalty activist. The book details Sister Prejean's work with survivors of murder victims and also makes both a religious and political case against executions. Although readers may ultimately disagree with the author, they can have no doubt about her stance on the death penalty or her reasons for opposing it.

The movie *Dead Man Walking*, however, which has been both a critical and box office success, fails to deliver the same unequivocal abolitionist punch as the book. Indeed, despite the author's statements that she "collaborated very closely with director/screenplay writer Tim Robbins in every line, every scene" of it, viewers are torn about whether or not this is even a film with an anti-capital punishment point of view. While many experience the movie as a strongly affecting statement against executions, others see it differently. One critic, for example, provoking a flurry of letters in the *Los Angeles Times*, went so far as to assert that Robbins tries "to manipulate audiences into a revenge mode." Another, Professor Hugo Bedau, celebrated for his books and articles on capital punishment, wrote in a letter to Sister Prejean that "if [*Dead Man Walking*] is a movie in opposition to the death penalty, I shudder at the thought of a movie intended to support [it]."

Some consider the disagreement over *Dead Man Walking's* message as virtue, proof of its "balance" and "evenhandedness." Although Wendy Lesser, author of *Pictures at an Execution*, criticized the film for other reasons, she asserted that Tim Robbins was "under no obligation to create a piece of anti-death penalty propaganda." Moreover, she said, his film should not be judged on his success in accomplishing that. While I agree with Lesser on this point, *Dead Man Walking* would have benefitted, without becoming mere agitprop, from adopting the book's more comprehensive take on the subject. Instead, Robbins' primary focus on the religious aspect of capital punishment leaves the audience clueless about the systemic inequities and arbitrariness that led Sister Prejean to abolitionist activism. And because the movie nun never gives direct voice to her death penalty opposition as a matter of principle, viewers are not sure exactly where she stands on the issue.

Given the high volume of today's law and order zeitgeist, the "balanced" *Dead Man Walking* is a lost opportunity to make an unambiguous statement against the death penalty. While several other capital punishment films are in the offing, including Sharon Stone's *Last Dance*, none will offer the confluence of art, politics, and talent that could have made *Dead Man Walking* a uniquely anti-death penalty movie. Whatever the movie's other achievements, its failure to translate the depth and breadth of the book's anti-execution position to the screen is disappointing.

NOTES & QUESTIONS

1.   When a book is brought to the big screen, the movie is invariably measured against the book on which it is based, and *Dead Man Walking* is no exception. Disappointed movie-goers tend to be those who, having read the book, expect to see a passionately abolitionist film adaptation. Instead, the story told on the screen is "balanced" in the sense that the suffering of the murder victims and the grief of their families is shown in vivid detail, as is the act of putting the offender to death, but the life circumstances of the offender or the fairness of the process by which he is selected for the death penalty are virtually ignored. Is this a true "balance," or was an important piece of the book's message omitted from the story told on the screen? What were your views on the death penalty before viewing the film? Did the screenplay move you in one direction or the other? Did it affect your pre-existing views on capital punishment?

2.   Matthew Poncelet, Sean Penn's character in *Dead Man Walking*, is not a real person. He is intended to be a composite of Patrick Sonnier and Robert Lee Willies, two death row inmates to whom Sister Helen ministered before and during their executions. The lawyer who represented both men, Millard Farmer, is critical of Director Tim Robbins for depicting Poncelet as racist and anti-Semitic. Farmer "knew the real death row inmate being portrayed. Farmer knew that the light in which Robbins was portraying the inmate's conduct was both unfair and unrepresentative of the many death row inmates Farmer has known and represented." Millard Farmer, Joe Nursey, Kimellen Tunkle & Steven Losch, *Death is Different: Reducing the Politically Acceptable Correct Executions Is Our Duty*, The Champion 19:9 (Nov. 1995) 9. Farmer writes that in contrast, Sister Helen's book "uses words to present the weaknesses of the persons described and, yet, recognizes the high personal dignity of each person portrayed . . . .[which] holds the book together and gives the book its power. The movie script pales greatly in comparison." *Id.* Do you agree that *Dead Man Walking* is a missed opportunity? Robbins purchased the intellectual property rights to the book. Does he have a duty to be faithful to the book's message in adapting it to the screen? Would the movie's message be diminished if it were more openly abolitionist?

3.   Compare Professor Haney's criticism of movies such as *Natural Born Killers* and *The Silence of the Lambs* with Shapiro's and Farmer's criticism of *Dead Man Walking*. Professor Haney argues that society is damaged by the depiction of criminals in film and news media "in what amounts to a social vacuum," based on empirical analysis of how criminals are portrayed in the news:

> We concluded that there was a heavy law enforcement and prosecutorial slant to the reporting, and that the stories focused repeatedly on particularistic details of the crimes themselves, to the exclusion of much else. Not surprisingly, perhaps, the most bizarre, heinous, or salacious details of the cases were the ones that received the most attention. We also found that "very little information was reported from which readers could develop a structural or contextual interpretation of the crime or any insight into the social historical roots of the defendant's criminality." Although we speculated that more balanced and complete news accounts of the causes of capital crime — ones that included more accurate information about the

influence of traumatic social histories and powerful social conditions — might lead to more informed public debate over the role of capital punishment in our system of justice, this perspective was rarely if ever presented in the stories we analyzed.

Craig Haney, *On Mitigation as Counter-Narrative: A Case Study of the Hidden Context of Prison Violence, in Symposium Issue: Death Penalty Stories*, 77 UMKC Law Review 911, 916-17 (2009).

Do you agree that the discussion of crime and punishment in the media is prosecution-slanted? Does media bias in reporting on crime and punishment issues have a negative impact on popular sentiment that may influence legislative policy? How else can one account for the excessive appetite for harsh punishment in the United States? Does Hollywood have a duty to provide a balanced message on social issues such as crime and punishment? Should it exercise better judgment in its depiction of crime and violence? To what extent are choices dictated by box office receipts? Can you envision a compelling anti-death-penalty story with popular appeal that does not involve an innocent protagonist?

G.   FORCED CONFORMITY AND THE HUMAN IDENTITY

Methods of criminal punishment attempt to strike a balance among societal goals which include retribution, deterrence, incapacitation, and rehabilitation. Most forms of punishment force a choice between one goal or another. The death penalty is retributive, but guarantees there will be no rehabilitation. Probation favors rehabilitation over retribution, while incarceration arguably advances the goals of incapacitation, deterrence, and retribution. The common aim of all punishments, however, is to enforce conformity with societal norms as reflected in the criminal law. There is a tension between that objective and the human dignity of offenders, who have the right to be treated as "uniquely individual human beings," rather than "as members of a faceless, undifferentiated mass." *Woodson v. North Carolina*, 428 U.S. 280, 304 (1976). To what extent does criminal punishment stifle the uniqueness which makes us human? How far should we go in our zeal to eliminate criminal behavior? If you put a clockwork in an orange, is it still an orange?

OIL AND WATER: WHY RETRIBUTION AND
REPENTANCE DO NOT MIX
Sherry F. Colb
22 Quinnipiac Law Review 59 (2003)

Many theorists probably have an instinctively negative response to the whole idea of therapeutic approaches to people who have engaged in criminal misconduct. Behavioral treatments for "bad" people, for example, have acquired a negative reputation in the popular media. Films like *A Clockwork Orange* suggest that such treatments are cruel and arbitrary. The nature of this reputation for cruelty, moreover, raises a second difficulty: perhaps operant conditioning is in fact a form of punishment. If so, might I be proposing that we substitute a cruel and arbitrary punishment for a more humane approach?

One could ultimately conclude that there is not much difference between behavioral treatment in a civil facility and criminal punishment in a prison. The U.S. Supreme Court has drawn an important constitutional line between the two, but some — including me — have criticized the line as artificial. Consider behavioral aversion therapy.

A Clockwork Orange critiques one kind of therapeutic approach to violence. Alex, the main character, a despicable person who savagely beats and rapes people for fun, is caught and held in a behavioral conditioning program in which he is given nausea-inducing drugs and then placed in front of a screen on which violent acts are depicted. Over time, he comes to have a visceral, nauseated reaction to violence, much as Pavlov's dogs began to salivate at the sound of a dinner bell. Alex then returns to the world, where he is unable to act violently, because of his conditioning. Since the world outside has not changed, however, he is vulnerable to the ubiquitous violence that may have made him the way he used to be in the first place. In addition, because the scenes of violence exhibited during his incarceration were accompanied by background music by his favorite composer, Beethoven, he is also robbed of his taste for "Ludwig Van." This is punishment indeed, and it changes its recipient into someone who literally *cannot* commit the crimes of which he used to be guilty.

Though the aversion therapy in *A Clockwork Orange* is punishment, [Professor Herbert] Morris would almost certainly not consider it a legitimate form of punishment. It does deliberately inflict suffering upon the subject in response to his past misconduct, and thus would perhaps satisfy some retributivists. It does not, however, bring suffering as a component of reaching out and mending a rift that the target has created between himself and society. It does not address and communicate with him at an intellectual or moral level, but rather uses his biological systems as an instrument (or a weapon) for altering his behavior. The fact that Alex's love of Beethoven is demolished in the process perhaps exemplifies the extent to which the experience of aversion therapy bypasses the conscious, intellectual, and autonomous being.

In real life, some physicians have used forms of aversion therapy to try to "cure" people of homosexuality. Such cures have not proven successful, and the entire enterprise of "reparative therapy" is ethically questionable and independently troubling. However, if it did succeed, its mode of operation would be to bypass the conscious mind and manipulate people without appealing to their higher natures. In this regard, we inflict suffering on a target as the means to his alteration rather than as a communicative act designed to convey condemnation and address and reach the target's moral sensitivities.

If communication is the goal of punishment, however, one must consider what it means to communicate moral outrage effectively. Presumably, simply stating "you did a bad thing" would not suffice, or punishment would be unnecessary. Though Morris is not a utilitarian, his model for retribution does appear to presuppose — as all deontological theories do — some core principles about human nature. It assumes, for example, that one can communicate with another's higher mental faculties as a means of recommending attitude adjustment. One purpose of punishment — the infliction of suffering as a just response to crime — is to speak with emphasis. As mentioned earlier, it is akin to a metaphorical exclamation point at the end of the sentence: "you have done wrong and offended our way of life."

NOTES & QUESTIONS

1. Professor Herbert Morris advocates humane and respectful punishment of those found guilty of crime and views the retributive value of punishment as an essential component of integrating the offender back into society. Yet he would presumably condemn aversion therapy because, "What must be aimed at is that the afflicted become autonomous not automatons. There must be freedom to disobey, for the moral price is too high that is paid in purchasing immunity from temptation and guaranteed conformity." *See* Herbert Morris, *A Paternalistic Theory of Punishment*, 18 American Philosophical Quarterly 263, 269 (1981). Do you agree? What is the "moral price" that Professor Morris deems too high?

2. Anthony Burgess writes in his novel, "It is as inhuman to be totally good as it is to be totally evil. The important thing is moral choice." Anthony Burgess, *A Clockwork Orange* 190 (1967). The seventeenth-century French author Francois de la Rochefoucauld said that a man does not deserve praise for his goodness unless he has the strength of character to do evil. Why is moral choice so highly valued? How does it compare to the social harm Alex committed before his conditioning "cured" him of his violent urges?

3. One of the advantages of examining social issues through literature, especially science fiction, is the ability to play "what if." *A Clockwork Orange*, paints a dark and disturbing picture of the involuntary use of operant conditioning to "rehabilitate" Alex's criminal mind. The late Professor Bruce Winick, widely known as a compassionate humanitarian, said, "Behaviorism, at least the radical behaviorism associated with B.F. Skinner — evoking the spectre of manipulative behavior modification of the *A Clockwork Orange* variety — has gotten a bad name." Bruce Winick, *Harnessing the Power of the Bet: Wagering with the Government as a Mechanism for Social and Individual Change*, 45 University of Miami Law Review 737, 739 (1991). He proposes a form of operant conditioning he describes as "wagering" to address behavioral problems. For example, the government would "bet" a drug addict $1,000 that he could not kick the habit for a specified period of time and would provide therapy, treatment, and drug testing to assist in achieving the goal of remaining drug-free for at least six months. If the individual failed, he would experience an agreed-upon sanction, perhaps a forfeiture of money paid into escrow (negative reinforcement). If the individual succeeded, he would receive his agreed upon reward, i.e. a job, or $1,000 cash (positive reinforcement). The offer to wager would have to be accepted by the addict, and thus would be the product of a voluntary choice, which would necessarily bring a higher degree of commitment to the endeavor and a correspondingly greater likelihood of success. The ethical issues are resolved by the requirement of a mutual agreement specifying treatment goals and procedures. How is this different from the behavioral therapy depicted in *A Clockwork Orange*? Considering that incarceration can cost upwards of $30,000 per person per year, do you see this as a practical alternative? Do you think such a system could effectively deal with violent offenders? What should be done with offenders who refuse to participate? If there is a consequence for refusal to participate, is participation truly voluntary? Is Professor Winick's proposal different from *A Clockwork Orange* in its nature or simply in degree? Where is the line between rehabilitation and destruction of free will?

4.   The films and literature discussed in this chapter grapple with the vexing question of what to do with the common criminal, regarded by today's society as the lowest of the low. The subject matter itself compels the artist to deal with themes common to great literature: struggle against conflict, man's inhumanity to man, and the triumph of the human spirit in the face of adversity. No other area of law presents as compelling a case for the study of the human condition and narratives that reveal both the frailties of mankind and the innate human dignity of each individual. By examining the treatment of the criminal in popular culture, we can gage the evolving standards of decency that mark our maturing society.

Part III

LEGAL SUBJECT AREAS

Chapter 9

TORT LAW

A. FILMOGRAPHY

A Civil Action (1999)

Erin Brockovich (2000)

The Insider (1999)

Philadelphia (1993)

The Verdict (1982)

B. TORTS IN POPULAR CULTURE

The tort seems to be everywhere in popular culture, even if its users recognize it only as a plot device. Both television and film use it as a vehicle to propel the plot, in comedies as well as dramas. From the slip on the ubiquitous banana peel or the icy sidewalk to the look in the side window by the nosy neighbor and the overly ambitious reporter, and on to the negligent shipment of the misassembled coffee maker and the house built over the intentionally buried toxic waste dump, the tort is grist for popular culture's story mill. Through their uses in narrative, however, tort stories do serve as a way for us to consider our relationships to one another and to reflect on our social responsibilities. Those are among the reasons torts continue to intrigue us and to form the basis of what seems to be a never-ending series of films, television episodes, and, sometimes, commercials. After all, many successful advertising campaigns are formed around slips, falls, and misadventures of the sort to which viewers can relate. Think about that talking duck ready to hand out cash to the forward-thinking insured person who has been injured.

Is the "tort film" a separate genre? At least one law and popular culture scholar thinks so.

CIVIL ACTION CINEMA
Anthony Chase
1999 Law Review of Michigan State University
Detroit College of Law 945 (1999)

While there are films touching upon such civil law issues as libel and slander, divorce, child custody, civil commitment, denaturalization, and no doubt others, I will focus on movies dealing with torts, what lawyers succinctly refer to as non-criminal wrongs. What I like to call *the master discourse of tort cinema* was established in four films made during the fifteen-year period between 1982 and 1997: *The Verdict, Class Action, Philadelphia*, and *The Rainmaker.* It is important to note the similarity between these four films, which taken together can be seen as expressing a single story or narrative, in spite of the fact that each film is directed by an individual stylist or auteur, respectively, Sydney Lumet, Michael Apted, Jonathan Demme, and Francis Ford Coppola. The force of generic conventions was sufficient to effectively restrain the otherwise strong personalities and cinematic idiosyncrasies of these four directors while working within the master discourse.

In *The Verdict*, Paul Newman plays Frank Galvin, a down on his luck, alcoholic, negligence lawyer who almost forgets to show for the case of a lifetime. Oddly, this cornerstone of tort cinema is most usually debated by lawyers and law professors as a film about ethics and professional discipline, rather than for the legal context of the film itself, its substantive law focus. Of course *The Verdict* is about good and bad lawyering. Not surprisingly, the film's audiences were at least as interested in whether Galvin would rally in time to save the day as they were in whether he had an obligation under the ABA Code of Professional Responsibility to notify his clients, for example, of a settlement offer. But the film is also, crucially in my view, about medical malpractice, one of the most important areas within the entire field of American tort law.

Galvin represents the family of a plaintiff who has suffered irreversible brain damage as a result of the way anaesthesia was administered during a routine medical procedure. In the movie's decisive scene, Galvin examines a nurse on the witness stand who effectively implicates the defendant physician in a plot to alter documents in order to hide his own responsibility for causing grievous harm. Galvin's closing argument to the jury — "Act as if you believe and faith will be given to you," — provides a remarkable restatement of Dean Prosser's general theory of torts: the courts are there to do justice but we have to believe in the system itself before we will take the risks, and go to the trouble, to make use of those courts.

Now there is, on the one hand, a certain similarity between *The Verdict's* story line and that of some criminal trial films. Take, for example, *True Believer*, in which James Woods plays Eddie Dodd, a down and out, formerly brilliant, now pot-smoking defense attorney available to any drug dealer who will take him on as counsel and can pay the fee in cash. Just as Frank Galvin gets that unique, dreamed of, potentially redemptive case, so does Eddie Dodd. For each lawyer, the big case moves gradually from the periphery of consciousness to the very center of their being. It becomes an obsession. Winning is not just winning any longer. Justice in a particular case, economic survival, professional prestige, personal salvation, and the credibility of the legal system itself, all hinge on their heroic struggle to see that the rule of law prevails.

But prevails over what? In *True Believer*, it is the cops and district attorney who set up Dodd's innocent client to take the fall for something he did not do. For them, the end justifies the means; they sacrifice an anonymous street kid and gang member in order to protect from public scrutiny the police department's own involvement with drug informants and drug dealers. The target of Galvin's advocacy in *The Verdict*, however, is quite different; physicians and the hospital where they practice medicine, the church hierarchy which funds the hospital, and the high-powered malpractice defense firm that represents them at trial.

Again, the stories themselves are structurally similar. Art critic Lawrence Alloway, in a very interesting essay on violent American movies, which was written to accompany a film series shown at the Museum of Modern Art in New York, points out that motion pictures "are dominated by conventions and can be grouped in cycles. . . . In movies the actors are as stereotyped as, say, the young hero or the old warrior types in Renaissance portraiture." Lawrence Alloway, *Violent America: The Movies, 1946-1964* 7 (1971). So the cross-generic (criminal law film/tort law film) superimposition of Eddie Dodd onto the silhouette of Frank Galvin should come as no surprise.

And we can even apply Alloway's offhand illustration to the particular iconography, if you will, of tort cinema. Just as we find "the young hero" in *Rainmaker's* Rudy Baylor, we can also see "the old (or aging) warrior," in *The Verdict's* Frank Galvin. "Situations," Alloway further argues, "are as recurrent in movies as the set themes of speeches in Seneca's plays, such as 'the simple life speech,' 'the haunted grove speech,' and 'the king must be obeyed speech,' to quote E.F. Watling." *Id.*

A highly significant example of the sort of recurrent situations identified by Alloway, but within the genre of tort films, is what might be described as the *how I almost didn't get the client* scene. In *The Rainmaker*, Rudy Baylor (Matt Damon) has to get past rusty gates and barking guard dogs to get the signatures of an exhausted mother and a war-injured veteran, who is "not right in the head," on a contingent fee agreement, so that he can represent their son who is dying of bone cancer. The latter, bleeding from the nose onto crucial documents, heroically signs his own name to the contract.

In *Philadelphia*, a homophobic attorney, played by Denzel Washington, actually rejects his first opportunity to represent HIV infected fellow-lawyer, Andrew Beckett, who has been fired from his prestigious law firm position for alleged "incompetence," right after being promoted within the firm. Crusading plaintiffs' rights attorney Jedediah Tucker (Gene Hackman), in *Class Action*, stands in line to get his client, whom he reels in by telling him that "these bastards think they do anything they want [but] they don't always get away with it . . . once in awhile people like us, this law firm, we stop them. This is going to be one of those times."

And in *The Verdict*, Frank Galvin tapes a note to his office door and goes to a bar to drink scotch and play pinball while his clients cool their heels in the hallway of a dingy office building where Galvin (former editor of the Boston College Law Review) stores his metal filing cabinets, but is generally too hung over to practice law (he has had four cases in court in the last three years). Again, *True Believer* is cut from the same cloth. Eddie Dodd is almost too stoned to answer the door to his office (where he now also lives in the back room) when an elderly Korean woman, mother of the falsely imprisoned Shu Kai Kim, comes to beg for Eddie's help. And just as Frank Galvin has a colleague and friend (Jack Warden) to sober him up just in time, and guide him along the way, Eddie Dodd has an idealistic young assistant, himself just graduated from the Michigan Law Review staff, who points Eddie in the right direction.

But what is crucially *different* about the tort film genre, or subgenre, as I suggested above, is the target, "who *they* are" as a grizzled Edmond O'Brien put it in Peckinpaw's *The Wild Bunch* — who its viewers can look forward to seeing impaled in the last act. Like every Criminal Law teacher, I spent years telling first year students that the reason the plaintiff in criminal law cases is always the government is that these are public, not private, actions. And movies, in their way, reflect the same reality; the villain of the piece in tort cinema is private power, not public.

So private parties, yes, but why villains? It makes perfect sense to ask why the master discourse of tort cinema, engraved frame by frame on public consciousness by *The Verdict, Class Action, Philadelphia,* and *The Rainmaker,* should have developed the way it did, *when* it did. We are now, and have been at least since Reagan's election in 1980, in a fourth period in the history of a developing regime of American tort law and litigation. This fourth, global capitalist, period seems to be one, on balance, of retrenchment in the state capitalist, Traynoresque transformation of tort liability — conservative backlash often peddled under the heading of tort reform. We might reasonably anticipate a tort cinema during this period which would mirror the current "structure of feeling" (as Raymond Williams would have put it) — the value system, in short, of a vigorous, anti-lawyer, anti-liability, corporate rollback of progressive tort law and practice.

But that is not what we have been getting from Hollywood torts. How come? Maybe the persistence of state capitalist tort values in the present period (see, e.g., anti-tobacco and anti-firearms litigation) is pushing pro-plaintiff motion pictures to the forefront. Maybe Hollywood is still run by communists (that, for the record, is a joke). Perhaps the movies enjoy something more than merely "relative autonomy" from the social and economic infrastructure (i.e., they are lost in space). But I can think of another explanation which seems to me better than these.

The targets on which these four films train their sights are, respectively, the medical profession and its defense bar, the automobile industry, employers who discriminate against minorities and the disabled in their hiring practices, and the insurance industry. In other words, basically, (crooked) corporate America. Eddie Dodd's world can easily be turned on its head and both the police and district attorneys, *True Believer's* nemeses, can be made into heroes, with a snap of the fingers (television, especially, does so night after night). But Frank Galvin's or Rudy Baylor's world? Corporations switching places with the victims of medical malpractice or insurance fraud, with the snap of the fingers? Now there is a challenge.

A steep challenge, to be sure, though not (depending on your view of business ethics) because corporations are inherently bad but, rather, because there do not seem to be readily available stories or narrative structures within which corporations can be fit in as champions. Somewhere, Fredric Jameson describes how the European novel had to go through a period analogous to what Marx described in economics as the stage of capital accumulation — only in the case of fiction, it is the stage of primitive accumulation of narratable forms. Corporate America in the movies seems to me a tad short on narratable hero figures and formations. From Robert Wise's *Executive Suite* in the 1950s through Oliver Stone's *Wall Street* in the 1980s, business has tended to look less like a public profession, than it has a highly specialized branch of organized crime.

Let us assume, for a moment, that this is actually the main stumbling block. "As persons appropriate from the common repertoire of legal schemes and resources," says Ewick and Silbey, "they are constrained by what is available, by legality as it has been previously enacted by others." Patricia Ewick & Susan S. Silbey, *The Common Place of Law: Stories from Everyday Life* 247 (1998). And just so with motion picture producers, story consultants, screenwriters, and directors making films about torts. Lots of models of lonely, struggling, lawyers who ultimately prevail on behalf of the little guy; but precious few scenarios in the script file which you would headline: *corporation makes good*. The corporate entity, according to buckskin lawyer and popular raconteur, Gerry Spence, "has been created to perform but one function: to seek profit. In the fulfillment of that objective, it is as mindless as any machine and as soulless as any cement mixer." Gerry Spence, *Give Me Liberty!: Freeing Ourselves in the Twenty-First Century* 76 (1998).

So what's a corporation to do? Two hours of a little girl spilling milk on her pinafore, while explaining that her daddy works for a lumber or chemical company which wants to make sure the grass the cows eat in the meadow is safe for animals so that milk will be safe for kids? Does that sound like something you would pay eight dollars to see? Even the thirty-second version provokes massive, home-based, channel surfing. Several pages into *Fortune* magazine's 1999 "Fortune 500" issue, Hoechst AG of Frankfurt, Germany, has a two-page spread whose theme is spelled out boldly: The chemical company is putting its heart into putting an end to heart and circulatory disease.

Better, obviously, than bravely committing your company to employment of slave laborers in Nazi Germany, for which Hoechst (along with Bayer and BASF, spokes in the wheel of death which was I.G. Farben) was convicted at Nuremberg and for this conduct, the pieces of the deceptively disassembled Farben chemical combine are now being sued around the world.

Could Hoechst's glossy business magazine advertising approach somehow imply a story line, the model for a narrative structure which could be incorporated into some new tort film discourse? Or, conversely, could new wine be poured into old wine skins? In Henry Hathaway's *Call Northside 777*, Jimmy Stewart, playing a crusading big city reporter, clears the name of mistakenly-jailed cop killer, Frank Wiecek (Richard Conte). Just as James Woods, in *True Believer*, clears his client's name and springs him from prison, and Stewart accomplishes the same trick in the Hathaway picture, could a reclusive and rather unsympathetic, old line Boston law firm attorney rise to the occasion, and clear the name of a victimized corporation, a company falsely accused of, say, poisoning the drinking water of a whole Massachusetts community?

I suppose that is one way of looking at Steven Zailian's 1998 motion picture, *A Civil Action*, which deals with a court case arising from leukemia deaths attributed to chemical pollutants contaminating the water supply of Woburn, Massachusetts. The attorney for Beatrice Foods, Jerome Facher, played by academy-award nominated, Robert Duvall, does get his corporate employers off the hook. And Jan Schlichtmann, played with remarkable conviction by John Travolta, does have some of the negative personal characteristics of Walter Mathau's William Gingrich in Billy Wilder's *The Fortune Cookie* — not a trial film but a tort film, certainly, and one which broke the tort film mold, so to speak, even before there *was* a mold. Many fans of Jonathan Harr's detailed legal account, on which *A Civil Action* is based (especially lawyers and law students), did not find the film nearly tough enough on the judge, the corporations, or Schlichtmann's opposing counsel. So one might regard the movie as an important new departure in tort cinema.

But one of the two corporations featured in the film, W.R. Grace & Co., did not see it that way. On the contrary, they even set up a web page on the internet to get the truth out, suggesting that Jonathan Harr's book effectively falsifies the truth, by what it leaves out. The film, according to the Grace web page, is no more honest than Harr's book and is, by implication, one more example of Hollywood liberal bias. Interviewed at Grace's headquarters in Boca Raton, Florida, by a *Miami Herald* business reporter, a Grace spokesperson expressed disappointment that the producers of *A Civil Action* failed to provide W.R. Grace with any opportunity whatever to help tell the story of the Woburn tragedy.

The remarkably deferential *Herald* reporter did not ask, for example, whether Grace felt Steven Spielberg should have granted the German government or, for that matter, a representative group of Nazi war criminals, an opportunity to edit the *Schindler's List* shooting script prior to production. But Grace's protests were themselves sufficient to make the point. *A Civil Action* picks on the same culprit as other mainstream tort films: corporate America. Thus, *A Civil Action* obeys the rules of the master discourse or genre code — and not just with respect to the crucial issue of villains and heroes either. The film also includes its own remarkable version of the mandatory, *how I almost didn't get the client* scene, one where Jan Schlichtmann actually has to park his Porsche by a highway bridge and climb down onto the muddy shoals of a polluted stream, in his expensive leather dress shoes, to see for himself just what has been done to the hapless residents of Woburn by Beatrice and W.R. Grace.

But there is one big difference between *A Civil Action* and the other tort films I have discussed here. To be sure, the dragon who must be slain by the lawyer/knight errant is, in all five films, as I have said, a private power broker or megathug. The thing is that in *A Civil Action*, unlike the other films, the bad guys win. As soon as I read that Harr's book was being made into a movie, I was both intrigued and perplexed by the enterprise. How could the end of *A Civil Action* be accommodated to the *is the jury limited in its damage award to the amount the plaintiff is seeking?* scene which, more or less, provides a stunning, and deeply satisfying, climax to the master discourse films? Conversely, if the facts were made to fit the fiction, cf., *Liberty Valance*: "When the legend becomes fact, print the legend," would the filmmakers actually have Beatrice and Grace both *lose*, even perhaps be forced to apologize, on screen, to the Woburn parents who lost their children, something which still has not happened, in fact, to this day?

As I see it, the filmmakers bit the bullet and let *the chips fall where they may*, or, better, actually did. The chemical polluters basically get off scot-free in *A Civil Action*, and it is the admirable (and I think quite heroic) but nevertheless defeated, nearly destroyed in fact, Jan Schlichtmann who ends up holding the bag. When he turns down what he regards as a pathetic settlement offer from Jerome Facher, Schlichtmann explains that a settlement would not be right, would not be fair to the children who died. Facher brutally responds that it stopped being about them the moment the first pleadings were filed. In the final scene, where Schlichtmann is shown as a petitioner in bankruptcy court, the presiding judge asks him what he has to show for all his years of high-flying trial lawyering, where are the objects by which people in our kind of society measure their personal worth? Clearly these are critical scenes.

Although it is not what Facher meant, in one profoundly important respect, the case *did* stop being about the children as soon as lawyers got involved, i.e., once the case was absorbed by the American legal process. Because that process, quite simply, is not about children, or facts, or personal responsibility, or justice, or anything remotely like that. It is about money. And corporations have more money than everyone else. They can pay their attorneys more and last longer and usually win; certainly when they are dragged into court, kicking and screaming, by the powerless.

John F. Kennedy was fond of quoting Harry Truman's remark that ten million Americans can afford to send lobbyists to Washington to look after their interests. Everybody else has to depend on the President of the United States. If most Americans have to depend on *tort law* to enforce their interests against corporate capitalism, they have not got a chance. That, I think, is the meaning of *A Civil Action*, and that is not something which can readily be fit into the reigning tort film paradigm — elaborated in *The Verdict, Class Action, Philadelphia*, and *The Rainmaker*. So, in this sense, *A Civil Action* does indeed cause a new wrinkle in the otherwise smooth fabric of the tort film genre. In this case, a non-fiction source helped replenish, indeed change the stock, piling up in the great storehouse of (tort cinema's) narratable forms. That is exactly how all literary and cinematic genres change over time, reflecting new, and sometimes bitter, realities.

At the same time, however, *A Civil Action* is not itself without cinematic precedent. Both with respect to its true life source and, significantly, its bleak conclusion, *A Civil Action* closely tracks Mike Nichols' *Silkwood*. Both films have the guts to name names, (Beatrice/Grace in *A Civil Action* and Kerr-McGee in *Silkwood*) and while one would not normally think of the Nichols' picture as a tort film, since it lacks lawyers and trials, it targets nuclear power in the same way that each of the tort films I have discussed arraigns a particular company or industry.

The climax of *Silkwood* comes when Karen Silkwood, attempting to deliver key documents (about Kerr-McGee's doctoring of atomic fuel rods) to a waiting *New York Times* reporter, is apparently run off the road in her Honda and killed.

Amazing Grace floods the soundtrack as Nichols reveals this appalling conclusion to the Karen Silkwood story. Although Karen herself, through her decision to join the union and her commitment to stopping Kerr McGee in its tracks may, in a sense, have been lost, but then found, the documents she was carrying that night have never been found. In 1979, a federal court required Kerr-McGee to pay the Silkwood estate 10.5 million dollars in damages as a consequence of the corporation's negligent treatment of Silkwood on the job.

Between Silkwood's death in 1974, and the 1983 release of Nichols' film about her battle for plant safety, another film was made about the nuclear power industry and this one too seemed based on Silkwood's experience. In *The China Syndrome*, released in 1979, virtually simultaneously with the Three Mile Island near-meltdown, a television station employee is shown driving at high speed to get photographs documenting plant construction fraud to a public regulatory hearing on nuclear power plants. He too is run off the road and killed, and in this fiction film, even less ambiguity marks who is responsible for the deadly vehicular ambush.

Some critics might tend to regard *Silkwood* and *The China Syndrome* as poor examples of precursors to *A Civil Action* since they are less "tort films" than "conspiracy films." Catching some of the same flack directed toward Oliver Stone's *JFK*, the two nuclear power films may be written off as further examples of what historian Richard Hofstadter, in a very different context, called "the paranoid style of American politics." But it is important to recall for the moment a simple fact, familiar to any lawyer, that the essence of conspiracy is not secrecy — let alone paranoia — but, rather, *agreement*. In other words, what makes a conspiracy charge so appealing to prosecutors is that it can be made out simply by providing sufficient evidence that two or more individuals have entered into an agreement to commit a crime. The defendants do not have to actually commit the crime itself - the agreement is the conduct part of the crime of conspiracy.

What *China Syndrome*, *Silkwood*, and *A Civil Action* have in common is just this sense of agreement, the notion that the people who run the television stations, the courts, the regulatory agencies, and industries which are hazardous to your health have basically entered into an agreement to make sure that nothing is allowed to threaten the bottom line, i.e., profits. Law does not have a chance when confronted with this agreement, this horizontal plane of combined social action, also termed "social class."

Describing the process by which Karl Marx became a Marxist, the author of *Delightful Murder*, quoted earlier, records that while still a young man, Marx discovered a contradiction between this ideal [Hegelian] notion of the state and the fact that the *Stande* (estates) represented in the provincial diet of the Rhineland strove to "drag the state down to the level of the idea of private interest." In other words, as soon as he tackled a current political problem — namely, the new law on the theft of wood — he came up against the problem of social classes. The state, which ought to embody the "general interest," seemed to be acting merely on behalf of private property, and, in order to do this, was violating not only the logic of law but even some obvious principles of humanity.

And when a serious journalist and filmmaker tackle a current tort problem, like that of the Woburn catastrophe, they come up against the problem of social classes.

The Massachusetts court, which should have embodied the general interest of the Commonwealth, violated not only the logic of law but even some painfully evident principles of humanity, in effectively insulating chemical companies from any real responsibility for the harm they caused. In *A Civil Action*, Jan Schlichtmann is compelled to relearn the same early lesson taught to Marx, in the nineteenth century, by the new law on the theft of wood. It seems to be a lesson that we are unable, or perhaps unwilling, to learn once and for all. In *A Civil Action*, Jan Schlichtmann takes to heart Frank Galvin's advice, "Act as if you believe. . . ." and, as a consequence, his life virtually disintegrates. By contrast, the master discourse represents (in dialectical tension) both a fantasy about the tort system and the dream of a better world.

NOTES & QUESTIONS

1. Does Professor Chase convince you that interpretative themes tend to run through "tort films," at least those tort films made in the past two to three decades? What about tort films made before 1980? If not, do you see any similarities of theme or structure in tort films that would lead you to believe they are a film genre? As you watch the films discussed in this chapter and other pop cultural tort narratives, what, if anything, do you think binds them together? Professor Chase continues his discussion in *Movies On Trial: The Legal System on the Silver Screen* (2002). For another view of the tort film genre, see Michael McCann and William Haltom, *Review Essay: Ordinary Heroes vs. Failed Lawyers — Public Interest Litigation in Erin Brockovich and Other Contemporary Films*, 33 Law & Social Inquiry 1045 (2008).

2. Think about films that networks offer up as "made for television movies." If these movies include torts as the issue that drives the plot, could they constitute a genre as well? The website "TV Tropes and Idioms" suggests that the familiar "Lifetime Movie of the Week" can follow certain themes that appeal to a particular demographic — for example, domestic violence, child care, divorce, and single parent issues. *See* http://tvtropes.org/pmwiki/pmwiki.php/Main/LifetimeMovie OfTheWeek. Could "made for television movies" seize on such themes as well? Consider in this regard a "made for television movie" such as *A Cry for Help: The Tracy Thurman Story* (Lifetime, 1989), based on the case of a woman who was attacked and nearly killed by her ex-husband despite the fact that she had a restraining order against him. The local police refused to assist her, and she filed a lawsuit against the city, claiming a violation of her civil rights. *See Thurman v. City of Torrington*, 595 F. Supp. 1521 (D. Ct., 1984). The case raised awareness of the reluctance of police departments to intervene in domestic violence cases and resulted in the passage of Connecticut's Family Violence Act of 1986 (Thurman's Law). Are such television movies driven by the human interest story, the tort issue, the desire for ratings, one or more of these, or all three?

3. Unfortunately, many Lifetime movies are not available on DVD. What do you think accounts for this embargo?

C. TORTFEASORS, VICTIMS, WITNESSES, AND ATTORNEYS

Tracing out the "truth" in a pop cultural work can be difficult, especially since the film, television show, or novel presents its own point of view and wants to persuade the viewer or reader of the rightness of that point of view. This difficulty is evident in the much-discussed *A Civil Action*, a film focusing on attorney Jan Schlictmann, played by John Travolta, who develops and pursues a complicated tort claim. One could argue that Schlichtmann is not a particularly sympathetic figure, and not simply because he fails to see the signals that taking the case to trial rather than settling is not a good strategy. Or one could argue that Schlichtmann is a heroic but tragic figure, who sacrifices his career for his clients (though perhaps he need not have done so). But one certainly has sympathy for the clients, who are suffering tragic health problems. These plaintiffs allege that they are the victims of someone's actions — the question is whose. One also can view the behavior of the defendant companies named in *A Civil Action* with a jaundiced eye. These companies seem to have acted improperly and put the local residents' health at risk.

At first glance, the film seems to lay out a rather unsophisticated "David and Goliath" story. But, as Steve Greenfield, Guy Osborn, and Peter Robson point out, the movie is somewhat more complex, and troubling, than we might expect. In their opinion, the film suggests both the upside and the downside of big-ticket speculative litigation. Schlichtmann achieves a settlement with one of the corporate tortfeasors but not the other. He also files for bankruptcy and considers committing suicide. More fundamentally, does Schlichtmann succeed in making the companies legally responsible to the community? Perhaps he does not or cannot. As Greenfield, Osborn, and Robson put it, "The difficulties of framing and winning a legal case are related to issues of causation, and evidence of poisoning, and the vast cost of bringing such an action, is stressed throughout." Steve Greenfield, Guy Osborn, & Peter Robson, *Film and the Law* 69 (2001).

NOTES & QUESTIONS

1. Is it possible to see past the images of the plaintiff's lawyer, whatever you might think of him, in *A Civil Action*, and the case he builds for his clients, to the case that the defendants' attorneys are building for their clients? Do films such as *A Civil Action* "stack the deck" against the defendants, persuading you that being a plaintiff's attorney is morally preferable (if not financially preferable) to being a member of the defense bar? Consider another film in which the potential defendants might actually be as attractive, or almost as attractive as the plaintiff: the 1982 film *Absence of Malice*. In that film, Megan Carter, a reporter for a Miami newspaper played by Sally Field, writes an article about a local businessman named Michael Gallagher, played by Paul Newman, based on false information fed to her by a U.S. Attorney. The businessman may have a cause of action for defamation. In a crucial (and famous) scene, the newspaper's attorney explains to Megan what "public figure" status and "absence of malice" mean. If the businessman is a public figure, he would have to show actual malice or reckless disregard on the part of the paper when it published the article (*see Curtis Publishing Co. v. Butts*, 388 U.S. 130 (1967); *Associated Press v. Walker*, 389 U.S. 28 (1967)), but if he is a private figure,

he would only have to meet the negligence standard (*see Gertz v. Robert Welch, Inc.,* 418 U.S. 323 (1974)).

2. Films about torts often discuss settlements and awards in the millions of dollars. Do you think it is difficult for viewers to contemplate such astronomical payments without feeling even a little envious of the victims? Or do you think viewers can feel sorry for the real individuals behind the characters (assuming the films are based on true stories)? After all, the characters on the screen have been "cleaned up" for viewing. Does Hollywood give a vaguely accurate picture of the pain and suffering that tort victims like those in *A Civil Action* or the other films discussed in this chapter undergo?

3. Wanting one's day in court — as opposed to an apology — is often the stated reason for filing a lawsuit. However, for the tort victim, the road to filing the lawsuit can be very long, and the considerations can be profound and profoundly felt. For many people, the offer of a settlement, even a relatively small one, can outweigh the dangers of an adverse jury verdict. But settlements do not necessarily make exciting film or television scenes, so we do not often see them dramatized, except as run-ups to more heart-pounding courtroom confrontations, as in *A Civil Action* or *The Verdict*. In addition, a confrontational scene, pitting an angry plaintiff's lawyer, or victim, against a previously powerful defendant, can be profoundly cathartic. For many people, a "day in court" does not simply represent a right they believe they have. It represents a rite of passage. When they see it dramatized on screen, they celebrate an emotional victory with the character who obtains it.

Thus, depending on the narrative, the fictional tort victim can represent the experience of the viewer, and the treatment the victim receives can symbolize the treatment the viewer thinks she can expect. Victory often comes in the form of money, sometimes with an apology. Rarely does the lawyer hop up to remind the joy-filled plaintiff that she will have to share a third or more of her check with him. That would be too great a dose of reality intruding into Hollywood happiness.

Happiness, and a happy ending, is often the key to the tort film narrative. Consider that many of the actions brought in tort films are, frankly, difficult for plaintiffs to win. Consequently, the defendants must look not simply negligent, but recklessly, relentlessly, evil, and their attorneys must be caught in the wildest of unethical schemes.

4. How do filmmakers evoke particular reactions about tort victims in their films? Here is one noted critic's response concerning the film *The Verdict*.

PATTERNS OF COURTROOM JUSTICE
Jessica Silbey
28 Journal of Law and Society 97 (2001)

At the climax — the trial toward which all of the film's energy has been directed — the camera hangs back from the activity in the courthouse, easily losing sight of and focus on the central character of the film, Francis Galvin (played by Paul Newman). He fades into the woodwork behind the plaintiff's table, is lost around the labyrinthine corridors of the courthouse, is blocked by the balconies and the columns inside the building. He is the underdog in this case of medical malpractice, an alcoholic plaintiff's attorney who has seemingly during the course of the film tragically bungled what would have been his first winnable case in over three years. The lack of the camera's focus on Galvin suggests his own weakness and his ambivalence toward the legal system which we learn bas cost him his job and his integrity due to corrupt colleagues from years past. He has become a pawn of the system, a stereotype of an ambulance-chaser, and as such, his figure and his lifestyle are completely dominated — taken over — by the structure of the courthouse.

The trial drags on for several days and straddles a weekend. With each witness, Galvin's case grows weaker and the anticipation of the trial's outcome bodes only tragedy. During the examination of these witnesses, the viewer-subject is made to simultaneously participate in and judge the trial's progress by being placed in critical roles and by cueing key relationships between the characters. Galvin's expert witness, for example, has been bought off by the defence to flee the jurisdiction and Galvin is instead stuck with an incredible general practitioner to counter the reputations of the world-renowned obstetricians who sit accused of malpractice. During the expert testimony, the judge, already angered by Galvin's poor performance, takes it upon himself to question the witness, a permissible if uncommon practice. During this exchange, the camera films the two men — the expert witness and the judge — in contrast. From the judge's bench, the camera teeters over the edge, looking down in a canted shot of the doctor, reinforcing his incredible testimony. From the witness stand, the camera looks up at the judge who peers over the side of his bench and who fills the screen as he fires harsh criticism down toward the witness and at his weak testimony. The close-up shots and the relational editing in this exchange neatly demonize both characters who both turn out to equally damage Galvin's sympathetic, however losing case. The viewer-subject is made uncomfortable in the position of witness and judge, unable to empathize with either character in this scene; in this alienating exchange, one strongly feels that the role of judge or expert will frustrate the legal system's hortatory goal.

In contrast, during the testimony of plaintiff's surprise rebuttal witness, Kaitlin Costello Price, the camera does not film her testimony from the judge's bench as if to criticize, but from the plaintiff's desk and the jury box as if in compassion and support. When Ms. Price gives her startling testimony — direct evidence of the obstetricians' malpractice — she is filmed close-up and straight on. The camera does not belittle her by filming her from above, nor does it aggrandize her from below. And despite the fact that the defence attorney, in all attempts to discredit her testimony, looms above her as she sits in the witness stand, the camera sides with Ms. Price, sitting on her shoulder as if in support and comfort. It is during this testimony when Galvin finally stands out in court. He does not look confident, however, but slumps behind plaintiff's desk biting his nails. Nevertheless, he figures centrally in this cross-examination of his own witness. The film sutures his expressions in between shots of Ms. Price as she testifies, of the judge as he sits back surprised at the serendipitous tum of events, and of the defence attorney Concannon as he fumbles about trying to positively spin her testimony in favour of his clients. The camera's movement between Galvin and Concannon, the judge and Ms. Price situates the dramatic tension in the credibility and control of Ms. Price's damning testimony. How will the jury judge this testimony?

NOTES & QUESTIONS

1. One of the issues that many critics of *The Verdict* bring up is that Frank Galvin does not discuss the settlement offer with his clients. He thinks he knows what they want. Putting aside for the moment any consideration of his breach of ethics, contemplate what plaintiffs want as a remedy at the end of a lawsuit. Do they want a great deal of money, even though a large settlement may never make them whole? Do they want an apology? An apology and money? The satisfaction of a "big win" and the knowledge that they have succeeded in publicly humiliating the defendants? An injunction? The knowledge that the defendants "won't do this again to anyone else," whatever "this" is? Two or more of these? Ultimately, what "side" do the creators of tort films, television episodes, and books seem to want us to take? Why?

2. For many people, injunctive relief seems the best way to remedy the situation, particularly in mass tort cases such as those portrayed in *A Civil Action* and *Erin Brockovich*. To someone who has not experienced the real costs of litigation — monetary, emotional, and practical — injunctive relief might seem to provide a happier ending than compensatory damages. For example, at the end of *A Civil Action*, the audience sees the Environmental Protection Agency using its substantial resources to resolve the case that Jan Schlictmann could not. However, Dan Kennedy, a reporter for the *New Republic*, points out that this ending is pure Hollywood:

> It makes for an uplifting conclusion to a decidedly downbeat story. It is also completely and utterly false. But, unlike most of the fictionalizations, exaggerations, and dramatizations in the transition from Jonathan Harr's best-seller to the Hollywood screen, the tale of Schlichtmann and the EPA is likely to have a lasting — and distorting — effect on the moviegoers who saw the film over the past few months. The notion that it took one lone ranger to force an uncaring, unresponsive government bureaucracy to act may resonate. But it's not true — or, at least, it wasn't in Woburn.

Dan Kennedy, "Civil Inaction," *New Republic*, 15 Mar. 1999, 13.

Do such happy endings dangerously skew public views about the reach of the law and the ability of lawyers to enact social justice? Or is this belief justified, even if it does not always come to fruition? Do you think films normally tend to fictionalize endings, even of films based on real stories, to make then "happy"? If so, what images do such changes send to viewers about their likelihood of success in the legal system? Are such dramatic liberties justified because a film only has a couple of hours to make its point? Because its purpose is primarily entertainment? Because the studio runs a disclaimer at the beginning of the movie, warning viewers that some or much of a film "based on a real story" is still fictionalized?

3. *Philadelphia*, a powerful film about an attorney who becomes a plaintiff after he reveals that he suffers from AIDS and then loses his job at a law firm, focuses not solely on the plaintiff, Andrew Beckett, played by Tom Hanks, and his relationship with his former employers, but on his relationships with others around him, including the attorney he eventually hires, Joe Miller, played by Denzel Washington. Not only does the film center on a trial, it also spawned at least one lawsuit for misappropriation. The family of attorney Geoffrey Bowers, who died of AIDS, argued that the filmmakers used his story as the basis for the movie. *See* Terry Pristin, "*Philadelphia* Screenplay Suit to Reach Court," *New York Times*, 11 Mar. 1996, D1. The parties eventually settled the case. *See* "*Philadelphia* Makers Settle Suit," *New York Times*, 20 Mar. 1996, B6. Other lawyers have since said the Beckett story is similar to theirs. *See* Tony Perry, "Gay Lawyer's Suit Offers a Real-Life *Philadelphia*," *Los Angeles Times*, 17 Feb. 1994, A1.

What effect do you think seeing articles about "real-life" Andrew Becketts might have on viewers, particularly if the facts of their life stories seem to fit so closely to Beckett's? Suppose that the case at bar is one of misappropriation in which the plaintiff needs to show that the defendant has (1) used a protected aspect of the plaintiff's identity (name or likeness, or some other protected attribute) (2) for a commercial or other exploitative purpose and the defendant has no news reporting or other protected interest in the use of plaintiff's identity, and cannot establish a link between the use of the plaintiff's identity and legitimate public interest or concern and (3) without the plaintiff's permission. If a number of attorneys fit the "Beckett" profile, or even two or three, is a jury more or less likely to believe that the film is "based on" the plaintiff's experiences? Or might it depend on other evidence?

4. Some films present both tort and constitutional issues, and we can have some trouble (and fun) distinguishing between the two. Consider *Deliberate Intent* (2000), a television movie based on the Rodney Smolla book about the case a family brings against the publishers of a book that explains how to bring off a successful "hit." In this movie, a hit man uses the publication, and the publishers of the book try to defend their publication on the grounds that the First Amendment protects speech. Professor Smolla, hired by the family of the victims, argues that the First Amendment does not protect speech whose sole aim is to commit a crime. *See Rice v. Paladin Enterprises*, 128 F. 3d. 233 (1997). This movie highlights the issue that directors, video game manufacturers, and other cultural workers often face if they produce violent entertainment. To what extent are they liable if consumers of the entertainment they produce copy the violence and reproduce it in real life? The answer is normally that the First Amendment protects the creators of entertainment from liability for "copy cat crimes." *See, e.g., Herceg v. Hustler*, 814 F. 2d 1017 (5th Cir. 1987).

5. Torts also occur regularly in novels, even if they are not the major point of the plot. John Grisham's *The King of Torts* (2003), for example, focuses on an ambitious attorney who uses insider information to try to create a career as a tort lawyer. Jonathan Harr's non-fiction book *A Civil Action* (1996) also tells a story of torts litigation. Mary Whisner of the University of Washington Law Library has prepared a useful page of resources related to *A Civil Action. See* http://lib.law.washington.edu/ref/civilaction.htm.

But torts can pop up unexpectedly in literature, just as they do in real life. For example, think about the number of torts committed in mystery novels in which amateur detectives seem to trespass, listen in on phone conversations, and misrepresent themselves with great abandon. For more torts, check out the wonderful "The Myth of the Reasonable Man," by A. P. Herbert, from his

Uncommon Law (1935). This fictional case is available in numerous anthologies, one of the most recent being *Law in Literature: Legal Themes in Short Stories* (Elizabeth V. Gemmette ed.1995). In this essay, Herbert humorously discusses the principle of the "reasonable woman" and the principle of reasonable care. *See also* here (http://www.oocities.org/bororissa/rea.html).

D. POPULAR CULTURE PRESENTS: THE TORT ON TRIAL

As it does with any other legal story, when a film or other pop cultural narrative actually presents a tort claim, it must, of course, shrink the tedious weeks and months of pre-trial preparation into a much shorter amount of time. Just as it combines characters for dramatic effect, it must convey the essence of a tort action with a few dramatic scenes, or even in one exciting confrontation. When the point is entertainment, procedural and substantial rules take a back seat to the story. One might then ask to what extent the pop cultural presentation of a legal proceeding distorts the viewer's understanding of what might go on in an actual lawsuit over a defamation claim, a products liability action, or a toxic tort lawsuit.

1. Breach of Duty of Care

In the following excerpt, Professor Leslie Bender presents a feminist alternative to the traditionally understood duty of care. As you read the excerpt, consider how the feminist alternative would affect a work of popular culture — which requires a recognizable villain — and whether popular conceptions of tortfeasors might interfere with the adoption of her duty of care.

FEMINIST (RE)TORTS: THOUGHTS ON THE LIABILITY CRISIS, MASS TORTS, POWER, AND RESPONSIBILITIES
Leslie Bender
1990 Duke Law Journal 848

"Responsibility" and "responsible" have several different meanings. I want to suggest that the meaning of "responsibility" in tort law is too thin. We can improve the tort system by rethinking the values underlying legal responsibility and making legal responsibility more multi-dimensional, more contextual, and more informed with insights from feminist theory. . . . I recommend the expansion of our legal account of responsibility to include a holistic, needs-based, caregiving response. . . . In order to achieve this end, the meaning of responsibility in law would include a commitment, in advance of harm, to protecting and caring about the health and safety of other people. . . .

Tort law has been weighted down by a language and value system that privilege economics and costs. Every time there is an injury, we determine legal responsibility by asking about the dollar and efficiency costs of paying for the harms and/or of avoiding them. Questions of cost have consistently been our first or second inquiry in cases of mass torts by corporate defendants.

As harms from mass tort have become more widespread, legal analysis in tort law has become desensitized to the individuals and groups of people harmed. The more people who are injured or subjected to the risk of injury, the more tort law dehumanizes people generally, views them as statistical risks, and sees their injuries as costs of economic growth and progress. If this kind of legal thinking is inconsistent with our core values, we must reject it out-right as violative of human dignity and equality. Instead, we can require corporate defendants, corporate officers, and courts to be more socially and personally responsible.

A. Meanings of Responsibility

Responsibility can be divided temporally into two types of categories: pre-event (prevention-based) responsibility and post-event (response-based) responsibility. . . .

The pre-event account of responsibility is important because it indicates who ought to be held responsible if something occurs. Pre-event or prevention-based responsibility is tied to the notion of power. The power to decide and take action entails a responsibility for the decisions made and action taken (or not taken). With power comes responsibility. They are inseparable. Prevention-based responsibility in mass tort derives from the power to choose (in a human agency sense) to impose risks on the health and safety of others or to perform activities that cause harm. One who "responsibly" exercises this power chooses to prevent harm, to minimize or eliminate risks to others created by activities or products, to gather information, to advance learning about the consequences of corporate actions, and to stress the values of health, safety, and human dignity. In wanting people to act more responsibly, we want them to choose to act with more care and reflection about the possible effects of their conduct and decisions on others. This is particularly true in dealing with potential harms caused by the actions of corporations. For-profit corporate activities are conducted with considerable input and pre-planning, which affords corporations more opportunities for intervention before harm is caused. We want this exercise of power to occur before there is harm (pre-event), so that there will be no harm. . . .

To compel people imbued with this power to take responsibility for the consequences of their actions and decisions, mass tort law as well as criminal law must be constructed in a manner that imposes personal liability on the individuals with the power to make decisions or select among actions. The process of requiring people to take responsibility also requires that the corporation as a whole be held responsible. . . .

Post-event responsibility ought to mean more than making reparations. A different notion of responsibility arises out of our interconnectedness as human beings, and it has to do with responding to the needs of someone through interpersonal caregiving — it means "taking care of." Although this account of responsibility seems completely absent from the law, it remains central to our life experiences. . . .

[C]orporate harm-causer/mass-tort victim relationships are analogous to those within the family to the extent that they involve responsibility.

Family members have an initial interpersonal responsibility of care for one another. At a minimum we understand this responsibility as an obligation to take care of or care for a family member who is unable to care for herself. Likewise, once the legal system determines that a corporation is liable or responsible for a harm, it has an obligation to remedy the harm and to take care of the people harmed. By shifting to a post-event meaning of responsibility that includes both a reparations sense and a caring sense, we can alter the way that the legal and corporate worlds function. . . .

NOTES & QUESTIONS

1.   Which model of responsibility better facilitates storytelling — pre-event or post-event? Think about this question first in terms of popular culture. How does the narrative set up the villain? Specifically, how do we know in *A Civil Action* that Grace and Beatrice are "bad" corporations, rather than simply businesses that made a mistake? Would it have been enough for Pacific Gas & Electric to have inadvertently polluted the town in *Erin Brockovich*? Why is it important in *Class Action* that Maggie Ward's client intentionally ignored information about the dangers inherent in the design of its cars? How does *The Verdict* manage to make the Catholic Archdiocese a "bad guy," and why? Why are defendants portrayed as not caring about the people they have injured?

2.   Now think about the difference between pre-event and post-event responsibility in terms of an actual trial. Put yourself in the shoes of the plaintiff's attorney. Your job is to tell the jury a story that moves them to punish the defendant and award substantial damages to your client. How would this goal best be accomplished — by trying to prove that the defendant violated its pre-event responsibility to the victims or by focusing instead on its post-event responsibility of care-giving? Is the trial narrative compatible with the popular one?

3.   How do you think judges can best respond to the effects that popular culture may have on jurors' impressions about how the law actually works? Through jury instructions? Should potential jurors have to watch videos before they are empanelled? Should they have to sign pledges assuring judges and counsel that they understand that they are jurors in an actual trial and not participating in an episode of *The Good Wife* or *Drop Dead Diva*? Consider the following Ohio jury instruction:

   1. ADMONITION. It is now my duty to give you what is called "The Admonition". This is a standing court order that applies throughout the trial. I will try to remind you of The Admonition at every recess, but if I forget to remind you, it still applies. Ladies and gentlemen, you (may be) (have been) selected as jurors in this case. We (will take) (have taken) the time to seat a neutral jury so this case can be decided based just on what goes on in the courtroom, and not on outside influences. You are required to decide this case based solely on the evidence that is presented to you in this courtroom. It is my role as the judge to determine what evidence is admissible and what is not admissible. It would be a violation of your duties, and unfair to the parties, if you should obtain other information about the case, which might be information that is not admissible as evidence. You must carefully listen to all the evidence, and evaluate all of it. Do not reach any conclusions until you have heard all the evidence, the arguments of the

attorneys, and the judge's instructions of law. Otherwise you will have an incomplete picture of the case. Do not discuss this case among yourselves or with anyone else. The reason for this is you might be given information or an opinion that could alter the way in which you view the evidence or the instructions or even how the case should come out. Such an opinion or conclusion would be based on an incomplete or inaccurate view of the evidence and therefore would be clearly unfair.

2. WARNING ON OUTSIDE INFORMATION. In addition, you absolutely must not try to get information from any other source. The ban on sources outside the courtroom applies to information from all sources such as family, friends, the Internet, reference books, newspapers, magazines, television, radio, a computer, a Blackberry, iPhone, smart phone, and any other electronic device. This ban on outside information also includes any personal investigation, including visiting the site, looking into news accounts, talking to possible witnesses, re-enacting the allegations in the (Complaint)(Indictment), or any other act that would otherwise affect the fairness and impartiality that you must have as a juror.

3. **WARNING ON OUTSIDE INFLUENCE. The effort to exclude misleading outside influences information also puts a limit on getting legal information from television entertainment. This would apply to popular TV shows such as *Law and Order*, *Boston Legal*, *Judge Judy*, older shows like *L.A. Law*, *Perry Mason*, or *Matlock*, and any other fictional show dealing with the legal system. In addition, this would apply to shows such as *CSI* and *NCIS*, which present the use of scientific procedures to resolve criminal investigations. These and other similar shows may leave you with an improper preconceived idea about the legal system. As far as this case is concerned, you are not prohibited from watching such shows. However, there are many reasons why you cannot rely on TV legal programs, including the fact that these shows: (1) are not subject to the rules of evidence and legal safeguards that apply in this courtroom, and (2) are works of fiction that present unrealistic situations for dramatic effect. While entertaining, TV legal dramas condense, distort, or even ignore many procedures that take place in real cases and real courtrooms. No matter how convincing they try to be, these shows simply cannot depict the reality of an actual trial or investigation. You must put aside anything you think you know about the legal system that you saw on TV.**

4. WARNING ON OUTSIDE CONTACT. Finally, you must not have contact with anyone about this case, other than the judge and court employees. This includes sending or receiving e-mail, Twitter, text messages or similar updates, using blogs and chat rooms, and the use of Facebook, MySpace, LinkedIn, and other social media sites of any kind regarding this case or any aspect of your jury service during the trial. If anyone tries to contact you about the case, directly or indirectly, do not allow that person to have contact with you. If any person persists in contacting you or speaking with you, that could be jury tampering, which

is a very serious crime. If anyone contacts you in this manner, report this to my bailiff or me as quickly as possible.

5. CONCLUSION. You should know that if this Admonition is violated, there could be a mistrial. A mistrial means that the case is stopped before it is finished and must be retried at a later date. This can lead to a great deal of expense for the parties and for the taxpayers, namely you and your neighbors. No one wants to see money, especially tax dollars, wasted. If a mistrial were to be declared based on a violation of this Admonition, the juror responsible could be required to pay the cost of the first trial, and could also be punished for contempt of court.

[Boldface added by editors.]

Taken from the *Ohio State Bar Association Jury Instructions*, available at http://www.lawriter.net/NLLXML/getcode.asp?statecd=OH&codesec=Undesign atedJURY%20ADMONITION&sessionyr=2009&Title=i&version=1&datatype= OHOSBAJI&cvfilename=ohohosbajicv2009TopicIUnprefixedC.htm&docname= JURY+ADMONITION&noheader=0&nojumpmsg=0&userid=PRODSG&Interf ace=CM.

4. Consider Professor Bender's assertion that corporate officers who make crucial decisions should be held personally liable for their actions. How well would this construct work in popular culture? What about a real trial? Is the difference clear in any of the movies examined in this chapter or any other works of popular culture with which you are familiar? Does it matter to the audience whether the corporation or individual is financially responsible? Could the ending of any of the movies be satisfying for an audience if it were clear that the individuals who were responsible for the injuries are likely not to be considered legally responsible? How does the need for an identifiable villain affect the public's notions of tort responsibility?

5. If you believe that one of the goals of our tort system is (or ought to be) prevention of future injury, how do you think popular culture contributes to this goal? In particular, do the ways in which these narratives portray the defendants as having breached a duty of care positively or negatively influence real people? Or does popular culture have no influence on real people?

2. Causation

Often, the most difficult part of a tort case is proving that the defendant's breach of her duty of care was the proximate cause of the plaintiff's injury. The following article examines the root of some of the legal difficulties, particularly in toxic tort cases, such as those portrayed in *A Civil Action* and *Erin Brockovich*.

GUARDING THE GATE TO THE COURTHOUSE: HOW TRIAL JUDGES ARE USING THEIR EVIDENTIARY SCREENING ROLE TO REMAKE TORT CAUSATION RULES

Lucinda M. Finley

49 DePaul Law Review 335 (1999)

Vigorously exercising their role as evidentiary "gatekeepers" — a task assigned to them by the United States Supreme Court in Daubert v. Merrell Dow Pharmaceuticals, Inc., 509 U.S. 579 (1993) — federal trial judges in products liability cases have been doing far more than screening proposed expert testimony to determine admissibility. The Daubert gatekeeper power has become a potent tool of tort lawmaking. Under the guise of admissibility determinations, federal judges have been making significant substantive legal rules on causation by substantially raising the threshold of scientific proof plaintiffs need to get their expert causation testimony admitted, and thus survive summary judgment. While the decisions purport to be no more than deferential nods to the criteria of science, judges have actually been making legal rules about what types and strengths of scientific evidence are necessary in order to prove causation. The emerging legal rule is that plaintiffs' experts must be able to base their opinions about causation on epidemiological studies, and that these studies standing alone must show that the population-wide risk of developing the disease in question, if exposed to defendants' products, is at least double the risk without exposure.

In the process of developing this legal rule, judges in products liability cases have been making profoundly normative judgments about the social allocation of risk and who should bear the burden of scientific uncertainty or controversy — injured people or manufacturers of the products alleged to have caused those injuries? Few of the opinions announcing or applying this emerging causal proof standard acknowledge awareness of the normative nature or implications of their decisions. Thus, an important underlying policy debate remains submerged. Should the rules of the tort system put the onus for uncertainty about the risks of a product on the manufacturer who has marketed it, perhaps without sufficient testing or warning? By doing so, causation rules would enhance the tort policies of deterring marketing of relatively untested products and promoting expanded research on both the effectiveness and hazards of drugs and medical devices. The tort system would also align itself more with the public health protective values that govern the FDA regulatory arena, where a drug is presumed not safe for marketing unless the manufacturer can prove its safety. Or, should the tort system instead embrace the conservative values of the scientific discipline of epidemiology, whose internal disciplinary standards start with a hypothesis of lack of risk, and demand stringent statistical proof of a doubling or tripling of the risk of a disease before entertaining the possibility of a causal association? Judges have been using their evidentiary gatekeeper power to squarely align tort law with the conservative causal normative principles of epidemiology, thus moving the law sharply away from the more consumer protective social policies about risk embodied in the safety regulatory system.

While adopting substantive changes in causation law through the rubric of evidentiary admissibility decisions, judges have also frequently conflated admissibility decisions and sufficiency of evidence decisions. This has effected another profound but concealed change in tort law. Judges have applied Daubert to subject each item of expert proof proffered by plaintiffs to substantive causation law scrutiny, to see if it, standing alone, would prove both general and specific causation. If the scientific studies underlying an expert's opinion are not alone sufficient, then the expert's testimony is deemed inadmissible. This stands in stark contrast to traditional and proper practice, which sees the admissibility of evidence as a question quite distinct from the sufficiency of evidence to meet a plaintiff's burden of proof. The sufficiency inquiry is supposed to view plaintiffs' evidence in its entirety to see if, taken as a whole, it would support a conclusion that causation is more likely than not. By calling what is really a sufficiency of the evidence determination an admissibility decision, judges are using their evidentiary gate-keeper power to close the gate on plaintiffs' opportunities to have their proof evaluated as a cumulative whole. This subtly but substantially increases plaintiffs' burden of proving individual causation, and it also furthers the trend in toxic tort cases to shift the allocation of power away from juries to judges. Because a trial judge's decision to exclude evidence is reviewed under the lenient abuse of discretion standard of review, this new heightened substantive standard of causation and judges' applications of it are largely insulated from meaningful appellate review. . . .

NOTES & QUESTIONS

1.   What exactly is the problem Professor Finley describes? Is it truly a "problem," or simply an inherent and correct part of the plaintiff's burden to prove causation in a tort case? Now consider the "problem" in works of popular culture which center on the story of the plaintiff's attorney gaining justice for his or her clients. Do you find the plaintiff's higher burden more fitting in a dramatic context? Less?

2.   According to Professor Finley, judges now tend to demand that expert testimony establish that the defendant's actions caused twice the risk that the plaintiffs develop a specific disease than the risk faced by the general population. Do works of popular culture seem to provide a higher or lower standard? In other words, do the stories make the proof of causation so strong that it seems as if the defendant made it even more than twice as likely that the victims would contract illness because of the defendants' activities? Or is the story furthered by lesser evidence, which is still taken as enough to satisfy the legal case being portrayed?

3.   What effect, if any, might these cinematic standards of proof have on actual legal cases? Consider the role of jury instructions in a court case and whether a jury understands the legal standards well enough to apply them correctly. Might it be just as easy for a jury to turn to the "knowledge" they have acquired from popular culture? Might a juror think she is applying the standard articulated by the judge but really substitute the one she thinks she already "knows" from popular culture? Or are people able to distinguish easily between fiction and reality?

4.   Professor Finley asserts that judges are unaware of the normative implications of their high admissibility standard for expert testimony in tort cases. Does the entertainment industry face the same sort of normative implications in its

depiction of torts in popular culture? If so, does its ignorance pose a greater or lesser problem than judges'?

5.   Is Professor Finley's "consumer protection" model attractive to you? Should popular culture act as a consumer protector? Can it? Consider movies like *Erin Brockovich* and *A Civil Action*, where causation seems obvious, and how they raise public awareness of the problems. Is such a portrayal harmful to real tort cases, where the evidence of causation tends to be less obvious? What about movies like *The Verdict* or *Philadelphia*, where defendants show deliberate indifference to the victims or cover up evidence of their negligence? Is it too dangerous to rely on popular culture to set the tone for consumer protection? Does the entertainment industry have sufficient checks on its power to persuade?

6.   In *Erin Brockovich*, causation is quite plainly an important component of the narrative tension — the plaintiffs' attorneys must prove it to win their cases. How important is it in the other movies? For example, in *Philadelphia*, is it important to prove that Andrew Beckett's injury (discharge from his job) was directly caused by his firm's discrimination against him as a gay man with AIDS? In *The Insider*, does the tension arise from the viewer's doubt about whether Jeffrey Wigand will be able (or willing) to deliver proof of Big Tobacco's bad behavior or doubt about whether the network will stand behind the story?

7.   How does popular culture dramatize the causation problem? Generally, causation is the most tedious part of a case because it often relies heavily on dry expert testimony. Thus, in *A Civil Action*, the defendants strike a fatal blow to the plaintiffs' case by convincing Judge Skinner to bifurcate the proceedings so that the jury must sit through weeks of testimony about how contaminants might enter a drinking water supply and find causation before they ever hear the more sympathetic and moving stories of the victims themselves. How do the filmmakers avoid boring the audience in the same way the lawyers bored the jury? In finding other ways to dramatize the plight of the plaintiffs to the movie audience, do the filmmakers do a disservice to real tort plaintiffs by making laypeople more accustomed to seeing the victims' tragedy portrayed cinematically?

8.   According to Professors Graham and Maschio, "[p]opular film serves as a cultural text. When we look at a group of films on any given subject, we are also viewing a record of the culture that produced those films. Generally, films produced for mass or popular consumption reflect the dominant culture's ideology." Louise Everett Graham & Geraldine Maschio, *A False Public Sentiment: Narrative and Visual Images of Women Lawyers in Film*, 84 Kentucky Law Journal 1027, 1028 (1995). Is this statement correct? Does a film "reflect the dominant culture's ideology"? If it does, does every audience member take away the same meaning? Would everyone who saw it describe the story the same way? By the same token, should every juror who views the evidence "correctly" come to the same conclusion about the defendant's culpability? If so, why do we have juries?

3. Injury and Compensation

Both in real cases and in popular culture, one of the most important things a plaintiff's attorney must do is encourage the fact-finder to feel sympathy toward her client. In an excerpt in Chapter 7 of this text, Professor Jeffrey Abramson discussed various jury stories available in popular culture. In the following excerpt, he contemplates two distinct narrative treatments of tort compensation that might differently affect a jury's — or an audience's — perception of tort victims as deserving of compensation.

THE JURY AND POPULAR CULTURE
Jeffrey Abramson
50 DePaul Law Review 497 (2000)

Let me call the first narrative the populist or Jacksonian story. In this narrative, as much as the common people would prefer to stay out of politics and off juries, sometimes they are simply needed to clean out a corrupt system. The common person responds to the moral heroism of deserving victims whose water, air, or lungs have been poisoned by corporate giants. The moral claims of the victims are so overwhelming, the behavior of the corporations so arrogant, that even lawyers are transformed by civil litigation from sleazy sharks into crusaders for a cause. This populist depiction of the morality tale inside many a civil trial has been the central story line in a cluster of recent hits. The first example is *A Civil Action*, a nonfiction account of the jury trial of W.R. Grace and Beatrice Foods for causing the cases of childhood leukemia in Woburn, Massachusetts, by contaminating the town's wells with carcinogenic chemicals. The second is *Erin Brockovich*, about one woman's discovery of how Pacific Gas and Electric Company poisoned the water of a California town and then conspired to cover up its torts. The third example is *The Runaway Jury*, the Grisham novel about corrupt Big Tobacco executives trying to buy a jury in an anti-smoking trial.

The timing of these "David and Goliath" books and movies on civil trials is itself interesting. Since the 1970s, a second narrative, the Hamiltonian one, has told the most popular stories about civil litigation. This story is all about the stupidity of setting economic policy through jury trials. Victims are rarely deserving and always litigious, lawyers prey upon the unfortunate, jurors are in over their heads, junk science breeds junk lawsuits, damage awards are a crap shoot, and the rich just cannot get justice. Hamiltonian stories are the mirror image of populist ones: the corporation or the doctor is the victim of unsavory lawyers serving shoddy victims. As to juries, the reigning Hamiltonian punch line is that "the only difference between TV juries and real juries is 50 IQ points." . . .

Mark Galanter and others have pointed out that the Hamiltonian story about civil justice is often impervious to empirical evidence that civil juries are not as anti-business and anti-doctor as the plot line demands. The narrative has some of the staying power of folklore, anchored into a deep belief structure about the essential immorality of damage awards that sever the connection between work and reward. . . .

NOTES & QUESTIONS

1. Do you agree with Professor Abramson's assessment of *A Civil Action* and *Erin Brockovich* as "Jacksonian"? What exactly makes them so? Can you imagine a Hamiltonian take on the stories in these films?

2. Is it possible for popular culture to be evenhanded, or must it take one side or the other? Do you think that evenhandedness is its function? Why or why not? If evenhandedness is not its function, and the result is a particular effect on the viewer, how could judges and lawyers overcome the effect?

3. How would you characterize the other movies discussed in this chapter or other works of popular culture about torts — Jacksonian or Hamiltonian? Consider when the works appeared. Do you discern any trends? Can such an analysis of popular culture tell us anything meaningful about widespread attitudes toward compensation in real tort cases? If you were an attorney representing one of the parties in a large tort suit, would you be concerned with such trends?

4. Professor Abramson cites research indicating that real juries are not influenced by the Hamiltonian narratives they receive in popular culture because they continue to award significant damages to plaintiffs. Is this reasoning sound? He goes on to argue that the Hamiltonian narrative has "the staying power of folklore." Is Abramson suggesting that people recognize and embrace it as pure fiction? If so, does that mean that people can also distinguish between the fiction of the Jacksonian narrative and the reality of an individual case?

5. How do the films discussed in this chapter or other popular culture about torts portray the victims' injuries? Be specific about how they are communicated. Is it in a scene of the victim talking to her lawyer? Where does such a conversation take place? Is she shown testifying in front of a jury? Or is the incident portrayed visually? What reasons might the filmmakers have for these choices? Does the different mode of communication adversely affect jury trials, where it is impossible to render a real-time depiction of the injury for the jurors?

6. If the narrative is centered around the lawyer as protagonist, how do the filmmakers account for the fact that the lawyer becomes involved well after the actual injury has occurred? In other words, if the movie starts with the lawyer, by the time we meet the victim, the incident is already past. How does an injury inflicted in the past fit into the narrative of the litigating the case?

7. Do filmmakers manipulate audience sympathy to make up for a perception that the victims themselves are really responsible for their own injuries? If this assertion seems far-fetched, consider the following:

> Perhaps no assumption about the civil jury is so universally accepted as the belief that juries are highly sympathetic to injured plaintiffs. Opinion surveys, business and insurance industry briefs, and court opinions reflect beliefs that juries naturally take the side of the injured plaintiff. Research on civil juries, however, provides evidence that jurors and the public are inclined to question the credibility and claims of plaintiffs who bring personal injury lawsuits.

Valerie P. Harris & Juliet Dee, *Whiplash: Who's to Blame?*, 68 Brooklyn Law Review 1093, 1094-95 (2003).

Where do these popular views of plaintiffs come from? Are jurors able to distinguish the tort victims portrayed in films from the ones they see in the courtroom? What about films based on true stories, like *A Civil Action* and *Erin Brockovich*? Could the secondary role of the victims in popular culture have something to do with juries' dismissal of real plaintiffs' injuries? Or does popular culture lead jurors to feel more sympathetic even to victims of less sensationalistic torts?

8.   Does the focus on sympathetic plaintiffs bypass the larger social considerations at stake in popular culture? Think about the types of tort cases that are likely to be considered interesting enough to be made into mass entertainment. They tend to have some larger social impact: toxic pollution that threatens entire communities (*A Civil Action* and *Erin Brockovich*); product liability suits that cause grievous injury to many people (*Class Action*); discrimination (*Philadelphia*); health care negligence (by the Catholic Church, no less) (*The Verdict*). Are these stories about the plaintiffs or about greater social harms that affect all of us?

9.   According to the authors of *Film and the Law*, relying on the stories of individual victims to build narrative sympathy for the protagonist, in this case the plaintiffs' attorney, can cause us to ignore remedies with a more widespread and positive social impact. "One issue that comes to the fore in both *A Civil Action* and *Erin Brockovich* is the question of remedies and the weakness of the law in providing some defence for the community. This is shown by the concentration on individual cases and monetary compensation as the prime remedy wants. There is [a] tension between what the law can provide, in terms of a remedy, and what the community wants." Greenfield, Osborn, & Robson, supra, at 93. Does popular culture have a responsibility to present remedies with a broader social impact?

10.   The same authors claim that the movies' reliance on monetary remedies to the exclusion of other forms of compensation parallels corporate thinking, wherein the costs of tort liability are calculated against the profits to be obtained by engaging in tortious activity. Do you agree? If audiences become accustomed to seeing tort cases resolved with financial remuneration, are they likely to begin viewing all injuries as monetarily compensable? Are they? How else can one make reparations for causing bodily or emotional injury?

11.   Think about the use of "bean counting" in *Class Action*. Recall that Maggie Ward, one of the attorneys for the defense, discovers that her client's chief risk-assessment manager was aware of a design flaw in the car they manufactured whereby if the car were rear-ended while engaging its left-turn signal, its gas tank would explode. The risk-assessment manager had determined that the cost of fixing the flaw would exceed the cost of paying victims of the likely explosions. This information, along with other ethical lapses by her colleagues, causes Ward's transformation from a hard-nosed defense attorney to a woman with a conscience who deliberately throws the defense's case. How realistic do you find this portrayal of corporate practices? If you find it plausible that corporations let the cost of compensating an injured public drive their actions, where does your knowledge of such corporate practices come from? Is it influenced by popular culture? By media

scrutiny of one or two particularly high-profile cases? Are law-abiding large corporations themselves the victims of popular attitudes derived from portrayals of tort cases in popular culture that need an identifiable villain?

E.   THE IMPACT OF TORT MOVIES ON THE LAW

In this section, we consider the connection between popular culture depicting tort cases and the current trend toward tort reform.

THE AMERICAN CIVIL JURY FOR AUSLÄNDER (FOREIGNERS)
Neil Vidmar
13 Duke Journal of Comparative & International Law 95 (Summer 2003)

Legal practitioners and scholars whom I encounter in my travels outside the borders of the United States frequently challenge me to explain the "crazy," "outrageous" system by which we allow groups of untutored laypersons to decide civil disputes. Invariably, they bring up Liebeck v. McDonald's Restaurants, P.T.S. Inc., 1995 WL 360609 (D.N.M. 1994), the McDonald's case in which a civil jury in New Mexico awarded a woman $160,000 in compensatory damages and $2.7 million in punitive damages just because she spilled coffee on herself. My inquisitors are frequently surprised to learn that for years McDonald's had kept its coffee many degrees hotter than home-brewed coffee or the coffee of its competitors; that for over five years it had been aware of the problem of serious burns resulting from the coffee through over 700 complaints but had never consulted a burn specialist, reduced the temperature of its coffee, or warned consumers; and that the seventy-nine-year-old woman who was injured suffered second and third degree burns to her private parts. They are also surprised to learn that the plaintiff had tried to settle the suit for a much more modest amount before trial, initially around $20,000 to cover her medical expenses, and that the jury's punitive damage award was equal to two days' worth of the McDonald's corporation's profits from selling coffee. Finally, almost everyone is ignorant of the fact that the trial judge subsequently reduced the punitive damage award to $480,000 for a total award of $640,000, and that the case was later settled for an undisclosed, presumably lesser, amount.

One source of misunderstanding in the McDonald's case is incomplete media reporting about the details of the case. This problem is endemic with media coverage of jury awards. A number of studies have carefully documented the fact that mass media newspapers and television tend to report jury awards selectively, focusing on large awards, ignoring small awards and defendant verdicts, and not providing complete details about issues put to the juries or matters preceding trial or following the jury verdict. In addition, industry groups generally opposed to the tort system frequently distort information about jury awards in order to further their political agendas. Moreover, some legal commentators who have made claims about the legal system may be less than informed about the empirical realities of jury behavior. . . .

E. Assessing Damages

It is jury damage awards that get the attention of the news media and the public. It is safe to say that the McDonald's case would have gained no attention from the media if the award had only been several thousand dollars. Studies indicate that media coverage is heavily skewed toward cases involving large damage awards. Of course, this skews public perceptions of the jury. . . .

In a major study of 1992 verdicts in a sample of the largest urban state courts, Brian Ostrom and his colleagues concluded that the typical jury award was "modest." The median jury verdict, including punitive damages, was $52,000; however, because of some very high awards, the arithmetic mean of those awards was much higher, $455,000. About eight percent of awards exceeded $1 million and the mean amount of the awards varied by case type, with malpractice, products liability, and toxic torts generating the largest awards on average. In contrast, automobile and premises liability cases had much lower awards.

Many of the same jurisdictions were assessed again in 1996. The median amount of the jury award for plaintiffs who won at trial was $35,000, with about nineteen percent of winners receiving over $250,000, and an estimated seven percent receiving $1 million or more. Of a total of 5060 jury trials in which the plaintiff prevailed, there were only 212 cases (about four percent) that resulted in punitive damages. Of these, about twenty-two percent involved intentional torts and forty-nine percent involved contract cases. In tort cases considered as a whole, the median punitive award was $27,000 compared to a median punitive award in contract cases of $76,000. . . .

G. Jury Consideration of Insurance and the Effects of Damage Awards

Is there any validity to the claim that jurors are profligate with defendants' or their insurers' money? Critics of the jury system might argue that juries are irresponsible because the jurors see the money award coming from the rich person or corporation and do not consider the aggregate impact of large awards on financial costs that must be borne by all of society. As a general rule, these claims about jury profligacy are not only unsupported by systematic research, but findings suggest just the opposite — that juries tend to be very skeptical of plaintiffs' claims about damages. . . .

A substantial body of systematic empirical studies indicates that the American civil jury system is not as erratic or unreasonable as portrayed in the media. Whether it involves issues of liability, responses to experts, attention to the judge's instructions, or damage awards, the civil jury performs much better than many people believe. If this were not so, surely the civil jury would have been abandoned, or at least drastically curtailed, despite the guarantee of the right to jury trial in the U.S. Constitution and the constitutions of individual states. American society could not afford the caprice and craziness ascribed to juries. Examined from this pragmatic perspective, it should not be surprising that the empirical research into the performance of the civil jury yields a generally positive picture, especially when considered in the context of the formal and informal controls on errant verdicts. . . .

NOTES & QUESTIONS

1. What might account for the downward trend in amounts of jury awards noted by Professor Vidmar? In making this assessment, be as specific as you can. For example, if you believe political factors are primary, consider what might have generated and contributed to the political movement. If you believe it is a product of popular culture, try to identify specific examples. Be as critical as you can about the role of popular culture in the decline of tort plaintiffs' awards.

2. Is the news media entirely to blame, as Professor Vidmar suggests? Is it more at fault than popular culture, such as the movies examined in this chapter? How do you distinguish between the news accounts of the McDonald's case and film versions of real cases like *A Civil Action* and *Erin Brockovich*?

3. Despite the downward trend in tort damages noted by the author, tort reform continues to enjoy substantial political support. For example, some members of Congress have supported a large surtax on lawyers' contingency fees and/or the federalization of virtually all class actions. Constituents have lobbied to replace jury awards for certain types of injuries with compensation funds set up by acknowledged mass tortfeasors. For a discussion of these reforms and the concomitant attacks on tort plaintiffs from the perspective of the Association of Trial Lawyers of America, a plaintiffs' bar advocacy group, see David S. Casey, Jr., *A Time to Fight, Trial*, Sep. 2003, 9. What do you make of such tort reform proposals, especially in light of Vidmar's claim that tort awards are actually on the decline? If popular perceptions of tort awards are skewed, how did they get that way? Is it irresponsible of Hollywood to produce entertaining movies about huge jury awards? Or is it up to movie-goers to distinguish between fact and fiction? What about other forms of popular culture?

4. Stephen Daniels and Joanne Martin argue that "[t]he future of punitive damages is in doubt because of the political success of the interest groups wanting changes in the civil justice system" even though "a punitive damages explosion . . . does not in fact exist." Stephen Daniels & Joanne Martin, *Punitive Damages, Change, and the Politics of Ideas: Defining Public Policy Problems*, 1998 Wisconsin Law Review 71, 71-73. If the authors are correct that there is not a problem of outrageous punitive damage awards, what is driving the political interest groups? Why rally behind a cause that does not really exist? What role does popular culture play in this political movement?

5. How important is the actual size of the award in works of popular culture about torts? In *A Civil Action*, the jury finds no liability on the part of Beatrice. The plaintiffs settle with co-defendant Grace for a total of $8 million — of which each family receives $375,000, with an additional $80,000 payable after five years. Legal expenses eat up $2.6 million of the settlement, and legal fees are $2.2 million. *See* Jonathan Harr, *A Civil Action* 453 (1995). The Reverend Bruce Young, who advised some of the victims, was furious and disgusted with the settlement. "This was a case I thought would have some real importance," he said. "It never happened." *Id.* at 452. Does Rev. Young's reaction affect whether you believe the plaintiffs were victorious? Do you think he was happy with the hugely successful book and movie that brought the case to the attention of a large audience? Should we have to rely on popular culture for this aspect of justice?

6. If you believe that popular culture predisposes the public against large corporations, how do you account for the statistics cited by the authors? If they are correct in their assessment of public attitudes toward tort plaintiffs, is it safe to say popular culture has no effect on public perceptions?

F. THE "MESSAGE" MOVIE

One research study suggests that viewers exposed to the anti-smoking message in *The Insider* may be more receptive to anti-smoking messages generally. Other studies of public receptivity to messages about smoking in popular culture have examined "pro-smoking" messages. The authors of the following excerpt compare reactions to *The Insider* and to *Erin Brockovich* (the "control" movie).

PUBLIC REACTION TO THE PORTRAYAL OF THE TOBACCO INDUSTRY IN THE FILM *THE INSIDER*
Helen G. Dixon, David J. Hill, Ron Borland & Susan J. Paxton
10 Tobacco Control 285 (2001)

Steve Kottak, a spokesman for Brown and Williamson in the USA, is quoted as saying of *The Insider*: "We regard ourselves as an ethical company and a responsible company. This movie has set us back in that regard." However our results indicate that before viewing the film, people's perceptions of the ethics and honesty of a tobacco industry executive were low relative to other professions. These findings parallel those of another Australian survey. As far as the movie promoting a more negative perception of the ethics of the tobacco industry goes, there was little room to move. People's baseline attitudes to the industry made a significant contribution to explaining their industry at post-film.

Erin Brockovich had parallels with *The Insider*, in that a major plot element was about a large business covering up the health impact of their [sic] products on the community. Our results suggest both films may have promoted a generalized perception of the power of big business, and subjects in both conditions showed similar agreement with the statement, "there should be greater penalties for companies whose products cause sickness or death" at post-film.

While viewing *The Insider* only accounted for a small (but significant) proportion of the variance in the dependent variables assessing attitudes toward the tobacco industry at post-film, it should be remembered that the effects observed are the result of a single exposure to anti-tobacco content in a movie. A study that captured the cumulative effects of repeated exposure to negative (or positive) depictions could be expected to show more substantial and lasting change. We found that the post-film survey items that focused on content specific to *The Insider* tended to elicit differences between viewing conditions. Subjects who saw *The Insider* tended to hold more negative perceptions of business conduct by the tobacco industry and show less community acceptance of the tobacco industry at post-film than those who saw *Erin Brockovich*. Another issue that received considerable attention in *The Insider* (but not *Erin Brockovich*) was that of news media bowing to pressure from big business. People who saw *The Insider* tended to agree more strongly that "when big companies are involved, news media aren't always free to present things as they are."

INTENTIONS FOR SMOKING

A most interesting finding is that *The Insider* may have promoted a reduction in intentions to smoke in the future among subjects that persisted for up to two weeks. Compared to the barrage of positive smoking images in films, *The Insider* represents a drop in the ocean. Yet the presence of this small effect for intentions suggests that if people were more recurrently exposed to anti-tobacco content in movies there may be potential for a more substantial and lasting cumulative impact on attitudes toward smoking. Our survey was of people aged 15 and over, who self-selected to see this film. It would be of interest to assess whether this film would promote an anti-smoking message to adolescents, who continue to be a challenging group to influence not to smoke. Evaluation results for anti-tobacco industry campaigns in the USA suggest that demonisation of the tobacco industry may be effective at promoting an anti-smoking message to youth audiences.

PERCEPTIONS OF SMOKING PREVALENCE

While people may be influenced by depictions of actors smoking in films, our results indicate viewers may not attend to the frequency of these depictions. Contrary to content analysis showing elevated smoking prevalence in films, a minority of subjects felt more people smoke in films than in real life. Cultivation theory predicts that people who consume a lot of media will hold perceptions of reality that reflect those of the media environment. In Australia, population smoking rates declined between 1989 and 1992, stalled between 1992 and 1995, then continued to decline. Smoking rates in popular movies increased during this period. We found that people who perceived "real world" smoking rates to have increased over the past 10 years watched movies more frequently than those who did not hold this perception. This finding points to the role movies may play in normalising smoking.

NOTES & QUESTIONS

1. What accounts for the difference — if there is one — between works of popular culture about torts and reality? What impact might portrayals of the legal system as a barrier to justice have on popular perceptions of law in reality? Are people less likely to expect a just outcome in real life if they receive the message from popular culture that the legal system impedes justice?

2. How much does the concept of "justice" have to do with how the stories are actually presented? In other words, think about all the ways in which the popular culture you have encountered "teaches" what the just result should be — its portrayals of the plaintiffs' attorneys, the defendants and their attorneys, the victims and their injuries. Do the same rules apply to "teaching" fact-finders the just result in real cases? Does real justice for tort victims depend on whether the plaintiff's attorney is attuned to current popular culture? Consider the Ohio jury instruction you read above, the narrative and other techniques you now know about

that creators use to tell stories, and other mechanisms used to sway viewers. Given that pop culture is so prevalent, and that it infiltrates so much of our lives, do you think that winning or losing a case, particularly a case tried to a jury, is mostly a matter of telling a good story?

Chapter 10

CRIMINAL LAW

A. FILMOGRAPHY

Fracture (2007)

The Ox-Bow Incident (1943)

A Place in the Sun (1951)

Presumed Innocent (1990)

The Thin Blue Line (1988)

B. INTRODUCTION

Initial reactions to the materials in a law school course in Criminal Law are often different than the initial reactions to the materials in other courses. Students have been subjected to innumerable stories about criminal law and criminals, and as a result they perceive the cases presented in law school as somehow familiar. The cases capture students' imaginations, and students frequently begin their criminal law studies eager to read "real" stories about crime.

Yet students' hunger is often not fully satisfied by the appellate opinions in their criminal law casebooks. Students perceive something is missing in these edited and fragmented texts about criminal law doctrine. Students rightfully believe that lurking beneath the surfaces and edges of appellate opinions are powerful, complex, and consuming stories which are usually not well served by the partial renderings in the facts presented in the opinions. These stories have numerous themes: stories about guilt and innocence; punishment, revenge, and redemption; whodunits and mysteries — some solved, others not; stories about notions of guilt and innocence that are more shaded and subtle than the law often allows; meanings more literary than legal; stories about character and motivation; stories about behaviors caused by environments; stories that provide fuller comprehension of the unfolding of events; stories about integrity and strength; and stories about systemic corruption, about the probabilities and possibilities of justice, and about justice gone haywire too. These are narratives that the opinions seldom reach.

Further, the appellate cases studied in law school purposefully minimize the drama of engrossing, complex, and often ambiguous narratives at the core of many criminal law stories. This dumbing-down of facts is often strategic; the narrow legal issues reviewed on appeal must not be subsumed by the compelling power of narrative. Appellate opinions dissect fragments or cross sections of a story, and appellate judges parse out from their opinions complex renderings of "character," "plot," "settings," "style," and "narrative time." The strange is made familiar; the story, intentionally flattened. It is the law and the doctrinal analysis that are placed in the foreground; the factual narrative is merely a springboard for legal analysis.

Pop cultural storytelling, especially in quality commercial films, routinely turns the legal world upside down. The plot-driven and character-based stories are now crucial. The law and the precise cataloging of facts in terms of legal doctrine are suspended; narrative is no longer subservient to doctrine. The lens of the story widens literally and figuratively. Constraints, conventions, and limitations placed upon storytelling in judicial opinions fall away; the popular storyteller attempts to capture a different truth than the appellate judge. Narratives emerge from beneath doctrine, and seem to take shape attempting to capture the imagination of the reader or viewer.

This chapter looks at several of these popular versions of law stories. It is divided into three main sections: The Players as Legal Actors, Legal Storytelling in Criminal Trials, and Popular Melodramas about Criminal Law. The excerpts may assist readers to better explore systematically the discrete and characteristic aspects of popular storytelling about criminal law.

C. THE PLAYERS AS LEGAL ACTORS

1. Defendants and Criminals

LEGAL FICTIONS: IRONY, STORYTELLING, TRUTH, AND JUSTICE IN THE MODERN COURTROOM DRAMA
Christine Alice Corcos
25 University of Arkansas at Little Rock Law Review 503 (2003)

Apart from pointing out the easy manipulation of the legal systems available to such unscrupulous defendants as Leonard Vole [*Witness for the Prosecution*] and Frederick Manion, [*Anatomy of a Murder*] the author or film-maker can also criticize the legal system by demonstrating that it fails from the beginning in its quest for justice by bringing the "wrong defendant" to trial. The "wrong defendant" may be a totally innocent person, or he may be someone whose morality is immediately apparent to the observer, and who, though he may be literally guilty, is ethically innocent of the charges.

Presumed Innocent and the Lawyer as the Accused

With the choice of defendant, particularly when the defendant is a lawyer, the conflicts of fact merge with the conflicts of belief to create a dramatic whole. Both the lawyer as ethical chameleon and the lawyer as defendant are popular choices for the author wishing to examine the contrast between law and justice in the legal system.

The image of the lawyer, expert in the manipulation and control of the legal system, as the accused in a criminal trial (particularly murder) is an obvious choice for the author wishing to present an ironic situation. . . .

The confusion of roles is a major component of the dramatic irony present in *Presumed Innocent*, and the spectacle of the lawyer-manipulator as accused-manipulated is a particularly striking one. From the cynical title (Rusty Sabich is clearly not presumed innocent by anyone except the real killer and arguably his lawyer) and his opening "I am a prosecutor" voice-over in the film, Sabich swings between the extremes of judge and judged, between accuser and accused. Sabich's superior, Raymond Horgan, assigns the murder case to him because "you're the only guy I can trust." In reality Sabich is "the only guy" likely to be loyal enough to him to cover up Horgan's involvement with the dead woman. Horgan equates "trust" with blind loyalty: the prosecutor who should be assigned the case is Horgan's political enemy — an enemy who ironically becomes the prosecuting attorney in Sabich's case. Yet Horgan does not trust Sabich enough to tell him the truth about the dead woman or about his and the dead woman's involvement with the judge. Further, Horgan lies on the stand in a final effort to cover up his own involvement and implicate Sabich.

Rusty's experience as a prosecutor seems to lead him completely astray once he becomes the defendant. His very definite opinions about how to obtain a conviction should alert him to the dangers of his own appearance on the stand, yet he insists to Sandy Stern, his attorney, that "the jury wants to hear me say I didn't do it." Stern is reluctant; defense attorneys in general prefer not to let their clients testify because the client may say something in an unguarded moment that the attorney cannot control, allowing the prosecutor an opportunity to attack the defense's entire case. Stern's own choice is for Rusty's wife, Barbara, to plead his case, but Sabich indicates that he believes his wife will not be a good witness. His sixth sense about testimony seems to guide him clearly but inexplicably here. Although Rusty believes (ironically) that his wife would not be a good witness because she is emotionally unstable, the truth is that she would not be a "good witness" because she committed the crime. Although Stern tells the judge that Sabich is "an integral part of our defense," Sabich loses every tactical argument that he has with Stern. Stern controls the defense completely, like a good attorney. Sabich the wily prosecutor becomes Sabich the client unable to make effective decisions in his own defense.

Rusty's voice-over in the opening scene establishes the irony of his situation: "I am a part of the process of accusing, judging, and punishing." Normally, he can only do the first — accusing; as the defendant, first accused, then exonerated, he ends by doing the second — judging — because the first is denied to him. Like a jury that "can't decide on truth," because of the identity of the real killer, Rusty can never do the third — punishing. Without that decision, no resolution is possible. Sabich's entire experience demonstrates that the very system to which he has devoted his life cannot uncover the truth necessary to resolve the question of guilt. Others (Sabich's lawyer, his police officer friend, the real killer, the district attorney) intervene to prevent crucial evidence from being presented to that jury. What does his ordeal teach Rusty? That the system works only for those who know how to manipulate it. The presumption of innocence is not merely untrue; it is irrelevant. . . .

NOTES & QUESTIONS

1.   One often-exploited "stock" story in popular culture concerns the wrongfully accused defendant. The film *Presumed Innocent*, as Professor Corcos observes, provides one version of this story. Here, this narrative theme is given an ironic spin as the prosecutor becomes the wrongfully accused defendant and feels the force of betrayal by the system which he has, until this time, used to his strategic advantage. Other versions of this story are numerous and prevalent in pop cultural storytelling and especially in popular films, including several suggested for this chapter. *The Ox-Bow Incident*, for example, is a gripping World War II-era film in which a posse of men in the early American West reconstitutes itself as judge and jury. The group votes 21-7 to hang three men for the murder, only to learn that the supposed murder victim is still alive and those who shot and wounded him have been captured. Overall, the film is a cautionary tale about disregarding the rule of law. For a provocative discussion of the film, see Robert Louis Felix, *The Ox-Bow Incident*, 24 Legal Studies Forum 645 (1999).

The approaches to the theme of the wrongfully accused defendant and the tonality of the storytelling are diverse. Contrast, for example, the humor of *My Cousin Vinny* (1992) with the realism of the fictional *12 Angry Men* (1957) or the mystery of Hitchcock's *The Wrong Man* (1956), which is based upon a real case and is discussed in Chapter 5 of this text. Despite their fundamental differences, these films compel our imaginative attention. Why do you think there is still such a recurring power and narrative satisfaction in retellings of this basic tale? Do we believe or suspect that the systematic processes of the law often do not work effectively, and that we wrongfully convict innocent defendants or let the guilty go free?

2.   Reflect upon your personal experiences: Have you ever been accused of committing a wrongful or criminal act that you did not commit? Have you ever been wrongfully punished? How did you respond? With anger and indignation? What, if anything, did you learn from your experiences? Does this story still stay with you? Does it affect your perceptions about whether there is usually fairness and justness, or are results often random and outcomes often unjust?

3.   Corcos observes that when Rusty Sabich, the prosecutor, is placed on trial for murder in *Presumed Innocent* and becomes the defendant, he desires to tell his story to the jury and testify on his own behalf. His shrewd defense attorney, Sandy Stern, does not want Sabich to testify, and advises even this court-savvy defendant against it. Juries usually want to hear the defendant's side of the story, and are disappointed when the defendant chooses not to testify. Nevertheless, criminal defendants are usually passive, and defendants do not usually testify at trial. Defendants characteristically rely upon the presumption of innocence and the inability of the prosecutor to prove the defendant's guilt beyond a reasonable doubt. This strategy, however, often makes for a less-than-satisfactory resolution in popular culture. Consequently, we are far more likely to see defendants testifying in films. Are the narrative certainties of film and the closure usually provided by most popular culture more satisfying than the problematic resolutions of many criminal trials?

4. In *Presumed Innocent* we learn that it is Barbara, Sabich's calculating wife, who has plotted and carried out the murder of Carolyn Polhemus. Likewise, the documentary *The Thin Blue Line* provides the satisfaction of narrative closure and resolution by strategically placing the dramatic confession of David Harris at the end. Without the careful selection and placement of these narratively structured and plot-driven events, assuming some component of uncertainty and irresolution remained, would we be compelled and drawn in by these stories? Does this suggest any strategies that a criminal defense attorney should follow in telling the defendant's story at trial?

5. In *Presumed Innocent*, defendant Sabich acts on his own behalf outside the courtroom. He is not a passive defendant. He participates actively in an independent investigation of the crime and draws upon his friends, e.g., Detective Lipranzer, to better understand the circumstances of the crime. Akin to a private investigator in a detective story, Sabich gradually develops his own theories of what happened and why. Note that this investigative function is not an activity usually undertaken by criminal defendants. It is the job of many defendants merely to remain largely passive, to not speak to the authorities without their attorney's permission, and to carefully follow the instructions and advice of their attorney, allowing their character and identity to be shaped by the attorney's storytelling at trial; the narrative strategies at trial depend upon the investigations undertaken by the attorney. Contrast, for example, the investigation undertaken by Sabich in the fictional *Presumed Innocent* with the investigations undertaken by the defense attorneys in The Thin Blue Line. Randall Adams, the defendant, is a passive, wrongfully accused victim trapped in a television-program nightmare over which he has no control. Does this discomforting imagery suggest the plight of the defendant in a typical criminal case, subjected to the power of the machinery of the state?

CONVICTS, CRIMINALS, PRISONERS AND OUTLAWS: A COURSE IN POPULAR STORYTELLING
Philip N. Meyer
42 Journal of Legal Education 129 (1992)

In "The Outlaw as Eve," the first of two papers, student ("C") uses anecdotal material to engage the reader in her analysis of popular cultural depictions of women as murderers, criminals, and outlaws in course materials. . . . There is the power of a student's discovering the authority of a first-person storytelling voice grounded in the particularity of experience rather than in the abstraction of theory. The journal begins:

> I went to school with a murderer. Two weeks before graduation, the police discovered the mother's body in the trunk of the family car, where it had rested while my schoolmate commuted to class each day. I attended a private Catholic girls' high school. The student was convicted and sentenced to Niantic Prison for Women, from whence presumably she received a high school diploma. My story has a point — the only murderer I ever knew personally was female, and very much like me, yet in the literature of criminality, women infrequently appear as direct or deliberate, as so-called cold-blooded murderers.

In her analysis, C observes that although female murderers are occasionally portrayed as "queens or warriors, pseudo-males, operating in their stead," female roles in criminality are generally archetypal and fall into two categories. There is the "evil stepmother of fairy tales, grasping and jealous," who "dominates the night psyche of many a child." And there is "Eve the primal temptress [who] preserves women's roles as both 'helpmate and temptress' and accounts for female evilness while maintaining her dual status as desirable and subservient. . . . Eve evokes ambivalence at once attractive and repugnant, compelling a response to our very nature." C places the female characters in course materials within her framework. Her journal is replete with subtle observations and a deftly accurate analysis of plots and characters.

Other students perceived and analyzed gender issues in their journals. In an untitled seminar journal, "H" explores sexual stereotyping, comparing the characters of Barbara in Turow's *Presumed Innocent*, Daisy in Fitzgerald's *Gatsby*, and Maria in Wolfe's *Bonfire*. H puts some nice vitriolic salsa on her prose, distinguishing characters in a voice often heard in a courtroom but seldom in classroom discussions of appellate cases. She contrasts Barbara, prosecutor Rusty Sabich's melancholy wife, with Daisy and Maria:

> The misogyny evident in the picture of Barbara, however, is of a newer, more invidious type than that found in the other novels. Daisy and Maria are the classic bimbos who find definition in their attractiveness to men. Barbara is a new stereotype: the "have it all" woman who is miserable.

Unlike Daisy and Maria, Barbara is capable of plotting and carrying out a murder: Barbara's crime is planned and motivated. She puts her prodigious brain power to work and plans the killing, "a byzantine scheme[,] as a way to both free and punish her husband." Barbara's physicality also distinguishes her from Daisy and Maria: "She is first seen laying on her bed with sweat clinging to her back after an aerobics workout. Our first view of Daisy, by contrast, finds her languishing on a couch which she has not left for hours. Maria, encumbered by her tight clothes and teetering on her high heels is likewise not a picture of vigorous physicality."

Nevertheless, H concludes that ultimately Barbara is just as sexist a creation as Maria and Daisy:

> Although Barbara, with her brains, her middle-class work ethic, and her independence from her husband seems far removed from the bright young things that Daisy and Maria become, she still is much like them in that she will never have to face justice. This could be due to a certain squeamishness on all three authors' part with the idea of women suffering for their crimes. Such an attitude is grounded in paternalistic notions of protecting women from life's rigors and with the idea that women, like children, are not really responsible for their actions and thus should not have to answer for them.

The course materials (stories) crystallize analysis that, I think, would be far more abstract and diffuse in, for example, theoretical discussions in a seminar on "Feminism and the Law." *Presumed Innocent* provides an excellent basis for thoughtful and animated discussion of sexuality and sexual conduct in the professional environments that law students and practicing attorneys inhabit. Again, academic purists and traditionalists might denigrate the propriety of allowing such discussion to take place within the law school curriculum. I doubt, however, that these discussions would take place elsewhere. . . .

NOTES & QUESTIONS

1.   Professor John Denvir, a longtime law and popular culture scholar, observes: "Students better understand this new language [of popular film] than their book-bound teachers. While legal scholars are more adept in reading written texts than their students, we quickly find that our video-sophisticated students are much better trained in 'reading' films. Therefore, film helps to level the pedagogical playing field to the advantage of teacher and students alike." John Denvir, *Legal Reelism: The Hollywood Film as Legal Text*, 15 Legal Studies Forum 195, 196 (1991).

2.   Do you agree with the student comments in the previous excerpt regarding gender stereotyping in popular culture? Are these stereotypes especially prevalent and pernicious in depictions of women criminals and defendants? Do you believe that, similarly, attorneys in courtroom storytelling at criminal trials rely upon stereotypical notions of defendants' character, grounded in stereotypical notions of behavior and archetypal models of character and behavior? Do the evidentiary and temporal limitations upon storytelling in the courtroom, e.g., rules of evidence pertaining to relevance and limitations upon character evidence, facilitate and encourage the use of stereotypes that engage jurors' preconceptions?

3.   Student "C" in the previous excerpt observes that, in the particularities of her experience, a female classmate at a private girls' Catholic school who murdered her mother was "female, and very much like me." Yet in popular culture, female criminals are depicted as "other," and seldom appear as deliberate and cold-blooded murderers. Perhaps we are more comfortable with female murderers who fall into certain categories that offer comforting distance. "C" identifies three archetypes: "the queen or warrior, pseudo-male"; "the evil stepmother of fairy tales, grasping and jealous [who] dominates the night psyche of many a child"; and "Eve the primal temptress." Do you agree that most female murderers can be conveniently slotted into one of these three categories? How might you categorize the character or identity of Barbara Graham in *I Want to Live!* (1958)? Does she fit neatly into one of the categories suggested by "C" in her journal? How might you describe her character and identity? Note that *I Want to Live!* is, purportedly, largely a fact-based dramatization, and perhaps a dramatic precursor to *The Thin Blue Line*. It is based upon the real trial and conviction of Barbara Graham for a murder occurring in 1953. Note that, as in the film, Graham was tried for and convicted of murder. Her conviction was affirmed by the California Supreme Court, and the U.S. Supreme Court refused to hear the case. Graham was executed on June 3, 1955.

4.   Student "H" perceives that the stereotyped depictions of defendants and criminals in popular storytelling result from the fantasies and projections of male authors and filmmakers. Implicitly, there is misogyny, intentionality, and a certain gendered pleasure at work in these artistic renderings of character. Do you agree? Are these characters versions of male fantasies? Or is the depiction of these characters as defendants and criminals aesthetically compelling because they are

psychologically accurate? Do you think that attorneys representing defendants at trial rely on similar stereotypical notions?

2. Adversaries: Defense Attorneys and Prosecutors

DEFENDING THE INNOCENT
Abbe Smith
32 Connecticut Law Review 485 (2000)

The truth is a complicated thing in criminal defense. I learned this early on as a public defender. During the initial training for new defenders, one of the senior lawyers shared a story. He was representing a man who maintained innocence about a series of thefts. The man claimed that he had nothing to do with the crime — instead, an enormous talking chicken had done it. The lawyer thought the client had a mental health problem and referred the case to the office's social services unit. Fortunately, he also asked an investigator to look into it. By doing so, the lawyer learned that on the day of the thefts there had been a promotional event for a newly opened fast-food restaurant specializing in fried chicken. As part of the event, the restaurant had hired a man to wear a chicken suit and hand out flyers. Several witnesses confirmed that they saw this "chicken-man" in possession of several of the stolen items near the location where the thefts had occurred.

I understood this anecdote to be a broad institutional lesson, the sort that gives rise to a number of maxims: Truth is stranger than fiction; don't be too quick to judge; you never know; and, most importantly, investigation is central to good defense work. I also understood it to suggest that the truth may not always be the most convincing or credible story, and, while the truth in this case led to the client's vindication, there may well have been other effective defense theories that could have been employed.

The best criminal defense lawyers have some sense of what the truth is, but are not hamstrung by it. Good criminal trial lawyers know how to use various aspects of the truth in order to construct a compelling narrative — one that jurors will accept, or one that will at least raise reasonable doubt. But, generally, criminal defense lawyers cannot and must not spend much time or energy worrying about the truth. After all, most criminal defendants are not innocent, and the truth is usually not helpful to the defense. When a crime is caught on videotape, this usually means a guilty plea.

By and large, I find the defense lawyer's relationship to the truth liberating. I like being unfettered by what "really happened." I like being free to craft my own story. I like putting the evidentiary pieces together in a puzzle of my choice. Criminal defenders are not mere lawyers; we are creative artists. Good defenders can make something of nothing and nothing of something. . . .

As defenders construct a theory of the case, much of their energy is spent trying to put the "truth" out of their minds. It can be disheartening to look at a police report with its damning account of your client's commission of a crime. You want to throw up your hands and say, how the hell am I supposed to defend against these charges? But, then you remind yourself: These are simply the allegations; they don't have to be taken at face value; there are many ways to raise questions and doubts about what is being alleged.

In some cases, the theory of defense may be that the truth of what happened is an existential question. Life is complicated. People are complicated. Memory is complicated. Motive is complicated. Sometimes defenders start believing that truth is itself illusory. No one can ever know what really happened in anything. Life is the movie *Rashomon.* . . .

When one undertakes a professional obligation to represent criminal defendants — the vast majority of whom are probably guilty — it seems quaint at best to suddenly start talking about innocence. After all, only Abraham Lincoln built a career representing only innocent clients. It is no easier for the factually innocent client to profess his or her innocence.

Of course, the problem with the defender's new-found embrace of truth in this posture is that truth is no simpler when a client is factually innocent than in a more typical case. The truth — even when it supports innocence — is often murky and complicated and may not make a very good story. . . .

Defending the innocent is no more noble than defending the guilty, no more honorable, no more virtuous; the calling of criminal defenders is to represent the guilty and innocent alike. But, the burden of defending the innocent is an extraordinary burden. It is constant and unrelenting. It is both a professional burden and a deeply personal one. It poses a challenge to everything I believe in, including myself.

NOTES & QUESTIONS

1. Criminal defense attorneys have ethically and morally complex professional relationships with "the truth" and, simultaneously, with their clients. In the preceding excerpt Professor Smith says of the defense attorney's relationship to the "truth": "The best criminal lawyers have some sense of what the truth is, but are not hamstrung by it." Smith finds this relationship "liberating." Is there something troublesome about the characterization? What, precisely, is the source of the discomfort for you, if any? Do the ethics of defense practice, or rationales about systematic checks and balances, provide sufficient insulation so that truth-telling takes a backseat to the interests of the client and to the primacy of the defense attorney's obligation to serve the client's interests without being "hamstrung"?

2. The defense attorney's complex role with respect to "the truth" is occasionally captured in popular culture. Scott Turow's Sandy Stern (played by Raul Julia in the movie version of *Presumed Innocent* and depicted in numerous Scott Turow novels) is a professionally competent and, usually, "ethical" defense attorney. Yet, in the film and novel versions of *Presumed Innocent*, Stern crosses ethical boundaries to prevent the truth from emerging at trial and to shape the evidence that does emerge into narrative. For example, in addition to conducting masterful cross-examinations of prosecution witnesses that disassemble the prosecution's case, in an *ex parte* conversation Stern threatens Judge Lytle, who presides over Sabich's trial, with the disclosure of a criminal investigation file that implicates the Judge in accepting bribes in complicity with the murder victim. This threat may compel the

Judge to dismiss the charges against Sabich after the close of the prosecution's case, and before Stern attempts to present the "B File" (including evidence of Lytle's corruption) as evidence to the jury. Why would an attorney risk his career in order to vindicate his client, especially a client whom he may not believe is innocent of murder? Why would Turow bend his plot upon the unethical conduct of his sympathetic and heroic defense attorney? Is this an exaggeration to push the plot forward? Are all criminal attorneys criminal when the stakes are sufficiently high? Does Turow exaggerate for the sake of dramatic effect? But is Stern's conduct really an exaggeration that is so far-fetched in the high-stakes games of legal storytelling in the courtroom in notorious criminal trials? Note that risky and professionally suspect conduct may not be limited exclusively to the actions of defense attorneys. Some prosecutors have equally complex and suspect relationships with "the truth." Prosecutor Douglas Muldur, recently a distinguished member of the Texas defense bar and sometimes featured on Court TV, is quoted by Adams' attorney in *The Thin Blue Line* to the effect that any good prosecutor can convict a guilty man, but it takes a great prosecutor to convict an innocent one.

3. The complexities of defense attorneys' roles and their professional relationships with the truth and with clients are often not explored in the flat and simplified narratives pervasive in popular culture. Television programs, especially serials such as *Perry Mason*, come immediately to mind. These provide formulaic plots and consistent characters to viewers desiring heroes and villains, and unproblematic, untroubling themes and plotting. These stories are, perhaps, merely the stuff of entertainment incorporating the inherent drama and conflict of the courtroom. For example, defense attorney Perry Mason is skillful, not corrupted; he is a truth-teller, a heroic and virtuous attorney. There is never anything problematic or troubling in Mason's relationships to his clients or to the truth; it is "the truth" that invariably emerges in the courtroom drama. Likewise, consistently heroic defense attorneys are often depicted in popular films.

PROFANE LAWYERING
James R. Elkins
http://myweb.wvnet.edu/~jelkins/mythweb99/profane.html

Webster's Seventh New Collegiate Dictionary defines profane: not concerned with religion or religious purposes — secular; not holy because unconsecrated, impure, or defiled — not sanctified; serving to debase or defile what is holy — irreverent; not among the initiated; not possessing esoteric or expert knowledge. The verb profane means to treat (something sacred) with abuse, irreverence, or contempt, to desecrate, violate. To debase by a wrong, unworthy, or vulgar use. . . .

Criminal lawyers, one suspects, are most accustomed to profane speech. Jerry Kennedy, the working man's lawyer in George Higgins's novel, *Kennedy for the Defense*, in his first meeting with Emerson Teller, a young man charged with homosexual solicitation of a police officer is questioned by his client about whether he thinks he "can get this cleared up?". . . Emerson tells Kennedy he was framed by the police officer. And Kennedy responds:

> Right. . . . And I was sculpted into my present graceful shape by a
> maniacal genius of a topiary gardener. Now, I did not haul my ass up here

this morning [from his vacation] to hear you tell me how you got framed and you're innocent and so help you God, you are the victim of a malevolent society. I came up here so you can tell me what happened. You tell me what happened. I will tell you whether you were framed, or whether there is some way I think maybe you got a shot at getting off, or whether you should hang down your head and cry and tell the judge that you ain't gonna do it again and you don't know what possessed you, you did it this time. I will also tell you what any one of those things is liable to cost you, and you will give me some money, and I will proceed. Or else you won't, and I won't. Clear? . . .

George V. Higgins, *Kennedy for the Defense* 65, 98-99 (New York: Ballantine, 1980). . . .

Lawyers are sometimes profane in speech, but they can also live profane lives. When lawyers tell stories about irreverent machinations of law, and their own lack of concern for justice, they become part of this profane world. The pull of this world and stories that defile are common in the hallways of buildings devoted to law.

Consider now [novelist and lawyer] George V. Higgins' introduction to Jerry Kennedy [the protagonist in *Kennedy for the Defense*]:

I have a client named Teddy Franklin. Teddy Franklin is a car thief. He is thirty-two years old, and he is one of the best car thieves on the Eastern Seaboard. Cadillac Ted is so good that he is able to support himself as a car thief. He has been arrested repeatedly, which is how he made my acquaintance, but he has never done time. That is because I am so good. It is also because Teddy is so good.

This is the way, Mack, Jerry Kennedy's wife describes her husband, according to Jerry Kennedy:

If you ask Mack what kind of lawyer I am, she will tell you that I am the classiest sleazy criminal lawyer in Boston, even if I am standing right there. This is not flattering, perhaps, but she knows I will not argue with her. I go to my office to make a living, not to make a life. My life is at home.

George V. Higgins, *Kennedy for the Defense* 1, 13 (1981).

Jerry Kennedy is not a bad man or a bad lawyer but he is working with some profane notions about lawyering, notions that may get him into trouble before all is said and done.

To profane law [to tell its profane stories, to treat law in a debased, irreverent way] violates one myth of professional life even as it identifies and configures another myth — that of the street-smart realist.

We profane only that which can be held sacred. Profanity of language is made possible by the beauty and inventiveness of language. If we had no poetry, no poetic rendering of experience, no word-shaped image of world and human sentiment, we could utter no profanity. In the absence of sacred sensibilities we would not experience outrage when we speak of what lawyers do in the name of law. . . .

NOTES & QUESTIONS

1. Professor Elkins provides illustrations of how, at least in popular legal fiction, the defense attorney's language begins to adapt to the world that he inhabits. He begins to sound like the criminals and defendants he represents, as if he is an insider within this world, able to see deeply into the thought processes of his clients and "speak their language." In doing so, the defense attorney in contemporary popular culture may begin to embody or inhabit the shadow world or underworld of the defendant. The compelling dialogue and street language of George V. Higgins' defense attorney Jerry Kennedy provide vivid examples. Like Sandy Stern, Jerry Kennedy is a recurring protagonist in a series of popular, successful and critically well-reviewed novels. Higgins is regarded as a master of dialogue and vernacular. It is unsurprising that in addition to his life as a novelist, Higgins practiced as both a prosecutor and defense attorney in Boston prior to his death. (He was also co-owner of a favorite bar and lawyer's hangout in Cambridge, Massachusetts.) Is Kennedy's street language (profane language) merely the fancy of a fiction writer or the idiosyncratic personal style of one novelist/attorney? Do criminal defense attorneys (and indeed other practitioners) tend to adopt the cultural coloration of the clients they serve?

2. A significant question is whether criminal defense attorneys adopt more from their clients' identities and through their professional relationships with their clients than merely language and style. Do they begin to assume moral ambiguity, if not engaging directly in the criminal activities of their clients? Is this perception embodied in a relatively recent shift in popular perceptions of defense attorneys in popular film? Is it also a characteristic of criminal law practice? Professor Richard Sherwin perceives the shift in identities of the defense attorneys in recent films from the idealizations of the heroic defense attorneys in earlier times. For example, in Martin Scorcese's *Cape Fear* (1991), defense attorney Sam Bowden is transformed from the heroic protagonist attorney and moral family man in the original film adaptation of J. Lee Thompson's novel (1961) into a far more complex and morally ambivalent character, who has suppressed evidence that would assist his client, engaged in adulterous behavior, and attempted to cover up his personal and ethical lapses and criminal misconduct. This may fit audience expectations in a different age. Richard K. Sherwin, *Cape Fear: Law's Inversion to Cathartic Justice*, 30 University of San Francisco Law Review 1023 (1996). Do you believe that this transformation of cinematic identity of criminal defense attorneys in popular culture anticipates cultural transformation in the identity of the typical criminal defense practitioner?

3. Professor J. Thomas Sullivan observes, "What is likely is that, for the most part, the inherent goodness of [Abraham] Lincoln and Atticus Finch is reserved for history, both in films and in our collective consciousness. This might mean that the adversarial system is due for reconsideration, if not revision. It may also mean that we have lost our innocence as an audience and society or that the problem of moral and legal guilt will remain a difficult one for clients, lawyers, and filmgoers struggling to understand how the defense attorney can represent a guilty defendant." J. Thomas Sullivan, *Imagining the Criminal Law: When Client and Lawyer Meet in the Movies*, 25 University of Arkansas at Little Rock Law Review 665, 680 (2003). Unlike Sherwin, Sullivan locates our unease with the role and tactics of the defense attorney in the fact that not only does the criminal defense attorney represent clients who are guilty, but also the defense attorney knows this to be so. Do you agree with Sullivan's observation? Has this always been the case? Why do you think our popular perceptions of the defense attorney have changed in recent years? Can you recall notorious criminal trials that may have reshaped popular perceptions of the role of the criminal defense attorney?

4. It may be that the defense attorney can speak no language except the profane language of the criminal client. However, it may also be that the successful defense attorney may be remarkably adept at translating this language into the embedded narratives of the trial and into the language of the law when the time is appropriate. In 1991, the reputed mobster Louis Failla was accused in a Racketeer Influenced and Corrupt Organizations Act (RICO) conspiracy prosecution of plotting the death of the father of his grandson (Tito Morales) under orders by the capo of the Connecticut faction of the Patriarca crime family (Billy "The Wild Guy" Grasso). Various incriminating conversations between Failla and the mobsters had been recorded on surveillance tapes by the FBI. Failla's attorney was Jeremiah Donovan, a former federal prosecutor. Donovan's task was a difficult one. He developed the theory that Failla only pretended to go along with the mobsters and pointed to a "subtext" in Failla's interactions with the mobsters. In his two-hour closing argument Donovan spoke the voices of various characters, including the gravelly voice of the defendant-turned-protagonist Failla, while quoting from transcripts of surveillance tapes. He literally created a new story. In the end, he had something that sounded "like a movie plot." Jeremiah Donovan, *Some Off-the-Cuff Remarks About Lawyers as Storytellers*, 18 Vermont Law Review 751, 756 (1994).

PROSECUTORS, PREJUDICES, AND JUSTICE: OBSERVATIONS ON PRESUMING INNOCENCE IN POPULAR CULTURE AND LAW
Christine Alice Corcos
34 University of Toledo Law Review 793 (2003)

In Scott Turow's world, prosecutors are the individuals least likely to presume anyone innocent as a matter of law or as a matter of fact — even though they are required by the canons of legal ethics not to prosecute anyone they believe might not in fact be guilty. Indeed, Turow's novel [*Presumed Innocent*] sketches for us the archetypal prosecutors who represent the best and worst of both real and fictional district attorneys (DAs), all of whom struggle with the question to some degree. In each archetype there is enough truth to cause some real concern about whether justice can be done, and seen to be done. In addition, *Presumed Innocent* presents us with a world in which many prosecutors intentionally or unintentionally, backed by the force of the state, destroy lives. They are not the heroes they should be; the heroes that Rusty thought he recognized when he first became a prosecutor. Only by leaving the world of the prosecutor does he fully discover this, although at the beginning of the novel he has his suspicions.

If we compare Turow's characters to prosecutors we hear and see in daily life, then the concern whether justice can be done deepens. Thus, *Presumed Innocent* continues to be relevant in any examination of both real and media justice. The film, of course, compresses many of Turow's complicated written images into more easily digestible visual chunks, but I would argue that it does not lessen the novel's impact. Fifteen years after its publication, *Presumed Innocent* remains an indictment of the legal system and suggests that one of our most honored principles — the presumption of innocence — is honored more in the breach than in the observance. . . .

NOTES & QUESTIONS

1.   Prosecutors and defense attorneys may not have precisely parallel roles or obligations. The defense attorney represents the interests of his client. The prosecutor, however, represents "the people" or "the state." What is the meaning of this distinction? Does it suggest that the prosecutor has a higher calling, and theoretically a greater interest in truth-telling than the defense attorney? That his obligations are not to effective storytelling but to doing justice? Pragmatically, the resources available to the prosecutor, e.g., police investigators, ability to question witnesses, etc., are vast compared to the investigatory resources available to the typical defendant. This often results in an imbalance of power. Does the prosecutor have an obligation of fair dealing and full disclosure in criminal cases? Or may a prosecutor properly adhere to a gamesmanship model as long as he does not violate ethical rules of conduct?

2.   Like George V. Higgins, Scott Turow was a former federal prosecutor before becoming a popular novelist and sometime criminal defense attorney. He speaks with the authority of his experiences. His depictions of prosecutors in *Presumed Innocent* and, indeed, in all his novels, are at best ambivalent. In *Presumed Innocent*, prosecutors are often careerist (the cold-hearted and venal Carolyn Polhemus comes to mind) or willing to cut corners and readily engage in ethically suspect conduct to obtain a conviction (Nicco della Guardia). Prosecutors are willing to sell out loyal subordinates to advance politically, or for revenge for personal or professional slights (Raymond Horgan). Further, they are often blatantly incompetent and lazy in their investigatory work and even in their courtroom practice (Tommy Molto). At least in Turow's Kindle County, prosecutors are often deeply entrenched in the shadows of criminality. Given these images, do you agree with Professor Corcos' assessment that, "if we compare Turow's characters to prosecutors we hear and see in daily life, then the concern whether justice can be done deepens"? Do you agree that *Presumed Innocent* "continues to be relevant in any examination of both real and media justice"? Or are these depictions of prosecutors in both the novel and film versions of *Presumed Innocent* merely fabrications, creating fictional antagonists to fuel popular narrative and propel stories forward toward dramatic and surprising resolutions that are not possible in the world of legal practice where, in fact, most criminal defendants brought to trial are guilty?

3.   There is clearly a counter-trend in popular culture as well. There are heroic prosecutors who, unlike the prosecutors in Turow's Kindle County, are committed to the emergence of truth, protectors of the public and cognizant of the rights of defendants. *Law & Order*, so popular as a prime-time television series that its original production stretched a full twenty years, tells the stories of heroic prosecutors with great moral integrity and legal acumen. These prosecutors are,

and remain, remarkably attractive characters psychologically, professionally, and physically (despite the passage of time). These prosecutors seek truth and justice and practice the law with scrupulous ethics. Unlike Turow's Kindle County prosecutors, seldom, if ever, do the trustworthy prosecutors on *Law & Order* cross ethical boundaries or sacrifice to expediency, avarice, or careerism in their noble calling to obtain the truth ethically. Why do these images still appeal to the viewer as consumer of television images? Why are they still so persuasive and compelling? Is it simply that we need these heroic archetypes in our popular narratives, as counterpoint to the dark stories of revelation and exploration of the shadow world of criminal practice? Further, the legal issues in *Law & Order*, although dramatically transformed, are well researched, and some law professors even employ episodes as texts in their classes. Does this program, with its images of truth-telling prosecutors, suggest more accurate representations of truth-telling prosecutors of competence and integrity and provide more accurate storylines for dramatization of what usually transpires within the criminal law system?

D. LEGAL STORYTELLING IN CRIMINAL TRIALS

As previously observed, films provide a unique mechanism for critical reflection on the dynamics of legal cultural storytelling, especially storytelling in criminal trials. That is:

> Lawyers are popular storytellers who operate in an aural and visual storytelling culture. Lawyers tell imagistic narratives constructed upon aesthetic principles that are closely akin to the principles that control the formulation of plot-structure in commercial cinema. We tell stories with hard driving plot-lines and clear themes that are readily distilled. We shoot our films from the fixed perspective of protagonist-clients.

Philip Meyer, *Visual Literacy and the Legal Culture: Reading Film as Text in the Law School Setting*, 17 Legal Studies Forum 73 (1993).

Here, we explore these perceptions: (1) through the theoretical concerns of a law professor analyzing Errol Morris' *The Thin Blue Line*; (2) through the observations of a "skeptical" law student in a seminar on "Law and Popular Storytelling" imagining the work of a criminal lawyer in relationship to the work of the filmmaker Errol Morris in *The Thin Blue Line* and to the work of the detective in Roman Polanski's film noir masterpiece *Chinatown* (1974); (3) through observations on how a skilled attorney in a "real" criminal case converts evidence into cinematic images in a narrative closing argument that intentionally implicates and draws upon "mob" stories from popular film; and, finally, (4) through the perceptions and wisdom of Jeremiah Donovan, a shrewd and self-reflective criminal law practitioner formulating his closing argument, who is profoundly aware of the interpenetration of legal and popular culture in criminal trial practice. Donovan further observes how and why he strategically attempts to incorporate popular storytelling practices at trial to the advantage of his client.

LAW FRAMES: HISTORICAL TRUTH AND NARRATIVE NECESSITY IN A CRIMINAL CASE
Richard K. Sherwin
47 Stanford Law Review 39 (1994)

When truth defies certainty and becomes complex, justice requires difficult decisions on the basis of that doubt. The struggle between shifting cognitive needs and legal duty is commonplace, and without a way to question how a given narrative shapes and informs our desire for certain and tidy justice, that desire, and competing ones, cannot be adequately understood. As a result, the kind of justice operating in a particular case at a given cultural juncture may remain confused or hidden from view. The emergence in our time of a post-modern narrative of justice, one that is spontaneous, contingent, and irrepressibly messy, provides a case in point. The challenge is to tap the salient cultural storylines, both familiar and newly emerging, that give meaning and coherence to uncertainty, so that when a case demands, we can feel sure enough in our reasonable doubt.

In some of what follows, I shall be arguing uphill, in favor of complexity, insinuating ambivalence about the kind of order legal stories typically create. I shall approach the disorder that lurks beyond the bounds of these well-told tales. Perhaps more unforgivable, I shall question whether the specific tale of Randall Dale Adams might be less tidy than we'd prefer. What if the modernist penchant for dichotomies that produces starkly polar choices like guilt/ innocence, frameup/ frameup undone, injustice/injustice corrected — the very mindset that gives us such satisfaction in seeing justice's scales finally balanced — were part of the problem? I want to suggest that the simplicity of these polarities, and the calm they induce, are at least partly responsible for making us leave things out. The messy things. The things that leave a sense of disorder and lack of control, the unsettling things we refuse to see or discuss. These are the things that make it hard to make legal decisions, decisions that can have irrevocable effects upon the body and soul of a person: prison, prison life, perhaps even death. No less grave, they are decisions that could lead to erroneous acquittal and the recurrence of violence by the liberated defendant. It is precisely because the stakes are so high that I want to examine how we might guard against facile resolutions without getting mired in indecision and meaninglessness. In particular, I want to explore a form of postmodern legal storytelling that can serve a sustainable sense of justice as well as order. But to follow this path we must learn to question our own complicity in making truth appear overly neat and coherent. Thus, rather than share in the triumph of having seen the system set straight, we must ask ourselves whether we are not accomplices in a form of reality-making that let the Adams frameup occur in the first place and that could let similar frameups occur in the future.

Uncontrollable disorder within the criminal justice system is an admittedly disturbing topic, and I don't enjoy dwelling on it any more than you do. But surely it is a good thing to increase our awareness of how we deal with the omnipresent possibility of disorder, as well as the possibility that conflicting legal stories may simultaneously be true. This sort of knowledge helps us guard against deception by others, and by ourselves, and better enables us to distinguish credible from incredible narratives. In criminal law, where lives hang in the balance of a tale, this ability is critical. . . .

NOTES & QUESTIONS

1.   Professor Sherwin speaks of a tension or struggle between a desire for a "certain and tidy justice" and an "emergence . . . of a postmodern narrative of justice" that is "spontaneous, contingent, and irrepressibly messy." What, exactly, does Professor Sherwin mean? Can you translate Sherwin's observation into an example that makes the abstract generalization come alive? Often, the word "postmodernism" appears in critical and scholarly writings on law practice. What is "postmodernism"? Do you believe that there is tension between "modernist dichotomies" such as "guilt/innocence" required for legal determinations in the courtroom, and how we now perceive stories as relativistic, "spontaneous, contingent, and irrepressibly messy"? Are legal outcomes in trials often a function of the power of the storyteller to construct and tell an effective and compelling narrative that matches the evidence introduced at trial? Could we say this has always been the role of the trial attorney in our advocacy system?

2.   Do you believe that trials are about the possibility of "objective" understandings that are not dependent upon the perspective and skill of the story-teller? Are courtroom battles in our system about unearthing and determining the truth? Or are you already a hardened and cynical postmodernist, comfortable with the notion that determinations of guilt and innocence are often based primarily upon who is the more effective storyteller, and who has the most resources to engage in investigations for evidence connected to artful and manipulative narratives?

3.   The stories that emerge at trial depend upon evidence that is developed in factual investigations. How are these investigations undertaken? Does the selection of a narrative theme shape the facts uncovered by the investigation that will be converted into evidence at trial? For example, consider the police investigation and prosecutorial decisions that resulted in the conviction of Randall Adams for murder in *The Thin Blue Line*. The reinvestigation by the filmmaker Errol Morris as developed in the movie points to a different culprit (David Harris). As you sit as a viewer as if upon a jury and observe the powerful storytelling practice of Errol Morris, are you persuaded that David Harris is clearly the murderer? How does Morris shape his story? What narrative and strategic choices does he make? What is the powerful theme that drives his construction of the narrative? Is it, as Professor Sherwin suggests, a story about "a frameup"? Is it a story about "actual innocence"?

4.   In *The Thin Blue Line*, what forces or presumptions shape the investigation by the police, anticipate the prosecutor's theory of the crime, and shape the trial story? Is it important that David Harris is an adolescent who cannot receive the death penalty? Or that he is a soft-featured and well-spoken young man from Texas while Randall Adams is a drifter from the Midwest? That the police desire to close the case quickly and condemn a cop killer to death for the murder? That the prosecuting attorney desires to maintain his excellent winning percentage (his "batting average") in jury trials?

5. Once the investigation targets Randall Adams, police and prosecutors seem intransigent and unwilling to change their theory of the case. What are the psychological and pragmatic forces that prevent the police and prosecutor from acknowledging the possibility that Randall Adams may not be the culprit?

6. Assume, as Sherwin suggests, that Morris' version of the story is about a "frameup." The new evidence uncovered by Morris (often first-hand testimony from the various legal actors, including the testimony of David Harris confessing to the crime placed at the end of the picture as the denouement) is extremely powerful. Why do the defendant's attorneys not conduct a similarly efficient and thorough investigation? How are they blocked and thwarted in their efforts by the prosecutor and the police? Is their failure to uncover evidence based upon a lack of resources? Did the prosecutor act unethically in the trial and investigation, or was he merely acting in accord with the gamesmanship model of adversary proceedings?

7. Assume you are now the prosecutor, and Randall Adams seeks postconviction relief. Would you challenge the authenticity of the confession by David Harris? Would you attack his credibility? Assume Harris' "confession" on the tape recording was introduced as new evidence at an evidentiary hearing. What, if any, counter-story might you tell? What, if any, counterarguments would you make against reopening the case based on Harris' alleged confession?

8. Are any crucial narrative pieces of the story omitted from Morris' version of the story? For example, is there a time on the night of the killing that is not accounted for by either the testimony of Randall Adams or David Harris? What, if anything, do you think occurred during this missing "gap" in time? Why is the time line of events not fully developed?

VISUAL LITERACY AND THE LEGAL CULTURE: READING FILM AS TEXT IN THE LAW SCHOOL SETTING
Philip N. Meyer
17 Legal Studies Forum 73 (1993)

Skepticism

I proposed hypothetical questions to contextualize our viewing of several films: Do trials ever reveal the "truth" of the past? Is this their primary function? Or are lawyers merely narrativist tricksters? Is it, as one seminar participant observed, only "God who really knows what happened?" Does the trial serve primarily other functions, ". . . such as resolving the controversy, releasing emotions, providing a sense of coherence — not necessarily between the event and the outcome, but between the outcome and what happened at the trial itself[?]"

Alternatively, as the cognitive theorist Jerome Bruner has argued persuasively, is the storytelling (narrative) mode discrete from the empirical (paradigmatic) mode of proof? Are stories formed by clever and devious aesthetic arrangements connected by the aesthetic tissue of verisimilitude? Although events may "happen," are the causes (the hows and whys of events) ever "knowable"? Can we, for example, ever look inside someone's mind to determine "intent" or "state of mind"? Do rules of procedure and evidence unduly circumscribe and artificially constrain trial narratives? Are lawyers an ethnocentric sub-culture of popular storytellers particularly subject to the professional self-delusion that cognitive theorists have termed "the original attribution error"?

In exploring this constellation of discussion questions and themes, thoughtful participants reveal in their journals additional features of visual literacy. Doug C. titles his exploration of the storytelling role of the lawyer "Truth In and Out of Chinatown." The journal compares *Chinatown* and Errol Morris' *The Thin Blue Line* as presenting visual metaphors for the lawyer's role in the storytelling process. "Chinatown" is the title of Roman Polanski's movie; it is also Doug's elliptical reference and response to conflicting images of the lawyer's storytelling role.

Initially, Doug's introduction states, somewhat apologetically, that his paper reflects a "familiar" seminar discussion theme:

> . . . [C]an the truth of a past event be known? Is an "objective" reality possible, or is every past occurrence only possible of interpretation within the context of the observer's unique unrepeatable perspective of the event?

Doug discusses this theme with a certain detachment and indignation, reflective of the attitudes of many bright seminar participants. That is, Doug's answer to this question is, implicitly, obvious. Stories, especially aural and visual stories, cannot and do not reveal truth. We live in an imagistic, fragmentary and subjective world, and our "stories" are intrinsically imaginative reconstructions.

> . . . [S]ince there is no recount[ing] of events that we can accept as absolutely true . . . we are forced to create systems of "truth substitutes" as alternatives and thus "truth" becomes definable only within the systems that we create. . . .

"Truth" is literally dependent upon the placement and angle of the camera:

> A popular example: last spring Tate George propelled the UCONN Huskies basketball team into the NCAA Final Eight by a "buzzer beating" last second shot. But was the shot "good"? The best view provided by CBS cameras' "Super Slo Mo" replays appears to indicate that Tate's hand touching the ball when the shot clock on the same screen indicated no time was remaining . . . this replay became the "truth substitute" to which the announcers latched onto and their pronouncement was that UCONN stole a victory. But in the case of Tate's shot, accepting a camera replay as the best "truth substitute" probably doesn't get us any closer to the absolute truth than the version espoused by any random ticketholders. Perhaps if God were a Husky fan, He might inform us that two molecules that connected Tate's hand to the basketball ceased to "touch" one another (in some atomic sense) with a nanosecond of time remaining in the game. However, anything short of such a divine vision will contain all the inherent defects that "truth substitute" systems suffer from. That is, belief in the truth becomes synonymous with belief in the system.

Doug's observations reflect a knowing cynicism that he shares with many seminar participants about the nature of their chosen profession and the limited possibilities of such a narrative-based system's providing "justice" that is ultimately any more than narrative resolution or denouement:

> . . . As a general rule, the justice system seems to favor the "knowable" version of the truth. Lawyers tend to believe the opposite. By their behavior and their beliefs, lawyers view the truth as "unknowable" and as an unapproachable ideal. Thus a lawyer might say that the judicial system is not a search for truth but a forum for the exposition of competing versions of what-the-hell happened in a given event.

Doug states his belief that "leaving aside examples where it is so clear that an account of an event is 'true' or at least so clear that no one wants to bother arguing about it — 'the truth' is 'unknowable.' Since there is no way 'truth' can be definitively proven, the role of the lawyer is not to aid in the search for truth, which according to him is an oxymoronic phrase anyway, but to arrange any and all facts available to produce the story that best suits his client's needs." Errol Morris's *The Thin Blue Line* is a "persuasive illustration" of how easily stories are manipulated and how readily we succumb to the call of our own stories:

> In the movie, truth is not static or fixed, but is malleable enough to bend according to the teller of the story. . . . The movie's premise achieves the effect of creating horrible unease in the hearts of viewers.

Detective mysteries, particularly cinematic detective stories, provide an effective visual metaphor for a contrasting idealization of how the "justice" system (a "truth-substitute" system) supposedly works.

> How do detectives fit into this scheme? . . . Each is faced with a past event that is open to dispute; a crime, mystery, or confusing or unexplained incident. Both must "reconstruct" the event for an audience. But here the detective and lawyer part company. The lawyer's motivation is not necessarily to find the truth; instead he is motivated to come up with a reasonable version of a story, consonant with the facts, that best serves his client's needs and in turn his own. In contrast, the . . . detective traditionally wishes to find the truth, or the least distorted version of truth available.

Detectives can be "roughly categorized into two groups; those that primarily ponder on the past and those that act within the present." In the first "genre" — akin to the way truth is uncovered in the judicial system — passive truth-finders "parse through all available information and establish not the best but the only explanation":

> . . . [A]n event leaves behind facts that are indelible and unique as a fingerprint. The mere inspection of existing clues would expose a wolfhound, a poisonous snake climbing a rope bellringer, or a murderous orangutan. Though cloaked in enticing packaging, this view of the the way the world operates is mostly stage theatrics and . . . borders on campiness.

A second type of truth finder is an "active participant" in the process. Jake Gittes in Polanski's *Chinatown* is an example of a detective in this genre:

> Gittes is quick-witted and bright but not of [Sherlock] Holmesian intellect. Instead, Gittes' genius appears to be not in finding out what the hell

happened but in making things happen. Since the case before him is not laid out like an intricate puzzle, Gittes must resort to oldfashioned investigative work and during his meddling, dames scream, punches are thrown, and guns blaze in the night. Gittes is a human monkey wrench and despite being confused as to what his role should be, since he isn't sure of anything including why he was initially hired, he throws himself into a vague conspiracy hidden against the gauzy southern California landscape

Jake seems to be aware that he will not always find clues merely by obtaining a superior vantage point but that clues must be dislodged by his very presence. . . . In Chinatown Jake is as much a part of the overall plot as the crime itself.

As much as *Chinatown* tends to resemble how truth is actually unearthed, the movie is still faithful to, and thus somewhat limited by its adherence to the notion that, truth is "knowable." This commitment to a clean, tidy universe is understandable in a commercial sense, since moviegoers are unlikely to flock to see a movie with no resolution, or worse, one whose conclusion is that truth is unknowable. Although Chinatown challenges commercial orthodoxy in certain ways, its iconoclasm is limited to sending the message that the search for truth and justice is not rewarded (can it be its own reward?) and the act of doing good will only result in getting your new girlfriend killed in the end.

Errol Morris' *The Thin Blue Line* presents a contrasting metaphor about the "nature of truth" although, Doug observes, the movie's ending is "at odds with the overall message":

Morris sets out to show that all stories are hopelessly subjective, and that truth cannot be found, except in the ending of the movie Morris betrays his own thesis. By concluding his film with David Harris's vague, ambiguous "confession," Morris has arranged the facts and interviews to produce the inevitable conclusion that Randall Adams is innocent and Harris is guilty. While I do not argue with the merits of this conclusion (anyone who saw the movie would have to agree that Harris is guilty as sin), the overall point of the movie is lost. Morris sets out to establish that all interpreters of events rely on their particular perspective; this is why no two accounts of an event can be absolutely similar and why the past only exists according to the storyteller's will. But by choosing to place Harris' confession at the end, Morris has made a conscious decision to have the story come to a conclusion that points to an obvious "truth"; that Harris is guilty. The theme of storyteller as creator of truth becomes an incestuous one, as Morris appears to fall prey to the same folly as those that he tries to expose.

Other participants, like Doug, revealed similar attitudes about stories, particularly visual and aural stories. Participants were deeply skeptical about the possibilities of such stories' revealing "truth" especially when these stories were embedded in the formulaic procedural maze and evidentiary constraints of the judicial process. This cynicism is, perhaps, partially a product of three years of immersion in the exclusively paradigmatic culture of law school that devalues and deemphasizes narratives. Simultaneously, participants — subjected to a continual barrage of visual and aural stories in a popular culture filled with advertising, television, radio, politics, sound-byte news — often felt deceived by stories and popular storytellers. Although extremely thoughtful and perceptive, they were sensitive to manipulation and tended to disbelieve their eyes and ears. The heightened awareness and critical acuity of many students was often accompanied by a hardened detachment, cynicism, and refusal to suspend disbelief. Many participants, like Doug, are truly suspicious of all visual narratives including "actual" video shots of such events as the Tate George shot or the Rodney King beating. These images, often edited into fragments and sound bytes that are deceptive and decontextualized from the events themselves, are perceived as "truth substitutes" that do not capture or reflect externalities or totalities. Many upper-level law students no longer trust narrative explanations; they are frozen into narrative disbelief. The filmic texts provided an opportunity to reflect systematically on this deep skepticism.

Passivity, detachment, cynicism and, I fear, resentment and anger, are also deeply ingrained features of the new visual literacy. . . .

NOTES & QUESTIONS

1.   As the preceding excerpt suggests, Professor Sherwin is not alone when he speculates that the process of narrativization of evidence in the criminal trial through legal storytelling may not always lead to discovery of "the truth." Doug C. and other law students in a "Law and Popular Storytelling" class likewise perceived inherent limitations on legal storytelling in criminal trials, and shared the postmodernist cynicism or skepticism identified by Sherwin. Do you share Doug C.'s belief that "truth" is often dependent upon "the placement of the camera" (perspective) or the shrewdness of attorney-storytellers' tactical and rhetorical strategies and the theatrics of the courtroom?

2.   Doug C. also argues that, in attempting to provide a clear narrative resolution by selecting David Harris' confession as the final piece of the narrative puzzle, Errol Morris "falls prey to the same folly as those that he tries to expose." That is, in attempting to fulfill the narrative expectations of his audience and provide a clear resolution and message, Morris betrays his underlying "postmodernist" message. How might Morris have restructured his story to more fully convey this message? How do you think the audience might have responded to a film without a clear narrative resolution?

3.   Stylistically, Errol Morris blends "real" interviews with reconstructions akin to a low-budget television program and clips from fictional movies. Why is there an intentional montage of fictional and non-fictional material in the narrative mix? Why does Morris employ an intentionally eloquent Phillip Glass musical score? Do all these seemingly irreconcilable aesthetic pieces clash or fit together? What do you think Errol Morris is trying to "say" with this strangely eclectic mix of source materials, and through his visual style and editing choices? Do these choices intentionally draw the viewer's attention to the interpenetration of legal and popular culture and, simultaneously, invite reflection upon how we construct our stories and meanings on the storyboards of our own imaginations?

4. Richard Pryor, the late African American comedian and storyteller, observed, "I went down to the courthouse looking for justice, and that's what I found: Just us! I went to the jails, and who's serving time? Just us! So who gets justice in this country? Right again? Just us!" Richard Pryor, *Is It Something I Said?* (Reprise Records 1975). Statistically, there seems to be evidence supporting Pryor's observation regarding prosecution, conviction, and incarceration of black Americans. For example, the U. S. Bureau of Justice Statistics estimates an 18.6% chance that an African American (male or female) will be imprisoned over the course of his or her life, but only a 10.0% chance that a Hispanic American will be imprisoned and a 3.4% chance that a white American will be imprisoned. U.S. Department of Justice, Bureau of Justice Statistics, *Prevalence of Imprisonment in the U. S. Population, 1974-2001* (Aug. 2003, NCJ 197976). The Bureau of Justice Statistics also produces yearly reports estimating the current number of state or federal prisoners of different races. In 2009, there were an estimated 1,548,7000 prisoners, of whom 591,700 (approximately 38%) were African American. U.S. Department of Justice, Bureau of Justice Statistics, *Prisoners in 2009* (Dec. 2010, NCJ 231675). The U. S. Census Bureau, meanwhile, reports that only 12.6% of the U. S. population is African American (*State and County Quick Facts*, available at http://quickfacts.census.gov/qfd/states/00000.html). Note that the films discussed in this chapter generally pertain primarily to white (Caucasian) attorneys telling the stories of white (Caucasian) defendants. African American storytellers are seldom lead characters in pop cultural stories, especially commercial entertainment films marketed to mass audiences. Why is there a shortage of stories featuring these characters in popular films? Are commercial audiences less able to understand fully narratives outside of their own experiences or to empathize fully with characters whose ethnicity, personal circumstances, and experiences are unlike their own?

WHY A JURY TRIAL IS MORE LIKE A MOVIE THAN A NOVEL
Philip N. Meyer
28 Journal of Law & Society 133 (2001)

Converting Evidence and Argument into Story

In trials to a jury, effective advocates often convert the more fragmented structures of rule-based analytical arguments into unitary and focused narratives. The analytical arguments are structured through logic and inference. Clinical paradigms for teachers of trial advocacy accurately articulate the sequence of steps that the trial attorney employs to create the analytical structure of a trial argument. First, the advocate converts the more abstract terminology and categories of legal elements into factual propositions. Some of these factual propositions are crucial and highly problematic and contested. Others are not. The advocate in structuring argumentation and proof at trial must establish the linkage between evidence introduced at trial and the crucial and relevant underlying factual propositions by identifying generalizations that connect the evidence to the factual propositions.

For example, I analyzed the trial of a federal criminal case (brought under the federal RICO conspiracy statute) charging a defendant with conspiracy in the attempted murder of another person. The problematic element of the charge was whether the defendant, a reputed mobster and member of a crime family, intended to murder that person. That is, the crucial legal issue was the question of defendant's "intent," the mens rea component of the crime. The most probative evidence of defendant's intent was his promise to the head of the crime family that he would kill the third person. The "logical" or "inferential" legal argument presented by the prosecution may be diagrammed in accordance with the clinical model presented for analyzing inferential arguments by Moore, Bergman, and Binder as follows:

Evidence: Defendant promised the mob boss that he would kill the third person.

Generalization: When a defendant promises another person that he will kill a third person, the defendant usually intends to kill the third person.

Especially when:

1. The defendant is a member of a "crime family."

2. The defendant is "deathly afraid" of the person to whom he has made the promise.

3. The defendant knows that the person to whom he has made the promise has a compelling motive for wanting the third person dead.

4. The defendant conspires with other members of the "crime family" about how to accomplish the killing.

The defendant responds with counter-propositions ("except whens") that make the prosecution's argument less likely to be true. These counter-propositions must also be supported by evidence submitted at trial. Thus the logic of defendant's counter-argument may be set forth as follows:

Defendant's "Except Whens":

1. Defendant is not receiving much benefit from being a member of the crime family and does not participate in the family's day-to-day activities.

2. Defendant has a close personal relationship with the third person.

3. Defendant does not really mean what he says and is lying about his true intentions to buy time for the third person.

4. Defendant is prone to hyperbole and exaggeration about his criminal intentions.

5. Defendant has failed to carry out the execution even when he has been alone with the third person and has had the opportunity to do so.

The attorney, hypothetically, could have presented evidence at trial, and structured his argument in just this way, as a series of logical counter propositions. Like many, perhaps most, effective attorneys these days, however, he did not choose to do so. Instead, he converted the "except whens," and the evidence supporting these propositions, into an aesthetically compelling narrative similar in tone, structure and content to many hard, linear, protagonist-driven Hollywood cine-myths. The evidence introduced at trial had been presented as if "story-boarded" and was then recapitulated in closing argument in the form of a three-part structure of a popular, compelling, and entertaining "Mafia movie." Theme, character, conflict, and narrative structure were intentionally proximate to filmic counterparts about the mob, and the story of the tender-hearted mobster had numerous historical, cinematic antecedents. Furthermore, the attorney nested his storytelling in these cinematic models. The story had many of the characteristics of a popular Hollywood mob fable filled with irony and humor, and attempted to fulfill the audience's expectations and understandings about American crime families derived from popular film.

Evidence is converted into story on the spine of a hard narrative structure that is "thematic." The theme is like the "stock" themes and repetitive stories of Hollywood entertainment fables. Here the theme is that of a redemption plot, where the protagonist moves from selfishness towards selflessness and ultimately sacrifices himself to a larger cause. The classic Hollywood version of redemption story is, perhaps, *Casablanca* where the protagonist, Rick, a strong but selfish man, moves from cynicism to romantic love and then, at the moment of crisis, sacrifices himself in service of a larger cause.

I have called the "title" of the defendant's version of the thematic trial story "Desperate For Love" and explained the plot as the story of a weak but kind man torn between the love of his Mafia family on the one hand and the love of his "real" family on the other. His dilemma and his internal psychological conflict and the outer plot conflict are resolved at the denouement. Like Rick, the protagonist in *Casablanca* who moves from great selfishness towards love of another and then towards self-sacrifice within the confines of three hard narrative acts, the protagonist, defendant Louie Failla, moves through a similar psychological arc, along the well-trodden character through-line and narrative progression of the contemporary almost-hero.

The perspective of the storyteller, the defendant's attorney, like the director's perspective in *Casablanca*, is focused upon Louie's psychological transformation that is intimated through his responses to the pressures of external events. Like the audience in *Casablanca*, the jurors respond to Louie's psychological transformation. Also, in the end, like Rick in *Casablanca*, Louie, the protagonist/defendant, a weak but kind man, gains strength and sacrifices himself, stringing along his adopted mob family and pretending to participate in the murder conspiracy while, in fact, protecting his son-in-law from the mob. . . .

It is my belief that trial storytelling genre conventions — the rules of evidence, the time constraints of the trial itself, the focus on arranging testimony and events into clear narrative progressions that complement juror expectations, and the focus upon events taking place on a shared and external narrative landscape — all shape the defendant's character in the trial story to take the imaginative form of the protagonist in a Hollywood genre film. . . .

NOTES & QUESTIONS

1.   Attorneys construct arguments based upon evidence entered at trial. Attorneys are very careful about the evidence that is entered and carefully shape the way their audience derives inferences from this evidence. Trial attorneys do not have the opportunity, outside of opening statements and closing arguments, to speak directly to their audience and explain the significance of the evidence. It is up to the audience (jurors or judges sitting as fact-finders) to ascribe meaning through inferences. How, precisely, does the audience make these inferences? Professor Richard Sherwin identifies such terms as the "schema" and "script." A script, for example, is a model of behavior embodying our normative expectations (how people go about their "normal" everyday lives and activities). Sherwin illustrates the "script" for ordering a meal in a restaurant. *See* Sherwin, *supra*, 50. The plots of stories, however, are typically about "conflicts" that are violations or breaches of customary or normative cultural scripts and explorations of the consequences of these violations.

2.   Sherwin further identifies "metaphors, stereotypes, narrative genres, and recurrent plot lines" as additional cognitive tools that jurors employ to decode meaning through customary patterns. *Id.* at 51. Recently, there has been an expansive and rapidly developing interdisciplinary literature by legal academics decoding how jurors interpret and convert the evidence at trial into meaning, and then formulate these stories to match verdict categories. For example, Professor Neal R. Feigenson draws upon work in social psychology and observes:

> Connecting the schematic analysis and the particular story are the cognitive frameworks we use to understand the social world. These implicit knowledge structures and inferential habits constitute the audience's "common sense" about how the world works and why people behave as they do. They shape the audience's cognitive and emotional responses to the facts and thereby guide the audience's interpretation of both the facts and their legal significance. . . .

Neal R. Feigenson, *On Social Cognition and Persuasive Writing*, 20 Legal Studies Forum 75, 75 (1996).

3.   Pop cultural stories, especially film stories, may provide (or illustrate) the "macro" templates upon which attorneys graft or "storyboard" evidence at trial. These stock stories are often "mythic." Can you identify one or more of these popular "stock" stories and identify the controlling myths that have been used in recent notorious criminal trials by both defense attorneys and prosecutors?

4.   In Errol Morris' *The Thin Blue Line*, various witnesses testify for the movie audience, and the director intentionally splices in (cuts to) internal images that are television-like reconstructions or "clips" — sequences of images — from old movies. These internalized narrative templates reveal a great deal about how the various witnesses reconstruct "reality" and imaginatively configure events into narratives that often seem like part of familiar movie plots. What are your core myths, and are they embodied in popular films? Do films similarly influence your world view? How might these stories influence you and predispose you to accept certain types of narratives?

SOME OFF-THE-CUFF REMARKS ABOUT LAWYERS AS STORYTELLERS

Jeremiah Donovan
18 Vermont Law Review 751 (1994)

This two-month trial provided an enormous amount of material to work from. If you listen to the tapes used in this trial, you would say to yourself, "This is not real life — this was written by a radio writer." The FBI intercepted a mob initiation ceremony, but it sounded as if it had been written for radio. It was responsorial, much like the old Latin mass, "Io voglio . . . io voglio . . . entrare . . . entrare . . . in questo orginazione . . . in questo orginazione." It sounded like a Latin prayer. When they burned the picture of the saint, you could hear the crackling of the fire on tape. I mean, this ceremony has been handed down from sixteenth century Sicily so you expect it to be dramatic. However, what was equally dramatic was all the activity surrounding it. Afterwards, after all the cleaning up and goodbyes, you hear the steps of the final participant going to the door, the door squeaks open, and then, to the empty room, you hear someone say, "No one will ever know what went on here today — except for us and the fucking Holy Ghost." Then you hear the door slam, and you imagine fifty FBI agents in the surveillance van shouting,

"Hurray!" Louis and Jack would reminisce not only about all the things that got the other defendants in trouble at trial, but also about their young days. These included some of the most wonderfully tender but obscene reminiscences about adolescent life such as going out on dates in the late 1930s and early 1940s. They were just wonderful pieces of evidence.

This extraordinary evidence caused a divorcement between reality and what was portrayed in the course of the trial, between what happened in the real world and the evidence that the jury saw. Professor Sherwin talked earlier today [at a Vermont Law School conference devoted to the consideration of narrative and the law] about taking a videotape, computerizing it, and looking at it over and over and over until the reality begins to change. In this trial that is exactly what happened. The evidence was so dramatic and so interesting that one got the sense that these things did not take place in the real world at all and that Billy Grasso was a character rather than a real dead person.

This struck me most strongly after the Government introduced an exhibit of a board with about a hundred human bones mounted on it. These tiny little bones, some of them, but not all, were alleged to be the remains of some poor guy who had the indiscretion to engage in an affair with the wife of an unindicted co-defendant on the lam. After the bones were introduced, I walked by the clerk's table one day where the bones were laying underneath all the other exhibits: videotapes, papers, documents, and boxes on top of this fellow's bones. Nobody had any sense whatsoever that these were once a man.

One of the corporeal acts of mercy is to bury the dead. I got a plastic bag, covered the bones, and put them in a corner of the courtroom. I realized at this point that nobody was thinking of reality, nobody was thinking, "These are a person's bones." They were props in a drama. That realization helped me with my final argument because I could make that argument into a story, something that sounded like a movie plot.

When I talk to juries in my closing argument I think back to my bachelor days, and the jury is my date. We just saw a movie and we're drinking coffee and talking about the movie. I talk about the trial as if it were the film we saw. "Do you remember the part where Sonny Castagno was testifying? Remember he said. . . ." As I do this, I talk directly to a particular juror. It doesn't seem to embarrass the juror. "Remember the part where Sonny Castagno said that he was going to give Jackie Johns a call that night? Do you know why that was so important? Do you know why? Did you follow it? Well, wait a second, before I get to that, let's talk about something else," and then I'll talk about something else. Now the jurors are dying to know why I think what Castagno said was so important. At the end, when I finally come back to it, they will be all ears.

These final arguments always have three parts, just as my talk to you today has three parts, because final arguments must be very carefully structured. The problem is, if you are not talking from notes it is hard to keep the structure of the argument in your mind. But if they always have three parts, you will always know where you are. So if you get carried away at some point, you nevertheless remember, "I'm still in part two."

Professor Meyer finds my storytelling cinematic. I never thought or realized that it was cinematic; however, I now see that he is right. I don't necessarily tell the story chronologically, rather I tell portions of the story or simply a dramatic segment of the story in order to illustrate a point. What happens once I begin telling the story is that I can relax since I know it. I've just watched the movie, and spent the last two months trying this case. The little details that I need to make the story vivid, to make the story come alive, are those details I've struggled with for the last two months to get in through my witnesses or through cross-examination of the Government's witnesses. Since these things are fresh in my mind I can relax during the course of retelling the story. I notice that juries tend to relax as well: they sit back and seem to enjoy the story that I'm retelling. After all, they've just seen the movie too.

NOTES & QUESTIONS

1. Jeremiah Donovan contrasts appellate arguments with closing arguments to a jury. Describing trial argumentation when the attorney speaks to the jury in a closing argument, Donovan employs the analogy of a conversation with a girlfriend on a date after a movie. Donovan stresses that his conversation is intentionally interactive or "dialogic," and the tone is intimate. That is, the attorney is retelling the story as if to his date, the juror. But he has another purpose in mind — he is not simply telling the tale for entertainment. Thus Donovan presents implicitly the image of the trial attorney as seducer. Do you find this image troubling or problematic? If so, identify the source of your discomfort.

2. Donovan also speaks of the "divorcement between reality and what was portrayed in the course of the trial, between what happened in the real world and the evidence that the jury saw." In addition, he emphasizes the visuality of the

evidence converted into images in a trial narrative, presented to evoke the "real" world. Donovan bifurcates what occurs in the courtroom (what is admitted into evidence) from some more objective determination of what may have happened outside the courtroom. Implicitly, this assessment affirms law student Doug C.'s skeptical postmodern perspective and his belief that the attorney's quest at trial is not for truth, but rather for a form that achieves a purpose and provides a "truth substitute" that affirms the system and serves his client's interests. Do you agree?

3.   Donovan speaks of a three-part narrative structure that undergirds, and is characteristic of, his closing arguments. Such a structure is also characteristic of other popular narratives, including traditional three-act plays and the three-part movements of the typical popular Hollywood film. According to Donovan, reliance upon this structure liberates him from the limitations of a strict and literal chronology. Stories can then seemingly move more freely in time, e.g., through flashbacks and flashforwards, within the set pieces of this structure. Likewise, events can be revealed to fit the rhythms of the storyteller and the needs of the story, rather than shaped artificially or limited by chronology. That is, narrative time in courtroom storytelling is not "real" time. Likewise, chronology is not the primary ordering principle in movies. Narrative time is more complex than in the stories presented in appellate cases, or in how students are typically allowed to retell the facts of a case in the law school classroom. Why do you think there is this difference?

4.   What interesting or unusual narrative strategies or techniques do law-related films employ to convey or reveal the passage of time? Do these techniques help or hinder the viewer to better understand the story? Do they make the story more compelling or persuasive? How might some of these techniques be useful to the legal storyteller in a criminal trial?

E.   HEROES, VILLAINS, AND VICTIMS IN POPULAR MELODRAMAS ABOUT CRIMINAL LAW

ARE THE CHARACTERS IN A DEATH PENALTY BRIEF LIKE THE CHARACTERS IN A MOVIE?
Phillip N. Meyer
32 Vermont Law Review 877 (2008)

The story [in a cinematic melodrama] is, at its positivist core, a melodrama about the confrontation between good and evil, the heroic protagonist battling against the evil villain.

Within this archetypal battle, Alfred Hitchcock suggests that the depiction of the character of the powerful villain is as important as that of a protagonist hero. Nevertheless, despite the power of the villain, the hero must in the end defeat the villain and the forces of antagonism; "melodrama denotes a story that 'ends on a happy or at least a morally reassuring note.' " Neil Feigenson, *Legal Blame* 90 (2000), quoting David Thorburn, "Television Melodrama," *in Understanding Television* 73 (Richard P. Adler ed. 1981). As Peter Brooks notes, melodrama requires the "prosecution of the good, and the final reward of virtue." Under Brooks' requirements, however, there is additional room in the outcome for determination of the victor: "The ritual of melodrama involves the confrontation of clearly identified antagonists and the expulsion of one of them." Peter Brooks, *The Melodramatic Imagination* 17 (1976).

The filmmaker and literary theorist Michael Roemer observes that the viewer of melodramatic and "positivist" popular film always roots for the hero and against the villain. . . .

> Popular story shows us as we are supposed to be and wish to see ourselves. Like the community itself, it represses what tragedy includes. By projecting evil onto the other, it purges us of our dark and dirty secrets, frees us from self-division, and fosters *communitas* by giving us someone to hate and fear. . . . [W]ithout a destructive threat — whether it be divine or human — there *is* no story. Most narratives begin when something goes wrong, and evil is often the energy that drives it forward.

Michael Roemer, *Telling Stories: Postmodernism and the Invalidation of Traditional Narrative* 281-82 (1995).

NOTES & QUESTIONS

1.   At its core, *Fracture* is a Hollywood version of classical melodrama, featuring the ultimate confrontation between good and evil. Anthony Hopkins portrays Ted Crawford, a wealthy aeronautical engineer who shoots his wife after he discovers her having an affair with a police detective. He then represents himself at trial for attempted murder, pitted against a young deputy district attorney, Willy Beachum. Hopkins cleverly (if problematically) shapes the plot so that the paramour, the police detective, investigates the shooting and arrests Hopkins, who has exchanged his murder weapon for the detective's gun.

In *Fracture*, Hopkins seemingly revisits another iteration of his Academy-Award-winning role as the criminal mastermind Hannibal Lecter, depicting an intellectually resourceful and "archetypal" villain in the battle of good and evil. Is Ted Crawford an effective villain because of Hopkins' acting skills? What is it that makes the audience suspend its disbelief and enjoy Hopkins' villainy? Does the audience anticipate from the beginning of the movie that Crawford will be convicted and punished, and that justice will prevail in the end? Is there an ironic playfulness and intellectual detachment in Hopkins' performance that makes us forget the obvious artifice of the plot? Would *Fracture* work as a melodrama if Ted Crawford got away with murder and outsmarted the protagonist, beating the system at the end?

2.   Alfred Hitchcock famously observed that, "the more successful the villain, the more powerful the story." In *Fracture*, Ted Crawford, the villain, initiates the plot and gives it shape and dimension, as villains in melodrama inevitably do. Indeed, for most of the movie he seems to have the upper hand against Beachum. Did you anticipate before the ending *how* the film's plot would climax and resolve and how Beachum would defeat Crawford at the end? If so, when did you figure out the ending?

3. Near the end of the movie, Ted Crawford trips up, as villains inevitably do. The hero finally gains the upper hand when he understands how Crawford has duped him, and he reverses the game by drawing upon Crawford's arrogance and hubris, just as Crawford had drawn on Beachum's egotism and distraction. Within the narrative logic of the movie, the mistake that Crawford makes, leading to his second prosecution, is to take his wife off life support equipment after he is acquitted of attempted murder, in violation of a court order. Crawford's actions causing his wife's death enable Beachum to re-prosecute Crawford, this time for his wife's murder, rather than the initial charge of attempted murder.

Commenting upon the movie, in response to a review in *The New York Times*, a lawyer writes:

Good film, not as bad as some

I enjoyed it in spite of my status as a lawyer. The murder prosecution could not have depended on the order [Beachum] got, for two reasons: (1) Hopkins was not served with the order, and (2) violation of an order is an offense in itself, but doesn't change otherwise legal conduct into homicide. The significance of Hopkins' wife dying is that it completed the elements of homicide, a different offense from the one for which Hopkins was tried. For double jeopardy purposes, the order dismissing the attempted murder charge was the equivalent of an acquittal; jeopardy "attaches" when the jury is sworn, and only a mistrial would end the trial without precluding a retrial. The problem I had with the plot had to do with the suppression of Hopkins' confession. I'm fairly certain that a motion to suppress a confession has to be heard before trial.

— morey21, Berkeley, CA.

When you, as law students, watch the movie, do you, like this lawyer-commentator, watch the movie as a legal expert attempting to test the logic of the plot against your understanding of Criminal Law and Procedure? That is, do you apply a close "reality critique" and test the film for legal accuracy as an important part of your evaluation of and response to the movie? Does viewing the movie as a legal expert blunt your admiration of Crawford's criminal "mastermind" intelligence? Likewise, do you critique Beachum's legal strategies? Do you also critique his ethical decisions?

4. In *Fracture*, Ryan Gosling plays a conflicted and sometimes unsympathetic hero: Willy Beachum is a young prosecutor who anticipates leaving the District Attorney's office to obtain a lucrative position in private practice. Beachum is distracted by his new job possibilities and his anticipated future, and he fails to investigate the crime completely before proceeding to trial. He is extremely confident that he can easily convict the non-lawyer Crawford, who is representing himself at trial. In taking on Crawford at trial, he falls into Crawford's trap. Beachum is not, initially, a compelling adversary for the shrewder Crawford. He is clearly a flawed protagonist, lazy and distracted, but he is not corrupt or unethical. For example, he does not choose the shortcut of planting evidence to obtain a conviction. In melodrama, it is important to differentiate the ethics of the hero from the ethics of the evil antagonist and to allow the viewer to identify with, and root for,

the hero. Beachum gathers strength as he devotes himself to defeat Crawford. He follows through with his obligation to prosecute and convict the evil, powerful, and playfully sinister villain. He sacrifices his career aspirations and finds his true calling as a prosecutor. Recalling the discussion in Chapter 3 of this text, we might say he is redeemed. Do you, as law students, identify with the education and redemption of the striving and careerist Beachum?

5.   The legal proceedings and courtroom that frame the story provide the battleground for the struggle between Beachum and Crawford. Could a similar battle between good and evil have taken place in a different setting in another Hollywood melodrama? On a lawless outpost in a western melodrama? Or in a distant galaxy in a melodrama about intergalactic invaders? Is *Fracture* compelling to you because it takes place, primarily, within the familiar context of the legal proceedings?

"WHAT A WASTE: BEAUTIFUL, SEXY GAL, HELL OF A LAWYER": FILM AND THE FEMALE ATTORNEY
Carolyn L. Miller
4 Columbia Journal of Gender and Law 203 (1994)

Attorneys themselves have . . . noticed the effect of media images on the practice of their profession. In light of the popularity of the television drama *L.A. Law*, "[a] trial lawyer needs a theme, just like they use in the show. . . . Don't just try to get facts across to a jury, because facts often fall on deaf ears. [A lawyer has] to hit them with a theme, so it burns itself on their minds." Mark Maiselli, "Lawyers Agree *L.A. Law* Is Less Boring Than Life," *The New York Times*, 6 Oct. 1991, CN6. . . .

[I]mages of attorneys in film affect not only those practicing attorneys who complain of the theatrical expectations raised in jurors by *L.A. Law*, but also the law students whose understandings of their future in this profession will be impacted by its primary framing within the four corners of a television or movie screen.

Despite their incredible influence, there is no requirement that [such] fictionalized accounts of lawyering be accurate, or even be held accountable for their consequences. The danger arises when these distorted depictions are adopted by viewers as representative of the legal sphere, which then impacts their later interactions with, and expectations of, lawyers and the law. "Erroneous information in popular culture may damage the ability to make correct assessments of institutions and policies, and may even affect the law itself." David A. Harris, *The Appearance of Justice: Court TV, Conventional Television, and Public Understanding of the Criminal Justice System*, 35 Arizona Law Review 785, 786 (1993). Harris notes five implications of these inaccurate portrayals: unattainably high standards for police, public perception of a violent world, exaggeration of the negative results of committing crime, elevation of whites as the archetypal victims of crime, and reduction of the law to a series of technicalities. One more implication should be added to this list: denigration of women as capable attorneys, and the inability of women attorneys to be capable human beings.

Female attorneys in film have been presented as an oxymoron; they have two identities — "female" and "attorney" — which cannot logically coexist. Initially, these characters are introduced as successful and bright legal practitioners; however, their personal lives are empty, which in the film's sexual economy means they are unmarried. This conflict between professional success and personal "failure" is resolved in favor of reasserting male privilege in the legal sphere, and returning women to the private, domestic sphere in which they should feel more comfortable. This return is marked by the destruction of the professional capacity of the female attorney. The oxymoronic puzzle is solved: these characters, robbed of their legal identities, are now only "women."

The reality of this imagistic bias has thus far been ignored by scholars of legal culture. Friedman doesn't refer to a single media image of a female attorney in his seminal work. Lawrence M. Friedman, *Law, Lawyers, and Popular Culture*, 98 Yale Law Journal 1579 (1989). Chase, in his "survey" of such images, makes a single, passing reference to a woman attorney in his mention of the film *Jagged Edge*, which he includes only to give belated credit to the actor Peter Coyote for his portrayal of an unethical District Attorney in that film. Anthony Chase, *Lawyers and Popular Culture: A Review of Mass Media Portrayals of American Attorneys*, 1986 American Bar Foundation Research Journal 281, 288 (1986). These authors, of course, are not completely to blame. They are simply analyzing Hollywood's productions, which have maintained the traditional association of men with the public, social, and legal world, while women remain at home as the supportive spouses. Women entering the legal profession — staking claim to "public" spaces like the courtroom, the negotiating table, and the corporate board room — are implicitly crossing this invisible line between the gendered public and private spheres. This realignment doesn't come without a price.

Dominant cinema, as represented by mass-market Hollywood-produced films, has selected a particular image of the female attorney — one whose gender identity compromises her professional abilities — which draws upon the power of the "myth," as described by Claire Johnston:

> Myth then, as a form of speech or discourse, represents the major means in which women have been used in the cinema: myth transmits and transforms the ideology of sexism and renders it invisible — when it is made invisible it evaporates — and therefore natural.

Claire Johnston, "Myths of Women in the Cinema," *in Women and the Cinema: A Critical Anthology* 409 (Karyn Kay and Gerald Perry eds. 1977). . . .

In *Presumed Innocent*, a 1990 film based on the novel by Scott Turow and directed by Alan J. Pakula, the previously separate identities of "female victim" and "female attorney" are collapsed; the murder victim is the attorney, and she is dead before the filmic narrative begins. In this film, the destruction of identity of the female attorney is complete and irreversible. In further contrast to the earlier films, the violence against the professional and sexual identities of the female attorney is waged by the hand of a superficially supportive but inwardly jealous wife. Women become the agents of their own demise, and are the tools of the cinematic resituation of the woman in the private, domesticated sphere.

In *Presumed Innocent*, although the female attorney, Carolyn Polhemus (Greta Scacchi), is violently murdered before the narrative begins, she remains a sexualized presence throughout. In the moral framework of this film, it is her sexuality which caused the violence: "the lady was bad news." Almost every male character in the film had a sexual relationship with this ambitious and talented attorney: District Attorney Raymond Horgan (Brian Dennehey); the Assistant District Attorney assigned to investigate her murder, Rusty Sabich (Harrison Ford); and the judge presiding over this case (Paul Winfield). All cinematic images of Carolyn are in the past, and with the exception of the child abuse case are the hazy sexual recollections of Rusty. Through his investigation he recalls images of their affair, first of desire and then of rejection, with the entire relationship controlled by her. She is sexually powerful, and performs the "physical and spiritual castration" which Paglia claims all men fear. For this power, as with all other filmic female attorneys, she is punished. . . .

The female attorneys of [movies such as] *Presumed Innocent* are not the role models for a new generation of emerging female law students and lawyers; they are a shadow of our worst nightmares. They are the imagistic manifestation of the demise of feminism, cinematic proof that women attorneys cannot have both professional and personal lives.

NOTES & QUESTIONS

1. Carolyn Miller focuses on the female murder victim, Carolyn Polhemus, in her article. But it is Rusty Sabich's wife Barbara, a non-lawyer pursuing a graduate degree and also the mother of Rusty's beloved son, who is the villain in *Presumed Innocent* and gets away with murder. How does Barbara compare with Ted Crawford, the villain in *Fracture*? Both are wronged spouses who take revenge upon a female victim. Both are depicted as extremely intelligent and calculating. Is Barbara a more complex and human character than Ted Crawford? How so? Do you have more sympathy for Barbara than for Ted? Why? The melodramatic plot of *Fracture* requires that Ted be defeated by the protagonist and receive his comeuppance at the end of the movie. In *Presumed Innocent*, Barbara is not convicted or punished for her crime. Is this ending troubling or problematic? Is the fact that Barbara escapes punishment somehow more permissible because of her gender? Or is it because the genre of the movie and the narrative logic of the story compel a more complex ending? Would the plot be as effective if Barbara were arrested for murder, convicted, and punished? Is it that, unlike Ted Crawford in the simple melodrama *Fracture*, Barbara is not the primary character in the film, and her fate is not the viewer's dominant concern? Assuming *Presumed Innocent* is not just a simple melodrama, how would you characterize its genre? In retrospect, how would you categorize the genres (or types) of plots presented by the other movies identified in this chapter? How do genre and theme influence and implicate the construction of the various plots?

2. Miller questions whether women today can "envisage a world, either in image or in reality, in which women can simultaneously occupy personal and professional spheres, a world in which the concept 'woman lawyer' is not effectively an oxymoron. . . ." She claims that popular films typically "resituate" women predominantly "in the private domestic sphere," and she identifies Carolyn Polhemus, the murder victim in *Presumed Innocent*, as a primary example. Is this so? In many ways, isn't Carolyn an extremely effective "woman lawyer" who, unlike Rusty Sabich's wife Barbara, does not reside primarily in the "domestic sphere"? Carolyn employs her heightened sexuality purposefully to her own advantage to advance her career in a male-dominated profession. But how is she so different from the corrupt and sexually predatory male attorneys in *Presumed Innocent*, whose sexual appetites similarly shape their behavior in the workplace?

3.   The fearless, hard-driving, highly sexualized and beautiful female attorney now seems almost a stock character often appearing in popular stories about the law. Why do you think there are so many of these characters, especially in stories about criminal law? Are these characters primarily the product of a predominantly male fantasy, as one student observed in an excerpt from a paper excerpted earlier in this chapter? Or does the appearance of these lawyer characters as both victims and victimizers reveal something else about changing images of women and women professionals?

4.   Reconsider the character of Nikki Gardner, the mid-level associate in *Fracture* who becomes romantically entangled with her underling, Willy Beachum. Does Nikki Gardner fit the stereotypical image of the oxymoronic "woman lawyer" who can't seem to sort out her personal and professional lives? Or is Gardner simply a woman in power who is, like the male attorneys in *Presumed Innocent*, drawn sexually to a successful and dashing young attorney in her office? When Crawford reveals at trial that the signed confession Beachum depended on is "fruit of the poisonous tree," demonstrating Beachum's inattention, Gardner exhibits her influence in the firm by keeping Wooton Sims' upset senior partner at bay. Which image of Gardner, susceptible woman and victim or powerful attorney, does this interaction further?

5.   How do the courtroom scenes and legal proceedings portrayed in *Fracture* further Miller's sense of the law being reduced to "a series of technicalities"? *Boston Globe* film critic Wesley Morris called the film a "preposterous courtroom thriller," and the movie's ending a "shrugging legal plot twist." Does the fact that the audience gets closure only through a legal technicality make the justice Beachum brings for Crawford's crime less satisfying? How so? Why is it necessary to provide this dramatic closure? Contrast the characters of the two female victims in *Fracture* and *Presumed Innocent*. Does *Presumed Innocent* intimate that it is, in part, Polhemus' own hyper-sexuality and provocative and risky sexual behavior that results in her becoming a victim? In *Presumed Innocent* is there an intimation that Polhemus is, in part, also a villain, a dark "noire" character implicated in her own demise? Specifically, Miller recalls Detective Lipranzer's misogynistic observation, "[t]he lady was bad news." Apparently, at least from the detective's perspective, she got what she deserved.

6.   Does the character of Nikki Gardner, who dismisses Beachum in his hour of need, represent the hardened, heartless corporate attorney, or a wise associate washing her hands of a needlessly complicated, if emotionally compelling, situation? Does Beachum, in his arrogant inattention to the evidence in his last case as a prosecutor, come across as the cocky young lawyer with one foot out the door

toward greener pastures, or as a prosecutor with a good track record who is caught off guard by an unexpected evidentiary twist?

CREATIVE MALPRACTICE: THE CINEMATIC LAWYER
William G. Hyland, Jr.
9 Texas Review of Entertainment and Sports Law 231 (2008)

[E]mpirical evidence demonstrates that the primary way people learn about lawyers is through watching narrative films, rather than relying upon news or documentaries. Fictionalized portrayals of lawyers form the views and opinions of the public. . . .

[Due in part to this fact], lawyers are in the midst of a decades-long battle to preserve their wilting reputation and the public's trust. According to a 2005 Gallup Poll, a mere 18% of the public rated lawyers high or very high in ethics and honesty. The percentage of Americans who give lawyers high ratings for honesty has fallen from an unimpressive 27% in 1985 to 17% in 1994. Another poll revealed that 95% of Americans would not recommend that their children enter the legal profession. . . .

Popular culture reflects the general attitudes of society. The public's intense distaste for lawyers is now accurately reflected in film. At the heart of the problem is the alienation of the public to lawyers, a public who view lawyers with suspicion and resentment. The negative portrayal of lawyers in the movies has had a devastating effect on the public's perception of the legal profession. . . .

This negative imagery has widespread implications that have been theorized and documented extensively for the past several decades by sociologists and psychologists. These experts have found: "that legal films do form unconscious yet lasting biases and preconceptions in potential jurors, who then cannot function impartially within the system. Biases also create a mistrust of the law, which can lead to a failure of justice." The issue then becomes how much of an impact this has on the law? . . .

In a perfect world, the duty of a juror is to return a verdict after weighing all of the evidence and applying the law to the facts presented. This decision-making process is of high interest to sociologists and jury consultants who study the field of law and psychology. In fact, psychologists have attempted to deconstruct juror decision-making for decades, often turning up conflicting results. The interest in the field derives from the extreme unpredictability of juries.

It should be equally important to trial lawyers because of the damaging images perpetuated by Hollywood. Empirical research has shown that jurors' personal lives play a huge part in their decision-making process. Even though the law presumes each juror to be a proverbial tabula rasa, they unavoidably have their own biases that stem from their life experiences. The following was declared in an editorial written by a *Florida Sun Sentinel* reporter who was called to jury duty:

> Like most citizens, I get my ideas about courtrooms and trials from the
> screen. Later, sequestered in the jury deliberation room, some of us will

wonder about the details of the trial and ask each other, "Shouldn't the lawyers have done this or that? That's what they do in the movies."

The author concluded that "the basic procedure and thus the basic drama of trial by jury is more faithfully reproduced in our screen fictions than one would think."

Hollywood's general rebuttal involves one of two arguments: 1) movies merely reflect public perception, but do not cause it; and 2) the influence of a singular film on a thinking, rational person is overblown. Hollywood executives maintain that films do not shape perception; they simply mirror the values of society at large.

While producers and executives generally admit that movies have become harsher in content and tone over the last three decades, they deny that this harshness has significantly influenced society. Instead of defending their art, they simply deny its impact. They insist that film, ephemeral by nature, does not consequently impact our society. Dark films, they argue, merely reflect the unpleasant realities around us. Those who blame Hollywood simplistically confuse cause and effect and scapegoat the messenger.

NOTES & QUESTIONS

1. William Hyland, Jr., opines that since the late 1960s, movies have perpetuated the image of corrupt, unethical lawyers. He claims that this "corrosive imagery" reflects "an aura of institutional distrust that seeped its way into cinema" after the Watergate scandal. William G. Hyland, Jr., *Creative Malpractice: The Cinematic Lawyer*, 9 Texas Review of Entertainment & Sports Law 231, 236 (2008). As a result, Hyland suggests that after Watergate, the "vision of the noble lawyer-statesman began to dim" as "attorneys on the big screen [were] portrayed as corrupt or incompetent. They tended to be rude, crass, selfish, greedy and exercised poor judgment in affairs of the heart." *Id.* at 249.

Hyland offers *Fracture* as one of many examples of this trend. He argues that the film "perpetuates the negative stereotype of an arrogant prosecutor about to dump his office for the greener pastures (and money) of corporate law." Hyland also cites as evidence the "alluring corporate associate (another example of negative female portrayals)" and the manner in which Wooton Sims "unceremoniously withdraws its job offer after Beachum botches the prosecution." *Id.* at 270. Do the attorneys portrayed in *Fracture* further this supposed trend toward attorneys portrayed as corrupt and profit-driven? What about Beachum's seemingly last-minute connection with his "calling" as a prosecutor? Does the fact that Beachum has the opportunity to manipulate false evidence into the record, but decides at the last minute to take honesty and the consequences over an easy win, at all revamp the image of a corrupt and opportunistic lawyer? None of the other recent dramatic films in this chapter, including *Presumed Innocent* and the docudrama *The Thin Blue Line*, depict criminal law practitioners (lawyers and judges) as primarily noble, heroic, and truth-seeking. They are often depicted as self-deceiving, flawed, or corrupt. Indeed, criminal law practice is depicted as occurring on a shadowy landscape, where truth is beyond knowing, and success is measured exclusively in terms of victory in the courtroom regardless of the costs. Is this merely a recent trend and a misperception fostered by popular stories? Or is it an embodiment of the "realities" of criminal law practice?

2.   In his article, Hyland describes the "cultivation effect," and the "influence of a film on a viewer's information, beliefs and attitudes":

> Cognitive psychology researchers concluded that there is a causal relationship, not merely a correlation, between film watching and belief formation. Their explanation is derived from what they term "heuristic processing" — snap judgments based on rules of thumb, such as "lawyers are sleazy." The research concludes that people typically do not "discount" information derived from fictional sources such as movies even though they are aware that movies do not supply factual information.

Hyland, *supra*, at 272.

Do you agree with Hyland that, although most people are aware that film portrayals are fictional and not based in reality, many nevertheless derive their opinions of the legal profession from television and movies? Could this negative portrayal of lawyers in film be responsible for the unending string of jokes pigeonholing attorneys as blood-sucking bottom-dwellers? Are individuals outside, or within, the legal profession no longer capable of envisioning attorneys instead as noble creatures? Is there still room for noble criminal law practitioners like Atticus Finch or Perry Mason? Would the public accept these traditionally heroic characters? Would a series of positive attorney "role-models" portrayed through film and television help recover the image of lawyer-as-agent-of-justice?

3.   How have your own experiences affected your understanding of attorneys and the legal profession? Did you have an image of "lawyer" in mind when you first came to law school? If so, how has your experience since beginning law school altered this image? Have you witnessed real trials and the work of "real-life" litigation attorneys since attending law school? Have you participated as a player in the legal system, working in criminal law practice during a summer internship or in a law school clinical program? If so, what have been your personal reactions to this practice? Have you been surprised by the work of real-life criminal law practitioners, or have they confirmed your expectations and prejudices based upon popular stories about criminal law? Are the lawyers and various players akin to the characters depicted in pop cultural stories about criminal law presented in this chapter?

4.   Other commentators have observed the close and often symbiotic relationship between legal and popular storytelling practices. Here is how one prominent legal novelist, former trial attorney, and law professor, puts it:

> What is happening? Well, in my view the line between the reality of lawyering and its fictional representation on television and in books [and in movies] has gone well beyond blurred. It isn't really a question of how lawyers and law are portrayed on television and in books [and in movies], because that depiction is merging with reality. . . . Almost everywhere we look, right now in popular culture, there is an almost complete merger of fiction and reality when it comes to law. Law has become entertainment, and entertainment law.

Lisa Scottoline, *Get Off the Screen*, 24 Nova Law Review 653, 656 (2000).

If this is so, is there a danger not only that the law will be distorted in the movies and other popular stories but also that real-life jurors will perceive law stories primarily as dramatic entertainment and reach determinations in real cases based upon the genre of the story and how they identify the roles of the various characters within this legal drama? Alternatively, do you think that popular stories could often more accurately portray the rules and procedures of criminal law and still work as entertainment?

5.   Law students, and their doctrine-bound law professors, are often perplexed or troubled by doctrinal and procedural errors depicted in popular movies like *Fracture*. Some legal academics dismiss pop cultural stories about the law and legal subjects because these stories could never unfold that way "in real life." But are there often compelling aesthetic reasons for these distortions of the law and exaggerations of legal characters in popular stories? After all, as noted in the first chapter of this text, the goal of popular movies is not, primarily, to educate viewers about the law but to engage and entertain viewers with compelling human drama. Based upon your criminal law and procedure course, is the doctrinal criminal law often too complex, and the procedures of criminal law too drawn-out and boring, to fit the audience's demands for plot-driven popular movies? Are distortions of criminal law inevitable as doctrine gives way to plot and character in popular stories about criminal law subjects?

GOOD GUYS AND BAD GUYS: PUNISHING CHARACTER, EQUALITY, AND THE IRRELEVANCE OF MORAL CHARACTER TO CRIMINAL PUNISHMENT
Ekow N. Yankah
25 Cardozo Law Review 1019 (2004)

Criminal law . . . continues to maintain the rigid dichotomy of good guys and bad guys. It is crucial that there be a clear allocation of virtue within the conflict. The state can impose punishment only if there is a clear dichotomy of good and evil. The state maintains the position of good guy. Placing the defendant within the realm of bad guys justifies the imposition of punishment.

Criminal law cannot recognize the moral ambiguity of film noir. If the criminal defendant's common humanity or the state's moral uncertainty were illustrated, the state would lose its moral right to punish. Witness the last-minute loss of nerve in the scheduled execution of Timothy McVeigh. The Federal Bureau of Investigation committed a blunder by failing to disclose 3000 pages of relevant material. No one in the Justice Department or the general public thought this material might exonerate the confessed terrorist McVeigh, but the image of professional incompetence made the Justice Department feel uneasy about taking a life. Only the virtuous have the right to execute.

Conceptualizing the state as good and the criminal as bad does more than justify our imposition of punishment. Imagining criminal offenders as a class of bad guys, cinematic villains who are living threats to all of us, allows us to distance ourselves from them. This image severs our common bond of humanity with the criminal defendants. . . .

Being human, we are given to making moral judgments about others' character. We base a great deal of our personal affections, admiration and blame on these judgments. We harbor cravings for a simple world where there are good guys and bad guys; a world where we know that good people do good and that the bad are punished.

When we translate our personal blaming practices into the criminal law, however, things go horribly awry. We begin to assume that those who are punished are unifaceted bad people and that the awesome power of the state should, replicating the personal sphere, make them pay for being bad people.

We ignore the critical difference between what is legitimate in personal moral judgment and political morality. We ignore the nagging truth that the state ought not permanently segregate and punish people because they are bad. When we premise punishment on character we give in to our thirst to get the bad guys. Though it is only too human, it quickly allows us to forget the common humanity of those we punish.

NOTES & QUESTIONS

1. Professor Yankah perceives the practice of criminal law and, presumably, storytelling in criminal law cases, as a form of melodrama. As observed in the initial excerpt in this section, in melodrama the plot is shaped to the conventions of the genre, and conflict is usually reduced to a battle of good against evil. There are clear heroes and villains; we identify with the hero and root for the hero to emerge triumphant at the end of the story. Do you agree with Yankah that melodrama is at the core of criminal practice? If so, then the defendant would be cast in the role of either protagonist/hero or antagonist/villain depending upon what legal actor (defense attorney or prosecutor) is telling the story. Is Yankah's position overstated? Do the compressions and simplifications of melodramatic plot lines provide adequate templates for narratives presented in the courtroom?

2. Some cultural works, traditionally novels but occasionally some films, focus upon careful investigations of character of the defendant. The question is not "whodunit" but why. In some criminal cases, determining the complexity of the thought processes, motives, and intentionality (*mens rea*) of the defendant is determinative in assessing culpability. For example, in the film version of Theodore Dreiser's novel *An American Tragedy* (1925), George Stevens' *A Place in the Sun*, the determinative issue is whether George Eastman (Montgomery Clift) intended to murder Alice Tripp (Shelly Winters) when they went boating together on Loon Lake. The trial focuses exclusively upon George's specific intent to murder Alice. Now recall your first-year criminal law course. Are there other relevant legal issues in addition to whether George acted with the premeditation and deliberation required for first degree murder? For example, did he commit any voluntary act that caused the harm? Was there concurrence between the *mens rea* and an action that resulted in her death? Knowing that Alice could not swim, and having taken her boating, and given the special relationship between Alice and George, did George have a duty to rescue Alice after she accidentally fell into the water? Is there sufficient circumstantial evidence to serve as the basis for Eastman's conviction and overcome the presumption of innocence that was so important in *Presumed Innocent*? The film and the arguments presented in the cinematic trial do not address these complex legal issues or explore the evidence of various levels of culpability that may result in conviction of lesser included offenses: second-degree murder, voluntary manslaughter, involuntary manslaughter, negligent homicide. Why does this flattening or compression into melodrama take place? Is it necessary to reduce the legal elements in the narrative to the simplest issues? Does this simplification and distortion of doctrinal law heighten the drama and intensify the conflict in the story, further compelling the imaginative attention of the audience? Would the plot work as well if the depiction of the legal issues were truer to "real life"?

In contrast, the criminal mind and intent of defendant Ted Crawford in *Fracture* seems to be clear: he intended to kill his wife. However, as the plot unfolds, the audience becomes less certain of Crawford's intentions. Did he intend to kill his wife, and accidentally wound her instead? Did he intend to hospitalize her, or did he envision her death and feel obligated to finish the job? Many other aspects of the plot are equally mysterious, such as the location of the murder weapon, Crawford's seemingly flawless ability to execute his carefully laid plans, and his seeming nonchalance at the arraignment and trial. Do Crawford's actions provide insight into his mental state?

3.   Does Hopkins' portrayal of the friendly and unflappable Crawford confuse the viewer, who is accustomed to the defendant in a homicide trial being portrayed as the quintessential bad guy? Crawford's motivations may not justify murder, but the audience cannot help but identify with his desire to publicly humiliate his wife's former lover. Likewise, Crawford's careful machinations are unexpected and intriguing, keeping the audience guessing why he would represent himself in an attempted murder trial and why he would attempt to endear himself to the young attorney prosecuting him. How does Crawford fit into the simple categorizations of a melodrama? Is he pure villain, or are there some aspects of his personality that make him more complex and even "likeable?"

4.   Reassess the "character" of defendant Rusty Sabich in the film version of *Presumed Innocent*. Rusty is a complex and flawed man. Nevertheless, he is a man of fundamental decency, and seemingly less corrupt than other legal actors in the drama (the judge who dismisses the case so that testimony will not emerge implicating himself in bribery, the ruthless yet ineffectual prosecutors, and even the victim of the murder, Carolyn Polhemus, who sleeps her way up the career ladder). In relationship to the other characters, it is with Rusty that the viewer identifies. We follow the story exclusively from his perspective or point of view. His valence is clearly more positive than negative. How would you describe Rusty's character? Does Rusty fit the simple and easy categorizations of melodrama (Yankah's duality of "good guys and bad guys")?

Chapter 11

CONSTITUTIONAL LAW

A. FILMOGRAPHY

First Monday in October (1981)

Gideon's Trumpet (1980)

The Pelican Brief (1993)

The People vs. Larry Flynt (1996)

Separate But Equal (1991)

B. INTRODUCTION

The Founding Fathers may not have anticipated the development, but by the first decades of the nineteenth century the Constitution had become a vehicle for discussing the nation's most pressing issues. The question of whether a law, procedure, or social practice was "unconstitutional" became part of the American political discourse. Then, too, the Supreme Court of the United States established itself as not only the third branch of the federal government but also the institution most responsible for tending to the Constitution.

The culture industry was as much aware of these developments as anyone else, and the industry might have been expected to bring constitutional questions and the Supreme Court into its individual pop cultural works. Hollywood, in particular, was the paradigmatic producer of popular culture, and it was accustomed to treating social issues in the cinema, albeit frequently in stylized and trivialized ways. "While Hollywood had traditionally defined its product as entertainment and has pooh-poohed 'message' filmmaking, in practice the industry has consistently relied on topicality as an ingredient for box-office success." Stephen Prince, *Political Films in the Nineties, in Film Genre 2000* (Wheeler W. Dixon ed. 2000).

And, indeed, engaging films, five of which are listed at the beginning of this chapter, concern constitutional issues and portray members of the Supreme Court. These "constitutional law films," more so than films related to other areas of law, overtly display political alignments, interrelate with dominant ideologies, and consider questions of social justice. At the same time, though, the number of "constitutional law films" is small. For purposes of the chapter at hand, it merits asking both how popular culture speaks to the Constitution *and* why this referencing is relatively infrequent.

C. POP CULTURAL CONSTITUTIONAL LAW

Viewers with constitutional law backgrounds might enjoy watching fictional films and pointing out how the drama in those films could translate into constitutional issues. The film *Whose Life Is It Anyway?* (1981), for example, tells the story of sculptor Ken Harrison, played by Richard Dreyfuss, who is confined to bed as a quadriplegic after a road accident and wishes his life would end. When his hospital refuses to end life-prolonging treatment, Harrison goes to trial and is supported by some of the hospital staff. Issues related to the "right to die" as part of a larger constitutional right of privacy hover over the drama. *See* Jean-Louis Baudouin, *Perspective Juridique*: Whose Life Is It Anyway? 26 McGill Law Journal 1076 (1981). The film *The Siege* (1998) portrays Arab terrorists detonating bombs in a school bus, a Broadway theater, and even the Manhattan FBI building, leading to the roundup and detention of all young Arab men who live in Brooklyn. The film to some extent prefigures the aftermath of 9/11 and also presents immense constitutional questions related to habeas corpus and due process. An FBI agent named Anthony "Hub" Hubbard, played by Denzel Washington, seems at first to agree with the aggressive police and military action, but Hubbard, blessed with a law degree, eventually sees the light and says government action of this sort will "shred the Constitution." For a fascinating treatment of Hollywood's long history of portraying Arabs negatively, *see* Jack G. Shaheen, *Reel Bad Arabs: How Hollywood Vilifies a People*, 588 Annals of the American Academy of Political and Social Science 171 (2003).

While articulating potential constitutional issues in fictional films can contribute to the appreciation of constitutional law, more revealing and less speculative renderings of constitutional law in the cinema are available in the various docudramas and dramatizations of actual cases which have made their way to the Supreme Court. As the film *Amistad* (1997) illustrates, these films have a tendency to discuss the constitutional issues in a very general way. The film portrays the legal battle growing out of an actual 1839 slave mutiny that ended up before the Supreme Court. *See United States v. L'Amistad*, 40 U.S. 518 (1841). Included in the film is the oral argument of former president John Quincy Adams, played by Anthony Hopkins, in which he pleads for the slaves' freedom. The film's budget was huge, distinguished actors appear at every turn, and historical events are more or less faithfully reported. But the filmmakers avoid anything resembling true constitutional argument or reasoning. Cinque, the leader of the slaves seeking their freedom in *Amistad*, inspired Adams with his deep respect for his ancestors. "Who we are *is* who we were," Cinque says. Adams, in turn, seems to prevail before the Supreme Court by invoking the Founding Fathers, naming the major ones in the process. It seems not to matter that the framed document on the wall of the Supreme Court's supposed courtroom is the Declaration of Independence rather than the Constitution.

The writers and producers of films such as *Amistad* defer to an iconic understanding of the Constitution. Icons, totems, and symbols in general can provoke reverential devotion, and true believers use them to reinforce their faith. In the American civic faith the Constitution often functions as a door that opens onto a belief in the American way of doing things. For many, the Constitution invites belief in the nation's freedom and commitment to justice. This iconic understanding of the Constitution actually emerged not long before the *Amistad* case. The politician Daniel Webster, to name only one especially prominent example, built his career on a professed love for the iconic Constitution. *See* David Ray Papke, *Heretics in the Temple: Americans Who Reject the Nation's Legal Faith* 4-8, 19-20 (1998).

Extreme veneration of the Constitution has declined in more recent decades, but the sense of the Constitution as an awe-inspiring whole remains much more powerful than any appreciation of particular phrases in the document or of anything resembling constitutional doctrine. As the remarkable legal realist Karl Llewellyn said in the 1930s, the American public's command of the Constitution manifested "pervasive ignorance and indifference as to almost all detail," but Americans, in his opinion, were loyal "in [the] first instance to a phrase, without more: 'The Constitution.' " Karl Llewellyn, *The Constitution As an Institution*, 34 Columbia Law Review 1, 23-24 (1934). Filmmakers are as likely to build their works on this generalized, iconic variety of constitutionalism as they are to explore anything more specific. Only a handful of films relate to actual constitutional law. Among those films, both canonizing and commodifying are common.

1. Canonizing Constitutional Law

Certain films, mostly in the civil rights area, tend to praise those seeking their constitutional rights and then second the constitutional pronouncements that recognize those rights. Films that follow this track include but are not limited to *Mr. and Mrs. Loving* (1996) and *Separate But Equal* (1991). The former is discussed at greater length in Chapter 12 of this text, which is devoted to Family Law. The film portrays the struggle of Mildred Jeter and Richard Loving to overcome Virginia's anti-miscegenation laws. The Supreme Court found those laws to be a denial of equal protection as guaranteed by the Fourteenth Amendment in *Loving v. Commonwealth of Virginia*, 388 U.S. 1 (1967). *Separate But Equal* is an excellent television mini-series dramatizing the litigation challenging the segregation of public schools and culminating in the Supreme Court decision in *Brown v. Board of Education of Topeka*, 347 U.S. 483 (1954). The mini-series starred Sidney Poitier in the role of Thurgood Marshall, the civil rights attorney who pursued and made the successful arguments before the Supreme Court.

Hallmark Hall of Fame's *Gideon's Trumpet* (1980) dramatizes the case culminating in the Supreme Court decision in *Gideon v. Wainwright*, 372 U.S. 335 (1963). Henry Fonda starred in the film as the sorry drifter Clarence Earl Gideon, who thought the failure to provide him with a lawyer during his trial was "unconstitutional." José Ferrer played the high-powered Washington D.C. attorney who represented Gideon on appeal, and John Houseman took the role of Chief Justice Earl Warren, giving him a bit of a British accent in the process. In the following excerpt, Corinna Barrett Lain discusses the way the decision in *Gideon* validated a national consensus and then how popular culture validated *Gideon*.

COUNTERMAJORITARIAN HERO OR ZERO? RETHINKING THE WARREN COURT'S ROLE IN THE CRIMINAL PROCEDURE REVOLUTION
Corinna Barrett Lain
152 University of Pennsylvania Law Review 1361 (2004)

C. *Gideon v. Wainwright*: A Piece of Storybook Americana

Decided in March 1963, *Gideon v. Wainwright* incorporated the Sixth Amendment right to counsel to the states, entitling all indigent felony defendants to a court-appointed attorney. In so doing, the Court in *Gideon* overruled its 1942 decision in *Betts v. Brady* and erased any doubts that a revolution in criminal procedure had begun. Unquestionably, *Gideon* was one of the most monumental criminal procedure cases ever decided — it guaranteed to state felony defendants "the most pervasive right," the one right defendants must have in order to meaningfully exercise any others. Moreover, because the vast majority of criminal defendants are indigent, *Gideon's* potential impact on the administration of criminal justice was truly astounding. Presumably for these reasons, Earl Warren considered *Gideon* to be the most important criminal procedure case his Court had decided and the third most important case of his tenure overall.

As important as it was, however, *Gideon* merits a place in the present analysis for another reason: it has been canonized by popular culture as a classic example of the Supreme Court's heroic, countermajoritarian role in the criminal procedure revolution. In part, *Gideon's* acclaim stems from the holding of the case — that even the poor are entitled to an attorney's help when faced with serious criminal charges. In part, however, *Gideon's* fame stems from the facts of the case itself. Clarence Earl Gideon was by all accounts "the least among men," a 51-year-old drifter with nothing more than an eighth-grade education and four felony convictions to his name. Gideon was not the dangerous sort, just a small-time gambler and thief; those who would later write about him would say he was "a perfectly harmless human being, rather likeable, but one tossed aside by life." When he was charged with breaking and entering a Panama City, Florida, poolroom, Gideon requested a court-appointed attorney to represent him at trial. The trial court denied his request. In the colloquy that has since become famous, Gideon challenged the trial court, claiming (mistakenly at the time), "the United States Supreme Court says I am entitled to be represented by counsel." Again, the trial court denied his request. Gideon went to trial without an attorney and was promptly convicted of the felony charge, receiving a five-year sentence. Having time on his hands and some experience in jailhouse legal matters, Gideon fastidiously pursued an appeal of his case, ultimately penciling a certiorari petition to the Supreme Court on lined sheets of paper from the Florida prison where he resided. All things considered, the Court could not have found a more perfect case to defend indigent felony defendants had it been looking for one — and the little-known truth is, it had been.

The rest, as they say, is history. The Supreme Court granted certiorari in Gideon's case and appointed one of Washington's most prominent lawyers, Abe Fortas, to argue on his behalf. It then vindicated Gideon's faith in the Court, refusing to allow the vagaries of personal finances determine a felony defendant's chances of prevailing at trial. As Earl Warren's biographer, Ed Cray, would later write, *Gideon* was "a piece of storybook Americana. . . . No tale so affirmed the American democracy. No story broadcast around the world so clearly proclaimed that not just the rich received justice in American courts." Ed Cray, *Chief Justice: A Biography of Earl Warren* 405-406 (1997). Even last year, as *Gideon* celebrated its fortieth anniversary, scholars reminisced about the pride they felt when the highest court of the land reached down to rescue the quintessential little man, Clarence Gideon. If ever the Supreme Court played the role of countermajoritarian hero, surely it played it here — or so we think.

Although *Gideon* was undoubtedly a heroic decision, our common perception of the Supreme Court's role there is only partly right; the Court may have rescued Gideon from the State of Florida, but it was hardly acting in the countermajoritarian fashion we tend to associate with the case. By the time the Court decided *Gideon*, all but five states — Florida, Alabama, Mississippi, North Carolina, and South Carolina — already provided counsel to indigent felony defendants, and those five were a less than prestigious lot in 1963. Even Florida provided counsel to indigent felony defendants in certain localities; it just so happened that Panama City was not one of them. Equally, if not more, telling of the nature of the Supreme Court's decision in *Gideon* was the fact that twenty-two state attorneys general joined together to file an amicus curiae brief on Gideon's behalf; Florida, by contrast, could muster only two to support its position. As contemporary observers recognized, it was nothing short of extraordinary for the top law enforcement officials of so many states to ask the Court to impose upon them a constitutional protection for criminal defendants.

Given the states' position on the issue, it should come as no surprise that *Gideon* was one of the most popular cases of the Warren Court era. Newspaper and television coverage praised the decision, as did the law review literature, which had long advocated that *Betts v. Brady* be overruled. Even the American Bar Association strongly supported *Gideon*, a remarkable endorsement given its previously critical stance on Supreme Court decisions that took power from the states. *Gideon* was so appealing, in fact, that it quickly became a part of pop culture, inspiring the best-selling novel *Gideon's Trumpet* in 1964 and, much later, a prime-time television movie with a handsome Henry Fonda playing the downtrodden Gideon role.

Among the Supreme Court Justices, too, *Gideon* was a popular decision. Indeed, of the five landmark cases discussed in this paper, it is the only one to have received the Justices' unanimous support, providing yet another indication of just how mainstream the Court's ruling was by 1963. Conservative Justices Clark and Harlan both had little difficulty voting to overrule *Betts*; in conference, Justice Harlan reportedly went so far as to say, "[*Betts*] is a freak, and we should get done with it." Even the Burger Court of the early 1970s — the Court known for launching a "counter-revolution" in criminal procedure — would embrace *Gideon*, unanimously extending its holding to misdemeanor cases where the defendant received jail time. In short, *Gideon*'s holding was agreeable to just about everyone, both in 1963 and in later, more conservative years.

Granted, much of *Gideon*'s appeal for the Warren Court Justices and others had to do with the doctrinal landscape at the time it was decided. Although *Betts* required the states to provide counsel to indigent felony defendants only in "special circumstances," the Court had found special circumstances present in every case it had reviewed after 1950. By the time the Supreme Court decided *Gideon*, it had even recognized as a special circumstance the complexity of legal issues involved, though lawyers would have found those issues to be "of only routine difficulty." Clearly, the Court had come to realize that a felony charge was, like a capital charge, its own special circumstance — a situation sufficiently perilous to justify the right to counsel. That being the case, it was easy to see why so many states urged the Court to overrule *Betts* and formalize the bright-line rule it had already implicitly adopted: more federal intrusion would actually mean less.

Equally significant were developments in the Supreme Court's appellate criminal procedure jurisprudence. In 1956, the Court had held that indigent defendants were entitled to a free transcript on appeal, leaving little doubt among commentators that indigent defendants were entitled to an attorney on appeal as well. Indeed, as Scott Powe's research has revealed, a majority of the Justices had already agreed on the right to appellate counsel in another case, *Douglas v. California*, well before *Gideon* was briefed and argued. Naturally, if indigent defendants had a right to counsel on appeal, they also had a right to counsel at trial, which perhaps explains why the Court carried *Douglas* over to the following term and decided it the same day as *Gideon*. In retrospect, then, Abe Fortas had the not-so-difficult job of convincing the Supreme Court to do what it was going to do anyway. No wonder Justice Douglas would remember Fortas' presentation as "the best single legal argument" he had heard in his thirty-six years on the bench; Gideon himself could have argued the case and still won without a fight.

No doubt, *Gideon*'s doctrinal inevitability explains much of its appeal among conservatives and law enforcement officials, yet there must have been more to it than that. Justice Harlan privately surmised that he would have been among the *Betts* dissenters in 1942, and the state attorneys general shared that sentiment, describing *Betts* as " 'an anachronism when handed down.' " The Court's opinion in *Gideon* also took the position that *Betts* was wrong when it was decided, so *Gideon*'s holding must have been more than just a product of doctrinal attrition. Changing ideology played a role too; in fact, that was most likely the reason the Court's jurisprudence had strayed from *Betts* in the first place. By 1963, however, it was only natural for the Justices to support the provision of counsel for indigent felony defendants as a matter of principle, and not just precedent. At the time, it was considered almost immoral not to. To understand why, one must again turn to the extralegal context in which the Court was operating.

Much of what has already been discussed regarding the impact of the civil rights movement on the Supreme Court's decision in *Mapp* applies with equal, if not more, force to its decision in *Gideon* just two years later. Though the events in Birmingham were still a month away when *Gideon* was decided, the civil rights movement had gained substantial support by the beginning of 1963 and the plight of black defendants in Southern courts had already begun to receive publicity. No doubt, the Supreme Court was thinking about the right to counsel in light of these developments; Gideon happened to be white, but the fact that only Southern states had refused to provide an attorney to indigent felony defendants made the connection impossible to ignore. For a Court presumably interested in protecting blacks from Jim Crow justice, extending the right to counsel to the states was attractive for two reasons. First and most obvious, it gave black defendants a sorely needed legal advocate to argue on their behalf. Second, and perhaps less obvious, it increased the opportunities for judicial oversight of suspect Southern courts. Appellate review of a defendant's conviction did little good if someone was not making motions and objections at the trial level, and most defendants needed an attorney to make that happen. In that regard, the Court's decision in *Gideon* served the same purpose as its habeas corpus ruling in *Fay v. Noia*, which coincidentally (or not) was decided the same day: both cases allowed federal courts to more easily scrutinize the treatment of black defendants by Southern criminal justice systems.

Even so, the civil rights movement was not the only factor contributing to the Court's ideological shift in favor of the right to counsel. By the late 1950s, the problem of poverty had begun to infiltrate the American consciousness, and with Michael Harrington's publication of *The Other America* in 1962, it moved to America's conscience as well. By all accounts, Harrington's book had an enormous impact on the national mood, though by 1962, Americans were in the mood to be sympathetic to the plight of poverty anyway. The late 1950s to early 1960s marked one of the strongest peacetime economies in recorded business cycle history, with record-breaking profits and wages as high as anyone could remember. At the same time, Americans were only a generation away from the Great Depression of the 1930s, so many knew how it felt to be poor through no fault of their own. In short, the early 1960s were a perfect time for the nation to turn its attention to the problem of poverty: the American public had wealth and was relatively open to the idea of sharing it.

As one might expect, the plight of poverty had captured the attention of majoritarian politics by the early 1960s as well. Though Lyndon B. Johnson would not formally declare war on poverty until January 1964, the executive branch began to focus on the problem as early as 1960, when John F. Kennedy campaigned on the country's callous disregard for its poor. In 1961, the Kennedy Administration turned specifically to problems faced by poor criminal defendants, establishing the Attorney General's Committee on Poverty and the Administration of Federal Criminal Justice — better known as the Allen Committee for its prestigious chairman, Francis A. Allen. In 1963, just weeks before *Gideon* was decided, the Allen Committee reported its findings. Presuming at the outset that poverty should be irrelevant in any "civilized administration of justice," the Committee recommended, among other things, federal legislation to adequately fund representation for indigent criminal defendants in federal courts. With the executive branch contemplating ways to ensure that the poor received assistance of counsel in federal courts, the Supreme Court had even more reason (as if it needed one) to do the same at the state level, where it mattered most.

Thus, for several reasons, *Gideon* was anything but an example of the Supreme Court swooping down to protect the underdog in the face of great opposition. Indeed, in light of the sociopolitical context of 1963, it is difficult to imagine the Court in *Gideon not* ruling as it did. In *Gideon*, the Supreme Court validated a well-established national consensus, suppressing Southern states that were out-of-step with the rest of the country's enlightened sense of fairness and equality by the early 1960s. As others have noted, this was the Warren Court's signature role. Still, it is more than a little ironic that the same legal assistance at issue in the Warren Court's most popular criminal procedure decision would also become the subject of its least popular criminal procedure decision three years later, *Miranda v. Arizona.*

NOTES & QUESTIONS

1. Pulitzer Prize-winning journalist Anthony Lewis' *Gideon's Trumpet* (1964) tells the story of Clarence Earl Gideon, but Lewis claims he himself did not realize how important the right of counsel was until watching the filming of the movie of the same name. At a symposium on indigent criminal defense in Texas, Lewis said:

> I thought I knew the case by heart. Then years later, I watched the filming of a movie on the case starring Henry Fonda as Gideon. The trial scenes were filmed in a former courthouse, south of Los Angeles. In Gideon's first trial, where he had no lawyer, one of the witnesses against him was a taxi driver who said Gideon had telephoned and asked to be picked up outside that pool room at two in the morning. The prosecutor asked the driver, "Did Mr. Gideon say anything when he got in the cab?" And the driver answered, "Yes. He said, 'Do not tell anyone you picked me up.'" Gideon, representing himself, did not cross-examine, leaving that damaging testimony un-touched. Now here we were in that Los Angeles courthouse, watching Gideon's second trial. The prosecutor asked the same question, and the taxi driver gave the same answer. But this time, Gideon's lawyer, Fred Turner, played by a skillful character actor, Lane Smith, cross-examined [the driver]. He asked, "Had he ever said that to you before?" "Oh yes," the taxi driver answered, "he said that to me every time I picked him up." "Why?" [asked Lane Smith] "I think it was some kind of woman trouble." And Lane Smith had a flower in his buttonhole, a touch that he invented himself. Ad-libbing, [he] walked over to the jury, winked, and said, "Well, we all know about that." The director said, "Cut." I turned to the person next to me, a stranger, and said, "My god, it really makes a difference to have a lawyer, doesn't it?"

Anthony Lewis, *Keynote Speech at Symposium on Indigent Criminal Defense in Texas*, 42 South Texas Law Review 1050, 1054-55 (2001).

2. In the preceding excerpt, Professor Lain says one reason for the acceptance of *Gideon* was the widespread belief that southern courts were biased, corrupt, and generally incompetent. A good number of Hollywood films incorporate this senti-ment, ranging from such classics as *Inherit the Wind* (1960) and *To Kill a Mockingbird* (1962) to more recent films such as *My Cousin Vinny* (1992) and *A Time to Kill* (1996).

3. For a relatively modest, made-for-television film, *Gideon's Trumpet* was surprisingly well-received. One prominent reviewer said the film was "absorbing," and Fonda's performance was "utterly convincing." John J. O'Connor, "TV: *Gide-on's Trumpet*, Landmark Rights Case," *The New York Times*, 30 Apr. 1980, C30. Why did viewers like *Gideon's Trumpet* as much as they did?

4. At the end of *Gideon's Trumpet,* a curious trio of "voices" is combined in a voice-over. The actor John Houseman speaks as Chief Justice Earl Warren, who is supposedly quoting United States Attorney General Robert F. Kennedy. The quotation suggests that, due to Gideon's efforts and because of the Supreme Court opinion, "the whole course of American legal history has been changed." Do you agree?

5. Scholars have disagreed regarding the extent to which rulings from the Supreme Court, especially those recognizing or expanding the rights of marginalized groups, change public attitudes. Might it be the case that when public attitudes change to a significant extent, the Supreme Court will then speak out for an end to discrimination against members of a given group? Professor William N. Eskridge, Jr. has argued that the Supreme Court is likely to extend constitutional protections to identity-based groups only after (1) the groups recognize themselves as such and (2) the public begins to appreciate the validity of the groups' demands. This general pattern is evident in the courts' recognition of rights for African Americans and for the disabled, and, Eskridge argues, the process is ongoing for gay men and lesbians. *See* William N. Eskridge, Jr., *Some Effects of Identity-Based Social Movements on Constitutional Law in the Twentieth Century*, 100 Michigan Law Review 2062 (2002). What do you think is the relationship between public attitudes, popular culture, and constitutional law?

2. Commodifying Constitutional Law

While film and popular culture might endorse and popularize constitutional law in positive ways, as in the previously discussed films involving civil rights, the culture industry's profit-seeking is every bit as powerful as its patriotism. Hence, Hollywood might well choose an intriguing case with constitutional questions and then alter the legal controversy and recharacterize the litigants in hopes of creating a film which will be successful at the box office.

A good example of such an undertaking involves the litigation leading to the Supreme Court's decision in *Hustler Magazine v. Falwell*, 485 U.S. 46 (1988). The plaintiff in the case was Jerry Falwell, a fundamentalist preacher and leader of the Moral Majority. The defendants were the pornographic *Hustler Magazine* and its outspoken, combative publisher Larry Flynt. Falwell took offense at *Hustler*'s satiric description of his sex act with his mother in an outhouse. At the bottom of the satire was the disclaimer "ad parody — not to be taken seriously." Speaking unanimously through Justice Rehnquist, the Supreme Court ruled that however offensive the satire was, it was entitled to First Amendment protection. A public figure such as Falwell, Justice Rehnquist said, could not recover damages without showing a false statement of fact which was made with actual malice.

The Hollywood version of the case constitutes a major portion of *The People vs. Larry Flynt* (1996), starring Woody Harrelson as Larry Flynt, Courtney Love as Flynt's wife Althea, and Edward Norton as Flynt's lawyer Alan Isaacman. The film ranges far and wife in Flynt's complicated and contentious life, complete with abundant nudity and salaciousness. The latter stages of the film emphasize the battle between Falwell and Flynt and include an extended scene in which Isaacman makes his oral argument before the Supreme Court and another scene in which he and Flynt receive the Court's unanimous decision in their favor.

In the following excerpt, Jennifer Peterson discusses the manner in which the film, directed by the renowned Czech-born Milos Forman, is pitched to the fetishistic attachment to individual expressivity at the heart of the liberal political fantasy of American freedom. She harshly criticizes those who reviewed or commented on the film.

FREEDOM OF EXPRESSION AS LIBERAL FANTASY: THE DEBATE OVER *THE PEOPLE VS. LARRY FLYNT*
Jennifer Petersen
29 Media, Culture & Society 377 (2007)

Our Flynt, our selves: the corporation as everyman

The film is highly open to being read as a rags-to-riches story, the rise, fall and ultimate triumph of Flynt the businessman. Yet few reviewers or commentators note the business aspect of Flynt. The majority focus solely on the movie as debate about speech, taste and expression, embodied in the character of Larry Flynt. In fact, the critics' reading of Flynt can be understood as a highly ideological (and perhaps moralistic) discourse on nation, liberal freedoms and formal equality. The movie portrays Flynt quashing the speech of his employees, summarily upbraiding or firing dissenters as he builds his publishing empire. Yet the reviewers uphold multi-millionaire Flynt as the "little guy" that the audience is (or should be) rooting for. It is notable, yet not noted in the public discourse, that Flynt has banked his first million before his first foray into the courtroom. The question of whether freedom of the press is limited to those who own one, to paraphrase an aphorism, is conspicuously not addressed in the majority of the media discourse. The discursive construction of free speech concerns as essentially a fight between individuals and the government is commonplace in US popular discourse. Yet the extent to which reviewers completely overlooked the tension between individual expression and business interests in the text, and were able to view the head of a successful corporation as emblematic of the "little guy" is remarkable.

The reviewers overwhelmingly equate Flynt and his predicament with theirs — and even the viewer's — associating the ability of ordinary citizens to make their speech heard with Flynt's, or at least willfully overlooking any difference between the two positions. This is underscored when Flynt is arrested for the second time and, amid questioning, turns to a journalist and demands, "Why do I have to fight for *your* rights?". . . .

In imagining an equivalence between themselves and Flynt, the journalists may be expressing their gratitude for the leeway they have in their work, but they are also over-interpreting their agency and influence. Flynt, as the owner of his press, was able to print (some of) what he wanted: he is limited by libel, obscenity and "fighting words" laws. Journalists face many more limits on what they can say, from publisher to editor. In practice, the rules of ownership trump rights of expression. Everything must be approved before it is written and vetted once it is. It is reasonable to assume the journalists "know" this, yet they overwhelmingly speak as if they did not (and perhaps fantasize that they act as if they did not).

Similarly, the final court case (in which Flynt appears before the Supreme Court) is often taken by the reviewers to be the moral statement of the film — if not its namesake — and to be proof that Flynt's actions paved the way for their own. This is expressed in reviewers' endorsement of a quote attributed to Flynt that noted that defending Flynt's right to satirize Falwell was equal to defending the freedoms of every American citizen. The equation of Flynt with everyman serves to equate our "freedoms" with those of the corporation. While the reviews (and the legal discourse in the film) focus on individual speech rights, those championed in the film appear to be the corporation's: the case before the Supreme Court was actually titled *Hustler Magazine vs. Falwell*, and turned on whether or not there could be a lower standard for finding emotional damages against media outlets than for proving libel. In essence, the case found that the First Amendment protects media outlets against civil damages suits brought by public figures. It is true that this is an important practical factor in allowing the press to print political satire and opinion. But it is also telling that a decision concerned with protecting media businesses from the economic costs of civil (private) lawsuits came to represent political and personal freedom of expression for so many reviewers: in one critic's words, the case represented a "crucial defense of American liberties.". . . The American liberties at stake are technically those of the corporation; the speech or "freedom" protected, celebrated, and equated with that of the viewers, is in fact that of a corporate entity. Of course, this is explicitly what the reviewers ideologically refuse to confront. It is not that the reviewers are blinded to, or unable to see, the differences between themselves and Flynt. Rather, their identification with Flynt the man becomes the center of a fantastic construction in which anyone's speech is equal to that of *Hustler* magazine's speech.

This willed equation of the speech printed in *Hustler* magazine with the speech of the average viewer equates the viewers' agency to a corporation's, overlooking the "abyss of technology" that separates a publisher's access to speech from an average citizen's. The desire to see speech rights in terms of the individual and of the speaker (rather than in terms of a public good, for example) is ideological in itself, a willed fantasy of the political community as one composed of equals in face-to-face dialogue with one another. This is a vision that fails to describe the way politics (and culture) function in large-scale societies. The ideas that large-scale media texts are expressions of an individual, and that media texts answer to individual needs and choices via the market, serve to keep the way we think about (and regulate) communication out of alignment with the way we do politics in a way that favors those in power and disables those at the margins.

In celebrating unfettered corporate speech as equivalent to American freedom or liberties, the reviewers further an equivalence between consumption and production. A private individual's right to purchase (or not) speech is equated with his or her right to speak. In the first trial of the movie, Flynt's lawyer instructs the jury that they do not need to like Flynt, but that they should like the fact that "you and I live in a country where we can make that decision for ourselves. . . . I can exercise my opinion and not buy it. I like that I have that right, and you should too." This discursive positioning is echoed by reviewers who equate the speech of producers with a consumer choice to buy or not to buy, in which Larry Flynt's right to speak is equated with the individual's right to ignore his speech or refuse to purchase it. Following this logic, any regulation of the producer is a regulation of the consumer's speech (understood as consumption of someone else's speech).

While it might seem woefully disempowering to characterize the average citizen's speech rights as exhausted by a consumerist choice to buy or not to buy someone else's (generally, a corporate entity's) speech, the reviewers and commentators do not take this position. Rather, they take cheer in *Hustler* Inc.'s ability to speak for them. Through over-identification with Flynt, the viewer is free to enjoy Flynt's agency to speak, earned through his status as owner of the means of production. In this, Flynt acts as a sort of Žižekian fetish-object. If one of the modern forms of misrecognition is of another's action as one's own, here we see a misrecognition of another's speaking agency as the subject's own. Flynt the person is misrecognized as acting for individuals, yet Flynt acts not as an individual but as the head of a corporation. This ability of corporate speech rights to stand in for individual ones is a key support to liberal traditions of negative speech rights. It is also, I would suggest, a major obstacle in arguing that regulatory reforms may further speech rights and opportunities for individuals. . . .

In refusing to see the antagonisms that underlie (and indeed drive the legal engagement with) speech rights, the commentators rhetorically construct a more perfect democracy than evidence would suggest actually exists. By acting on the assumption that there are equal opportunities to speak, the commentators engage in ideological fantasy, refusing to see antagonisms based on differential access to money, power and technology. By identifying with the man — and as I will argue in the following section, focusing on speech in terms of personal expression and taste — they engage in the ongoing liberal construction of politics as located in the personal rather than the structural or economic.

Express yourself! Speech is what makes you free

The reviewers, then, embraced the movie and, centrally, the character of Flynt in the movie. They over-interpret their freedom to speak/write under the law and choose to see the agency of corporate speech as proof of their own agency as individuals. I suggest that the idea of freedom of speech, equally shared by all, is a key support for a political fantasy of "freedom." This fantasy works by casting expression (and especially sexual expression) as the realm of agency, allowing individuals to willfully ignore issues of economy and structure (as irrelevant to their expression, the fantastic "true" area of freedom) as the givens, or reality.

By focusing on and over-investing in the idea of self-expression as the "true" realm or proof of freedom, we can construct a liberal ideal (fantasy) of freedom that offers pleasure in a sense of agency. The over-interpretation of the speech rights of individuals, via an ideological/fantastic view of the law and an equation of individual and corporate speech, allows individuals to invest in only one level of social life as *the* realm of "freedom." Issues of economic constraints, even the actual extent of the law, are evaded by the popular attachment to the fantasy of free expression. The very terms in which this idealized freedom is articulated trace the contours of a liberal political imagination (the citizen as individual unfettered by the state in the expression of his or her pure individuality). It is not so much that the idea of free speech hides economic issues or makes it impossible to see inequalities in power and access and effectivity of speech, as that we would rather believe in the fantastic individualist articulation of freedom. It is this that makes the attitude toward free speech displayed in the public discourse on *The People vs. Larry Flynt* that of the fetishist.

Freedom of expression is discussed as emblematic of the freedoms of the US as a liberal political system, and this emblematic freedom is articulated as a matter of taste and psychology. By casting this freedom in terms of taste and expression, the discourse suggests that liberal freedoms are located in what is typically considered the private or intimate realm, rather than the public realm of political economy or social justice. It follows that the evidence and exercise of this freedom is to be found in psychology and personal action. While these realms are not necessarily outside the political, by focusing solely on psychology and expression as the realms of freedom, it is easy to overlook material constraints on action.

One of the ways in which the movie is argued as proof of liberal freedoms is in the frequent reference to Milos Forman's biography in the reviews and debate surrounding the movie. Over and over again, commentators cite the fact that Forman's family perished in a Nazi concentration camp and that he grew up under Soviet communism as proof that he knows the true value of American liberties and has a proper appreciation of the nation. The movie is described as a celebration of the greater freedoms enjoyed by Americans than other peoples, and Forman's own experience in authoritarian regimes is cited as proof of the veracity of this message. His life and endorsement of American liberalism are proofs not only of the superiority of US liberalism, but even of US liberalism as the only option (other than totalitarianism): again and again he is described as being all too familiar with "the alternative" to American liberalism. This discursive limitation of the political universe to such unequal options naturalizes US liberalism as effectively the only choice, but still a choice. The political system in place in the US is the one anyone could/should choose. Implicitly, Americans have chosen well. As the political legitimacy of liberalism rests on the idea of individual choice, all politics must be the result of individual choices and personal preferences, even when there are no effective options. In fantastically casting all politics in terms of individual psychology, preference and choice, structural imperative is experienced as individual desire. In the process, individual agency is exaggerated.

This discursive equation of freedom with taste and expression (I would argue to the exclusion of structure) is not limited to concerns with the director's biography. In discussing the movie itself, and its political message, the reviewers and commentators frequently argued that the idea that Flynt embodies the "worst" speech is central to the movie's message: as Forman told a reporter, he wanted to make the point that the US rises "to its best when provoked by the worst." Flynt's speech is positioned as the worst, an example of the sort of extremity that must be tolerated in a "free society."

Yet, what type of provocation or extremity does Flynt represent in this discussion? At the same time as commentators term his speech the "worst" and a prime example of the sort of utterances that test the bounds of free society, they also describe his speech purely in terms of personal expression and taste. At one point in the movie, Flynt protests that all he is guilty of is bad taste. This line is picked up and reiterated by multiple reviewers. . . . According to this language, the issues at hand are aesthetic and cultural judgments, and the stakes hurt feelings and damaged sensibilities. The discussion of the movie suggests that the bounds that must be tested in a "free society" are those of decorum and taste (rather than those of the public good or justice).

This is far from an exceptional way of articulating freedom of expression: speech rights are often articulated in terms of self-expression, to the point that, in popular discussion (and regulatory decisions) on speech rights, there is no room for considering intersubjectivity, reception or effects. Expression is largely treated as a possession of the speaker in both popular political discourse and regulatory action.

NOTES & QUESTIONS

1. *Hustler*, itself an example of popular culture, published its satire of Jerry Falwell in the form of a bogus Campari Liqueur advertisement. Campari advertisements were widely distributed in the 1980s in a standard format. Each advertisement featured a photograph of a famous person and a discussion of his or her "first time," meaning, on one level, the first time he or she drank Campari and, on another level, the first time time he or she had sex. The following discussion appeared beneath Falwell's picture:

FALWELL: My first time was in an outhouse outside Lynchburg, Virginia.

INTERVIEWER: Wasn't it a little cramped?

FALWELL: Not after I kicked the goat out.

INTERVIEWER: I see. You must tell me all about it.

FALWELL: I never really expected to make it with Mom, but then after she showed all the other guys in town such a good time, I figured, "What the hell!"

INTERVIEWER: But your mom? Isn't that a bit odd?

FALWELL: I don't think so. Looks don't mean that much to me in a woman.

INTERVIEWER: Go on.

FALWELL: Well, we were drunk off our God-fearing asses on Campari, ginger ale, and soda — that's called a Fire and Brimstone — at the time. And Mom looked better than a Baptist whore with a $100 donation.

INTERVIEWER: Campari in the crapper with Mom . . . how interesting. Well, how was it?

FALWELL: The Campari was great, but Mom passed out before I could come.

INTERVIEWER: Did you ever try it again?

FALWELL: Sure . . . lots of times. But not in the outhouse. Between Mom and the shit, the flies were too much to bear.

INTERVIEWER: We meant the Campari.

FALWELL: Oh, yeah. I always get sloshed before I go out to the pulpit. You don't think I could lay down all that bullshit sober, do you?

Hustler, Nov. 1983, inside cover.

2. The Supreme Court's unanimous decision was delivered by Chief Justice Rehnquist and in a nuanced way spoke primarily to the conflict between the tort of intentional infliction of emotional distress and First Amendment protections. The latter, Rehnquist observed, do not depend on the motivations of the speaker. (Flynt had admitted under oath that he had hoped to undermine respect for Falwell and to question his integrity.) *Hustler's* satire of Falwell, Rehnquist added, was entitled to receive great constitutional solicitude because it involved a public figure, and, furthermore, discourse regarding a public figure should not be impeded because it strikes some as outrageous. Thoughtful commentaries on the opinion include: Paul A. LeBel, *Emotional Distress, the First Amendment, and This Kind of Speech: A Heretical Perspective on* Hustler Magazine v. Falwell, 60 University of Colorado Law Review 315 (1989), and Robert C. Post, *The Constitutional Concept of Public Discourse: Outrageous Opinion, Democratic Deliberation, and* Hustler Magazine v. Falwell, 103 Harvard Law Review 601 (1990).

3. How and why might one expect the culture industry to simplify the constitutional law embedded in Rehnquist's decision? In the excerpt printed above, Professor Peterson underscores the film's emphasis on an individual's effort to speak freely rather than on a magazine's determination to satirize a public figure. The individual freedom to speak freely, the film also suggests, is central in the entire notion of American freedom. Why might Hollywood filmmakers have gravitated to the theme of individual speech rights?

Professor Peterson also points out that the film invites reviewers to take Flynt's freedom of speech to be their own. Flynt, Petersen says, acts "as a sort of Žižekian fetish-object." The reference is to the theories of Slavoj Žižek, whose works include *The Plague of Fantasies* (1997). Žižek argues that in contemporary life the misrecognition of another's actions as one's own is both common and problematic.

4. The portrayal of Larry Flynt in *The People vs. Larry Flynt* fits with the endorsement of individualized First Amendment protections. While many took the actual Flynt to be a boorish, pig-headed egotist, he is portrayed in the film as a creative entrepreneur who made his way from rags to riches. Indeed, the earliest scenes in the film introduce Flynt as a humble boy from the hills of Kentucky who sells moonshine for a mere $1 per bottle. Later in the film, Flynt's equally humble parents visit their son in his palatial home and are impressed by the lavishness of his entertaining. Does the traditional rags-to-riches tale, the so-called "Horatio Alger myth," continue to be winning in the contemporary United States? *See* Richard Delgado, *The Myth of Upward Mobility*, 68 University of Pittsburgh Law Review 879 (2007).

In addition to emphasizing Flynt's rages-to-riches story, the filmmakers also portrayed other features of Flynt's life in ways that would make us more likely to sympathize and perhaps even identify with him. Flynt's love for the one-time exotic dancer Althea, for example, is portrayed as tragic. After they profess their undying love for one another and marry, she supposedly remains his loyal mate only to die young. When Flynt is shot by an unkown would-be assassin and left paralyzed as a result, he becomes, at least through the camera's eye, a virtual martyr for his cause. The Hollywood cinema is almost always character-driven, and Flynt, whatever he may be like in real life, becomes not only our protagonist but also our hero.

5.   When we first meet Attorney Alan Isaaacman in the film he is said to be a former public defender who is only 27 years old. Without much apparent aging, the character goes on to represent Flynt in his many cases and controversies, culminating in Flynt's appeal of adverse lower court decisions in the Falwell case. In reality, Flynt hired many lawyers over time, and while the real-life Isaacman was one of them, he differed from the attorney portrayed in the film. *See* Clay Calvert & Robert D. Richards, *Alan Isaacman and the First Amendment: A Candid Interview with Larry Flynt's Attorney*, 19 Cardozo Arts & Entertainment Law Journal 313 (2001).

D.   THE SUPREME COURT OF THE UNITED STATES

Films exist featuring the exploits of individual Justices of the Supreme Court of the United States, be those Justices fictional or actual. Hollywood gravitates frequently to narratives in which a single protagonist encounters difficulties, fights through those difficulties, and finds some resolution or closure before the final credits scroll. An individual Supreme Court Justice could serve as a protagonist as well as anyone else.

An older but intriguing film revolving around a fictional Supreme Court Justice is *A Stranger in Town* (1943). This film, discussed in a subsequent excerpt, features fictional Justice John Josephus Grant, played by Frank Morgan. A small-town attorney is struggling to stop the corrupt practices of town officials, but Grant, while on a duck-hunting trip, lends a hand. The notion of a Supreme Court Justice as a crime-stopper might give one pause, but if law professor Paul Armstrong, played by Sean Connery, could leave the lectern in *Just Cause* (1995) to stop crime (in the Everglades no less), a Supreme Court Justice should be able to leave the bench and do the same.

The most respected film concerning an actual individual Justice of the Supreme Court is *The Magnificent Yankee* (1950). The film portrays Justice Oliver Wendell Holmes during his twenty years on the Supreme Court. The film includes a few scenes in which Holmes orally delivers judicial opinions, but the narrative primarily concerns Holmes' private life with his wife Fanny. The couple was childless, and Holmes and his wife more or less treated Holmes' law clerks as the children they did not have. The film is moving in unanticipated ways, and Hallmark successfully remade the film in 1965 as part of the "Hallmark Hall of Fame" series.

The record is mixed, meanwhile, when the culture industry turns to portraying multiple Justices, much less the institution of the Supreme Court. Films, television series, and novels of this sort are few in number to begin with, and the handful of works that exist are disappointing. For the most part, they fail to appeal to critics and consumers alike. One reason for the culture industry's difficulties in portraying the Supreme Court is the institution's formality and authority. In the following excerpt, Professor Laura Krugman Ray discusses how *New Yorker* cartoons regarding the Supreme Court play off that perceived formality and authority in order to garner a chuckle or — more likely — a smile.

LAUGHTER AT THE COURT: THE SUPREME COURT AS A SOURCE OF HUMOR
Laura Krugman Ray
79 Southern California Law Review 1397 (2006)

E. Life at the Court

In addition to the cartoons that view the Court and its justices from the outside, a handful provide an inside perspective on life behind the bench. In these cartoons, the justices comment, usually to one another, on the nature of their job. None of the artists attempts to represent particular justices; these are generic characters, identifiable only by their surroundings or robes or the substance of their remarks. It is not always easy to distinguish cartoons about Supreme Court Justices from those about lower court judges, but educated guesses are possible. When, for example, a robed figure sitting in formal judicial chambers plucks at a daisy, saying "It's constitutional, it's unconstitutional, it's constitutional, it's unconstitutional," it seems a safe assumption that the 1965 cartoon is targeting the exercise of power by the justices of the Warren Court.

These behind-the-scenes cartoons suggest that the judicial life carries its burdens as well as its pleasures. A 1964 cartoon shows several justices headed for their courtroom, while one observes to another, "Decisions, decisions, decisions!" That good-humored lament about the work ahead is balanced by a later cartoon in which another justice walking through the Court building remarks exuberantly to a colleague, "Gorgeous day! Puts one in the mood for a landmark decision." Two cartoons by Al Ross deflate the notion of the justices' omniscience and power. In one, a justice responds to his colleague's question about the Court's opening ceremony with a confession of ignorance that most readers would share: "Now that you ask, I'm damned if I <u>do</u> know what 'oyez' means!" In the other, a justice turns to his colleague on the bench with a request to conceal his uncertainty from the public: "If you please, Mr. Justice, would you mind not saying, 'Of course we could be wrong?'" Like Justice Jackson's often quoted observation that the justices are "not final because we are infallible, but we are infallible only because we are final," both cartoons pierce the Court's aura of unquestioned authority.

Two other conversations between justices suggest both the breadth and the dangers of their work. The first has a justice answering his colleague's question with resignation: " 'What's on the docket?' Are you kidding? What <u>isn't</u> on the docket?" Coming in 1974, that response suggests a general awareness of the increasing scope of the issues before the Burger Court. The second cartoon, published almost thirty years earlier, depicts a justice with a black eye explaining its cause to his neighbor on the bench: "He said he considered our decision incompetent, delusive, and vindictive. Then he hung this mouse on me." At the date of publication, Chief Justice Fred Vinson had been in office barely three months, and the Court's 1946 term was just beginning. It is thus hard to tie this cartoon to any particular decision capable of inciting a member of the public to personal violence. In light of the timing and the artist — Peter Arno, famous for his *New Yorker* cartoons of elderly plutocrats and youthful showgirls — the cartoon seems to be using a Supreme Court justice as an easily recognizable foil for the story of the punch that produced the "mouse."

These diverse glimpses of the justices show them as fallible and vulnerable, not unlike the employees at less exalted workplaces who also have to cope with unending tasks, uncertainty, and occasionally severe criticism. The humor depends on the reader's basic perception of the Court's dignity and power in order to humanize its justices; no specific knowledge about the justices or their cases is necessary to get the joke, which usually operates by combining judicial formality with the language, customs, and limits of ordinary life.

NOTES & QUESTIONS

1.   While orally delivered jokes might be best characterized as "folk culture," published cartoons are most certainly a part of popular culture. Few comment directly on social issues or political controversies. Instead, cartoons tend to gently ridicule or satirize. In the United States, cartoons about law, courtroom proceedings, and lawyers are abundant.

2.   Cartoons in *The New Yorker* are directed not toward a mass audience but rather toward a decidedly bourgeois crowd. The magazine's cartoonists and readers take the cartoons to be especially witty and subtle. According to Professor Ray in the article excerpted above, the Supreme Court did not become a regular subject for humor in *The New Yorker* until the 1950s:

> In the decades following *Brown*, the cartoons began to increase in frequency and change in substance to reflect a growing awareness of the Court's constitutional decisions and their relevance to the usually prosperous and privileged lives of *New Yorker* readers. For the past half century, as the Warren Court transformed the jurisprudence of individual rights, the Burger Court modified that jurisprudence, and the Rehnquist Court turned in a more conservative direction, *New Yorker* cartoons have echoed in their own way the Court's increasing prominence in America's political landscape.

Ray, *supra*, at 1405-06.

3.   While readers of *The New Yorker* might have delighted in cartoons related to the Supreme Court, portrayals of the Supreme Court in films, television series, and published fiction remained few and far between. In the following excerpt, Adam Burton offers several explanations for why the Supreme Court remains largely invisible in popular culture.

PAY NO ATTENTION TO THE MEN BEHIND THE CURTAIN: THE SUPREME COURT, POPULAR CULTURE, AND THE COUNTERMAJORITARIAN PROBLEM

Adam Burton

73 UMKC Law Review 53 (2004)

1. The "People" Do Not Know the Nine Justices from the Three Stooges

Public opinion polls historically show a profound lack of public knowledge about the Supreme Court and the Justices who compose it. A 1989 poll showed that 54% of the respondents could name Judge Wapner, the presiding judge on the television show *The People's Court*, while only 9% could name Chief Justice William Rehnquist as a member of the Court. In 1995, more people could name the Three Stooges (59%) than could name three Justices (17%).

If these polls accurately reflect the public's knowledge of and interest in the Court, then the traditional absence of the Court from the channels of mass culture is no mystery. Hollywood could easily predict from the numbers that the public is disinterested in the institution and that television shows or movies about the Court likely would inspire equally little interest and generate correspondingly low box office figures or Nielsen ratings. On this view, the Court's image is protected from the searching and distorting glare of popular culture by a lack of public interest and awareness: to modify Perry's calculus, ignorance equals power.

Of course, that may be putting the cart before the horse. Awareness of the Court may be low precisely *because* of the body's absence from popular culture. As the Court itself recognized in *Dickerson v. United States* [2000], popular culture often serves as an educator, and a successful and prolonged representation of the Court in mass culture would probably spark public awareness in the institution. . . .

2. The Court is Removed From the Concerns of the People

A related explanation for the limited coverage of the Court in popular culture is that the people do not care what the Court does because they do not believe it affects their lives. Indeed, apathy toward the Court would be consistent with the public's apparent view toward politics in general, if historically low voter turnout is any indicator. The view that the Court does not in fact affect people's lives, even through monumental cases such as *Brown v. Board of Education*, has some academic support, although the empirical consequences of such cases is a matter of debate.

However, whether or not the Court has any actual effect on people's lives is a different question from whether people perceive the Court as such. The Court frequently serves as a minor character in films that touch on the implications of the Court's decisions for ordinary Americans, underlining the importance of the institution for the general public. The Court's decision in *Brown* was and is widely viewed as an important step in the civil rights movement, especially among Southerners who vented their opposition to segregation by displaying "Impeach Earl Warren" signs. Notwithstanding the views of segregationists, *Brown* continues to stand as a landmark of racial justice in the American consciousness and was lionized as such in the critically acclaimed 1991 television movie *Separate but Equal*, starring the archetypically classy Sidney Poitier.

Furthermore, the Court's abortion decisions constantly remind Americans of the Court's power to affect their most important life choices. Every year on the anniversary of *Roe v. Wade*, or when the Court decides a case calling *Roe v. Wade* into question, advocates on both sides of the abortion controversy demonstrate their views on Maryland Avenue and around the country. Representational popular culture supports the assertion that the Court is perceived as powerful and important. The Court's power to sustain or withdraw the right to abortion has resonated in film, inspiring a litany of films about the decision. The latest television movie on the subject, *Swing Vote*, shows the inter-chambers political maneuvering behind a fictional Supreme Court's crafting of a moderate abortion decision.

The Court's capital punishment jurisprudence also has spawned a number of films depicting the effect of the decisions on society. Following the Court's decision striking down the death penalty in *Furman v. Georgia*, *Terminal Island*, co-starring a young Tom Selleck, appeared in movie theaters. After the Court in the movie strikes down California's death penalty, voters pass an initiative to exile all first-degree murderers (both male and female) to the island of San Bruno, where they are free to do whatever they like except leave. Predictably, the rule of law breaks down, and the movie degenerates into an orgy of sex and violence. But the point is made that the Supreme Court's "liberal" death penalty decision paves the way for the breakdown of orderly society.

More recently, *The Pelican Brief* reestablished the "link between individual Justices and the decisions of the Court . . . in the public mind." Starring Denzel Washington as reporter Gray Grantham and Julia Roberts as law student Darby Shaw, *The Pelican Brief* centers on the assassination of two Supreme Court Justices. Like any diligent and crafty law student, Darby figures out that the culprit is a shadowy millionaire oilman who will do anything to protect his billion dollar oil fields from the grasping green hands of an environmentalist Court. The lesson is that big money turns on the Court's pen strokes.

Thus, it does not appear that the public underestimates the power of the Court to rule on issues that affect large segments of society.

3. The Court Really *is* Revered

The third possibility for the general lack of treatment of the Court in represen-tational popular culture is that the traditional explanation for the Court's legitimacy, namely, that the public reveres the Court as it does the Constitution, is accurate. Thus, the public's view of the Court as an unassailable paragon of virtue is exceptional in an otherwise irreverent age, and people leave the Court alone or depict it in glowing terms because, despite periodic criticism of judicial opinions, "residual Court-worship" and "judge-worship" exist among the American public.

The depictions of the Court in the 1930s might seem to draw this argument into question. However, even though the decisions of the Court were unpopular, and the popular culture reflected the public's disfavor with the Court, the public remained supportive of the institution and never seriously questioned either the legitimacy of judicial review or the commitment of the Justices to the principles of the Constitution. Even the Court's image as "nine old men" had been repaired in 1943, when MGM released *A Stranger in Town.* In that film, a small town attorney trying to break a ring of corrupt officials runs for mayor. His attempts to clean up the town's political system are frustrated until he gets help from a visiting fisherman, who turns out to be vacationing Supreme Court Justice Jon Josephus Grant. Thus, the Court, represented by the fictional Justice Grant, is a secretive and anonymous but benevolent force, a deus ex machina saving justice from politics.

Other films have portrayed the Court's most popular decisions, promoting the Court as a guarantor of justice. As noted above, the 1991 television movie *Separate but Equal* celebrated the Court's decisions ending segregation. In 1980, Henry Fonda and Jose Ferrer co-starred in *Gideon's Trumpet,* a well received television film dramatizing the litigation of *Gideon v. Wainwright,* in which the Court interpreted the Sixth Amendment as guaranteeing the provision of counsel at state expense for anyone accused of a felony.

More recently, the Court has been portrayed in reverential terms in *The People vs. Larry Flynt.* This Sony Pictures' 1996 film dramatizes the life of pornographer Larry Flynt and culminates in his successful First Amendment battle before the Court in *Hustler Magazine v. Falwell.* While feminist critiques attacked the film for making a hero out of Flynt, director Milos Forman claimed that the film was a "love letter to the Supreme Court" and that "the real hero of [the] film is . . . the Supreme Court of the United States." Following from Forman's vision, the on-screen Court is portrayed as serene and dignified, if not heroic. Even the on-screen Flynt, who throws oranges and spews profanities at lower court judges throughout the film, acts with relative decorum in the Supreme Court while his lawyer argues his case. The Court and its members, as the impartial, ultimate expositor of the Constitution, are thus automatically worthy of a respect that the lower court judges do not enjoy, and the film celebrates the Court as a defender of the Constitutional rights of even unpopular causes or despicable characters. . . .

Works depicting Justices as flawed characters have arguably distinguished between the individual member of the Court and the Supreme Court as an institution, sometimes showing the Justice in an unflattering light while simultane- ously upholding the Court as "an institution of dignity and authority." Showing the idiosyncrasies of personal disputes among the Justices as individuals is different from showing that these quirks result in arbitrary decisions or that Justices tailor their decisions to spite their colleagues, either of which might call into question the legitimacy of the institution. Likewise, showing that an individual Justice has personal political opinions and fixed moral guideposts is a far cry from accusing the Justices of regularly engaging in partiality in rendering decisions — this is the familiar academic distinction between high politics and low politics, and it in part explains why maintaining mystery is not essential for the Court to retain its authority.

However, showing the Justices as compromisers and dealmakers and not as principled decision-makers, i.e., showing the institutional processes of rendering a decision as no different in timbre than Congressional or Presidential legislative processes, might undermine respect for their decisions. . . . CBS and ABC premiered television shows about the Court as an institution in 2002. Both networks believed that public interest in the Court would support television shows illuminating the inner workings of the Court, dispelling the mystery of the tribunal's proceedings and exposing the Court's decision-making process as both a highly political and highly personal affair. *First Monday* producer, Donald P. Bellisario, explained the premise of the show: "I really wanted to pull the ol' curtain aside like Toto did and show the wizard behind it. Or in this case, the nine wizards." In this way, *First Monday* and *The Court* were poised to become fictional television versions of *The Brethren* [the popular "inside look" at the Supreme Court by Bob Woodward and Scott Armstrong, published in 1979], propagating the themes of that book to a more widespread and general audience and in the process damaging the Court's prestige.

Neither show quite lived up to *The Brethren* in style or critical acclaim. *First Monday* starred Joe Mantegna as the recently appointed, politically moderate Justice Joe Novelli and James Garner as mean-spirited conservative Chief Justice Thomas Brankin. *First Monday* portrayed the Court as the ultimate arbiter on serious issues, although it often addressed them in clichéd terms or with inappropriate caprice. In only thirteen episodes, the Court decides cases on capital punishment, teenage abortion, and the "three strikes law." CBS' impish Court also hears cases on whether dwarves are protected by the ADA and whether the First Amendment protects polygamists.

First Monday attempted to depict the Court's decision-making process in the style of NBC's popular drama about the President, *The West Wing*. *First Monday* portrayed the Court as unabashedly political, suggesting that the Justices' chambers are but settings for cigar smoke-filled backroom deals and that politics, not legal reasoning or precedent, is the only relevant factor in the resolution of a case. Furthermore, *First Monday* overemphasized the roles of the law clerks, who are portrayed as sexy, glamorous, and cocky.

Producer Don Bellisario admitted to taking liberties with accuracy in the interests of creating dramatic plots: "[Q]uite honestly, you're creating a TV series. You're trying to entertain." But the inaccuracies of the show were more than subtle, leading one television critic to quip, "Nothing about . . . *First Monday* is believable except the set." For example, *First Monday* implausibly shows one of the clerks discovering a botched autopsy report in a death row case, as if the clerks' job approximated that of Columbo or Magnum P.I., and the Justices ask obnoxious and arrogant questions directly of the parties, instead of the lawyers. But these factual inaccuracies were the least of the show's flaws. Most critics found the show's writing lacking, at times even laughable, and *First Monday* was cancelled on May 13, 2002, due to low ratings.

ABC's *The Court* fared even worse, even though critics favorably compared the show's writing to that of *First Monday*. Starring the likeable Sally Field as Justice Kate Nolan, a recently appointed moderate in an ideologically divided Court, *The Court* attempted to focus more on the inner workings of the Court than on the flurry of Constitutional issues dealt with in *First Monday*. The first episode of ABC's show dealt with the appointment of Kate Nolan to the Court. The popular governor of

Ohio, Nolan is appointed in only six hours despite her lack of a judicial record and her refusal to answer questions regarding her position on important issues. But the implication is that we can trust her to vote with her conscience and that we can trust her judgment. After all, this is no ordinary stealth candidate; this is Sally Field.

Like *First Monday, The Court* portrays the Justices as politically motivated actors, separating the Justices into "teams" of conservatives and liberals. *The Court* also raises questions concerning the important role of law clerks, although the young, good-looking, and competitive law clerks are portrayed as having "far too large an effect on the outcome of the cases." In the second episode, Justice Nolan makes a decision in an important case based on the misleading information of her ambitious young clerk, raising questions about who is really in charge of important Supreme Court opinions. Despite Ms. Field's best efforts, the show was cancelled after only three episodes and declining ratings.

While both *First Monday* and *The Court* ultimately failed to engage the audience in the same way that *The West Wing* has, their stance toward the Justices and the institution should lay to rest any arguments that the public still trembles in awe-struck deference to the Supreme Court. Most television commentators who reviewed the shows agreed that they failed because of poor writing, not because the Supreme Court is an inappropriate subject for television or because the Court should remain shrouded in mystery. At the same time, the airing of each show apparently does not augur a new era in popular culture with the Court as subject, as the popular culture has moved on to new subjects and a seemingly endless supply of reality shows. Nor does it signal that the Court's popular legitimacy is waning; neither program overtly questioned the institutional legitimacy of the Court, even though both occasionally depicted the Justices as bare-knuckled politicians. . . .

4. Popular Culture Stifles Public Debate

A fourth possibility for the dearth of treatment for the Court in popular culture is that the tawdriness of the culture itself discourages producers and consumers from paying attention to the institution. The Supreme Court cannot slake the public appetite for scandal and sex except on bizarre occasions, so producers turn elsewhere for subject matter. The world of the Court is filled with thinking and writing, which is not exactly the stuff of Perry Mason, or even Judge Judy. The Supreme Court and its discussion of arcane legal matters, which take time and concentration to grasp, fail to provide satisfying material for the culture of instant gratification. Popular culture could therefore only discuss the institutional values of the Supreme Court in a most cursory (or worse, inaccurate) fashion. The mission of Hollywood, and television in particular, is to entertain (and thereby keep the attention of consumers), not to educate.

There may be something to the claim that the culture of instant gratification has decreased the quality of public debate. But the major flaw of this argument is that we have not seen a major drop off from production of shows with the Court as subject matter in relation to earlier time periods with different cultural backdrops. Indeed, the popular culture of earlier time periods featured the Court no more often than today's. The popular culture media of earlier times were, of course, much different, but within those media the Court was not prominently featured.

5. Popular Culture, Social Utility, and Democracy

The social utility of popular cultural depictions of the Court in the modern mass media remains questionable. Exposing the Court as a policy-making body and increasing the general level of knowledge about the Court's proceedings might benefit democracy by fostering debate about the Court's place in the government. However, such depictions might also misinform the public about the Court in the interests of making it seem more dramatic, exaggerating the deficiencies of the body and its members. The public might also become more knowledgeable about the fictional Court than about the real Court and blur the line between the two. As Richard Sherwin put it, "[w]hatever the visual mass media touch bears the mark of reality/fiction confusion." Richard K. Sherwin, *When Law Goes Pop: The Vanishing Line Between Law and Popular Culture* 141 (2002). Neither exaggerating the heroism or deficiencies of the Court nor blurring the line between fact and fiction would serve to inform the public about the Court or inspire greater public accountability from the Court. There are two negative possibilities that might result from the exaggeration of the role that personal ideology plays in Court decisions. The first possibility is to legitimize the role of "low politics" in judicial decision-making. As Judge Harry Edwards has argued with regard to lower court judges, if the public expects the Justices to decide cases according to blunt partisan ideology, the Justices may be tempted to conform to this perception; the inappropriate politicization of the Court would thus become a self-fulfilling prophecy. This outcome is not likely, however, among Justices who take their role seriously. The second, and more likely, possibility is that Senators or the President might use widespread public perceptions of a Court run amok, propagated and dramatized in fictional images, to further their own careers at the expense of the judiciary. In 1968, President Nixon's Law and Order campaign played on popular discontent at the perceived overreaching of the Warren Court, especially in the field of criminal procedure. Today's Senate also vigorously pursues judicial appointments as a political and electoral issue. The point here is not to pass judgment on the propriety of increasingly politicizing judicial appointments — the Constitution surely anticipates such an outcome, and political struggle over appointments does not in itself decrease the likelihood that quality jurists will be appointed to the Court. Rather, the point is to illustrate the possible negative effects of distorted popular culture depictions of the Court to that process. Moreover, if the Court's appearances in popular culture mostly are limited to the rare occasions when the Court is involved in scandal, and popular culture serves as a tracker for the Court's mishaps, then maybe the absence of the Court from fictional television is a good thing.

Some critics argue that the Court might receive more public attention, and possibly more attention in popular culture, if oral arguments were televised. Then, the Court would receive fuller treatment in public discourse, as opposed to appearing only on the rare occasion of public scandal or other sporadic treatment. However, like C-SPAN for Congress, a C-SPAN for the Court's arguments is unlikely to attract a wide audience. To the extent that television news might air portions of oral arguments, it would likely dilute the arguments into ten-second sound bites, taking arguments out of context.

NOTES & QUESTIONS

1. The majority of prime-time television series fail within a year, but the abrupt failure of both *First Monday* and *The Court* in 2002 is nevertheless especially striking. Both series revolved around a fictional Supreme Court of the United States, and both series had established writers and producers and well-known, popular actors. To be sure, the series often portrayed members of the Supreme Court as politicized wheeler-dealers, but these portrayals may not have been as important in the series' inability to attract viewers as Burton suggests in the preceding excerpt. To what extent do you think continuing reverence for the Supreme Court as an institution contributed to the demise of *First Monday* and *The Court*?

2. In most of his discussion, Burton assumes that the culture industry's decisions regarding films, television series, and novels related to the Supreme Court derive from the public's limited awareness of the Supreme Court. As noted in the introductory chapter of this textbook and repeated in other chapters as well, the culture industry surely hopes its products resonate with the public's values and beliefs. However, it would be mistaken to take film and popular culture in general to be merely a mirror of public sentiments. What is the best way to conceptualize the relationship between popular culture and public sentiments?

3. Burton's final point is different from his first four points and goes less to the absence of Supreme Court portrayals in popular culture and more to the potential social utility of this absence. He suggests that portrayals of the Supreme Court could conceivably legitimize what he calls "low politics" in judicial decision-making and that Justices themselves might be tempted even more than they already are to decide cases politically. Burton also suggests that if there were more films and television showing a tawdry side of the Supreme Court, politicians would be able to further their careers by attacking the Supreme Court as a politically motivated institution hiding behind a supposedly neutral rule of law. Do you find these arguments persuasive?

4. In the following excerpt, Professor Laura Krugman Ray discusses portrayals of the Supreme Court in *First Monday in October* and *The Pelican Brief*. As the excerpt indicates, *First Monday in October* began as a Broadway play by Jerome Lawrence and Robert E. Lee and fits the romantic comedy model. It was easily adapted into a film of the same name starring Walter Matthau and Jill Clayburgh. *The Pelican Brief*, meanwhile, began as a mystery thriller written by best-selling novelist John Grisham. Hollywood adapted the novel into a film of the same name starring Julia Roberts and Denzel Washington. Both films are culminations in the process of transmogrification, which is a central feature in the production of popular culture and is briefly discussed in Chapter 1 of this textbook.

JUDICIAL FICTIONS: IMAGES OF SUPREME COURT JUSTICES IN THE NOVEL, DRAMA, AND FILM
Laura Krugman Ray
39 Arizona Law Review 151 (1997)

The Supreme Court as Battleground: *First Monday in October*

The most prominent Supreme Court play since *The Magnificent Yankee* is *First Monday in October* by Jerome Lawrence and Robert E. Lee, first produced on Broadway a generation later in 1978 and prophetic of Sandra Day O'Connor's appointment to the Court by President Reagan in 1981. Although *First Monday in October* anticipates history by placing a woman on the Court, it is scarcely an innovative or radical work. Like *Talk of the Town*, it draws heavily on the conventions of romantic comedy; unlike the earlier film, however, it has little interest in the institution of the Court except as a new setting for its traditional story.

Although the authors characterize their play as "a comedy-drama," it might more appropriately be described as an exercise in polarity. The first woman appointed to the Court is Ruth Loomis, a youthful circuit court judge from California who is athletic, orderly, and outspokenly conservative in her jurisprudence. Her opposite number is Dan Snow, the Court's senior Associate Justice, a dedicated liberal who cultivates a messy desk and, when not climbing mountains, exercises his sharp tongue. The play is organized around their mutual antagonism, which includes more than their basic ideological disagreement; she finds him arrogant, while he finds her priggish. In the first act, they spar over a First Amendment case, and Ruth questions Dan as he plays the part of the distributor of a pornographic film. In the second act, the disputed case is a shareholder suit against a large corporation, and this time Dan questions Ruth as the missing corporate president. Even the stage set emphasizes the characters' opposition. It consists principally of their judicial chambers, set "back to back," with a foreground area that serves as all of the other Court settings.

Despite its legal trappings and debates, *First Monday in October* is a variant of a familiar romantic comedy pattern: the man and woman meet in unusual circumstances, recognize their differences, and bicker relentlessly until they realize what the audience already knows, that they are a perfect match. Dan, who has been considering retirement from the Court, is energized by the news that Ruth has been appointed. He begins sniping at his new colleague even before she arrives, calling her "Lady Purity" and the "Mother Superior of Orange County" and preparing for battle. At their first meeting, in the Justices' robing room, they size each other up, and the stage directions make clear the future course of their relationship: "They look at each other with a full awareness of the gulf between them. Cryptic smiles cross each face: boy, are these two going to have a donnybrook!" Ruth rises to the occasion, challenging Dan's approach to First Amendment cases and accusing him of behaving "like a burlesque comic." By the end of the first act, Dan has acknowledged that she is "a worthy adversary," and he pays her the serious compliment of finding her "dangerous."

In the conventional comedies perhaps most perfectly embodied by the films pairing Katharine Hepburn and Spencer Tracy, the protagonists inevitably move toward a romantic resolution. Lawrence and Lee stop short of providing such an ending for their play, but they do give the relationship of Ruth and Dan some sexual overtones. By the second act, both Justices are romantically available; Ruth is a widow, and Dan's wife has filed for a divorce. In a conversation with Dan's law clerk, Ruth asks several increasingly suggestive questions: what does Dan do for recreation, what is his wife like, and, most revealingly, "[d]oes he ever talk about me?" Dan himself answers the last question when he describes for Ruth his wife's suspicions about the Justices' relationship:

> Dan. I think she thinks I spend so much time being furious at you I don't have enough energy left to be furious at *her.* You know — love-hate, hate-love. And I suspect she's got a hunch that I consider you attractive.
>
> Ruth. Well, there's no evidence to support *that* contention.
>
> Dan. I wouldn't be too sure.
>
> Ruth. I hope you'll assure Mrs. Snow that the mere fact one of your colleagues happens to be a woman. . . .
>
> Dan. That's no "mere" fact — it's a *towering* fact!

Ruth is sufficiently unsettled by this exchange to misinterpret Dan's movement toward her as an advance, but the stage directions make clear that he is only reaching for a book. Although the scene ends not with an embrace but with Dan's collapse from an apparent heart attack, it teases the audience by bringing to the surface the romantic subtext of the legal arguments between the Justices.

The audience remains, however, unclear about the nature of the relationship between Dan and Ruth because the play treats the "towering fact" of a woman Justice with ambivalence that borders on confusion. At her confirmation hearing, Ruth acknowledges that her gender will affect her opinions and that "[p]erhaps it's time for the majority of the population to have one voice in nine in the rulings of the Supreme Court." At the same time, she rejects the term "lady" and asks the senators "[w]hat has sex got to do with being a judge?" Dan seems similarly confused about how to treat a woman colleague, worrying when five Justices sit for the Court's annual photograph while Ruth stands; he has no difficulty, however, in asserting his seniority when the Justices march into the courtroom. The play adds another layer of confusion by identifying Dan with a jurisprudence of compassion and concern for the individual, while Ruth insists that Justices should be "dispassionate" in their search for "broad legal principles." It is hard to imagine within this framework what role Ruth envisions for the woman's voice on the Court, and the play offers no explanation.

Although Lawrence and Lee retreat from a romantic reconciliation of their protagonists, they provide instead the professional equivalent. When Ruth, having learned that her late husband was involved in misconduct connected with a pending case, decides to resign from the Court, Dan insists that it is her public duty to remain. He tells her that the "Court changes people" from flawed individuals to honorable judges; whatever their ideological and personal differences, they share a professional bond that is meant to replace or overshadow the romantic bond that has been dangled before the audience and withdrawn. The play ends with the two Justices cheerfully anticipating their battles over future cases and agreeing only, as Ruth says, that "[y]ou and I make each other possible." In place of the conventional kiss, there is a handshake before Ruth and Dan proceed, in order of seniority, into the courtroom; the scene might have been scripted as a deliberate contrast to *Talk of the Town*, where the couple instead escapes from the Court. There is, however, an even more important difference between the two resolutions. In the earlier work, Lightcap's chilly rationalism has clearly been moderated by his brush with emotion; in the later play, there is only a brief hint from Dan that Ruth's dispassionate approach to the law may have been softened by Dan's compassion. The point of the final scene is that the antagonists remain just that, what Dan has earlier described as "a pair of flying buttresses" which, supporting "opposite sides of a Gothic cathedral . . . keep the roof from caving in."

First Monday in October is less a play about the Court than it is an attempt to transpose the conventions of romantic comedy into the judicial workplace. This is made clear by the film version, adapted by the playwrights and released in 1981, which softens Ruth somewhat and contributes two new characters to the romantic aspect of the plot. Ruth is now courted by her late husband's law partner, while Dan's wife is present to demonstrate his lack of interest in their marriage. A gentler Ruth rides in the ambulance with Dan after his heart attack and, when he rejects her resignation, gives him a chaste kiss. While its romantic elements are enlarged, the legal elements of the plot are less clear and less accurate than in the play. The authors are understandably confused about the certiorari process, but they might on that ground have given less prominence to the battle over bringing the corporate misconduct case to the Court. Although both the play and the film treat the Court as an honorable and powerful institution, they are principally interested in it as a novel setting for a familiar story, a setting that defeats their intentions. As Supreme Court Justices, Dan and Ruth remain in a kind of dramatic limbo: too elevated for the ordinary resolution of romantic comedy, but too conventional for a plausible version of collegial relations at the Court. . . .

The Supreme Court as Target: *The Pelican Brief*

John Grisham's 1992 suspense novel, *The Pelican Brief*, is the first to hinge a plot on the composition of the Supreme Court and the first to locate the solution to murder in the Court's docket. Writing a decade after [Margaret] Truman [daughter of President Harry Truman and author of the murder mystery novel *Murder in the Supreme Court*], Grisham had several advantages in basing a plot on the Court. As a lawyer, he brought to his novel a more sophisticated understanding of the Court's role than the typical layperson, even an experienced Washington observer like Truman. More importantly, Grisham wrote after the defeat of Robert Bork's nomination to the Court had educated the public about the significance of a single Justice's vote. Not since Owen Roberts' celebrated "switch in time [that] saved Nine" helped to derail Roosevelt's court packing plan had the nation been forced to consider how the viewpoint of a single Justice might alter the legal landscape.

A national audience watched Robert Bork's confirmation hearings on television in

September 1987 with the sense that the Senate Judiciary Committee was about to make a choice that was not merely important but momentous. Bork had been nominated to fill the seat of Justice Lewis Powell, a moderate Justice generally considered a swing vote between the liberal and conservative wings of the Court, and thus it was generally assumed that his vote would determine the Court's direction. In the overheated rhetoric of such Bork opponents as Senator Edward Kennedy, the confirmation of Bork would threaten the basic civil liberties of all Americans. Bork's supporters inside and outside the Reagan administration countered that Bork's confirmation was essential to restrain the Court's dangerous and illegitimate tendency to rewrite the law in accord with its members' liberal policy preferences. The televised spectacle of the nominee responding to the senators' questions was accompanied by a fierce media campaign that insisted on the apocalyptic nature of the battle: the lives of all Americans would be directly affected by the confirmation or rejection of Robert Bork. Four years later, the confirmation hearings of Justice Clarence Thomas created another media spectacle, though this time the focus was less on the Court's balance than on the credibility of the nominee. Together the Bork and Thomas nominations dramatized for the American public the turbulent emotions and high stakes surrounding the selection of Supreme Court Justices.

Although *The Pelican Brief* is largely a novel of pursuit, the chase is set in motion by the problem of the Supreme Court's composition. Grisham's premise is that a wealthy entrepreneur appealing the injunction that prevents him from drilling for oil in a wildlife refuge has ordered the assassination of the Court's two environmentalist Justices in order to secure a more favorable bench. The entrepreneur, a heavy contributor to the incumbent President's election campaign, accepts the advice of counsel that two new conservative appointees will ensure a favorable decision worth millions of dollars. The novel's plot is a variation on the Bork scenario — the motive is financial rather than ideological — but it relies on the same assumption that a shift in Court membership will have immediate and predictable consequences. Grisham makes the point with some emphasis at the start of the novel, when a crowd of 50,000 angry demonstrators rings the Supreme Court on the first Monday in October, and we learn that "[t]hreats, serious ones, against the justices had increased tenfold since 1990." The link between individual Justices and the decisions of the Court is well established in the public mind.

The target of eighty percent of the death threats against the Court is Justice Abraham Rosenberg, a ninety-one year old liberal who, though paralyzed and weak after two strokes, still writes his own opinions and refuses to resign until a Democrat is elected President. Rosenberg's position on environmental issues is unequivocal: "the environment over everything." Justice Glenn Jensen, sixth among the Justices in death threats, is an erratic conservative who has drifted toward the left since his close confirmation vote six years earlier and who is now "fairly consistent in his protection of the environment." Jensen also has a secret life in which he takes Prozac for his depression and frequents a theater specializing in gay pornographic films. Although his fear of exposure has been largely replaced by the pleasure he takes in the challenge of evading detection, Jensen, like several of Truman's Justices, has a part of his life that he wants to keep from the public. In the violent political climate surrounding the Court, all of the Justices are closely guarded by FBI agents, though not well enough to prevent the assassinations of Rosenberg and Jensen by a highly skilled professional.

In the aftermath of the assassinations, the most perceptive detectives are not the law enforcement experts but the amateurs who understand the roles played by Rosenberg and Jensen on the Court. Justice Ben Thurow, a former federal prosecutor, tells his colleagues that the victims " 'were murdered for a reason, and that reason is directly related to a case or an issue already decided or now pending before this Court.' " Thurow proposes using the Court's law clerks "to solve the killings" by having them review the cases pending in the circuit courts, though the other Justices are skeptical. In fact, Thurow is on the right track. The case is solved by a second year law student at Tulane, Darby Shaw, who examines the pending appellate cases and finds one with the crucial element: not a strong ideological issue, but simply "a great deal of money." The angry protesters and the death threats against the Justices turn out to be red herrings. The motive is greed, that staple of detective fiction, though the solution is found in electronic data bases by someone who knows how to read the jurisprudence of the victims.

The Pelican Brief is thus a highly conventional novel that casts the Supreme Court as a source of financial benefits, much like the victim's will in a mystery novel by Agatha Christie or Ngaio Marsh, and a law student as the detective. What is new in Grisham's fiction is the grounding of motive in the substance of the Court's decisions and the related idea that the Court can be easily redirected by the expedient of substituting more congenial Justices for hostile obstructionists. In Rosenberg and Jensen, Grisham presents two varieties of obstacle. Rosenberg, the committed liberal, is determined to control his seat by withholding his resignation from a conservative President; Jensen, the erratic conservative, has become unpredictable and therefore a business risk for the entrepreneur who seeks certainty and control. The murders, carried out on advice of counsel, are thus a carefully researched business strategy. Grisham is a good deal less interested in working out the implications of his novel's premise than he is in detailing Darby Shaw's ingenuity in evading her pursuers, and the novel does not linger long over the Court and its docket. Nonetheless, *The Pelican Brief*, together with its popular film, has brought to a vast audience an image of the Court not as a powerful protector of constitutional rights but rather as a vulnerable institution subject to manipulation by sinister external forces bent on furthering their own financial interests through their mastery of the Court's jurisprudence.

NOTES & QUESTIONS

1. Professor Ray casts *First Monday in October* as a romantic comedy. This genre dates back at least to the Great Depression of the 1930s and in that era was sometimes called "screwball comedy." In the midst of the Depression, romantic comedies were able, at least momentarily, to relieve the anxieties of their fans. The films were humorous, promised happy endings, and even subtly conveyed the promise that social differences could be overcome. Some film historians identify *It Happened One Night* (1934), starring Clark Gable and Claudette Colbert, as the model for the literally hundreds of romantic comedies that followed. Two masters of the romantic comedy during the 1940s and 1950s were Spencer Tracy and

Katharine Hepburn, and their delightful *Adam's Rib* (1949) turns out to be law-related. The film concerns husband-and-wife attorneys, Adam and Amanda Bonner, played by Tracy and Hepburn, who end up on opposite sides in a prosecution for attempted murder and almost wreck their marriage in the process. *See* David Ray Papke, *Genre, Gender, and Jurisprudence in* Adam's Rib, *in Screening Justice — The Cinema of Law: Significant Films of Law, Order and Social Justice* (Rennard Strickland, Teree E. Foster & Taunya Lovell Banks eds. 2006).

2.   In the film version of *First Monday in October*, Justices Dan Snow and Ruth Loomis, played by Walter Matthau and Jill Clayburgh, banter and miscommunicate like the classic romantic comedy duo. Snow, a woolly liberal, calls the conservative Loomis "the Mother Superior of Orange County," and Loomis, referring to Snow's absolutist understanding of the First Amendment, says Snow "may want the absolute freedom to go straight to Hell." As the film goes on, Snow and Loomis develop respect, admiration, and affection for one another. Snow talks Loomis out of resigning from the Supreme Court in the midst of a scandal involving her late husband. When at the very end of the film Snow suffers a heart attack, Loomis coddles and nurses him, even at one point giving him a tender kiss. The filmmakers stopped short of passionate scenes involving the Justices, but it is not too much of a stretch to say they come to love one another. However, as the Justices' love for one another develops, any chance for robust debate regarding the Constitution or an extended comparison of political philosophies disappears. As David R. Shumway has argued, the love interest in a romantic comedy is effective as a mechanism for displacement. In *First Monday in October*, the characters' growing affection for each other displaces their politicized dialogue regarding the Constitution. *See* David R. Shumway, *Screwball Comedies: Constructing Romance, Mystifying Marriage*, Cinema Journal 30:4 (Summer 1991) 7-23.

3.   And alas, *First Monday in October* disappoints not only as a portrayal of the Supreme Court but also as a romantic comedy. As Ray notes in the preceding excerpt, the film is largely "an attempt to transpose the conventions of romantic comedy into the judicial workplace." The filmmakers place Snow and Loomis in an unusual place for romance, but their romance can hardly be consummated. To quote Ray, "As Supreme Court Justices, Dan and Ruth remain in a kind of romantic limbo: too elevated for the ordinary resolution of romantic comedy, but too conventional for a plausible version of collegial relations at the Court." Could the Supreme Court ever be the setting for a winning romantic comedy?

4.   Professor Ray characterizes *The Pelican Brief* as a murder mystery and compares it to the works of novelist Margaret Truman. The latter wrote a dozen popular mysteries in the 1970s and 1980s. The most relevant of these mysteries is *Murder in the Supreme Court* (1982). But while *The Pelican Brief* has elements of the murder mystery — would-be detectives answering the proverbial question of "whodunit" — it also fits within the thriller genre. In the later stages of John Grisham's novel law student Darby Shaw and journalist Gray Grantham dodge bullets and car bombs galore. As in the typical thriller, the main characters are repeatedly terrorized. Why do many delight in reading thrillers?

5. *The Pelican Brief* became even more of a thriller when adapted for the large screen. Alan Pakula was the chief screenwriter and director, and his earlier films included such cinematic thrillers as *Klute* (1971) and *All the President's Men* (1976). Before his death in 1998, Pakula had mastered the art of creating a cinematic sense of danger and paranoia. Some have argued that film is *the* medium that can most induce the kind of suspense one expects from a thriller. Skilled directors employ short takes, close-ups of panicked characters, and rapid physical movements to leave viewers on the edge of their seats. *See* Gordon Gow, *Suspense in the Cinema* (1968).

6. Despite the abundant talent of John Grisham and Alan Pakula and the presence of superstars such as Julia Roberts and Denzel Washington, *The Pelican Brief* failed to win over the critics. Richard Schickel said, "Mostly this is a movie about people getting in and out of cars, which either do or do not blow up when they turn on the ignition." Richard Schickel, "Running (Barely) on Empty," *Time*, 20 Dec. 1993, 62. Reflecting on how thrillers work, Schickel added, "They can be comforting when you're page-turning your paperback in economy class and all you're looking for is a gentle diversion. Movies, though, require something more than connective tissue, however handsomely rendered. They are a dramatic form, which implies a need for both ever-tightening menace and, ultimately, direct confrontations with evil's source." *Id.*

7. Genre is a major element in Hollywood's production process. Hollywood uses genre to advertize films and even to place films in sections of video rental stores. Not surprisingly, viewers routinely come to films with expectations based on the film's genre.

So be it, one might say, but does the reliance on genre help explain the paucity of films concerning constitutional issues or portraying the Supreme Court? The public's limited sense of the Constitution as an icon and of the Supreme Court as a formal, distant and even irrelevant institution are reflected in Hollywood's small body of "constitutional law films," but Hollywood's reliance on genre in the assembly line of film production could also be a factor. Generic works may be winning, but they rarely have a provocative, critical edge. When a romantic comedy devolves into a story of the affection bordering on love that politically opposite Justices develop for one another, thoughtful explorations of constitutional doctrine are unlikely. When a thriller keeps you on the edge of your seat as the assassins of two Supreme Court Justices attempt to add the film's heroes to their list of victims, insights about the working of the Supreme Court are too much to expect.

Chapter 12

FAMILY LAW

A. FILMOGRAPHY

Baby M (1996)

Kramer vs. Kramer (1979)

Losing Isaiah (1995)

Mr. and Mrs. Loving (1996)

The War of the Roses (1989)

B. MARRIAGE

The American style of marriage originated in the Anglo-Saxon tribal society. It included a betrothal through which the bride's family agreed to transfer the bride to the bridegroom in return for property ranging from token amounts to the truly substantial. After the Norman conquest and the increase in Christianity's importance, marriage passed into the hands of the church. Marriages through the church were also standard in the North American colonies, but after the founding of the American republic, civil marriage and common law marriage supplemented Christian ceremonies and covenants. In the present, Americans remain extremely fond of marriage. Nine out of ten say "I do" at least once during their lifetimes, and even the percentage of divorced Americans who remarry is on the rise.

Contemporary marriage law includes rules about how and when one might marry, but the same rules also make clear who may not marry and who may not marry whom. For much of the twentieth century, marriage law frowned on marriages between people of different races. Some western states barred marriages between whites and Chinese, and most of the southern states had statutes barring marriages between whites and African Americans. "More statutes banned miscegenation than any other form of racially related conduct." Kermit L. Hall, *The Magic Mirror: Law in American History* 157 (1989).

One might think struggles to overcome these restrictions would have provided the grist for dramatic films, but from the 1920s through the 1950s Hollywood refused to even portray marriages involving people of different races. As the following excerpt from an article by Alexandra Gil indicates, miscegenation was one of the subjects Hollywood had on its self-censorship list.

GREAT EXPECTATIONS: CONTENT REGULATION IN FILM, RADIO, AND TELEVISION

Alexandra Gil

2009 University of Denver Sports and Entertainment Law Journal 31

Debate over film censorship can be traced back to the beginning of film. Thomas Edison's *The Kiss* (1896), a twenty-second film depicting a man and a woman talking to each other cheek to cheek for about eighteen seconds and then sharing a chaste kiss, was met with hearty criticism for its then-risqué subject matter. Although the kiss itself was chaste, the camera's proximity to the two lovers was a good deal closer than that of the audience to a stage play, creating an uncomfortably voyeuristic experience for many who viewed kissing as strictly a private activity.

In 1915, the Supreme Court gave legitimacy to the censorship of film, writing in *Mutual Film Corporation v. Industrial Commission of Ohio* that films were in the same category as "the theatre, the circus, and all other shows and spectacles" which could be regulated under the police power without concern for freedom of expression. The court further explained, "We immediately feel that the argument is wrong or strained which extends the guaranties of free opinion and speech to the multitudinous shows which are advertised on the bill-boards of our cities and towns. . . ." After all, the court reasoned, the police power had successfully been exercised to regulate the exhibition of films in many states.

The legality of state censorship boards had previously been upheld without considering the potential free speech implications. Freedom of expression was not at issue in those cases, the court explains, because "the exhibition of moving pictures is a business pure and simple, originated and conducted for profit, like other spectacles, not to be regarded . . . as part of the press of the country or as organs of public opinion." Since the Ohio statute at issue in *Mutual Film* allows the exhibition of "such films as are in the judgment and discretion of the board of censors of a moral, educational, or amusing and harmless character," the court reasons that all the positive aspects of film will be retained while filtering out film's potential to attract a prurient interest. "They are mere representations of events, of ideas and sentiments published and known, vivid, useful, and entertaining no doubt, but, as we have said, capable of evil. . . ."

Though the Supreme Court's quick dismissal of films as potentially deserving of first amendment protection may seem harsh, it was in complete harmony with the many cases brought in state and federal courts at the time. Courts in many states upheld statutes that limited the rights of motion picture theater owners, requiring a license for their general operation and allowing a censorship board to review the content of films to be screened. In 1898, the Minnesota Supreme Court ruled: "In respect to theatrical exhibitions and amusements of similar character, a larger discretion on the part of municipalities is recognized than in the case of ordinary trades and occupations, both because they are liable to degenerate into nuisances, and also because they require more police surveillance, and police service." In 1909, an Illinois court ruled constitutional a Chicago ordinance which stated that "the chief of police shall not issue a permit for the exhibition of any obscene or immoral picture or series of pictures, but that he shall issue a permit, without fee or charge, for all pictures which are not obscene or immoral." In 1912, the Minnesota Supreme

Court extended its view of theaters as a potential nuisance to include motion picture theaters, allowing a small town to charge a $200 annual fee for any who wished to obtain a license to run a motion picture theater. "[E]xperience teaches that, where amusements are furnished for pecuniary profit, the tendency is to furnish that which will attract the greatest number rather than that which instructs or elevates," the court stated. "It must therefore be classed among those pursuits which are liable to degenerate and menace the good order and morals of the people, and may therefore not only be licensed and regulated, but also prevented by a village council."

In 1922, under increasing pressure from government and religious organizations, movie producers brought former Postmaster General Will Harrison Hays to Hollywood to head the newly formed Motion Picture Producers and Distributors of America (MPPDA). Lending credibility to the industry, Hays came out with the "Hays formula," a list of "Don'ts and Be Carefuls" for movie producers that accurately predicted which elements of a film state and local censors would find problematic. The original eleven "Don'ts" were: pointed profanity, licentious or suggestive nudity, illegal traffic of drugs, any inference of sex perversion, white slavery, miscegenation, sex hygiene and venereal diseases, actual childbirth, children's sex organs, ridicule of the clergy, and willful offense to any nation, race or creed.

By 1930, the combination of new sound technology and desperate producers scrambling to bring in audiences despite the devastating stock market crash precipitated the need for an updated Hays Formula. Scandalous ads became commonplace as the movies promised to deliver "brilliant men, beautiful jazz babies, champagne baths, midnight revels, petting parties in the purple dawn." Earlier films, though frequently also thematically questionable, were more easily dismissed because their lack of sound or color rendered them less lifelike. For example, an early MGM film, *Heart of a Painted Woman* (1915), is a love story about a prostitute who falls in love with a young millionaire who is on trial for killing another man with whom she had once been intimate. The addition of sound to already spicy plots proved to be the final straw for moviegoers. The Production Code of 1930, or Hays Code, provided a much more comprehensive list of what could and could not be shown onscreen.

Despite its thoroughness, the Hays Code lacked an enforcement mechanism. From 1930 until the Code was properly enforced in 1934, producers deliberately flouted the comprehensive yet unenforceable Code to create some of the most sin-filled movies in Hollywood history. This period is generally referred to as pre-Code because for five years, producers knew of and ignored the accepted norms and conventions in film production. Many are familiar with the sexual innuendo and suggestive films of Mae West, but even Jeanette MacDonald, who is best remembered today for her wholesome roles opposite Nelson Eddy, earned the nickname "Lingerie Queen," for her many bedroom scenes. A 1931 review lists MacDonald's "chief talent" as "an aptitude for undressing before the camera quickly and almost completely with becoming grace and without embarrassment."

Movie audiences became very familiar with bedroom scenes, bath scenes, and other excuses for actresses to be scantily clad. Pre-Code films were by and large more risqué in their depictions of women's state of undress and the sanctity of marriage, though not every film went as far as *Call Her Savage* (1932), which featured nearly every Code violation imaginable, including, "marital infidelity, interracial marital infidelity, sadomasochistic whipping, erotic frolicking with a Great Dane, prurient exposure of female flesh, kept women, femme-on-femme catfights, a demented husband who tries to rape his wife, prostitution, gigolos, and a pair of mincing homosexual waiters." Obviously, not every film provides as dramatic a departure from acceptable standards. *It Happened One Night* (1934) is also a pre-Code film, but its deviance from the Code is much more limited, much of it encompassed by Claudette Colbert's character's revelation: "I'll stop a car and I won't use my thumb!" Pulling up her skirt to reveal her leg, she proceeds to do just that.

Regardless of the degree to which producers chose to ignore the Hays Code, it quickly became clear that further change was needed in the film industry. "Thirty-six states pushed for greater censorship and regulation of films, Catholic organizations threatened to boycott the movies, and Hollywood's effect on national morality was suddenly a hot topic for debate." Already hit hard by the decline in movie attendance caused by the early years of the Depression, producers could not risk a further attack on their revenue. In addition, the recently inaugurated Franklin Delano Roosevelt made it clear that government intervention in the film industry was not out of the question. Addressing the issue of Prohibition, for example, one of Roosevelt's advisors wrote a letter to Will Hays, urging him to convince producers to tone down the onscreen drinking, lest the president be forced to intervene in the industry and tone it down himself. Although the threat of Federal censorship is veiled and almost reluctant, it is there.

In 1934, no longer able to ignore the looming threat of government intervention, Hollywood producers were forced to take action. On June 19, the Communications Act of 1934 officially became law, establishing Federal regulatory power over broadcast media — radio and television. With First Amendment protection of film still nearly twenty years away, the industry had to treat any threat of censorship as a legitimate threat. In July of 1934, the MPPDA created the Production Code Administration (PCA), an organization devoted to the enforcement of the Hays Code. Instead of merely providing guidance to filmmakers, as the MPPDA had since 1922, the new PCA issued a seal of approval to be displayed at the beginning of all Code-compliant films. Many theaters refused to exhibit films without the PCA seal of approval, which provided a serious incentive for producers to comply with the Code. In addition, the PCA was authorized to fine non-compliers up to $25,000 for each Code violation.

Although unpopular now, the Hays Code was welcomed in 1934. Addressing the issues of potential Federal censorship as well as a growing national resentment with the salacious content of films, the Code was seen by many as a wonderful example of industry self-regulation. A retrospective article in 1945 said of the Hays Code, "Cinema's wonderful self-regulation is a splendid example of how business can stay out of the government's 'paralyzing' clutches."

NOTES & QUESTIONS

1.   As recently as 1967, seventeen states, mostly in the South, continued to prohibit marriages between whites and African Americans. However, in that year the United States Supreme Court ruled in *Loving v. Commonwealth of Virginia*, 388 U.S. 1 (1967), that the Virginia statutes depriving citizens of different races of the right to marry violated the Fourteenth Amendment's guarantees of both due process and equal protection.

2.   Hollywood released *Guess Who's Coming to Dinner* in 1967, six months before the Supreme Court ruling in *Loving*. Although the film does not actually portray an interracial marriage, it certainly suggests the possibility. Joanna "Joey" Drayton, a young white woman played by Katharine Houghton, has fallen in love with Dr. John Prentice, an articulate African American doctor played by Sidney Poitier. Drayton brings Prentice home to meet her parents, played by Katherine Hepburn and Spencer Tracy. Most of the film portrays the nervousness of the older Draytons regarding the interracial romance and possible marriage. As old-fashioned as the film may seem today, the remake titled *Guess Who* (2005) is much more difficult to watch. It reverses the races of the young lovers, and the African American father of the would-be bride, played by the late Bernie Mac, is the staunchest opponent of the interracial union.

3.   Fortunately, Hollywood has told a grittier and more interesting story of interracial marriage in *Mr. and Mrs. Loving*, a dramatization of the actual Virginia case. The acting is captivating, with Timothy Hutton playing the role of Richard Loving and Lela Rochon playing that of Mildred Jeter Loving.

4.   Were the portrayals faithful to the real-life Richard Loving, a simple man of few words, or to Mildred Jeter Loving, an African American woman who grew up without even knowing of Martin Luther King, Jr.? Perhaps, but a film's accuracy is less important than its viability as a pop cultural artifact. Most Hollywood productions are character-driven. These characters need not be complex or conflicted, and, indeed, many film portrayals are stock. We recognize the characters as types or subtypes and journey with them through the plot. "It is always a character who takes steps, a character who makes choices, a character's responses that drive the story forward or spin it around in new directions. It is a character who overcomes, a character who changes or learns." Suzanne Shale, *The Conflicts of Law and the Character of Men: Writing "Reversal of Fortune" and "Judgment at Nuremberg*," 30 University of San Francisco Law Review 991, 999 (1996). "The classical Hollywood film presents psychologically defined individuals who struggle to solve a clear-cut problem or to attain specific goals. In the course of this struggle, the characters enter into conflict with others or with external circumstances. The story ends with a decisive victory or defeat, a resolution of the problem and a clear achievement or non-achievement of the goals." David Bordwell, *Narration in the Fiction Film* 157 (1985).

5.   Some have argued that the issue of same-sex marriage is comparable to the issue of interracial marriage in an earlier era. At the time of this writing, the states remain divided, with a half dozen allowing same-sex marriage but over forty saying same-sex marriage violates state public policy. The culture industry has produced a handful of narratives about same-sex marriages, with the television wing of the

industry perhaps leading the way. In Showtime's *Queer as Folk* (2000-05), for example, partners Michael and Ben tied the knot, and in the prime-time series *Brothers and Sisters* (2006-11) Kevin and Scotty married while California law briefly allowed it.

6. Hollywood seems likely to follow television's lead. Sensitive dramas with same-sex relationships include *Philadelphia* (1993), *Brokeback Mountain* (2005), and *The Kids Are All Right* (2010). Independent filmmakers have produced excellent documentaries concerning same-sex marriage, including but not limited to *Freedom to Marry: The Journey to Justice* (2004) and *Pursuit of Equality* (2005). A feature film concerning either a fictional or real-life same-sex couple's struggle to marry seems inevitable in the near future.

C. DIVORCE

Family law has come in recent decades to address new and unanticipated issues such as grandparents' rights, in vitro fertilization, and surrogacy, to name only three. But the old standby divorce law continues to be family law's most developed and active area. In the following excerpt, Michael Asimov discusses both the role of divorce in American life and the dramatic possibilities divorce affords in popular culture.

DIVORCE IN THE MOVIES: FROM THE HAYS CODE TO *KRAMER vs. KRAMER*
Michael Asimow
24 Legal Studies Forum 221 (2000)

Marital trouble and divorce are unpleasant but ever-present realities of modern life. These days, approximately one of every two first-time marriages ends in divorce, and the prospects for later marriages are even worse. Similar patterns apply throughout the first world. But this is nothing new. During the twentieth century, divorce has been a social and economic phenomenon of epic proportions. The divorce rate has advanced steadily, particularly after World War I and throughout the 1920s. It fell during the Depression, but spiked after World War II, stabilized (though at a much higher rate than before the War) during the 1950s, and shot upwards throughout the 1960s, 70s, and 80s. Divorce law reform was a subject of constant controversy during most of the century.

The reasons for the relentless advance in the divorce rate are not difficult to discover. The social stigma attached to divorce diminished steadily; the more people that got divorced and survived the experience, the more others wanted to follow in their footsteps. Divorce laws were liberalized. Perhaps most important, in the early part of the century and especially between WWI and WWII, a new paradigm for marriage took hold. In the old days, most people viewed marriage as a matter of social status and a lifetime commitment to furnish mutual financial and homemaking support. Long-term love and happiness might be an unexpected and welcome byproduct, but few people thought such things were essential. Under the new paradigm, people came to believe that marriage should bring happiness and personal fulfillment. Since marriage frequently fails to provide happiness and fulfillment to one or both partners, a great many marriages fail to meet expectations. Such marriages are doomed to disintegrate, and divorce generally follows.

At the same time, women reevaluated their roles and came to believe that they were socially and economically equal to men; they rejected the idea that men and women inhabited their own spheres, the woman at home and the man in the world. Women's economic opportunities improved, making divorce a realistic option for many more women. Women renounced the sexual double standard. They believed they were entitled to escape from dreary, loveless, or abusive marriages, and they thought they could manage economically without male support. As more and more women internalized these feminist sentiments, more of them decided to leave their marriages.

The eternal process of marital breakdown and divorce is full of dramatic possibilities. During the pre-divorce phase, the parties become increasingly incompatible and unhappy in their lives together. Frequently, there are complex and clandestine love affairs outside of marriage; deception, jealousy, and betrayal; emotional upheaval; disruption of the lives of children; and economic warfare. The routine of everyday life is shattered. During the post-divorce phase, one or both parties may find themselves physically and emotionally isolated; others turn to promiscuity. Forced out of the shelter of the household, many women find satisfying new careers; others find that the world of work holds nothing for them. Often one ex-spouse's standard of living rises while the other's plummets. One partner's true personality blooms when freed from the stifling constraints of marriage; another's joy of life is snuffed out. A high divorce rate insures that there are plenty of complex blended families with multitudes of stepchildren and ex-spouses.

This sort of highly dramatic material should be the subject of countless film scenarios, right along with such staples as romance, love, marriage, and childbirth. After all, a high percentage of adults have been divorced at least once; everyone else has friends or relatives that have been divorced. A substantial percentage of young people have experienced their parents' divorce. All of these people can empathize with the travails of fictional characters whose marriages disintegrate. And they should, therefore, be willing to buy tickets to dramatic or comedic movies that center on divorce.

These days, movies routinely dwell on the emotional and financial prequels and sequels to divorce. Divorce is the obvious and natural platform for numerous modern film stories: *Living Out Loud* (1998) focuses on the loneliness of a divorced woman; *Husbands and Wives* (1992) explores the struggles of two newly divorced couples; *As Good As It Gets* (1997) deals with the difficulties of single parenthood; *Music of the Heart* (1999) features a divorced woman who, by necessity, starts a fulfilling new career; *Mrs. Doubtfire* (1993) centers on a father's unusual tactics to live with his kids; *Stepmom* (1998) deals with the travails of two moms, the kids, and the dad; *The First Wives Club* (1996) features a group of embittered ex-wives out for a little revenge; a black woman is abandoned by her husband for a younger white woman in *Waiting to Exhale* (1995). And there are countless others. . . .

NOTES & QUESTIONS

1. Hollywood has told both sad and comic divorce stories. The sad tales often have special poignancy because marriages almost always start with professions of eternal love and dreams of profound contentment. Played by Kate Winslet, the character April Wheeler in *Revolutionary Road* (2008) reminds her husband Frank Wheeler, played by Leonardo DiCaprio, that at the beginning of their marriage they shared a secret: "We would be wonderful in the world." When marital sanctuaries prove illusory and divorce looms, viewers can be moved by the pain and disappointment. In the stirring *Too Far to Go* (1982), a film based on stories by John Updike and starring Blythe Danner and Michael Moriarty, flashbacks show the good times and the bad times in the marriage of Joan and Richard Maple. Love and trust give way to deep resentment and extramarital flings, and the Maples divorce.

Comic divorce films can be hilarious, in part because viewers know that things will work out well for the major characters. In Woody Allen's *Manhattan* (1978), for example, viewers laugh at the divorce-related troubles of Isaac Davis, played by Woody Allen himself. Davis's wife not only divorces him but also is hard at work on a book about what a loser he is.

2. *The War of the Roses* (1989) is an especially biting divorce comedy. In the following excerpt, Ira Lurvey, a California divorce lawyer, and Selise E. Eiseman, a Hollywood screenwriter, argue that the film is an especially revealing portrayal of the modern-day divorce process.

DIVORCE GOES TO THE MOVIES
Ira Lurvey & Selise E. Eiseman
30 University of San Francisco Law Review 1209 (1996)

If the multitude of divorce films produced during the past century has shown Hollywood to be ahead of reality, the quintessential divorce movie may be *The War of the Roses.* It shows not only the current state of the divorce process, but the illogic of continuing without meaningful change.

From its brilliant title, which can be interpreted to mean various things, to its black satire on Yuppie materialism and its devastating climax in the chandelier scene, *Roses* seems to sum up the present bleak state of the divorce process. If war is hell, *Roses* says, then divorce is worse!

Not without small irony, Danny DeVito, one of Hollywood's most talented and versatile character actors, elects here not only to serve as the film's director, but as the divorce attorney as well. As director, he presumably has put his imprint on the production. As the divorce attorney cum narrator, he tells us in effect that the process was totally outside his control.

It did not have to be that way. Instead of just shrugging away at various times in the plot when his increasingly hysterical client, Oliver Rose, requested legal acts or advice, DeVito could have tried to return moderation to the matter. The movie does not even try to suggest such a possibility. DeVito is a hired gun. Perhaps a wiser, more sensitive and perceptive gun than the usual stereotypic divorce lawyer, but a total mercenary nevertheless.

For those who may have forgotten, *Roses* is a story about the sheer horror of an uncontrolled divorce. As Oliver and Barbara Rose, Michael Douglas and Kathleen Turner show how wonderful it was to be young and beautiful and falling in love in the 60s. The days were filled with sunshine and promise; the lovers were filled with one another. Life was dreams and romance and soft strings of background music so well integrated to the whole that you only hear it when you listen closely. This was how boy-girl movies used to end.

In *Roses*, however, it is just the beginning. Marriage, the movie tells us, is just the overture to tragedy.

With time but seemingly little effort, Oliver becomes a successful lawyer. Barbara becomes an extraordinary housekeeper. At this point, it is *Stepford Wives* revisited. The couple has two children, who grow normally and healthfully and eventually move away to school or adulthood. It has been a "marriage of long duration."

Barbara now "awakens." Selling some of her "wonderful" liver pate to a neighbor, she realizes that true independence lies in self-employment as a caterer. Somehow, because there is a lot more plot yet to cover in only a short remaining time, this discovery leads Barbara to tell Oliver that she wants a divorce as well as the house and furnishings that she says she created during the marriage. Oliver presumably can keep his law practice.

As in reality, however, it does not end that simply. What follows is a series of escalating interactions between Oliver and Barbara so vicious and mean-spirited that it has made Roses a classic of what is wrong with the divorce process.

When the "war" is over, with the Roses swinging like pre-Darwinian apes from their prized chandelier, scorched earth as a policy of battle is made to seem a term of endearment.

The movie often is billed as black comedy. It has been critiqued as a satire on materialism. According to DeVito, no marriage ever is happy for long.

There may be a larger, and more constructive, message as well. Viewing the horror for the absurdity it is may teach that divorce is survivable if each spouse is willing to compromise.

Barbara states that she just wants the house because it represents her adult achievement. She remodeled it and picked the furniture. Oliver says the house should be his because he earned the money that permitted its purchase and development. *Roses* says that both are right and neither is: if spouses cannot share, neither will get anything.

The moral is both accurate and Draconian. It is accurate because it portrays what all too often is the result of modern divorce. It is Draconian because it discounts as worthless to mitigate human nature, both the role of the intelligent divorce lawyer and the entire legal process.

For example, what if Barbara was correct? What if she should have received the house and furnishings? What if Oliver was being unreasonable in seeking to deny them to her? Was the message of Roses that there is no recourse when one spouse is being unreasonable?

Perhaps that is why Roses has become so classic an example of the genre. Perhaps we face now an era (hopefully temporary!) when most persons have lost faith in any process mitigating the horrors of their personal lives and emotions.

DeVito as the seemingly hopeless divorce lawyer can do no more than stand by at the beginning and end to tell us the story, smoking a big, comforting cigar. Has a fascination with greed and self-absorption so clouded thinking that even the mythmakers of Hollywood cannot break through?

After one hundred years of examining the issue, is the ultimate message the movies have for us on the subject of divorce that clients will fiddle while lawyers' cigars burn? We moviegoers may have a right to expect much more from our beloved silver screen. . . .

NOTES & QUESTIONS

1. Lurvey and Eiseman seem to assume that Hollywood filmmakers have an obligation to critically contemplate divorce, divorce law, and divorce law reform. They speak of Hollywood's "clouded thinking" and suggest "moviegoers may have a right to expect much more from our beloved silver screen." What responsibilities does the film industry have to educate the public about law? What might viewers legitimately expect of their films? Hollywood's ultimate goal might be the production of dramatic, engaging films that will attract viewers and generate profits. As a result, Hollywood could be expected not to make a pitch for divorce law reform but rather to portray divorce in ways that capture viewers.

2. Lurvey and Eiseman suggest *The War of the Roses* might be best understood as a "black comedy," that is, a work in which naïve, inept, or pernicious characters find themselves part of a tragic farce that is both comic and horrifying. Why might black comedies be especially appealing to present-day filmgoers? *See* Max F. Schultz, *Black Humor Fiction of the Sixties* (1980).

3. As Lurvey and Eiseman mention, Danny DeVito's Gavin D'Amato in *The War of the Roses* is both Oliver Rose's divorce lawyer and the film's narrator. He is frustrated when his suggestions are ignored and the Roses' battle escalates. In reality, many real-life divorce lawyers take firm, managerial control of their divorce cases. Is this part of the reason that when the divorce process is complete, clients often end up disliking their own lawyers?

4. The best-known pop cultural divorce lawyer of the late-1980s and early 1990s was Arnie Becker. A conniving practitioner and insatiable womanizer, Becker was one of the featured lawyers in the popular prime-time series *L.A. Law* (1986-94).

TAKING *L.A. LAW* MORE SERIOUSLY

Stephen Gillers

98 Yale Law Journal 1606 (1989)

Today, an informal group of teachers of legal ethics, I among them, periodically meet to discuss how to teach the course. Inevitably, our discussions include scenes from *L.A. Law.*

My favorite episode . . . is one in which Arnie Becker, the firm's sometimes shallow (but always adept) divorce lawyer, meets with Lydia, a woman nearing forty who has decided to accept her husband's settlement offer. Lydia has come to Arnie because her original lawyer, Julia, had qualms about the settlement and urged Lydia to talk to Arnie about it. Lydia tells Arnie she does not want a fight. "I just don't want it to get into an ugly, pitched battle with name calling and recriminations," she insists. *L.A. Law* (NBC television broadcast, Sept. 15, 1986).

On the very morning of the day he meets Lydia, a gun-carrying former client threatened Arnie because he had not stopped her from accepting a settlement she now realized was too low. In the interim, the former client had learned that her husband had "another woman" and that they were living up in Bel Air while Arnie's former client was living out in Van Nuys. With the memory of that assault still painfully present and based on his years of experience as a divorce lawyer, Arnie tells Lydia that her husband surely has another woman. He urges Lydia to be more aggressive in protecting her economic interests. Lydia does not believe there is another woman or doesn't want to believe it — "My husband and I are not statistics," she declares, "we're individuals." Arnie responds: "For your husband, divorce is a fiscal inconvenience. But for you, this can be the most important financial decision that you'll ever make in your life."

At the conclusion of their meeting, Lydia is wavering. Citing "friendship to Julia" and "admiration for your principles," Arnie offers to review the proposed settlement agreement and tell Lydia his conclusions over lunch at a fancy restaurant that following Thursday. Meanwhile, without Lydia's knowledge, Arnie has his private detective surveil the husband. She succeeds in getting several eight by ten glossy photographs of Lydia's husband and the inevitable other woman in very compromising positions, all of which are meticulously described.

Arnie takes the glossies to the fancy lunch, where Lydia informs him that she has decided to accept the settlement offer. "In the long run, there are more important things than money," she insists. Tapping the envelope containing the glossies, Arnie muses that he will just put the "investigation" of her "husband's affairs, financial, otherwise" on hold. Predictably curious, Lydia asks if it will obligate her financially to look in the envelope. "In no way," Arnie assures, but then in a rare burst of compassion, he warns Lydia that "it may be painful." Of course she looks, then quickly escapes to the lady's room to give up her lunch, as nonchalant Arnie had previously told the investigator she would. Arnie summons the waiter for dessert.

In the next scene, a retributive Lydia, in a sit-down with her husband and counsel, can hardly contain her anger as she hurls insults and her pocketbook across the conference table. Arnie uses other, financial information the investigator obtained to force the husband to increase his offer considerably. The not-so-veiled threat is that otherwise the information will get the husband in trouble with the law. . . .

Afterwards, Arnie is pleased with himself ("we really socked it to them"), but Lydia is crying uncontrollably. She tells Arnie: "I think what you did was despicable. I'll never be able to look at him again with any kind of respect or affection." For Arnie, she says, it was "all so easy. . . . Just sock it to him and get the money. I lost my life, my children lost a family. And there's no amount of money that would compensate for that." Arnie asks Lydia if she wants to return the money. She does not. Having thereby proved his point to his own satisfaction, Arnie predicts that in two weeks Lydia will be recommending him to a friend. In two months, she will be inviting him to dinner. . . .

Client autonomy is an ethical issue. It is the analogue in law to informed consent in medicine. It is difficult to define and harder to teach. The episode I have just described (and my summary does not do it justice) is nearly perfect in presenting the autonomy issue in equipoise. Without his client's permission, Arnie Becker used an investigator to obtain a legally irrelevant but inflammatory fact — opposing counsel points out that in California the husband's affair has no bearing on the grant of a divorce or support obligations. Arnie then used that fact to get his client angry enough to fight for a larger settlement, employing weapons that would inevitably destroy the modicum of civility the couple still enjoyed and which Lydia had declared at the outset she wanted to retain.

Did Arnie exceed his authority when he connived to override his client's stated wishes in order to secure the money he truly (perhaps correctly) believed she would later regret not having? Should he have requested Lydia's authorization before hiring a detective to follow her husband? Did he give insufficient respect to Lydia's declaration that "there are more important things than money?" Did Arnie manipulate Lydia? Or did he save her? Whichever he did, did he act properly? . . .

NOTES & QUESTIONS

1.   Charles B. Rosenberg, a Los Angeles attorney, served as the legal advisor to *L.A. Law*. His assignment was to make the laws and legal proceedings in the series as accurate as they could be given the demands of creating engaging television drama. Rosenberg recognized that one of the keys to the series' popularity was the interesting characters. Viewers could feel sympathy, empathy, and antipathy for them. Arnie Becker and Douglas Brackman, Jr., McKenzie, Brackman, Chaney & Kuzak's penny-pinching managing partner, "are good examples of characters in whom the initial interest was generated by antipathy." Charles B. Rosenberg, *Inside* L.A. Law, ABA Journal, Nov. 1988, 57.

2.   Sleazy divorce lawyers who win a spot in our hearts are common in film as well. In *Liar Liar* (1997), Jim Carrey plays Fletcher Reede, a duplicitous divorce lawyer whose own marriage has ended in divorce. The running joke in the film involves the difficulty a divorce lawyer has telling the truth. In *Intolerable Cruelty* (2002), divorce attorney Miles Massey, played by George Clooney, bursts with pride over an antenuptial agreement he has developed that supposedly could never be challenged in court. However, the film does include a scene in which a husband

attempts to demonstrate his love for his wife by literally eating one of Massey's agreements. Would the work of his digestive juices constitute effective rescission?

D.   CHILD CUSTODY

Hollywood has for a century delighted in featuring child actors in its films, and one might assume films involving child custody fights would be perfect vehicles for the winning and sympathetic child. But while Hollywood films with child custody battles in them do include children, the films are mostly about the parents. Viewers of course worry about the child at the middle of a custody battle, but they are even more involved with the battling parents.

As the following excerpt indicates, Hollywood sometimes "modifies" the law in order to enhance the drama involving the battling parents. Surprising leeway exists in this regard because lay viewers have little knowledge of law's technicalities.

PEACE BETWEEN THE SEXES: LAW AND GENDER IN *KRAMER vs. KRAMER*
David Ray Papke
30 University of San Francisco Law Review 1199 (1996)

When scholars contemplate law and legal proceedings in popular culture, there is perhaps an inevitable tendency to turn to considerations of accuracy. Edward Bennett Williams, the famous trial lawyer, complained before his death that Perry Mason and a bevy of other fictional lawyers from prime-time television in the 1950s and 1960s created unrealistic expectations. With Mason always dramatically exonerating his innocent client and identifying the true perpetrator, clients, jurors, and others were invariably disappointed when real-life criminal defense lawyers proved much less resourceful. Even the very best of criminal defense lawyers, Williams noted, are lucky to win acquittals in the majority of their cases. More specifically, Charles and Mariann Pezella Winick have added that, although cross-examination is important to criminal trials, actual witnesses rarely break down on the stand and confess the way they often do in fictional television trials. Taking this variety of cultural criticism even one step further, Jon L. Breen argues explicitly that the "accuracy" of a trial in popular culture is a crucial issue in critical evaluation. Breen lists and thereby denigrates three especially inaccurate court-room novels: William Ard's *Hell is a City*, Harold R. Daniels' *The Accused*, and Barbara Frost's *Innocent Bystander.*

Both at the time of its release and more recently, *Kramer vs. Kramer* has itself prompted this type of criticism. After previously reviewing the movie and reporting on the popular hubbub it generated, Time doubled back to explore the child custody questions the movie addresses. Much of *Kramer vs. Kramer*, Time concluded, was "legally out of date.". . .

Criticism of this sort does no harm, and there is indeed something to be gained from alerting the citizenry to differences between the law and legal proceedings in popular culture and what might be understood as "real life." However, those who are determined to apply a legal truth test to popular culture or to *Kramer vs. Kramer* in particular, should also realize that the "legal inaccuracies" are not mistakes, much less attempts to dupe the lay public. Critics with a bent for noting "legal inaccuracies" should dismount the high horse of expertise and recognize that cultural conventions and prescriptions, much more than faithfulness to the law, shape works of popular culture.

In *Kramer vs. Kramer*, as previously suggested, law provides the movie's gender battlefield, and in particular, the producers employ a resurrected and misrepresented maternal preference standard. If one reviews the history of American child custody standards, one is struck by the amazing shifts with regard to gender. In the early Republic, when divorce was rare by modern standards and sometimes granted by legislatures rather than courts, child custody almost always went to the father. This paternal preference began to disappear in the mid-nineteenth century, and in the decades after the Civil War the "tender years" approach settled into place. Reflecting a Victorian sense that the mother was the true nurturer and care giver for children, the "tender years" doctrine resulted in custody awards to the mother whenever there was a contest over young children. Then, in still another striking shift in the second half of the twentieth century, this doctrine also gave way. Due to legal arguments couched with reference to state and federal equal protection standards, and more generally to shifting gender norms, courts moved to a gender-neutral standard and attempted to determine which custodial option would be in the "best interests of the child." A few states seemed stalled in the Victorian Age, but Justice Brennan's stern words in an opinion invalidating an Alabama statute that made only husbands and not wives susceptible to alimony, should have provided pause:

> Legislative classifications that distribute benefits and burdens on the basis of gender carry the inherent risk of reinforcing the stereotypes about the "proper place" of women and their need for special protection. . . . Thus, even statutes purportedly designed to compensate for and ameliorate the effects of past discrimination must be carefully tailored. Where, as here, the State's compensatory and ameliorative purposes are as well served by a gender-neutral classification as one that gender-classifies and therefore carries with it the baggage of sexual stereotypes, the State cannot be permitted to classify on the basis of sex.

By 1979, the year in which *Kramer vs. Kramer* was released, New York (the state where the movie is set) had abandoned maternal preference and moved to a "best interests" test, but you would never guess it from the movie. Attorney Shaughnessy, played by veteran actor Howard Duff, warns Ted Kramer that courts favor mothers in custody battles over young children. The task, Shaughnessy is certain, is to prove Joanna is an unfit mother. Shaughnessy also apparently overlooks the fact that the parties had already divorced (admittedly off-screen), and Ted had custody, so the issue was not custody per se but rather custody modification. Even assuming a maternal preference rule, modification hearings place great weight on maintaining child care continuity. Real law notwithstanding, fictional Judge Atkins sees things the way attorney Shaughnessy does. Atkins' award of custody to Joanna Kramer relies almost completely on the "tender years" approach. Atkins, in Shaughnessy's words, "went for motherhood right down the line.". . .

NOTES & QUESTIONS

1.   When *Kramer vs. Kramer* was released, members of the divorce bar pointed out the film's misleading characterizations of child custody law. *See Custody: Kramer vs. Reality*, Time, 4 Feb. 1980, 77.

2.   With good reason, Ted Kramer asks his attorney if the trial court decision might be appealed, but Shaughnessy discourages him by warning that on appeal he will have to put Billy on the stand. Parties, of course, do not testify in appellate proceedings, and the film in this sense continues to proffer legal inaccuracies. What themes might the legal inaccuracies in *Kramer vs. Kramer* enhance? Why might the producers have chosen to present the law as they did?

3.   The relationship of gender and child custody decisions has proven to be a gold mine for popular culture. Filmmakers and other producers of popular culture have used child custody battles to explore a wide range of issues regarding gender in contemporary society. In *The Good Mother* (1988), a divorced mother played by Diane Keaton loses custody of her daughter to her ex-husband after her lover innocently allows the daughter to touch his genitals. In *Striptease* (1996), a Florida stripper played by Demi Moore tries to enlist an infatuated Congressman in her struggle to regain custody of her daughter from her ex-husband. In *When Innocence Is Lost* (1997), a single mother returning to school loses custody when at trial her husband argues the child is better off in the care of his own mother than in day care. In *Stepmom* (1998), Jackie Harrison, a dying mother played by Susan Sarandon, learns to trust and respect her ex-husband's younger wife, played by Julia Roberts. Harrison and her ex-husband had proudly worked out their custody arrangements without the services of a lawyer, but Harrison now realizes that the lively, vivacious "stepmom" will assume parenting responsibilities after Harrison dies.

4.   Custody battles and their ramifications can also be the basis of comedy. In *Mrs. Doubtfire* (1993), a noncustodial father played by Robin Williams so desperately misses his children that he disguises himself as a nanny, one Mrs. Euphegenia Doubtfire. Distaining drag comedy, the remake of *The Parent Trap* (1998) revolves around twin girls, both played by Lindsey Lohan, and their successful efforts to reunite their divorced parents. The original custody decree for the girls — one to the father, the other to the mother — is an example of "split custody," that is, the awarding of the children to the parents almost as if they were assets to be divided.

5.   Prime-time television series have not only portrayed child custody fights but also found ways to combine serious drama and lighthearted comedy in the portrayals. Short-lived series such as *Civil Wars* (1991-93) and *Family Law* (1999–2000) featured small law firms specializing in family law and composed of lawyers with their own, sometimes quirky problems. In the first episode of the latter, one of the plot lines concerned the sad story of a recovering alcoholic who falls off the wagon and therefore abandons a custody fight. A second plot line, meanwhile, involved a silly couple battling over their deceased dog's ashes.

6.   In *Judging Amy* (1999–2005), a recently divorced lawyer played by Amy Brenneman leaves corporate practice in New York City and, in an unbelievably short period of time, becomes a family court judge in Connecticut. Her court seems

to have jurisdiction over everything from sobering juvenile justice matters to child custody disputes. The judge sometimes receives advice from her own mother, a know-it-all social worker played by Tyne Daley. The latter has three tips on how to be a good family court judge: (1) Pee before going on the bench, (2) Do not wear perfume, and (3) Make sure there is no food in your teeth. For an essay praising the fictional Amy Gray for her humane and compassionate "jurisprudence," see David Ray Papke, *Judging Amy, in Lawyers in Your Living Room!* 233-41 (Michael Asimow ed., 2009).

E. ADOPTION

The annual number of adoptions in the United States reached a high of approximately 175,000 in 1970, then dropped somewhat in the 1980s, and has now leveled out between 120,000 and 130,000 annually. However, adoption seems to have become a larger presence in the mass media and popular culture. Tabloids and television entertainment news shows have reported at great length on the efforts of celebrities such as Madonna and Angelina Jolie to adopt children in Africa. Not to be outdone, Hollywood has produced films with fictional adoptions that are inevitably complicated and difficult. These stories are ideal for dramatizing human hopes for fulfillment and connection.

The dramatic potential of a good adoption film notwithstanding, adoption films resemble child custody films in one important way: They tend to revolve around the trials and tribulations of adults rather than children. The films are tales of desperate childless couples seeking to adopt, depressed biological mothers wishing they had not placed a child for adoption, or both.

Sometimes Hollywood enhances its adoption stories even further by adding racial tensions to the plot. In *Losing Isaiah* (1995), for example, Khaila Richards, a young crack-smoking African American mother played by Halle Berry, accidentally loses her child after placing him in a trash pile. Sanitation workers find and rescue the child, and Margaret Levin, a white social worker played by Jessica Lange, adopts him. Still later in time, Richards reappears and wants her child back. She and her attorney expertly play the "race card" at trial, and a well-intentioned judge decrees that it is best for a child to be with his or her biological mother, especially if a racial issue is involved. In the following excerpt, Twila L. Perry argues that *Losing Isaiah* plays off a bias against African American mothers.

TRANSRACIAL AND INTERNATIONAL ADOPTION: MOTHERS, HIERARCHY, RACE, AND FEMINIST LEGAL THEORY
Twila L. Perry
10 Yale Journal of Law & Feminism 101 (1998)

The idea that Black parents must teach Black children how to survive in a racist society was not invented in response to the controversy over transracial adoption. Instead, this view represents the acknowledgment by many Black people of a long history of struggle to ensure that Black children are able to survive physically and emotionally in a racially hostile world. Many Blacks would agree that Black parents face unique challenges in raising Black children, and they celebrate the fact that generations of Black children have been successfully raised against the odds.

However, white society's view of Black women mothering Black children is often at odds with this perspective. A number of scholars have written exclusively about society's devaluation of Black mothers, noting the widespread stereotypes of the emasculating matriarch, the lazy welfare mother, and the licentious Jezebel. In recent conservative discourse, Black mothers are portrayed as raising a future generation of welfare cheats, violent criminals, and absent fathers.

I have argued elsewhere that the mothering of Black children by Black women has been devalued in both the public and the legal discourse surrounding transracial adoption. The media frequently presents the public with scenarios in which screaming, crying Black children are ripped from the arms of loving white foster parents who want to adopt them only to be returned to out of control, drug-addicted Black mothers destined to abuse them, or even kill them. Some legal scholarship advocating transracial adoption incorporates and reifies this approach to promote the argument that the use of race as a factor in adoption is harmful to Black children.

Films, in particular, have a long tradition of objectifying and misrepresenting the experiences of Black people, and they have, through both narrative and imagery, replicated and reinforced a negative portrayal of Black mothers. Films can tell a story about race and about the intersection of race and the law that can exert a powerful influence on society's view of what the law on a particular issue should be.

A recent movie, entitled *Losing Isaiah*, provides a potent example of the way in which the portrayal of Black mothers in film can be used to support the argument that the law should be structured to favor the adoption of Black children by whites.

The plot of *Losing Isaiah* involves a Black birth mother's attempt to reclaim her three-year-old son from a white middle class family with whom the child was placed for foster care shortly after birth. The white family is in the process of adopting Isaiah when his mother initiates the case for his return.

The movie opens with Isaiah's birth mother in a crack-induced daze. A voice from another room in a shabby tenement yells out, "Get that cryin' baby outta here!" Isaiah's mother staggers with her newborn son out into the street, where she places him in a garbage can while she goes in search of drugs. The next morning Isaiah is rescued by a sanitation worker seconds before he is crushed by the trash compactor of a garbage truck. A few hours later, Isaiah's mother wakes up from her drug-induced haze, remembers where she has left her baby and goes to retrieve him. Seeing that the garbage has been picked up, she assumes, without investigation, that Isaiah is dead and simply goes on with her life. Meanwhile, Isaiah has been placed with a warm, loving, white family with whom he thrives. They grow to love Isaiah and want to adopt him. Eventually Isaiah's birth mother learns that her son is alive. She enrolls in a drug rehab program, kicks her crack habit, and retains a lawyer to seek her child's return.

The movie abounds with negative images of Black mothers. In addition to Isaiah's mother, who left him in a garbage can, there is another young Black mother in the movie who treats her young son with coldness and crudeness. The only exception is in one scene in which the child is breakdancing. In that scene, and in that scene only, the mother beams with warmth and pride.

The central courtroom scene in the movie promotes numerous negative images of Black women and Black families. Isaiah's mother admits on the witness stand that her son was conceived by accident during an anonymous drugs-for-sex encounter. When asked by the judge whether she has anyone to assist her in the care of her son should he be returned back to her, Isaiah's mother replies that the only people she can rely on are also recovering crack addicts. The implication is that there is no family that is in contact with or cares about this young girl, no family that is thrilled that she has overcome her drug habit and is on the road to rehabilitating her life. The movie depicts no concerned and caring sisters, brothers, aunts, or uncles — no loving Black grandmother waiting to shower attention and affection on her newly discovered grandson.

In the end, the court returns Isaiah to his birth mother, who can only offer him a life of squalor and chaos. Her frustrations bring her to the brink of child abuse. Finally, in an ambiguous ending, she calls the white adoptive mother for help, and possibly to return Isaiah to her. In this way, Isaiah's mother confirms her own inadequacy and confirms that the white adoptive mother was the better mother after all.

Although Black women may often see themselves as successfully mothering against the odds, this is often not the perception of the larger society. The legal discourse on both foster care and transracial adoption, and the media images represented in a film such as *Losing Isaiah*, are examples of a widespread negative view of the competence of Black mothers in raising Black children. . . .

NOTES & QUESTIONS

1. In the final scene of *Losing Isaiah* the white adoptive mother and African American mother hug and then sit on the rug at a day care facility playing together with little Isaiah. Is the scene supposed to suggest the possibility of racial harmony?

2. Fifteen years after *Losing Isaiah*, Hollywood returned to something close to a transracial adoption in *The Blind Side* (2009). The film dramatizes the life of Michael Oher, who in a classic rags-to-riches story made his way from the slums to wealth and fame as a National Football League star. Along the way, Oher is taken into the home of Anne Tuohy, a pushy white woman played by Sandra Bullock. With the help of Don Yaeger, Michael Oher has told his story in *I Beat the Odds: From Homelessness to the Blind Side and Beyond* (2011).

3. Oher refers to Tuohy as "Mama," and she calls him "son," but technically speaking, there is no adoption. By the end of the film, Oher is almost eighteen; instead of adopting him, Tuohy and her husband have themselves named legal guardians. Does the film seem unduly paternalistic?

4. For some couples or individuals, adoption is not the first choice as a way to obtain a child. Since the 1980s, growing numbers of would-be parents have turned to surrogacy, but with such complex and sensitive arrangements, there is room for breakdowns. Just that happened in a prominent case involving William and

Elizabeth Stern, a childless New Jersey couple, and Mary Beth Whitehead, their surrogate. After the baby was born, Whitehead could not bear to part with her and fled to Florida. In general, the public took the Sterns' side in the controversy, but perhaps the following passage from Whitehead's book prompts some sympathy:

> The Sterns and the Infertility Center had told me I was doing a beautiful thing, but I wasn't. All the way through my pregnancy, I had tried to believe it. I had suppressed the reality; I had denied my feelings. I had not allowed myself to deal with it. But now I couldn't pretend anymore.
>
> I began to feel angry and defensive. My body, my soul, my heart, my breathing, my everything had gone into making this baby. What had Bill Stern done? Put some sperm in a cup. What had Betsy Stern done? Bought some clothes, a box of diapers, and a case of formula.
>
> All I did was sob and cry. I just couldn't stop crying. It just kept coming, and the emptiness I felt was something I never want to feel again.
>
> Eventually I fell asleep. Suddenly I opened my eyes. The room was dark, and I was lying in a pool of milk. The sheets were full of milk. I knew it was time to feed my baby. I knew she was hungry, but I could not hear her crying. The room was quiet as I sat up in the bed, alone in the darkness with the milk running down my chest and soaking my nightgown. I held out my empty arms and screamed at the top of my lungs, "Oh, God, what have I done — I want my baby!"

Mary Beth Whitehead (with Loretta Schwartz-Nobel), *A Mother's Story: The Truth about the* Baby M *Case* 25-27 (1989).

5. Not surprisingly, the culture industry saw dramatic possibilities in the Whitehead case. ABC Circle Films produced the three-hour *Baby M* in 1988. The film starred JoBeth Williams as Mary Beth Whitehead, and Williams' performance was highly praised. She received both an Emmy nomination for Outstanding Lead Actress in a Mini-Series or a Special and a Golden Globe nomination for Best Performance in a Mini-Series or Motion Picture Made for Television.

6. The film nicely dramatizes the major developments in the Whitehead case, including Whitehead's refusal to abide by a provision in the surrogacy agreement giving the Sterns the exclusive right to name the child. They chose the name Melissa, but Whitehead preferred the name Sarah and used that name when obtaining a birth certificate for the child. The New Jersey Supreme Court ultimately ruled that surrogacy contracts were unenforceable. *See Matter of Baby M*, 537 A. 2d 1227 (N. J. 1988). The ruling receives only minor attention in the film, but shortly before the final credits, a summary of the decision is scrolled on the screen. Can the cinema effectively present the written law?

Chapter 13

BUSINESS LAW

A. FILMOGRAPHY

Capitalism: A Love Story (2009)

Inside Job (2010)

Margin Call (2011)

Mind Over Money (2010)

Too Big to Fail (2011)

B. INTRODUCTION

Law students vary considerably in their prior exposure to, interest in, and knowledge of business and business law. Students range from complete business novices to undergraduate business or economics majors to MBAs or Ph.D. students in economics. Most law schools do not offer a single course titled Business Law and instead offer a set of related courses in the general area of Business Law. Typical foundational Business Law courses include Accounting for Lawyers, Agency Partnership & the LLC, Banking & Financial Regulation, Bankruptcy, Business Planning, Corporate Finance, Corporations, Economic Analysis of Law, Income Tax, and Securities Regulation. Typical intermediate Business Law courses include Antitrust, Arbitration, Commercial Transactions, Corporate Tax, Mergers & Acquisitions, Negotiation, Partnership Tax, Secured Transactions, and Venture Capital & Private Equity. Typical advanced Business Law courses include Advanced Corporate Law, Consumer Law, Commercial Drafting, and Derivative Securities Regulation, and some schools also offer clinics related to entrepreneurial law, securities litigation, and family businesses. If law students study at a university with a business school, they may take some number of cross-listed MBA courses and possibly public administration or policy school courses.

The phrase "business law" itself as colloquially used by laypeople is of course related to, yet quite often substantially different from, the above subjects that law schools typically offer as part of their Business Law curriculum. By business law, most non-lawyers mean simply the legal environment which businesses face in terms of consumer protection laws, contract law, financial regulations, commercial law, and product liability. Traditionally, business law involves the application of microeconomics (which deals with individual consumers and producers interacting in markets) instead of macroeconomics (which deals with aggregate fluctuations in employment, national income, and overall price indices) to analyze legal rules governing businesses. Due to what some call the Great Recession of the late 2000s, there has been more media coverage, popular culture, and public attention directed at what can and should our federal, state, and local governments do to smooth out dips in the business cycle in general and in particular stimulate business hiring, consumer spending, economic activity, and investor confidence. Ordinary people who live on Main Street also have come to realize that what bankers and other finance professionals who work on Wall Street do can have dire consequences and spillover effects on the non-financial sectors of an economy. There is a new angst, anxiety, and unease that people have over their economic futures and financial health reflecting their uncertainty over the competitiveness and economic health of American businesses and increased volatility of stock market prices.

Many business law courses have students read casebooks that contain appellate and Supreme Court opinions that often interpret relevant statutes. Almost always, business law professors offer some background about core business transactions and economic principles to provide underlying context about what is at stake or going on in the cases that students read. As with criminal law courses and cases, much of what makes business and business law compelling if not exciting are forced into a familiar emphasis upon doctrinal analysis of the law. Lost are the bigger-than-life characters, cautionary narratives of avarice, greed, temptation, and weakness of will, stories about life-long dreams realized or shattered, and tales of corporate bravery, espionage, intrigue, or whistle-blowing.

Popular culture depictions of business and business law naturally emphasize that which is entertaining and familiar. Movies and television shows focus typically upon flawed characters on transformative journeys often involving public shame and personal redemption. Business and legal details matter less than action, catharsis, and suspense. The projection of an affectively nuanced, rich, and textured multi-dimensional reality into an emotionally flattened, impoverished, and poor legal caricature for appellate case analysis is reversed by the popular culture retelling.

In children's books and much of popular culture, there is a tendency for popular cultural works about business law to become morality plays in which poor characters are benevolent, good-natured, hard-working, or smart and rich characters are bad, evil, lazy, or stupid. Familiar examples include the spoiled brats whose parents buy them whatever they want, Augustus Gloop and Veruca Salt from Roald Dahl, *Charlie and the Chocolate Factory* (1964), or the appalling wicked Dursleys from the Harry Potter books who shower Dudley, their son, with presents. Americans know and like stories about characters going from rags to riches, such as Horatio Alger, and characters who fall from wealth and grace due to alleged financial improprieties, such as Martha Stewart.

This chapter analyzes various works of popular culture that involve business and business law. There are two major sections that focus on, respectively, the corporation and the market economy. Of course, these two topics are naturally interrelated and quite intertwined together. It is nevertheless helpful to at least conceptually separate this pair of discrete subjects in an examination of how business law is portrayed in modern popular culture. Because the Great Recession of 2008-09 is hopefully a once in a lifetime sort of event, all of the movies featured in this chapter deal with it as do several notes and questions.

C. THE CORPORATION

1. Stockholders and Other Stakeholders

Popular depictions of businesses understandably focus on corporations because corporations are a ubiquitous part of modern daily life and society. As you consider the corporations portrayed in films discussed in this chapter and other portrayals of corporations in popular culture that you know about, think about whether the story being told about each corporation reflects how you and others view corporations. Are corporations in popular culture better or worse than real-world corporations? How so? Are corporations in popular culture more or less bureaucratic, caring, evil, indifferent, insidious, and inspiring compared to corporations you know? How do corporations from popular culture generally fare relative to your bank credit or debit card companies, local cable television or other public utility companies, Internet service provider, and cell or residential phone service providers?

FRAMING THE MARKET: REPRESENTATIONS OF MEANING AND VALUE IN LAW, MARKETS, AND CULTURE
Robin Paul Malloy
51 Buffalo Law Review 1 (2003)

Two films, *Wall Street* [1987] and *Other People's Money* [1991], contain significant scenes involving corporate stockholder meetings, and raise interesting issues about the nature of market values and the purpose of exchange. They also raise questions about the nature of the firm, the characteristics of ownership, and the community obligations of business. Both films involve a takeover bid by an investor seeking to break up a company as a way of enhancing stockholder value. The lead characters in each film make appeals to the stockholders, urging the stockholders to vote in favor of the takeover, and for liquidation of the firm in an effort to maximize stockholder value.

In *Wall Street*, Gordon Gekko, played by Michael Douglas, takes the center stage at a stockholder meeting held in the surroundings of a well-appointed convention center. In the room, there are plenty of well-dressed stockholders who are seated on chairs at the floor level, looking up to a platform stage upon which sits the president and his thirty-three corporate vice presidents. After the corporate president warns stockholders that Gekko is a destroyer of companies, and that they should reject any takeover offer from him, Gekko takes up the microphone, from the floor, and declares, "I am not a destroyer of companies, I am a liberator of them." Gekko goes on to tell stockholders to vote in favor of his takeover bid because he will make them rich. He tells them "greed is good, greed simplifies, greed clarifies, greed in all of its forms makes the marketplace work." He tells them to ignore the concerns of the inefficient management of the company, and to pursue their own self-interest, to follow their greed in the pursuit of wealth. The clarity of the self-interested pursuit of greed will bring them to a freedom that only Gekko can deliver.

Similarly, in *Other People's Money*, Danny DeVito, playing Larry the Liquidator, makes an appeal to stockholders to vote in favor of his takeover bid because he will make them money. He tells them that the company, while profitable, is worth more dead (liquidated) than alive. He tells stockholders to vote for making the best return on their money, and that they have no obligation to the employees of the company or to the community where its factory is located. Their only obligation is to make the best profit for themselves.

In contrast to these views, Gregory Peck, playing the role of the eighty-one-year-old founder and president of the New England Wire and Cable Company in *Other People's Money*, argues that a company is worth more than the value of its stock. He says that a business is about people. It is about people who work together pursuing a common purpose, and who share the same friendships and live in the same community. He cautions the stockholders to avoid selfish and greedy actions and instead asks them to vote with their feelings. He asks them to vote for the continuation of a profitable business. He asserts that a business is more than a collection of capital goods. He tells them that a business is a community.

In contrast to the scene from *Wall Street*, the stockholder meeting in *Other People's Money* occurs at the factory, and the film's director presents us with images of the "blue collar" town and workers who are present both inside and outside of the meeting. The meeting is not set in some sterile convention hall as in *Wall Street*, but is held in the very town that will be affected by closing the plant. The dispute is not about an inefficient management team; it is about a company that is no longer as productive as other investments because new technologies are cutting into its market. The common theme between these films is the same, however. Each involves the takeover of a company by a rational, but "heartless," Wall Street "money-man" declaring that the only obligation people owe one another is to maximize wealth in the pursuit of self-interest.

In both *Wall* Street and *Other People's Money*, the takeover advocates address the legal owners of the company, the stockholders, and tell them to maximize their wealth by voting to liquidate the companies while they are still valuable. In contrast, Peck's character frames the appeal differently. He basically asserts that a company has obligations to its "stakeholders," and not just to its legal owners. He positions the proper market analysis as including the community, the schools, residents, workers, and others that have contributed to the company over the years. The company is not simply a detached and impersonal capital good; it is more than a physical object; it is a web of interconnected interests and values. He argues that resource determinations should account for a broader set of interests than those reflected by legal owners simply pursuing self-interest. In part, therefore, Peck's character questions the value frame and the interpretive reference set by the wealth maximizing character, Larry the Liquidator. By changing the value frame and the interpretive reference, Peck's character can logically promote a different economic calculus.

In viewing these scenes, one gets a close-up look at the real tension between two different visions of the market. It becomes clear that the disagreements are as much, or more, about values as they are about facts. It is not just a debate about the profitability of the various companies in question, for instance, but about the values to be promoted and endorsed by a market economy.

These two film clips also deal with tensions surrounding the meaning of property. Both involve corporate takeovers, and, in a similar way, each raises fundamental questions about ownership and the corporate form. Each asks us to consider who owns a company — the stockholders, the management, the workers, the community? How does ownership relate to having a "stakeholder" interest? Are claims by the community in this type of situation any different than the ones made by fans when their favorite major league football or base-ball team threatens to pull out and move to a new city? Do corporations exist simply to maximize profit for the stockholders? Is there such a thing as good corporate citizenship? What is the basic nature and role of the firm in law and society, and how do alternative conceptions of the firm, and of the market, relate to matters of information costs, risk assessment and management, production costs, market price, firm valuation, and labor relations? These considerations set up an examination of the exchange relationships within the firm, and between the firm, its constituent parts, and the community. Understanding the relationships helps us establish a map or plan for a more detailed investigation of factors to address in legal reasoning and public policy making. . . .

CONFLICTS IN THE REGULATION OF HOSTILE BUSINESS TAKEOVERS IN THE UNITED STATES AND THE EUROPEAN UNION
Barbara White
9 Ius Gentium 161 (2003)

During the 80s, in the heyday of the hostile takeovers in the U.S., news organizations and show business media spotlighted attention on the community fallouts from the waves of mergers and acquisitions. Acquirers were often portrayed as voracious greedy vultures picking on firms in a manner that destroyed a valuable company and/or valued ways of community life and doing so solely for the purpose of making money. One merely needs to think of popular movies on the subject produced at the time to have a sense of public perception: *Big Business* (1988, Comedy, Lily Tomlin, Bette Midler — a corporate struggle over whether to close down a factory that will also destroy a southern town's way of life); *Other People's Money* (1991, Comedy, Danny DeVito — corporate raider's efforts to acquire a local company that is the lifeblood of a New England community); and the most notorious, *Wall Street* (1987, Drama, Michael Douglas, Charlie Sheen, Martin Sheen — young ambitious stock broker learns that his idol, a major corporate raider, is really and can only be greedy and unscrupulous in order to be successful.) Even in *Pretty Woman* (1990, Julia Roberts, Richard Gere), the hero, a successful, albeit ethically questionable, corporate raider, is psychologically redeemed when he decides to keep one corporate acquisition intact and build it up further instead of selling off its component parts for profit. These movies and others like them mirrored the sentiments held by the United States public at large regarding the disruption to corporations' and people's lives that the waves of corporate acquisitions and mergers had caused. News media gave similarly heartrending stories of families' and communities' lives in upheaval as a result of shifts in corporate winds.

Despite the popular sentiment of hostility towards (and fascination with) the corporate raiders and the concern for the disruption that such activities were perceived to cause, court decisions and legislative efforts to regulate hostile takeover activity did very little to address them. Roberta Romano, a leading U.S. scholar in takeover activity, found little or no evidence that state lobbyists or legislators were ever concerned for the negative impact on their communities or employment as a result of takeover activity.

NOTES & QUESTIONS

1. How realistic are these alternative visions of corporations in *Wall Street* and *Other People's Money?* If Professor Malloy is correct about stockholders having to choose between pursuing their self-interested greed versus fulfilling their community-interested obligations, what roles do and should corporate boards of directors, executives, employees, and managers play? Do these other corporate stakeholders or constituencies merely serve as faithful or unfaithful agents of stockholders? Compare both of these movies' scenes portraying animated stock-holder meetings, to probable apathy by most individual stockholders. In reality, will it be worthwhile for most individuals to spend enough of their scarce attention, effort, and time to become informed voting stockholders?

2. Should those corporate stockholders who choose to vote guard against being too myopic and greedy or too long-sighted and caring? Think realistically about what actually would happen if you let every corporation whose stock you own influence your ethics and life so fundamentally. Alternatively, are you really better off by remaining unmoved by the suffering of employees in corporations whose stock you own?

3. Both *Wall Street* and *Other People's Money* focus on how disruptive hostile takeovers can be to interests other than those of the stockholders. Professor Barbara White describes a number of similar popular portrayals of hostile takeovers. Consider other films discussed in this chapter, as well as any other popular business narratives with which you are familiar. How many of them, for purposes of more dramatic storytelling, focus on how corporate (mis)behavior causes misfortunes and negative consequences for identified and sympathetic victims' lives?

4. Is the separation of control and ownership that is typical of large, modern, publicly traded corporations a desirable governance structure for stockholders? Consider this perspective based upon stockholder happiness:

> However, once we frame "best interests" in terms of shareholders' psycho-logical needs, it is clear that the separation of ownership and control, and in particular the situation of shareholder passivity, acts as a barrier to — rather than facilitator of — shareholder happiness.

James McConvill, *The Separation of Ownership and Control Under a Happiness-Based Theory of the Corporation*, The Company Lawyer, 26 (2005), 35. How persuasive is framing stockholders "best interests" in psychological as opposed to financial terms likely to be? Should business law be designed to maximize stockholders' happiness? *See* Peter H. Huang, *Happiness in Business or Law*, 12 Transactions: The Tennessee Journal of Business Law 53 (2011). Do you think that business law should take into account how regulations impact investors' and others' confidence, emotions, and trust? *See* Peter H. Huang, *How Do Securities Laws Influence Affect, Happiness, & Trust?*, 3 Journal of Business & Technology Law 257 (2008). How do you feel about basing legal policy in general upon considerations of happiness? *See* Peter H. Huang, *Happiness Studies and Legal Policy*, 6 Annual Review of Law & Social Science 405 (2010); Peter H. Huang, *Authentic Happiness, Self-Knowledge, & Legal Policy*, 9 Minnesota Journal of Law, Science, & Technology 755 (2008). Should the rules of civil procedure take into account how people adapt emotionally? *See* Peter H. Huang, *Emotional Adaptation and Lawsuit Settlements*, 108 Columbia Law Review 50 Sidebar (2008). How about basing employment discrimination law upon happiness? *See* Scott Moss & Peter H. Huang, *How the New Economics Can Improve Employment Discrimination Law, and How Economics Can Survive the Demise of the "Rational Actor,"* 51 William & Mary Law Review 183 (2009). What about basing tort law upon happiness? *See* Rick Swedloff & Peter H. Huang, *Tort Damages and the New Science of Happiness*, 85 Indiana Law Journal 533 (2010). How do you feel about reforming law firms and law schools based upon considerations of happiness? *See* Peter H. Huang & Rick Swedloff, *Authentic Happiness and Meaning at Law Firms*, 58 Syracuse Law Reviews 335 (2008); Nancy Levit & Douglas O. Linder, *The Happy Lawyer: Making a Good Life in the Law* (2010).

5.   While people likely value their personal happiness over their financial wealth, do they mistakenly believe that increased financial wealth leads to increased personal subjective happiness? If people incorrectly forecast how increased financial wealth should lead to increased personal subjective happiness, then why is there no disconfirming feedback evidence to cause people to learn the error of their ways? Do people have different private versus public views about how their personal subjective happiness depends on their financial wealth?

6.   Corporations are often depicted in popular culture as very resourceful and powerful, but nefarious and up to no good. An example is the secretive and sinister Umbrella Corporation in the science fiction and horror thriller *Resident Evil* (2002) and its many sequels. Why do most American movies focus on portraying most corporations as being evil? Do corporations make good villains because they represent big and impersonal forces that are beyond any single individual's control? Is there a sense in popular culture of corporations being modern-day Goliaths and of those who do battle against corporations in popular culture being modern-day Davids? Do pop cultural portrayals of corporations as evil, faceless, and soulless entities merely satisfy people's existing suspicions about possible abuse of massive concentrations of power and wealth?

7.   Debra Schleef describes a face-to-face interview of a male, second-year business student at a prestigious private university in the Midwest, in which the student lionizes corporate raiders like Gordon Gekko, the fictional character played by Michael Douglas in *Wall Street*. According to the student:

You're supposed to hate those guys. Those guys are really good guys. They are helping people, consumer Americans. If a company gets broken up, and all the workers get fired, it's probably 'cause they're not producing as efficiently as they could. . . . The manager is responsible for maximizing shareholder return, getting as much money as possible. Where does he get off, taking a half percent off the bottom line and giving it to Meals on Wheels or something? [That] is theft.

Debra Schleef, *Empty Ethics and Reasonable Responsibility: Vocabularies of Motive among Law and Business Students*, 22 Law & Social Inquiry 619, 626 (1997). Do students become socialized in business and law schools to hold pro-business or pro-corporate views? How do business and law schools differ in terms of their entering and graduating students' beliefs and perspectives about business? Does taking business law courses make law students more sympathetic to corporate interests?

8. Consider this explanation of differences between owning stocks and owning call options written on those stocks:

From a legal perspective, a stockholder is entitled to any financial gains or losses from selling the stock in the future, to any periodic dividend payments, and to vote at annual shareholder meetings or special meetings. In contrast, a stock option holder is entitled only to any financial gains or losses from exercising or selling the stock option in the future. The stock option holder is not entitled to receive any periodic dividend payments, nor to exercise voting rights at shareholder meetings.

Peter H. Huang, *Teaching Corporate Law from an Option Perspective*, 34 Georgia Law Review 571, 576-79 (2000). Do you believe that most individual stockholders buy stocks in order to secure rights to dividends, get potential capital gains, or vote at stockholder meetings? Do you feel there should be a legal prohibition against explicitly trading in corporate voting rights? What do you think about corporate voting swaps, in which a "deal splits up stock ownership rights into corporate voting rights and financial rights, and then swaps those corporate voting rights for cash"? Id. at 578.

9. Consider how the actions of Gordon Gekko in *Wall Street* and others engaged in corporate takeovers are described:

The 1987 film *Wall Street* chronicled the pursuits of a corrupt and greed-driven raider who ruthlessly manipulated stocks, conducted insider trading, and contributed to the destruction of major corporations. Virtually all books on the subject chronicled the alleged abuses and arrogance of financial entrepreneurs engaged in both hostile and friendly deals.

John Pound, *The Rise of the Political Model of Corporate Governance and Corporate Control*, 68 New York University Law Review 1003, 1037 (1993). Does this portrayal of those who engage in corporate takeovers appear to be fair and unbiased? Could threats of hostile corporate takeovers discipline corporate management from indulging in managerial bonuses, salaries, perks, laziness, and self-dealing? Can, does, and should law-related popular culture differentiate between socially desirable and undesirable corporate takeovers?

10.   Consider this fact: many individual stockholders who have been victims of corporate misbehavior or securities fraud are not familiar with the intricacies of accounting, business, corporate finance, economics, and statistics. Similarly, most jurors are not familiar with the intricacies of accounting, business, corporate finance, economics, and statistics. Corporate directors and executives are of course more likely to be familiar with the intricacies of accounting, business, corporate finance, economics, and statistics. Does this difference have any impact on how most corporate wrongdoing or securities lawsuits ultimately get resolved? Is any such disparity reflected in popular culture regarding business lawsuits?

2.   Boards of Directors, Executives, and Managers

ON THE PROPER MOTIVES OF CORPORATE DIRECTORS (OR, WHY YOU DON'T WANT TO INVITE HOMO ECONOMICUS TO JOIN YOUR BOARD)
Lynn A. Stout
28 Delaware Journal of Corporate Law 1 (2003)

For those who do not see the humor in the suggestion that directors might be driven by fear of personal liability, a short primer on the nature and enforcement of directors' fiduciary duties may be instructive.

In brief, directors' fiduciary duties come in two basic flavors: the duty of care and the duty of loyalty. These two flavors reflect the fact that when people misbehave, they tend to do so in one of two common ways. First, they may misbehave by acting like fools (acting carelessly). Second, they may misbehave by acting like knaves (acting dishonestly).

The duty of loyalty is designed, in theory, to address the knavishness problem. Put more bluntly, the duty of loyalty addresses the possibility that directors might try to steal from their firms. The duty of loyalty discourages such theft by imposing liability on directors who enter unfair "interested transactions," meaning transactions between the firm and the director (or between the firm and some individual or entity in which the director has a personal interest) under terms that are unfavorable to the firm. It also penalizes directors who steal from their firms by "taking corporate opportunities" — business opportunities that, for a variety of reasons, ought to have gone to the firm.

A problem arises, however, when we look to the remedy that is normally granted when a court finds that a director has violated the duty of loyalty. When a director has participated in an unfair transaction with the firm, the usual remedy is to make the director pay a fair price. If the director has violated the duty of loyalty by taking a corporate opportunity, she must return to the firm any profits made from that opportunity. In sum, the remedy for a breach of the duty of loyalty is to make the director give back whatever she has stolen from the firm.

This is not the kind of threat to strike terror into a larcenous heart. As any parent can tell you, if the only punishment a child receives for stealing from the cookie jar is that she has to give back the cookies if caught, you can expect a lot of stolen cookies. For similar reasons, it is easy to suspect that the threat of being held liable for breach of the duty of loyalty is not the sole, or even the principal, reason most corporate directors do not steal from their firms. Although the duty of loyalty on first inspection deters corporate directors from stealing, closer analysis suggests that as a practical matter the rule does not have much bite.

This toothlessness is even more obvious in the case of the director's duty of care. In theory, corporate directors owe their firms a duty to manage those tens of trillions of dollars of corporate assets with the care of a reasonably prudent person. In practice (as any law student who has taken a class in corporations knows) the duty of care is ameliorated — some might say eviscerated — by a doctrine known as the business judgment rule. The business judgment rule is a legal presumption that a director has, in fact, met the standards of the duty of care. This presumption can only be overcome if a plaintiff can show that the director did not act "on an informed basis," "in good faith," or "in the honest belief that the action taken was in the best interests of the company." The last two elements (good faith and honest belief) usually go unchallenged in any case that does not involve the sort of conflict of interest that gives rise to a loyalty question. As a result, whether the business judgment rule applies to a particular director usually turns solely on whether that director bothered to "inform" herself before acting. Furthermore, the test for whether a director is uninformed is not mere negligence, but gross negligence.

The business judgment rule accordingly allows a director who makes even a minimal effort to become "informed" to make foolhardy decisions all day long, without fear of liability. And what about the rare case of the director who is found to have been uninformed? Even then, other barriers protect directors from personal liability. For example, Delaware corporation law allows corporations to adopt charter provisions that eliminate director liability for breach of the duty of care. A number of large corporations have taken advantage of this provision. In firms that have not, if a lawsuit claiming breach of director care is brought, the odds are that it will be settled, and either an insurance company will foot the bill (under a director's liability policy) or the corporation itself will pay (under an indemnity provision).

Taking these factors together, it is only a slight exaggeration to suggest that a corporate director is statistically more likely to be attacked by killer bees than she is to have to ever pay damages for breach of the duty of care. This reality of business life is well-recognized among corporate scholars. In response, several have suggested in recent articles that corporate directors exercise care not because they fear legal sanctions, but because they fear what might be called "social sanctions" — because they do not want to lose face, acquire a bad reputation, or become the object of disapproving glances and cutting remarks.

This is an intriguing argument. There are several reasons, however, to suspect that the fear of social sanctions may provide only a weak incentive for exercising care for most directors in most circumstances. While directors involved in more-spectacular corporate crimes (for example, a massive accounting fraud) can suffer unpleasant notoriety, allegations of garden-variety negligence or conflict of interest are far less likely to attract media attention. In most cases neither the general public, nor a director's immediate social circle, would know (much less care) whether she was doing a good job as a fiduciary. Similarly, it can be difficult for others to judge whether an allegation of breach of fiduciary duty has merit, or is simply an attempt to extract money from the director's liability insurer through the threat of a "strike suit." For these and other reasons, external sanctions — including not only legal sanctions, but also social sanctions — are inadequate to explain why a purely self-interested director would take her fiduciary duties seriously. . . .

NOTES & QUESTIONS

1.   How do popular culture and media coverage depict corporate directors? How do you feel toward Enron's board of corporate directors? What factors do you believe motivate desirable and undesirable behavior of corporate directors? Do you think corporate directors are more afraid of punishment in the form of financial and legal sanctions or loss of personal and social reputation? Do you believe that large monetary fines or even small jail sentences are more likely to deter malfeasance by corporate directors?

2.   Some corporate law scholars think that the business judgment rule safeguards against corporate directors, who acted competently even though corporate outcomes turned out badly, being mistaken to have acted negligently by judges, juries, and shareholders, all of whom typically have less business expertise and may also exhibit hindsight bias. This cognitive bias occurs when people are prone to exaggerate in hindsight what one knew in foresight. In other words, hindsight vision is 20/20. Do you find this explanation for having a business judgment rule convincing? Why does there not exist a similar type of rule for medical doctors and malpractice because legal fact finders, judges, and shareholders, all of whom also lack medical and surgical expertise, may exhibit hindsight bias?

3.   Consider Professor Lynn A. Stout's conclusions:

Most important, if we want the social institution of the board of directors to be effective, we should do our best to accomplish three things. First, we should try to ensure that directors receive social signals that will encourage them to adopt an other-regarding, rather than a purely self-interested, perspective — that will convince them that they ought to "do the right thing." Second, we should make sure that doing the right thing is not too personally costly for directors. Third, we should make sure that we pick the sort of people who want to do the right thing in the first place.

Lynn A. Stout, *On the Proper Motives of Corporate Directors (Or, Why You Don't Want to Invite Homo Economicus to Join Your Board)*, 28 Delaware Journal of Corporate Law 1, 24-25 (2003). Can corporate directors benefit from such continuing education programs as Stanford Law School's directors' college or directors' consortium? Would you like to serve on the board of directors of a corporation someday? Can a single member of a corporate board of directors have a good or corrupting influence upon other members of a corporate board of directors?

4.   How appropriate, helpful, and insightful was it for the movie *The Corporation* (2003) to apply a tool for psychiatrists and psychologists to make diagnoses of human psychiatric illnesses, the Diagnostic and Statistical Manual of Mental Disorders, Fourth Edition (DSM-IV), to corporations, and find that according to the DSM-IV, corporations display highly anti-social psychopathic "personalities"? Does

a corporation even have a personality and, if so, is that personality its corporate culture? Would it surprise you if most corporations and organizations in general had multiple personalities? Should lawmakers require that directors, executives, and managers of corporations undergo mandatory psychological counseling and therapy? *See* Jayne W. Barnard, *Narcissism, Overt-Optimism, Fear, Anger, and Depression: The Interior Lives of Corporate Leaders*, 77 University of Cincinnati Law Review 405 (2008).

5. Does the public take today's managerial chief executive officers to be more or less powerful business figures than their financial, deal-making counter-parts? Are corporate managers or investment bankers more sympathetic as business figures? According to Professor William W. Bratton, Jr., "Today's popular conception of the powerful business figure is not the managerialist chief executive officer but the capitalist deal maker — the financial entrepreneur or the investment banker. Characterized in the vocabulary of the new economic theory, these figures acquire power as transaction cost engineers. They conceive and initiate transactions, depriving the managerial beneficiaries of the more costly existing contracts of power and wealth." William W. Bratton, Jr., *The New Economic Theory of the Firm: Critical Perspectives from History*, 41 Stanford Law Review 1471, 1523 (1989). Do managers fit more comfortably within the public's conceptions of business than financial engineers of corporate transactions? Are most people more likely to identify with a corporate executive officer, such as Martha Stewart, or a financial entrepreneur, such as Ivan Boesky?

6. In the movie *Working Girl* (1988), Katherine Parker, played by Sigourney Weaver, an associate partner in mergers and acquisitions at Petty, Marsh, & Company, steals an idea for a merger deal from her assistant Tess McGill, played by Melanie Griffith. Do you feel that the gender of these characters made any difference, dramatically or in some other manner? Compare them with Caroline Butler, played by Teri Garr, in *Mr. Mom* (1983). She is a successful advertising executive who must overcome a lecherous boss, Ron Richardson, played by Martin Mull, and a sexist client. Another fictional businesswoman is J.C. Wiatt, played by Diane Keaton, in *Baby Boom* (1987). She is a management consulting executive who is forced to give up her career when she becomes a single mom and intolerant executives at Sloane Curtis & Co. demote her, but she ultimately triumphs upon founding her own gourmet baby food company. Do you feel that portrayals of businesswomen are typically less or more sympathetic than portrayals of business-men? Are they portrayed as equally competent in popular culture?

7. Professor Manuel A. Utset suggests:

[T]ime-inconsistent preferences can lead managers to engage in nibbling opportunism and gatekeepers to repeatedly procrastinate monitoring and disciplining managers, notwithstanding the fact that doing so defeats their long-term preferences. This time-inconsistent explanation of misbehavior helps explain, at least in part, the puzzling behavior of mid-level managers, accountants, and lawyers in the recent corporate scandals; in misbehaving, these actors appear to have risked far too much compared to the benefits that (even in the most optimistic scenarios) they could have expected to receive.

Manuel A. Utset, *Time-Inconsistent Management & the Sarbanes-Oxley Act*, 31 Ohio Northern University Law Review 417, 444 (2005).

Do you repeatedly plan to start a new diet in a few days in order to lose some weight and become healthier? Do you know a smoker who would like to quit but nevertheless smokes a couple of packs daily? Are you familiar with people who want to live comfortably in their senior years, but constantly spend over their monthly budgets before retirement? If people have self-control problems in their personal and private lives, could they also display self-control problems in their business and corporate lives?

8.   Besides Gordon Gekko in *Wall Street* and Larry the Liquidator in *Other People's Money*, there are many examples of business executives being portrayed as evil characters in popular culture. For example, Dick Jones, the senior vice president of Omni Consumer Products, murders another vice president, Bob Morton, when Morton threatens Jones' tenure in the science fiction movie *Robocop* (1987). Why do you believe that most American movies choose to portray most business executives as being at least unsympathetic, if not downright evil?

9.   Consider Professor Nancy B. Rapoport's analysis of whether *Titanic* (1997) or *The Perfect Storm* (2000) provides a more accurate metaphor for Enron:

> The metaphor most used to describe Enron's quick descent into chapter 11 has been "the perfect storm." That "perfect storm" metaphor irks me to no end. I maintain, and this essay is designed to illustrate, that what brought Enron down — at least as far as we know — wasn't a once-in-a-lifetime alignment of elements beyond its control. Rather, Enron's demise was a synergistic combination of human errors and hubris: a "Titanic" miscalculation, rather than a "perfect storm."

Nancy B. Rapoport, *Enron, Titanic, and the Perfect Storm*, 71 Fordham Law Review 1373, 1374-75. Before you started law school, how much did you know about what happened at *Enron? After seeing Enron — The Smartest Guys in the Room* (2005), do you feel that you understand much better than before about what happened at Enron? If you had been an employee working at Enron, do you feel that you would have wanted to believe that Enron stock was a good investment?

10.   In Professor Lynn A. Stout's analysis of why stockholders of publicly traded corporations permit boards of directors to control their corporation's assets, she makes the analogy that "as the legendary Ulysses served his own interests by binding himself to the mast of his ship, investors may be serving their own interests by binding themselves to boards." Lynn A. Stout, *The Shareholder as Ulysses: Some Empirical Evidence on Why Investors in Public Corporations Tolerate Board Governance*, 152 University of Pennsylvania Law Review 667, 669 (2003). Is Professor Stout's analogy convincing and helpful? Besides ceding their authority to boards of directors, are there other legal and non-legal mechanisms for stockholders to bind themselves from temptations? Assume that Professor Stout's analogy correctly describes a role played by corporate boards of directors. How can you explain the dominance and popularity of a model that focuses on corporate boards of directors as monitors who police against potential misbehavior by other corporate executives?

3. Individual Investors, Institutional Investors, and Securities Regulators

THE MECHANISMS OF MARKET INEFFICIENCY: AN INTRODUCTION TO THE NEW FINANCE
Lynn A. Stout
28 Journal of Corporation Law 635 (2003)

Real people, of course, are not always rational. Sometimes we are misled by our emotions, and sometimes we make foolish mistakes. The fundamental insight of behavioral finance is that human emotion and error can influence investment choices just as they influence choices to play lotteries or wear seat-belts. The trick, of course, is to figure out in advance just how this influence operates. To do this, behavioral finance theorists rely on the psychological literature, and especially on empirical studies of human behavior in experimental games, to identify predictable forms of "cognitive bias" that lead people consistently to make mistakes. They then examine whether these systematic biases can help explain or predict empirically observed market anomalies that cannot be explained or predicted by rational-actor-based traditional finance.

It is difficult to overstate just how rapidly the behavioral finance literature has grown over the past decade. Over one hundred papers and a number of books have been produced on the topic, which has also inspired specialty journals. Indeed, the number of behavioral finance papers being produced now rivals scholarly production in traditional finance.

At the same time, many of the behavioral finance studies that have captured public attention are not the sort that would convince a skeptic that the field necessarily has much to offer in terms of developing our structural understanding of securities markets. For example, one recent study reports that stock prices are significantly influenced by the lunar cycle, while another concludes that seasonal affective disorder (SAD) leads stock returns to rise and fall with the seasonal lengthening and shortening of daylight hours. A third "behavioral finance" theory that has been discussed in the national media — if not in a peer-edited journal — explains the late-1990s stock market bubble as a consequence of the increased use of antidepressants such as Prozac and Zoloft, with an attendant collective surge in investor optimism. (Sadly, this entertaining theory suffers from a number of flaws, most obviously its inability to explain the Crash of 2000 absent evidence the investing public suddenly and collectively "went off its meds.")

These sorts of studies have raised the profile of behavioral finance in the popular media. Unfortunately, they have also contributed to a perception among many theorists that behavioral finance is more suitable for dinner party conversation than for serious research. This perception has been rein-forced by the rather large number of cognitive biases that have been argued to influence securities prices, some of them quirky, some of them short-lived, and some of them apparently contradictory. The net result has been the wide-spread impression that while behavioral finance sometimes may be useful to arbitrageurs, it has little to offer theorists other than a prediction that securities prices sometimes depart from informed estimates of value in arbitrary and capricious ways.

This impression is unjustified. More careful review of the behavioral finance literature quickly reveals that, in addition to offering insights into the effects of seasonal and lunar cycles, behavioral finance can also help explain market phenomena that are far more enduring and consequential. . . .

NOTES & QUESTIONS

1.   How convinced are you that most small retail investors are prone to rely on cognitive biases, emotions, and heuristics in making investment decisions? Why do you think small retail investors do not learn from their investing errors? Do you believe that securities markets will eventually weed out small retail investors who do not make their stock picks rationally? Are large institutional investors, such as hedge funds, mutual funds, and pension funds, likely to have their own set of cognitive biases, heuristics, and emotional motivations for investment decisions?

2.   Professor Lynn A. Stout elsewhere states:

> American investors take it as a matter of faith that the brokers and mutual fund managers to whom they entrust their savings will use those funds to actually purchase securities on their behalf. They take it as a matter of faith that the corporations that issue securities really exist, have real assets, and make real profits. Because they have faith, American investors buy trillions of dollars of corporate equities each year, even when they are not quite sure what it is that they are buying. . . . This is not to say that American investors necessarily believe that corporate insiders and securities professionals are honest and dependable individuals. . . . At a minimum, however, American investors must sufficiently believe that the benefits of investing outweigh the risks. They must believe that the regulators are regulating, and the watchdogs are watching. . . . [T]hey must at least trust the system.

Lynn A. Stout, *The Investor Confidence Game*, 68 Brooklyn Law Review 407, 419-20 (2002). If she is correct, then erosion of investor confidence and trust in securities markets by corporate scandals is a serious economic, legal, and social problem. Do you believe that faith by small retail investors in American securities regulation can be and has been restored? Is there possibly a problem of small retail investors being overconfident in U.S. securities markets and securities regulation?

3.   Professor David A. Hoffman observes:

> [C]ourts hold purchasers of securities to something similar to a duty of care. Courts require investors to investigate their purchases, to coldly process risk, to disregard oral statements of optimism, and in general to be economically rational. If investors fail to meet these expectations, judges deny them the protection of the securities laws. In this way, courts impose on public securities investors a special kind of legal duty, novel in scope and, I will argue, ungrounded in principle.

David A. Hoffman, *The "Duty" to Be a Rational Shareholder*, 90 Minnesota Law Review 537, 538 (2006). Do you feel that most small retail investors are likely to behave as rational shareholders? Do you believe that courts treating small retail investors as if they were rational shareholders can lead small retail investors to become rational shareholders?

4. Consider this analysis of why irrational anxiety and exuberance of investors may persist over time for both small retail investors and institutional investors:

> As with Bill Murray's character, Phil, in the movie *Groundhog Day* [1993], noiseless feedback and stationary environments promote learning effects. But investing yields very noisy feedback because people can quite naturally (and perhaps even subconsciously) confuse their investment successes with financial insight and confuse their investment failures with bad luck. In addition, empirical evidence suggests that securities markets are highly nonstationary environments. . . .

> Although securities markets are highly competitive, valuation in securities markets is an extremely subjective process. Emotional factors often influence the assessment of securities values across investors, just as emotions often affect subjective appraisals of the value of residential properties across home buyers and home owners. In fact, because securities, unlike consumer durables and real estate, are never consumed, securities markets, even more than other durable goods markets, involve subjective, often ephemeral and potentially very emotional anticipations of the future. Whereas reasonable people may agree on the past and the present (although there is reason to be skeptical of even these propositions as evidenced by the well-known fallibility of eyewitness testimony and memory), reasonable people often disagree on the future, both in terms of the set of contemplated outcomes and their various relative likelihoods. People are repeatedly caught off guard upon the realization of previously subjectively unforeseen contingencies.

Peter H. Huang, *Regulating Irrational Exuberance and Anxiety in Securities Markets*, in *The Law and Economics of Irrational Behavior 506-07* (Francesco Paresi & Vernon Smith eds. 2005). Can learning by investors be problematic? Does investing most resemble a video game that you can learn how to play optimally after many repeated iterations or a game of chance such as a slot machine or blackjack at which you can improve but can never learn to master completely? Can you think of reasons why investors would be unable to learn how to invest better over time?

5. Do you feel that most investors are motivated to believe they are smart when they make a lot of money investing and to believe they are unlucky when they lose a lot of money investing? Do you think that these are other personal contexts in which most people have motivated beliefs: "my spouse and kids love me," "my colleagues and neighbors like me," and "God is looking out for me, my family, and friends"? Can and should legal policy do anything to correct people's motivated beliefs?

6. Do such movies as *Boiler Room* (1992) and *Rogue Trader* (1999) depict settings that foster an individualistic type of a lone gun-slinger mentality? Do you find it surprising that sexual harassment lawsuits alleging hostile workplace environments have been filed and settled against male-dominated stock broker-

ages? Are you surprised: (a) men are more overconfident than women; (b) male stock investors trade more frequently than female stock investors; and (c) male stock investors do worse financially than female stock investors?

7.   Are securities brokers and professionals more or less likely than average people to be overly competitive, exploitive, opportunistic, and self-regarding? Do securities employers look to hire employees who enjoy taking risks, are indifferent toward risk-taking, or averse toward risk-taking? What sort of personality types do you think are more likely to enter and stay in securities professions?

8.   Consider this account of moody investing:

> There is experimental evidence of systematic differences between two psychological processes that people utilize to construct their preferences, namely valuation by calculation and valuation by feelings. Recent research in psychology and the neurosciences reveals that humans comprehend and face risk utilizing two fundamental systems, one analytic and the other experiential. Of course, in practice, "reason and emotion are intertwined as the threads in an oriental carpet." But, moody investing refers to investing that is (at least, partially) non-cognitive. . . . Affect and images crucially shape people's attitudes towards securities and their judgments concerning securities. On the positive affect side, in 2000 and 2001, a $3-million advertising campaign in European and Asian magazines and newspapers introduced a series of global mutual funds alongside fashion supermodels. . . . On the negative affect side, perceived dangers of genetically manipulated organisms can stigmatize biotechnological stocks. . . . Finally, a recent event study documented that positive abnormal returns and increased trading volume followed a company's Super Bowl television commercials.

Peter H. Huang, *Moody Investing and the Supreme Court: Rethinking Materiality of Information and Reasonableness of Investors*, 13 Supreme Court Economic Review 102-05 (2005). Do you believe that cognitive or moody investing more accurately describes how most retail small investors actually behave? Do securities issuers and other professionals intend for their communications with investors to affect investors' cognitions or moods? If investors are less aware of how securities advertisements, communications, and disclosures affect their moods than their cognitions, then can and should securities regulators be more worried about cognitive or moody investing?

9.   Professors Steven J. Choi & Adam C. Pritchard argue that:

> If cognitive defects are pervasive, will intervention help? Even well-intentioned and fully rational regulators may find it difficult to solve the problem of cognitive illusions among investors. Disclosure, the prevailing regulatory strategy in the securities markets, may not protect investors if cognitive biases prevent them from rationally incorporating the information disclosed into their investment decisions. More fundamentally, if everyone suffers from cognitive defects, doesn't that also include the commissioners and staff of the SEC?

Steven J. Choi & Adam C. Pritchard, *Behavioral Economics and the SEC*, 56 Stanford Law Review 1, 5-6 (2003). How can, does, and should law and regulatory policy balance concerns over the relative decision-making and judgment competencies of investors as opposed to securities regulators? *See also* Stephen J. Choi, *Behavioral Economics and the Regulation of Public Offerings*, 10 Lewis & Clark Law Review 85 (2006).

10.   Consider this analysis of some online brokerage ads:

Television commercials by online securities brokerages not only emphasized the personal control, ease, and profitability of such trading, but also were rich in emotional imagery. . . .

A Discover Brokerage Direct television commercial about online trading depicted a conversation between a passenger and a stock-trading tow-truck driver, who states, "That's my home. Looks more like an island. Technically, it's a country." Another television commercial included a stock-trading teenager, who owned his own helicopter. A series of Schwab commercials featured such celebrities as former teenage Russian tennis star Anna Kournikova. An E*TRADE advertisement claimed "that on-line investing is 'A cinch. A snap. A piece of cake' "). . . .

Peter H. Huang, *Regulating Irrational Exuberance and Anxiety in Securities Markets*, in *The Law and Economics of Irrational Behavior, supra*, 511-13 (2005). What is one's likely reaction upon seeing these sorts of television commercials depicting individuals being able to "get rich very quickly" via online investing? Were you amused, placed in a good mood, and more likely to look into how to be an online stock investor? How would you have reacted if you had also seen sad, vivid, and visceral depictions of unlucky online investors or day traders losing their shirts, life savings, retirement nest eggs, or kids' college education funds?

D.   THE MARKET ECONOMY

1.   Commerce or Greed?

There is a long tradition of questioning the capitalist market system of economic organization in particular and various forms of economic thinking in general. As early as 1790, Edmund Burke said in *Reflections on the Revolution in France*: "The age of chivalry is gone. That of sophists, economists, and calculators has succeeded; and the glory of Europe is extinguished for ever." More recently, 1972 Nobel Laureate and economic theorist Kenneth J. Arrow stated: "One of the oldest critiques of economic thinking has been its perceived disregard of the deeper and more sacred aspects of life." Kenneth J. Arrow, *Invaluable Goods*, 35 Journal of Economic Literature 757, 757 (1997). Even more recently, the blockbuster film *Avatar* (2009) raised the issue of the social appropriateness of valuation by markets of scarce indigenous natural and environmental resources. Consider the following excerpt about market values in scenes from two very different movies.

FRAMING THE MARKET: REPRESENTATIONS OF MEANING AND VALUE IN LAW, MARKETS, AND CULTURE

Robin Paul Malloy

51 Buffalo Law Review 1 (2003)

One scene from the film Class Action [1991] involves a discussion of cost and benefit analysis related to the question of repairing a defect in an automobile that a company has on the market. This scene is reminiscent of the Ford Pinto litigation, and is reflective of the more recent rash of lawsuits involving allegedly defective Firestone tires. In the film, the automobile in question has a defective turn signal switch that causes sparks to ignite the vehicle in certain types of collisions. The sparks cause the vehicle to explode, and a number of plaintiffs are suing the company for burns and deaths. In this particular scene, the company president explains to the corporate lawyers that statistical studies were done by the company indicating that it would be cheaper to deal with potential lawsuits than to recall and fix all of the cars. "It's a simple cost and benefit analysis." Thus, the company knowingly chose to leave the defective cars on the market and allow people to be injured and killed. . . .

Disney's *Pocahontas* [1995] presents the contrast of two competing frames of reference for market analysis. One view, put forward by the character of John Smith, is based on a belief in science, technology, and the separation of man from the natural world. The other view, represented in the character of Pocahontas, is grounded in a connection to nature, and based on an emotive sense of belonging and a non-monetary sense of value. The scene, therefore, positions tension between two competing value frames and different sets of interpretive references.

In one particular scene, Captain Smith is alone with Pocahontas in the woods. He is telling her about his home in London, and explaining the way in which the English will show Pocahontas and her people how "to make the most of their land." He explains how England has civilized "savages" all over the world and showed them how to industrialize and make progress. Smith sees the land and its resources in terms of the ability to commodify them for purposes of economic gain and wealth maximization. Pocahontas responds that her people already know how to make good use of the land, and that they are not savages just because they are different from the English. She explains the connection between nature and her people, and wonders if Smith can ever understand the value of the land without calculating its monetary worth.

In a sense *Pocahontas* reiterates the theme of each of the other films [*Class Action, Wall Street, Other People's Money*, and *Do the Right Thing*]. Each reflects a deeply contested public discourse regarding the nature of market life. Each contests assertions of ownership and of the pursuit of self-interest as a sustainable and worthy criterion for social organization. Each raises questions of valuation and of participation in the decision-making process. Each offers competing frames and references and challenges us to develop supportable and persuasive justifications for invoking one frame rather than another. Similarly, each provides us with an understanding of the way in which alternative cultural-interpretive frames promote different potential distributions, as well as competing meanings and values.

Collectively, these scenes from selective contemporary film illustrate, at a popular culture level, the highly contested interpretive conflicts represented in modern legal and economic discourse. Debates concerning these same issues fill law reviews, law school curriculums, courthouses, and legislative hearings. Gaining a better understanding of these discursive tensions, and their implications for law and market economy, requires an interpretive approach to law and economics. Furthermore, once we understand the framing and referencing conflicts that ground these interpretive conflicts, we can employ a variety of social science tools to assist us in clarifying and enlightening the process of pragmatic legal decision-making.

CRUELLA DE VIL, HADES, AND URSULA THE SEA-WITCH: HOW DISNEY FILMS TEACH OUR CHILDREN THE BASICS OF CONTRACT LAW
Michael A. Baldassare
48 Drake Law Review 333 (2000)

"Nicholas, time for bed."

"Daddy, let's make a deal."

"I'm listening."

"If I'm quiet, can I play Batman for ten minutes?"

"Okay, but only for five minutes."

"It's a deal, daddy."

Actually, it is a contract. Nicholas offers peace and quiet in exchange for ten minutes of play time. I counter-offer with five minutes. Nicholas accepts. There is ample consideration: Nicholas gets to kill Mr. Freeze a few more times, and I can maybe get up on my reading for conflict of laws. At four years old, Nicholas is a fierce negotiator. He is well versed in the basics of contract law. To think, all he did to gain this wealth of knowledge was watch Disney videos.

This Essay explores how Disney films teach our children the basics of contract law. Each Part begins with the general fact-pattern of a film, then offers legal analysis of the dialogue and actions of the characters. This reveals the contractual lessons children learn from each film. Many of the contracts discussed are oral and thus teach children the seminal lesson that few classes of contracts must be in writing. However, a close analysis reveals the contractual lessons of these films are more complex.

Part II analyzes *The Little Mermaid* and its contractual lessons: offer, acceptance, consideration, and novation. Part III deals with *Hercules* and its lessons: accord and satisfaction, liquidated damages, and the implied covenant of good faith. Part IV analyzes *101 Dalmatians* and the contractual issues that drive the plot: the non-binding nature of preliminary negotiations, the proper rejection of an offer, and the implied duty of good faith.

NOTES & QUESTIONS

1. Do you find some forms of cost-benefit analysis to be disturbing or unavoidable? Do you engage in cost-benefit analysis in your own personal decisions, such as whom to date, marry, and have children with; or which job offer to accept; or how and where to live? Do you believe that often cost-benefit analysis is more a form of rationalization undertaken after the fact in order to justify a decision that has already been made, as opposed to a form of rational analysis undertaken before the fact in order to come to a decision that still remains to be made?

2. Consider this discussion of market metaphors:

> For some people, markets can evoke negative images of unsympathetic robber barons and selfish capitalists exploiting hard-working laborers, and the infamous scene in the film *Wall Street*, in which Gordon Gekko made the notorious speech about how greed is good. Such depictions make for colorful stories of and reflect suspicions toward markets. Academic and professional lawyers routinely tell stories, make analogies, and use metaphors, as do academic and professional economists. Human cognition at its heart involves narratives, analogies, and metaphors. Of course, there are limits to the appropriateness or aptness of market metaphors. There are related negative or positive metaphors about marketing. To be sure, there are positive metaphors about markets with the most famous being Adam Smith's notion of an invisible hand.

Peter H. Huang, *Emotional Reactions to Law and Economics, Market Metaphors, and Rationality, in Theoretical Foundations of Law and Economics of Irrational Behavior*, 163, 173-74 (Mark D. White ed. 2009).

Do you find such economic metaphors as the marketplace of ideas persuasive in advocating freedom of expression or speech? Is the so-called market for ideas likely to be competitive with low or no barriers to entry? Is it more likely to be instead monopolistic or oligopolistic with high barriers to entry and hard to beat incumbent advantages? In other words, "though there is a 'market' for ideas, it is one that is institutionally sticky and requires entrepreneurial activity to give it life. For this reason, intellectual history is necessary but not sufficient." Steven M. Teles, *The Rise of the Conservative Legal Movement: The Battle for the Control of the Law* 3-4 (2008). The recent Supreme Court case *Citizens United v. FEC*, 130 S. Ct. 876 (2010), which recognized the right of corporate political speech, implicitly assumes the marketplace of ideas must be protected. That opinion also makes untenable assumptions regarding the economic and legal realities of corporations. *See* Anne Tucker, *Flawed Assumptions: A Corporate Law Analysis of Free Speech and Corporate Personhood in Citizens United*, 61 Case Western Law Review 497 (2011).

3. There is a whole cottage industry of popular trade books by economists for laypeople that apply microeconomic principles to real-world non-economic situations. The success of Steven D. Levitt and Stephen J. Dubner's international best-seller *Freakonomics: A Rogue Economist Explores the Hidden Side of Everything* (2009) led inevitably to a sequel: Steven D. Levitt & Stephen J. Dubner, *SuperFreakonomics: Global Cooling, Patriotic Prostitutes, and Why Suicide Bombers Should Buy Life Insurance* (2010). It also spawned a number of books with similar titles of fill-in-the-blank-nomics, such as Joshua Gans, *Parentonomics: An Economist Dad Looks at Parenting* (2009); Paula Szuchman & Jenny Anderson, *Spousonomics: Using Economics to Master Love, Marriage, and Dirty Dishes* (2011); Claire Shipman & Katty Kay, *Womenomics: Work Less, Achieve More, Live Better* (2010); Joel Waldfogel, *Scroogenomics: Why You Shouldn't Buy Presents for the Holidays* (2009). Similar books written by economists include: Tyler Cowen, *Discover Your Inner Economist: Use Incentives to Fall in Love, Survive Your Next Meeting, and Motivate Your Dentist* (2008); three by Robert H. Frank, *The Darwin Economy: Liberty, Competition, and the Common Good* (2011), *The Economic Naturalist's Field Guide: Common Sense Principles for Troubled Times* (2010), and *The Economic Naturalist: In Search of Explanations for Everyday Enigmas* (2008); three by Tim Harford, *The Logic of Life: The Rational Economics of an Irrational World* (2009), *Dear Undercover Economist: Priceless Advice on Money, Work, Sex, Kids, and Life's Other Challenges* (2009), and *The Undercover Economist: Exposing Why the Rich Are Rich, the Poor Are Poor and Why You Can Never Buy a Decent Used Car!* (2007); four by Steven E. Landsburg, *The Big Questions: Tackling the Problems of Philosophy with Ideas from Mathematics, Economics, and Physics* (2009), *More Sex is Safer Sex: The Unconventional Wisdom of Economics* (2008), *Fair Play* (1997), and *The Armchair Economist: Economics and Everyday Life* (1995); and Richard B. McKenzie, *Why Popcorn Costs So Much at the Movies and Other Pricing Puzzles* (2008). Have you heard about and/or read any of these books? Do you find them amusing, compelling, disturbing, eye-opening, helpful, insightful, or strange?

4. In the movie *Star Trek: First Contact* (1996), Captain Jean-Luc Picard, played by Patrick Stewart, explains how economics in the twenty-fourth century differs from that of the twenty-first century. In the future people are no longer motivated by the pursuit of money, but rather by the good of mankind. Dr. Zefram Cochrane, played by James Cromwell, who is the twenty-first-century inventor of the warp drive, bristles at being called heroic, stating instead that his motivation for inventing warp drive was merely to make money. Consider this viewpoint on the relationship between greed and capitalism offered by Professor Eric Posner:

> Shylock is a threat to capitalism. Capitalism needs moderation, not excess; far-sightedness, not cunning; self-interest, not greed. *The Merchant of Venice* posed the question of how the creatures of the market can be kept from undermining it, for recall that Shylock's remedy would spell the end of the merchant of Venice. The answer, for dramatic purposes anyway, lay in the law, albeit in the bizarre legal formalism of Portia. This formalism, though a satire, foreshadowed the practices of modern judges, who must draw on legal resources to produce just or preferred outcomes. The use of emotional language in addition to formalistic language is an overlooked aspect of this tradition, and the tensions it produces are condensed in the concept of greed, which is both the basis of and threatening to the institutions that judges are supposed to defend.

Eric A. Posner, *The Jurisprudence of Greed*, 151 University of Pennsylvania Law Review 1097, 1132 (2003). If there is a fundamental tension between greed and commerce, how should judges, juries, and lawmakers navigate this underlying opposition? Can judges, juries, and lawmakers affect people's characters? Should judges, juries, and lawmakers affect people's characters?

5. Do children really learn contract law basics from watching Disney videos? If so, is this a good thing for children, parents, and society? Do children learn about not just contract law, but also ethics, morality, and relationships? Baldassare continues:

> Disney does not deserve all the credit. The myths upon which many of these films are based already contained the contracts examined in this Essay. However, the presentation of these lessons in Disney films is significant for two reasons. First, the lessons are accessible to children long before they can read. This enables them to begin learning the basics of contract law much earlier than they would otherwise. Second, even when children learn to read, they are not likely to read the same story as often as younger children watch the same video.

Id. at 357. How convincing do you find the two reasons for the power of Disney films? Does it make a difference that when little children read books or listen to oral stories adults are involved? Is it troubling that most children who watch Disney videos are also likely to want Disney merchandise and toys associated with the videos? *See* Daniel Acuff & Robert Reiher, *Kidnapped: How Irresponsible Marketers Are Stealing the Minds of Your Children* (2005); Susan Linn, *Consuming Kids: Protecting Our Children from the Onslaught of Marketing and Advertising* (2005); Juliet B. Schor, *Born to Buy: The Commercialized Child and the New Consumer Culture* (2004); and Betsy Taylor, *What Kids Really Want That Money Can't Buy* (2003).

6. Do you believe that people are capable of unbiased cost-benefit analysis? Are what counts as costs and benefits fixed and immutable over time or culturally and socially constructed for a particular time? Can otherwise reasonable people differ in their assessments over what should count as costs and benefits, as well as what sorts of techniques are best for estimating or measuring costs and benefits? Do you find judicial opinions and regulatory decisions more or less trustworthy if they engage in cost-benefit analysis? *See* Robert H. Frank, *Why Is Cost-Benefit Analysis So Controversial?*, 29 Journal of Legal Studies 913 (2000).

2. Capital Markets and Initial Public Offerings

Much of the dotcom stock market boom involved unprecedented first-day stock price spikes of Initial Public Offerings (IPOs). In this next section, Professor Christine Hurt analyzes IPOs.

MORAL HAZARD AND THE INITIAL PUBLIC OFFERING
Christine Hurt
26 Cardozo Law Review 711 (2005)

Rising skepticism among the public has created a backlash against corporations, underwriters, analysts, and mutual funds that has resulted in numerous investigations, civil and criminal, into various trading practices, some of which have been around in various forms for years. At the same time, the number of individual investors participating in the capital markets has grown substantially, highlighting the discrepancies in investing opportunities between Wall Street regulars and retail investors.

One of the first trading practices to come under regulatory and shareholder fire was the initial public offering (IPO) process, which has revealed itself to be undemocratic at best and manipulative at worst. During the late 1990s and early 2000s (the "1999-2000 Boom"), a growing number of companies "went public," making the transition from being privately owned to having shares traded and owned by public investors. During the 1999-2000 Boom, IPOs generated $65 billion each year, compared with $8 billion per year in the 1980s.

Among those companies going public were an increasing number of companies without a significant history of positive earnings. However, the prices of shares of these companies were skyrocketing in value during the first hours or days of the offering. Although large first-day returns of IPO shares have been reported for decades, the first-day returns during this period were unprecedented. However, most individual investors were never buyers of original IPO shares. In the presence of very high demand for shares in almost any IPO, underwriters allocated the majority of original IPO shares to regular customers, mostly institutional investors, and few retail investors are able to buy these shares until they were resold by an original buyer. Because of the high demand for IPO shares, any investor who was offered the opportunity to buy original IPO shares at the offering price was buying an almost guaranteed first-day profit.

Unfortunately, the majority of the shares issued in IPOs in the last few years did not retain that initial profit, and the share price eventually plummeted, resulting in a loss for the retail investor who purchased in the aftermarket. For every person inside the IPO loop who sold high, a retail investor bought high. What at first seems to be a very respectable process, managed by the most elite investment banks, analysts, and venture capitalists substantially conforming to existing securities laws, turns out to be a Wall Street sponsored "pump-and-dump" scheme.

Historically, taking a company public was the equivalent of receiving the Good Housekeeping Seal of Approval; not only was the company a success story, but Wall Street was vouching for its potential for all the investing public to see. However, after the end of the most recent IPO boom, investors are beginning to realize that Wall Street was very willing to sell its stamp of approval for the opportunity to use a company's IPO for personal gain. In the 1999-2000 Boom the investing public fell victim to the oldest trick in the IPO order book: The Pump-and-Dump. Together, existing securities laws and industry customs have worked together to create a system that not only routinely excludes the small investor from seizing the opportunity to be an original buyer of IPO shares but also cleverly attracts the same investor to purchase these same shares in the aftermarket, locking in a profit for the fortunate original buyers. . . .

Securities laws universally condemn "pump-and-dump" schemes whereby insiders and underwriters hype a company's stock and create an illusion of high demand, then sell their shares once the public has accepted the hype and bought the stock. Wall Street generally derides these activities, assigning them to "microcap companies," internet scams and telemarketing ventures. Disturbingly, the movie Boiler Room [2000] juxtaposes a fly-by-night investment banking firm staffed with loud, aggressive men of varying ethnic backgrounds without Ivy League educations against Wall Street investment banking firms staffed with sophisticated, WASP-ish MBAs. Of course, the former firm engages almost exclusively in illegal pump-and-dump schemes. Divorcing these stereotypes from the actual behavior, imagine a scenario in which any group of underwriters and company insiders tout the value of a stock, create arrangements whereby other industry insiders create demand in the stock in return for cheap stock, and then sell their shares shortly after a successful IPO. This scenario, which describes the U.S. IPO process, is a pump-and-dump scheme.

Each step in the IPO process, when performed by industry players acting in their self-interest, creates an ingenious method to extract wealth from the retail investor. Because industry custom and legal practices combine together to restrict supply and generate demand, IPO share prices may increase substantially, allowing both issuer and industry insiders to sell early and realize profit. However, the average IPO stock will then see a dramatic decrease, leaving the retail investors with built-in losses. . . .

NOTES & QUESTIONS

1. Do small retail investors actually understand the above types of details about how the IPO process worked? Should greed and irrational exuberance by investors be considered in regulating IPOs?

2. Check out http://www.pbs.org/wgbh/pages/frontline/shows/dotcon/, which is a companion website to the PBS *Frontline* television program *Dot Con*, which aired on January 24, 2002, and explore some of the hyperlinks on that website to read additional online resource materials about IPOs. After doing so, what do you think of the legality and morality of how many investment banks conducted IPOs in 1999-2000?

3. Does disclosing potential conflicts of interest by securities analysts who also work at investment banks actually lead to investors being more trusting and securities analysts feeling more justified in engaging in hyperbole? In other words, do you think a danger exists that upon disclosure about potential conflicts of interest, audience members feel that speakers are less prone to exaggerate, but speakers feel they can exaggerate more than previously because their audience has been duly warned of their potential conflicts of interest. *See Conflicts of Interest: Challenges and Solutions in Business, Law, Medicine, and Public Policy* (Don A. Moore et al. eds. 2005). Is investor confidence and trust in IPO markets only a cognitive decision?

4. How easy will it be for corporate America to restore investor confidence and trust in IPO markets? Do people who get rich in IPO markets do so because of their superior abilities, hard work, or personal and social connections?

5. Have you watched any of the following financial news programs: *The Wall Street Journal Report with Maria Bartiromo*, in national syndication; *Closing Bell* with Maria Bartiromo, on CNBC; James Cramer's *Mad Money*, on CNBC; *The Suze Orman Show*, on CNBC; *Squawk Box*, on CNBC; and *Market Wrap* with Ron Insana, on MSNBC? Is it easy to distinguish between entertainment and information on these shows? Does watching these programs make you less or more likely to buy or sell corporate stocks? Do some commentators on these shows appear to be unbiased cheerleaders for corporate America? Is it likely that stock analysts who appeared on such programs and recommended buying particular stocks during the last bull market contributed to irrational exuberance? Do you trust anchors of these shows to be knowledgeable and unbiased? What do you think about financial news hosts becoming celebrities, media darlings, and popular icons?

6. The PBS *Frontline* television show *Secret History of the Credit Card* (Nov. 23, 2004) has a companion website at http://www.pbs.org/wgbh/pages/frontline/shows/credit/more/ that provides additional online resource material about credit cards. Explore some of the hyperlinks on that website. Congress passed and President Barack Obama signed into law the Credit Card Accountability Responsibility and Disclosure Act of 2009 to deal with many of the dubious business practices that credit card companies engaged in to trick and trap unwary credit card users that are detailed in the PBS program.

Leo Gottlieb Professor at Harvard Law School and bankruptcy law expert Elizabeth Warren, featured in the PBS show, co-authored with her daughter Amelia Warren Tyagi, a former McKinsey consultant, the book *The Two-Income Trap: Why Middle Class Mothers and Fathers Are Going Broke* (2003). Professor Warren has been an outspoken critic of credit card companies, chaired the Congressional Oversight Panel that oversaw the Troubled Assets Relief Program (TARP) banking bailout, and was Assistant to the President and Special Advisor to the Secretary of the Treasury for the newly created Consumer Financial Protection Bureau under the Dodd-Frank Wall Street Reform and Consumer Protection Act.

7. There is a debate as to whether improving economic and financial literacy is desirable or even possible. *See* Jayne W. Barnard, *Deception, Decisions, and Investor Education*, 17 Elder Law Journal 201 (2009); Lauren E. Willis, *The Financial Education Fallacy*, 101 American Economic Review 429 (2011); Lauren E. Willis, *Evidence and Ideology in Assessing the Effectiveness of Financial Literacy Education*, 46 San Diego Law Review 415 (2009); Lauren E. Willis, *Against Financial Literacy Education*, 94 Iowa Law Review 197 (2008). Also, explore these websites about financial education or planning: http://www.practicalmoneyskills.com/english/index.php (Decision Education Foundation); http://corp.financialengines.com/ (Financial Engines) and http://www.whatsmyscore.org/ (The Saint Paul Foundation, What's My Score). Do you find these websites amusing, confusing, educational, or informative?

3. Securities Markets and Fraud

According to Professors Jennifer H. Arlen and William J. Carney, "Fraud on the Market usually occurs when agents fear themselves to be in their last period of employment." Jennifer H. Arlen & William J. Carney, *Vicarious Liability for Fraud on Securities Markets: Theory and Evidence*, 1992 University of Illinois Law Review 691, 693. Do securities markets mitigate corporate and securities fraud of directors and managers who are in their last period of employment?

DEAL PROTECTION PROVISIONS IN THE
LAST PERIOD OF PLAY

Sean J. Griffith

71 Fordham Law Review 1899 (2003)

Another negative net present value project that managers in their last period of play may consider is securities fraud. Professors Arlen and Carney have shown that last period incentives may drive "fraud on the market" schemes. In securities law, "fraud on the market" consists of issuing false statements to increase or maintain the firm's stock price. A manager's mid-stream incentives generally do not favor committing fraud on the market because at some point the statements are likely to be revealed as false, causing the paper gains in stock price to vanish. Moreover, when the statements are revealed as false, the manager is likely to be fired. Yet fraud on the market occurs, Professors Arlen and Carney argue, as a result of the last period problem:

> [A]n agent generally will not commit Fraud on the Market so long as his future employment seems assured. When the firm is ailing, however, an agent's expectations of future employment no longer serve as a constraint on behavior. In this situation a manager may view securities fraud as a positive net present value project. Aside from criminal liability, in a last period the expected costs of fraud (civil liability and job loss) are minimal, while the expected benefits of fraud may have increased. As remote as the prospects for success may seem, these benefits include possible preservation of employment as well as the value of the manager's assets related to the firm's stock, if by committing fraud he is able to buy sufficient time to turn the ailing firm around.

Jennifer H. Arlen & William J. Carney, *Vicarious Liability for Fraud on Securities Markets: Theory and Evidence*, 1992 University of Illinois Law Review, 691, 702-703 (1992).

Managers facing the failure of their business may thus prefer to risk lying to the market, potentially incurring legal liability, than to suffer the immediate and certain consequences of the market's reaction to the truth — that is, the further decline of their share price and creditworthiness and the further degradation of their business prospects.

Far from academic abstraction, these concerns can be seen to motivate several of the recent accounting scandals, including Enron and WorldCom. Putting aside the apparent self-interest of Enron's chief financial officer, the use of off-balance sheet financing activities seems to have been directed towards the end of keeping news of Enron's increasing losses from the market until a turnaround in the company's fortunes occurred. The turnaround never came, the financing activities revealed management as dishonest, and the company failed. Similarly, the dishonest financial reporting of WorldCom may be seen as management's attempt to conceal the truth about a fast-failing company long enough for a market turnaround (or an extension of credit) to save their jobs. Again, they failed.

Another corporate law last period problem occurs when a company is sold, as in a "bust up" acquisition. In the film Wall Street, for example, Michael Douglas portrayed a prototypically loathsome raider, proposing to buy Blue Star Airlines, auction its fleet of airplanes, fire its employees, and use its pension fund to finance the acquisition, thus plunging the fictional company into a paradigmatic last period scenario. In such situations, ordinary mid-stream constraints will not operate with their usual force and may not operate at all. Blue Star managers and directors will be indifferent to product market constraints because the firm, ceasing to operate as a going concern, will no longer take products to market, indifferent to capital market constraints because the firm will no longer need to raise capital, indifferent to labor market constraints because there will be no more hirings or promotions, indifferent to the market for corporate control because control has already been wrested from them, and indifferent to intra-firm norms because the firm will soon be extinct. Faced with the destruction of the firm and, perhaps, the end of their careers, directors and managers are freed from the concerns that ordinarily constrain their decision-making and may therefore be more apt to behave foolishly or selfishly. . . .

NOTES & QUESTIONS

1. How do the requirements of apartment complexes that renters pay their monthly rents on the first of each month or that renters pay one month's rent in addition to a cleaning deposit upon moving into their apartments affect renters' incentives regarding paying their last month's rent? Can you see why corporate directors and managers can have perverse incentives for engaging in corporate malfeasance or securities fraud if their employment or their corporation is near its end?

2. You can find "detailed information relating to the prosecution, defense, and settlement of federal class action securities fraud litigation" at http://securities.stanford.edu/, a public database provided by Stanford Law School. This website also contains articles, reports, and research studies about how federal class action securities fraud litigation changed after passage in 1995 of the Private Securities Litigation Reform Act (PSLRA). Explore some of these resources. After doing so, do you think that this public database succeeds at correcting some misimpressions that people are likely to have about federal class action securities fraud litigation based upon sensationalist documentaries or media coverage and fictional accounts in popular culture?

3. Are an individual's political beliefs likely to be highly correlated with that individual's sympathy for securities plaintiffs or defendants? Do you think a focus on apocryphal widows and orphans as defrauded securities plaintiffs by journalists, politicians, and regulators is more than just merely a theatrical device? Do you find talk of wanting securities markets to be a level playing field to be mere rhetoric? Could a level playing field drain itself?

4. Do securities markets reward hard work, pure chance, or private information? Is the movie *Wall Street* representative of popular culture in the way it depicts insider securities trading as being evil and immoral?

5. What did you think about Martha Stewart being prosecuted for insider securities trading? Did Martha Stewart declare her innocence of being engaged in

insider securities trading in order to commit securities fraud against her stockholders?

6.   In the last scene of the movie *Wall Street*, Bud Fox, played by Charlie Sheen, goes up the steps of the New York state court building instead of the United States federal court building. But the federal government, and not any individual state government, oversees the regulation of securities markets; any securities fraud that Gordon Gekko and Bud Fox would have committed in the movie *Wall Street* would have been a federal, not state, offense. This means that Fox is entering an incorrect building, assuming that he is on his way to help the Securities and Exchange Commission or the Justice Department convict his former mentor. This minor inaccuracy relates to the issue of whether legal accuracy matters in popular culture. Did you notice this mistake? Do you believe that most viewers of the movie knew of this error? Would they be less inclined to believe the business and legal accuracy of the rest of the story told in the movie if they were informed of these mix-ups?

4.   Derivatives Markets and Debacles

DERIVATIVES ON TV: A TALE OF TWO DERIVATIVES DEBACLES IN PRIME-TIME
Peter H. Huang, Kimberly D. Kraviec & Frank Partnoy
4 The Green Bag 257 (2001)

On March 5, 1995, the CBS newsmagazine 60 *Minutes* broadcast a story about derivatives, focusing on Orange County. Reporter Steve Kroft introduced derivatives as "too complicated to explain, but too important to ignore," and described derivatives as "highly exotic, little understood, and virtually unregulated." 60 *Minutes* concluded its introduction to derivatives by noting that "some people believe they're [derivatives] so unpredictable they could bring down the world banking system." The show opened with aerial images of picturesque Orange County: birds flying over the blue Pacific, palm treelined homes with pools, yachts, a plush golf course, and sandy beaches, under the sun.

Throughout the program, Kroft and his guests likened derivatives to gambling, repeatedly emphasizing that derivatives are essentially bets. This analogy is misleading because buying certain derivatives is like buying insurance against an accident, while not buying those derivatives is essentially betting on the accident not happening. The interviewees (primarily private and public fund managers) also emphasized the complexity of derivatives. Kroft claimed that, no matter who they interviewed and no matter how hard they tried, viewers and investors were unlikely to understand derivatives. A Painesville, Ohio councilman and two female treasurers from Ohio school districts corroborated this point by claiming that they had purchased derivatives without realizing that they had done so and without understanding the risks involved. To emphasize this point, Kroft exhibited the coupon rate formula for one Orange County derivative contract, a formula that obviously would appear impossibly complex to a viewer unfamiliar with derivatives (but could have been explained step-by-step).

The program continued to liken derivatives investing to complex science by stating that Wall Street hired "rocket scientists" with mathematics or physics Ph.D.s, but no finance background, neglecting to note that Wall Street also hired many finance Ph.D.s (or even salesmen with little technical training). Kroft compared rocket scientists to genetic engineers and derivatives to Frankenstein's monsters.

60 *Minutes* concluded by suggesting ominously that viewers may already own derivatives in mutual funds or pension plans without realizing it. In the parting shot, Kroft queried the Ohio councilman as to where the money that his city treasury had lost in derivatives went. After several moments of embarrassed silence, the councilman was forced to admit that he had no idea. Unfortunately, neither did 60 *Minutes*' producers.

On February 8, 2000, the PBS show *NOVA: Trillion Dollar Bet* described the discovery of the Black-Scholes option pricing formula and its use by LTCM [Long-Term Capital Management]. The show opened with aerial images of Chicago and trading in the pits of the Chicago Mercantile Exchange, while stating the golden rule of capitalism: "if you want to make money, you have to take risks."

NOVA explored the tension between much modern financial theory, exemplified by economist Merton Miller's explanation of the random walk theory of stock prices and the efficient markets hypothesis, and the views held by many professional traders that it is possible to predict market prices and thus "beat the market." This view was stressed by one trader's explanation of the importance of fear, human judgment, intuition, and psychology. Financial economist Zvi Bodie articulated the view that traders may succeed due more to luck than skill.

NOVA provided a good overview of the history of options pricing and the development of modern options pricing models. Paul Samuelson, for example, discussed early attempts to price options, referring to a precise option pricing formula as the "Holy Grail." The *NOVA* commentators described the shortcomings of early financial models, which attempted to capture mathematically a typical investor's risk preferences, emotions, and guesses about other investors' expectations. The problem with such models, as Bodie explained, is that they required unobservable inputs.

Scholes described the great contribution to the field made by Fisher Black and Scholes: eliminating all unobservable variables from the model except one: the riskiness of the underlying stock. By depicting synchronized moving colored graphs, the show clearly explained and illustrated the crucial ideas of dynamic hedging and portfolio replication.

Robert Merton then explained his continuous-time version of the Black-Scholes model. *NOVA* successfully countered the fearful reactions television viewers often have to mathematical formulae by devoting significant time to the formula itself. The show depicted Merton writing the stock call option pricing formula, while Samuelson and Miller explained the formula's importance. To illustrate the formula's impact on financial markets, *NOVA* depicted traders using the formula to price options and hedge risks. The program concluded its historical overview of options pricing by describing how Scholes and Merton won the Nobel Prize in economics for their option pricing models.

NOVA, unlike 60 *Minutes*, emphasized the use of options for hedging purposes, rather than painting derivatives as risky vehicles used only for speculation. The commentators described options as a form of insurance that effectively controls risk and explained the risk transfer and risk allocation effects of derivatives.

NOVA then detailed the circumstances surrounding the creation of LTCM, emphasizing the role that the founders' reputations played in attracting investors to the fund. For example, *Wall Street Journal* reporter Roger Lowenstein described the awe LTCM's founding members inspired on Wall Street, and other commentators explained that the most prestigious investors, banks, and institutions competed to invest in LTCM. Lowenstein noted that many institutional managers felt honored to meet and invest with Merton and Scholes, modern finance's high priests, whose models they had studied in business school.

NOVA succinctly and clearly educated viewers about both LTCM's investment strategy and the secrecy it employed in its operations. The program described LTCM's search for deviations from historical pricing relationships across global markets and emphasized LTCM's phenomenal early returns (while showing Scholes golfing on lush courses). The show then described the Asian crisis while explaining that LTCM's many bets diverged instead of converging, causing large losses.

NOVA introduced the issue of systemic risk by having Lowenstein explain the great fear that markets would seize up if LTCM attempted to dump or unwind its huge positions. The show then revisited the financial models versus human judgment debate by describing the Federal Reserve-brokered private bailout of LTCM. A question posed by Fed Chairman Alan Greenspan — "How much dependence should be placed on financial modeling, which for all its sophistication, can get too far ahead of human judgment?" — and statements by Peter Fisher, Greenspan's deputy, indicated that models do not always work. In contrast, Scholes asserted that many things, including bad luck, could be responsible for LTCM's difficulties and that the models themselves were not necessarily to blame.

NOVA concluded that the Black-Scholes model continues to be used in complex financial markets as a powerful tool for managing risk, but that the model assumes functioning markets and is not a crystal ball. The piece ended with Samuelson observing that there always is room for judgment. . . .

Overall, coverage of LTCM was more accurate than coverage of Orange County. There are several possible reasons for this difference. First, 60 *Minutes* and *NOVA* have different target audiences. Because 60 *Minutes* is a popular show that reaches a wide audience with divergent backgrounds and educations, its producers necessarily strive for non-technical stories appealing to most viewers. Alarmist stories painting derivatives as dangerous, incomprehensible, and capable of mass destruction are more likely to attract viewers' attention (and win ratings) than are more balanced stories accurately educating the public about derivatives. *NOVA*, on the other hand, is a PBS program aimed at more sophisticated viewers with an interest in the sciences.

The intervening five years between the two shows may also account for the differential coverage. Both the size of derivative markets and media coverage of derivatives increased substantially during that period. Consequently, derivatives were less foreign to most people in 2000 than they were in 1995, and the general public may have had the interest and the ability to understand more sophisticated coverage by 2000.

It is important to emphasize the dangers of one-sided, inaccurate television reporting like that in the 60 *Minutes* show on derivatives. A 60 Minutes viewer without prior knowledge of derivatives would necessarily view derivatives as risky gambles capable of wreaking havoc on both individual investors and the financial system as a whole, while providing few or no social benefits. Because these viewers can also be voters, jurors, shareholders, legislators, or judges, their inaccurate, negative opinions can greatly impact derivatives use and regulation. A simple description on television of a derivative in a context familiar to most consumers (for example, a homeowner's option to prepay her mortgage without penalty and thus reduce her total borrowing costs) would be far more educational, though certainly less entertaining.

60 *Minutes* focused exclusively on speculation and failed to mention the many beneficial uses of derivatives, including hedging for improved risk management. Nor did it discuss "regulatory arbitrage," the use of derivatives to avoid taxes or other regulations.

In addition, by failing to distinguish OTC (Over-the-Counter) derivatives which are not traded on exchanges from exchange-traded derivatives, 60 *Minutes* implied that the dangers highlighted in the show applied equally to all derivatives, a patently false conclusion. These two markets differ in ways that are difficult to overemphasize. In fact, nearly all of the derivatives characteristics discussed in the show apply only to OTC derivatives, and not to exchange-traded derivatives. OTC derivatives represent a relatively new market that is largely unregulated. Because there is often no active market for a particular OTC derivative, there is less liquidity and less transparency in that market. Consequently, OTC derivatives end-users must perform their own pricing and marking-to-market, a fairly costly function that requires relatively sophisticated programming and investment skills. Additionally, OTC derivatives present credit-risk problems that exchange-traded derivatives do not, because the exchange clearinghouse acts as the counterparty in all exchange trades. Many OTC derivatives end-users, however, feel that the many benefits of custom-tailored derivatives outweigh these costs.

60 *Minutes'* closing segment suggesting that money lost in derivatives transactions had somehow mysteriously disappeared revealed that the show's producers failed to understand that derivatives investment is a zero-sum game. Every dollar one party loses trading derivatives is gained by the counterparty. The wealth lost by the Ohio municipality did not disappear; it was redistributed to a smarter or luckier counterparty.

In contrast to 60 *Minutes*, NOVA's derivatives coverage was educational and raised many controversial issues. First, it raised the issue of whether LTCM had unwisely accepted too much risk, ensuring a disaster if markets did not behave as predicted, or whether the market behavior was so unforeseeable that none of the carefully constructed market risk models could anticipate its occurrence. An analysis of this issue has implications reaching far beyond the problems LTCM faced. The capital-at-risk model most market participants use to evaluate their positions' riskiness does not account for very low probability events that might disrupt capital markets, a criticism often raised by those who argue for greater regulation of derivative markets.

NOVA also raised the issue of whether derivatives implicate systemic risk concerns. The Federal Reserve's involvement in LTCM's "bail-out" was precipitated by fears that attempts to unwind LTCM's positions in an already illiquid market would cause or contribute to an illiquidity driven crash. Although no federal funds were used in LTCM's private bailout, a taxpayer bailout, like that of the U.S. Savings and Loan industry, implicates difficult policy questions. The whole economy may suffer if the government doesn't prevent a systemic crisis. A government bailout, however, presents a definite moral hazard problem because the benefits of more risk-seeking accrue only to private parties, while the costs are shared by society generally.

Finally, *NOVA* raised important questions about professional investors' increasing reliance on mathematical models to predict market prices. If market prices reflect unpredictable human behaviors and attitudes far more than they reflect any evidence of intrinsic value, then computer-generated trading may ignore some of the most important determinants of market prices. NOVA thus concluded by raising a debate with important implications regarding the roles of specialists, market makers, floor traders, and physical exchanges generally — a debate further intensified by major technological innovations changing how capital markets operate. . . .

NOTES & QUESTIONS

1. The companion website for the *NOVA* television show *Trillion Dollar* Bet is at http://www.pbs.org/wgbh/nova/stockmarket/ and provides additional online resource materials about derivatives markets. Explore some of the hyperlinks on these websites. After doing so, what do you think about derivatives markets?

2. What, when, and where had you heard about derivatives before today? Did you realize that examples of straightforward derivatives in the movies include the orange juice futures in *Trading Places* (1983) and the stock options that the villain in *Mission Impossible* II (2000) wanted instead of cash from the CEO of a biotech company?

3. Did you believe that derivatives markets have some connection to mathematical derivatives from calculus? Do you find mathematical discussions, references, or subjects confusing? Do you feel that mathematical and quantitative analysis improves, obfuscates, or is divorced from legal and policy discourse?

4. Do American people, politicians, and regulators have a love-hate relationship with numbers and quantification? On the one hand, numbers are seductive because they imply some degree of measurability, order, predictability, and precision in our lives. On the other hand, numbers are often seen to be and criticized for being arbitrary, inhuman, rigid, and subjective. Can and should legal and public policy combat innumeracy? Does popular culture feed a common public desire to believe in a fundamental tension between art, humanities, and literature versus mathematics, science, and technology?

5. Do depictions of business law, economics, and finance in popular culture have a special responsibility to be at least not misleading, if not accurate? How do reactions to popular culture related to business law, economics, and finance compare to reactions to popular culture related to medicine or science? Might non-physicians and non-scientists realize that they lack medical and scientific expertise and training, while people who are not experts in, nor even trained in business law, economics, and finance believe they are nonetheless knowledgeable about business law, economics, and finance?

6. Do you feel that disclosure about CEO compensation, including stock options, will help investors make better-informed choices about which corporate stocks to buy or sell? Do you think disclosure about CEO compensation, including stock options, will cause CEO compensation to decrease? Do you think shame or guilt among CEOs over their compensation, including stock options, is likely to last for a shorter period of time than envy or jealousy by employers, shareholders, and the public over CEO compensation, including stock options? *See* Peter H. Huang & Christopher J. Anderson, *A Psychology of Emotional Legal Decision Making: Revulsion & Saving Face in Legal Theory & Practice*, 90 Minnesota Law Review 1045 (2006).

7. There is a branch of corporate finance and management strategy known as real options analysis that applies concepts and theories about options to analyze situations that involve exercising or preserving various options upon learning information. Examples of real options include buying a house, getting married, having children, and litigation. *See* Joseph A. Grundfest & Peter H. Huang, *The Unexpected Value of Litigation: A Real Options Perspective*, 58 Stanford Law Review 1267 (2006); Peter H. Huang, *Lawsuit Abandonment Options in Possibly Frivolous Litigation Games*, 23 The Review of Litigation 47 (2004); and Peter H. Huang, *A New Options Theory for Risk Multipliers of Attorneys' Fees in Federal Civil Rights Litigation*, 73 New York University Law Review 1943 (1998).

8. Much of the media coverage of the Great Recession focused on the ubiquitous roles certain types of derivative securities including credit-default swaps and mortgage-backed securities played in both the creation and bursting of the American housing bubble. Do you feel that such media coverage really explained the how, what, and why of such derivatives? Is that too much to ask of the popular press in the age of sound bites and Bloomberg-style television in which there is a continual scroll of real-time updated (inter)national quantitative financial data below or alongside the speaking anchor or reporter?

9. The book *Too Big to Fail* (2009) and the HBO documentary film based upon it do a good job of explaining the moral hazard of government bailing out banks and other financial institutions that lost huge amounts of money from speculation in mortgage-related derivatives betting that residential home prices would keep going up indefinitely. How much of a role do you think fears of an economic meltdown played in Congressional passage and public acceptance of the Troubled Assets Relief Program (TARP)?

10. Is fear or panic ever a good impetus to promulgate regulation? Does it matter if the fear is disproportionate, genuine, imagined, justified, or manipulated? What roles can and do popular culture and media coverage about business and business law play in dispelling fears or spreading rumors? What role can such positive affect as pride play in policy and regulations? *See* Peter H. Huang, *Diverse Conceptions of Emotions in Risk Regulation*, 156 University of Pennsylvania Law Review PENNumbra 435, 442-444 (2008).

5. Markets, Monetary Commensurability, and Capitalism

DANGERS OF MONETARY COMMENSURABILITY: A PSYCHOLOGICAL GAME MODEL OF CONTAGION
Peter H. Huang
146 University of Pennsylvania Law Review 1701 (1998)

Incommensurability claims have been in vogue of late in the legal academy. But, as with many instances of legal scholarship drawing on other academic disciplines, something often gets lost in the translation or (mis)application of ideas from other fields of inquiry. In this case, the idea of incommensurability comes from the philosophical literature, in particular, discussions of practical reasoning. There is much intuitive appeal to incommensurability claims, as vividly illustrated by the reader's or audience's reactions to such choice situations as those forcibly contemplated in *Sophie's Choice* or made in *Indecent Proposal*. Yet, perhaps because of the strong emotional resonance or moral outrage these "desperate exchanges" or "double binds" evoke in us, they may be mere fanciful, atypical hypotheticals and not real-life decisions faced every day by individuals, legal decisionmakers, or policy analysts who are engaged in so-called "cool" rational deliberation. . . .

The idea that any particular language constrains both a communicator and her audience should not be surprising, especially to multilingual individuals. Thus, the notion that people who have been exposed to the discourse of monetary commensurability might think and behave differently from those who have not is certainly plausible and a real possibility. Furthermore, there is evidence that students of economics act differently in experimental situations than students not exposed to economics. For example, a well-known study revealed that first-year economics graduate students are more apt to free-ride in experiments requiring private contributions to public goods. First-year economics graduate students also had difficulty with the meaning of "fairness" and basing their decisions on considerations of "fairness." This study has been criticized, however, for not controlling for age and gender differences between the "noneconomic" control groups (undergraduates and high school students with equal numbers of males and females) and the economics graduate students (predominantly older males). Another study, not subject to this particular criticism, investigated the effect of enrolling in an introductory microeconomics course at Cornell University on the answers to questions about a pair of hypothetical ethical dilemmas. The control group was an introductory astronomy class. There were two subject groups, one taught by an economist who specialized in the field of industrial organization and taught some rudimentary game theory, and one taught by a development economist who did not include any instruction on game theory. Students completed a survey during the first and last weeks of class. This survey consisted of four questions: two questions about losing or finding an envelope containing $100 and an individual's name and phone number, and two questions about receiving delivery of ten personal computers but only being billed for nine. Students indicated the probability that they would be honest, as well as their perceived probability that others would be honest. Because the above study design has a potential drawback of students understating the "undesirable" effects of their education to themselves and others, another complementary study design involved actual choices in experimental games with monetary payoffs. Students played a game involving cooperativeness, namely, the well-known prisoner's dilemma. The prisoner's dilemma is a two-person, one-shot game in which each player chooses to cooperate or defect.

The key feature of the prisoner's dilemma is that defecting is a dominant strategy for each player in that it yields higher payoffs to either player than does cooperating regardless of how the other player behaves. Both players defecting, however, results in the lowest total monetary payoff of all of the four possible outcomes. Thus, the prisoner's dilemma provides a setting to investigate the conflict between individual and social or group rationality (assuming the game is one-shot and there is common knowledge of players' rationality and preferences). Frank et al. found that the probability of an economics major defecting is about 0.17 higher than that of a non-economics major defecting when the subjects were not allowed to make promises about what they would do. When such promises, which were unenforceable due to their anonymity, were allowed, there were virtually no differences in defection rates. An exit questionnaire revealed that while 31% of the economics students explained their behavior solely with respect to features of the game, only 17% of the non-economics students did so. Finally, the study revealed that: (1) expectations about the other player's choice strongly influence a player's behavior; and (2) even holding expectations constant, economics students defect at a significantly higher rate than do non-economics students.

Other studies have found that economics majors behave significantly more like the neoclassical economics model predicts than do non-economics majors in ultimatum bargaining games. These are two-person games in which the first player (the allocator) has to propose how to divide a sum of money (ten dollars in the experiments) between that player and another player (the receiver), who can accept the proposed split, or refuse, in which case both players get nothing. The fact that these games are one-shot should rule out reputation and repetition effects. Standard economic theory predicts a division of $9.99 to player one and only $0.01 to the other player. But, experimental research found that fifty-fifty splits are the most commonly made proposal by allocators, while receivers will reject very one-sided proposals as being unfair. In both the role of allocator and receiver, economics (or commerce) majors acted more like standard economic theory predicts than non-economics majors (or psychology students). This experimental design assigned allocator and receiver roles through a preliminary word game, which might have led allocators to feel they deserved a bigger split than receivers did because they "earned" their position. This issue has been addressed in two well-known related studies, which replaced the word game with a coin flip game. Further, the above findings are robust with respect to the size of the monetary payoffs involved and the nationality of the subjects involved.

What do all of these findings mean? They certainly provide support for two propositions: (1) Economics is a language that affects the behavior and expectations of speaker and listener; and (2) there is a tendency for economics models to become self-fulfilling, although this is not always the case.

The issue of whether or not exposure to monetary commensurability by itself, as opposed to more generally the language of economics, affects behavior is not resolved by the above findings, however, because all of the above experiments investigating the impact of economics instruction are joint tests of not only the behavioral impacts of learning about monetary commensurability, but also the behavioral impacts of learning about other aspects of the language of economics, such as the assumption of rationality in the sense of the pursuit of self-interest. . . .

What is perhaps most disturbing about commensurability to incommensurabilists is commensurability with money because it is argued that money is a one-dimensional cardinal scale which flattens out and impoverishes the multidimensional contours and richness of life. But such a one-dimensional view of money is by no means universal, as evidenced by the findings of economic sociology and behavioral economics. Of course, the same criticism of projection of multiple dimensions of reality into a single dimension of analysis already applies to utilitarianism in general, even when utility functions are not expressed in wealth, but only are reducible to abstract "utils." . . .

NOTES & QUESTIONS

1.   Are some people troubled by explicit monetary commensurability being different from implicit monetary commensurability because the former leaves no "wiggle room" while the latter preserves possibilities for being deliberately ignorant, imprecise, or vague about monetary commensurability and trade-offs? Do you view your experience with American legal education as fostering a belief in explicit and universal monetary commensurability? Why do some people find monetary commensurability morally disturbing, while others do not?

2.   Professor Holly Doremus is concerned about whether our consumer society is compatible with environmental values that respect nature:

> Frugality strikes me as perhaps the most difficult of the indirect environmental values to develop in today's America. Indeed, I wonder whether today it is properly considered "conventional" at all, in the wake of the "greed is good" 1980s, with conspicuous consumption considered nearly patriotic and the Vice-President arguing publicly that while energy conservation may be a "personal virtue" it is not one the government should encourage. Nonetheless, frugality is not an entirely forgotten value. A movement has developed to celebrate and encourage "voluntary simplicity," and prominent commentators have argued that endless consumption, far from proving satisfying, is a barrier to a happy, fulfilling life. For those who adopt it, frugality can apparently provide considerable personal satisfaction and can encourage environmentally responsible behavior.

Holly Doremus, *Shaping the Future: The Dialectic of Law and Environmental Values*, 37 U.C. Davis Law Review 233, 252 (2003). Do you share her concerns? What roles do and can portrayals of business and consumption in popular culture have in shaping our environmental values?

3. Consider this observation about our attitudes toward wealth maximization:

> We find evidence of manipulation of the belief set in our popular culture toward wealth maximization; examples include . . . the notion that "greed is good" from the famous line in the Hollywood movie *Wall Street*, and the adage, "If you are so smart, why aren't you rich?" Advertisements consist of nothing but attempts to modify belief sets, by everything from providing simple information to more active influence through suggestion of counter-factual rules (e.g., if you owned this car, the opposite sex would love you). The consumer society is fueled by the notion that one should acquire ever fancier and more sophisticated physical possessions. The consumer society "works" even if consumers do not actually consume or enjoy the objects that they buy, so long as consumers purchase.

William H. Widen, *Spectres of Law & Economics*, 102 Michigan Law Review 1423, 1439 (2004). Are corporations likely to last in a competitive market system if they only sell products that consumers are induced to purchase via commercial advertising, peer pressure, social conformity, and sophisticated marketing, but do not actually consume or enjoy? Do you really enjoy or even actually consume all that you purchase? *See* Tim Kasser, *The High Price of Materialism* (2002). Does a market society require that its consumers perpetually want products they will not like? *See* Juliet B. Schor, *The Overspent American: Why We Want What We Don't Need* (1999). Do people living in modern societies face overwhelmingly too many choices in their lives? *See* Barry Schwartz, *The Pardox of Choice: Why More Is Less* (2004). Should a government enact legal and public policy to pursue higher social well-being, even if that means less gross domestic product? *See* Derek Bok, *The Politics of Happiness: What Government Can Learn from the New Research on Well-Being* (2010); Carol Graham, *The Pursuit of Happiness: An Economy of Well-Being* (2011).

4. *Capitalism: A Love Story* criticizes the current American economic system and more generally capitalism. Using clips from *Jesus of Nazareth*, documentary filmmaker Michael Moore asks if capitalism is a sin and whether Jesus would be a capitalist, who wanted to maximize profits, deregulate banking, and have the sick pay out-of-pocket for pre-existing conditions. He asks if one could patent the sun and questions how the brightest American youth are drawn towards finance and not science. He proceeds to Wall Street asking for non-technical explanations of derivative securities in general and credit default swaps in particular. Both a former vice-president of Lehman Brothers and current Harvard University economics professor Kenneth Rogoff fail to clearly explain either term. Moore thus concludes that our complex economic system and its arcane terminology exist simply to confuse people and that Wall Street effectively has a crazy casino mentality. Do you find Moore's arguments compelling? How about his unique style of documentary-making and usual ambush interviews? Are you more or less convinced of his thesis because of his particular style?

5. The PBS NOVA episode *Mind Over Money*, which originally aired on April 26, 2010, asks whether markets can possibly be rational when people clearly are not. In posing this question, the show offers an entertaining, yet quite informative survey of elements of behavioral economics and finance. Its companion website, at

http://www.pbs.org/wgbh/nova/body/mind-over-money.html, provides additional re-source materials concerning the role of emotions in financial decision-making. Does it matter for law and policy how people make their financial judgments and decisions? If so, then how and if not, then why not?

6. The documentary *Inside Job* and its companion website http://www.sonyclassics.com/insidejob/ present a compelling argument in five parts of how the American financial services industry has systematically and systemically corrupted the United States government and in so doing brought about changes in banking practices and legal policies that led directly to the Great Recession. Are you convinced by this argument? Did you find the movie to be unexpected in any way? Would you be surprised to learn about some minor factual inaccuracies in this film? Would that make a difference in your views about business law?

7. The documentary *Chasing Madoff* tells the tale of Harry Markopolos' multi-year crusade to expose the multi-billion dollar Ponzi scheme perpetrated by Bernie Madoff. Alleged victims of this massive fraud include the celebrity couple of Kyra Sedgwick (of *The Closer* on TNT) and Kevin Bacon (of such films as *Apollo 13* (1995), *Sleepers* (1996), and *Mystic River* (2003)). The Dodd-Frank Wall Street Reform and Consumer Protection Act included a broad set of whistleblower provisions under which the Securities and Exchange Commission adopted specific rules and procedures to incentivize potential whistleblowers by way of cash rewards and protection from retaliation. Is a choice to become a whistleblower typically a good career move? How hard is the decision to be a whistleblower? How do most business law whistleblowers currently fare?

8. *Wall Street: Money Never Sleeps* (2010), the lackluster sequel to the iconic and often quoted *Wall Street* (1987), did not do as well commercially as its predecessor. The second *Wall Street* film tells a tale of revenge and redemption that has the Great Recession as its backdrop. Its moral is that love has more power than money. Do you find the original or the sequel to be more compelling or memorable as a parable about capitalism, money, and power? Is either film temporally appropriate and a reflection of its own time? What do you think would be the audience reactions if the films came out at other times than they did and in particular if a movie similar to *Wall Street* were to appear today, or a movie similar to its sequel had appeared back in 1987?

9. What do you think of the metaphors of Darwinian selection and the "survival of the fittest" applied to market actors? Should law and policy strive to protect market actors who are likely to be preyed upon by other market participants? Do market participants who are not the fittest nonetheless play a valuable social role of providing liquidity to more fit or informed market actors? *See* Gregory La Blanc & Jeffrey J. Rachlinski, *In Praise of Investor Irrationality, in The Law and Economics of Irrational Behavior* 570 (Francesco Parisi & Vernon L. Smith eds. 2005).

10. Markets are merely one out of many possible ways to allocate resources and organize economic activity. Other common possible resource allocation mechanisms include auction, bribery, coercion, "first-come, first-serve," force, intelligence, litigation, meritocracy, physical appearance, random assignment, seniority, strength, "women and children first," and many voting procedures, such as approval voting, Borda count, Condorcet method, majority voting, plurality voting, range voting, and weighted voting. What do you think of these alternatives? Do you feel that markets and their attendant emphasis on autonomy, empowerment, freedom of choice, and personal responsibility fit more comfortably with individualistic versus collectivistic societies? For what particular kinds of scarce items do markets work particularly well or badly? Do you seem to notice that parties who are well-off in terms of initial endowments of resources tend to favor markets or voluntary exchange and vice versa? Do you realize that the form of economic organization governing any particular situation is variable and is chosen by governments and people? Similarly, sellers often engage in market design to maximize profits or some other goal. Can you think of examples from popular culture of non-market mechanism design?

Chapter 14

INTERNATIONAL LAW

A. FILMOGRAPHY

Death and the Maiden (1994)

In the Name of the Father (1993)

Judgment in Berlin (1988)

Music Box (1989)

Storm (2009)

B. CHARACTERISTICS

While popular culture has in the past not tended to pay much attention to the difference between international law and comparative law, or to the niceties of extra-territoriality, it has begun to focus more and more on the clash of legal cultures. In many ways, international law seems made for pop cultural examination. For one thing, much tension exists in the ways that nations interpret the underlying disputes that make up much of the legal conflict that emerges in international legal tribunals. For another, the fact that international tribunal decisions are binding only on the parties means that conflicts may continue or recur. Conflicts that fuel international legal feuds — over territorial boundaries, resources, and war crimes, to name just a few reasons that nations take their arguments to court — are juicy opportunities for films, television miniseries, and blockbuster novels, and a wonderful opportunity for popular culture to explore and educate the public.

In everyday speech, international law is the law that governs the relationships existing between and among countries. Its rules originated in Roman and canon law but coalesced with the rise of the Renaissance states. In order of importance, the sources of international law are treaties (which can be either bilateral or multilateral and may or may not be "self-executing"), customary law, learned works, and case law (which has persuasive but not precedential value). Because of its deep respect for and regular reliance on scholarly writings, international law is particularly suitable for academic study.

An entity claiming nationhood must prove that it has a defined territory, a stable population, a functioning government, and the ability to engage in foreign relations. These four elements are the sine qua non of sovereignty and, in bifurcated political systems like those of Australia, Canada, and the United States, help to define and distinguish the roles of the states (or provinces) and the federal government.

Because only nations can assert rights and take on duties under international law, individuals, partnerships, corporations, and others are barred from the field. Nevertheless, their claims and concerns can and often have been asserted in international tribunals by countries acting on their behalf (usually in the aftermath of a war). Since 1945, such interests also have been championed by an ever-growing number of INGOs, or international non-governmental organizations. Specifically recognized by Article 71 of the United Nations Charter, INGOs have become particularly important advocates of human rights.

Although a lawyer appearing on behalf of a government in an international court is called an "agent" rather than an "attorney," he or she has the same duties as the government lawyer who appears in a domestic court. Unlike domestic courts, however, international courts cannot hear a case unless both parties agree. Likewise, international courts lack the enforcement powers possessed by domestic courts. These are obvious and serious weaknesses, and have severely limited the utility of international courts. They also explain why governments often resort to such extra-judicial processes as conciliation, mediation, and arbitration and some-times opt to take their arguments directly to the "court of international public opinion."

C. INTERNATIONAL CRIMINAL COURTS AND THE RIGHTS OF THE ACCUSED

What rights do parties (particularly the criminally accused) have under international law? In the 2009 film *Storm*, an Australian prosecutor named Hannah Maynard takes on the task of convicting a man accused of killing innocent Bosnian civilians. But her case seems to evaporate when her star witness must admit that he has fabricated his testimony. The prosecutor comes under pressure to continue the case, but the judge in charge believes the manner in which she seeks out witnesses and files motions unnecessarily delays the proceeding and may be prejudicing the defendant. The case becomes a web of deceit and deception, with any number of well meaning and not-so-well meaning individuals repeatedly telling Maynard that they were not certain whether they should tell her what they knew and/or when they should tell her. Knowledge of bad acts, unwillingness to testify, unwillingness to cooperate, and ultimately, a distrust of the entire process continually threatens to scuttle Maynard's entire case against the accused. But the ultimate question remains: is he actually guilty? And to whom does Maynard owe her loyalty? To her witness? To the untold hundreds who died? To the system? Or to the truth, however one defines truth?

The International Criminal Court, which meets at the Hague, and of which Hannah Maynard is a part, makes its procedures and rules public at http://www.icc-cpi.int/Menus/ICC/Legal+Texts+and+Tools/.

Among the rights that it tries to balance are those of the criminal defendant and those of the witnesses who are sometimes extremely unwilling to come forward. Consider in particular in this regard Section III of the Rules of Procedure and

Evidence of the International Criminal Court, Adopted by the Assembly of States Parties, First Session, New York, 3-10 September 2002 (Official Records ICC-ASP/1/3), which discusses the rights and protection of victims and witnesses and Section V of the same Rules on jurisdiction and admissibility.

NOTES & QUESTIONS

1.   *Storm* examines the difficulty of prosecuting individuals accused of war crimes when the atrocities are so heinous that accusers might manufacture evidence in order to see the defendants convicted. These accusers truly believe, like Paulina Escobar in the film *Death and the Maiden*, that the ends justify the means. Like Gerardo Escobar in *Death and the Maiden*, Hannah Maynard wonders whether she will be able to prosecute the defendant successfully once she learns that her star witness has fabricated his testimony. But are Maynard and Escobar's situations precisely similar? Maynard, while part of the international legal regime set up to try war crimes, is a prosecutor from a particular member state. Escobar is now part of his country's administration.

2.   Part of Hannah Maynard's problem is that she fails to vet her witness. But as she points out to her superiors, the area of the Balkans in which the atrocities are alleged to have occurred is a dangerous and difficult place to investigate. She necessarily took some of his testimony on faith. Given the situation in the area, was she justified in doing so? To what extent can or should prosecutors who prepare war crimes trials take the testimony of witnesses "on faith"? After all, these individuals often come forward reluctantly and at great risk to their own lives? How likely is it that they might be lying about their experiences? Consider the debate over the testimony of a young woman, later identified as the daughter of the Kuwaiti Ambassador to the United States, that Iraqi troops had thrown Kuwaiti babies from their incubators and taken the equipment back to Iraq. Physicians contradicted her report, but it fueled calls for what became Operation Desert Storm. *See* "Doctors Reportedly Deny Iraqis Took Away Babies' Incubators," *L.A. Times*, March 16, 1991, at http://articles.latimes.com/1991-03-16/news/mn-164_1_babies-incubators. The resulting journalistic confusion became a scene in the film *Live From Baghdad* (HBO, 2002).

3.   Some academics have begun to question the veracity of testimony given before truth commissions and tribunals and procedural guarantees available to the accused. *See* Alexander Zahar, *The Problem of False Testimony at the International Criminal Tribunal for Rwanda* at http://www.heritagetpirdefense.org/papers/Alexander_Zahar_The_problem_of_false_testimony_at_the_ICTR.pdf. Do you think such problems are more systemic in international criminal tribunals than in domestic criminal trials? Note that Dr. Zahar is assisting in the defense of Dr Radovan Karadžiæ, who is currently facing charges before the International Criminal Tribunal for the Former Yugoslavia. *See* http://www.law.mq.edu.au/html/staff/azahar.htm. Do Dr. Zahar's consulting activities change your opinion of his scholarly writings?

4.   With regard to the depiction of international and comparative law, consider the 1997 film *Red Corner*, in which U.S. citizen Jack Moore, played by Richard Gere, finds himself wrongly accused of murder. While the American embassy in

Beijing monitors the situation, its options for intervening directly are limited. In addition, political reasons cause it to tread warily. As a result, Moore finds himself at the mercy of his hosts.

A country that does not treat foreigners well, however, runs the risk that other countries will do likewise to its citizens. Thus, the principle of reciprocity often helps to mitigate extreme conduct. In addition, where a country has formally granted rights to foreign nationals (either by treaty or under its own law), embassies have much greater leverage.

Ironically, the United States has consistently failed to live up to its obligations under the 1963 Vienna Convention on Consular Relations, 21 U.S.T. 77, 596 U.N.T.S. 261, which requires foreign officials to be notified whenever one of their citizens is arrested. Although the International Court of Justice (ICJ) has ordered the United States to abide by the treaty, *see Case Concerning Avena and Other Mexican Nationals (Mexico v. United States of America)*, 2004 I.C.J. 12, 43 I.L.M. 581, the United States Supreme Court has declined (at least for the moment) to give effect to this judgment. *See Medellin v. Dretke*, 544 U.S. 660 (2005). For a further discussion, compare Vicki S. Jackson, *World Habeas Corpus*, 91 Cornell Law Review 303 (2006) (applauding the ICJ's decision) with Julian G. Ku, *International Delegations and the New World Court Order*, 81 Washington Law Review 1 (2006) (criticizing the ICJ's decision).

5. In *Red Corner*, defense attorney Shen Yuelin, played by Ling Bai, tells Moore that if he pleads innocent, he will undoubtedly be found guilty, sentenced to die, and executed within a week (with his family billed for the cost of the bullet used to kill him). Thus, his only hope is to plead guilty, admit his crime, and humbly accept his punishment. Does this mean that there is no presumption of innocence in the Chinese legal system, or merely that the Chinese legal system only tries those who are guilty?

6. Criminal justice systems typically are designed to serve four specific functions: truth-finding, punishment, restitution, and rehabilitation. In movies about American courts, truth-finding normally is deemed the most important, while in Red Corner the filmmakers suggest that the Chinese legal system places a premium on rehabilitation. How accurate is either of these views?

7. Suppose the situation in *Red Corner* were reversed, and Moore were a Chinese defendant in a United States courtroom. In what ways would the story have changed?

D. EXTRATERRITORIALITY

In the film *Judgment in Berlin*, Martin Sheen plays Herbert J. Stern, the New Jersey federal district judge who presided over the trial of Hans Tiede and Ingrid Ruske. In August 1978, the two East Germans had escaped to West Berlin by diverting a Polish airliner. Incensed, the Soviet Union demanded that the pair be severely punished as hijackers, and the United States hoped that Stern would conduct a quick trial, hand down a suitably harsh verdict, and thereby put the incident to rest. But Stern refused to be rushed and in time concluded that American law guaranteed Tiede and Ruske a trial by a jury of their peers.

Consider the film's depictions of the various interests at work. While they are exaggerated to some extent, the Cold War certainly dictated that the U.S. government be rather more sensitive to political concerns than it might have been otherwise. Consider also the scene in which Judge Stern's wife confronts him with their family's treatment at the hands of the Germans during World War II, telling him that she does not think he can be impartial. She raises an important question that continues to concern us today — to what extent does the Holocaust inform and control decision-making in legislatures, in courts, and in policy-making, as well as in forming public opinion, even when we may not be aware that it is doing so?

UNITED STATES v. TIEDE
86 F.R.D. 227 (U.S. Ct. Berlin 1979)

STERN, JUDGE.

The Prosecution's basic position is that the United States Constitution does not apply to these proceedings because Berlin is a territory governed by military conquest. The Prosecution maintains that the question whether constitutional rights must be afforded in territories governed by United States authorities outside the United States depends on the nature and degree of association between such territories and the United States, and that the relationship between the United States and Berlin is such that the Constitution does not apply in proceedings in Berlin.

As a corollary to this position, the Prosecution contends that everything which concerns the conduct of an occupation is a "political question" not subject to court review. Thus, it states in its brief: "Berlin is an occupied city. It is not United States territory. The United States presence there grows out of conquest, not the consent of the governed. The United States and the other Western Allies have, over time, made political judgments to turn over to the Berliners control of important institutions and functions of governance. But these decisions reflect political judgments, not legal necessity."

The Prosecution further argues that this Court is not an independent tribunal established to adjudicate the rights of the defendants and lacks the power to make a ruling contrary to the foreign policy interests of the United States. This, it contends, follows from the fact that "United States occupation courts in Germany have been instruments of the United States occupation policy."

It was not until 1951 that the state of war was formally ended. It was not until 1955 that sovereignty was returned to the German people everywhere in the Western zones of occupation excepting, of course, Berlin. It is against this background that we must evaluate the claim of the Prosecution that the civilian German population in Berlin in 1979 may be governed by the United States Department of State without any constitutional limitation.

The Prosecution maintains that any rights to which the defendants are entitled must be granted by Secretary of State [Cyrus] Vance, or they do not exist at all: "The basic point is this: a defendant tried in the United States Court for Berlin is afforded certain rights found in the Constitution, but he receives these rights not by force of the Constitution itself . . . , but because the Secretary of State has made the determination that these certain rights should be provided." Further, the Prosecution argues, such rights would be granted not because of constitutional dictates, but because they would be in accord with our longstanding foreign policy.

Pursuing its thesis that this Court is nothing more than an implementing arm of the United States' foreign policy, the Prosecution instructs the Court that the Secretary of State has determined, as a matter of foreign policy, that the right to a jury trial should not be afforded to the defendants. The Prosecution's brief asserts: "The conduct of occupation is fundamentally different from the exercise of civil government in the United States. The actions of an occupying power, from necessity, may be inconsistent with the wishes or attitudes of the occupied population. In short, the assumptions and values which underlie the great common law conception of trial by jury do not necessarily have a place in the conduct of an occupation. Whether it does in a particular situation is quintessentially a political question, to be determined by the officers responsible for the United States conduct of this occupation, and not by this Court."

The Court finds the Prosecution's argument to be entirely without merit. First, there has never been a time when United States authorities exercised governmental powers in any geographical area — whether at war or in times of peace — without regard for their own Constitution. *Ex parte Milligan*, 71 U.S. (4 Wall.)2 (1866). Nor has there ever been a case in which constitutional officers, such as the Secretary of State, have exercised the powers of their office without constitutional limitations. Even in the long discredited case of In re Ross, 140 U.S. 453, 11 S. Ct. 897 (1891), in which American consular officers were permitted to try United States citizens in certain "non-Christian" countries, the Court made its decision under the Constitution — not in total disregard of it. The distinction is subtle but real: the applicability of any provision of the Constitution is itself a point of constitutional law, to be decided in the last instance by the judiciary, not by the Executive Branch.

This fundamental principle was forcefully and clearly announced by the Supreme Court more than a century ago in *Ex parte Milligan*, 71 U.S. (4 Wall.) 2, 120-21, (1866):

> [The Framers of the American Constitution] foresaw that troublous times would arise, when rulers and people would become restive under restraint, and seek by sharp and decisive measures to accomplish ends deemed just and proper; and that the principles of constitutional liberty would be in peril, unless established by irrepealable law. The history of the world had taught them that what was done in the past might be attempted in the future. The Constitution of the United States is a law for rulers and people, equally in war and in peace, and covers with the shield of its protection all classes of men, at all times, and under all circumstances. No doctrine, involving more pernicious consequences, was ever invented by the wit of man than that any of its provisions can be suspended during any of the great exigencies of government. Such a doctrine leads directly to anarchy or despotism, but the theory of necessity on which it is based is false; for the government, within the Constitution, has all the powers granted to it,

which are necessary to preserve its existence; as has been happily proved by the result of the great effort to throw off its just authority.

Although the Supreme Court was reviewing the power of military commissions organized by military authorities in the United States during the Civil War, the wisdom of the principle set forth above is nowhere better demonstrated than in this city, during this occupation, and before this Court.

The Prosecution's position, if accepted by this Court, would have dramatic consequences not only for the two defendants whom the United States has chosen to arraign before the Court, but for every person within the territorial limits of the United States Sector of Berlin. If the occupation authorities are not governed by the Constitution in this Court, they are not governed by the Constitution at all. And, if the occupation authorities may act free of all constitutional restraints, no one in the American Sector of Berlin has any protection from their untrammeled discretion. If there are no constitutional protections, there is no First Amendment, no Fifth Amendment or Sixth Amendment; even the Thirteenth Amendment's prohibition of involuntary servitude would be inapplicable. The American authorities, if the Secretary of State so decreed, would have the power, in time of peace and with respect to German and American citizens alike, to arrest any person without cause, to hold a person incommunicado, to deny an accused the benefit of counsel, to try a person summarily and to impose sentence — all as a part of the unreviewable exercise of foreign policy. This Court does not suggest that the American occupation authorities intend to carry the Prosecution's thesis to its logical conclusion. Nonetheless, people have been deceived before in their assessment of the intentions of their own leaders and their own government; and those who have left the untrammeled, unchecked power in the hands of their leaders have not had a happy experience. It is a first principle of American life — not only life at home but life abroad — that everything American public officials do is governed by, measured against, and must be authorized by the United States Constitution.

As the Supreme Court made clear in *Ex parte Milligan*, the Constitution is a living document to be applied under changing circumstances, in changing conditions and even in different places. This Court finds devoid of merit the suggestion that the Prosecution has no constitutional obligations or that this Court lacks the competence to inquire into those obligations. The Constitution of the United States manifestly applies to these proceedings.

Second, the Court rejects the Prosecution's contention that, even if the Constitution applies to these proceedings, it is the State Department rather than the Court which interprets the Constitution.

It is clear, because the Constitution applies to these proceedings, that the defendants have the right to due process of law. Due process requires that if the United States convenes this Court, it must come before the Court as a litigant and not as a commander. The Secretary of State, in establishing a court, appointing a judge, and then electing to appear before it as a litigant, delegates his powers to the Court. Thereafter, the United States may, and indeed it should, press strongly for its views. It may argue them and, if it is so authorized, may appeal from an adverse decision. It may not, however, compel that its views be victorious. Thus, the responsibility falls solely upon the Court to declare the requirements of the Constitution in this proceeding.

The sole but novel question before the Court is whether friendly aliens, charged with civil offenses in a United States court in Berlin, under the unique circumstances of the continuing United States occupation of Berlin, have a right to a jury trial. This Court is not concerned with the procedures to be used by a United States military commission trying a case in wartime or during the belligerent occupation of enemy territory before the termination of war. This case does not involve the theft or destruction of military property. Nor does it involve spying, an offense against Allied military authority or a violation of the laws of war. Further, this Court does not sit as an international tribunal, but only as an American court.

The defendants are German citizens. It is of no moment whether they be deemed citizens of the Federal Republic or of the German Democratic Republic because the United States is at peace with, and maintains diplomatic relations with, both states. Thus, in law, the defendants are friendly aliens. They are not enemy nationals, enemy belligerents, or prisoners of war. The defendants are charged with non-military offenses under German law which would have been fully cognizable in the open and functioning German courts in West Berlin, but for the withdrawal of the German courts' jurisdiction by the United States Commandant.

The Court takes judicial notice that the occupation regime in existence in Greater Berlin in 1979 is unique in the annals of international relations. Berlin has played, and is destined to play in the future, a special role in the preservation of the free world. The genesis of the occupation is to be found in belligerent occupation, but the relationship between the "occupiers" and the "occupied" in Greater Berlin has undergone fundamental changes since Berlin was initially occupied in 1945 by force of arms. The Court therefore rejects the Prosecution's suggestion that the obligations of the American occupation authorities to the people of Berlin are to be determined solely by rules of law applicable to belligerent occupation of enemy territories.

The parties have extensively briefed and argued whether, in the setting of this case, the Constitution requires a jury trial. The Court finds that none of the precedents cited are dispositive of the issue and that the Constitution requires that these defendants be afforded a trial by jury.

The Prosecution seeks to distinguish most prior decisions dealing with the rights of an accused in occupation courts from the instant proceeding on the ground that the prior adjudications concerned the rights to be afforded to American citizens, whereas the defendants here are aliens. Although it is true that most of the cases discussed concerned prosecutions of American citizens abroad, the Court finds the purported distinction unpersuasive in the context of a trial of friendly aliens, accused of non-military offenses, in Berlin in 1979. The Prosecution conceded in oral argument that in its view aliens, as well as citizens, enjoyed the same "non-rights" in this Court; that is, neither need be afforded a trial by jury. More importantly, whatever distinction may still be permissible between citizens and friendly aliens in civil cases, the Fifth Amendment to the Constitution requires, in terms admitting of no ambiguity, that "no person" shall be deprived of life or liberty without due process of law; similarly, the Sixth Amendment protects all who are "accused," without qualification. Finally, it appears to the Court that the United States is precluded from treating these defendants less favorably than United States citizens, not only by its own Constitution, but also by [the 1963 Tokyo Convention], an international agreement [on aerial hijacking] to which the United States is a party.

Therefore, this Court believes that these defendants should be afforded the same constitutional rights that the United States would have to afford its own nationals when brought before this Court. In sum, this Court does not hold that jury trials must be afforded in occupation courts everywhere and under all circumstances; the Court holds only that if the United States convenes a United States court in Berlin, under the present circumstances, and charges civilians with non-military offenses, the United States must provide the defendants with the same constitutional safeguards that it must provide to civilian defendants in any other United States court.

NOTES & QUESTIONS

1. Did Judge Stern reach the right conclusion, i.e., the United States Constitution was applicable to the citizens of West Berlin? Or should he have deferred to the executive branch, as the prosecution urged? If he had, what would have been the practical consequences for the defendants? And to what extent would his decision have been binding on future American courts?

2. After reading Judge Stern's opinion and viewing the film, do you have the sense that he was engaging in "result-oriented" judging? If so, is this a basis for criticizing him and invalidating the decision?

3. In an interview with Deutsche Welle, a German television and radio network, Judge Stein, who resigned from the federal bench in 1987 and returned to private practice in New Jersey, discusses parallels between the *Tiede* case and the situation of prisoners held at Guantanamo Bay. Judge Stein says, "State took the position that they had the right to define what rights the defendants had, because Tiede and Ruske were neither U.S. citizens nor on U.S. territory, but stood before an occupational court, a conquerer's court so to speak, the kind of court they have now instituted at Guantanamo, where the same issues (concerning defendants' rights) have percolated up." *See* http://www.dw-world.de/dw/article/0,,3587971,00.html.

Do you see parallels between the detained East Germans and the detainees at Guantanamo? Consider the question posed by the film *The Response* (2008), starring Kate Mulgrew, Peter Riegert, and Sig Libowitz as three JAG officers required to rule on the fate of an enemy combatant. Mr. Libowitz, an actor, conceived of the film while studying at the University of Maryland Law School; he used actual Gitmo transcripts as the basis for his script. Two of the officers make their decisions known at the end of the film. One decides that the detainee should continue to be held; the second thinks he should be released. The "lady or the tiger" ending asks you (and the JAG officer left undecided) to tip the balance. What rights should a non-citizen have in a U.S. court but in territory not within U.S. borders?

E.   REPARATIONS OR TRUTH COMMISSIONS?

In recent years, countries emerging from civil wars, dictatorships, and the like have often convened so-called "truth commissions" or "reconciliation commissions" to achieve national closure. To encourage abusers to come forward and tell their stories, such entities normally are empowered to grant witnesses amnesty or immunity. When victims learn what happened to them, they obtain this information at the expense of their right to reparations. Critics of the commissions sometimes suggest this sacrifice is too great and that the commissions provide cheap justice.

The play *Death and the Maiden* (1990) by Chilean writer Ariel Dorfman provocatively explores truth commissions and those affected by them. It contemplates the extent to which a reconstituted democracy might and should turn its back on the victims of the regime it replaced. In the film adaptation of the play, the lawyer Gerardo Escobar, played by Stuart Wilson, agrees to serve as a member of the commission in an unnamed third-world country. While doing so will presumably help his nation to heal, it leaves his wife Paulina, played by Sigourney Weaver, with no ready means of avenging her rape at the hands of Dr. Roberto Miranda, a former government official. Played by Ben Kingsley, Miranda may or may not be guilty of the crime.

ON DORFMAN'S *DEATH AND THE MAIDEN*
David Luban
10 Yale Journal of Law & the Humanities 115 (1998)

Of course the Investigating Commission isn't going to do it [bring Paulina's torturer to justice], because political realities make that impossible. The fledgling democracy dangles from a chain of compromises and constraints. Democracy in return for amnesty. A truth commission in return for confidential findings. The army in its barracks, but still armed and watchful and menacing. An investigation, but only for victims who are dead, because living victims may still be dangerous to their tormentors, and their tormentors are still dangerous to the democracy. Paulina knows these realities but rejects them; Gerardo accepts them. Perhaps he even approves of them. As he tells Paulina, "A member of the president's Commission . . . should be showing exemplary signs of moderation and equanimity. . . ."

In his image of his mission, Gerardo ironically is not very far from Roberto Miranda, who lectures him when Paulina is out of the room: "She isn't the voice of civilization, you are. She isn't a member of the president's Commission, you are." Later, the doctor insists that "the country is reaching reconciliation and peace."

Gerardo, it seems, has an optimistic view of his mission and of the nation's future. During the dictatorship, he took deadly risks as an activist, but he was lucky: Paulina never revealed his identity under torture. If she had, she tells the doctor, someone would be investigating Gerardo's murder rather than the other way around. Because he was lucky, Gerardo never had a personal reason to abandon his belief in happy endings. If the truth be known, he has avoided unpleasant knowledge that might shake his optimism.

For example, after Paulina's release, Gerardo never asked her exactly what they did to her. He told himself that it would be better for her that way, just as he told himself a few hours ago that lying to Paulina about whether he had accepted the President's invitation would be better for her. Both times, actually, Gerardo did what was better for him. To Paulina, "human rights violations" means rape and having her face shoved into a bucket of her own shit and electric current burning her genitals so that she can never have a baby. To Gerardo, much as he loves her, "human rights violations" remains a deeply emotional, but essentially abstract, legal category. He has vowed to devote his career to justice, but to do that he needs to believe in happy endings. He needs to believe that the living can put the past behind them. He is a lawyer, and law itself, implicitly promising to lift us out of the state of nature, rests on those beliefs. Otherwise, law can never end the chain of violence. As Doctor Miranda tells Paulina, "someone did terrible things to you and now you're doing something terrible to me and tomorrow somebody else is going to — on and on and on."

When Gerardo explains to Paulina which cases his Commission is entitled to investigate, he can't bring himself to use the ugly and impolitic word "murder." Instinctively, he finds a euphemism: He speaks of "cases that are beyond — let's say, repair." Only murder, he seems to think, is beyond repair; only death is irreversible. Paulina bitterly echoes, "Beyond repair. Irreparable, huh?" And he replies, "I don't like to talk about this, Paulina."

Of course he doesn't. How can he harbor any hopes for their marriage if the damage his wife sustained, which was less than murder, turns out to be irreparable? And how can he harbor any hopes for a democratic society if the damage to all the dictatorship's other living victims is irreparable? Gerardo cannot cope with Jean Amery's observation, based on his own experiences at the hands of the Gestapo: "Anyone who has suffered torture never again will be able to be at ease in the world. . . . Faith in humanity, already cracked by the first slap in the face, then demolished by torture, is never acquired again." Jacobo Timerman, tortured for thirty months by the Argentine police during the Dirty War, confesses: "I cannot prevent the memories of the tortures from spreading themselves over my daily life — like a jigsaw puzzle that a neat and careful child spreads piece by piece over the floor of his room." To go on, Gerardo needs to hold the concrete physical reality of torture and humiliation, the jigsaw puzzle, at arm's length.

Perhaps that is why Gerardo is so shocked at the sight of Roberto Miranda, bleeding from a head wound, helplessly bound to a chair in Gerardo's own living room, gagging on Paulina's underpants stuffed in his mouth. When Gerardo has collected himself, he says: "Paulina, I want you to know that what you are doing is going to have serious consequences." To which she replies ironically: "Serious, huh? Irreparable, huh?"

What is irreparable, and what is not? Can a society be repaired unless its killers, rapists, and torturers are named and exposed? Can it be repaired if its killers, rapists, and torturers are named and exposed? That is the overarching question of transitional justice; it may even be the overarching question of life in human society. Just as no relationship can survive in the complete absence of truth, no relationship can survive in the complete absence of lies, nor in the complete absence of forgiveness. . . .

Gerardo wants to heal his nation by doing justice. What did Paulina want when she took Doctor Miranda captive? At first, she tells Gerardo, she wanted to torture him in every way that they tortured her. Then she wanted to rape him, perhaps with a broom handle. But finally, she says:

> I began to realize that wasn't what I really wanted — something that physical. And you know what conclusion I came to, the only thing I really want? I want him to confess. I want him to sit in front of that cassette recorder and tell me what he did — not just to me, everything, to everybody — and then have him write it out in his own handwriting and sign it and I would keep a copy forever — with all the information, the names and data, all the details. That's what I want.

Now, at last, we know what the trial is about. Paulina wants to do the legal justice work of the Investigating Commission — the work that politics prevents it from doing.

Well, Paulina is hardly the first vigilante with that idea. As Felix Frankfurter once warned, "There can be no free society without law administered through an independent judiciary. If one man can be allowed to determine for himself what is law, every man can. That means first chaos, then tyranny." *United States v. United Mine Workers*, 330 U.S. 258, 312 (1947) (Frankfurter, J., concurring) Taking justice into your own hands is dangerous; even Paulina admits at one point that she "still had a doubt" that Miranda is the right man. Gerardo, a lawyer to the core, entirely agrees with Frankfurter:

> *Gerardo*: You know that I have spent a good part of my life defending the law. If there was one thing that revolted me in the past regime it was that they accused so many men and women and did not give the accused any chance of defending themselves, so even if this man committed genocide on a daily basis, he has the right to defend himself.

Paulina does not bother to point out that Gerardo is admitting that the previous regime's denial of due process revolted him more than what they did to his wife. Instead, she drops a bombshell:

> *Paulina*: But I have no intention of denying him that right, Gerardo. I'll give you all the time you need to speak to your client, in private.

If we wanted to treat Dorfman's characters allegorically, Paulina would be named "Memory" and Gerardo "Due Process." Gerardo must be the doctor's defense lawyer, because only due process stands between the doctor and the accusing, possibly inaccurate, power of memory.

But Dorfman's characters are not mere allegories, and Gerardo, a man of compassion as well as a lawyer, worries that due process alone may yield the wrong outcome:

> *Gerardo*: There's a problem, of course, you may not have thought of, Paulina. What if he has nothing to confess?

> *Paulina*: Tell him if he doesn't confess, I'll kill him.

Gerardo: Paulina, you're not listening to me. What can he confess if he's innocent?

Paulina: If he's innocent? Then he's really screwed.

Paulina may sound heartless, but she is merely stating a straightforward fact about every system of criminal justice in the world. Due process is entirely consistent with wrong verdicts, in which case, if you're innocent, you're really screwed. As Robert Cover has reminded us, the rule of law is not merely due process, impartially administered rights, or textual interpretation. The rule of law is channeled violence, and even when it works punctiliously, innocent people are occasionally screwed. Paulina may understand the meaning of due process better than Gerardo. Due process will not stop her from blowing a hole in Roberto Miranda's head if he refuses to confess to crimes he may never have committed. To Gerardo's credit, he wants something more than due process.

To achieve that something more, he makes unauthorized use of the testimony he has just elicited from Paulina. The truth commissioner metamorphoses into the defense lawyer, and Gerardo supplies Miranda with details from Paulina's tape to include in his confession. After all, the doctor pleads, "I need to know what it is I did, you've got to understand that I don't know what I have to confess. . . . I'll need your help, you'd have to tell me." Truth can always be coopted to ulterior purposes; as every lawyer knows, ulterior uses of truth are the only uses adjudicatory systems recognize. Adjudication's aim is closure. Factfinding is only an instrument of closure; and to the extent that institutional truth-seeking obstructs closure, all legal systems avoid it. . . .

Actually, Paulina doesn't want truth and justice purely for their own sakes either. Three times during the play she explains what else she wants: She wants Schubert back — her favorite composer, unbearable to her for the past fifteen years. What does Schubert represent to Paulina?

"There is no way of describing what it means to hear that wonderful music in the darkness," she tells Gerardo, "when you haven't eaten for the last three days, when your body is falling apart. . . ." Schubert, with what she calls his "sad, noble sense of life," represents the civilization outside the torturers' basement — the entire world of art and science and philosophy, of beauty and meaning, of humanity. When the doctor first played the music, and talked to her about music, science, and philosophy, she wildly supposed that he was different from the others, that the two of them shared civilization and were in that way different from the vile and foulmouthed soldiers who tortured and mocked her.

But then he betrayed her. In Polanski's film version, she describes her horror the first time she heard the doctor, her healer, slowly taking his pants off to rape her. The civilized doctor, it turns out, was just another savage, and when he raped her and talked filth to her, he took civilization away. Now she means to get it back. . . .

Polanski's film version of *Death and the Maiden* ingeniously dramatizes the morbid connection between sexuality and violence by reversing roles: When Paulina takes Roberto prisoner, she bends very close to him, she straddles him, she presses her face to his ankles to bite off the electrical tape she is using to bind his legs. As he gapes at her, she lifts her skirt, removes her underpants, and crams them into his mouth to stifle his yells.

What I am suggesting is that Dorfman meant his title, *Death and the Maiden*, to serve double duty: first, as a metaphor for the torture doctor and Paulina; second, as an emblem of both the noble and the base sides of the civilization that Paulina wants to recover. The torture doctor, Dorfman seems to suggest, raped Paulina because of his civilization rather than in spite of it. It is, after all, a civilization that enshrines pornographic images of Death raping the Maiden in the world's great museums, in the Uffizi and the Prado. The implicit question, then, is whether Paulina should want civilization back.

I don't mean to suggest that the answer is obviously no, and I certainly don't mean to suggest that Schubert's quartet is tainted by connections between a title Schubert never gave it and pictures he never saw. To the degree that civilization includes works as unambiguously beautiful as Schubert's D minor quartet, Paulina is right to want it back. Nevertheless, the question is a legitimate one because of the ambiguously beautiful, morally problematic, images that emerge from masculine civilization's id — what Roberto calls "the swamp." Few artists transcribe that id as faithfully as Hans Baldung Grien, and few images represent the swamp as purely as the *Death and the Maiden* motif. Like Schubert, Paulina may have never seen pictorial versions of *Death and the Maiden*, just as she never laid eyes on her rapist [because he had blindfolded her]. Significantly, music, the most immediate and least representational of the arts, becomes Paulina's emblem for civilization; she entertains no doubts about its worth and beauty, just as she entertains no doubts about the entirely aural evidence that Roberto Miranda is the man who raped her. Dorfman invites us to question her certitude on both counts — of Miranda's guilt and of civilization's innocence.

To some it will seem mistaken to focus on specifically sexual human rights abuses, and to infer connections between political rape and culture. Like Dorfman, I disagree. In their book on the Argentine dirty war, John Simpson and Jana Bennett report that junior officers placed bets on who could bring back the prettiest girls to torture and rape. This, I think, is not simply one random horror story out of many that might be told. The Serbian "rape motels" in Bosnia have focused attention on the systematic infliction of rape and forced impregnation as specifically political crimes. The Statute of the International Criminal Tribunal for former Yugoslavia added rape to the standard list of crimes against humanity, and includes "causing serious bodily or mental harm to members of the group," an offense that includes rape, in the definition of genocide.

Of course, soldiers raping civilians is nothing new, nor is the political use of rape to terrorize civilian populations. Shakespeare's *Henry V* brings the French town of Harfleur to its knees by threatening to let his men rape at will if he has to take the town by force. What seems genocidal in the Bosnian Serb strategy is the calculated effort to make the Muslim women outcasts in their own culture by despoiling them and impregnating them with unwanted babies.

Political rape exploits a constellation of traditional values and shadowy fantasies in patriarchal societies. First among these is the value placed on chastity and a woman's yielding of her sexuality exclusively to her husband or proper mate;

ineluctably, the rape victim has been shamed as well as tortured because her rapist has made her sexuality common. She is sullied goods. At every moment of her ordeal she expects death, but she also anticipates that if she survives she will never be entirely her own woman, nor even her husband's. For that matter, nothing she says or does can completely dispel the menfolk's lingering suspicion that she liked it at least a little bit. (Do the pictures not illustrate what men guess but seldom say — that maidens enjoy their trysts with Death?) Rape drives its victims to the margin of a patriarchal community, and in that way it weakens the community as a whole. In Bosnia, shunning has been the terrible fate of too many rape victims and their bastard children. Gerardo has never admitted to himself that Paulina was raped as well as tortured fifteen years ago. The reasons are as obvious to Paulina as they are to us.

When, like Paulina, the victim is a political activist, her rapists humiliate her further by demonstrating that she is only a body to be used at their pleasure, not a citizen with political rights and ideals and will. Of course, all political torture aims to teach its victims, men as well as women, that they are nothing but passive bodies in pain, not the active shapers of destiny they had fancied themselves. That is how torture works as an instrument of state. But when the victim is a woman and the torture is rape, her humiliation becomes triply political. Like a male victim, she is passive rather than active and subjugated rather than victorious. But, in addition, her rapists expel her from the recent and still-fragile world of women's political emancipation into a history-nightmare — a nightmare of traditionalist society in which, or so the rapists want to teach her, she was never anything more than [a] cunt. Political rape humiliates her male comrades as well. The same cultural habits that make chastity valuable and rape shameful to its victims obligate men to protect their women's honor. The man who fails stands exposed and impotent. Again, Gerardo has never admitted to himself that Paulina was raped as well as tortured fifteen years ago. The reasons — all the reasons, not only her shame, but his as well — are as obvious to Paulina as they are to us. And that returns us to the question of whether Paulina should want civilization back, contaminated as it is with swampland fantasies of *Death and the Maiden.*

Well, Paulina at least gets her Schubert back; in Polanski's film version she compromises her demand for justice and spares Doctor Miranda. In the final scene, Gerardo and Paulina attend a concert performance of the *Death and the Maiden quartet,* and *Doctor Miranda* is there, too. As they sit down, Paulina's eyes briefly meet the doctor's. "Then she turns her head and faces the stage."

Just as she accepts the bad in civilization along with the good, she accepts the compromises of transitional justice. Dorfman seems to suggest that in the end they may be one and the same compromise: an agreement to leave the fascists untouched in return for democratizing a civilization of which they too can approve. (The play is more ambiguous than the film, for there Dorfman ends the penultimate scene with Paulina still undecided about whether to spare the doctor. And in the final concert scene we don't know whether the doctor is present in the flesh or only in Paulina's fantasy.)

In the play, Dorfman's directions for the final scene require "a giant mirror which descends, forcing the members of the audience to look at themselves. Selected slowly moving spots flicker over the audience, picking out two or three at a time, up and down rows." The mirror is an interesting and powerful device. For one thing, it reminds us, the audience, that we are akin to a jury: Judgment of Miranda, but also of Paulina and Gerardo, is a task Dorfman charges to us.

More importantly, however, the mirrors and spotlights force us to confront our own complicity. Dorfman presumably had in mind a Chilean performance in which the spotlights may well have picked out actual torturers in the audience — torturers in the best circles of society, torturers who by agreement of their peers will never be brought to justice.

It once seemed to me that this sensational idea would be merely melodramatic in a British or American theater. Although I haven't seen the stage version, I now think differently. A North Atlantic audience may not include rapists, torturers, murderers, or beneficiaries and accomplices of dirty war. But a North Atlantic audience contains many — perhaps everyone, certainly me — who can't decide whether sparing the doctor would represent a happy ending or not. That seems embarrassing enough.

NOTES & QUESTIONS

1. Why does Paulina let Dr. Miranda go rather than kill him? Is it because her need for vengeance has been satisfied, or because at the moment when she must act she cannot overcome her own doubts as to his culpability? One commentator has suggested that the answer lies somewhere in the middle:

> After a long dark night of the soul, she lets her suspect go. Was he guilty? We don't know, but we suspect so. Has she gotten what she needed from the episode, that is, some kind of emotional satisfaction? We think so. Should she have done what she did? She explains that she does not trust the government, including her husband, who is part of the administration, to do justice for her and her fellow victims. She prefers to put her faith into her own personal truth commission. But can she trust that what comes out of her prisoner's mouth is truth? Perhaps all she really needed was to exert some kind of control over her own life and over her prisoner's. The power of life and death is, after all, the ultimate power — the power we give to our judicial system. Can the South African government trust that what those brought before it confess is true? The truth commissions had safeguards; they had ways to test the veracity of those brought before them. But could their safeguards have failed? Possibly. Does it matter?

Christine Alice Corcos, *Prosecutors, Prejudices and Justice: Observations on Presuming Innocence in Popular Culture and Law*, 34 University of Toledo Law Review 793, 811-12 (2003).

2. Professor Teresa Godwin Phelps frequently invokes the themes of Dorfman's play in her treatment of truth commissions in Argentina, Chile, El Salvador, and South Africa. She suggests, "History shows us that revenge cycles end when the victims cede the right to take revenge to the state and the state properly fulfills this duty." Teresa Godwin Phelps, *Shattered Voices: Language, Violence, and the Work of Truth Commissions* 5 (2004).

F. TERRORISM

Since 9/11 — the horrid terrorist attack in 2001 — the United States has been engaged in a war on terrorism that has forced a national debate over how to balance civil rights and public safety. Yet in other countries this discussion had been going on for many years. In England, for example, the "Northern Ireland question" had often led officials to take shortcuts that were later justified on the grounds of national security.

In the following excerpt the authors summarize the problems in the hasty prosecutions and convictions of the Guildford Four and Maguire Seven.

MISCARRIAGES OF JUSTICE IN THE WAR AGAINST TERROR

Kent Roach & Gary Trotter
109 Penn State Law Review 967 (2005)

The Guildford Four were convicted of murder in 1975 for pub bombings by the IRA in 1974 that killed seven people. An appeal taken in 1977 failed on the basis that alibi evidence, including claims by others that they had committed the bombings, was not convincing given the confessions. In 1989, the Home Secretary referred the case back to the Court of Appeal after new scientific evidence was discovered indicating that police reports were not taken contemporaneously with the alleged confessions. New evidence also emerged about an alibi witness and other exculpatory evidence that was not disclosed. In 1989, the convictions were quashed after the Director of Prosecutions decided not to contest the convictions of the four: Paul Hill, Carole Richardson, Gerald Conlon, and Patrick Armstrong. A public inquiry also was made into the case, and the case was subsequently dramatized into a movie, *In the Name of the Father.*

The Guildford case was also related to that of the Maguire Seven, who were convicted in 1976 of possessing explosives. The convictions rested on the basis of forensic tests that showed traces of nitroglycerine, even though no explosives were found. The Maguire Seven included Gerald Conlon's aunt, Anne Maguire, and his father, Giuseppe Conlon, who died in prison in 1980. Gerald Conlon, part of the Guildford Four, allegedly confessed to the police that his aunt had taught him how to make bombs. Most of the Maguire Seven were sentenced to terms of imprisonment of fourteen years. In 1987, the Home Secretary refused to refer the Maguires' case to the Court of Appeal on the basis that he had no doubts about the scientific evidence linking them with explosives. Subsequent tests carried out at the behest of the public inquiry, however, revealed the possibility of innocent contamination, as well as the fact that not all of the scientists' notes had been disclosed to the defense at the original trial. In 1991, the Home Secretary referred the case back to the Court of Appeal with the Director of Public Prosecutions conceding that the convictions were unsafe. The Court of Appeal quashed the convictions on the basis "that the possibility of innocent contamination cannot be excluded and on this ground alone, we think that the convictions of all the appellants are unsafe and unsatisfactory. . . ." The Maguires insisted that no explosives had been found in the house and complained that the Court of Appeal's innocent contamination theory did not constitute a full exoneration.

The May public inquiry sided with the Maguires over the Court of Appeal by endorsing statements by the Maguires' counsel that the "Crown's case, as presented at trial was so improbable as to be frankly incredible." Lord May explained the wrongful conviction as following from frequent references in the Guildford Four trial to the Maguires' residence as a "bomb factory." He concluded:

> [T]he "bomb factory" assumption pervaded the entire case and was allowed to obscure the improbability of what was alleged against the Maguire Seven. I do not criticize the jury: the context of the prevailing bombing campaign and the atmosphere of the trial are likely to have made it impossible for them to make a wholly objective and dispassionate appraisal of the admissible evidence alone.

In less diplomatic terms, the jury was influenced by tunnel vision, fear, and stereotypes. The connection between the Guildford and Maguire cases illustrates how the cell nature of modern terrorism, when combined with unreliable interrogations and forensic evidence, can lead to multiple and related miscarriages of justice. . . .

NOTES & QUESTIONS

1. What is it about effective terrorism in and of itself that might contribute to the likelihood of flawed and biased police investigations and prosecutions?

2. Are Irish terrorists who plagued Great Britain in the 1970s and 1980s comparable to Muslim terrorists in the contemporary United States? President George Bush and members of his administration for the most part described the struggle in the United States and elsewhere as a "war on terror." However, some have questioned the appropriateness of this characterization, noting that it indicts a methodology rather than the social composition or ideological program of those on whom we are warring.

3. As the preceding excerpt by Professors Roach and Trotter suggests, the story of the Guildford Four was dramatized for the big screen. The film *In the Name of the Father* starred Daniel Day-Lewis as defendant Gerald Conlon and Emma Thompson as determined defense lawyer Gareth Pierce. The following excerpt from an article by Professors Steve Greenfield and Guy Osborn considers the argument that the filmmakers were reckless in the way they made the actual case into a film.

PULPED FICTION? CINEMATIC PARABLES OF (IN)JUSTICE
Steve Greenfield & Guy Osborn
30 University of San Francisco Law Review 1181 (1996)

Some of the criticisms were fairly mundane or semantic — for instance the issue of whether or not Gerry Conlon did in fact bring some sausages to his Auntie Annie is not particularly material or interesting. Other points have included the "false" depiction of Gerry and Giuseppe Conlon sharing a cell at times during their sentence. In fact, current practice dictates that persons convicted of such offenses do not share cells with anyone, let alone members of their own family, and the two were only in the same prison at the same on a very limited number of occasions. The film also lacks substantial portions of Gerry Conlon's visit to England — noticeably the amount of time he spent in Southhampton before moving to London. However, as Robert Kee notes:

> Some inaccuracies about the Belfast life and family of the Daniel Day-Lewis/Jerry Conlon character are reasonably acceptable as part of that artistic license with which the producers seek to justify their treatment of the whole story. These instances are no more important than the inevitable physical differences in having an actor portray a real person.

Robert Kee, "In the Name of the Father," *The Times (London)*, 6 Feb. 1994, § 6 at 3 (movie review).

Another problematic area is the portrayal of Gareth Pierce and, in particular, her role in discovering the evidence that effectively leads to the freeing of the Four. Early in the film she is introduced and identified by the camera moving from the wig on the passenger seat in the car to her face — instantly showing her legal credentials. However, not only was the use of the barristerial wig factually incorrect in that Pierce was in fact a solicitor, her heartfelt plea at the end of the film to the court of appeal in fact could not have happened, as she did not have a right of audience to appear in such a court. The evidence she is said to have discovered that forms the basis of her plea was unearthed by the Avon and Somerset police, and not — as the film depicts — by Pierce.

Some of the more fundamental criticism relating to *In the Name of the Father* was based on a claim that the film exacerbated the persistent feeling in some quarters that the Four were in fact guilty. *The Daily Telegraph* emphasized this point when reporting on the acquittal of the three police officers charged with conspiracy to pervert the course of justice:

> Until now the received view of the Guildford Four, at least since they were released by the Court of Appeal in 1989, is that they were all innocent victims of a scandalous miscarriage of justice who spent many years in prison for crimes they did not commit. The acquittal of the three ex-policemen, and some of the new evidence heard in the course of their Old Bailey trial, suggests there are reasonable grounds for suspecting that two of the Guildford Four, Mr. Patrick Armstrong and Mr. Gerry Conlon, might have been guilty after all. This raises the disturbing possibility that the real miscarriage of justice in their case occurred when they walked free.

Iris Bentley, quoting *The Daily Telegraph*, *in* Let Him Have Justice 67 (1996).

This notion that the Four were after all responsible lies at the heart of much of the film's criticism. There is no doubt that a persistent theme running throughout the Irish miscarriage of justice cases is not that the police had caught the wrong people but had merely been overeager in the investigation and collection of the evidence. This theme neatly ignores the central arguments concerning the reliability of confession evidence and the methods employed by the police to obtain them. By permitting appeals on the basis of unreliable scientific evidence, or corrupt police notes, the dispute concerning police behavior is never addressed. While police brutality was never admitted in court, oppressive police actions are shown in the film as being part of the interrogation process.

The interrogation scene involves several police officers who are surrounding Conlon in an interrogation room. The scene starts with the senior officer talking to another police officer, who has already observed Conlon, outside of the room where Conlon is being questioned. The following exchange takes place:

> Senior Officer: "Is he leading us up the garden path?"
>
> Other Officer: "I dunno . . . I can make him confess."
>
> Senior Officer: "Well why don't you have a word in his ear? You live in the same town; he'll understand you."
>
> Other Officer: "Will you have the bomber?"
>
> Senior Officer: "Our job is to stop the bombing."

As both officers enter the cell, there is an atmosphere of brooding menace. While the other officers talk quietly in background, the junior one circles Conlon, and whispers in his ear softly:

> Police Officer: "I'm gonna shoot your da."
>
> Conlon: "What did you say to me?"
>
> Police Officer: "Little Bridie will have no daddy. I'm gonna shoot Giuseppe."

Conlon then becomes hysterical and has to be restrained by the other officers, including the Senior Officer, who reassures him that no one will harm his father. Meanwhile, the officer who has made the threats leaves the cell, dementedly pointing a gun at his own head. Conlon breaks down completely and says: "Give me the [expletive] statement, for [expletive] sake give me the statement, give me a pen. Right there's my [expletive] name there, you can write what you like."

The film also acknowledges the position of the police when the members of the Balcombe Street gang are arrested and confess to the Guildford and

Woolwich bombings. The hard-natured, cynical, IRA terrorist McAndrew is used to contrast with a more sympathetic portrayal of Conlon; Sheridan makes his Gerry Conlon the archetypal loveable Irish rogue, while McAndrew is the murderous Republican psychopath that we read about in the tabloid press.

By laying the blame for the bombings firmly with others, Conlon and Hill's alibi is accepted, and they are shown to be in London at the time of the bombing. The film asserts their innocence and has no difficulty with the notion that while the Balcombe Street gang may have been primarily responsible, the Guildford Four may also have been involved. . . .

In the Name of the Father lays the blame squarely at the door of the police officers, who both bully the evidence from the Four and lie in court. An important point that the film does draw out is the extent to which the confession evidence is used to drag others into the frame:

Frighteningly, the effect of duress does not stop with the person who is subjected to it and in the case of Gerry Conlon and the others of the Guildford Four, things they said were used to enmesh Gerry's father, his Aunt Annie Maguire and five other relatives and friends who collectively became known as the Maguire Seven.

Michael Mansfield & Tony Wardle, *Presumed Guilty* 82 (1994). The police corruption is compounded when they find the "real" bombers. . . .

It is the existence of the jury that deflects much of the potential criticism, for it is a group of the accused's peers who have determined their guilt, not the police officers or politicians. The process is potentially pure, but it has been corrupted from within at both ends [and] actually enhanced. . . . After all, the

Guildford Four are freed at an appeal hearing, indicating the ability of the system to correct original mistakes. The implication is that if the defense had been shown a copy of the alibi evidence, the Four would not have been convicted in the first instance. Fault lies clearly with those conducting the prosecution, not with the process itself. . . .

In the Name of the Father portrays the police in a . . . brutal light: eager to obtain a conviction through applying undue pressure. The desirability of admitting unsupported confessional evidence is not raised as an issue — rather, the emphasis is on the Four being able to demonstrate their innocence through the introduction of alibi evidence. The overriding view is of a system, basically sound, but subject to corruption by the infamous "few bad apples." Eventually the process can defeat this attempt to pervert the system, and the innocent, in the case of the Four, are freed. . . .

The superhero lawyer Gareth Pierce played by Emma Thompson makes an interesting addition to the genre. Like Cher [in the movie *Suspect* (1987)] she is female, but more importantly, she is shown to single-handedly save the Four through her quick-wittedness in deliberately asking for the "wrong" file. This information was actually discovered by the investigating police force, and this final portrayal is interesting. As Simon Jenkins notes, it is in many ways the pivotal point of the film — the instant when the Four finally obtain justice. Pierce, ostensibly a quiet and unassuming person, is portrayed by Emma Thompson, as Jenkins writes:

> Hair aflame with anger, she screams at the Old Bailey judge whose own words . . . are taken from the court report. Thompson's words are pure fiction. Conlon's alibi was actually supplied to the defence during the appeal by police investigators. Solicitors (sadly) do not yet appear in the Old Bailey. They certainly do not appear wigless and screaming. Much else in the film, as Robert Kee has pointed out, is a "farrago of rubbish."

Simon Jenkins, "Stories that Get in the Way of Facts," *The Times (London)*, 12 March 1994, 16.

Conclusion

The issue of using films in such a way to depict real events is undoubtedly contentious. Some commentators have argued that filmic portrayal is actually damaging if it is not accurate:

> The fictional presentation of the Guildford case in the feature film *In the Name of the Father* suggested the appeal rested on the discovery by defence lawyers of an alibi statement which had never been seen before, marked "Not to be seen by the defence." In this and in other respects too numerous to mention, the film was a travesty of the facts, which manages to weaken the drama of what really happened.

David Rose, *In the Name of the Law* 339 (1996).

It may however be the case that by going beyond the minutiae of detail, film may in fact be immensely important in terms of raising the consciousness of the general public. . . . A major strength of *In the Name of the Father* is its gloves-off account of the events that led to the dreadful miscarriage of justice perpetrated against the Guildford Four. While some have claimed that the only authentic way to portray such events is by means of the documentary, with no subjectivity to cloud the "truth," as [Alexander] Kluge notes this also is not a guarantor of accuracy or authenticity of representation:

> A documentary film is shot with three cameras: (1) the camera in the technical sense; (2) the filmmaker's mind; and (3) the generic patterns of the documentary film, which are founded on the expectations of the audience that patronizes it. For this reason one cannot simply say that the documentary film portrays facts. It photographs isolated facts and assembles from them a coherent set of facts according to three divergent schemata. All remaining possible facts and factual contexts are excluded. The naive treatment of documentation therefore provides a unique opportunity to concoct fables. In and of itself, the documentary is no more realistic than the feature film.

Alexander Kluge, *A Perspective* 4 (1988).

What makes the [film] important is not found in a semantic debate about minutiae of detail, but rather through a wider view of [its] worth in terms of raising consciousness or awareness of the issues that pervade [it].

NOTES & QUESTIONS

1. Professors Greenfield and Osborn compare the portrayal of Gareth Pierce by Emma Thompson in *In the Name of the Father* to that of attorney Kathleen Riley by Cher in *Suspect* (1987). Is the comparison an apt one? While the former film is a fictional version of an actual case, the latter is fiction pure and simple. Furthermore, attorney Riley is hardly portrayed as an independent, resourceful lawyer. She would never have succeeded as a public defender in a murder case without the help of a sympathetic juror who leaves the courtroom to undertake detective work and ultimately becomes her lover.

2. More generally, Greenfield and Osborn seem willing to grant the filmmakers substantial "artistic license" in adapting the story of the Guildford Four for the screen. Judging whether a film dramatizing real-life events plays too fast and loose with what really happened is a difficult task. The definition of a "documentary" is hardly fixed and seems largely to stand for any film that is not totally fictional. *See* James Monaco, *How to Read a Film: The Art, Technology, Language, History, and Theory of Film and Media* 429 (1981). Some commentators use the term "docu-drama" to suggest pop cultural works that wander too recklessly from the facts. "Of course, the godfather of the docudrama was Orson Welles's historic radio program *The War of the Worlds* (1938), whose documentary techniques were so lifelike that hundreds of thousands of listeners thought we really were being invaded by Martians." *Id.* at 398. In more recent years, hundreds of made-for-television movies have been "docudramas." For a fine treatment of the actual facts in the *Guildford Four* case, see Kent Roach and Gary Trotter, *Miscarriages of Justice in the War Against Terrorism, supra*, 177-79.

3.   Does *In the Name of the Father* suggest that a defendant caught up in a trial like the one depicted in the film cannot get justice because of the nature of the times? Does the public really want security at the expense of liberty? Does the film suggest how the English legal system can redress the balance, or does it merely serve as an indictment while failing to provide any alternatives?

4.   The court depicted in the film is a "Diplock court," a type of tribunal in which the ordinary protections afforded a British citizen are not available to the defendants (who are residents of Northern Ireland). The Diplock courts were named after the report that recommended their adoption, which in turn took the name of its chairman, Lord Diplock. *See* Matthew S. Podell, *Removing Blinders from the Judiciary: In re Artt, Brennan, Kirby as an Evolutionary Step in the United States-United Kingdom Extradition Scheme*, 23 Boston College International and Comparative Law Review 263, 267-68 (2000).

Such courts, of course, are difficult to square with at least two international treaties to which the United Kingdom is a party: the International Covenant on Civil and Political Rights, Article 14, § 3(g), which guarantees that criminal defendants shall not be compelled to testify against themselves or confess guilt), and the 1950 European Convention on Human Rights and Fundamental Freedoms, 213 U.N.T.S. 222, which in Article 6 provides:

> In the determination of his civil rights and obligations or of any criminal charge against him, everyone is entitled to a fair and public hearing within a reasonable time by an independent and impartial tribunal established by law. Judgment shall be pronounced publicly, but the press and public may be excluded from all or part of the trial in the interests of morals, public order or national security in a democratic society, where the interests of juveniles or the protection of the private life of the parties so require, or to the extent strictly necessary in the opinion of the court in special circumstances where publicity would prejudice the interests of justice.
>
> 1.   Everyone charged with a criminal offence shall be presumed innocent until proved guilty according to law.
>
> 2.   Everyone charged with a criminal offence has the following mini-mum rights:
>
>   a)   to be informed promptly, in a language which he understands and in detail, of the nature and cause of the accusation against him;

b)   to have adequate time and facilities for the preparation of his defence;

c)   to defend himself in person or through legal assistance of his own choosing or, if he has not sufficient means to pay for legal assistance, to be given it free when the interests of justice so require;

d)   to examine or have examined witnesses against him and to obtain the attendance and examination of witnesses on his behalf under the same conditions as witnesses against him;

e)   to have the free assistance of an interpreter if he cannot understand or speak the language used in court.

The British Parliament enacted the Human Rights Act in 1998 in order to give effect to the European Convention. Its Article 6, entitled "Right to a fair trial," reads as follows:

1.   In the determination of his civil rights and obligations or of any criminal charge against him, everyone is entitled to a fair and public hearing within a reasonable time by an independent and impartial tribunal established by law. Judgment shall be pronounced publicly but the press and public may be excluded from all or part of the trial in the interest of morals, public order, or national security in a democratic society, where the interests of juveniles or the protection of the private life of the parties so require, or to the extent strictly necessary in the opinion of the court in special circumstances where publicity would prejudice the interests of justice.

2.   Everyone charged with a criminal offence shall be presumed innocent until proved guilty according to law.

3.   Everyone charged with a criminal offence has the following minimum rights:

   (a)   to be informed promptly, in a language which he understands and in detail, of the nature and cause of the accusation against him;

   (b)   to have adequate time and facilities for the preparation of his defence;

   (c)   to defend himself in person or through legal assistance of his own choosing or, if he has not sufficient means to pay for legal assistance, to be given it free when the interests of justice so require;

   (d)   to examine or have examined witnesses against him and to obtain the attendance and examination of witnesses on his behalf under the same conditions as witnesses against him;

   (e)   to have the free assistance of an interpreter if he cannot understand or speak the language used in court.

Notice that neither the Convention nor the Act specifically discusses whether it is impermissible to draw adverse inferences from a defendant's silence. Why is this, and what are the consequences of the omission? *See* Mark Berger, *Reforming*

Confession Law British Style: A Decade of Experience with Adverse Inferences from Silence, 31 Columbia Human Rights Law Review 243 (2000).

5.   Despite the lessons taught by the Guildford Four case, the United Kingdom continues to struggle in balancing the rights of the accused with the need for security. In the wake of the July 2005 London train bombings, jittery police officers mistakenly shot and killed a Brazilian electrician because they thought he was a terrorist, leading to yet another public examination of the subject. *See* Tod Robberson, "Britons Question Anti-Terror Agenda: Proposals Seen as Unnecessarily Restrictive," *St. Paul Pioneer Press*, 9 Oct. 2005, 5A.

G.   EXTRADITION

In the film *Music Box*, lawyer Ann Talbot, played by Jessica Lange, jumps to her father's defense (Mike Laszlo, played by Armin Mueller-Stahl) after the United States government accuses him of being a Nazi war criminal. Yet as the evidence of Laszlo's guilt keeps growing, Talbot finds it increasingly difficult to remain convinced of his innocence. That her client is also her father only compounds her confusion over what is demanded of her as a lawyer, daughter, and human being. As noted in previous chapters of this text, Hollywood films tend to be character-driven narratives. Major characters are psychologically defined early in the film, and then they struggle with events, other characters, *and* themselves in the course of the film.

THE CONFLICTS OF LAW AND THE CHARACTER OF MEN: WRITING *REVERSAL OF FORTUNE* AND *JUDGMENT AT NUREMBERG*
Suzanne Shale
30 University of San Francisco Law Review 991 (1996)

Although not all movies terminate their story according to the same principles, in Hollywood, by and large, they do. The conventional Hollywood story form adopts the narrative mode of the classical tradition, in which the story firmly concludes with a sense of satisfying completeness. What makes us feel that sense of satisfaction, of desirable closure? The answer lies in the play of the main components of Hollywood narrative we have already identified: character, action, conflict, and change. The protagonist's struggle to achieve her goal, and the transformative effects of this odyssey, must have reached some resolution before we feel that matters have been brought to a close. Part of the pleasure of watching a movie is to learn what the protagonist's goal may be and then look forward to finding out how or, indeed, whether she achieves it.

Courtroom dramas rarely end immediately when the trial ends. There is almost always more to be resolved, a scramble of loose ends, a belated epiphany, a final twist or unanticipated denouement. While some trial movies merely require a brief epilogue, a dotting of i's and crossing of t's, the majority still have some story distance to go. *A Few Good Men* closes, unusually, as the lawyer walks from the courtroom. *In the Name of the Father* ends soon after the trial comes to a close, but cannot resist an epilogue referring to the lives of the characters as they continued beyond the confines of the film narrative. In *Judgment at Nuremberg*, Judge Haywood has still to have important discussions with Hans Rolfe and Ernst Janning, and Madame Bertholt has still to retreat from him, before his story ends. In *Let Him Have It*, we have still to witness Derrick Bentley's execution before the film closes. In *Reversal of Fortune*, Claus has a meeting with Dershowitz and one last bad joke to go. In *Music Box* and, famously, in *Witness for the Prosecution*, the story has still to turn a crucial twist before the meaning of the film's trial events is made clear. Indeed, the ending in *Witness for the Prosecution* subverts the meaning of the entire preceding narrative.

Each film closes at that point in the narrative when all of the key elements of the protagonist's story have reached a resolution. The ending of the trial will coincide with the ending of the movie only where the trial itself has resolved the last of the major dramatic conflicts the story has set in motion. *In the Name of the Father* can finish shortly after Gerry Conlon's appeal hearing secures his release from custody because we have already seen how the miscarriage of justice and his experiences in prison transform the innocent Conlon from a callow youth to a man of judgment and determination. Judge Haywood's story continues beyond his tribunal verdict because *Judgment at Nuremberg* is about Judge Haywood and his attitude toward justice. His verdict is only the beginning of a sequence in which we come to see and understand the spirit of the man and the full import of his decision. *Music Box*, the tale of a woman lawyer defending her father who is accused of concealing his fascist past, does not close its story at the end of the trial because the film is about the age-old conflicts between love and duty, and loyalty and truth. In *Music Box*, the trial is not supposed to resolve the underlying dramatic conflict. It is in the story to provide the most strenuous and symbolically significant test of the daughter's loyalty, as she wavers between her desire to believe that her father is innocent and her fear that he is not. *Witness for the Prosecution* is as much a story about the testing of a great advocate as a story about the trial of the defendant. At the end of the criminal trial, Charles Laughton's advocate's greatest challenge — the unfamiliar humiliation of having been deceived — is yet to come. . . .

NOTES & QUESTIONS

1. By calling into question the memories of the government's witnesses and challenging the authenticity of its evidence, Talbot is able to keep her father out of the hands of his pursuers. Yet after she does so, she discovers that he is, in fact, guilty. Does this make her a villain, a hero, or simply a lawyer who has done her job? *Compare* Jonathan R. Cohen, *The Culture of Legal Denial*, 84 Nebraska Law Review 247 (2005) (criticizing lawyers for failing to take their clients to task) *with* Abbe Smith, *Defending Defending: The Case for Unmitigated Zeal on Behalf of People Who Do Terrible Things*, 28 Hofstra Law Review 925 (2000) (suggesting that defense attorneys must do everything in their power to help their clients).

2. Consider as well the relevance of Rule 3.3 of the ABA Model Rules of Professional Conduct. It requires a lawyer to take reasonable remedial measures when she has misled (or allowed others to mislead) a tribunal. Should Talbot be subject to discipline under this rule? Might the narrative imperatives preclude any such discipline *in the film*, given the emphasis on the daughter's blind love for her father?

3. Assuming that Talbot turns over the evidence that proves her father's guilt, is it too late for the United States to bring a new proceeding against Laszlo? If it is too late, might another country initiate a proceeding against him? Could it bring its own action and demand his extradition? Should it do so? Is there some point at which such prosecutions are simply brought too late (witnesses die, memories fade?) Consider the case of John Demjanjuk, a Seven Hill, Ohio, ironworker originally deported to Israel in the 1980s and convicted, only to be set free and returned to the U.S. Then, at the age of 89, he was deported to Germany, convicted, and sentenced to 5 years in prison. *See* Jack Ewing and Alan Cowell, "Demjanjuk Convicted For Role in Nazi Death Camp," *New York Times*, 12 May, 2011 (http://www.nytimes.com/2011/05/13/world/europe/13nazi.html).

Beyond considerations of viable national jurisdiction, consider the jurisdiction of the International Criminal Court, which was created in 1998 and sits at The Hague. Could the International Criminal Court try Laszlo? *See* Steven Feldstein, Comment, *Applying the Rome Statute of the International Criminal Court: A Case Study of Henry Kissinger*, 92 California Law Review 1663, 1666, 1727 (2004) (noting that the court has jurisdiction only over events occurring after July 1, 2002 and, in any event, "is not meant to serve as a common court of judgment for even medium-level perpetrators. Its governing statute and historical legacy both point to the same conclusion: that the court's objective is to try the highest-level perpetrators of the most heinous crimes.")

INDEX

[References are to sections.]

[References are to sections.]

[References are to sections.]

[References are to sections.]